# For Reference

**Not to be taken from this room**

# ANTISEMITISM

# ANTISEMITISM
## A HISTORICAL ENCYCLOPEDIA
## OF PREJUDICE AND PERSECUTION

## VOLUME 2: L–Z

Richard S. Levy, Editor

A B C ● C L I O

Santa Barbara, California    Denver, Colorado    Oxford, England

4-20-2006
WW
$ 92.50

Library of Congress Cataloging-in-Publication Data is available from the Library of Congress

Antisemitism : a historical encyclopedia of prejudice and persecution /
    Richard S. Levy, editor.
        p. cm.
Includes bibliographical references and index.
ISBN 1-85109-439-3 (hardback : alk. paper) — ISBN 1-85109-444-X (ebook)
1. Antisemitism—Europe, Western—Encyclopedias. 2. Antisemitism—History—Encyclopedias.
I. Levy, Richard S. II. Title.

DS146.E8A58 2005
305.892'4'009—dc22          2005009480

06 05 04 03 02 01   10 9 8 7 6 5 4 3 2 1

This book is also available on the World Wide Web as an eBook. Visit abc-clio.com for details.

ABC-CLIO, Inc.
130 Cremona Drive, P.O. Box 1911
Santa Barbara, California 93116–1911

This book is printed on acid-free paper.
Manufactured in the United States of America

# CONTENTS

*Contributors and Their Entries, xiii*
*Introduction, xxix*

ANTISEMITISM
A HISTORICAL ENCYCLOPEDIA OF PREJUDICE AND PERSECUTION

# CONTRIBUTORS
# AND THEIR ENTRIES

**John Abbott**
*Purdue University Calumet*
Hammond, Indiana
    Agrarian League
    Memminger, Anton (1846–1923)
    Oberammergau Passion Play
    Ratzinger, Georg (1844–1899)
    Riehl, Wilhelm Heinrich (1823–1897)

**Ernst Baltrusch**
*Friedrich-Meinecke-Institut, Free University
  Berlin*
Berlin, Germany
    Roman Empire
    Roman Literature

**Henryk Baran**
*University at Albany, SUNY*
Albany, New York
    Doctors' Plot (1953)
    Leskov, Nikolai Semenovich (1831–1895)
    *Protocols of the Elders of Zion* on Trial
    *Rabbi's Speech, The*
    Solzhenitsyn, Aleksandr (1918–  )

**Lawrence Baron**
*San Diego State University*
San Diego, California
    Hollywood, Treatment of Antisemitism in
    Night of Broken Glass (November 1938
      Pogrom)

**Boris Barth**
*University of Konstanz*
Konstanz, Germany
    Versailles Treaty

**Scott Beekman**
*Ohio University*
Athens, Ohio
    Pelley, William Dudley (1890–1965)

**Dean Phillip Bell**
*Spertus Institute of Jewish Studies*
Chicago, Illinois
    Court Jews
    Expulsions, Late Middle Ages
    Host Desecration
    Jud Süss (Joseph ben Issachar Süsskind Op-
      penheimer), (1692–1738)
    Middle Ages, High (1096–1343)
    Middle Ages, Late (1343–1453)
    Prague Massacre (1389)
    Rindfleisch Massacre (1298)
    Shabbetai Zevi
    Sorcery/Magic
    Yellow Badge

**Steven Beller**
*George Washington University*
Washington, D.C.
    Degeneration
    Herzl, Theodor (1860–1904)
    Nordau, Max (1849–1923)
    Weininger, Otto (1880–1903)
    Zionism

**Joseph W. Bendersky**
*Virginia Commonwealth University*
Richmond, Virginia
    Armed Forces of the United States
    Moseley, George Van Horn (1874–1960)
    Patton, Gen. George (1885–1945)

**Doris L. Bergen**
*University of Notre Dame*
Notre Dame, Indiana
    Churches under Nazism
    Deutsche Christen
    Institute for the Study and Eradication of
    Jewish Influence on German Church Life

**Lena Berggren**
*Umeå University*
Umeå, Sweden
  Sweden

**Katell Berthelot**
*National Center for Scientific Research*
Aix en Provence, France
  Misanthropy

**Burton J. Bledstein**
*University of Illinois at Chicago*
Chicago, Illinois
  Norris, Frank (1870–1902)
  *Passing of the Great Race* (1916)
  Twain, Mark (1835–1910)

**Susan R. Boettcher**
*University of Texas, Austin*
Austin, Texas
  *Entdecktes Judenthum* (1700, 1711)
  Reformation (1517–1648)
  Supersessionism

**Dorothee Brantz**
*German Historical Institute*
Washington, DC
  Kosher Slaughtering

**Edward Bristow**
*Fordham University*
New York, New York
  Alliance Israélite Universelle
  White Slavery

**Matthias Brosch**
*Independent Scholar*
Hamburg, Germany
  Bayreuth Circle
  Dinter, Artur (1876–1948)
  German Racial Freedom Party
  *Handbook of the Jewish Question (Anti-semites' Catechism)*
  *Jews and the German State, The* (1861)
  *Myth of the Twentieth Century, The* (1930)
  *Sin against the Blood* (1917)
  Yellow Star

**Micha Brumlik**
*Johann Wolfgang Goethe University*
Frankfurt, Germany
  Schopenhauer, Arthur (1788–1860)

**Randall L. Bytwerk**
*Calvin College*
Grand Rapids, Michigan
  Streicher, Julius (1885–1946)
  *Stürmer, Der*

**Vicki Caron**
*Cornell University*
Ithaca, New York
  Alsace

**Jolene Chu**
*Jehovah's Witness Holocaust-Era Survivors Fund*
Patterson, New York
  Jehovah's Witnesses

**Geoffrey Cocks**
*Albion College*
Albion, Michigan
  Psychoanalysis

**Richard I. Cohen**
*Hebrew University*
Jerusalem, Israel
  Gobineau, Joseph Arthur de (1816–1882)
  Jew Bill (1753)
  Renan, Ernest (1822–1893)
  Toland, John (1670–1722)
  Wandering Jew

**Gaby Coldewey**
*Humboldt University*
Berlin, Germany
  LANC–National Christian Defense League

**Brian Crim**
*University of Maryland University College*
Adelphi, Maryland
  Jew Census (1916)
  Roth, Alfred (1879–1940)

**Philip A. Cunningham**
*Center for Christian-Jewish Learning at Boston College*
Chesnut Hill, Massachusetts
  Gospels

**Peter R. D'Agostino**
*University of Illinois at Chicago*
Chicago, Illinois
    Coughlin, Charles E. (1891–1979)
    *Cross and the Flag, The*
    Smith, Gerald L. K. (1898–1976)
    Winrod, Gerald B. (1900–1957)

**Peter J. Davies**
*University of Huddersfield*
United Kingdom
    Le Pen, Jean-Marie (1928– )

**Manfred Deselaers**
*Center for Dialogue and Prayer in Oświęcim-*
    *Auschwitz*
Oświęcim, Poland
    Höss, Rudolf (1901–1947)

**Carol Diethe**
*Middlesex University*
London, United Kingdom
    Förster-Nietzsche, Elisabeth (1846–1935)

**Betty A. Dobratz**
*Iowa State University*
Ames, Iowa
    White Power Movement

**Hans-Jörg Döhla**
*University of the Saarland*
Saarbrücken, Germany
    Almohad Persecution

**Marc Dollinger**
*San Francisco State University*
San Francisco, California
    African American–Jewish Relations
    Black Nationalism
    Farrakhan, Louis (1933– )
    Immigration and Naturalization Laws
    (U.S.)
    Multiculturalism
    Nation of Islam
    New Left
    *Secret Relationship between Blacks and Jews,*
    *The*
    Student Nonviolent Coordinating
    Committee (SNCC)

**William Collins Donahue**
*Rutgers University*
New Brunswick, New Jersey
    Fontane, Theodor (1819–1898)
    *Garbage, the City and Death, The*
    *Jews' Beech, The* (1842)
    Mann, Thomas (1875–1955)

**Gilles Dorival**
*University Aix-Marseille I*
Aix-en Provence, France
    Origen (ca. 185–ca. 251 or 254)

**Michael Dreyer**
*Northwestern University*
Evanston, Illinois
    Frantz, Constantin (1817–1891)

**Elizabeth A. Drummond**
*University of Southen Mississippi*
Hattiesburg, Mississippi
    Class, Heinrich (1868–1953)
    German Eastern Marches Society
    *If I Were the Kaiser* (1912)
    Pan-German League
    Schemann, Ludwig (1852–1938)
    Treitschke, Heinrich von (1834–1896)

**Albrecht Dümling**
*Center for Research of Antisemitism, Technical*
    *University of Berlin*
Berlin, Germany
    Music, Nazi Purge of Jewish Influence in

**Simone Duranti**
*Scuola Superiore S. Anna*
Pisa, Italy
    *Manifesto of the Racial Scientists* (1938)
    October Roundup (Rome, 1943)
    Preziosi, Giovanni (1881–1945)
    Racial Laws (Italy)

**Richard K. Emmerson**
*Medieval Academy of America*
Cambridge, Massachusetts
    Antichrist

**Frank Felsenstein**
*Ball State University*
Muncie, Indiana
    Caricature, Anti-Jewish (Early)
    Hogarth, William (1697–1764)
    Pork
    *Punch*
    Rowlandson, Thomas (1756–1827)

**Lars Fischer**
*King's College London*
London, United Kingdom
    Feuerbach, Ludwig (1804–1872)
    Hegel, G. W. F. (1770–1831)
    *Jewish Question, The* (1843)
    Léon, Abram (1918–1944)
    Mehring, Franz (1846–1919)
    Young Hegelians

**Samuel Fleischacker**
*University of Illinois at Chicago*
Chicago, Illinois
    Kant, Immanuel (1724–1804)

**Saul S. Friedman**
*Youngstown State University*
Youngstown, Iowa
    Slave Trade and the Jews

**Yvonne Friedman**
*Bar-Ilan University*
Ramat-Gan, Israel
    Peter the Venerable (ca. 1092–1156)

**Sandra Gambetti**
*College of Staten Island, CUNY*
Staten Island, New York
    Alexandrian Pogrom
    Apion
    Arch of Titus
    Bar Kochba Revolt
    Claudius (10 BCE.–54 CE)
    Diaspora Revolt (115–117 CE)
    Manetho

**Evelien Gans**
*Netherlands Institute for War Documentation*
*University of Amsterdam*
Amsterdam, the Netherlands
    Netherlands in the Twentieth Century

**Richard S. Geehr**
*Bentley College*
Waltham, Massachusetts
    Aryan Theater
    Kralik, Richard von (1852–1934)
    Lueger, Karl (1844–1910)
    Müller-Guttenbrunn, Adam (1852–1923)

**Jay Howard Geller**
*University of Tulsa*
Tulsa, Oklahoma
    Bubis, Ignatz (1927–1999)
    German Democratic Republic (East Germany)
    Germany, Federal Republic of (West Germany)

**Alexandra Gerstner**
*Free University Berlin*
Berlin, Germany
    German National White Collar Employees
        Association (1893–1934)

**Simone Gigliotti**
*Victoria University of Wellington*
Wellington, New Zealand
    Eichmann Trial
    Holocaust
    Wannsee Conference

**Hermann Glaser**
*Technical University of Berlin*
Germany
    Theater, Nazi Purge of Jewish Influence in

**Elaine Rose Glickman**
*Independent Scholar*
Houston, Texas
    Haman

**Ivo Goldstein**
*University of Zagreb*
Zagreb, Croatia
    Croatia
    Croatia, Holocaust in
    Pavelić, Ante (1889–1959)
    Ustasha

**Richard J. Golsan**
*Texas A&M University*
College Station, Texas
  Crimes against Humanity (French Trials)
  Fascist Intellectuals (French)

**David G. Goodman**
*University of Illinois*
Urbana, Illinois
  Fugu Plan
  Japan

**Julie V. Gottlieb**
*University of Sheffield*
Sheffield, United Kingdom
  British Union of Fascists
  Webster, Nesta (1876–1960)
  Women and British Fascism

**Keith R. Green**
*University of Illinois at Chicago*
Chicago, Illinois
  Steiner, Rudolf (1861–1925)
  Theosophy

**Kim M. Gruenwald**
*Kent State University*
Kent, Ohio
  Colonial America
  Stuyvesant, Peter (1592–1672)

**Michael Hagemeister**
*European University Viadrina*
Frankfurt an Order, Germany
  Liutostanskii, Ippolit (1835–1915/1918?)
  Nilus, Sergei (1862–1929)
  Pranaitis, Justinas (1861–1917)
  *Protocols of the Elders of Zion*

**Michaela Haibl**
*University of Vienna*
Vienna, Austria
  Doré, Gustave (1832–1883)

**Murray G. Hall**
*University of Vienna*
Vienna, Austria
  Bettauer, Hugo (1872–1925)

**Rita Haub**
*Archivum Monacense Societatis Jesu*
Munich, Germany
  Jesuit Order

**Peter Hayes**
*Northwestern University*
Evanston, Illinois
  Aryanization (Germany)
  German Big Business and Antisemitism
    (1910–1945)

**Ludger Heid**
*University of Duisburg*
Duisburg, Germany
  *Ostjuden*

**Armin Heinen**
*Historical Institute, Technical University of*
  *Rhineland-Westphalia*
Aachen, Germany
  Iron Guard

**Jonathan M. Hess**
*University of North Carolina*
Chapel Hill, North Carolina
  Dohm, Christian Wilhelm von
    (1751–1820)
  Fichte, J. G. (1762–1814)
  Michaelis, Johann David (1717–1791)
  State-within-a-State

**Laura Higgins**
*University of Illinois at Chicago*
Chicago, Illinois
  Jung, Carl Gustav (1875–1961)

**Klaus Hödl**
*Center for Jewish Studies, University of Graz*
Graz, Austria
  Masculinity

**Christhard Hoffmann**
*University of Bergen*
Bergen, Norway
  Berlin Movement
  Christian Social Party (Germany)
  Henrici, Ernst (1854–1915)
  Neustettin Pogrom (1881)
  Stoecker, Adolf (1835–1909)

**Colin Holmes**
*University of Sheffield*
Sheffield, United Kingdom
    Boer War (1899–1902)
    British Brothers League
    *Cause of World Unrest, The*
    Gwynne, H. A. (1865–1950)
    Hobson, J. A. (1858–1940)
    Webb, Beatrice (1858–1943)

**Klaus Holz**
*Evangelisches Studienwerk e.V. Villgst*
Schwerte, Germany
    Anti-Zionism in the USSR
    "Jewish" Press
    Purges, Soviet

**Brian Horowitz**
*Tulane University*
New Orleans, Lousiana
    Russia, Imperial

**Gregor Hufenreuter**
*Free University Berlin*
Berlin, Germany
    Central Association of German Citizens of
        Jewish Faith
    League against Antisemitism
    Stauff, Philipp (1876–1923)

**Jack Jacobs**
*John Jay College, CUNY*
New York, New York
    Marx, Karl (1818–1883)
    Socialists on Antisemitism

**Stephan Jaeger**
*University of Manitoba*
Winnipeg, Manitoba, Canada
    Varnhagen von Ense, Rahel Levin
        (1771–1833)

**Christoph Jahr**
*Humboldt University*
Berlin, Germany
    Pückler, Count Walter von (1860–1924)

**Paul B. Jaskot**
*DePaul University*
Chicago, Illinois
    Degenerate Art
    Eichmann, Adolf (1906–1962)
    Himmler, Heinrich (1900–1945)
    *Schwarze Korps, Das*

**Robert D. Johnston**
*University of Illinois at Chicago*
Chicago, Illinois
    Frank, Leo (1884–1915)
    Ku Klux Klan (1915–1941)
    Populist Movement
    Watson, Tom (1856–1922)

**Jeremy Jones**
*Executive Council of Australian Jewry*
Sydney, Australia
    Australia

**Jonathan Judaken**
*University of Memphis*
Memphis, Tennessee
    Action Française (1899–1945)
    Barrès, Maurice (1862–1923)
    Camelots du Roi (1908–1936)
    Drumont, Édouard (1844–1917)
    France (1789–1939)
    *France juive, La* (1886)
    Maurras, Charles (1868–1952)
    Sartre, Jean-Paul (1905–1980)
    Stavisky Affair (1933–1934)

**Gema A. Junco**
*Florida International University*
Miami, Florida
    Spain under Franco (1938–1975)

**Rainer Kampling**
*Seminar for Catholic Theology, Free University
    Berlin*
Berlin, Germany
    *Adversus Iudaeos*
    Capistrano, John of (1386–1456)
    Chrysostom, John (349–407)
    Deicide
    *Demonstratio Adversus Iudaeos*
    *Dialogue with Trypho*
    Iconography, Christian

**Carsten Kretschmann**
*Johann Wolfgang Goethe University*
Frankfurt am Main, Germany
    Boniface Society for Catholic Germany
    Rohling, August (1839–1931)
    *Talmud Jew, The*
    Ultramontanism

**Alfred Kube**
*Historical Museum Bremerhaven*
Bremerhaven, Germany
    Göring, Hermann (1893–1946)

**Lisa Moses Leff**
*Southwestern University*
Georgetown, Texas
    Fourier, Charles (1772–1837)
    Gougenot des Mousseaux, Henri
       (1805–1876)
    Infamous Decree (1808)
    Proudhon, Pierre-Joseph (1809–1865)
    Toussenel, Alphonse (1803–1885)
    Veuillot, Louis (1813–1883)

**Russel Lemmons**
*Jacksonville State University*
Jacksonville, Alabama
    *Angriff, Der*
    German National People's Party
    Goebbels, Joseph (1897–1945)
    Hugenberg, Alfred (1865–1951)

**Jeffrey Lesser**
*Emory University*
Atlanta, Georgia
    Brazil

**Jay Levinson**
*Independent Scholar*
Jerusalem, Israel
    Cuba

**David W. Levy**
*University of Oklahoma*
Norman, Oklahoma
    Dewey, Melvil (1851–1931)

**Richard S. Levy**
*University of Illinois at Chicago*
Chicago, Illinois
    Ahlwardt, Hermann (1846–1914)
    Antisemites' Petition (1880–1881)
    *Antisemitic Correspondence*
    Antisemitic Political Parties (Germany,
       1879–1914)
    Antisemitism, Etymology of
    Anti-Zionism
    Böckel, Otto (1859–1923)
    Fritsch, Theodor (1852–1933)
    Glagau, Otto (1834–1892)
    *Judaism as an Alien Phenomenon*
       (1862–1863)
    Liebermann von Sonnenberg, Max
       (1848–1911)
    Marr, Wilhelm (1819–1904)
    *Mirror to the Jews, A*
    *Our Demands on Modern Jewry*
    *Victory of Jewry over Germandom, The*
       (1879)
    *Word about Our Jews, A* (1880)

**David Isadore Lieberman**
*Brandeis University*
Waltham, Massachusetts
    Evolutionary Psychology
    Herder, J. G. (1744–1803)
    Musicology and National Socialism
    Nietzsche, Friedrich (1844–1900)

**Albert S. Lindemann**
*University of California, Santa Barbara*
Santa Barbara, California
    Beilis Case (1911–1913)
    Chmielnicki Massacres (1648–1649)
    Damascus Blood Libel (1840)
    Disraeli, Benjamin (1804–1881)
    Dreyfus Affair
    Jewish Question
    Mosley, Oswald (1896–1980)
    Mussolini, Benito (1883–1945)
    Rothschilds

**Jay Lockenour**
*Temple University*
Philadelphia, Pennsylvania
    Ludendorff, Erich (1865–1937)
    Ludendorff, Mathilde (1877–1966)
    Ludendorff Publishing House

**Kevin Madigan**
*Harvard Divinity School*
Cambridge, Massachusetts
    Augustine of Hippo (354–430)
    Church Councils (Early)
    Church Fathers
    Constantine, Emperor (274–337 CE)
    Gregory the Great, Pope (590–604)
    *Judensau*

**Ellen Martin**
*Johann Wolfgang Goethe University*
Frankfurt/Main, Germany
    Pfefferkorn, Johannes (1468/1469–1522)

**Jonathan Marwil**
*University of Michigan*
Ann Arbor, Michigan
    Antisemitism, Accusations of
    Lindbergh, Charles (1902–1974)

**David A. Meier**
*Dickinson State University*
Dickinson, North Dakota
    Militia Movement

**Gerd Mentgen**
*Arye Maimon Institute for the History of the
    Jews, University of Trier*
Trier, Germany
    Crusades

**Matthias Messmer**
*International Research and Consulting Centre*
Fribourg, Switzerland
    Ukraine, Post-Soviet

**Brigitte Mihok**
*Center for Research of Antisemitism, Technical
    University of Berlin*
Berlin, Germany
    Antonescu, Ion (1882–1946)
    Romania, Holocaust in

**Victor A. Mirelman**
*West Suburban Temple Har Zion*
River Forest, Illinois
    Argentina
    Buenos Aires Pogroms (1910, 1919)
    Tacuara

**Richard Mitten**
*Weissman Center for International Business,
    Baruch College, CUNY*
New York, New York
    Austria
    Waldheim Affair
    Wiesenthal-Kreisky Controversy

**Douglas Moggach**
*University of Ottawa*
Ottawa, Ontario, Canada
    Bauer, Bruno (1809–1882)

**Birgitta Mogge-Stubbe**
*Rheinischer Merkur*
Bonn, Germany
    Dühring, Eugen (1833–1921)
    *Jewish Question as a Racial, Moral, and Cul-
    tural Problem, The*

**Jonathan Morse**
*University of Hawaii at Manoa*
Honolulu, Hawaii
    Belloc, Hilaire (1870–1953)
    Chesterton, G. K. (1874–1936)
    Eliot, T. S. (1888–1965)
    English Literature of the Twentieth Century
    Pound, Ezra (1885–1972)
    Wharton, Edith (1862–1937)

**Gary Saul Morson**
*Northwestern University*
Evanston, Illinois
    Dostoevsky, Fyodor (1821–1881)

**Johann Baptist Müller**
*University of Stuttgart*
Stuttgart, Germany
    Stahl, Friedrich Julius (1802–1861)

**Cary Nathenson**
*Northwestern University*
Evanston, Illinois
    Film Industry, Nazi Purge of Jewish Influ-
    ence in
    Film Propaganda, Nazi

**Hannah Newman**
*Independent Scholar*
Ariel, Israel
    Aquarius, Age of
    Bailey, Alice A. (1880–1949)
    Blavatsky, Helena P. (1831–1891)
    Devi, Savitri (1905–1982)
    Invocation, The Great
    Jewish Force
    New Age
    The Plan of the Hierarchy
    *Secret Doctrine, The* (1888)

**Sören Niemann-Findeisen**
*Hamburg University of Economics and Politics*
Hamburg, Germany
    Wells, H. G. (1866–1946)

**Donald L. Niewyk**
*Southern Methodist University*
Dallas, Texas
    Social Democratic Party (Germany,
       1875–1933)
    Weimar

**Dietrich Orlow**
*Boston University*
Boston, Massachusetts
    National Socialist German Workers' Party
    Nazi Party Program

**Steven Paulsson**
*University of Oxford*
Oxford, United Kingdom
    Boycott of 1912 (Poland)
    Dmowski, Roman (1864–1939)
    Ghetto Benches
    Hlond, August (1881–1948)
    Jedwabne
    Kolbe, Maksymilian (1894–1941)
    Moczar, Mieczysław (1913–1986)
    National Democrats (Poland)
    Poland (1918–1989)
    Poland since 1989
    Purge of 1968 (Poland)
    *Twilight of Israel, The* (1932)

**John T. Pawlikowski**
*Catholic Theological Union*
Chicago, Illinois
    Pius IX, Pope (1792–1878)
    Pius XII, Pope (1876–1958)
    Vatican Council, First (1869–1870)
    Vatican Council, Second (1962–1965)

**Anton Pelinka**
*University of Innsbruck*
Innsbruck, Austria
    Vogelsang, Karl von (1818–1890)

**Edward Peters**
*University of Pennsylvania*
Philadelphia, Pennsylvania
    Innocent III (1160/61–1216)
    Inquisition
    Lateran Council, Fourth (1215)
    Raymund of Peñafort (1175/1180?–1275)
    Talmud Trials

**Fritz Petrick**
*Historical Institute of Ernst Moritz Arndt*
    *University*
Greifswald, Germany
    Best, Werner (1903–1989)

**Larry L. Ping**
*Southern Utah University*
Cedar City, Utah
    *Debit and Credit* (1855)
    Freytag, Gustav (1816–1895)

**Wendy Plotkin**
*Arizona State University*
Tempe, Arizona
    Restrictive Covenants

**Michael Posluns**
*St. Thomas University*
Fredericton, New Brunswick, Canada
    Canada

**Pamela M. Potter**
*University of Wisconsin*
Madison, Wisconsin
    *Judaism in Music* (1850, 1869)
    Wagner, Cosima (1837–1930)
    Wagner, Richard (1813–1883)

**Alfredo Mordechai Rabello**
*Hebrew University*
Jerusalem, Israel
    Justinian Code (Corpus Iuris Civilis)
    Theodosian Code

**Benjamin Ravid**
*Brandeis University*
Waltham, Massachusetts
    Ghetto

**Ian Reifowitz**
*Empire State College, SUNY*
Old Westbury, New York
    Bloch, Joseph Samuel (1850–1923)

**Helmut Reinalter**
*University of Innsbruck*
Innsbruck, Austria
    Freemasonry

**Paul Reitter**
*Ohio State University*
Columbus, Ohio
    Benn, Gottfried(1886–1956)
    Billroth, Theodor (1829–1894)
    Book Burning (May 10, 1933)
    George, Stefan (1868–1933)
    Lanz von Liebenfels, Jörg (1874–1954)
    List, Guido von (1848–1919)
    Mahler-Werfel, Alma (1879–1964)
    Rosenberg, Alfred (1893–1946)
    Self-Hatred, Jewish

**Johannes Rogalla von Bieberstein**
*University of Bielefeld*
Bielefeld, Germany
    Judeo-Bolshevism

**Daniel Rogers**
*University of South Alabama*
Mobile, Alabama
    Historians' Controversy
    Neo-Nazism, German

**Stefan Rohrbacher**
*Institute for Jewish Studies, Heinrich Heine University*
Düsseldorf, Germany
    Hep-Hep Riots (1819)

**Susan Rosa**
*Northeastern Illinois University*
Chicago, Illinois
    Balzac, Honoré de (1799–1850)

**Emily Rose**
*Princeton University*
Princeton, New Jersey
    Hugh of Lincoln
    Ritual Murder (Medieval)
    Simon of Trent
    Usury
    Well Poisoning
    William of Norwich (d. 1144)

**Vadim Rossman**
*University of Texas*
Austin, Texas
    Rozanov, Vasilii (1856–1919)
    Russia, Post-Soviet
    Russian Orthodox Church (ROC)

**Bernd Rother**
*Federal Chancellor Willy Brandt Foundation*
Berlin, Germany
    Auto-da-Fé
    Ferrer, Vincente (1350–1419)
    Pure Blood Laws
    Spain, Riots of 1391
    Torquemada, Tomás de (1420–1498)

**Jens Rybak**
*University of Bielefeld*
Bielefeld, Germany
    Arndt, Ernst Moritz (1769–1860)

**Jeffrey L. Sammons**
*Yale University*
New Haven, Connecticut
    Biarritz (1868)
    Heine, Heinrich (1797–1856)
    Heine Monument Controversy
    Raabe, Wilhelm (1831–1910)
    Young Germany

**Karl A. Schleunes**
*University of North Carolina*
Greensboro, North Carolina
Boycott of Jewish Shops (Germany, 1933)
Nazi Legal Measures against Jews (1933–1939)
Nuremberg Laws (1935)
Purge of the German Civil Service (1933)

**Charlotte Schönbeck**
*Pedagogical University of Heidelberg*
Heidelberg, Germany
  Physics, "German" and "Jewish"

**Ralph Schoolcraft III**
*Texas A&M University*
College Station, Texas
  Bardèche, Maurice (1909–1998)
  Brasillach, Robert (1909–1945)
  Céline, Louis-Ferdinand (1894–1961)
  Darquier de Pellepoix, Louis (1897–1980)
  Rebatet, Lucien (1903–1972)

**Alexander Schürmann-Emanuely**
*Independent Scholar*
Vienna, Austria
  LICA—International League against Anti-
    semitism

**Frederick M. Schweitzer**
*Manhattan College*
Bronx, New York
  Zündel, Ernst (1939– )

**Alyssa Goldstein Sepinwall**
*California State University, San Marcos*
San Marcos, California
  Grégoire, Henri-Baptiste (1750–1831)
  Voltaire, François-Marie-Arouet de
    (1694–1778)

**Esther Shabot**
*Excelsior*
Mexico City, Mexico
  Mexico

**Milton Shain**
*University of Cape Town*
Cape Town, South Africa
  South Africa

**Amy Hill Shevitz**
*California State University, Northridge*
Northridge, California
  Adams, Henry Brooks (1838–1918)
  General Orders No. 11 (1862)
  Restricted Public Accommodations,
    United States
  Seligman-Hilton Affair (1877)
  United States

**Frederick J. Simonelli**
*Mount St. Mary's College*
Los Angeles, California
  American Nazi Party
  Carto, Willis (1926– )
  Christian Identity Movement
  Liberty Lobby
  Rockwell, George Lincoln (1918–1967)

**Helmut Walser Smith**
*Vanderbilt University*
Nashville, Tennessee
  Center Party
  Konitz Ritual Murder (1900)
  *Kulturkampf*
  Xanten Ritual Murder (1891–1892)

**Roderick Stackelberg**
*Gonzaga University*
Spokane, Washington
  Bartels, Adolf (1862–1945)
  Chamberlain, Houston Stewart
    (1855–1927)
  Förster, Bernhard (1843–1889)
  Hentschel, Willibald (1858–1947)
  Lagarde, Paul de (1827–1891)
  Lange, Friedrich (1852–1917)
  Lienhard, Friedrich (1865–1929)
  *Völkisch* Movement and Ideology

**Michael E. Staub**
*Bowling Green State University*
Bowling Green, Ohio
  Rosenberg Trial

**Roni Stauber**
*Stephen Roth Institute, Tel Aviv University*
Tel Aviv, Israel
  Auschwitz Lie
  Faurisson, Robert (1929– )
  Holocaust Denial, Negationism, and Revi-
    sionism
  Institute for Historical Review (IHR)
  Irving, David (1938– )
  *Leuchter Report*

**Alan E. Steinweis**
*University of Nebraska*
Lincoln, Nebraska
  Nazi Cultural Antisemitism
  Nazi Research on the Jewish Question

**Norman A. Stillman**
*University of Oklahoma*
Norman, Oklahoma
  Arab Antisemitic Literature
  Arab Boycott
  Arafat, Yasir (1929–2004)
  Constantine Pogrom (1934)
  Farhud (1941)
  Hamas
  Hussaini, Mufti Hajj Amin al- (1895–1974)
  Iranian Revolution
  Islam and the Jews
  Islamic Diaspora
  Islamic Fundamentalism
  Khomeini, Ayatollah (1902–1989)
  Mohammed (ca. 570–632)
  Muslim Brotherhood
  Nasser, Gamal Abdel (1918–1970)

**Kenneth Stow**
*University of Haifa*
Haifa, Israel
  Agobard (779–840)
  Expulsions, High Middle Ages
  Middle Ages, Early (430–1096)
  Paul
  Visigothic Spain

**Werner Suppanz**
*University of Graz*
Graz, Austria
  Christian Social Party (Austria)
  Linz Program (1882)
  Pan-Germans (Austria)
  Schönerer, Georg von (1842–1921)

**Adam Sutcliffe**
*University of Illinois*
Urbana, Illinois
  Barruel, Augustin (1741–1820)
  Diderot, Denis (1713–1784)
  *Memoirs Illustrating the History of Jacobinism*
    (1797–1803)
  Philosemitism

**Mark Swartzburg**
*University of North Carolina*
Chapel Hill, North Carolina
  Aryan Paragraph
  Germanic Order
  Rathenau, Walther (1867–1922)

Reventlow, Ernst zu (1869–1943)
"Three Hundred," The
Thule Society

**John F. Sweets**
*University of Kansas*
Lawrence, Kansas
  Vichy

**Marcia G. Synnott**
*University of South Carolina*
Columbia, South Carolina
  *Numerus Clausus* (United States)

**Guillaume de Syon**
*Albright College*
Reading, Pennsylvania
  J Stamp
  Restitution (Switzerland)
  Switzerland

**Bożena Szaynok**
*Wroclaw University*
Wroclaw, Poland
  Kielce Pogrom (1946)
  Stalinization of Eastern Europe
  Slánský Trial

**Melissa Jane Taylor**
*University of South Carolina*
Columbia, South Carolina
  Evian Conference
  Long, Breckinridge (1881–1958)
  Oswego Camp

**Susanne Terwey**
*Humboldt University*
Berlin, Germany
  Britain (1870–1939)
  Maxse, James Leopold (1864–1932)

**Tatjana Tönsmeyer**
*Humboldt University*
Berlin, Germany
  Hlinka Guard
  Slovakia, Holocaust in
  Sudeten Germans
  Tiso, Jozef (1887–1947)

**Leif P. Torjesen**
*California State University, Dominguez Hills*
Carson, California
   Heidegger, Martin (1889–1976)

**William Totok**
*Study Group for the History and Culture of East*
   *Central and Southeast Europe*
Berlin, Germany
   Romania (1878–1920)
   Romania, Post-Soviet

**Aryeh Tuchman**
*Anti-Defamation League*
New York, New York
   Circumcision
   Dietary Laws
   Duke, David (1950–  )
   Internet
   Talmud

**Tzvetan Tzvetanov**
*Free University of Berlin*
Berlin, Germany
   Bulgaria, Holocaust in
   Dahn, Felix (1834–1912)

**Istvan Varkonyi**
*Temple University*
Philadelphia, Pennsylvania
   Freud, Sigmund (1856–1939)
   Kraus, Karl (1874–1936)
   Schnitzler, Arthur (1862–1931)

**George Vascik**
*Miami University*
Hamilton, Ohio
   German Peasant League
   German Students, Association of
   Hahn, Diederich (1859–1918)
   Tivoli Program (1892)
   Sombart, Werner (1863–1941)
   Wagener, Hermann (1815–1889)

**Nadia Valman**
*Parkes Centre for the Study of Jewish/Non-Jewish*
   *Relations, University of Southampton*
Southampton, United Kingdom
   *Coningsby* (1844)
   Dickens, Charles (1812–1870)
   Dracula

   English Literature from Chaucer to Wells
   Svengali
   Trollope, Anthony (1815–1882)

**Petr Vašíček**
*Independent Scholar*
Berlin, Germany
   Polná Ritual Murder (1899)

**Jeffrey Veidlinger**
*Indiana University*
Bloomington, Indiana
   Stalin, Joseph (1879–1953)
   USSR

**Brian E. Vick**
*University of Sheffield*
Sheffield, United Kingdom
   Christian State
   Dining Society, Christian-German
   Grimm, Brothers
   *Verjudung*

**Clemens Vollnhals**
*Hannah Arendt Institute for the Study of*
   *Totalitarianism, Technical University Dresden*
Dresden, Germany
   Gemlich Letter
   Hitler's Speeches (Early)
   Hitler's *Table Talk*

**Dirk Walter**
*Münchner Merkur*
Munich, Germany
   Culture-Antisemitism or Pogrom-Anti-
     semitism? (1919)
   Desecration of Cemeteries and Synagogues
     in Germany since 1919
   German Racial League for Defense and De-
     fiance
   Pudor, Heinrich (1865–1943)
   Scheunenviertel Pogrom (1923)

**Henry Wassermann**
*Open University of Israel*
Tel Aviv, Israel
   Caricature, Anti-Jewish (Modern)
   *Fliegende Blätter*
   *Gartenlaube, Die*
   *Kladderadatsch*
   *Simplicissimus*

**Horst Weigelt**
*University of Bamberg*
Bamberg, Germany
    Lavater, Johann Kaspar (1741–1801)

**Richard Weikart**
*California State University, Stanislaus*
Turlock, California
    Eugenics
    Racism, Scientific
    Social Darwinism

**Gerhard L. Weinberg**
*University of North Carolina*
Chapell Hill, North Carolina
    Hitler, Adolf (1889–1945)
    Hitler's "Prophecy" (January 30, 1939)
    *Mein Kampf*

**Wolfgang Weiss**
*University of Munich*
Munich, Germany
    *Jew of Malta, The*
    Shakespeare, William (1564–1616)

**Edith Wenzel**
*Institute for Germanistics and General Literary Sciences, Technical University of Rhineland-Westphalia*
Aachen, Germany
    Passion Plays, Medieval

**Edward B. Westermann**
*School of Advanced Air and Space Studies*
Montgomery, Alabama
    Commissar Order
    Einsatzgruppen
    Order Police

**Cornelia B. Wilhelm**
*University of Munich*
Munich, Germany
    German-American Bund

**Benn Williams**
*University of Illinois at Chicago*
Chicago, Illinois
    Vallat, Xavier (1891–1972)

**George S. Williamson**
*University of Alabama*
Tuscaloosa, Alabama
    Fries, Jakob Friedrich (1773–1843)

**Andreas Winnecken**
*Reha-Zentrum Soltau*
Soltau, Germany
    Youth Movement (German)

**Victoria Saker Woeste**
*American Bar Foundation*
Chicago, Illinois
    American Jewish Committee and Anti-defamation Efforts in the United States
    *Dearborn Independent* and *The International Jew*
    Ford, Henry (1863–1947)

**Ulrich Wyrwa**
*Center for Research of Antisemitism, Technical University of Berlin*
Berlin, Germany
    1848
    Emancipation
    Burschenschaften

**Krista Zach**
*Institute for German Culture and History in Southeast Europe*
Munich, Germany
    Codreanu, Corneliu Zelea (1899–1938)
    Cuza, A. C. (1857–1946)
    Goga, Octavian (1881–1938)

**Lizabeth Zack**
*University of South Carolina, Spartanburg*
Spartanburg, South Carolina
    Algeria
    Régis, Max (1873–1950)

**Karl Zieger**
*University of Valenciennes*
Valenciennes, France
    Zola, Émile (1840–1902)

# L

## Lagarde, Paul de (1827–1891)

Although Paul de Lagarde held a chair in Oriental studies at the University of Göttingen, he thought of himself as a theologian whose mission was to promote the spiritual and political regeneration of the German nation. His essays combining nationalistic religiosity with a vituperative antimodernism and antisemitism were collected in a volume entitled *Deutsche Schriften* (German Writings) in 1878 and reissued in an expanded edition in 1886. Appearing in several different versions up to 1945, this book exercised considerable influence within the growing *völkisch* (racist-nationalist) movement before and after World War I, and it was widely regarded as one of the foundational texts of the Third Reich.

Born Paul Anton Boetticher, Lagarde lost his mother at birth and suffered under the constrictive upbringing of his narrow-mindedly sectarian father, leaving him with lifelong feelings of homelessness and bitterness. His unhappy childhood helped to form a hypersensitive, stubborn, abrasive, and self-righteous personality, giving rise to professional conflicts and disappointments that further nourished his belligerence. Adoption by his maternal great-aunt in 1854 led to his change of name and an accompanying sense of rebirth. Unable to obtain a university post after completing his doctorate at the University of Berlin, partly as a result of his cavalier attitude toward accepted scholarly practices, he taught at a Berlin preparatory school for several years before landing a professorship at Göttingen in 1869.

Lagarde's personal and professional frustrations colored his political views and turned him into a fierce critic of the political, religious, and educational institutions of the newly founded German Empire. He admired Otto von Bismarck's aristocratic personality and leadership in the wars of unification but faulted the chancellor for a number of "failings," above all for neglecting to recognize and act on the threat to authentic Germanity supposedly arising from the spread of Jewish influence. Although he distinguished between Jewry and individual Jews (who could, in his view, become good Germans by giving up their Jewishness), he regarded the Jewish religion as an atavistic form of Asiatic paganism. He blamed the Jews for inventing the stock market, which enabled capitalists to accumulate unprecedented wealth without assuming the obligations that landownership entailed. He portrayed the German *Mittelstand* (lower middle class) and peasantry as victims of capitalism. Capitalist excesses promoted socialism, a form of internationalism that served the purposes of the Jewish conspiracy that Lagarde imagined to be at work throughout Europe.

From his paranoid perspective, the Alliance Israélite Universelle, an organization founded in Paris in 1860 to defend Jews against discrimination, was, in fact, designed to prevent Jews from becoming good members of their host societies, thus serving the same function as the Jesuit order for Catholics. Like many antisemites who advocated assimilation as a way of eradicating Jewish identity, Lagarde favored the establishment of a Jewish state, to which those Jews who would not renounce their Jewishness could be deported. Aware that his antisemitism could jeopardize his academic credibility, he made a distinction between *Antisemitismus* and *Judenfeindschaft* (antisemitism and Jew-hatred), declaring that though he was proud to be an antisemite, he was not an enemy of the Jews.

Repeating a favorite antisemitic trope, Lagarde declared that the real problem lay in the innocence and simple-heartedness of Germans, who were easily duped by Jewish guile. He deplored the fact that so many of his compatriots (namely, German progressives) had become cosmopolitans alienated from their own national essence. According to Lagarde, that essence lay in a characteristically German idealism—the pursuit of a moral imperative, an attitude diametrically opposed to the materialism and commercialism represented by Jews. Only the development of an authentically German religion could fully unite the German people behind a nationalistic agenda. He advocated a Christianity freed of all Jewish, Greek, and Roman accretions and based on the teachings of Jesus without the modifications introduced by Paul, the Catholic Church, or the Protestant Reformation. Unlike the majority of völkisch religious reformers, who venerated Martin Luther, Lagarde criticized Luther for eliminating bishops and priests, adopting the Paulist doctrine of justification by faith, retaining the Old Testament, and bringing about the religious division of Germany. The Counter-Reformation, in turn, had made the Catholic Church the enemy of all nations. Although he sought to join religion and politics in a common national cause, he paradoxically called for the separation of church and state in Germany so that the decadent churches could die a natural death.

Lagarde also proposed numerous other reforms, consistently opposed to such modernizing forces as democracy, liberalism, rationalization, urbanization, and secularization. His call for a unified German national community freed of the Jewish presence found devoted followers in such völkisch propagandists as Houston Stewart Chamberlain, Theodor Fritsch, and Heinrich Class of the Pan-German League. But even the moderate conservative Thomas Mann admired Lagarde and acknowledged his influence.

—*Roderick Stackelberg*

***See also*** Alliance Israélite Universelle; Capital: Useful versus Harmful; Chamberlain, Houston Stewart; Class, Heinrich; Fritsch, Theodor; Lienhard, Friedrich; *Mirror to the Jews, A;* Paul; Sombart, Werner; *Victory of Jewry over Germandom, The; Völkisch* Movement and Ideology
***References***
Lougee, Robert W. *Paul de Lagarde, 1827–1891: A*

*Study of Radical Conservatism in Germany* (Cambridge, MA: Harvard University Press, 1962).
Stern, Fritz. *The Politics of Cultural Despair: A Study in the Rise of the Germanic Ideology* (Garden City, NY: Anchor Books, 1965).

# LANC–National Christian Defense League

Romania's LANC—the Liga Apărării Naţional Creştine (National Christian Defense League)—was founded by A. C. Cuza in 1923 and pursued a clearly antisemitic agenda that contributed significantly to the worsening of Jewish-Romanian relations. Following World War I, Romania nearly doubled its territory with the annexation of Transylvania, Bukovina, and Bessarabia. Simultaneously, it enlarged its minority populations, especially Hungarians, Germans, and Jews, which, in turn, increased the anxiety levels of Romanian nationalists and antisemites. Meanwhile, the postwar economic dislocations further undermined Romanian small farmers. These grievances and tensions provided the fodder for nearly continuous election campaigning by antisemitic groups and parties, among them LANC.

LANC opposed Romanian citizenship or naturalization for Jews. It also agitated against critical journalists and leftist political organizations. The Right, however, weakened its effectiveness by splintering into three major groupings in 1927. LANC, whose core membership was composed of secondary school and university students, was not represented in parliament in 1927 and 1928. In 1930, however, it once again began to gain influence, mobilizing new members and voters with antisemitic propaganda. It appealed to the peasantry, alienated by the old parties' inability to deal with structural problems in agriculture, by promising to expropriate Jewish property on behalf of small farmers. In some regions, young peasants engaged in pillaging and physically abused Jews. Unable to win many seats in parliament, LANC nevertheless changed the climate of the institution by means of its brutally aggressive interventions; these included actual physical attacks on other deputies, such as the one carried out on a member of the Jewish Party (which led to the ouster of LANC representatives from parliamentary sessions). Unlike the Iron Guard, however, LANC avoided a total dissolution. Also unlike the Iron Guard, LANC's aggressive antisemitic activities were seemingly spontaneous rather than centrally organized, and its members did not attempt to assassinate Romanian politicians. But LANC's violence-prone, blue-clad paramilitary certainly intimidated the Jewish population.

After Hitler gained power in 1933, LANC began cooperating more closely with Romanian German Nazis. At Hitler's invitation, Cuza led a Romanian delegation to Berlin, from which LANC received financial support. Hitler's access to power changed the political situation in Romania, too, as German and Jewish deputies ceased cooperating in the defense of minority rights. In 1935, LANC joined with Octavian Goga's National Agrarian Party to form the National Christian Party (PNC), which supported the exclusion of Jews from national economic life, the imposition of a *numerus clausus* (maximum number) in the professions and state-owned firms, and a scrutinizing of Jews' citizenship status. Even though the PNC won less than 10 percent of the vote in 1937, King Carol II asked Goga to form a government. During the brief life span of his government, Goga oversaw the destruction of the democratic press and the passage of significant antisemitic legislation. By 1939, as a result of the new laws, nearly one-third of the Jews of Romania—most from regions annexed after World War I—lost their citizenship and were thereby excluded from the educational system and the practice of many professions.

—*Gaby Coldewey*
*Richard S. Levy, translation*

**See also** Cuza, A. C.; Goga, Octavian; Iron Guard; Romania

**References**

Heinen, Armin. *Die Legion "Erzengel Michael" in Rumänien: Soziale Bewegung und politische Organisation—Ein Beitrag zum Problem des internationalen Faschismus* (Munich, Germany: Oldenbourg, 1986).

Livezeanu, Irina. *Cultural Politics in Greater Romania: Regionalism, Nation Building and Ethnic Struggle, 1918–1930* (Ithaca, NY: Cornell University Press, 1995).

# Lange, Friedrich (1852–1917)

Friedrich Lange was a nationalistic and antisemitic German journalist who founded the Deutschbund (German Union) in 1894, an elitist, conspiratorial organization dedicated to *völkisch* (racist-nationalist) objectives, including the exclusion of Jews from German society. Drawing its membership from the educated upper middle class and organized in the form of a secretive fraternal lodge (open only to men before 1914), the Deutschbund had only 1,100 members organized into fifty-four regional or local affiliates in 1910. But it exercised an influence beyond these small numbers; one important example was the impact it had on the longtime head of the Pan-German League, Heinrich Class, who credited the Deutschbund with forming his völkisch worldview.

A preparatory school teacher who had earned a doctorate in ancient philosophy from the University of Göttingen in 1873, Lange turned to journalism in the 1880s, becoming the editor of the conservative Berlin newspaper *Tägliche Rundschau* (Daily Review) in 1890 and of the hypernationalist *Deutsche Zeitung* (German Newspaper) in 1895. A collection of his essays was first published as *Reines Deutschtum* (Pure Germanness) in 1893 and reissued in several expanded editions in the course of the following two decades.

The Deutschbund was founded, in part, as a reaction to the evident failure of the antisemitic political parties of the 1880s and 1890s to gain a mass following. Lange criticized their rowdy brand of antisemitism (*Radauantisemitismus*) and the exclusive reliance on antisemitism (*Nur-Antisemitismus*) in their party programs. He hoped that a less personal, less agitational, and less negative and envy-driven form of antisemitism would have a broader appeal to influential Germans. Antisemitism, he wrote, was only one expression of a comprehensive völkisch worldview that put the principle of racial heredity at the center of all efforts to strengthen German ethnicity (*Volkstum*). A harsh critic of parliamentary politics, he rejected the creation of a völkisch or antisemitic party in favor of a strategy of infiltrating all major parties and social and cultural institutions. Notwithstanding his "unpolitical" stance, he joined in founding the

Reichswahlverband (Reich Election Association) in 1902, which grew into the Reichsverband zur Bekämpfung der Sozialdemokratie (Reich Association for the Struggle against Social Democracy) in 1904.

Lange's proposed solution to the Jewish Question did not differ from the programs of the antisemitic parties. German Jews were to be deprived of citizenship, and foreign Jews (as well as Slavs and Latins [Welschen]) were to be deported. To Lange, the Jewish Question was not a matter of "whether" but only of "how." The Deutschbund also became a leading purveyor of the concept of racial hygiene, calling for a prohibition on marriage for the mentally and physically handicapped and other undesirable groups. In many ways, Lange's vision of a völkisch state anticipated the Third Reich. The Deutschbund was one of the few völkisch organizations that was not dissolved by the Nazis in 1933.

—*Roderick Stackelberg*

**See also** Antisemitic Political Parties; Class, Heinrich; Eugenics; Fritsch, Theodor; Pan-German League; *Völkisch* Movement and Ideology

**References**

Bohrmann, Hans. "Lange, Friedrich." In *Neue Deutsche Biographie,* vol. 13 (Berlin: Duncker and Humblot, 1982), 554–555.

Levy, Richard S. *The Downfall of the Anti-Semitic Political Parties in Imperial Germany* (New Haven, CT: Yale University Press, 1975).

Pulzer, Peter G. J. *The Rise of Political Anti-Semitism in Germany and Austria.* Rev. ed. (Cambridge, MA: Harvard University Press, 1988).

## Lanz von Liebenfels, Jörg (1874–1954)

The only full-length study on the writer Jörg Lanz von Liebenfels bears the title *Der Mann, der Hitler die Ideen Gab* (*The Man Who Gave the Ideas to Hitler* [1958]). This title is something of an overstatement, based on the hypothesis that during an extended stay in Vienna before World War I, Hitler probably read articles by Lanz in various antisemitic newspapers, as well as in the author's own journal. In addition, young Hitler might have visited Lanz around 1909. The phrase *might have* is appropriate here because only Lanz's accounts, written after Hitler had become famous, testify to the encounter, and, as will soon be clear, Lanz the witness lacked great credibility.

In journalistic writings and in his best-known book, *Theozoologie oder die Kunde von den Sodoms-Äfflingen und dem Götter-Elektron* (Theozoology, or the Study of the Little Sodom-Monkeys and the Gods' Electron [1905]), Lanz advanced an extravagant form of racism. As the title suggests, he combined pseudoscience with grandiose Theosophical and mystical conceits in confabulations on racial hierarchy. He believed in the cosmic superiority of Aryan peoples and that their mingling with other races represented the greatest problem of the age.

Above all, Lanz was a charlatan. A native Viennese, he was born Joseph Adolf Lanz in 1874. When he was nineteen, he joined—as the novice Brother George—the Order of the Cistercians of the Chapter of the Holy Cross in the Vienna Woods. He became an ordained priest in 1899. But a year later, he left the order because of "growing nervousness" and established the Order of the New Templars, the main principle of which was racial purity.

Lanz then undertook to change his identity. He altered his date and place of birth and conferred a fake doctorate on himself, smuggling all this apocryphal information into Vienna's official registry. He also changed his name to Baron Adolf Georg (Jörg) von Liebenfels, Ph.D. Apparently, his mother, whose maiden name was Hoffenreich, had Jewish ancestry. So beyond wanting to feed his megalomania, Lanz needed to bring his own heritage into line with his ideology.

If Lanz might have acted as Hitler's mentor, he clearly had mentors of his own, most notably the mystical antisemite Guido von List. In fact, Lanz belonged to the List Society and eventually became part of List's own order, the Armanship. He established his Aryan supremacist journal *Ostara* in 1905, shortly before Hitler arrived in Vienna. It ran, though not continuously, until 1928, totaling just over 100 numbers, most of which Lanz wrote himself. After the war, the journal carried a telling subtitle, "The Empire of the Blond People."

Until that time, antisemitism was no more prominent in Lanz's work than were general claims about the superiority of blond, blue-eyed

*Völker* (peoples) and admonitions against the tainting of Aryans through "Mongol" or "Negro" blood—Jews, for Lanz, belonged to the "Mediterranean peoples." In *Ostara* articles such as "Race and Woman and Her Predilection for a Man of a Lower Nature" (1909) and "The Love and Sex Life of Dark and Blonde People" (1910), for instance, Lanz persistently worried the theme of miscegenation, for which he held German women partially responsible (as the former title implies). Because, in his opinion, Jews wanted to remain a separate *Volk,* he did not treat them as a particularly dire threat.

That position changed with the loss of World War I, which he blamed on the Jews. He reconfigured his main motifs accordingly. Still fixated on sex between German women and "Negroes," he now attributed that problem to Jewish conspiracies. In 1921, for example, he wrote, "The Jew wants to violate, to ruin completely our German race; that's why he throws German women to the Negroes in the Rhineland."

After World War II, Lanz bragged about—and in all likelihood exaggerated—his influence on Hitler. In everyday life, however, he came across differently. He was treated more as a curiosity than as someone who helped pour the intellectual foundation for mass murder. "At home," his nephew Luigi Hoffenreich recollected, "we only called him 'Cuckoo.'"

—*Paul Reitter*

*See also* Austria; Hitler, Adolf; List, Guido von; Theosophy; *Völkisch* Movement and Ideology
**References**
Daim, Wilfried. *Der Mann, der Hitler die Ideen Gab: Von den religiösen Verirrungen eines Sekteriers zum Rassenwahn des Diktators* (Munich, Germany: Isar Verlag, 1958).
Goodrick-Clark, Nicholas. *The Occult Roots of Nazism: Secret Aryan Cults and Their Influence on Nazi Ideology* (New York: New York University Press, 1994).

## Lateran Council, Fourth (1215)

The Fourth Lateran Council was convened by Pope Innocent III for the purpose of reforming the Latin Christian Church and society and recovering the Holy Land, lost to Saladin after 1187. The council was held at the Lateran Palace complex in Rome between November 11 and November 30, 1215, and was the largest, most productive, and most influential church council of the Middle Ages. Its canons 67 through 70, which pertained to Jews, defined several important aspects of Jewish identity in Christian Europe for centuries.

Innocent announced the council in a circular letter in April 1213, giving the participants what was, at the time, an extraordinary two and one-half years to prepare for their participation. Around 5,000 people eventually attended, so large a number that the council was usually referred to simply as the Great Council. The seventy canons and the call for another crusade produced by the council virtually redefined Latin Christianity for the next three and one-half centuries.

Canons 67 through 70 reflected the hostile perceptions of contemporary Judaism held by Innocent III and others. They strictly regulated Jewish moneylending (67), prescribed distinctive Jewish dress (68), forbade Jews to appear in public on certain Christian holy days (68), criminalized Jewish expressions deriding Jesus and Christianity (68), prohibited Jews from holding public office and exercising power over Christians (69), and prohibited Jewish converts to Christianity from continuing to use Jewish rites (70). By including these restrictions among the massive statements of doctrine and discipline of the council, Innocent III contributed substantially to the significant reduction of Jewish status in Christian Europe that would characterize the following three centuries.

—*Edward Peters*

*See also* Church Councils (Early); Crusades; Innocent III; Middle Ages, High; Usury; Yellow Badge
**References**
Bolton, Brenda. "A Show with a Meaning: Innocent III's Approach to the Fourth Lateran Council, 1215." In *Innocent III: Studies on Papal Authority and Pastoral Care* (Aldershot, UK, and Brookfield, VT: Ashgate, 1995), XI.
Kuttner, Stephan, and Antonio Garcia y Garcia. "A New Eyewitness Account of the Fourth Lateran Council," *Traditio* 20 (1964): 115–178.
Moore, John C. *Pope Innocent III (1160/61–1216): To Root Up and to Plant* (Leiden, the Netherlands, and Boston: Brill, 2003), 228–252.

Tanner, Norman., S.J. *Decrees of the Ecumenical Councils.* Vol. 1, *Nicaea to Lateran V* (Washington, DC: Georgetown University Press, 1990), 227–272. The canons are translated in this work.

## Lavater, Johann Kaspar (1741–1801)

The Zurich theologian and man of letters Johann Kaspar Lavater was a European celebrity because of both his wide-ranging literary output and his communication skills. Among his large circle of correspondents was Moses Mendelssohn, whom he met three times in Berlin on his "grand tour" (1763–1764). In 1769, Lavater dedicated his annotated translation of Charles de Bonnet's *Philosophical and Critical Inquiries Concerning Christianity* to Mendelssohn, whom he challenged either to refute Bonnet's proofs of Christianity or to do "what Socrates would have done, had he read this book and found it irrefutable" (120). During the following months, the two engaged in a heated, closely followed controversy that played out in letters, journals, and monographs.

The exact interpretation of Lavater's challenge is still debated today. Generally, it is seen as a well-meant but rather awkward attempt at conversion. Some see it as his attempt to engage Mendelssohn in a dialogue concerning faith or immortality. Yet another theory suggests that it was not a traditional attempt to convert Mendelssohn to one of the Christian confessions but rather an invitation to turn to the Messiah of the Scriptures.

Salvation history (*Heilgeschichte*) and, especially, eschatological-apocalyptic themes produced in Lavater a lively theological interest in Judaism. Like many of his contemporaries, he was deeply convinced that the imminently expected millennium would not occur before "the entire Jewish nation" had turned to Christianity or at least that the beginning of the "thousand-year Reich" was tied to a general conversion of the Jews. He voiced this expectation often and eloquently in *Views of Eternity* (*Aussichten in die Ewigkeit*) and his major life's work, the *Physiognomic Fragments* (*Physiognomische Fragmenten*), in which he also made several minor observations concerning Jews. (To do justice to these, it is necessary to refer to the original German text because later editions and translations leave out much or include numerous additions.) He treated the subject first in a section on "national and family physiognomies," the existence of which he had no doubts about. He confessed to only a "very slight knowledge of nationality" and thus relied on others' observations, "contributing nary a mite of his own observations" (4: 267). He quoted a handwritten message from his friend the poet Jakob Lenz. The Jews, according to Lenz, "carry with them the signs of their Oriental homeland into the four corners of the earth," namely, "short, curly black hair and a brown complexion." Their Oriental origin also accounted for their "rapid speech and the hectic, frantic nature of their actions." Lenz also thought that they "in general, possessed more gall than other men." Lavater opined that "the national character of the Jewish countenance included a pointy chin, thick lips, and a well-defined middle line of the mouth" (4: 272–274).

In the fifth section of his traversal of the individual components of the human face, Lavater dealt with the nose, which he thought was the sign of "taste, sensibility, and feeling" (2: 98). Adopting a view that had been widespread since the fifteenth century, Lavater declared that Jews possessed "for the most part, hawk noses" (4: 258). He made a more serious nasal observation in his "hundred physiognomic rules," which, because of possible misuse, was not printed in his lifetime (posthumously published in English in 1804). There, he maintained that noses "arched in the upper part" indicated "fearful" and "voluptuary" character traits. Although he did not relate this passage specifically to Jews, such an association was likely for readers of the *Physiognomic Fragments,* in which there were abundant illustrations of Jewish profiles with hook noses. One illustration was captioned "a hard-hearted rabbi" (4: 367). With observations such as this, Lavater was simply repeating a discriminatory cliché.

Nevertheless, it would be unjust to judge Lavater as anti-Jewish or antisemitic. He sought and recognized the face of God in the face of every human being. Moreover, when Moses Mendelssohn asked him, in 1775, to intervene on behalf of the sorely pressed Jews of the Swiss commacnes of Endingen and Lengly, Lavater responded successfully.

—*Horst Weigelt*
*Richard S. Levy, translation*

**See also** Caricature, Anti-Jewish (Early); Dohm, Christian Wilhelm von; Kant, Immanuel; Michaelis, Johann David; Philosemitism

**References**
Luginbühl-Weber, Gisela. "' . . . zu thun, . . . was Sokrates gethan hätte': Lavater, Mendelssohn und Bonnet über die Unsterblichkeit." In *Das Antlitz Gottes im Antlitz des Menschen: Zugänge zu Johann Kaspar Lavater.* Edited by Karl Pestalozzi and Horst Weigelt (Göttingen, Germany: Vandenhoeck and Ruprecht, 1994), 114–148.
Wechsler, Judith. "Lavater, Stereotype, and Prejudice." In *The Faces of Physiognomy: Interdisciplinary Approaches to Johann Caspar Lavater.* Edited by Ellis Shookman (Columbia, SC: Camden House, 1993), 104–125.

# Le Pen, Jean-Marie (1928– )

When he emerged as a significant player on the French political scene in the early 1980s, Jean-Marie Le Pen displayed strong antisemitic prejudices and went out of his way to make them public. Le Pen followed in a long line of demagogues on the French Far Right. From Gen. Georges Boulanger and Maurice Barrès in the late nineteenth century to Charles Maurras and the leaders of the fascist leagues in the interwar years and Marshal Philippe Pétain and Pierre Poujade in the 1940s and 1950s, France has had its fair share of racists.

But the situation that Le Pen found himself in during the 1980s was different. Society had moved on. No longer was the Jewish Question the dominant issue for those on the Far Right wishing to engage in "racial warfare." For various reasons (the sheer number of North Africans working in France, the color of their skin, and the unflattering stereotypes that had begun to emerge), the "immigrant question" had superseded the Jewish Question. Le Pen and his party, the Front National (FN), have been highly effective in their concerted campaign of hostility toward immigrants, but the suspicion of Jews (French and non-French) regarding his antisemitism persists.

Le Pen and his party have employed a variety of strategies. On one level, they have courted scandal and controversy by making the most outrageous claims. In 1987, the FN leader stated that the Holocaust was a "point of detail" in the history of World War II; in 1988, he derided the government minister Michel Durafour by calling him "Durafour-*Crématoire*"—an allusion to Hitler's gas ovens. And in 1990, he was accused of preparing the political climate that gave rise to the desecration of Jewish graves in the southern town of Carpentras.

The casual observer might conclude that Le Pen is prone to the occasional gaffe, but, in fact, for Le Pen, "all news is good news." He has always survived and sometimes even flourished on the back of negative press. Some observers contend that the FN executes a bizarre publicity stunt every September (when the French political year recommences). The stunt often involves a Jewish element. Le Pen, a man who has made a career out of smashing taboos, is able to detect a "Jewish conspiracy" in every corner and to exploit the publicity thus engendered.

On another level, however, Le Pen and his party have been more covert. They have developed a coded language that has sought to hide the finer points of their antisemitic discourse. Thus, when Le Pen talks about "the lobby," he is talking about the Jewish leadership, and when he uses the phrase "cosmopolitan plot," he is often referring to a Jewish organization. Using this kind of language has enabled him to connect with his natural constituency on the racist Right, and it has, at the same time, helped him to deflect criticism and reduce the number of occasions he is asked to appear in court to defend himself. Le Pen has also argued, as a last line of defense, that his movement includes a number of French Jews in its ranks and thus cannot possibly be antisemitic.

In 2002, Le Pen ran for the French presidency and caused a political earthquake by reaching the second round of balloting for that office. There was never any possibility of him becoming head of state, but the presence of an enthusiastic antisemite in the knockout phase of the election was a startling reminder that France had not yet buried its prejudiced past. What is at least as disturbing is that a small percentage of French Jews,

A young girl waves a French flag during a demonstration at the Pantheon, central Paris, April 28, 2002. Thousands of protesters joined the demonstration called by the Jewish student association and the International League against Racism and Antisemitism (LICRA). (Reuters/Corbis)

perhaps as many as 5 percent (or 20,000 voters), actually backed him in the election. In a period of intense friction between Arabs and Jews, they reasoned that the FN leader was the only candidate promising the mass expulsion of North African immigrants, thus aiding French Jews in their quest for security.

—*Peter J. Davies*

**See also** Action Française; Barrès, Maurice; France; Maurras, Charles; Stavisky Affair; Vichy
**References**
Davies, Peter J. *The National Front in France: Ideology, Discourse and Power* (London: Routledge, 1999).
Marcus, Jonathan. *The National Front and French Politics* (Basingstoke, UK: Macmillan, 1995).
Simmons, Harvey G. *The French National Front: The Extremist Challenge to Democracy* (Boulder, CO: Westview Press, 1996).

## League against Antisemitism

In the 1880s, Germany's antisemitic political parties succeeded in mobilizing sizable sectors of the lower middle class. Their goal of undoing Jewish emancipation posed a danger not only to Jews but also to the liberal political and social values of many other middle-class Germans. Responding to the threat, representatives from the liberal and left-liberal political parties and private individuals of the educated and propertied elite formed the League against Antisemitism (Verein zur Abwehr des Antisemitismus, or Abwehr-Verein) in January 1890.

Although there were always a considerable number of Jewish members in the organization, leadership of the Abwehr-Verein remained in the hands of non-Jewish intellectuals, who continued to set the tone for the forty-three years of its existence. That this was a gentile initiative was clear from the inaugural announcement of the league, signed by 535 Christians who declared it a matter of honor for the German people and especially for Christians to combat the un-Christian activities of the antisemites that menaced the well-being of the fatherland. The fight against antisemitism and the defense of the rights of Jews were not the primary objectives. Rather, the league worked to safeguard the public sphere of the German Empire and to uphold the rule of law. Although it never functioned as a Jewish interest group—a constant and entirely predictable accusation of the antisemites—the Abwehr-Verein made it one of its important goals to turn the de jure equality of Jewish citizens, including the freedom to practice their religion, into a practical reality. Repeatedly, members of the league who sat in the Reichstag and state parliaments admonished the government to live up to the constitution and to appoint qualified Jews to civil service and military positions.

As was the case with the Central Association of German Citizens of Jewish Faith, the Abwehr-Verein attributed antisemitism to intellectual backwardness and believed that the struggle against antisemitism had to be fought with the honorable weapons of public enlightenment. To this end, in 1892, the league began publishing the *Antisemites' Mirror* (*Antisemiten-Spiegel*), a handbook of reliable information about the antisemitic parties, interest groups, and press. Further, its weekly newspaper, brochures, pamphlets, and public lectures countered the propaganda of the antisemites, presented logical arguments against their racist theorizing, and generally endeavored to present them in the worst possible light. A free correspondence service regularly provided German newspapers with accurate information about the activities of the antisemites. At election time, the candidates of the Conservative Party received special attention, especially after the party adopted an antisemitic plank in its Tivoli Program (in 1892).

At the outbreak of World War I, it was hoped that the loyal service of Jews to their German fatherland would put an end to antisemitism once and for all. But by the close of 1915, the league leadership regretfully recognized that it would have to struggle on against antisemitic calumnies. Supportive of Weimar democracy, the organization continued to condemn antisemitism as a fundamental danger to the German people and polity. It presented the antisemites as unpatriotic because they damaged Germany's reputation abroad and hindered its conduct of foreign policy, including attempts to ameliorate the harsh conditions imposed by the Versailles Treaty.

Overcoming a serious economic crisis during the period of German hyperinflation, the Abwehr-Verein kept producing a steady list of publications, including the *Abwehr-ABC* and numerous enlightenment works aimed at a mass audience. Members and leaders spoke out against the rising number of cemetery and synagogue desecrations and against acts of physical violence that victimized Jews. In the ending phase of the republic, the National Socialists and their radical racist antisemitism stood at the center of the organization's antidefamation work. For the Reichstag elections of 1930, the league campaigned under the slogan "No votes for Nazis," holding Germans who voted for the National Socialist German Workers' Party (NSDAP) responsible for the ultimate decline of the country.

Mounting threats from the Nazis drove the Abwehr-Verein to assume a defensive posture. The direct combat with fascism gave way to a behind-the-scenes attempt to influence the opinion of important people. To the end, the organization kept faith in the powers of reason, justice, and truth to defeat Nazism. After the Nazis assumed power in January 1933, the Abwehr-Verein ceased all activity, voluntarily disbanding on July 7, 1933.

—*Gregor Hufenreuter*
*Richard S. Levy, translation*

**See also** Antisemitic Political Parties; Central Association of German Citizens of Jewish Faith; Desecration of Cemeteries and Synagogues in Germany since 1919; Emancipation; National Socialist German Workers' Party; Racism, Scientific; Tivoli Program; Versailles Treaty

**References**

Suchy, Barbara. "The *Verein zur Abwehr des Antisemitismus* (1)—From Its Beginnings to the First World War," *Leo Baeck Institute Year Book* 28 (1983): 205–239.
———. "The *Verein zur Abwehr des Antisemitismus* (2)—From the First World War to Its Dissolution in 1933," *Leo Baeck Institute Year Book* 30 (1985): 67–103.

# Léon, Abram (1918–1944)

Biographical information on Abram Léon is sketchy, provided by a fellow member of the

Trotskyite Fourth International, Ernest Mandel, in the introduction to the first edition of Léon's posthumously published *Materialist Concept of the Jewish Question* (1946). Léon was born Abraham Wajnsztok in Warsaw in 1918. His family returned to Poland after a failed emigration to Palestine between 1924 and 1925 and finally settled in Belgium in 1926. There, Léon became an activist in the socialist Zionist youth organization Hashomer Hatsair (the Young Guard) and, according to Mandel, also chaired the Belgian Zionist Federation for a year. In 1940, already in contact with the Trotskyites and increasingly disenchanted with Zionism, he presented his *Theses on the Jewish Question,* a first draft of the published text he finally completed in December 1942, to his associates in Hashomer Hatsair. By the time of the German invasion of the Lowlands in May 1940, he had abandoned Zionism and finally thrown in his lot with the Trotskyites. He helped reestablish the movement's illegal Belgian organization during the Occupation, acting as its political secretary; editing its periodical, *Lenin's Way;* and maintaining the organization's international contacts. Arrested in Charleroi in June 1944, he was viciously tortured before being deported to Auschwitz, where he died in the gas chamber later that year.

Léon's economist reductionism was clearly overdetermined by his wish to purge himself of Zionism's formative influence on him. Far from being the logical result of an impartial "materialist" analysis along Marxist lines, his anti-Zionism was, in fact, the impulse that had led Léon to embark on his supposedly Marxist analysis in the first place, and hence, it fundamentally shaped (and constrained) his particular brand of materialist analysis from the outset. He radicalized Marx's contention that the religious identity of Jewry was a reflection of its distinct socioeconomic function, by concluding that Jews maintained a distinct identity only where they played a distinct socioeconomic role.

Thus, he contended, everywhere the Jews were discernible as an entity, they also formed a separate class, and any animosity toward them was invariably a reflection of a genuine class antagonism. Jewry's socioeconomic role was, in fact, integral to precapitalist societies. With the emergence of capitalism proper, it lost this role. In the West, capitalism had afforded the integration and assimilation of the Jews. Elsewhere, it had rendered Jewry's previous socioeconomic role precarious without allowing the Jews to integrate. Now that capitalism was heading toward its ultimate demise, the absorption of the displaced Jews was beyond its reach altogether. Imperialism translated this failure into an ideology of superiority vis-à-vis the Jews as an ostensible antirace at home, a notion that complemented its view of racial superiority with regard to colonized peoples.

At that moment in history, Léon argued, modern antisemitism differed from previous forms of anti-Jewish animosity that had expressed a genuine class antagonism. It was the utter groundlessness of the current persecution of the Jews, however, that would prompt the working class, parts of which initially subscribed to antisemitism, finally to overcome its reservations regarding the Jews.

Léon's analytical approach does not seem to have placed him in a privileged position as he grappled with his own desperate situation. Otherwise, he could hardly have made the astonishing claim, while the Nazis' Final Solution unfolded around him, that nothing substantial would ultimately change for the Jews if Hitler disappeared.

—*Lars Fischer*

**See also** Jewish Question; Marx, Karl; Socialists on Antisemitism; Zionism
**References**
Léon, Abram. *The Jewish Question: A Marxist Interpretation.* Introduction by Ernest Germain [Ernest Mandel]. (Mexico City: Ediciones Pioneras, 1950).

# Leskov, Nikolai Semenovich (1831–1895)

Nikolai Leskov was one of Russia's most important prose writers. A master of the short story, he was noted for his sophisticated handling of narration, his stylistic virtuosity, and the diversity of plots and characters he presented, often drawn from little-known social and ethnic milieus. His attitude toward Jews and the Jewish Question has been a subject of considerable debate, principally centered on several short stories in which the main characters are Jewish.

The complexity of Leskov's prose, especially his use of multiple narrators, argues for caution in trying to extract an ideological message from his fiction and attempting to judge to what degree the views of his protagonists coincided with their creator's. Still, there is little doubt that the stories "Rakushanskii melamed" (The Melamed of Österreich [1878]) and "Zhidovskaia kuvyrkollegiia" (Yid Somersault [1882]) exploit and reinforce anti-Jewish stereotypes. In the 1878 story, the *melamed* (religious school teacher) Skharia has acquired wealth thanks to his learnedness that "kills the spirit," his reputation for holiness (derived from a superstitious, fanatical adherence to ritual), and his rascally business practices. The 1882 story, "the most vicious thing Leskov ever wrote" (McLean 1977, 422), is an extended anecdote about how a trio of Jewish conscripts in Tsar Nicholas I's army feigned an inability to fire a gun, how repeated beatings failed to convince them to abandon their trickery, and how they were finally "cured" by a clever Russian soldier. Although representatives of other ethnic groups are also presented in uncomplimentary terms, the story emphasizes the pervasiveness of Jewish trickery, treats the beatings matter-of-factly, and refers to the pogroms of the early 1880s in a way that shifts the blame from the victimizers to the victims.

These two texts may be contrasted with "Vladychnyi sud" (Episcopal Justice [1877]), in which Leskov strongly condemns the forced conscription of Jewish children during Nicholas I's reign and the hapless Jewish protagonist, a bookbinder threatened with the loss of his son, is transformed by the end of the narrative into a near saint (and a Christian convert). Even here, however, Leskov's attitude toward Jews is ambiguous: his narrator is surely right to criticize the Jewish community's manipulation of conscription rules for the benefit of the powerful and the wealthy, yet his rhetoric is more vehement than the situation calls for ("the limitless cruelty of Yid falsehood and trickery, practiced in all possible ways").

"Melamed" and "Somersault" contrast strikingly with Leskov's sympathetic discussion of Jewish religious holidays and other aspects of Judaism in nearly thirty newspaper pieces. There is also his remarkable pamphlet *The Jew in Russia: Some Notes on the Jewish Question* (which appeared, unsigned and in limited circulation, in 1884 and was republished in 1919 as *The Jews in Russia*). Commissioned by a group of prominent Petersburg Jews, it was presented as a private report to the Pahlen Commission, charged with developing measures to prevent a repetition of the pogroms of 1881. In this piece, Leskov strongly defended the Jewish community against hostile accusations and called for Jews to be given full equality before the law: if Russia would "start to treat her Jews as a mother and not as a stepmother, then they would . . . become her loyal sons." Finally, there is the didactic "Tale of Theodore the Christian and His Friend Abraham the Hebrew" of 1886, a reworking of a medieval text. Set in fourth-century Byzantium, the story offered so clear-cut a message of tolerance and full equality between Jews and Christians that it provoked Konstantin Pobedonostsev, the reactionary procurator of the Holy Synod, to prevent its distribution in mass editions.

—Henryk Baran

*See also* Dostoevsky, Fyodor; Emancipation; Jewish Question; Pobedonostsev, Konstantin; Pogroms; Russia, Imperial

**References**
Edgerton, William B. "Review of *Nikolai Leskov* (Hugh McLean)," *Comparative Literature* 3 (1980): 313–318.
McLean, Hugh. *Nikolai Leskov: The Man and His Art* (Cambridge, MA: Harvard University Press, 1977).
Safran, Gabriella. *Rewriting the Jew: Assimilation Narratives in the Russian Empire* (Stanford, CA: Stanford University Press, 2000), chap. 3.

## Leuchter Report

An allegedly scientific document that was first published in Canada in 1988, the *Leuchter Report* determined that the facilities in the Auschwitz, Birkenau, and Majdanek concentration camps were incapable of mass annihilation. The author, Fred Leuchter of Boston, claimed to be a specialist in constructing and installing execution apparatus in U.S. prisons. He was hired by the German Canadian Holocaust denier Ernst Zündel to be an expert witness at his trial in April 1988; Zündel was prosecuted by the Canadian government both in 1984 and 1988 for knowingly disseminating false information on the Holocaust. Before the trial, with Zündel's financial assistance, Leuchter spent eight days in Poland, where he visited Auschwitz, Birkenau, and Majdanek and illegally collected "forensic samples," mainly bricks and cement fragments for chemical analysis. Based on his findings, the alleged blueprints of the camps, and the samples, he claimed that gas chambers in these camps were never used for mass extermination.

The allegation that the gas chambers in Nazi concentration camps in general and in Auschwitz in particular were used only for disinfection purposes was not new. It was raised a few years after the war by one of the first European Holocaust deniers, the French fascist Maurice Bardèche, and from then on, it appeared in numerous Holocaust denial publications.

During Zündel's trial, it was established that Leuchter's claim to be an engineer was fraudulent, and the court rejected his testimony as an expert witness. In addition, after the trial, researchers and educators, notably Shelly Z. Shapiro, revealed that Leuchter had misled the court about his knowledge of the characteristics and effects of the gas used to exterminate Jews, Zyklon B. It was also revealed that he had no experience in the construction of gas chambers. Yet even though the report's "science" and its author's credentials have been exposed as bogus, the *Leuchter Report* continues to impress people who ought to know better. Even a German minister of justice, Eberhard Engelhardt, once called the document "scientifically correct," and it was only after many angry protests that he admitted his error.

In spite of the facts, the *Leuchter Report,* like many antisemitic frauds, took on a life of its own among antisemites and Holocaust deniers and became a landmark of great significance in the history of Holocaust denial. It was espoused by deniers such as Robert Faurisson and David Irving, who characterized it as a major breakthrough for those "seeking the truth" because now their claim had allegedly been proved scientifically.

—*Roni Stauber*

*See also* Auschwitz Lie; Bardèche, Maurice; Faurisson, Robert; Holocaust Denial, Negationism, and Revisionism; Irving, David; Zündel, Ernst

**References**

Lipstadt, Deborah E. *Denying the Holocaust: the Growing Assault on Truth and Memory.* Reprint ed. (New York: Plume, 1994).

Shapiro, Shelly. *Truth Prevails: Demolishing Holocaust Denial: The End of "The Leuchter Report"* (New York: Beate Klarsfeld Foundation, 1990).

## Liberty Lobby

The Liberty Lobby was founded in 1957 by antisemitic agitator and publisher Willis Carto as an umbrella organization for his many publishing, business, political, media, and propaganda enterprises. Carto's monthly *Liberty Letter* was the lobby's initial publication and circulated widely within ultra-right-wing and neo-Nazi circles. As his following grew, Carto diversified into specialized publications. *Liberty Lowdown* gave special "inside news" to generous financial contributors; *Western Destiny* concentrated on matters of race and geopolitics; the *Washington Observer* gave his unique take on national politics, with special emphasis on the machinations of the left-wing conspirators Carto saw as controlling most of the nation's affairs. Strong anti-Israel positions appeared regularly in all Liberty Lobby publications.

By the mid-1960s, the Liberty Lobby flourished as the largest and most active generator of ultra-right-wing literature in the United States. Carto's holdings included facilities to publish books, magazines, newspapers, pamphlets, broadsides, and flyers. Although its publications were never as crude as the literature published by George Lincoln Rockwell, Carto's close friend and contemporary, the Liberty Lobby generated a consistent flow of material that attempted to mask raw antisemitism by presenting it as an objective revision of history. This thrust was particularly evident in Carto's obsession with disseminating Holocaust denial material.

In 1966, Carto bought the over-the-hill *American Mercury,* once the most highly regarded right-wing publication in the country. In 1975, he gave the Liberty Lobby's eighteen-year-old *Liberty Letter* a major facelift, renaming it the *National Spotlight* and bringing it out as a well-illustrated magazine. The *National Spotlight* (the name was later shortened to *Spotlight*) continued to promote Carto's antisemitic and racist beliefs without the overt crudity that marked similar publications. That restraint earned it greater market acceptance than comparable productions. The Liberty Lobby continued to lead other similar organizations in media innovation, venturing into syndicated radio programming in the 1970s and moving on to the Internet in the 1990s.

—*Frederick J. Simonelli*

**See also** Carto, Willis; Holocaust Denial, Negationism, and Revisionism; Internet; Militia Movement; Rockwell, George Lincoln; White Power Movement

**References**

Flynn, Kevin, and Gary Gerhardt. *The Silent Brotherhood* (New York: Signet, 1990).

Mintz, Frank P. *The Liberty Lobby and the American Right: Race, Conspiracy and Culture* (Westport, CT: Greenwood Press, 1985).

## LICA—International League against Antisemitism

LICA—the Ligue Internationale contre l'Antisémitisme, or International League against Antisemitism—was founded in Paris in 1928 at a time when antisemitism was a presence in daily political life and the basis of mass movements. Its founder, Bernard Lecache, gathered around himself a host of celebrities: Albert Einstein, who had already had a foretaste of antisemitism in Germany; the feminist Séverine; writers and performers such as Josephine Baker, the Countess Noailles, Romain Rolland, and Joseph Kessel; and the politicians Edvard Beneš, Tomàš Masaryk, and Léon Blum. By 1931, LICA numbered over 10,000 members. Activists conducted a campaign of enlightenment regarding antisemitism. They also formed self-defense groups to protect individuals who were the frequent targets of racist and radical-rightist attacks.

When the Nazis assumed power in Germany in 1933, the league concentrated its efforts on caring for refugees and counteracting the effects of Nazism on French political life. It was at this juncture that Sigmund Freud and George Bernard Shaw joined the organization. During World War II, whenever possible, members joined the ranks of the Resistance or the Free French of Charles de Gaulle. Committed enemies of the Nazis, several active members of LICA were deported and murdered.

After the war, LICA's mission focused on stopping human rights violations before they started. This program included pursuing the history of the Shoah and working for the abolition of the statute of limitations on crimes against humanity. It also entailed intervening in current French colonial policies and against racist attacks on minority groups and the denial of their rights anywhere in the world.

One of the league's greatest successes came shortly before the outbreak of World War II, when the French government, responding to LICA's demand, adopted legislation that made it possible to prosecute racist defamation. The tightening of these laws in July 1972 conferred special status on the organization, allowing it to represent victims of racist defamation and discrimination in court—a significant achievement.

In 1979, recognizing a more universal task, the organization renamed itself the League against Racism and Antisemitism (LICRA). Today, it pursues the general aim of achieving a humane existence and a just society for all, regardless of religion, heritage, or legal status. *The Right to Live,* the longtime journal of the league, devotes itself to discussions of the rights and problems of minorities, discrimination against those minorities, and the ways and means of overcoming injustice in society. LICRA's jurists continue to work on expanding antiracist legislation. The organization's teaching members offer seminars on the Shoah and on current events. One of LICRA's most recent accomplishments is the founding of the European School for Human Rights, which promotes a conscious engagement in the struggle for the rights of humanity.

—*Alexander Schürmann-Emanuely*

**See also** Crimes against Humanity (French Trials); France; Freud, Sigmund; Vichy

**References**

Allali, Jean-Pierre, and Haim Musicant. *Des Hommes libres: Histories extraordinaires de l'histoire de la LICRA* (Paris: Bibliophane, 1987).

Vérard, René. *Jean Pierre-Bloch: Un Français du monde entier* (Orléans, France: Corsaire, 1997).

## Liebermann von Sonnenberg, Max (1848–1911)

An extreme nationalist, militarist, and accomplished orator of the patriotic school, Max Hugo Liebermann von Sonnenberg played a key role in the creation of party-political antisemitism in the German Empire. He was born into a landless noble family in West Prussia and served in the 1870–1871 Franco-Prussian War but then fell victim to the crash of 1873 and was forced to resign from the army when he could not meet his debts. Aggrieved at the loss of his military career and blaming unnamed "usurers," he began to participate in the politics of protest, helping to organize the Antisemites' Petition in 1880 and joining the Berlin Movement in the following year. This uneasy alliance of radicals and conservatives that aimed at loosening the left-liberal grip on the capital's politics gave him practical experience in organization and antisemitic agitation, which he used to form his own political apparatus. His grassroots "reform club," the German National Union (Deutscher Volksverein), lasted just long enough to afford him prominence at the international antisemitic congresses of the early 1880s and, in 1889, to also found the German Social Party (Deutschsoziale Partei). Liebermann used this institutional base to navigate the treacherous currents of antisemitic politics in the German Empire. He sat in the Reichstag from 1890 until his death in 1911 and remained the movement's most durable and visible spokesman.

With his class and nationalist credentials and his solicitude for the respectability of the antisemitic enterprise, Liebermann typified the conventional, socially acceptable form of political antisemitism of the period. He rapidly became a fixture in what the historian George Mosse aptly termed the "interlocking directorate of the Right." Liebermann regularly addressed the raucous meetings of the Agrarian League pressure group, cultivated the antisemitic Association of German Students, and served as a high-profile, trusted member of the racist-nationalist Pan-German League. In his speeches to these groups, in the Reichstag, and on the campaign trail, he espoused a middle-of-the-road antisemitism. The disenfranchisement of the Jews, achieved within the framework of German law, was the substance of his program. Political agitation, the growth of the antisemitic movement, and the election of antisemites to the Reichstag would enable the passage of legislation to remove Jewish influence from German public life. Unlike the radicals in the movement and at its fringes, Liebermann insisted that no revolutionary changes in the German economy, educational system, or cultural life needed to be considered. He repeatedly used his authority to keep antisemitic radicals and rowdies at bay. In 1894, for example, he wrested control of the antisemites' major newspaper, the *Antisemitic Correspondence* (*Antisemitische-Correspondenz*), away from Theodor Fritsch. Fritsch's dabbling in religious "purification" movements that would replace or at least de-Judaize Christianity threatened to alienate the antisemites' powerful conservative allies, according to Liebermann.

When the Nazis wrote the history of this early period of political antisemitism in Germany, they did not acknowledge Liebermann as a founding father. They viewed his stodgy Protestant conservatism and antilabor politics as errors (that Adolf Hitler rectified). Unwilling to recruit the "traitorous" Catholic and working-class masses of the population, Liebermann's conventional antisemitism resulted in an isolated movement with too narrow a social base to accomplish any part of its program.

—*Richard S. Levy*

**See also** Agrarian League; Antisemites' Petition; *Antisemitic Correspondence;* Antisemitic Political Parties; Berlin Movement; Fritsch, Theodor; German Students, Association of; Pan-German League

**References**
Levy, Richard S. *The Downfall of the Anti-Semitic Political Parties in Imperial Germany* (New Haven, CT: Yale University Press, 1975).
Massing, Paul W. *Rehearsal for Destruction: A Study of Political Anti-Semitism in Imperial Germany* (New York: Harper and Brothers, 1949).

## Lienhard, Friedrich (1865–1929)

Friedrich Lienhard was an Alsatian German novelist, dramatist, and publicist who devoted his career to promoting conservative and nationalist values in a variety of genres. He saw himself as a defender of "German idealism" and traditional literary forms against modernistic aesthetic movements such as naturalism or expressionism, as well as political movements of the Left. His publications reached a wide middle-class readership in the late imperial era and in the 1920s, but his literary reputation did not long survive his death in 1929.

Lienhard strongly identified with the conservative literary reaction against foreign influences in Germany in the 1890s, particularly the naturalism of Émile Zola and the psychological realism of Henrik Ibsen. Frustrated by his failure to achieve literary success, Lienhard coined the catchphrase *los von Berlin* (away from Berlin) in 1903 and settled in the central German town of Weimar. From there, he issued a steady stream of lamentations about the degeneration of German life and literature as a result of the growing dominance of modern urban intellectual culture in which Jews played what he considered a disproportionate role. With Adolf Bartels, he founded the short-lived nativist *Heimatkunst* (art of the homeland) movement to promote a more "natural" literary form than the allegedly artificial, theoretical, and hypercritical output of the literary avant-garde. Lienhard preferred, however, to characterize his own literary endeavors as *Höhenkunst* (art of the highlands). From a synthesis of Protestant Christianity, German classicism, and Nordic Germanicism, he sought to create a usable ideology for mass consumption, which he disseminated in his six-volume *Wege nach Weimar* (Paths to Weimar [1905–1908]). His most popular novels were *Oberlin* (1910) and *Der Spielmann* (1913), which appeared in numerous editions up to 1940. He also wrote several bombastic historical dramas in the Wagnerian mode.

Lienhard's antisemitism derived from his equation of Jewishness with modernism and materialism. He did not hesitate to label as Jewish all movements that he defined as materialistic, whether philosophical, aesthetic, or political, even when a majority of their proponents or practitioners were not of Jewish origin. He ascribed the rise of political doctrines such as liberalism and socialism, as well as the growing secularization of society, to the inordinate influence

of Jews. His refusal, however, to accept racial or biological determinism, which, in his view, represented just another form of materialism, led to a break with his erstwhile collaborator Adolf Bartels. Nor did he subscribe to the conspiracy theories with which right-wing extremists sought to justify their campaign of violence and assassination after World War I.

Yet while advocating spiritualism, quietism, and Jewish assimilation, Lienhard continued to disseminate antisemitic attitudes after the war as editor of the conservative Protestant monthly *Der Türmer* (The Watchman in the Tower). He viewed the Jewish Question as a test of Germany's strength to assert its own character in the face of alien influences. Despite his rejection of racial determinism, he shared the racist assumption that the presence of a separate Jewish community in Germany constituted a major social problem.

—*Roderick Stackelberg*

**See also** Bartels, Adolf; Chamberlain, Houston Stewart; Lange, Friedrich; Zola, Émile
**References**
Stackelberg, Roderick. *Idealism Debased: From Völkisch Idealism to National Socialism* (Kent, OH: Kent State University Press, 1981).

# Lindbergh, Charles (1902–1974)

Charles Lindbergh always denied that he was an antisemite. His reputation for being one, however, warrants his inclusion in an encyclopedia devoted to the subject of antisemitism. It also raises questions about the use of the term.

In the aftermath of his first visit to Germany in 1936, Lindbergh often praised German accomplishments in military aviation. And in 1938, he received a medal from the German government for his own aeronautical efforts, notably the 1927 cross-Atlantic flight.

But the primary evidence for thinking Lindbergh was antisemitic came in a speech he delivered under the auspices of the America First Committee in Des Moines, Iowa, on September 11, 1941. In that speech, which opposed U.S. involvement in the war already under way in Europe, Lindbergh singled out the British, the Roosevelt administration, and the Jews as the "major agitators for war." Although he sympathized with the Jews' desire for "the overthrow of Nazi Germany," Lindbergh expressed concern over "their large ownership and influence in our motion pictures, our press, our radio, and our government."

Rage over those comments was widespread, fueled by the memory of his earlier remarks about Germany. The America First Committee itself was divided and embarrassed, and Lindbergh's reputation was severely damaged. In giving voice to a stereotype frequently uttered by well-known antisemites in Europe and the United States, he had, it seemed, announced who he really was.

But had he? No one who ever knew Lindbergh thought him antisemitic. Nor had he ever spoken before—or would he again—about Jews. These negatives, of course, prove nothing; they do, however, require that the words, their context, and the man himself be more carefully considered.

The debate over American involvement in the war was the bitterest war debate ever conducted in the United States. Fear, suspicion, and hyperbole were its hallmarks. Two of the groups Lindbergh mentioned, the British and the Roosevelt administration, were widely thought to want the United States to enter the war. To have believed in 1941 that the Jews also favored U.S. entry made sense, even though a poll would have shown that the Jewish community was divided over the question. The stereotype, moreover, of Jewish power and influence was not without truth, as is often the case with stereotypes. Jews did control most Hollywood studios, own the premier newspaper in the United States, and occupy important positions in the Roosevelt administration. One could, therefore, imagine they had influence. Lindbergh did and believed that he was simply reporting facts. His critics assumed he was deliberately espousing and inducing prejudice. As Rabbi Irving F. Reichart of Temple Emanu-El of San Francisco commented, "Hitler himself could not have delivered a more diabolical speech" (Berg 1998, 428).

Lindbergh never apologized for his remarks. He believed that what he had said was true, and he would not disavow the truth to gain public approval. Naive, impolitic, and self-confident to a fault, he did not suppose that words that others used for their purposes, and still others interpreted for theirs, could not be used for his own. He suffered greatly for making this mistake. But his critics, then and now, have continued to make their own mistake in thinking that words, unexamined for their context, can tell us what is in a soul.

—*Jonathan Marwil*

*See also* United States
*References*
Berg, A. Scott. *Lindbergh* (New York: G. P. Putnam's Sons, 1998).
Cole, Wayne S. *Charles Lindbergh and the Battle against American Intervention in World War II* (New York: Harcourt Brace Jovanovich, 1974).

## Linz Program (1882)

The Linz Program of September 1, 1882, was the initial political and ideological platform for the German-National Association (Deutschnationaler Verein), which had been founded three months earlier by, among others, Georg von Schönerer, the Pan-German deputy to the Reichsrat (parliament); the writer Engelbert Pernerstorfer; the (Jewish) physician Viktor Adler; the lawyer Robert Pattai; and the German-National historian Heinrich Friedjung. That future representatives of the Social Democratic Party Adler and Pernerstorfer, as well as the future Christian Social deputy Pattai, were among its initiators proves that, at that time, bourgeois German-Nationalist, Social Democratic, and even Christian Social ideologies were not considered incompatible. What made cooperation possible was the mutual antagonism of these elements toward the dominant economic liberalism.

The intended function of the Linz Program, however, was to unify the heterogeneous elements of the German-National movement. The focus of its eleven articles was the reinforcement of German supremacy in Austria, as well as a stricter separation of the Austrian and Hungarian parts of the empire. According to the Linz Program, the German language was to become the official language of Austria (Cisleithanian lands): every civil servant had to be able to speak German, and German was to become a compulsory subject in all elementary schools. Demands such as these were amplified by the call for a state treaty to strengthen the alliance with the German Empire. These pronouncedly nationalist planks of the Linz Program were accompanied by politically liberal statements that favored the extension of suffrage and freedom of expression, as well as economically antiliberal measures to render the state "independent of financial powers." Among these were implementation of a progressive income tax, establishment of a common customs area for the Habsburg and German Empires, nationalization of railways and insurance companies, and restrictions on female and child labor.

The original programmatic statement of 1882 made negative reference to "financial powers" (*Geldmächte*); this could be read both as explicit anticapitalism and implicit antisemitism. In 1885, Schönerer removed any lingering doubts by adding a twelfth article that pointedly called for the "elimination of Jewish influence in all spheres of public life" as an "indispensable" precondition for the other reforms advocated in the Linz Program. The explicit injection of antisemitism in the program marked an important moment in the history of the German-National movement, when, under Schönerer's growing influence, a liberal form of nationalism succumbed to the more extreme form of racist (*völkisch*), ethnically based nationalism.

It is fair to say that the original focus of the Linz Program had been national and socioeconomic, with "racial" questions playing a quite minor role. The explicitly antisemitic Article 12 of 1885, however, led in a different direction and provoked the withdrawal of Adler and Pernerstorfer. Schönerer had achieved his goal—but at a cost. The Linz Program could no longer serve as the foundation for a broadly based German-National party.

—*Werner Suppanz*

*See also* Austria; Christian Social Party (Austria); Pan-Germans (Austria); Schönerer, Georg von
**References**
Pauley, Bruce F. *From Prejudice to Persecution: A History of Austrian Anti-Semitism* (Chapel Hill: University of North Carolina Press, 1992).
Sottopietra, Doris. *Variationen eines Vorurteils: Eine Entwicklungsgeschichte des Antisemitismus in Österreich* (Vienna: Passagen, 1997).

## List, Guido von (1848–1919)

Part Pan-German propagandist, part mystagogue, Guido von List authored a number of books that proclaimed the supremacy of the Aryan race. They included his first success, the two-volume novel *Carnuntum* (1888), as well as *Deutsche-Mythologische Landschaftsbilder* (German-Mythological Landscape Portraits [1891]), *Ostaras Einzug* (Ostara's Arrival [1896]), and *Das Geheimnis der Runen* (The Secret of the Runes [1908]), which, according to an eyewitness account, Hitler read and praised shortly after it appeared. Through these works, List acquired a devoted following, and this, in turn, enabled him to found several semisecret societies or mystical orders, among them: the Armanship (in 1907)—according to List, the Armans were a pre-Christian "noble race of people"—and the High Armans' Revelation (in 1911). These organizations had contact with (and invite comparison to) other nationalistic antisemitic groups of the time. In 1907, List's disciples brought the Viennese Guido von List Society into being. But above all, List is known as the popularizer of the swastika as the "secret" symbol of an "invincible" Aryan savior.

Born in 1848, List spent his life in Vienna. Although, as mentioned, his first literary success came in 1888, his career as a writer took a decisive turn toward the prolific fifteen years later, when he temporarily went blind. He believed that, while blind, he had epiphanic visions, which revealed to him the true meaning of old Germanic symbols. He immediately attempted to gain official recognition for his new knowledge by submitting a manuscript to the Austrian Imperial Academy of the Sciences in 1903. Its rejection failed to deter him. In such works as *Die Rita der Ariogermanen* (The Rite of the Aryo-Germans [1909]), he presented himself as the true custodian of old Germanic laws and called for their revival. More specifically, he proposed that as a ritual humiliation the donkey ride for adulterous women be instituted, along with the requirement that all Jews wear a special "Jewish hat."

In contrast to his more famous Austrian contemporaries Karl Lueger and Georg von Schönerer, List never advocated a coherent antisemitic political program or became formally in-

ein Starke von oben·

Portrait of Guido von List pictured in front of the swastika he helped popularize. His Nordic mysticism may have influenced Adolf Hitler in his Vienna years. (Charles Walker/Topfoto/The Image Works )

volved in politics. And unlike his acolyte Jörg Lanz von Liebenfels, he had no scientific pretensions. But race was one of his central themes. And he railed against the threat of miscegenation as vehemently as any exponent of biological antisemitism, if also in more oracular terms. Although List's idiosyncratic antisemitism belongs in its own category, that category connects directly with larger, more fateful modes of antisemitism. For an obvious example, it fed into the antisemitic organization that made his secret Aryan symbol into one of the world's most recognizable icons.

—*Paul Reitter*

**See also** Austria; Bayreuth Circle; Hitler, Adolf; Kralik, Richard von; Lanz von Lanz, Jörg; Lateran Council, Fourth; Lueger, Karl; Pan-Germans (Austria); Schönerer, Georg von; Thule Society; Yellow Badge

**References**
Goodrick-Clark, Nicholas. *The Occult Roots of Nazism: Secret Aryan Cults and Their Influence on Nazi Ideology* (New York: New York University Press, 1994).
Haman, Brigitte. *Hitler's Vienna: A Dictator's Apprenticeship* (London and New York: Oxford University Press, 1999).

## Lithuania

The earliest record of Jews in Lithuania, known as the Litvaks, comes from a Jewish cemetery in Eišiškės where a tombstone with a date of 1170 is located. In 1388, Vytautas the Great, Grand Duke of Lithuania, granted Jews who had immigrated from the West a charter of privileges, making them free and dependent on the ruler's justice, rights similar to those enjoyed by the gentry. Through most of their history in the land, Jews remained deeply immersed in their own vibrant, religiously based culture, taking little part in the life of the larger polity. Although, thanks to their ties to Jewish communities all over Europe, they served as a cultural conduit between western Europe and Lithuania during the Middle Ages, they spoke Yiddish rather than Lithuanian and related to the Christian population only in the economic sphere. By the late fifteenth century, Jews had prospered enough to purchase the right to sell alcohol and salt, take tolls on bridges, and collect custom duties. With their rise came the first signs of active prejudice. In 1495, Grand Duke Alexander (r. 1492–1506) expelled the Jews from Lithuania, confiscated their wealth, and paid his debts with the proceeds. By 1503, Alexander, now also king of Poland (r. 1501–1506), allowed them to return to Lithuania but did not restore their property.

Early Lithuania produced a number of myths about the Jews that persisted into the twentieth century. Lithuanian peasants believed that Jews had supernatural powers to subvert the effects of the sacraments; they lacked souls and had congress with the devil. Spoken Lithuanian makes use of the diminutive, which, although linguistically neutral, can also have a comical or derisive connotation. Thus, the word *žydas* (Jew) can be transformed into *žydelis* (little Jew), not a term of endearment. Lithuanian folk culture produced a plethora of sayings, jokes, and warnings about Jews.

By the seventeenth century, Lithuanian Jews

began to live in separate Jewish quarters, and their activities as moneylenders, pawnbrokers, and jobbers allowed them to establish the first bank in Vilnius. Jews usually dealt with the Polonized nobility and burghers. In their contact with the Lithuanian peasantry, the economic realm was the most likely point of friction. For example, until 1890, when the Russian government instituted a state monopoly on vodka, Lithuanians knew the Jews primarily as tavern owners and associated them with various other exploitative middleman functions. The Jewish population living in ethnographic Lithuania rapidly expanded in the nineteenth century because of the caarist government's creation of the Pale of Jewish Settlement, which limited Jews to the western provinces of Russia and further restricted them to urban areas. In the cities and towns, they engaged in vocational trades, which led to an ever-increasing tension between non-Jewish and Jewish craftspeople.

The nineteenth century also spawned an extreme form of integral nationalism reinforced by religious intolerance. Some of the activists of the Lithuanian national revival began to write antisemitic articles in underground newspapers such as *Auszra* (Dawn) and *Varpas* (Bell). With articles including "Us and the Jews" and satirical pieces such as "Why the Jews Don't Eat Pork," these activists perpetuated the image of the Jew as the Other. Lithuanians saw Jews as dishonest merchants and, more important, as foreigners. Although the Poles and Russians were the objects of much popular hatred, Lithuanians still considered them people, but "Jews were Jews"—belonging to a special category all their own. Unlike the Poles or the Russians, Jews were a minority without a state to protect them and therefore were especially vulnerable to discrimination.

Modern antisemitism intensified as the Lithuanian national revival began to gain strength in the 1860s. Seeking an end to Russian domination, activists demanded national equality, the reestablishment of a Lithuanian press, and the preservation of their language. "Lithuania for the Lithuanians" became their motto. Because many secularized Jews (a small minority of the Jewish population) identified with Russian culture, the Lithuanian nationalist press began to

portray Jews in general as traitors to the national cause, parasites who fostered Russification.

In 1918, Lithuania gained its independence, but along with freedom, a new, disturbing element entered into the relationship between Jews and Lithuanians. Most Jews had remained indifferent to the establishment of a democratic Lithuania, but a very few had participated in the attempt to establish a communist government. This action, no matter how unrepresentative of the Jewish population as a whole, fueled a new, popular, and ultimately destructive stereotype—the Jewish Bolshevik.

But there were many hopeful signs accompanying the birth of a sovereign Lithuania as well. After independence, Jews started to participate in Lithuania's political and cultural life as never before. The prime minister of the first government, Augustinas Voldemaras, appointed the president of the Vilnius Jewish Society, Jakov Vygodski, as the country's first minister of Jewish affairs, an entirely new departure. The government guaranteed Jews full civil rights, as well as the right to use Yiddish when dealing with public and governmental institutions. Jewish minority rights, part of the system of treaties ending the world war, were more far-reaching and longer lasting in Lithuania than in most of the other new and reborn states of eastern Europe. The president of Lithuania, Antanas Smetona regarded Jews as an integral part of Lithuania because they had participated in Lithuania's wars for independence, and served in the Lithuanian government. Nachman Rachmilevicz, a member of the Lithuanian Seimas (parliament), remarked, "If there is a portion of the Lithuanian population that is loyal in body and soul to Lithuania, it is the Jews" (in Atamukas 1998, 126.) Comparing the treatment of Jews beyond the borders in Poland, Lithuanian Jewish leaders were fond of describing their situation as a veritable paradise for Jews.

However, these promising new beginnings did not survive the 1920s. With the rise of right-wing political elements, serious economic problems, and tense relations with neighboring countries, the initial euphoria surrounding Jewish-Lithuanian relations evaporated. The government abolished the Ministry of Jewish Affairs and prohibited the use of Yiddish to conduct official business. In 1922, Rytas (Morning), an educational society, called for the expulsion of Jews for "bringing Bolshevism to Lithuania." The first evidence of organized antisemitism occurred in 1923 when Jewish stores were tarred with antisemitic slogans in several Lithuanian cities. In 1926, the government forbade the activities of the Jewish councils, which sought to represent the autonomous rights of native Jews. By 1927, the paramilitary fascist Geležinis Vilkas (Iron Wolf) organized as an antidemocratic, anti-Jewish, fascist underground force in Lithuania. Publicly, the most antisemitic organization was the Verslininkų Sajunga (Businessmen's Union). In its newspaper, the union propagated the notion that Jews had caused Lithuania's economic problems as far back as the Middle Ages. In 1934, the students of Kaunas University booed the noted psychiatrist Lazar Gutman at his inaugural lecture, delivered in the Lithuanian language, with chants of "Down with Jews!" In the winter of 1935, rumors of Jewish ritual murder precipitated a round of attacks on Jewish businesses. By the late 1930s, some extreme nationalists began calling for Lithuania to imitate Hitler's Germany. In this atmosphere, anti-Jewish incidents multiplied in both urban and rural areas. Officially, the Lithuanian government denounced manifestations of antisemitism, but it did little to stop them.

—*Virgil Krapauskas*

See also Judeo-Bolshevism; Lithuania, Holocaust in; Lithuania, Post-Soviet; Middle Ages, High; Pale of Settlement; Russia, Imperial; Sorcery/Magic; Versailles Treaty

**References**
Atamukas, Solomonas. *Lietuvos yd kelias: Nuo XIV amiaus iki XX a. pabaigos.* [The Way of Lithuanian Jews: From the 14th Century to the End of the 20th] (Vilnius: Alma littera, 1998).
Greenbaum, Masha. *The Jews of Lithuania: A History of a Remarkable Community, 1316–1945* (Jerusalem: Grefen, 1995).
Rastenis, Vincas. "Jews in Lithuania." In *Encyclopedia Lituanica.* Edited by Simas Suziedelis (Boston: Kapočius, 1972).

# Lithuania, Holocaust in

Lithuanians today are concerned with being labeled a nation of "Jew shooters." Although a small percentage of Lithuanians actively engaged in the pogroms and killings during World War II, many more participated in the bureaucracy and apparatus of the German killing machine. Too few Lithuanians resisted the Nazis.

Modern Lithuanian historians, such as V. Brandišauskas, have attributed their compatriots' role in the Holocaust to five factors: (1) vengeance against Jews who had collaborated with the Communists during the 1940–1941 Soviet occupation, (2) the opposing views of the pro-Soviet Jews and the pro-German Lithuanians, (3) traditional antisemitism, (4) the rise of fascism in the 1930s, and (5) individual criminal actions.

The Molotov-Ribbentrop Pact of 1939 between Nazi Germany and the Soviet Union produced two results that influenced Lithuanian participation in the Holocaust: it eventually led to the incorporation of Lithuania into the Soviet Union, and it delayed the Final Solution on Lithuanian soil until 1941 when German forces drove out the Soviets. The German invasion forced Jews to look to the Soviet Union for salvation, whereas Lithuanians looked to Germany for liberation. Although most Lithuanians realized that the Germans had no intention of restoring Lithuania's independence, they had already experienced deadly oppression at the hands of the Soviets, who deported and killed a great number of civilians. Many believed (falsely) that the Jews constituted a majority of the Communists who sent Lithuanians to their deaths, finding in this belief a rationale for the pogroms that took place as the Soviets retreated; these were, they claimed, no more than just acts of vengeance against the Soviet agents responsible for a Lithuanian genocide. In fact, only a small percentage of Lithuanian Jews were Communists. The vast majority of Jews killed during the Holocaust were innocent victims who had nothing to do with the Soviet atrocities perpetrated against both Lithuanians and Jews.

With the advance of the German Wehrmacht into the Baltic states in the summer of 1941, the special operational units of the SS—the Einsatzgruppen—organized and implemented the destruction of Lithuanian Jews. Although most Lithuanians remained indifferent bystanders, the question naturally arises as to what extent Lithuanians actively participated in the killing of Jews. Exact numbers of perpetrators will probably never be established. However, some infamous acts of Lithuanian complicity in the Holocaust are part of the historical record, such as the massacre by Lithuanian partisans of over fifty Jews at the Lietūkis garage in Kaunas on June 27, 1941. (Some believe that Lithuanians played only a minor role in the Lietūkis atrocity, claiming instead that the Germans present during the massacre were the real culprits.)

A controversy still exists as to the role of the Lithuanian Activist Front (LAF) in the Holocaust. Officially the LAF was organized to restore Lithuania's independence by driving out the Soviet occupiers, but the LAF was pro-German and received approval from the German government to organize. In a declaration of June 22, 1941, the LAF proclaimed, "Let us free Lithuania forever from the Jewish yoke . . . the fateful hour has arrived to finally settle scores with the Jews." The LAF held the entire Jewish population collectively responsible "for the Sovietization of Lithuania" in the previous year.

In an attempt to reestablish independence, Lithuanians simultaneously sought to curry favor with the Nazis by organizing 13,000 partisans, some willingly, others forcibly, into police battalions. Eventually, several of these units took part in murders throughout eastern Europe. Tragically, the June 1941 uprising of Lithuania against the Soviets did not achieve national independence but rather initiated one of the darkest chapters in Lithuania's history. Nazis and their Lithuanian collaborators killed Jews in over 200 killing sites. In the Paneriai forest, outside of Vilnius, an estimated 70,000 Jews were murdered. Among the concentration camps in Lithuania, the VII and IX Forts near Kaunas were the most deadly. Germans and Lithuanians shot thousands of Jews from Lithuania and also those deported from elsewhere in Europe. Although there were exceptions, the country's influential Roman Catholic clergy did virtually nothing to stop this.

By August 1941, the Germans declared Lithuania "cleansed of Jews," except for the ghettos in Vilnius, Kaunas, and Šiauliai. For the next three years, the Jews there provided slave labor for the German war economy. Disease, deportation, and executions gradually emptied the ghettos; the remaining survivors were eventually transferred to death camps, where they were killed. Only a few hundred Lithuanian Jews survived to the end of the war in 1945.

—*Virgil Krapauskas*

*See also* Einsatzgruppen; Holocaust; Judeo-Bolshevism; Lithuania; Lithuania, Post-Soviet; Order Police; Stalinization of Eastern Europe
**References**
Eidintas, Alfonsas. *Zydai, Lietuviai ir Holokaustas* (Jews, Lithuanians and the Holocaust) (Vilnius: Vaga, 2002).
Greenbaum, Masha. *The Jews of Lithuania: A History of a Remarkable Community, 1316–1945* (Jerusalem: Grefen, 1995).

## Lithuania, Post-Soviet

The Nazis and their collaborators exterminated more than 90 percent of all Lithuanian Jews, as high a mortality rate as anywhere in Nazi-held Europe. In 1989, there were about 12,400 Jews in Lithuania; by 1997, only 5,000 remained. Many emigrated to Israel. Since the fall of the Soviet Union, Lithuania has lifted the restrictions placed on Jewish cultural and religious life by the Communists, and today, Lithuanian Jews have several social and cultural organizations. Among the various Jewish museums, the most important is the Vilnius Gaon Jewish State Museum. Slowly, Lithuanians are recognizing "Litvak" culture as an integral part of the Lithuanian cultural scene, and the government of Lithuania now has denounced all forms of antisemitism.

But "antisemitism without Jews" remains a feature of Lithuanian life. In 1995, President Algirdas Brazauskas officially apologized to Israel for the Holocaust, but the media angrily criticized him for "humiliating himself unnecessarily." On the national Day of Repentance and Apology in 2000, the bishops of Lithuania lamented that, even then, antisemitic manifestations were occurring in Lithuania. Swastikas, slogans of "*Juden 'Raus*" (Jews out!), and other graffiti have appeared on public buildings. Vandals have desecrated Jewish gravesites, and newspaper articles have essentially denied the extent of the

Holocaust in Lithuania. Serious scholars have tried to prove that many of the Lithuanians who participated in the Holocaust were, in fact, Germans dressed up as Lithuanians, and others claim that only a small criminal element was involved. Some officials have even called for Jews, who collaborated with the Communists between 1940 and 1941, to be put on trial for crimes against humanity.

Although most Lithuanians do not interfere with Jewish cultural and religious life, they often talk privately about the "Jewish mafia," whose members, everyone "knows," rule the world with their money even though they do no work. One often hears statements such as, "Well, what do the Jews want from us?" Fringe political organizations, including the Lithuanian National Socialist Unity Association and the Logic of Life Party, imitate Nazis with their symbols, rhetoric, and behavior. The newspaper *Respublikos varpai* (Bell of the Republic) regularly prints antisemitic articles. Even the legitimate press is not immune from antisemitism, at times portraying the Jews as the terrorists in the Arab-Israeli conflict. When Israeli and Lithuanian sports teams compete, Lithuanian fans often taunt Jewish athletes.

More disturbing than antisemitic vandalism is the growth of a crude form of political populism. Political parties such as the Lithuanian Freedom Union are gaining votes and influence among the Lithuanian electorate. Street orators with simple answers to complex economic and social problems blame Jews for the poverty of post-Soviet Lithuania. Some members of the Lithuanian parliament accuse the government of accepting blame for the Holocaust simply to appease American Jews and thus gain entrance into the European Union and the North Atlantic Treaty Organization (NATO). Today's Lithuanian Jews fear that, for all of the progress in Jewish-Lithuanian relations, the antisemitism that surfaced in the nineteenth century still has a grip on some elements of state and society.

—*Virgil Krapauskas*

**See also** Holocaust Denial, Negationism, and Revisionism; Judeo-Bolshevism; Lithuania; Lithuania, Holocaust in

**References**

Alperavičius, Simonas, and I. Lempertas. *Jewish Community of Lithuania* (Vilnius: American Joint Distribution Committee, 2001).
Puišytė, Rūta, and Darius Staliūnas, eds. *Jewish Life in Lithuania* (Vilnius: Zara, 2001).

## Liutostanskii, Ippolit (1835–1915/1918?)

A Roman Catholic priest and then briefly a Russian Orthodox monk, Ippolit Liutostanskii became known as the author of antisemitic pamphlets and one of the most stubborn purveyors of the blood libel. His biography is difficult to reconstruct because rumor and speculation surround the person of this "pathological liar" (Klier 1995, 423). Liutostanskii was responsible for some of the speculation himself: for example, he asserted that he was a convert from Judaism and a former rabbi. The rest was the work of his enemies.

The son of a Polish nobleman from the district of Kovno, Ippolit took the name Fulgentius when he entered the cloister in Telsze; he became a priest in 1864. In 1868, because of serious moral lapses, he was defrocked, brought before a court, and charged with perjury and attempted rape. The outcome of the trial is not known, but in the same year, he converted to Russian Orthodoxy and was admitted to the Moscow Theological Academy.

In 1876, Liutostanskii left the clergy and embarked on his career as an antisemitic writer with a pamphlet on a grandiose scale: *The Question of the Use by Jewish Sectarians of Christian Blood for Religious Purposes, in Connection with Questions of the General Attitudes of Jewry to Christianity*. In the work, which appeared with full scholarly apparatus, he sought to demonstrate that adherents of fanatical Jewish sects practiced ritual murder. The book unleashed a fierce controversy. The well-known Hebraist Daniil Khvol'son showed that Liutostanskii did not even know the Hebrew alphabet and that he plagiarized the relevant writings of Polish, German, and Russian authors. But under slightly altered titles, the book lived on, appearing in several editions; it was translated into Bulgarian in 1898 and German in 1934. It was alleged that Liutostanskii had offered to sell the manuscript, instead of publishing it, to the Moscow rabbi Solomon Minor.

His magnum opus appeared in 1879. *The Talmud and the Jews* was an "encyclopedia" of anti-Jewish legends and falsifications, from ritual murder and the alliance with the Antichrist to modern secret societies striving for world domination. For source material, he relied not only on the Talmud but also on the "authentic" testimony contained in *The Rabbi's Speech,* which was, in fact, a scene taken from Herrmann Goedsche's novel *Biarritz* (1868). In volume two of the third edition of the work, which appeared in 1904, Liutostanskii excerpted the imaginary *Program for World Conquest by the Jews*—which would later be better known as the *Protocols of the Elders of Zion. The Talmud and the Jews* went through several editions and eventually comprised seven volumes. When sales lagged, after the initial *succès de scandale,* Liutostanskii endeavored to revive them by spreading the rumor that Jewish circles tried to offer him a lavish bribe to prevent publication.

At the height of the pogroms in Russia in 1882, Liutostanskii published a surprising repudiation of his anti-Jewish stance, titled *A Contemporary View on the Jewish Question.* Prior to publication, however, he had circularized leading Jewish figures and rabbis to offer the book to them for distribution. Further, he offered to institute public readings in defense of the Jews in several Russian cities. Jews saw this as no more than blackmail and rejected the offer, whereon Liutostanskii renewed his attacks.

Despite all his efforts to make his anti-Jewish polemics profitable, he remained a poor man and died in obscurity. The exact date of his death is not known, but the year 1915 is mentioned in some accounts. According to another unreliable report, Liutostanskii was shot by the Cheka (the secret political police), a victim of the "Red Terror" in Moscow in September 1918.

—*Michael Hagemeister*
*Richard S. Levy, translation*

**See also** Antichrist; *Biarritz;* Pogroms; *Protocols of the Elders of Zion; Rabbi's Speech, The;* Ritual Murder (Modern); Rohling, August; Russia, Imperial; Russian Orthodox Church; Talmud; *Talmud Jew, The;* Talmud Trials

**References**
Hagemeister, Michael. "Ljutostanskij, Ippolit." In *Biographisch-Bibliographisches Kirchenlexikon,* vol. 23. Edited by Traugott Bautz. (Nordhausen, Germany: Bautz, 2004). Available at http://www.bautz.de/bbkl/l/ljutostanskij_i_i.shtml. (Accessed February 27, 2005).
Klier, John D. *Imperial Russia's Jewish Question, 1855–1881* (Cambridge: Cambridge University Press, 1995).

## Ljotić, Dimitrije (1891–1945)

Dimitrije Ljotić was the leader of Zbor, a fascist movement founded in 1934 in Yugoslavia. In his speeches and pamphlets, as well as a number of articles published in newspapers close to the movement (*Otadžbina, Naša borba, Bilten JNP Zbor*) in the years leading up to the outbreak of World War II, Ljotić advocated the abolition of parliamentary democracy and the promulgation of a corporatist constitution as a solution to the country's political problems. Toward the end of the 1930s, his rhetoric adopted overtly antisemitic themes.

Born in Belgrade in 1891 to a well-known family with close ties to the Karadordević dynasty, Ljotić graduated from the Law School of the Belgrade University, after which he spent a year in Paris on a state scholarship. It was during that year, according to his memoir, that he encountered the political ideas of Charles Maurras, whom he described as a "rare shining spirit" and whom he prized as his most important intellectual influence. Ljotić rushed back to Serbia in 1914 to fight in World War I. The ideas he discovered in Paris, as well as the victory of the Serbian peasant military over the Austro-Hungarian, German, and Bulgarian armies, transformed the young Ljotić into an enthusiastic Yugoslav, a proponent of an integral Yugoslav nationalism that was, in his view, the only way to overcome the centrifugal forces at work in the Balkans. This goal, he was certain, could not be achieved with parliamentary democracy and its attendant political turmoil. Disappointed by the lack of progress toward achieving his vision for Yugoslavia, Ljotić turned to organizing several like-minded groups based in Serbia, Bosnia, and Slovenia into Zbor, a new political organization that pressed for a genuine corporatist reform along the lines of Italian fascism.

The major obstacle to Yugoslav fusion, according to Ljotić, was the parliamentary system, and it was there that he saw the "Jewish spirit" working in destructive ways. Capitalism and parliamentary democracy were Jewish inventions, he asserted, and in fighting against them, one by necessity had to be anti-Jewish. In addition, he described the Jews as "dissolving acids" working against cohesion among European nations. To forge a nation, one had to fight off the Jews. Ljotić's antisemitic rhetoric, influenced by traditional Orthodox Christianity and modern right-wing ideologies, was more directly a product of his dedication to establishing an integral Yugoslav national identity. The continuing failure of this project only intensified his antisemitism.

Zbor was unable to win a single seat in the parliament, gaining less than 1 percent of the vote in the elections of 1935. But despite the political marginality of his movement, Ljotić's antisemitic discourse increasingly gained currency in the latter part of the 1930s, as Yugoslavia gradually came to be dominated economically by the Axis powers. Some of his most rabidly antisemitic publications date from this period; the most significant of these was *Drama savremenog čovečanstva* (The Drama of Contemporary Humankind [1940]), a pamphlet describing a Jewish global conspiracy in the style of the *Protocols of the Elders of Zion*. By the outbreak of World War II, a solid body of antisemitic literature was available to Yugoslav readers, and Ljotić was considered an expert on the Jewish Question.

In April 1941, Nazi Germany and its allies invaded and partitioned Yugoslavia. Soon, a puppet government was set up in Serbia under the leadership of Milan Nedić. Ljotić preached collaboration with the Germans; although he himself did not assume any political position under Nedić, some other members of Zbor did, becoming government ministers. From the summer of 1941, the Nazi authorities increasingly depended on the local anticommunist militias, dominated by the men from Zbor, to curb the communist resistance and round up and deport Serbian Jews. Ljotić lived in Belgrade through the war and was killed in a car crash in Slovenia in 1945, while fleeing from the victorious communists.

—*Emil Kerenji*

*See also* Fascist Intellectuals; Holocaust; Jewish Question; Maurras, Charles; Mussolini, Benito; *Protocols of the Elders of Zion*
**References**
Stefanović, Mladen. *Zbor Dimitrija Ljotića, 1934–1945* (Belgrade: Narodna Knjiga, 1984).

## Long, Breckinridge (1881–1958)

Born on May 16, 1881, in St. Louis, Missouri, Samuel Miller Breckinridge Long had a lengthy career in the U.S. Department of State, during which, in the 1940s, he worked to impede Jewish immigration to the United States. He received his bachelor's degree from Princeton University in 1904 and his law degree from St. Louis Law School (now Washington University in St. Louis) in 1906, after which he was admitted to the Missouri bar. In 1912, Long married the wealthy Christine Graham.

Although he was politically unsuccessful in his native Missouri, Long was an influential Democrat who contributed to both Woodrow Wilson's and Franklin D. Roosevelt's presidential campaigns. In 1917, after Wilson's reelection, Long was appointed as the third assistant secretary of state. In that post, he primarily oversaw Foreign Service appointments. From 1920 to 1933, he returned to Missouri to practice international law and ran twice, both times unsuccessfully, for the Senate. After Roosevelt's victory, Long was appointed ambassador to Italy in 1933. During his time in Italy, he supported neutrality and isolation for the United States, believing that a European war was on the horizon and that his nation should remain uninvolved in the conflict at all costs. Long was recalled from Rome in 1936 over disagreements pertaining to the Italian invasion of Ethiopia. After the outbreak of war in 1939, he feared that Britain would drag the United States into the conflict. Only after the fall of France in 1940 did he see isolationism as no longer a viable option.

From 1940 to 1944, Long again served as assistant secretary of state, but this time he was the supervisor of its Immigration Visa Division. During his tenure, he continually opposed efforts to increase immigration, largely out of a fear that Nazi agents were entering the United States disguised as refugees. The consensus among historians today is that the actual problem of fifth column activity was significantly less important than Long led people to believe. Enemy espionage could have been dealt with by means other than further restrictions on immigration policy. In November 1943, Congress began considering a rescue effort to save the remaining Jews trapped in Europe. Long testified before the House Foreign Affairs Committee that such an effort was unnecessary and noted that the United States alone had accepted nearly 580,000 refugees within the preceding decade. In reality, the number of Jewish refugees admitted to the United States from all of Europe was an estimated 138,000.

Although Long boasted that he made every effort to help refugees, he actually took all the steps available to him to hold back their immigration; he even went so far as to argue that immigration could be halted altogether, especially if consuls employed any number of suggested pretexts in order to postpone the granting of visas for as long as possible. Breckinridge Long's political career ended when he was dismissed by Secretary of State Cordell Hull at the end of 1944. He died on September 26, 1958.

—*Melissa Jane Taylor*

**See also** Evian Conference; Holocaust; Immigration and Naturalization Laws; United States

**References**

Breitman, Richard, and Alan Kraut. "Anti-Semitism in the State Department, 1933–44: Four Case Studies." In *Anti-Semitism in American History*. Edited by David A. Gerber (Chicago: University of Illinois Press, 1986), 167–197.

Wyman, David. *Paper Walls* (Amherst: University of Massachusetts Press, 1968).

## Ludendorff, Erich (1865–1937)

Erich Friedrich Wilhelm Ludendorff was born on April 9, 1865, in Kruschevnia in what was then the Prussian province of Posen. He rose to prominence in the Prussian army before World War I. After Erich Falkenhayn was replaced by Paul von Hindenburg as chief of the General Staff in 1916, Ludendorff was promoted to first quartermaster general, a position that gave him virtually unfettered control over Germany's economy and military operations. Hindenburg and Ludendorff steadily increased their control over all aspects of the war effort, so that by 1917, it is fair to speak of a military dictatorship in Germany. Most studies of Ludendorff confine themselves to his policies during this period of dictatorship and to his decision to seek an armistice with the Allies in late September 1918.

But Ludendorff's postwar career is also noteworthy. After the German defeat in World War I, he became a central figure in right-wing politics during the early years of the Weimar Republic. He participated in the planning of the Kapp-Lüttwitz Putsch in 1920 and marched alongside Hitler during the latter's Beer Hall Putsch in 1923, escaping punishment in both cases by trading on his military fame. During Hitler's imprisonment, Ludendorff assumed a leadership position in the National Socialist Freedom Party and, although he rarely attended its sessions, he was one of the party's delegates to the Reichstag until 1925. He ran as the Nazi Party's presidential candidate in 1925 but received a mere 286,000 votes (1.1 percent of the total cast).

Ludendorff's political engagement was powerfully shaped by his growing conviction that "supranational powers" (Jews, the Catholic Church, and Freemasons) had been responsible for Germany's defeat in 1918 and its subsequent suffering. In this "unholy trinity," Ludendorff claimed to have found the "key to world history." Numerological insights, he claimed, uncovered the hand of Jews and Freemasons in the Russian Revolution of 1905, the outbreak of war in 1914, and the French occupation of the German Ruhr in 1923. The individual integers in each of those dates add up to fifteen, which made them "Jehovah-years" and therefore particularly auspicious for "kabbalistic" activities, according to the former general. Again on the basis of numerology, Ludendorff predicted that the supranational powers would unleash a world war aimed at the final destruction of Germany in the year 1932.

Ludendorff also came increasingly under the influence of Mathilde von Kemnitz, whom he made his second wife in September 1926. He wholeheartedly adopted her anti-Christian *Deutsche Gotterkenntnis* (Germanic understanding of God) as his faith and engaged, for the rest of his life, in a fierce struggle with the Catholic Church in his adopted homeland, Bavaria.

In 1926, Ludendorff parted ways with Hitler, who was unwilling to support his extreme anti-Christian views; thereafter, he faded into political insignificance. He cultivated a small following in the Tannenberg League and around his publishing house, Ludendorffs-Volkswarte-Verlag (Ludendorff's Peoples' Watch Tower Publishing), which churned out antisemitic, anti-Catholic, and anti-Freemason screeds at a feverish pace. The Tannenberg League sought to achieve the "unity of blood (racial inheritance) and faith (holy perception)" and to carry on the struggle against the supranational powers, "Juda, Rome, and their accomplices in Freemasonry" (Fricke 1968, 2: 668–671) The group's critique of National Socialist policy toward the Vatican led to its banning in 1933, although Ludendorff continued to be revered by many Nazis.

Erich Ludendorff died in Munich on December 20, 1937. Hitler honored "the commander in chief," as Ludendorff liked to call himself, by attending the lavish state funeral held a few days later.

—*Jay Lockenour*

*See also* Freemasonry; Hitler, Adolf; Ludendorff, Mathilde; Ludendorff Publishing House; National Socialist German Workers' Party; New Age; Sorcery/Magic; *Völkisch* Movement and Ideology; Weimar

**References**

Fricke, Dieter, ed. *Die bürgerlichen Parteien in Deutschland.* 2 vols. (Berlin: das europäische Buch, 1968).

Goodspeed, D. J. *Ludendorff: Soldier, Dictator, Revolutionary* (London: Hart-Davis, 1966).

## Ludendorff, Mathilde (1877–1966)

Born Mathilde Spiess on October 4, 1877, in Wiesbaden to a Protestant minister and his wife, Mathilde showed an interest in science and, with some interruption, studied medicine, specializing in psychology and women's health. She was married to the scientist Gustav Adolf von Kemnitz from 1904 until his death in 1917.

Mathilde von Kemnitz moved in right-wing circles after World War I and achieved notoriety for her numerous publications on religion and the occult, beginning with *Triumph des Unsterblichkeitswillens* (Triumph of the Immortal Will [1922]). From her residence in Tutzing, outside Munich, she corresponded with the National Socialists there as well as with Erich Ludendorff, who had moved from Berlin to nearby Ludwigshöhe in 1920. She and Ludendorff married in September 1926.

Mathilde Ludendorff fancied herself a philosopher and espoused a doctrine she called *Deutsche Gotterkenntnis* (Germanic Understanding of God). According to her, races were distinguished not so much by their physical characteristics as by their unique spiritual existence. All religious faiths could be classified as either religions "of light" or "of the pit" (*Schacht*). Religions of the pit, such as Christianity and Judaism, demanded sacrifice and obedience of their followers and worshiped vengeful and capricious deities. "Light" religions, such as that allegedly practiced by the Germans' Nordic ancestors, allowed their faithful to live in harmony with the natural world and to achieve "self-fulfillment" through a healthy relationship with the spiritual world. Ludendorff also claimed that her faith was unique among contemporary religions for achieving a harmony between religion and science.

In her writings, she emphasized the pernicious activities of Jews, whose God "demanded the enslavement and plunder of all peoples." Freemasons and Catholics were further targets of her wrath. The Catholic Church, she argued, strove for world domination at the expense of people's religious freedom but thereby only furthered the project of Jews, who had penned the holy texts of Christianity. In one of her most widely circulated publications, *Die Erlösung von Jesu Christo* (1931), published in England by the "Friends of Europe" as *Getting Rid of Jesus Christ* (1937), Ludendorff claimed that the "myth" of Jesus and his teachings were cobbled together by Jewish authors using fragments of Indian religious teachings. Christianity, therefore, was not only a human fabrication, it was also unsuited to the Mediterranean peoples and later the Scandinavians who would become its principal practitioners. Christianity ultimately served the interests of Jews, according to Ludendorff, because it convinced Europeans to subscribe to Jewish doctrine (the Old Testament) and to worship the Jew Jesus.

In November 1946, Mathilde managed briefly to revive her society, now cleverly disguised, with the removal of the sensitive words *Deutsch* and *Ludendorff* from its name, as the Bund für Gotterkenntnis (L) (League for the Understanding of God). Her publishing house, the former Ludendorff Verlag, also resumed business under a new name in 1949. However, her notorious work and infamous name had made her too many enemies over the years, and Ludendorff became the target of an investigation by de-Nazification authorities. In 1950, she was classified as a "major offender" for her antisemitic views and forbidden to write or speak publicly for seven years.

A court lifted the ban in 1954, but this did not end Ludendorff's troubles with the democratic government of West Germany. The activities of the Ludendorff Movement, founded in 1959 as the political counterpart of the League for the Understanding of God, attracted the attention of the Interior Ministry, which banned both groups as antisemitic and antidemocratic in May 1961. Mathilde Ludendorff died on May 12, 1966, but her organization lives on under the scrutiny of the German constitutional protection authorities.

—*Jay Lockenour*

**See also** Freemasonry; Germany, Federal Republic of; Ludendorff, Erich; National Socialist German Workers' Party; New Age; *Völkisch* Movement and Ideology; Weimar

**References**
Martini, Winfried. *Die Legende vom Hause Ludendorff* (Rosenheim, Germany: Leonhard Lang, 1949).

## Ludendorff Publishing House

Ludendorffs-Volkswarte-Verlag (Ludendorff's Peoples' Watch Tower Publishing) was the company operated by Erich and Mathilde Ludendorff to disseminate their racist, nationalist, and antisemitic ideas. The company published the official newspaper of Erich Ludendorff's Tannenberg League as well as its monthly journal, *Am Heiligen Quell* (At the Holy Spring), which espoused the principles of Mathilde Lu-

dendorff's *Deutsche Gotterkenntnis* (Germanic Understanding of God) doctrine. The distinguishing feature of the countless pamphlets, books, newspapers, journals, and other materials that issued from the publishing house was a preoccupation with the world-spanning conspiracies of the "supranational powers": Judaism, Catholicism, and Freemasonry.

Despite the Nazi-imposed ban on the Tannenberg League in the summer of 1933, the publishing house continued to operate with Heinrich Himmler's blessing. Subscribers of the now illegal publication *Ludendorffs-Volkswarte* were informed that they could satisfy their thirst for knowledge with (the less political) *Am Heiligen Quell,* which became a biweekly publication. Although *Am Heiligen Quell's* distinctly anti-Christian themes were occasionally at odds with the official policies of the regime, its circulation rose throughout the 1930s. After Erich Ludendorff's death in 1937, the regime's mandate to tone down anti-Christian rhetoric in the interest of domestic harmony during the war and the eventual withholding of paper supplies by government fiat served to marginalize the publication.

Under Allied occupation, Mathilde Ludendorff and her son-in-law, Franz Freiherr Karg von Bebenburg, resumed the publishing house's operations under various names, settling finally on Hohe Warte (Lofty Watch Tower) in October 1949. Ludendorff initially succeeded in convincing Allied authorities that her prewar publications had opposed National Socialist racial policies by pointing to a few prominent critiques of Hitler, including her husband's outlandish work *Hitler's Betrayal of the German People to the Roman Pope* (1931). Mathilde Ludendorff was eventually investigated and condemned as a "major offender" by a de-Nazification court, but she saved the publishing house by transferring control of it and all of her works to her son-in-law. Her success was only temporary, however, because an investigation of the company's private correspondence in 1961 led to the conclusion that it, along with the League for the Understanding of God, was engaged in spreading antisemitic propaganda. Both were banned until 1977, when a Bavarian court overturned the 1961 ruling. Hohe Warte Publishing is now located in Pähl in Upper Bavaria and peddles its wares over the Internet.

—*Jay Lockenour*

***See also*** Freemasonry; Germany, Federal Republic of; Himmler, Heinrich; Ludendorff, Erich; Ludendorff, Mathilde; National Socialist German Workers' Party; *Völkisch* Movement and Ideology; Weimar

**References**

Borst, Gert. "Die Ludendorff-Bewegung, 1919–1961." Dissertation, University of Munich, 1969.

## Lueger, Karl (1844–1910)

Austria's "uncrowned king of Vienna" during his term as the city's mayor (1897–1910), Karl Lueger has since become enshrined in popular Viennese folklore. A prominent bronze statue in Vienna's first district has long been part of the municipal landscape, and a portion of the famous Ringstrasse is named after him.

Lueger was an unsystematic but potent and influential antisemite. Rather late in his career, he once answered criticism about his lack of sincerity about the Jewish Question by remarking, "I decide who is a Jew," the words for which he is most remembered. More than anyone else, he legitimized antisemitism in Austrian politics, and his more aggressive successors built on the foundations he laid down.

The son of a custodian at the Vienna Polytechnic Institute, Lueger received an elitist education—unusual for a person of his lowly social origins—at the private preparatory Theresianum and at the University of Vienna. He was an outstanding student, became a doctor of law in 1870, and opened a law office in Vienna's third district. In 1875, he ran for the municipal council as a liberal and won.

The 1870s were years of decline for Austria's ruling Liberal Party after the crash of 1873. During these turbulent times, Lueger gradually drifted away from the Liberals, seeking a new party and experimenting with a variety of political alliances. In 1890, he became the undisputed leader of the fledgling Christian Social Party after the death of its founder, Karl von Vogelsang. Under Lueger, the Christian Socials became Austria's first successful party of mass politics. Al-

most from the beginning, antisemitism was a central theme of his campaigns. He played on the fears and deeply rooted prejudices of his initially lower-middle-class constituents—"little people" who felt threatened by the influx of Jews from the Habsburg Empire's eastern provinces.

Three times in 1895 and 1896, Emperor Franz Joseph withheld the necessary sanction for Lueger to become Vienna's mayor because he disapproved of him as a demagogue, an antisemite, and an anti-Hungarian. But a compromise was finally reached, and Lueger was sworn in as mayor in April 1897. In that post, he municipalized privately owned utilities and transportation. He experimented with various forms of antisemitism—sometimes economic, sometimes racial, occasionally religious. Although he was duty-bound to uphold the equality of all the emperor's subjects, he nonetheless often managed to circumvent these restrictions, and there was never any doubt where his true sentiments lay.

Lueger introduced a number of political innovations of an antisemitic nature. The Christian Socialist women's movement, which he claimed to have created, was outspokenly antisemitic, openly demonstrating against Jewish-owned stores. During his tenure, antisemitic children's literature was introduced into Vienna's elementary schools, Jewish schoolteachers were discharged, and Jewish municipal officials were denied promotion. An annual literary prize funded by the provincial diet (controlled by the Christian Social Party) was awarded to the most promising "Aryan" playwright, and this work was performed in the party theater. Lueger, mindful of the need to control information, repeatedly attacked the "Jewish" press. He endorsed the ritual murder canard in parliament, both before and after he became mayor. He was not above using antisemitism as a tool of physical intimidation. At a large Christian Social rally in late 1905, Lueger himself threatened violence against the leader of the Social Democratic Party, Viktor Adler, a convert from Judaism, as well as other Socialists on the basis of their Jewish heritage; they had dared to demonstrate, peacefully, for universal male franchise.

Although ill health increasingly prevented his more active participation, Lueger condoned until his last days the aggressive antisemitism of his followers, such as Ernst Schneider and Hermann Bielohlawek. His most notorious admirer was Adolf Hitler, who nonetheless faulted his antisemitism for its lack of racial foundation. Lueger's continuing image in the minds of his apologists is that of "the respectable antisemite" who only attacked the worst "Jewish excesses." Such apologists discount Lueger's malicious demagogy and ignore the precedent his antisemitism created and legitimized and whose violent potential would be amply demonstrated after 1918.

—*Richard S. Geehr*

**See also** Aryan Theater; Austria; Christian Social Party (Austria); Hitler, Adolf; "Jewish" Press; Ritual Murder (Medieval); Ritual Murder (Modern); Vogelsang, Karl von

**References**
Boyer, John W. *Political Radicalism in Late Imperial Vienna* (Chicago and London: University of Chicago Press, 1981).
———. *Culture and Political Crisis in Vienna* (Chicago and London: University of Chicago Press, 1995).
Geehr, Richard S. *Karl Lueger: Mayor of Fin de Siècle Vienna* (Detroit, MI: Wayne State University Press, 1990).

Martin Luther exerted great influence on the relations between Christians and Jews. His angry denunciations of Jews and Judaism in his last years have been used for racist political causes he would not have fathomed. (Library of Congress)

## Luther, Martin (1483–1546)

For someone whose opinion of Judaism was formed in the almost complete absence of experience with any Jews, Martin Luther has had an immense influence on relations between Jews and Christians. In part because he inherited the conventional views of his age and in part because of the clarity and forcefulness of his own additions to those views, Luther's role in the history of Christian anti-Judaism has been enigmatic, notwithstanding his stature within the history of the theological position that the Jews' damnation is the necessary foil to the salvation of the Christian church. The purely historical inquiry into Luther's place in the theological tradition was overshadowed in the nineteenth and twentieth centuries by religious and, more often, nationalistic interests, alternately allying the great Reformer with a variant of racial antisemitism unknown in the early modern period and distancing him from a theological anti-Judaism common to the era.

Born to newly bourgeois parents, Luther was the product of a number of dominant religious and cultural strains of late medieval Saxony. Educated at Erfurt and ordained in the Order of Augustinian Hermits, Luther became professor at Wittenberg, where he devoted himself to biblical studies in a search, as he would later describe it, for a righteous deity. He read his Bible Christologically, in keeping with the prevailing exegetical methods. Thus, he saw Jesus Christ as the sole and necessary fulfillment of ancient Israel's pious expectations. It was the Jews who first articulated the messianic hope at the core of the Christian faith.

For Luther, as for most adherents of the Christian tradition before him, Jewish piety was the indispensable foundation of the Christian covenant. He often spoke of the holy Jews of antiquity, identifying with them in their unwavering trust in the absolute benevolence of their Lord. For Luther, as for the Israelites, the privileged knowledge of God was as a redeemer, and the people's certainty of that quality took the form of trust (*fiducia,* in Latin), a confidence in divine redemptive power unavailable to those outside the covenant. What God had revealed, God would fulfill; thus, redemption remained the expectation to the adherents of both covenants. The crucial difference between the two was in the realm in which that redemption was expected to be realized. Whereas the Jews expected their redemption to recapitulate their deliverance from Egyptian bondage, specifically in the expulsion of Roman dominance and the restoration of control over their land, the Christian community understood redemption in otherworldly terms and thus saw a heavenly eschaton (end of the world) as the field of redemption. In subscribing to this view, Luther shared an outlook forged among the persecuted communities of the ancient church.

The second influence on Luther's thought was the apostle Paul, principal formulator of the theology of the New Covenant replacing the old. In Luther's view, Paul taught that the Old Covenant was one of works and the new was one of love of God and neighbor. In proclaiming a gospel of love, Paul's Jesus repudiated the works-righteousness of contemporary Jewish sects, teaching that the ancient trust in a benevolent redeemer was the only possible path to salvation. Amid the apocalyptic anxiety of first-century Palestine, where an ever-intensifying scrupulosity in observance seemed the only means to achieving an ever-receding divine protection, the Pauline proclamation was a bold demand to disregard externals in favor of inward disposition.

The Pauline message seemed to address Luther's deepest concerns, as he saw the Catholic Church of his own time in the same light in which Paul saw the Judaism of his. Over the centuries, the Western church had developed a system of "good works" and devotional practices intended to draw believers into "cooperating" with grace in order to earn their salvation. The principle at work was the doctrine that certain good deeds would bring their agents *merit* in the eyes of God and thus serve as steps toward a deserved salvation. For Luther, as for all Evangelical theologians after him, the weight of original sin was too great to allow any human deed, no matter how good it may be in human terms, to appear to God as anything but sin. And those who saw their works as good, both in themselves and by divine reckoning, were all the more culpable of the sin of pride.

Although directed toward the theologians and seekers of perfection within the Catholic Church, Luther's view implicated contemporary Jewry as well. The deniers of Jesus' messianic role merited the dispersal that was their lot after the destruction of the Temple in 70 CE (a view dating from the beginnings of the Christian church); further, they were punished still more for their faithlessness by having as their only alternative a church structure that only duplicated, mutatis mutandis, the system of works that the Pharisees and others had advocated. Hence, the system of meritorious "works" being promoted by the Catholic Church was no different from the focus on external forms of purity dismissed by Paul. Among theological adversaries, Luther used the term *Pelagian* for the Catholic program, after the fourth-century heretic condemned by Augustine, but elsewhere and ubiquitously, he used the term *Judaizing* when referring to the pursuit of perfection via external works.

Set within this context, the term *Judaizing* served rhetorical needs without necessarily feeding anti-Jewish feeling among his followers: it effectively evoked a Pauline image without implicating any contemporary Jews. The latter, in Luther's view, had little reason to adopt a "false" Roman Christianity that promised no more redemption than the Temple and purity cults of the first century had.

Luther has been credited with a more notorious role in the history of antisemitism than his own work warrants. The ferocity of his pronouncements during his final decade had the effect of setting him off as a model of intolerance in the interest of a Christian society. Whether these statements represent the "true Luther" is an unanswerable question, but it needs to be set within the larger topic of whether opposition to Judaism is a structural component of Christian thought.

More elusive and provocative is the question of Luther's understanding of ancient Judaism and of the divine role within that worldview. In reading the prophets, Luther found a wrathful deity regularly displeased with Israel's inability to conform to revealed law. To Luther, the correlation of human incapacity and divine wrath structured the divine-human relationship, insofar as the true purpose of the law was to reveal the inability, because of original sin, to fulfill it. Those who failed to see the law serving this diagnostic use and who strove to fulfill its demands were self-deceived and incurred the divine wrath articulated in the prophetic books. In minimizing the weight of original sin, both Jews and perfection-seeking Catholics excluded themselves from grace.

—*Ralph Keen*

***See also*** Augustine of Hippo; Melanchthon, Philipp; *On the Jews and Their Lies;* Paul; Reformation; Roman Empire; Supersessionism; Usury

***References***

Brosseder, Johannes. *Luthers Stellung zu den Juden im Spiegel seiner Interpreten* (Munich, Germany: M. Hueber, 1972).

Lewin, Reinhold. *Luthers Stellung zu den Juden* (Aalen, Germany: Scientia Verlag, 1973).

Oberman, Heiko A. *The Roots of Anti-Semitism in the Age of Renaissance and Reformation.* Translated by J. Porter (Philadelphia: Fortress Press, 1984).

# M

## Mahler-Werfel, Alma (1879–1964)

Perhaps the most famous muse of the twentieth century, Alma Mahler-Werfel was married to Gustav Mahler, Walter Gropius, and Franz Werfel, in that order. Moreover, Mahler-Werfel flirted with Gustav Klimt before she met Mahler, and after Mahler's death, she entered into a more substantial liaison with Oskar Kokoschka. Although two of her three husbands were Jews—Mahler and Werfel—she harbored various anti-semitic sentiments, which she recorded in her diaries and letters and also frequently expressed in conversation.

Mahler-Werfel was born into a Viennese artist's family in 1879. Her father was Emil Schindler, a respected, if not stellar, painter. At a young age and perhaps as a result of having grown up around mediocrity in a culture that worshiped artistic genius, Mahler-Werfel developed a strong attraction for greatness. She appreciatively read Friedrich Nietzsche's ideas about the need for a brave new type of man. And, of course, she consistently sought out great artists, using her looks (which do not come across as extraordinary in photographs) and her bold personality to attract them. Needless to say, her success rate was high.

Yet Mahler-Werfel experienced much frustration. A talented composer in her own right, she gave up her artistic undertakings at Gustav Mahler's insistence. Compelled to live through the works of her husbands and partners, she often felt that these men were not doing enough. In Werfel's case, she ascribed his artistic limitations to a Jewish background. Indeed, she once remarked that he would never write "pure German" prose because he was a Jew. She also commented spitefully on his appearance, confiding to her diary, "He [Werfel] has once again shrunk to the small, hateful, corpulent Jew—my first impression."

These depictions were fairly generic, turn-of-the-twentieth-century Viennese antisemitic stereotypes. Much worse and much more upsetting to Mahler-Werfel's largely Jewish circle of interlocutors was her apparent respect for Hitler and the Nazis. She maintained, for instance, that "the Allies are weaklings and degenerates," that "the Germans, including Hitler, are supermen," and that "the humanistic, liberal cause is lost, and the blond beast will triumph." Moreover, in front of fellow exiles and much to Franz Werfel's displeasure, she made what one of her friends called "unbearable jokes at the Jews' expense." She also tried to downplay the extent of Jewish suffering in Europe. As late as 1944, she asserted that the concentration camps boasted excellent medical care and that the Red Cross was conscientiously looking after the prisoners.

How earnestly meant were such statements? It is hard to tell because they come to us as fragments of recounted conversations. But most eyewitnesses seem to have felt that Mahler-Werfel was at least partly serious when she disparaged Jews, belittled their mistreatment, and spoke in rapturous tones about Germanic heroism. And her husband Werfel took her claims about Nazis seriously enough to become agitated over them.

Notwithstanding her obvious singularity, her sentiments were not quite as unique as they might seem. After all, in 1933, Thomas Mann wrote in his diary, "The revolt against Jewish things might have my understanding to a certain extent," even though he was married to a convert from Judaism at the time and had been for over fifteen years.

—*Paul Reitter*

*See also* Austria; Freud, Sigmund; George, Stefan; Hitler, Adolf; Masculinity; Nietzsche, Friedrich; Weimar
**References**
Keegan, Susanne. *The Life and Times of Alma Mahler-Werfel* (New York: Viking, 1992).
Mahler-Werfel, Alma. *Gustav Mahler: Memories and Letters.* Selected and translated by Basil Creighton (New York: Viking, 1946).

## Manetho

Manetho is the Greek name by which we identify an Egyptian priest who flourished in the first half of the third century BCE. We do not know his Egyptian name. Manetho was very likely the first learned Egyptian to write in Greek (or translate into Greek) the history and traditions of his country. None of his works has survived in complete form, but we learn of them through titles mentioned and excerpts quoted by later authors. According to one of those, Josephus—a Jewish priest who, at the end of the first century CE, wrote extensively on the Jews—Manetho, in his *History of Egypt,* included both officially recorded and undocumented stories about the Jews, the latter negatively portraying them and meant to be alternative versions of the biblical story of the Exodus.

According to the officially recorded story, people from Asia, named the Hyksos, invaded Egypt and ruled it harshly for several generations from the city of Avaris, until they reached an agreement with King Tutmoses and left the country to settle in Asia, where they founded Jerusalem. According to the popular story, King Amenophis expelled the lepers from Egypt because they prevented him from seeing the gods. Under the leadership of Osarsiph, a priest of Heliopolis, these people gathered in Avaris and then made an alliance with the Hyksos, calling them back from Jerusalem. Together, they ransacked the country, showing no respect for the Egyptian gods; at that point, Osarsiph changed his name to Moses. Eventually, Amenophis was able to push them all into Asia. Josephus praised the authenticity of the first story and contemptuously dismissed the second as unreliable. Greek and Roman historians knew other versions of this same story, making possible its diffusion and elaboration throughout the Mediterranean world.

On the strength of these stories, modern scholars have labeled Manetho history's first antisemitic writer. However, some scholars regard the authorship of the second story as not altogether certain. More important, they suggest that Josephus's commentary may have been intended to persuade his readers to accept his own anti-Jewish reading of the text and that the identification of the Jews with both the Hyksos and the lepers was his invention. A recent interpretation raises the possibility of further Jewish textual embellishments, thus casting considerable doubt on whether Manetho should be considered an antisemite.

—*Sandra Gambetti*

*See also* Roman Empire; Roman Literature
**References**
Gruen, Erich S. *Heritage and Hellenism: The Reinvention of Jewish Tradition* (Berkeley: University of California Press, 1998).

## *Manifesto of the Racial Scientists* (1938)

Promulgated on July 13, 1938, in Italy and published in all the national papers on the following day, the ten proposals enunciated in the *Manifesto degli scienziati razzisti* (Manifesto of the Racial Scientists) represented the Fascist Party's official theoretical position on race. The regime showed how much importance it gave the *Manifesto* by attempting to pass off the document's proposals as the consensus arrived at by deliberations within the scientific community. Purportedly written by a group of Fascist intellectuals, lecturers within the Italian universities and coordinated by the Ministry of Popular Culture, the *Manifesto* was, in fact, put together by Guido Landra, a lowly teaching assistant in the Anthropology Department of Rome University and future functionary of the Racial Office.

The document, also referred to as *Il Fascismo e i problemi della razza* (Fascism and Racial Problems), covered not only the Jewish Question but Fascist racial policies in general, beginning with the affirmation that human races exist on a hereditary basis. Centering racism and antisemitism on biological principle was a new departure for the Fascists. Until that time, their movement had been content to stigmatize Jews and others on the basis of inferior "spiritual and moral" qualities. Although the *Manifesto* conceded that "the racial concept is a purely biological one," it saw no conflict with traditional forms of antisemitism, including that grounded in Catholic doctrine; biological racism was just another weapon in the struggle against the Jews. The fourth of its ten principles maintained that the Italian population was, in its majority, "of Aryan descent and Aryan in its civilization." It followed from this axiom that it was absolutely necessary to protect the racial purity of Italians from contamination.

The *Manifesto,* when taken together with the *Protocols of the Elders of Zion* and a few other documents, served as the ideological starting point for the most extreme hate campaign that the Fascist press had yet indulged in. Its final paragraphs presented a program for Italians. They were to profess racism, distinguish and safeguard the nation from all the non-European races, and regard "Orientals" and Africans as enemies (thereby legitimizing Italy's colonial enterprises). In the ninth paragraph, the document affirmed that "Jews do not belong to the Italian race. . . . The Jews were the only population group never assimilated in Italy because they bore non-European racial traits, absolutely alien—and, of course, inferior—to the racial origins of the Italians."

The *Manifesto of the Racial Scientists* is often made light of by historians, particularly because of its shady genesis and because it appeared to be no more than an opportunistic concession by Benito Mussolini to his German ally. But the document had serious consequences. It provided a basic programmatic document for the Fascist Party's educational and propaganda agencies down to the intermediate level. It affected the behavior and attitudes of ordinary party members and, perhaps, of ordinary Italians toward the so-called inferior races. Most important, the *Manifesto* paved the way to its own logical corollary, the Racial Laws of November 1938 that sought to separate Jews from the rest of the population, forbade intermarriage, and proscribed Jews from the economic, cultural, and professional life of the nation.

—*Simone Duranti*

*See also* Mussolini, Benito; Preziosi, Giovanni; *Protocols of the Elders of Zion;* Racial Laws; Racism, Scientific
**References**
Felice, Renzo de. *The Jews in Fascist Italy.* Translated by Robert L. Miller (New York: Enigma Books, 2001).
Michaelis, Meir. *Mussolini and the Jews: German-Italian Relations and the Jewish Question in Italy, 1922–1945* (New York: Clarendon Press, 1978).

# Mann, Thomas (1875–1955)

Thomas Mann's attitude toward Jews and his fictional Jewish characters are two quite different, if obviously related, matters. Throughout his life, Mann, like many of his contemporaries, held to the belief that there were certain characteristic Jewish qualities, though he usually defined these in positive terms, including adaptability, intellect, and cosmopolitanism. (Such an "essentialist" mind-set is more likely to give offense today than in Mann's own time.) "The Jews have something special," he opined in the 1921 essay *On the Jewish Question,* "which makes them appear stranger than their noses: an inborn love of intellect. This love has often made them leaders in the sins of humanity, but it also renders outsiders, freethinkers, artists, and writers their friends and debtors" (Mann, *Gesammelte Werke,* 1974, 13: 475; translated by the author). Mann regarded himself as "a convinced and incontrovertible 'philosemite'" (in Kurzke 2002, 192). Prior to World War I, he expressed the conviction that assimilation—meaning Europeanization, encouragement of baptism, and mixed marriage—was the best way to ensure that Germans and Jews continued a mutually beneficial relationship. Mann held that Jews provided an indispensable European cultural stimulus, the leaven, so to speak, so essential to German culture. Though he was repelled by east European Jews and their version of German—a disdain shared by many cultured Germans and German Jews of his day—he came to value the eastern Jews in their own right once their existence became threatened by the Nazis' antisemitic propaganda and subsequent murderousness. Where once he had rejected Zionism in favor of assimilation, he now endorsed it.

Mann's official pronouncements on Jews and Judaism were generally positive, but his diaries contain some ugly remarks, usually in relation to Jewish rivals or opponents. The worst of these may be the entry of April 10, 1933, in which his anger at the literary critic Alfred Kerr became a qualified affirmation of some early Nazi restrictions on Jews: "That Kerr's spirited and poisonous gibberish about Nietzsche is excluded is no misfortune in the final analysis; nor is the removal of Jews from the judiciary" (in Kurzke 2002, 205). In a letter, Mann described successful journalists as possessing "practicality, cunning, subtle and shameless irreverence, impertinence . . . the art of making oneself popular, the 'ass kissing'—all the vulgar characteristics which make Jews so suitable to this profession" (in Heilbut 1995, 374). Despite such utterances, the suggestion that Mann nurtured a secret antisemitism (akin to his half-hidden homosexuality) while only appearing to be a friend of the Jews is, in the end, not supportable. Scholars who do not fully exonerate Mann of the charge of antisemitism refer rather to the author's "ambivalence" regarding Jews.

Many people thought Mann was Jewish himself, perhaps because he married into a family of prominent assimilated Jews. Nazi literary critic Adolf Bartels repeatedly claimed he was a Jew. Mann responded that he was not but took pains to point to his mixed heritage (Portuguese on his mother's side) as an occasion to celebrate the miscegenation, as he put it, that would continue into his children's generation and beyond. In a way, though, Mann did see himself as a Jew: on several occasions, he suggested an analogy between the artist and the Jew. This point is perhaps overeagerly taken up by those keen to play down his bigoted remarks, trying to pass them off as a kind of self-criticism.

The two major turning points in Mann's life, from a political perspective, were his belated support of the Weimar Republic in 1922 and his exile from Nazi Germany, beginning in 1933. From 1936 on, he actively began to make antifascist speeches, to urge the United States and other democracies to allow more Jewish immigration, to condemn antisemitism forthrightly, to make known the atrocities of the Holocaust, and

to support individual Jews in need. On a regular basis, he made special recordings for the British Broadcasting Corporation (BBC) to be broadcast into Nazi Germany to encourage resistance and enlighten his compatriots.

Mann's fictional representation of Jews is a different matter because, though it was clearly informed by the author's belief in a particular Jewish essence, it necessarily lived a life of its own. Whereas Mann endeared himself to many by championing the cause of Jews in his later years, his fiction must be judged on its own merits or, rather, by the shifting standards of taste that currently include a heightened sensitivity to depictions of Jews. Mann's oeuvre contains both extremely positive images of Jews, such as Doctor Sammet in *Königliche Hoheit* (*Royal Highness* [1909]), and rather negative ones, such as the Baroness von Stein in *Der Wille zum Glück* (*The Will to Happiness* [1896]). With regard to the characters Chaim Breisacher and Saul Fitelberg from *Doktor Faustus* (1947), Mann admitted that, lacking positive Jewish figures to balance them out, his novel might encourage "simpler readers" to view this representation as antisemitism. Frequently, Leo Naphta, the "Jewish Jesuit" and brilliant debater from *The Magic Mountain* (1926), is grouped among Mann's questionable Jewish characters. However, given the author's trademark use of irony and the noted complexity of his prose in general, it would seem inadvisable simply to isolate a single figure from the larger narrative context for assessment.

The real scandal in Mann's oeuvre remains the novella *Wälsungenblut* (*Blood of the Wälsungs* [1906]), which tells the story of two upper-class Jewish twins, Siegmund and Sieglinde, who attend a performance of Wagner's *Valkyrie* and, in imitation of the Germanic figures they so ardently wish to become, commit incest. The original version of the novella concludes with another motivation for the incest—the desire to cheat Sieglinde's gentile fiancé of his sexual prerogatives. Siegmund lapses into a crude Yiddish-laced German (Judendeutsch), exclaiming, "We have begoniffed him—the goy!" Mann withdrew the novella for a number of years and replaced the final sentence (for aesthetic reasons, he said), but the story retains undeniable antisemitic clichés, even if one seeks to balance it against Mann's celebrated *Joseph* tetralogy (1933–1943), which presents very positive, if largely secularized, fictions of key narratives from the Hebrew Bible.

—*William Collins Donahue*

**See also** Bartels, Adolf; Immigration and Naturalization Laws; Jewish Question; Nazi Cultural Antisemitism; *Ostjuden;* Philosemitism; Weimar; Zionism

**References**

Heilbut, Anthony. *Thomas Mann: Eros and Literature.* (Berkeley: University of California Press, 1995).

Kurzke, Hermann. *Thomas Mann: Life as a Work of Art.* Translated by Leslie Willson (Princeton, NJ: Princeton University Press, 2002).

Stern, Guy. "Thomas Mann und die jüdische Welt." In *Thomas Mann Handbuch.* Edited by Helmut Koopmann. 2nd ed. (Stuttgart, Germany: Kröner, 1995), 54–67.

## Marr, Wilhelm (1819–1904)

Wilhelm Marr was never the important man he thought he ought to be. Heinrich von Treitschke called him a "windbag," and Karl Marx regretted having had to meet him, "despite all precautionary measures." "Immature boaster," "conceited ass," "subterranean literat," "poisonous snake"—this is only a partial list of insults hurled at him during his long life and afterward. Even the Nazis found him too flamboyant and suspected—mistakenly—that he was a Jew. Although he saw himself as too idealistic, too revolutionary, too principled ever to prosper in this world, almost everyone else saw the shallow journalist, the natural-born conspirator, and the opportunist prone to shabby tricks.

Appearances notwithstanding, Marr is one of the most important figures in the history of antisemitism before Hitler. He "reinvented" the word *antisemite* to describe a new sort of politics. His best-selling *Victory of Jewry over Germandom* (1879) popularized the idea of the Jewish world conspiracy while insisting on a racial conception of the Jewish Question. He made the first attempt to organize antisemitism into a political party and to inject it into a wide range of political, cultural, and social issues. He might well be thought of as the first antisemite.

The son of a famous theater actor-director, Marr was brought up in Hamburg in lower-middle-class surroundings. His formal education ended in 1839 with certification as a commercial clerk. He went to work for a firm in Vienna before moving on to Switzerland in 1841, where he gave up commerce for political agitation among the German artisans there. Under the influence of the Young Hegelians, Bruno Bauer, and the communist Wilhelm Weitling, Marr became a militant atheist, radical democrat, and revolutionary conspirator. The Swiss expelled him in 1846, and after further expulsions from several German states, he reluctantly returned to Hamburg. There, he started his own satirical newspaper and became a leading ultraleftist in the Revolution of 1848, during which he at least tacitly supported Jewish emancipation.

But the failure of the revolution soured Marr on the democratic potential of the German masses. After the coup d'état of Louis Napoleon in December 1851, he "resigned" from the democratic movement, went through a personal crisis, and turned away from his previous belief in the ideas of the Enlightenment, the French Revolution, and German idealism. In need of better answers to questions about the direction of history and his personal role in the world, Marr seized on a new vocabulary and a new set of metaphors in the infinitely flexible, pseudoscientific doctrines of racism. He soon began pondering skulls and cubic capacities of brain pans, looking for clues to explain "the undoubted precedence of the Caucasian Race" (Marr 1852, 116–117). The size and shape of heads, rather than what was in them, now counted most for Marr.

Thus primed to become a full-blown racist, he became one in the Americas of the 1850s. In the United States (which he loved) and in Central America (which he loathed), he became a white supremacist and an advocate of various eugenics schemes. But unable to establish his fortune in the New World, he returned once again to Hamburg in 1859 to take part in the revival of reform politics. Between 1862 and 1863, he was ostracized by his former democratic political associates because he wrote and spoke on behalf of black slavery and against Jewish and proletarian emancipation. In his Voltairean *Mirror to the Jews*

(1862), he maintained that Jewry, a state-within-a-state and an alien tribe with unpalatable racial characteristics, would find it impossible ever to become truly German; Jews did not deserve equal rights. But Marr was premature. Interest in the Jewish Question was slight, and the book struck no sparks.

He did not return to the subject until 1879, although he wrote incessantly on many other themes. In the intervening years, he had failed in business; divorced his first, rich, Jewish wife; and lost another wife in childbirth and a third to a fellow antisemite. In Berlin during the 1870s, he could not acclimatize himself to modern journalistic practices and eked out a living writing for any newspaper that would have him. An embittered failure, Wilhelm Marr then wrote the pamphlet that was instrumental in the politicalization of antisemitism. The tone of the *Victory of Jewry over Germandom* is one of unrelieved pessimism, in harmony with its author's thwarted ambitions. He clothed his personal grievances about journalism, his economic woes, and his general lack of significance in familiar rhetoric. His charges regarding the Jews' mendacity, ethical inferiority, instinctive hatred for all non-Jews, and unwillingness to do hard physical labor—Marr himself never did any—were already familiar to his readers. But he went further by placing Jewish evil in a racial, conspiratorial, and world-historical context. A political action program, implicit in the book, became explicit in his next pamphlet, swiftly turned out in late 1879—*Elect No Jews!* (subtitled *The Way to Victory of Germandom over Jewry*). His attempt to organize the resentments of the urban lower middle classes into the first specifically antisemitic political party, the Antisemiten-Liga (Antisemites' League), failed as quickly as had most of his other ventures. Although once again denied personal success, Marr left his mark on subsequent history by alerting powerful elements in Germany to the potential of antisemitism as a tool of political mobilization.

Irascible and impossible, Marr was soon cast aside by a younger generation of antisemitic activists. In the remaining quarter century of his life he found no role to play in their parties or politics. He died in obscurity in 1904.

—*Richard S. Levy*

*See also* Antisemitic Political Parties; Antisemitism, Etymology of; Bauer, Bruno; Emancipation; Eugenics; *Mirror to the Jews, A;* Racism, Scientific; State-within-a-State; Treitschke, Heinrich von; *Victory of Jewry over Germandom, The;* Voltaire, François-Marie-Arouet de; Young Hegelians

**References**

Levy, Richard S., ed. *Antisemitism in the Modern World: An Anthology of Texts* (Lexington, MA: D. C. Heath, 1991).

Marr, Wilhelm. *Anarchie oder Autorität.* (Hamburg, Germany: Hoffmann and Campe, 1852).

Zimmermann, Moshe. *Wilhelm Marr: The Patriarch of Antisemitism* (New York: Oxford University Press, 1986).

## Marx, Karl (1818–1883)

Karl Marx knew relatively little about Jews or Judaism. Although both of his parents were of Jewish origin, Marx was baptized in the Lutheran Church when he was six years old, did not receive a Jewish education, and is not known to have evinced interest in Jewish affairs as an adolescent. However, when he was studying at the University of Berlin, he became friends with the Young Hegelian Bruno Bauer, who was a lecturer in theology at the university. In 1842 and 1843, Bauer published several pieces on the Jewish Question. Marx read the works of his onetime teacher and responded to them.

The Jews of Prussia were not legally emancipated at that time, and Bauer maintained that civil emancipation alone would not make Jews free. The first step toward freedom, he believed, would take place when Jews recognized that their religious beliefs were preventing them from becoming free and when they therefore rejected those beliefs. Bauer, in sum, believed that Jews would have to give up Judaism before they could become liberated.

Marx disagreed with Bauer's perspective on this issue. In March 1843, he informed his friend Arnold Ruge, another Young Hegelian, that the leader of the Jewish community of Cologne had asked him to write a petition on behalf of the Jewish community to the Prussian provincial diet and that he wanted to accede to this request. Bauer's view of the Jews, Marx wrote to Ruge, struck him as too abstract.

Marx's most famous reply to Bauer, *On the*

Jewish Question (*Zur Judenfrage*, written in the fall of 1843 and published in 1844), has been interpreted by some commentators as an antisemitic tract. Seen in context, however, it is an (additional) indication that Marx actually favored the political emancipation of the Jewish community and thus differed sharply from the overwhelming majority of the antisemites of his day on the critical issue confronting Prussian Jewry. An often overlooked fact is that the political position staked out by Marx on the question of civil emancipation had more in common with that of Bauer's Jewish critics than with Bauer's hostile view of the matter.

Marx underscored that there was a distinction between political emancipation and human emancipation and that Jews were entitled to the former. In *The Holy Family,* which appeared a year or so after his response to Bauer, he and his coauthor, Friedrich Engels, went significantly further and actually suggested that the modernity of a given state could be judged by the extent to which Jews had been granted equal political rights within it.

Marx's forthright support for the political emancipation of the Jews, however, was most assuredly not accompanied—either in the 1840s or later in his career—by sympathy for Jews per se, for Jewry, or for Judaism. In the same letter in which he informed Ruge that he intended to intervene on behalf of the Jewish community of Cologne, he also proclaimed "the Israelite faith" to be "repugnant."

After the mid-1840s, Marx never again devoted significant time or energy to the so-called Jewish Question. However, he made use, both in his published writings and in personal correspondence, of deplorable anti-Jewish slurs and regularly described individuals of Jewish origin using highly distasteful epithets. Nevertheless, since Marx's writings of the early 1840s are his only extended pieces on the Jewish Question and since the position he took on civil emancipation in these pieces was both shared by leading German Jews and rejected by opponents of the Jewish community, the allegation that Marx was an antisemite should not be sustained.

—*Jack Jacobs*

**See also** Bauer, Bruno; Christian State; Emancipation; Feuerbach, Ludwig; Hegel,

**References**
Avineri, Shlomo. "Marx and Jewish Emancipation," *Journal of the History of Ideas* 25 (1964): 445–450.
Carlebach, Julius. *Karl Marx and the Radical Critique of Judaism* (London: Routledge and Kegan Paul, 1978).
Silberner, Edmund. "Was Marx an Anti-Semite?" *Historia Judaica* 11 (1949): 3–52.

## Masculinity

In the course of the nineteenth century, the image of the Jewish male as effeminate became one of the most strident stereotypes concerning Jews. This anti-Jewish prejudice was backed by arguments from a particularly wide variety of modern disciplines with scientific pretensions, making it appear almost irrefutable. The image of the unmanly Jew rested on a complex set of presuppositions evolving at the intersection of culture and nature, of scientific evidence and popular myth. The idea had a long history, dating back as far as antiquity, and it gained new currency in the Middle Ages when (male) Jews were accused of ritually killing infants in order to use their blood to stop their own menstruation. In the nineteenth century, the stereotype of the feminine Jew was further corroborated by its parallel development with prejudices against other socially marginalized groups, such as homosexuals.

The effeminate Jew stereotype had several layers, each contributing to its resiliency. At the cultural level, traditional Judaism's division of male and female roles in everyday life was of great importance to the dissemination of the prejudice. In the culture of Diaspora Judaism, Jewish women were ideally in charge of providing the family income, whereas Jewish men were supposed to dedicate themselves to religious study. This preoccupation tied men to indoor activities and made them assume a passive role ordinarily reserved for women in many other cultures. Viewed from this perspective, Jewish men performed female tasks and were therefore feminine.

Even more powerful arguments in the forging of this stereotype stemmed from medicine and physical anthropology. The major task of nineteenth-century anthropology was to collect data on physical measurements and to employ them to explain peoples' "nature." The data allegedly demonstrated that the physical constitution of Jewish men was similar to that of women: their short stature, the shape of their heads, the length of their arms in comparison to the size of their torsos, and so on. Male Jews, as well as women, seemed to be smaller and more fragile than gentile males. But the supposed physical resemblance of Jewish men and the female population and the perceived differences between Jewish and non-Jewish men went beyond externals, adversely influencing the Jews' societal position. These differences served as markers of Jewish "backwardness"—compelling evidence of "arrested development." As a result of their less developed bodies, male Jews, as well as "savages," were deemed unqualified to assume the same social status as gentile men.

Another physical factor indicating the male Jews' assumed femininity—and consequently, another impediment to their equal social standing—was their narrow chest measurement. This physical "handicap," it was widely argued, rendered them unfit for military service and thus disqualified them from performing a quintessentially male social task. "Flat feet," which impaired their ability to march, was another frequently adduced reason for excluding Jews from military service.

The peculiar speech patterns of the Jews, the supposed result of other anatomical disabilities, reinforced the notion of deficient masculinity. The so-called (big) Jewish nose produced a unique bone and muscle structure that simply made it impossible for them to produce the same sounds as non-Jews, rendering their speech largely incomprehensible. Additionally, they were said to speak faster than other people and be prone to gibbering, "exactly like women." Jews, utterly unlike Caucasian males, were also considered especially susceptible to the "female diseases," such as hysteria, neurasthenia, and nervousness. Finally, ritual circumcision had long been thought of as reducing one's manliness, therefore explaining the cowardice historically attributed to "feminized" Jews.

These physical and anthropological peculiari-ties of the Jews—the products of inherited prejudice and supported by modern science in that era—provided a long list of pretexts for denying Jewish males the opportunity to fulfill a traditionally male role and to be regarded by non-Jews as fully qualified to exercise the rights of citizenship. Refuting this negative stereotype and fighting against its consequences became one of the central projects of the Zionist movement, which sought to replace the "effeminate Jew" with the "muscular Jew."

—*Klaus Hödl*

*See also* Circumcision; Degeneration; Homophobia; Jew Census; Racism, Scientific; Ritual Murder (Medieval); Sorcery/Magic; Zionism
**References**
Gilman, Sander. *The Jew's Body* (New York: Routledge, 1991).

## Maurras, Charles (1868–1952)

Charles Maurras was born on April 28, 1868, in the small fishing village at Martigues, near Marseille, into a middle-class Provençal family that was strongly Catholic and royalist. Although personally agnostic, he developed a lifelong adherence to the church as a pillar of French civilization and to monarchism for the principle of leadership that gave consistency to his political doctrines. When he was six, his father died; at fourteen, he went deaf; and two years later, he left for Paris, the bastion of cosmopolitan modernity—all formative experiences for the man who would become a principal theorist of "integral nationalism." Antagonistic to the Third Republic and its liberal values, Maurras targeted his exclusionary patriotism at four groups that he defined as "anti-France": Jews, Protestants, Freemasons, and *métèques* (foreigners). Frenchness was defined in opposition to these groups and to Germany and England in the name of Latin, Roman, Catholic values and in the name of classicism and clarity.

First achieving notice as a literary critic associated with the neoclassicism of the École Romane (school of classical studies), he rose to prominence at the height of the Dreyfus Affair with his defense of Colonel Hubert Henry, who committed suicide in 1898 after it was revealed that he was the key forger of evidence against Alfred Dreyfus. The next year, he helped found Action Française, a leading voice on the extreme Right for the next half century, providing it with a coherent cultural, social, and political program. Classical aesthetics would restore the order of taste, beauty, and harmony to Catholic France, the only legitimate heir of the Latin world. The Catholic Church and its ceremonies would instill social values and ensure truth, and the monarchy would guarantee national unity, grandeur, and continuity.

In a series of books, Maurras drew on analyses of French decadence by thinkers such as Hippolyte Taine and Paul Bourget, and he developed a systematic cure for it. He rejected the Enlightenment's assumption of the natural goodness of man as false, as he did the heritage of the French Revolution—republicanism, individualism, and parliamentary democracy. He called instead for the restoration of national unity through the hereditary king, hierarchical but decentralized institutions of order on the provincial level, the reconstruction of the patriarchal family, and corporate structures that united workers and bosses within various sectors of industry.

He firmly defended clericalism, classical ideals, and Western civilization against barbarism and Orientalism, and he urged state antisemitism to purge the nation of contamination. From his perspective, Jews were the ultimate source of the Protestant Reformation that instilled a belief in individual conscience, which led to the destruction of Christendom and the rise of anarchic liberalism. Like the Masonic lodges, the Jewish secret cabal sought to replace legitimate rule with its own dominion. Antisemitism also served as a rallying point for all groups opposed to the republic and was, therefore, a central organizing principle of his integral nationalism.

In 1938, Maurras was elected to the prestigious Académie Française. After the defeat of France in 1940, he supported Marshal Philippe Pétain, the Vichy government, and the National Revolution that actualized many of his ideas. He was sentenced to life imprisonment and national degradation after the Liberation. On hearing the verdict, he famously declared, "It is the revenge of Dreyfus!" thus punctuating his lifelong struggle. He was released in March 1952 for medical reasons and died in November of that year, leaving behind a body of doctrine that continues to exert influence today.

—*Jonathan Judaken*

*See also* Action Française; Dreyfus Affair; France; Freemasonry; Ljotić, Dimitrije; Vichy

**References**
Carroll, David. "The Nation as Artwork: Charles Maurras and the Classical Origins of French Literary Fascism." In *French Literary Fascism: Nationalism, Anti-Semitism and the Ideology of Culture* (Princeton, NJ: Princeton University Press, 1995).
Weber, Eugen. *The Action Française: Royalism and Reaction in Twentieth-Century France* (Stanford, CA: Stanford University Press, 1962).

## Maxse, James Leopold (1864–1932)

The British journalist James Leopold Maxse was one of the most prolific and outspoken British antisemites of his time. From 1893, Maxse owned and edited the Conservative *National Review* (NR), using the monthly publication to voice his antisemitic views. He warned readers against the "International Jews" because they were deeply involved in pro-German intrigues in Britain and, alternatively, "German Jews" in England who stopped at nothing to foster their pro-German intrigues. Even though he stressed that he was writing for the man in the street, the NR's readership was actually to be found in the suburban, upper-class villas; major subscribers were Conservative politicians and journalists.

In December 1911, Maxse commenced an antisemitic campaign on the strength of vague claims that the "International Jew" was manipulating the press in order to bring England and Europe under the German yoke. But he soon turned from alleged Jewish wire-pulling to the use of antisemitism as a means of discrediting government policy and defaming leading politicians. During World War I, when Maxse's antisemitism reached its peak, he accused international Jewry of pushing—and the government of allowing itself to be pushed into—a pro-German policy that entailed the negotiation of an early end to hostilities. The existence of a powerful and sinister Jewish influence employed for destructive purposes in the life of the nation was an unquestioned article of faith for Maxse and his readers.

The implicit questioning of prevailing rules for citizenship, the *Jus Soli,* and the positing of the dual nature of Jews were further components of Maxse's antisemitism. He strictly distinguished between "good, national Jews" and "unpatriotic, dangerous international Jews." The distinction was unstable and arbitrary, however, depending on Maxse's criteria at any given moment. The national Jew could be capriciously turned into an "International Jew." National Jews were at times held hostage for the scheming of their international brethren and threatened with dire consequences should they fail to put a stop to their alleged Jewish anti-British and pro-German machinations.

Maxse was no original thinker, and therein lies his historical importance. He took his themes from the mainstream Conservative press, primarily the *Times* (London). He can be usefully studied as a kind of seismograph, registering the intensity of anti-Jewish sentiments within a certain segment of British society. His characteristic combination of racial antisemitism with Germanophobia can be seen as paradigmatic for the British discourse on Jews during his period.

—*Susanne Terwey*

*See also* Britain; Gwynne, H. A.; Webster, Nesta
**References**
Hutcheson, John A. *Leopold Maxse and the "National Review," 1893–1914: Right-Wing Politics and Journalism in the Edwardian Era* (New York: Garland, 1989).
Terwey, Susanne. "Stereotypical Bedfellows: The Combination of Anti-Semitism with Germanophobia in Great Britain, 1914–1918." In *Uncovered Fields: Perspectives in First World War Studies.* Edited by Jenny Macleod and Pierre Purseigle (Leiden, the Netherlands: Brill, 2004), 125–141.

## May Laws

The anti-Jewish pogroms between 1881 and 1882 in the Russian Empire marked the beginning of the reversal of the state's century-old effort to promote Jewish acculturation, integration, and assimilation. Under the year-long administration (May 1881 to May 1882) of Minister of Internal Affairs Count N. P. Ignatiev, an attempt to segregate Jews from non-Jews was inaugurated.

The initial concern of the regime was that socialist agitators were responsible for the pogroms. When police investigations failed to confirm this belief, Ignatiev reverted to prejudices he had long held toward the Jews. Chief among them was the belief in "Jewish exploitation," the claim that Jews avoided productive work and sought to live at the expense of their Christian neighbors through such activities as petty trade and tavern keeping. The pogroms, in this analysis, were the response of the backward, inarticulate masses to the burden of exploitation. The remedy was to be sought in separating Jews from their neighbors—specifically, by removing Jews from the countryside and from peasant villages where their exploitation was most highly developed.

Ignatiev sought justification for this change of policy by convoking local commissions in the provinces of the Pale of Settlement to examine the relations between Jews and non-Jews. These Ignatiev Commissions were charged with the task of answering questions that amounted to a virtual bill of indictment against Russian Jewry:

1. What aspects of Jewish economic activity had an especially harmful influence on the life of the native population?
2. What practical difficulties were encountered in those localities, given the existing legislation on the Jews, regarding the sale and lease of land, trade in alcohol, and usury?
3. What changes in the existing legislation were necessary to prevent evasion of the law by the Jews, and what legal and administrative measures should be taken in order to neutralize the harmful influence of the Jews in the economic life of the country?

The commissions were ordered to submit their findings to the Jewish Committee, which Ignatiev created within his ministry under the direction of his deputy D. V. Gotovtsev. The members of the commissions, appointed by the governor, offered a diverse and contradictory set of recommendations for resolving the Jewish Question—some even recommended the abolition of the Pale of Settlement. Ignatiev consistently misrepresented these responses, claiming that there was unanimous support for removing Jews from the countryside. The Gotovtsev Committee prepared a draft law that would have done precisely that by expelling Jews living in rural areas and by banning them from tavern keeping, a livelihood that supported hundreds of thousands of rural Jews.

However, leaks about the committee's deliberations engendered a widespread debate in the press and mobilized the elite secular Jewish leadership in St. Petersburg, grouped around the financier Baron G. O. Gintsburg, to block Ignatiev's initiatives. Faced with growing opposition, Ignatiev recognized that he would be unable to secure ratification of the proposed new rules by the State Council, the usual legislative course. Instead, he sought the approval of the Committee of Ministers, presenting the rules as temporary, emergency measures. But even this course met opposition from his fellow ministers, led by Minister of Finance N. Kh. Bunge, who warned of the economic harm the rules would produce. Other ministers pointed out that the worst pogroms had been in the cities, where Ignatiev now proposed to relocate the Jews driven out of the countryside.

Ignatiev argued, in turn, that the government had to be seen to be taking some action to prevent future pogroms if it was to retain the confidence of the general population. A compromise was agreed on, resulting in the promulgation of four rules:

1. As a temporary measure prior to a general review of the laws concerning the Jewish population, Jews were forbidden to settle anew outside the towns and shtetls, with the exception of existing Jewish agricultural colonies.
2. All purchases, mortgages, and leases of land located outside the towns and shtetls were suspended on a temporary basis.
3. Jews were forbidden to carry on trade on Sundays and on the twelve major feasts of the Orthodox Church.
4. Rules 1 through 3 applied only to the Pale of Settlement.

The Ministry of Finance also agreed to oversee more closely the existing laws that governed Jews in the tavern trade. The regulations were published as temporary laws at the beginning of May 1882, thus becoming known as the May Laws. Ignatiev himself fell from power within the month over an unrelated issue.

The May Laws acquired a sinister reputation in Russian Jewish historiography, despite the attenuated form in which they ultimately appeared. In fact, their negative impact has been much exaggerated. An early judicial ruling found that they did not apply to the Russian-governed Kingdom of Poland. They did not affect Jews who already lived in the countryside but only new settlement. They did not apply to shtetls, the small market towns where many Jews lived. Capricious interpretations of the May Laws, highlighted by the historian S. M. Dubnow, were usually overturned by the Russian Senate, the highest court of appeal. In the decade following the promulgation of the May Laws, the Jewish population of the countryside actually increased in numbers.

Nevertheless, the May Laws endured until the fall of the tsarist regime. They marked a turn toward segregation in Russia's Jewish policy and were an expression of a fundamental distrust in the higher spheres of the Russian administration of the economic activities of all Jews, be they rich bourgeois or the pauperized, "exploiting" masses.

—*John D. Klier*

**See also** Jewish Question; Pale of Settlement; Pogroms; Ratzinger, Georg; Russia, Imperial; Russian Orthodox Church; Usury

**References**
Dubnow, S. M. *History of the Jews in Russia and Poland.* 3 vols. (Philadelphia: Jewish Publication Society of America, 1916–1920).
Loewe, Heinz-Dietrich. *The Tsars and the Jews: Reform, Reaction and Antisemitism in Imperial Russia, 1772–1917* (Reading, UK: Harwood Academic Publishers, 1993).
Rogger, Hans. *Jewish Policies and Right-Wing Politics in Imperial Russia* (London: Macmillan, 1986).

## Mehring, Franz (1846–1919)

Although initially a left-liberal journalist sympathetic to the Social Democrats, Franz Mehring became a staunch antisocialist in the late 1870s. Subsequently, he returned to the left-liberal fold, editing the *Berliner Volks-Zeitung* from 1884 to 1890 before finally joining the relegalized Social Democratic Party in 1891. Mehring wrote editorials for the party's theoretical organ, *Neue Zeit* (New Era), for nearly two decades and was editor in chief of the renowned *Leipziger Volkszeitung* from 1902 to 1907. He is best known for his massive history of the German labor movement (1897–1898) and his Marx biography (1918), both of which are still indispensable sources; he also edited the early writings of Marx (including *On the Jewish Question*) and Engels in 1902. Moving leftward in the party, he immediately joined the radical opposition against the war and was interned without trial for several months in 1916.

It has generally been argued that Mehring's highly ambiguous pronouncements on antisemitism and matters Jewish made him an exception among his staunchly "anti-antisemitic" socialist peers. His publication of and enthusiasm for *On the Jewish Question,* as well as his obsession with the harmful nature he ascribed to philosemitism (the term generally used to denote anti-antisemitism in imperial Germany), have usually been cited as evidence against him. Philosemitism purported to defend the Jews only in order to defend the capitalist order, he argued. His critics suggested that Mehring stood alone with this interpretation and was even publicly taken to task for it, especially by Eduard Bernstein, the foremost exponent of evolutionary socialism. That Mehring wrote more extensively than any of his peers on matters Jewish and that his denunciation of philosemitism was singularly vitriolic has underscored the notion of his exceptional role.

But few of his peers wrote as extensively on any issue as Mehring did on this one or several others, and his critiques of other phenomena were generally no less vitriolic. It is worth noting that his extensive coverage of the Jewish Question resulted, in part, from his role as the Berlin correspondent for the *Neue Zeit,* compelled as he was to churn out weekly editorials on current affairs. Moreover, the philosemitism discourse was, in fact, widely accepted by German (and European) socialists. Nor was Mehring's appreciation of Marx's *On the Jewish Question* as exceptional as generally suggested. That said, his untenable claim that Marx, too, had been an avowed "antiphilosemite" and his enthusiasm for Bruno Bauer did spell out the implications of this discourse in an original and particularly stringent way.

There can be no doubt that Mehring used *On the Jewish Question* as substantiation for his own anti-Jewish prejudices and that he used the philosemitism argument to evade an unambiguous condemnation of antisemitism. The argument not only provided cover for his animosity toward Jews but also made the expression of that animosity an antiphilosemitic duty. Yet on balance, in none of these respects was Mehring genuinely at odds with the notions and practices prevalent within German Social Democracy during the imperial era.

—*Lars Fischer*

**See also** Bauer, Bruno; Jewish Question; *Jewish Question, The* (1843); Marx, Karl; Philosemitism; Social Democratic Party

**References**

Fischer, Lars. "'Es ist überall derselbe Faden, den ich spinne': Annäherungen an Franz Mehrings Haltung zu Antisemitismus und Judentum." In *Dem freien Geiste freien Flug: Beiträge zur deutschen Literatur für Thomas Höhle.* Edited by Thomas Höhle, Dieter Bähtz, Manfred Beetz, and Roland Rittig. (Leipzig, Germany: Leipziger Universitätsverlag, 2003), 129–154.

———. "Social Democratic Responses to Antisemitism and the Judenfrage in Imperial Germany: Franz Mehring, a Case Study." Dissertation, University College London, 2003.

Wistrich, Robert S. "Anti-Capitalism or Antisemitism? The Case of Franz Mehring," *Leo Baeck Institute Year Book* 22 (1977): 35–51.

## Mein Kampf

While in prison in 1924 after the failure of his attempted coup of November 1923, Adolf Hitler dictated to Rudolf Hess the first part of a book that was entitled *Mein Kampf* (*My Struggle*) and was published by the Eher Verlag, the Nazi Party's publishing house, in 1925. A second part was dictated to Max Amann and issued in December 1926, with a 1927 copyright. The two parts were combined into a one-volume edition in 1930, although they continued to be available separately. By 1945, the Eher Verlag had sold many millions of copies, and Hitler had collected enormous royalties.

An English-language edition of the full text of *Mein Kampf,* with an introduction and annotations, was published by Reynal and Hitchcock in 1939. A translation with a different introduction and notes was issued by Houghton Mifflin in 1943 and has been repeatedly reprinted since. Hitler dictated a further book in 1928 but did not publish it; this text was published in German in 1961 and in English translation in 2003.

In *Mein Kampf,* Hitler set forth a survey of his life before 1914 as he wanted it known, with special emphasis on the political lessons he claimed to have acquired as a young man in Vienna. He explained his view of World War I, his own role in it, the reasons for Germany's defeat, and the beginnings of his participation in what became the Nazi Party. In considerable detail, he outlined his beliefs about the domestic and foreign policies Germany should have been following instead of those that had been adopted by the kaiser's Germany and those that were being suggested by others on the political scene at the time he was writing. The racial interpretation of world history, the insistence on a one-party state, the conviction that Germany had to conquer vast territories for settlement, and the vehement anti-semitism—all the characteristics of his rule after 1933—were set forth in *Mein Kampf* for all to see. Hitler also explained his sense of how politics and propaganda should be carried out in furthering the goals he advocated.

In spite of all the distortions in the account of his own past as well as the preposterous character of the aims he set for Germany, the book provides extremely useful insights into the man. Some believe Hitler to have been essentially an opportunist and a national leader of a traditional type. However, it is far more conducive to an understanding of the policies he adopted once in power if one recognizes that Hitler largely believed what he wrote and tried to act on those beliefs when he had the opportunity to do so. Such a reading of *Mein Kampf* in no way precludes the possibility that when in power, as in his years of striving for power, there would be occasions for opportunistic hesitations, compromises, and alignments, but it allows one to see that these efforts were undertaken in the expectation of furthering the goals Hitler had originally set for himself and Germany.

—*Gerhard L. Weinberg*

*See also* Austria; Hitler, Adolf; Lueger, Karl; National Socialist German Workers' Party; Racism, Scientific; Schönerer, Georg von; Social Darwinism; Wagner, Richard; Weimar

**References**

Jäckel, Eberhard. *Hitler's "Weltanschauung": A Blueprint for Power.* Translated by Herbert Arnold (Middletown, CT: Wesleyan University Press, 1972).

Weinberg, Gerhard L., ed. *Hitler's Second Book* (New York: Enigma Books, 2003).

Wiener Library. "The Story of *Mein Kampf.*" *Wiener Library Bulletin* 6 (1952), 31–32.

# Melanchthon, Philipp (1497–1560)

A humanist and theologian of the early Lutheran Reformation, Philipp Melanchthon was educated at Heidelberg and Tübingen. At both universities, he was exposed to the dominant strains of Scholasticism as well as the beginnings of Renaissance humanism. Unusually adept at languages, he gained the attention of senior scholars early on, and in 1518 (with some influence from his great-uncle Johann Reuchlin), he was called to fill the first professorship of Greek at the recently established university at Wittenberg. There, he became a close ally of Martin Luther and continued his education by acquiring a degree in biblical studies. He became an articulate formulator of doctrine and an influential mentor to generations of students. Melanchthon helped shape the curriculum of secondary schools and universities throughout Germany, and his services on behalf of education earned him the honorific title, which he shares with Hrabanus Maurus, of Preceptor of Germany. An advocate of scientific and historical studies, he oversaw the publication of classical texts, biblical commentaries, and grammars and lexicons in Greek and Hebrew.

Despite full participation in the legacy of theological anti-Judaism, Philipp Melanchthon never exhibited the active intolerance found in Martin Luther, nor did he devote much effort to the conversion of the Jews. (Library of Congress)

With a rare clarity of thought and language, Melanchthon wrote some of the seminal texts of the Lutheran tradition: the *Loci Communes,* the *Augsburg Confession,* and manuals for ordination and parish visitations, as well as topical pamphlets and dozens of treatises. Theologically one with Luther in most respects, Melanchthon saw in the Catholicism of his own time a form of religion corresponding to the legalistic Judaism of the first century. Rather than inspire and guide outward observance, religious law served to reveal to a person the full extent of original sin; the Gospel, in turn, promised the comfort of divine forgiveness for those who acknowledged their sinfulness and despaired of pleasing God. Thus, a particular view of Judaism, more specifically of the Mosaic law and original sin, was a necessary component of Melanchthon's theology. That the broader Jewish tradition did not share this view

was only proof, in Melanchthon's view, of the stubbornness of the unregenerate.

Despite full participation in the legacy of theological anti-Judaism, Melanchthon never exhibited the active intolerance found in Luther; neither does he seem to have devoted much effort to the cause of converting Jews to Christianity. Rather, he projected popular prejudices on Christian "Judaizers," advocates of legalistic forms of Christian piety. For Melanchthon, as for Luther, the essence of Christianity was a liberation from codes governing outward actions to a life of gratitude for freedom from law, achieved with the atonement on the cross. The Judaizers of Melanchthon's time included the Anabaptists, for imposing biblical customs in their communities: the Catholics, for demanding outward observances in the sacramental-penitential system of meritorious "works"; and finally, fellow Lutherans, for capitulating, in the interest of peace, to pressure from Catholic powers by allowing certain Roman practices to be reinstated. Thus, despite an apparent indifference to the presence of Jews in his own time, his work, both structurally and rhetorically, capitalized on inherited prejudices.

—*Ralph Keen*

**See also** Luther, Martin; Reformation; Reuchlin, Johann
**References**
Oberman, Heiko A. *The Roots of Anti-Semitism in the Age of Renaissance and Reformation.* Translated by J. Porter (Philadelphia: Fortress Press, 1984).
Scheible, Heinz. *Melanchthon: Eine Biographie* (Munich, Germany: C. H. Beck, 1997).

## Memminger, Anton (1846–1923)

Through the Wilhelmine era, the Würzburg-based publicist and newspaperman Anton Memminger brought to German agrarian politics a populist orientation consistently marked by antisemitic appeals. Born into a constable's family in Straubing, Bavaria, Memminger enjoyed a brief stint at the University of Würzburg before embarking on a journalistic career. He started out on the political Left, working for democratic and social democratic newspapers in Würzburg and Nuremberg. His public call to the democrats and liberals of the world to aid the destitute Ludwig Feuerbach in 1872 did little to improve the ailing philosopher's fortunes, but Memminger did garner some notoriety when he delivered a prominent oration at Feuerbach's funeral the following year. By 1873, Memminger's controversial articles had earned him a series of libel suits. When these led to a nine-month prison sentence, he fled to Switzerland, where he remained for five years. He later claimed that his Swiss sojourn "fundamentally cured" him of his "internationalist cosmopolitan attitude."

Returning to Germany, he wrote a handful of books, including a polemic against free trade, an antisemitic tract, and several pieces on railway promotion schemes. He also traveled to Vienna to work on Karl von Vogelsang's *Christian Social Monthly.* In 1882, he took over editorship of a floundering Munich daily, recasting it as "a Christian-German People's Paper" championing the cause of Germany's *Mittelstand* (lower middle class). In 1886, former colleagues from the democratic *Würzburger Journal* described him as typifying the new age of "journalistic mass production": "He writes today for the democrats, tomorrow for the conservatives; in the mornings an article of antisemitic vilification flows from his pen, while in the afternoons, now overflowing with tolerance, he offers consolation. At nine o'clock he is Ultramontane, at ten o'clock liberal— in short, his pen resembles the disreputable carded ladies who prostitute themselves for payment" (*Würzburger Journal,* July 22, 1886).

For the rest of his career, Memminger would use the "Jew democrats" of the *Journal* as prominent foils in his agitation. In 1886, he acquired a Würzburg paper, the *Neue Bayerische Landeszeitung,* which soon gained Bavarian-wide notoriety for its inflammatory mixture of antisemitism and agrarianism. In 1893, as rural discontent exploded across Germany, Memminger played a leading role in Bavaria's rambunctious peasant movement. Spurning overtures to affiliate outright with the Prussian-based Agrarian League, he instead helped launch the Franconian Peasants League (Bauernbund), which merged with other Bavarian peasant leagues in 1895.

Memminger's relationship with other league leaders, especially the anticlerical radicals of Lower and Upper Bavaria, was frequently stormy; behind the scenes, he maintained a wide correspondence with more like-minded leaders from the antisemitic agrarian movements of central Germany, including Hesse, Saxony, and Thuringia, in hopes of eventually forging an agrarian party. From 1903 to 1906, he served in the Bavarian Diet, combining reformist appeals with attacks on Jewish business practices and dire warnings about the growing presence of *Ostjuden* (eastern European Jews) in Bavaria's vacation resorts. These speeches also drew from his one arguably original contribution to antisemitic thought—*Der Talmud* (1897), a lurid exposé masquerading as a scholarly study.

In 1909, Memminger and other Franconian leaders split from the Bavarian Peasants League, affiliating with the newly formed German Peasants League (Deutscher Bauernbund), a Germanwide venture intended as a liberal alternative to the Agrarian League. In this new organization, Memminger denounced Prussia's Junkers as well as the Jews, while blaming Germany's mounting troubles on its departure from Otto von Bismarck's tried-and-true path. Several books issued from Memminger's later years; the suggestively titled *Swastika and Star of David* (1922) largely indulged his lifelong fascination with occultism. Memminger died of complications from a carbuncle in 1923. His three sons, August, Thomas, and Anton, had already taken over operations of the *Neue Bayerische Landeszeitung,* which was published well into the Nazi years.

—*John Abbott*

**See also** Agrarian League; Antisemitic Political Parties; Feuerbach, Ludwig; German Peasant League; *Ostjuden;* Ratzinger, Georg; Riehl, Wilhelm Heinrich; Talmud; Vogelsang, Karl von

**References**

Abbott, John. "Peasants in the Rural Public: The Bavarian *Bauernbund,* 1893–1933." Dissertation, University of Illinois at Chicago, 2000.

## Memoirs Illustrating the History of Jacobinism (1797–1803)

The five volumes of the *Mémoires pour servir à l'histoire du jacobinisme* (*Memoirs Illustrating the History of Jacobinism*) by the French Jesuit exile Abbé Augustin Barruel make no mention of Jews in an elaborately paranoid account of the supposed conspiratorial origins of the French Revolution. Nonetheless, this foundational text in the history of modern conspiracy theories constitutes a key chapter in the prehistory of the emergence of similar fantasies focusing on Jews in the later nineteenth century, culminating with the *Protocols of the Elders of Zion.*

The Jacobins currently terrorizing France, Barruel argued in his preface, could not have appeared out of thin air. He promised to expose their lengthy conspiratorial history—and also their plans for the future, which, if not stopped, would result in the utter destruction of society. The principal authors of the conspiracy, he claimed, were Voltaire, Jean-le-Rond d'Alembert, and King Frederick II of Prussia, who had secretly planned to destroy Christianity through such methods as the publication of the *Encyclopedia,* the crushing of the Jesuits, and the recruitment of thousands of coconspirators, including Joseph II of Austria and Catherine II of Russia. These "sophists" had formed an alliance with the Freemasons, whose antireligious conspiratorial origins Barruel traced back to the medieval Knights Templars. The final and most utterly evil group in this triple conspiracy, however, were the Bavarian Illuminati, under their satanic leader Adam Weishaupt. Jacobinism had emerged out of the union of these three groups, with the aim of utterly crushing the church and concentrating all power in the conspirators' hands. Barruel's *History* was soon translated into all the major European languages, bringing its author considerable money and fame, and it remained an influential text among anti-Masonic conspiracy theorists into the twentieth century.

The association of Jews with this theory was first raised in a mysterious letter received by Barruel in August 1806, purportedly from a Napoleonic captain in Florence, Jean-Baptiste Simonini. Barruel's excellent book, Simonini wrote, had overlooked one crucial element: the conspiracy of the Jews, who had secretly founded both Freemasonry and the Illuminati and planned to dominate the world and enslave all Christians within a hundred years. The letter may have been a forgery designed to heighten anti-Jewish sentiment at the time of the Assembly of Jewish Notables in Paris. The letter was not published, however, until 1878, together with an article by another Jesuit, Grivel, who claimed that Barruel had, in an unpublished text, demonstrated the existence of a conspiratorial alliance between the Jews and the Knights Templars dating back to the fourteenth century. This assertion cannot be verified, however. It also seems possible that Simonini's letter was itself a creation of the 1870s.

—*Adam Sutcliffe*

*See also* Barruel, Augustin; *Biarritz;* Diderot, Denis; Drumont, Édouard; Freemasonry; Gougenot des Mousseaux, Henri; Infamous Decree; Jesuit Order; *Protocols of the Elders of Zion;* Voltaire, François-Marie-Arouet de; Webster, Nesta

**References**

Cohn, Norman. *Warrant for Genocide: The Myth of the Jewish World Conspiracy and the "Protocols of the Elders of Zion."* New ed. (London: Serif, 1996).

Hofman, Amos. "Opinion, Illusion and the Illusion of Opinion: Barruel's Theory of Conspiracy," *Eighteenth-Century Studies* 27 (1993): 27–60.

## Mexico

As of 2004, the Jewish community of Mexico numbered 40,000, out of a total population of 102 million. This modern community is well organized, with strong institutions, and in general has not suffered from antisemitically motivated acts of violence against individuals, institutions, or property. However, traditional Christian prejudices toward Jews, combined with specific historical trends and situations, have produced sporadic episodes of antisemitism in the media, among intellectuals, and in daily life as well.

During the late 1920s and 1930s, antisemitic outbursts centered on economic, nationalistic, and racial themes. Groups such as the Anti-Chinese and Anti-Jewish National League (1930) and the Association of Honorable Traders, Industrialists, and Professionals (1933) lobbied the government to restrict Jewish immigration. In May 1931, 250 Jewish peddlers were expelled from the Lagunilla market in Mexico City, and on June 1, 1931, proclaimed the National Day of Commerce, demonstrators protested the presence of Jews in commercial life.

Registering the influence of Nazi propaganda, the race issue gradually became dominant among right-wing groups such as the Mexican Revolutionary Action, which operated through its paramilitary Camisas Doradas (Golden Shirts). Antisemitic press campaigns and pressure on the government peaked in 1938 and 1939, thanks to the activism of the Pro-Race Committee and the National Union of Veterans of the Revolution. Typically, up to that point in Mexican history, antisemitism entered into national politics from the Right.

But after the Six Days' War of 1967, antisemitism also began to take hold on the Left. In the following decades, periods of national crisis were often punctuated with anti-Jewish sentiments expressed strongly in the media. In the aftermath of the earthquake in Mexico City in 1985, for example, Jewish factory owners were accused of profiting from the disaster, letting their workers die while saving their property. In the 1980s, during the Israeli invasion of Lebanon, and in the 1990s, during the first intifada and Gulf War, anti-Jewish commentary and antisemitic graffiti on university campuses featured traditional stereotypes that went well beyond criticism of Israeli policies.

The second intifada revived antisemitism and anti-Zionism in Mexico, and the events that followed September 11, 2001, strengthened these trends. Even though there is no significant Muslim presence in Mexico, anti-Americanism has strong support in the general population and on the Left. Israel is frequently depicted as the partner or pawn of the biggest imperialist country and oppressor of the Palestinian people. Although there were no physical attacks on Jews, over 130 antisemitic incidents were reported in 2002, a dramatic rise over previous years. Most took the form of E-mail threats, graffiti, and anti-Zionist demonstrations in which some well-known political figures took part.

Tribuna Israelita, the human relations council of the Jewish community, actively works to counter antisemitism and anti-Zionism through a program that includes the publication of articles in the national press; meetings with representatives of the government, political parties, and the mass media; and participation in radio and TV interviews. Beginning in 1995, representatives of the community and Tribuna Israelita helped fashion a statute calling for the elimination of all forms of discrimination, particularly antisemitism and xenophobia. On April 10, 2003, the Mexican Congress unanimously wrote these provisions into federal law.

—*Esther Shabot*

**See also** Anti-Zionism; Argentina; Brazil; Cuba
**References**
Gleizer Salzman, Daniela. *México frente a la immigración de refugiados judios, 1934–1940* (Mexico City: INAH: Fundación Cohen, 2000).
Porat, Dina, and Roni Stauber, eds. *Antisemitism: World Report 1995* (New York: American Jewish Committee, 1995).

## Michaelis, Johann David (1717–1791)

One of eighteenth-century Germany's leading Protestant authorities on ancient Judaism, Johann David Michaelis was a major voice in the debates over Jewish emancipation unleashed by Christian Wilhelm von Dohm's treatise *Über die bürgerliche Verbesserung der Juden* (On the Civic Improvement of the Jews [1781]). In an influential essay published in his *Orientalische und exegetische Bibliothek* (Oriental and Exegetical Library), a prominent organ of biblical criticism, Michaelis spoke out vehemently against Dohm's proposal for granting rights to Jews, arguing that their corrupt character would resist any and all measures of reform.

Michaelis studied in his native Halle before beginning a long, distinguished career as an Orientalist at the newly founded University of Göttingen. He was one of the first scholars to use knowledge of Arabic, Aramaic, and Syriac to illuminate the Hebrew Bible. His interpretation of Scripture also made liberal use of contemporary empirical sciences, drawing on geographic, historical, and archaeological writings to read the Bible much as one would approach profane texts from antiquity. Michaelis sought to study the Hebrew Bible on its own terms, as a historical document of ancient Israel. The author of many seminal works and biblical translations, Michaelis helped define the field of historical biblical criticism. Reprints of his writings in Germany and translations into English, French, Dutch, and

Danish solidified his influence through the nineteenth century.

As an expert on ancient Judaism, Michaelis also took an interest in contemporary Jewry. In a review of Gotthold Ephraim Lessing's *Die Juden* (The Jews [1749]), a drama that broke with tradition to present a Jew as a noble character, Michaelis complained that finding nobility of character in a Jew was utterly implausible. In one of his earliest published writings, Moses Mendelssohn expressed amazement at encountering such views in a scholar and accused Michaelis of using his professional position to "degrade our oppressed nation" (in Hess 2002, 107). In his critique of Dohm's proposals for Jewish emancipation in 1782, Michaelis stuck by his original views, claiming that both Judaism and the Jews' character were incompatible with citizenship. Citing their moral corruption, proclivities toward crime, and the clannish nature of Judaism as insurmountable obstacles to integrating Jews into the modern state, he claimed that granting them rights would risk transforming Germany into a "defenseless, despicable Jewish state" (in Hess 2002, 173). In this context, he drew on the discussions of race and racial difference that had emerged in the 1770s, claiming Jews were an "unmixed race of a more southern people" (in Hess 2002, 53) that even in ten generations would never have the bodily strength to perform military service. Arguing in this manner, he challenged the vision of "regeneration" central to Dohm's plea for emancipation, and he did so as a theologian, explicitly invoking his expertise on ancient Judaism. Reprinted by Dohm in 1783, Michaelis's polemics were frequently cited in the ensuing debates over Jewish emancipation.

—*Jonathan M. Hess*

**See also** Dohm, Christian Wilhelm von; Emancipation; Racism, Scientific

### References

Hess, Jonathan M. "Johann David Michaelis and the Colonial Imaginary: Orientalism and the Emergence of Racial Antisemitism in Eighteenth-Century Germany," *Jewish Social Studies* 6, no. 2 (2000): 56–101.

———. *Germans, Jews and the Claims of Modernity* (New Haven, CT, and London: Yale University Press, 2002).

## Middle Ages, Early (430–1096)

It is commonly believed that Jews in early medieval Christian Europe enjoyed relative safety. Supposedly well-disposed rulers protected them, as did a church that honored what historical literature calls the Augustinian theory. In fact, the early Middle Ages were a time of severe threat, especially from churchmen but no less from secular rulers, who often expelled Jews or, in the case of Visigothic Spain, forced them to convert. An established Jewish civil status provided a degree of stability. Early medieval Jews descended from Jews who possessed Roman citizenship and were considered permanent residents, not foreigners, and hence entitled to various rights and privileges.

Roman law eventually disappeared. By the seventh century, only abridgments (for example, the book called the *Breviary of Alaric*) were used in places such as Spain, yet in law, Jews were still *cives* (people with civic rights). They were also a "recognized people," a *gens,* eligible to receive a charter of *tuitio* (special privilege), which was given to individuals, usually merchants, vouchsafing safe conduct and freedom from tolls. Eventually, all legal statuses changed, with feudal statuses of direct dependency replacing ancient citizenship. This new order automatically excluded Jews, since all dependents (or vassals) had to swear oaths as Christians. As Jews settled in towns along the Rhine River from the late ninth century, they were also confused with foreign merchants, and like the latter, they had to depend on group privileges for the right to live in a given locale. The same tuitio charter that once signaled special privilege became the basic set of privileges defining a Jewish communal presence, eventually making Jews wholly dependent on rulers.

The church offered no great respite. The letters of Gregory the Great from the late sixth century document early churchmen forcing Jews to convert and confiscating Jewish communal structures, including synagogues. Bishop Agobard of Lyons forbade Jews to dine with Christians, for those Christians might then dine with a priest, which would, in turn, make him impure and lead to the contamination of communicants. About 1100, the French abbot Guibert de Nogent told pornographic stories of Jews who made priests spill their seed on the Eucharist. The fear of defilement by Jews through contact was rampant. Jews were said to work sympathetic magic with waxen images, a precursor of the twelfth-century charge of ritual murder. Churchmen were also petrified by the idea of Judaizing, meaning doing anything Jews might do—an anxiety harking back to Paul in Galatians 4 and 5 and I Corinthians 10, where Paul said that those who participate in or imitate Jewish rites contaminated the Christian altar and should be expelled like Ishmael, the son of Hagar, Abraham's biblical concubine. These so-called Judaizers were eventually confused with the Jews themselves. Centuries later, the image of the Jews as Ishmael served the legal scholar Oldradus in constructing a theoretical scenario justifying expulsion. By no later than about 1000, the motivation to prevent contamination led to church canons demanding nearly complete segregation. Ecumenical councils in the late twelfth and early thirteenth centuries made this preexisting legislation binding on the entire church. Segregation's goal, achieved through laws of special dress and the prohibition of the employment of Christian domestics, was to prevent Jews from ritually endangering eucharistic purity.

As for the so-called Augustinian theory of witness, it was not one of toleration or of Jewish witness to Christianity's origins pure and simple. Each reference to witness in Augustine's writings contextualizes that Jews are *capsarii,* or slaves who bear the (Christian) master's books. Following Augustine, popes cited Psalm 59:12, which speaks of not killing Jews. But this citation was a prooftext, signifying a complex policy of toleration and restraint. Nobody took it at face value, not, at least, until Pope Benedict XIV in his bull of 1751 intimated precisely that it should be taken literally.

Jews themselves lived in small communities and never exercised real power, notwithstanding various legends asserting that they were princes and rulers in Narbonne. Nor were they high officials, although some frequented royal courts; the often heard claim of a royal-Jewish accord lacks substance.

Internal Jewish life under these conditions is well reflected in a rhymed prose narrative in Hebrew, the *Scroll of Ahimaaz,* a tale of origins and pride that reveals what Jews studied and what re-

lations they had with Jews beyond Europe—Ahimaaz lived with and described Jews in Oria (far southern Apulia in Italy)—including Byzantium and the land of Israel. Ahimaaz's women are sometimes forceful, his fathers "cherish" their daughters, and most heroes practice (positive) magic. When Rabbi Jacob Tam (d. 1171) said, no doubt playfully, that from Bari goes forth the Torah and the word of the Lord from Otranto, he knew that his ancestors had immigrated from these Apulian cities, northward to the Rhineland—with their learning, which great scholars such as Solomon Yitzhaki (Rashi), would later perfect.

Jewish communal organization was commensurate with the small communities found throughout what is today northern and southern France and the Rhineland, as well as Italy and Spain. Jews reached England only with William the Conqueror in 1066; apparently, no Jews lived in Scandinavia or the Low Countries, and Poland's great Jewries date only from the sixteenth century. A Hebrew text from about the early eleventh century in the Rhineland refers to a theory of government by consensus of the governed. People were to "enter into a *herem,*" meaning a common oath to set aside a particular district as a place where certain rules were enforced (not excommunication)—what the English later called the domain where the king's writ runs (hence, a judicial district). Christians justified these districts by likening them to the eternal body of Christ, with the kingdom eventually perceived (in imitation) as a mystical political body. Jews obviously could not do this, and in the long run, they failed to develop a satisfactory political theory, especially a theory of representation, however close to one the concept of a consensual herem was. Guided by rabbinic scholars, until about the thirteenth century, Jews viewed the community as a court originating with a mythical founding scholar. Theoretically—the rabbinic pressure for this is explicit—such a court might overrule any deliberative body.

Still, Jewish communities thrived. Commerce developed, and so did schools. The Talmud, essentially legal discussions edited in Asian Mesopotamia between about the third and seventh centuries, was also assimilated to European realities. New glosses (in the eleventh century) led to extensive commentary (from the twelfth), enabling Jewish daily and communal life. The First Crusade of 1096 dramatically interrupted this process. Marauding bands, including nobles, but not the formal crusading army led by a bishop, wreaked havoc among the Jewish communities. Numerous instances of Jews dying to sanctify God's name—often suicides, preceded by parents slaughtering children and spouses—particularly perplexed Christians. So, too, did the return to Judaism by those forcibly converted to Christianity during the mayhem, which Christians branded as apostasy. These events and the memory of them fostered by Christians served to entrench the lessons already to be found in the writings of John Chrysostom, Agobard of Lyons, and Guibert de Nogent: Jews were immoral, and excessive contact with them menaced the purity of Christian society.

An opposing school or, more precisely, a complementary one said, following Paul in Romans, that Jews had an integral role to play in Christian society as harbingers of the end of days. This view, commensurate with the Jews' status as citizens in later Roman law, was espoused by Gregory the Great despite his equal concerns about Jews and Judaizing, and it was enshrined by Pope Alexander II in 1063 when he wrote that because Jews always accepted Christian rule, they were not to be considered active enemies like the Saracens, and, hence, merited protection and the right to live peacefully. In 1096, this irenic vision came under permanent threat, as did Jewish lives themselves, no matter how much Jews might culturally and economically thrive thereafter and no matter how many periods of quiet might intervene between one attack or expulsion and another.

—*Kenneth Stow*

*See also* Agobard; Augustine of Hippo; Chrysostom, John; Crusades; Expulsions, High Middle Ages; Gregory the Great, Pope; Lateran Council, Fourth; Paul; Ritual Murder (Medieval); Sorcery/Magic; Visigothic Spain; Yellow Badge
*References*
Cohen, Gerson D. "Esau as Symbol." In *Jewish Medieval and Renaissance Studies*. Edited by Alexander Altman (Cambridge, MA: Harvard University Press, 1967), 19–48.

Gilchrist, John. "The Perception of Jews in the Canon Law in the Period of the First Two Crusades," *Jewish History* 3, no. 1 (1988): 9–25.
Stow, Kenneth. *Alienated Minority: The Jews of Medieval Latin Europe* (Cambridge, MA: Harvard University Press, 1994).
Ta-shema, Israel. "Ashkenazi Jewry in the Eleventh Century: Life and Literature." In *Ashkenaz: The German Jewish Heritage*. Edited by G. Hirschler (New York: Yeshiva University Museum, 1988), 23–57.

## Middle Ages, High (1096–1343)

During the High Middle Ages, European culture reached an impressive pinnacle. Characteristic of Europe from the late eleventh through the early fourteenth centuries were: urbanization; "the commercial revolution"; territorial expansion; advances in science, schools, and universities; increasing social mobility; and the emergence of national state powers, particularly England and France. It was in this era that the church also flourished, extending its reach and developing an elaborate internal structure. One of its chief concerns in this phase of its history was the identification and suppression of heresy, which naturally led to an intensive interest in the Hebrew language and the practice of Judaism.

Europe was home to a growing Jewish population as well. In the midst of rapid and far-reaching changes in social, cultural, political, and economic life and perhaps as a result of them, anti-Judaism surfaced in a variety of forms, one of which was overt physical aggression. Violence against the Jews erupted frequently in the High Middle Ages, but no event was more severe or has been more discussed than the massacres of the Jews that took place during the First Crusade, at the very outset of the era. Scholars debate the overall effects on the Jewish community, but the vivid and detailed chronicle accounts leave a stark impression of the extent of the carnage and the precarious position of the surviving Jews in much of Europe for the rest of the period.

According to one recent interpretation, two phases of anti-Judaism are visible in the High Middle Ages: the first hinged on the foreign nature of an immigrant Jewish population and the related perception of Jews as religious dissidents; the second focused on the image of Jews as hos-

Illustration of Jews being burned in Cologne, after a woodcut by Wohlgemuth. Violence against the Jews erupted frequently in the High Middle Ages, but none was as severe or widespread as the massacres that took place during the First Crusade. (Stapleton Collection/Corbis)

tile toward European Christian society, not just as religious nonconformists but also as economic competitors, allied to the barony, and as historic enemies (Chazan). Throughout the Middle Ages, contact between Christians and Jews was unavoidable. Conflict could be overt, leading to violence, or latent, making possible some degree of integration and normal daily relations.

Despite the great advancements that have been collectively termed the Renaissance of the Twelfth Century, Jews were increasingly marginalized in theological and learned discourse. The preexisting *Adversus Iudaeos* tradition remained dominant, further enhanced by a string of polemical works that cast Judaism as the antagonist of Christianity. Indeed, slowly crystallizing elements of Christian doctrine set the scene for expanded anti-Jewish accusations. As the Eucharist became more fully a Christian sacrament during the High Middle Ages, alleged Jewish desecration of the host surfaced and became widely publicized. By steal-

ing and attempting to defile the host, Jews, it was alleged, were actually attesting to the power of the Eucharist, thus corroborating the church's message: namely, that the real presence of Jesus was in the consecrated wafer. Tales of divine intervention that resulted in the apprehension and lethal punishment of Jews, as well as the establishment of pilgrimage sites, fostered correct Christian belief and by the same token cast Jews as increasingly nefarious. It was in this period, as well, that Jews began to be accused of acts of ritual murder. The charges typically alleged that Jews first abducted and then tortured and murdered Christian children to use their blood for religiously prescribed rites, especially for the baking of Passover matzah. Many Jews died as a result of these constantly recurring fantasies.

A number of church councils also had significant legal impact on the Jews, whose activities and appearance were ever more closely monitored and controlled. The Third Lateran Council of 1179, for example, prohibited Jews and Muslims from having Christian servants and extended a general ban on usury. At the same time, however, measures were enacted to protect Jews from forcible conversion and physical assault. With the Fourth Lateran Council in 1215, significant and ominous legal precedents were established: Jews were prohibited from usurious excesses, even as crusaders had the interest they owed on any debts remitted; they were forced to identify themselves by wearing a yellow badge; and they could not hold public office or appear in public on Easter and other Christian festivals. Converts from Judaism were ordered to desist from any form of Jewish practices.

As the church strengthened its hold on European life and particularly through the agency of the mendicant orders, Jews experienced increasing hostility. Many mendicants became noted for their skill and interest in Hebrew, but they used this knowledge to preach openly against the Jews and against their rabbinic writings. Jewish literature was extensively censored and attacked, on the pretext that the rabbinic texts blasphemed Christianity. The Talmud was "put on trial" and burned in Paris in 1240 and in many other places as well. The desire to convert the Jews led to forcible disputations, such as the one that took place in Spain in 1263 when the convert Pablo Christiani debated Rabbi Moses ben Nahman (Nahmanides).

Throughout the High Middle Ages, Christian imagery—in a preliterate age—depicted Jews as involved in magic, theft, and deception and thirsting after Christian blood. A variety of graphic representations fashioned them as demonic, criminal, and blind to true religion. Jews were often physically segregated in their own quarters, although official ghettoization did not begin until the end of the Middle Ages. There were also some attempts to protect Jews. Indeed, after the violence of the Crusades, it was clear that they required governmental protection. Efforts in this regard, however, often took the form of making Jews into "servants of the chamber," by definition a weak and dependent status that contributed to the popular contempt in which Jews were held; like the clergy and women, they could not bear arms. The political and social turmoil experienced by the emerging nation-states

of England and France also had disastrous effects on the security of Jews. England expelled them in 1290. In France, the Blois blood libel of 1171 led to the burning of thirty-one Jews and was a prelude to increasing marginalization. In 1181, Philip Augustus had all the Jews of Paris arrested and then ransomed for a large sum of money; in 1236, there were serious riots in Anjou and Poitou, and in Brittany, the violence culminated in 1240 in another expulsion. A blood libel case in 1247 and host desecration charges in 1290 ultimately led to the sweeping expulsion of 1306.

It would be a mistake to assume that the history of anti-Judaism in the High Middle Ages was limited to Christian Europe. Although at times faring better under Muslim rule, Jews living in the orbit of Islam also experienced discriminatory treatment and general insecurity. Defined as a "people of the book," the Jews were conceived of as a protected but second-rate population and were forced to endure a number of social and cultural humiliations, such as wearing distinguishing clothing and paying special taxes. With its emphasis on orthopraxy as opposed to orthodoxy, Islam was less concerned with heresy than medieval Christian Europe was. Although they were sometimes treated better than Christians, Jews could expect no more than toleration, and this, too, occasionally gave way to oppression and massacre, as in Granada in 1066 and the Almohad persecutions of the twelfth century in Spain and North Africa.

—*Dean Phillip Bell*

**See also** *Adversus Iudaeos;* Almohad Persecution; Crusades; Dominican Order; Expulsions, High Middle Ages; Ghetto; Host Desecration; Iconography, Christian; Islam and the Jews; *Judensau;* Lateran Council, Fourth; Masculinity; Peter the Venerable; Rindfleisch Massacre; Ritual Murder (Medieval); Sorcery/Magic; Talmud; Talmud Trials; Usury; Yellow Badge

**References**
Baron, Salo W. *A Social and Religious History of the Jews.* Vol. 11 (Philadelphia: Jewish Publication Society of America, 1952).
Chazan, Robert. *Daggers of Faith: Thirteenth-Century Christian Missionizing and Jewish Response* (Berkeley: University of California Press, 1989).
———. *Medieval Stereotypes and Modern Antisemitism* (Berkeley: University of California Press, 1997).

Cohen, Jeremy. *The Friars and the Jews: The Evolution of Medieval Anti-Judaism* (Ithaca, NY: Cornell University Press, 1982).

———. *Living Letters of the Law: Ideas of the Jew in Medieval Christianity* (Berkeley: University of California Press, 1999).

Cohen, Mark R. *Under Crescent and Cross: The Jews in the Middle Ages* (Princeton, NJ: Princeton University Press, 1994).

Langmuir, Gavin. *Toward a Definition of Antisemitism* (Berkeley: University of California Press, 1990).

Stow, Kenneth R. *Alienated Minority: The Jews of Medieval Latin Europe* (Cambridge, MA: Harvard University Press, 1992).

## Middle Ages, Late (1343–1453)

The anti-Jewish outbursts of the High Middle Ages grew in intensity and scope during the later Middle Ages, a period that has frequently been defined by historians as one of decline and decay in the position of the Jews. Wandering and mendicant preachers continued to dispose the populace negatively toward the Jews. Increased agitation against Jewish moneylending and usury combined with tense political and social situations in many late medieval cities and towns to spark massacres, expulsions, and elaborate restrictive legislation. These factors reinforced the growing marginalization of Jews that had been under way for centuries. Added to the charge that they practiced a heterodox religion, they were also frequently accused of more secular sins—subverting the common good and harming ordinary folk. Caught in the web of escalating political tensions between the nobility, the emperor, and the cities, German Jewry was manipulated, attacked, and "pawned" in a series of regional and urban expulsions that covered much of the German-speaking world from the middle of the fourteenth century until the middle of the sixteenth century. The lack of strong centralized government in central Europe, a shrinking economy, and protracted feuds and wars left little chance for solid or consistent policies or protection, even had this been desired by the powerful.

In France, there were general expulsions throughout the fourteenth and fifteenth centuries and massacres in 1380. The persecutions of 1338 and 1347 throughout Alsace and in Germany in the late 1330s and during the Black Death hinged on charges that the Jews were poisoning wells and plotting the downfall of Christian religion and government. In Spain, the end of the fourteenth century witnessed violent anti-Jewish preaching that led to demands for the destruction of synagogues and murderous attacks on Jewish communities. The wave of violence in 1390 and the subsequent forced conversions in 1391 bequeathed significant problems with *conversos* (New Christians) during the entire fifteenth century.

The immiseration of the Jews seemed irreversible. Promising social and economic mobility during the fifteenth century was soon curbed by anti-Jewish legislation in late medieval Spain. In 1412 in Castile, Jews were required to live in special quarters, were not allowed to hold the honorific title "don," and were forbidden to serve as tax farmers. In 1449, riots in Toledo led to the first Pure Blood Laws, excluding all men of Jewish ancestry from holding municipal office there. The conversos issue, combined with purity-of-blood legislation, tense social relations, and the later establishment of the Inquisition, resulted in numerous and significant trials of New Christians, accusations of Judaizing, and increasingly negative attitudes toward the remaining observant Jews, who were accused of trying to sway conversos back to Judaism. Significant regional expulsions in the 1480s turned out to be only a prelude to the final expulsion of some 200,000 Jews in 1492, effectively emptying the Iberian Peninsula of its ancient Jewish population by the early sixteenth century.

Another initially hopeful sign also proved disappointing. With the Renaissance came a renewed interest in the Hebrew language and the appearance of Christian Hebraists. But this interest, even when it led to calls to preserve and protect Jewish literature, did little to slow the enthusiasm of radical churchmen seeking to burn rabbinic writings and convert the Jews. Anti-Jewish preaching, greater "knowledge" of Judaism, and theological disputations (in which Jewish participants were extremely vulnerable to retaliation)—all these substantiated for Christian scholars the claim that Christians had definitively supplanted Jews as God's chosen people. Attitudes toward Jews alternated between fear and disdain.

Written out of history and increasingly ghettoized, Jews lived in habitual insecurity, subject to the whims of individual rulers and the volatile hatreds of the mob.

Fervent preaching against the Jews in a language accessible to simple people was at least as influential as sophisticated theological arguments in the hardening of rejectionist attitudes. One particularly persuasive preacher of the period was Bernardino of Sienna. Drawing from a rich store of economic, criminal, communal, and medical metaphors and arguments, Bernardino likened the Jews to a plague attacking the body of the civic commune and all of Christendom:

> Money is the vital heat of a city. The Jews are leeches who ask for nothing better than the opportunity to devour an ailing member, whose blood they suck dry with insatiable ardor. When heat and blood abandon the extremities of the body to flow back to the heart, it is a sign that death is near. But the danger is even more imminent when the wealth of a city is in the hands of the Jews. Then the heat no longer flows, as it does normally, towards the heart. As it does in a plague-ridden body, it moves towards the ailing member of the body; for every Jew, especially if he is a moneylender, is a capital enemy of all Christians. (In Robert Bonfil, *Jewish Life in Renaissance Italy,* 1994, 24.)

Familiar accusations of host desecration and ritual murder originated earlier in the Middle Ages, but each had a significant further development in the late Middle Ages. The most famous case of an alleged ritual murder was that of Simon of Trent (in 1475). Young Simon became the subject of a folk song, "*Vom heiligen Simon,*" that served to broadcast the guilt of the Jews far and wide in a preliterate age. According to the song, the Jews, in their great need for Christian blood, sent for a Christian child. As was also typical of many of the cases of host desecration, a disgruntled Christian acted as intermediary, arriving in the Jewish quarter with "the goods"—the pious son of a cobbler. The "contemptuous Jews," because of their great blindness, tortured and murdered the boy, using his collected blood

to bake their Passover bread, which was then distributed to many lands. The song described how the Jews read anti-Christian statements from the (imaginary) tractate *Agoyim*. In the end, however, they were punished for the cruel shedding of innocent blood, and miracles occurred in the name of the martyred Simon.

The focus of the song and of the accusations more generally were on the alleged criminal and inhuman acts of the Jews. But a number of elements in this and other stories of heinous crime synthesized older and newer stereotypes that have since appeared and reappeared as the so-called Jewish Question. First, Jews work with traitorous Christians to achieve their ends. Second, Christian victims are required for Jewish ritual and practice; Judaism thus becomes the exact and deadly antithesis of Christianity and Jews the remorseless enemies of Christians. Third, the Jewish actions not only reflect general animosity toward Christianity but also give birth to the fantasy of a union of Jews operating across borders and dedicated to fearful evil.

—*Dean Phillip Bell*

**See also** Alsace; Capistrano, John of; Expulsions, Late Middle Ages; Ghetto; Host Desecration; Inquisition; Jewish Question; Middle Ages, High; Passion Plays, Medieval; Prague Massacre; Pure Blood Laws; Ritual Murder (Medieval); Simon of Trent; Spain, Riots of 1391; Supersessionism; Usury; Well Poisoning

**References**

Beinart, Haim. *The Expulsion of the Jews from Spain.* Translated by Jeffrey M. Green (Oxford: Littman Library of Jewish Civilization, 2002).

Bell, Dean Phillip. *Sacred Communities: Jewish and Christian Identities in Fifteenth-Century Germany* (Leiden, the Netherlands, and Boston: Brill, 2001).

Breuer, Mordechai. "The 'Black Death' and Antisemitism." In *Antisemitism through the Ages.* Edited by Shmuel Almog and translated by Nathan H. Reisner (Oxford: Pergamon, 1988).

Foa, Anna. *The Jews of Europe after the Black Death.* Translated by Andrea Grover (Berkeley: University of California Press, 2000).

Meyer, Michael A., Brenner, Michael, Breuer, Mordechai, and Graetz, Michael., eds. *German-Jewish History in Modern Times.* 4 vols. (New York: Columbia University Press, 1996), especially vol. 1, *Tradition and Enlightenment: 1600–1780.*

Roth, Norman. *Conversos, Inquisition, and the Expulsion of the Jews from Spain* (Madison: University of Wisconsin Press, 1995).

Stow, Kenneth R. *Alienated Minority: The Jews of Medieval Latin Europe* (Cambridge, MA: Harvard University Press, 1992).

Trachtenberg, Joshua. *The Devil and the Jews: The Medieval Conception of the Jew and Its Relation to Modern Anti-Semitism* (Philadelphia: Jewish Publication Society of America, 1943).

## Militia Movement

The militia movement in the United States draws together hundreds of diverse groups seeking to preserve their vision of an American society based on traditional ideals and, especially, on limited government. The movement's self-image stems from a mythic understanding of the role of the American militias in the Revolutionary War. Collectively xenophobic, anticommunist, anti-Catholic, antisemitic, and racist, the movement's social-intellectual outlook owes much to the nineteenth-century Ku Klux Klan (KKK) and twentieth-century Christian Identity movement. Christian Identity anticipates a biblical apocalypse and calls on members to prepare by storing food and weapons. An elaborate Identity theology links the KKK to several of the diverse elements of the militia movement in the United States.

During the second half of the twentieth century, the militia movement remade itself around the concept of the "patriot" movement. Contrary to the more public and confrontational style of the KKK, the U.S. militia movement shied away from public exposure in favor of survivalist and isolationist activities. Militia tactics ranged from relatively nonviolent acts, such as the refusal to pay income taxes and calls for secession from the United States, to highly visible armed standoffs with government agencies.

In the late 1970s and 1980s, the Posse Comitatus sought to appropriate the image of the militia of the American Revolution. Its newsletter declared the United States had fallen under the control of international Jewry. The group's founder, Henry Beach, a veteran of pro-Hitler organizations in the 1930s, claimed that the United Nations had taken control of the election of federal officials and that the Federal Emergency Management Agency would serve as the instrument for imposing the new world order in the United States. Typical of subsequent militiamen, the Posse members believed they were involved in a struggle against an international conspiracy to deny average citizens their rights. One of their seminal texts was the novel *The Turner Diaries* (1978) by William Pierce, who, under the pseudonym Andrew Macdonald, described an underground white army conducting a brutal revolution against the so-called Zionist Occupied Government (ZOG), located in Washington, D.C. Behind ZOG, according to Posse and Identity adherents, stands world Jewry, communists, and those who would defile the white race.

In the 1990s, the loosely constructed movement defined itself around prominent organizations, individuals, issues, and events: the Posse Comitatus; John Trockman and his Militia of Montana; William Pierce; the death of Gordon Kahl in Arkansas; the shoot-out at Ruby Ridge and the assault on David Koresh's Branch Davidians in Waco, Texas; and the Freemen standoff in Jordan, Montana. The article of faith uniting these disparate elements is a fundamental, deeply embedded distrust of the government. The ideas of America's Founding Fathers, they are certain, have been irreparably subverted. According to militia supporters, the U.S. government no longer represents the interests of the American people or protects the freedoms enshrined in the Constitution and Bill of Rights. These so-called patriots commonly see agents of this conspiracy against liberty in all branches of the U.S. military and law enforcement (from the level of county sheriff all the way up to the Federal Bureau of Investigation). Their paranoid style connects the militia to many other groups on the radical Right and to those who still find inspiration in the *Protocols of the Elders of Zion*. In their battle against the new world order, militia supporters oppose any sort of gun control. They are antigay and against abortion rights; they call for the repeal of the Federal Reserve Act and the Internal Revenue Code.

What degree of support the militias enjoy in the broad American public is difficult to ascertain. It is fair to say, however, that the bombing of the Murrah Federal Building in Oklahoma

City, with its clear links to the militia, seriously diminished whatever public sympathy might have existed for the movement. That die-hard supporters insist on holding the government responsible for the Oklahoma City bombing has probably not helped their cause.

For up-to-date information about the militia movements in the United States, various reputable watchdog groups, including the Anti-Defamation League of B'nai B'rith and the Southern Poverty Law Center, continually track their activities and monitor their publications. These efforts have revealed the existence of hundreds of militia-related Internet sites. Militia-related propaganda continues to circulate, primarily via newsletters, radio broadcasts, mass mailings, and videotapes and over the Internet.

—David A. Meier

See also American Jewish Committee and Antidefamation Efforts in the United States; Christian Identity Movement; Internet; Ku Klux Klan; Pelley, William Dudley; *Protocols of the Elders of Zion;* United States; White Power Movement

**References**
Barkun, Michael. *Religion and the Racist Right: The Origins of the Christian Identity Movement.* Rev. ed. (Chapel Hill: University of North Carolina Press, 1996).
Bennett, David H. *The Party of Fear: From Nativist Movements to the New Right in American History* (Chapel Hill: North Carolina University Press, 2001).
Stern, Kenneth S. *A Force upon the Plain: The American Militia Movement and the Politics of Hate* (New York: Simon and Schuster, 1996).

## Mirror to the Jews, A

*A Mirror to the Jews* (*Der Judenspiegel* [1862]) marked a critical moment in the journey of its author, Wilhelm Marr (1819–1904), from ultra-Left revolutionary to racist antisemite. In the same year he brought out this argument against equal rights for Jews, he published an attack on the idea of proletarian emancipation and a defense of the institution of black slavery. *Der Judenspiegel* owed its existence to the local politics of Marr's Hamburg hometown, providing the excuse for the famously splenetic author to let off steam and settle petty personal grudges. Aside from his musings on eugenics, bolstered by his travels in North and Central America during the 1850s, there seemed to be little new in the substance of his anti-Jewish opinions. But the notions of Jewish mendacity, ethical inferiority, instinctive hatred for all non-Jews, and arrogant adherence to a hollow religion—all ideas that could be found in Voltaire or the Young Hegelians—were given a pointedly racial character by Marr. "[Judaism] and its precepts are nothing but products of [the Jews'] consciousness, their particularities are manifestations of their organism" (in Zimmermann 1986, 116–118). The onetime apostle of liberty announced that he would not lend his pen to the cause of Jewish emancipation. Because of the Jews' incompatible "tribal peculiarities," emancipation was unwarranted and would probably provoke a hostile reaction on the part of the masses. He was certain that the people intuitively distrusted Jews as an alien race, as did 90 percent of Germans of all classes. Marr advanced his own Hamburg experience as decisive proof of his view. Jews, recognizing their peril at the hands of popular forces, had flocked to the reaction after the revolution of 1848, not only for safety's sake but also to reap the rewards won for them by idealistic radicals such as himself. Emancipation would simply act as an invitation for Jews to control everything; its motive, he now realized, was to facilitate the pursuit of their material interests. Marr thus voiced one of the central fears of those who, a few years later, would call themselves antisemites—that Jewish emancipation would reverse the power relations between Jews and Germans, leading ultimately to the "Victory of Jewry over Germandom," as his best-seller of 1879 put it. Emancipation, for the Jews, was not an idealistic struggle for freedom but a grab for naked power.

As often was the case in Wilhelm Marr's career, his timing with *A Mirror to the Jews* was faulty. The decade of the 1860s was not especially receptive to discussions of the Jewish Question. The author had to publish the work at his own expense; it roused a flurry of interest in Hamburg and then vanished swiftly from public view. After such an indifferent reception, Marr waited seventeen years before venturing to raise these issues again, doing so then in a vastly altered political and economic environment.

—Richard S. Levy

**See also** Emancipation; Marr, Wilhelm; *Victory of Jewry over Germandom, The;* Voltaire, François-Marie-Arouet de; Young Hegelians
**References**
Zimmermann, Moshe. *Wilhelm Marr: The Patriarch of Anti-Semitism* (New York: Oxford University Press, 1986).

## Misanthropy

In antiquity, the charge of misanthropy was leveled against the Jews for the first time at the beginning of the third century BCE, in a text written by the Greek ethnographer Hecataeus of Abdera; it can be found, as well, in Latin literature until the beginning of the second century CE, in Juvenal's fourteenth satire. According to the extant sources, only twelve writers (at most) may be said to have accused the Jews of misanthropy during the period, but this is not a good indicator of how widespread the belief was. Ethnic stereotypes were common in the ancient world, and some other peoples were characterized as hostile toward foreigners in an even harsher way. But the accusation of misanthropy was formulated exclusively against the Jews.

*Misanthrôpia* or *apanthrôpia*—translated in English as *misanthropy*—is not only a Greek word but also a Greek concept. In opposition to the traditional view that the charge of misanthropy was originally an Egyptian anti-Jewish theme stands the argument that the origin of the accusation is Greek. Hecataeus—who was not hostile toward Jews and expressed surprise at their "somewhat misanthropic and inhospitable mode of life" (Diodorus 40.3.4)—related their misanthropy to the traumatic experience of expulsion from Egypt because of their differing religious rites. His etiological explanation is similar to the one Plato gave of misanthropy in general (*Phaedo,* 89d).

The misanthrope was a common figure in Greek theater during the fourth and third centuries BCE, where he was never a barbarian but rather a Greek who refused to take part in the life of the polis and to interact with his fellow citizens. Thus, qualifying the Jews as a misanthropic people implied that they belonged to the Greek world. This was actually the case in Alexandria, the place where Hecataeus made his ethnographic investigations: all Jews, many of whom served in the Ptolemaic armies, were considered Hellenes. Nevertheless, from the second century BCE onward, in the tense context of military conflicts between the Hasmonean dynasty and Hellenistic cities in Palestine, the charge of misanthropy became much more malevolent and was used as an argument for harming Jews (see Diodorus 34–35.1.1–5). In Latin literature, the charge appears mainly in texts written after the Jewish war against Rome, always in a pejorative way.

In general, the charge of misanthropy is connected to three factors: (1) a negative perception of Jewish dietary rules; (2) a negative perception of the Jewish refusal to take part in cultic celebrations that were an integral part of Hellenistic political life; and (3) the idea that Jews rejected basic human duties such as showing the way to the foreigner, giving fire or water to those in need, and so on. Only two texts refer to the ritual murder of foreigners. The prominence of the charge of misanthropy at certain times and in certain places can be explained by a combination of political factors and philosophical influences (mainly Stoic-Peripatetic universalistic humanism).

—*Katell Berthelot*

**See also** Alexandrian Pogrom; Dietary Laws; Manetho; Ritual Murder (Medieval); Roman Empire; Roman Literature
**References**
Berthelot, Katell. *Philanthrôpia judaica: Le débat autour de la "misanthropie" des lois juives dans l'Antiquité* (Leiden, the Netherlands: Brill, 2003).
Schäfer, Peter. *Judeophobia: Attitudes towards the Jews in the Ancient World* (Cambridge, MA: Harvard University Press, 1997).
Stern, Menahem. *Greek and Latin Authors on Jews and Judaism.* 2 vols. 5th ed. (Jerusalem: Israel Academy of Sciences and Humanities, 1998).

## Moczar, Mieczysław (1913–1986)

Mieczysław Moczar, born Mikołaj Demko, was a member of the pre–World War II Polish Communist Party and joined its successor, the Polish Workers' Party, shortly after its formation in 1942. During the war, he was a partisan with the Communist People's Guard and People's Army.

After the war, he became head of the secret police for Lodz. He displayed a talent for surviving the various changes of regime and party line, serving during the Stalinist period (1948–1956) as district governor of Olsztyn and then as chairman of the Białystok District Council. In 1964, he founded the Union of Fighters for Freedom and Democracy, a veterans' organization, heading a group nicknamed the "partisans": this became his power base. In the same year, he became minister of the interior, in charge of the secret police nationally.

Moczar had already displayed antisemitic views while holding his post in Lodz: he expressed the opinion that the number of Jews in the security apparatus was excessive and was undermining the party's credibility. Later, as head of the partisans, he advocated "national Communism" or "Endo-Communism"—a mix of *Endek* (National Democrat) and Communist ideas—as a way of enhancing the party's popularity. Moczar was the chief instigator of the "anti-Zionist" purge in 1968, which he may have believed would open the way for him to take the top job. If so, his plan failed. In 1968, he was demoted to party secretary, and he filled various other posts until his death.

—*Steven Paulsson*

**See also** Anti-Zionism; National Democrats; Poland; Purge of 1968; Stalinization of Eastern Europe

**References**

Steinlauf, Michael C. *Bondage to the Dead: Poland and the Memory of the Holocaust* (Syracuse, NY: Syracuse University Press, 1997).

Stola, Dariusz. *Kampania antysyjonistyczna w Polsce, 1967–1968* (The Anti-Zionist Campaign in Poland, 1967–1968) (Warsaw: Instytut Studiów Politycznych Polskiej Akademii Nauk, 2000).

## Mohammed (ca. 570–632)

Islam's prophet and founder did not originally hold negative views about Jews and Judaism. As a young man, Mohammed had probably met a good number of both Jews and Christians. His native city of Mecca was a center of mercantile activity along the caravan route linking Yemen to the south, where frankincense and myrrh and other luxury commodities were produced, with

the Byzantine provinces of the Levant to the northwest and the Sasanian Empire to the northeast. According to Islamic tradition, he had traveled with caravans into Byzantine Syria and was impressed by the piety of Christian monks. Moreover, the caravan route passed through Arabian oases that had major Jewish settlements. Most historians agree that Mohammed probably encountered Jewish and Christian merchants who acted as amateur missionaries from whom he absorbed basic monotheistic notions. Mohammed believed that Jews, Christians, and others had received divine revelations in their own languages, which the one supreme God had sent through prophets. When he began to receive his own revelations in Arabic, he challenged his pagan opponents to go and ask the Children of Israel, who would confirm the truth of his own revelations. Internal evidence in the Koran suggests that he may have been encouraged in his early preaching by monotheist mentors. However, when Mohammed went to Medina in 622, at the invitation of the Arab tribes there that converted to his new faith, he came into daily contact with a large, organized Jewish community that had no part in inviting him. The encounter changed his—and Islam's—attitudes toward Jews for the worse.

Historians differ on the precise nature of Mohammed's conflict with the Medinese Jews and the circumstances surrounding their opposition to him. Many Western scholars have argued that Mohammed arrived in Medina expecting to be accepted by the Jews there as a prophet sent by God; when he was rejected by them, the scholars contend, he turned against them out of pique, driving out two tribes—the Banu Qaynuqa and the Banu 'l-Nadir—and massacring the third—the Banu Qurayza. This scenario is unlikely. Mohammed was certainly aware that Jews and Christians did not recognize each other and that many Christian sects considered one another anathema. He may, however, have hoped that the Jews of Medina would give him some encouragement in his mission to the pagan Arabs. Instead, he met with fierce opposition. The Jewish scholars of Medina openly contradicted him, and he was particularly stung by their ridicule of what they considered his glaring errors in relating biblical and midrashic lore. They, who were, by his own admission, the recipients of a divinely revealed Scripture, were attacking him on the very level at which he was most vulnerable, the all-important revelatory level. Mohammed became convinced that the Jews' opposition to him was purely arrogance on their part.

With the faith of the true believer in his own inspiration, he came to the logical conclusion that whatever the Jews were citing to contradict him must be false. He may have heard the Christian accusation that the Jews had corrupted the text of their Scriptures. He had already been told by the Jewish convert to Islam 'Abdallah ibn Salam that the Bible contained prophecies foretelling Mohammed's coming. Like other Jewish renegades in both the medieval Muslim and Christian worlds, 'Abdallah proved his zeal for his adopted religion by exposing the falseness of his former coreligionists who either refused to see or suppressed those signs in their sacred texts that predicted the advent of Mohammed or Jesus, as the case may be. Koranic revelations, such as Sura 3:78, confirmed the belief that the Jews were misrepresenting their Scriptures, and the idea that Jews (and also Christians) had tampered with, made substitutions to, and altered their holy books became an article of later Islamic dogma.

Mohammed did not have sufficient strength to act against the Jews during his first two years in Medina, but shortly after his arrival, he promulgated a covenant for the governance of the town, which is often referred to as the Constitution of Medina. In this document, he confirmed the Jews as members of the Medinese community with rights and responsibilities alongside the Muslims but on the condition that they did not act wrongfully. This vague proviso was to provide the Arabian prophet with a legal avenue for changing Jewish status at a later date. In 624, after his first significant victory against the pagans of Mecca, Mohammed found a pretext to turn on the weakest of the Jewish tribes, the Banu Qaynuqa, who surrendered after a brief siege and were expelled from Medina. The following year, after a Muslim defeat by the Meccans, Mohammed accused the Banu 'l-Nadir of plotting against him (after being warned by a divine revelation) and expelled them as well. Their lands

were divided up among the Prophet and his followers who had gone with him from Mecca. Mohammed's own share brought him financial independence, and the booty formed the basis of the new Muslim state treasury. In 627, he attacked the last remaining Jewish tribe, the Banu Qurayza, on the very day that the final Meccan siege of Medina was abandoned. The casus belli was that the tribe had supposedly planned to make common cause with Mohammed's pagan enemies. After a twenty-five-day siege, the Qurayza surrendered, expecting to be exiled like the two Jewish tribes before them. Now stronger than ever, Mohammed showed no mercy. All the adult males—between 600 and 900 individuals—were beheaded in the central marketplace, and the women and children were enslaved.

In 628, Mohammed led his forces against the Jews of the Khaybar oasis, 95 miles northeast of Medina. After putting up a fierce resistance, the Khaybaris surrendered. The Banu 'l-Nadir who had taken refuge there were given no quarter, but the local inhabitants were guaranteed their lives and their property in exchange for an annual payment of 50 percent of their date harvest. Similar tributary agreements followed shortly thereafter with the Jews in the other oases of northwestern Arabia, and following the surrender of Mohammed's native town of Mecca and his supremacy over the entire Hijaz, Jews as well as Christians all over Arabia—from Yemen in the south to Yamama, Nejd, and Bahrain in the east—began to pay tribute, called *jizya,* to the new overlord. In 630, Mohammed received divine confirmation of this practice when the koranic verse was revealed to him enjoining Muslims to fight against the peoples of the Book "until they pay the *jizya* out of hand and have been humbled" (Sura 9:29). In 632, the year of his death, Mohammed established the precedent of making the jizya, which previously had been paid in kind, a poll tax.

Mohammed's attitudes toward Jews became increasingly negative during the last ten years of his life. Throughout the period of conflict in Medina, he received more and more revelations censuring the Jews as those who "pervert words from their meanings" and whom "Allah has cursed for their disbelief" (Sura 4:46). Other Koranic verses from this period denounce the Jews because "they hasten to spread corruption throughout the earth" (Sura 5:64) and accuse them, along with the polytheists, of being "the most vehement of men in enmity to those who believe" (Sura 5:82). But despite the fact that he believed that their Scriptures had, in some degree, been corrupted, he never questioned the basic validity of their religion. The Hadith, or Islamic tradition of the Prophet's words and deeds, attribute both hostile and benign pronouncements on the subject of Jews. The original recognition accorded them prior to his *Hijra* (hegira), or emigration to Medina, was never abrogated. Jews were to be fought against only until they submitted to Muslim rule as humble tribute bearers. Mohammed's sunna, or practice, in his attitudes toward and treatment of Jews, as indeed in all other things, set the precedent to be followed by the Muslims of future generations.

—*Norman A. Stillman*

*See also* Arab Antisemitic Literature; Islam and the Jews; Islamic Fundamentalism
**References**
Goitein, S. D. *Jews and Arabs: Their Contacts through the Ages,* 3rd rev. ed. (New York: Schocken, 1974).
Stillman, Norman A. *The Jews of Arab Lands: A History and Source Book* (Philadelphia: Jewish Publication Society, 1979).

## Mortara Affair

On June 23, 1858, police in Bologna, Italy, descended on the home of Momolo Mortara and Marianna Padovani and their seven children. Sent on orders of the local inquisitor, they had come to seize the Jewish couple's six-year-old son, Edgardo. The inquisitor, having determined that the boy had been secretly baptized, received instructions from the Holy Office of the Inquisition in Rome—headed by Pope Pius IX himself—to have the child taken. The church had long held that no baptized child of a Jewish family could remain with his parents, for they would exercise a pernicious influence on him. Whether the parents had authorized the baptism or even known about it was irrelevant from the church's perspective. Although the Mortaras were not then informed of who allegedly had baptized their son, they later learned that a former domestic servant, Anna Morisi, claimed to have secretly baptized Edgardo when, at age twelve months, he was ill. Whether she actually performed such a baptism in the Mortara's house remains a mystery, for she had other motives that might have led her to make such a charge.

Many similar cases of forced baptism followed by abduction by the police occurred in Italy in the first decades of the nineteenth century. What made the Mortara affair different was the international uproar that ensued. With separation of church and state being one of the main rallying cries of the Italian movement for national unification and with the primary obstacle being the continuing existence of the Papal States—of which Bologna was the largest city after Rome—the Mortara case offered champions of unification a golden opportunity to rally support. Moreover, Jews in western Europe were increasingly free to organize politically and to express their views through the expanding press. After the Damascus ritual murder case of 1840, the Mortara affair was the first major campaign of self-defense over which the international Jewish community organized. Indeed, the case led directly to the founding of the Alliance Israélite Universelle, the most important Jewish international self-defense organization in Europe.

Edgardo Mortara was taken directly from his house to Rome, where he was initially placed in the House of the Catechumens, established in the sixteenth century as a place to convert Jews and Muslims. But as the international protests grew—reaching as high as the French emperor and involving popular demonstrations in the United States, with 3,000 participants in San Francisco and 2,000 in New York—the pope himself began to play an active role. Indeed, Edgardo came to be treated as Pius IX's adopted son, and the pope withstood all the pressure, arguing that it was his sacred duty to prevent the child from returning to his Jewish family. Not even his redoubtable secretary of state, Cardinal Antonelli, who argued that holding on to the child would be a political disaster for the precarious position of the Holy See, could move him. Attempts by the Jewish community of Rome to petition the pope on the Mortaras' behalf were rejected.

A year after the Jewish boy was taken, the forces of Italian unification drove the cardinal legate out of Bologna and ended the pope's temporal dominion there, as in much of the Papal States. In January 1860, police of the new regime arrested Father Feletti, Bologna's inquisitor, at his Dominican monastery and charged him with the kidnapping of Edgardo Mortara. A few months later, the court acquitted him of the charge, ruling that he had acted according to the laws then in force. Edgardo had, by this time, been transferred to a Roman religious school run by the Canons Regular order at the Church of San Pietro in Vincoli, placed there by the pope himself. He was periodically shown off to visitors by Pius, who was eager to demonstrate that the boy was happy to have been plucked from his Jewish family and pleased to have found the true path to salvation.

Meanwhile, Momolo Mortara—a merchant of modest means—toured Europe to drum up support for the return of his son. With the Holy See now confined to the city of Rome and the surrounding area, the pope's position became tenuous. Momolo sought to take advantage of the pope's desperate need for all the diplomatic support he could get from France, Britain, and other countries. However, none of the efforts to apply pressure proved successful.

When Italian forces finally conquered Rome in 1870, destroying the last vestiges of the Papal States, Momolo Mortara hurried in to reclaim his son. Edgardo, however, now nineteen and not having seen his parents in a dozen years, had decided to become a priest. With the help of the monks of his monastery, he fled Rome just as his father was about to see him and then escaped Italy altogether. He did, indeed, become a priest, devoting much of his career to preaching throughout Europe in the several languages in which he was fluent, telling the inspirational story of how God plucked him from his Jewish family in order that he might attain true salvation.

The Mortara case not only had great significance for Jews but also played a role in the drama of Italian unification. The pope's refusal to heed the pleas of Napoleon III helped further undermine his support for the continued existence of the Papal States, which French troops were then helping to maintain. More generally, the refusal to return Edgardo contributed to the growing sense that the pope's role as temporal ruler, with his own police force, was an anachronism that could no longer be maintained.

Edgardo Mortara died in 1940 at age eighty-eight, in a Belgian abbey where he had lived for many years. He had reestablished contact with his mother in the 1870s—his father having died in the meantime—and in later years occasionally visited members of his family, whom he sought, unsuccessfully, to convert.

—*David I. Kertzer*

***See also*** Alliance Israélite Universelle; Damascus Blood Libel; Inquisition; Pius IX, Pope
***References***
Kertzer, David I. *The Kidnapping of Edgardo Mortara* (New York: Knopf/Vintage, 1997).
Korn, Bertram W. *The American Reaction to the Mortara Case, 1858–1859* (Cincinnati, Ohio: American Jewish Archives, 1957).

## Moseley, George Van Horn (1874–1960)

A highly decorated and respected military leader, Gen. George Van Horn Moseley was also one of the preeminent antisemites in the United States. This "survival-of-the-fittest" Darwinian espoused elaborate theories warning of an imminent Jewish danger to Western civilization. Moseley is usually depicted as an extremist, not truly representative of the army. Yet he was far from a peripheral figure, and the fundamental aspects of his "political biology" were present in army teaching, reports, and political engagements into the 1930s. Moseley, who became Douglas MacArthur's "most trusted subordinate" and President Herbert Hoover's confidant, was also an influential mentor to George C. Marshall, George S. Patton, and especially Dwight D. Eisenhower.

An archetype of the old officer corps, Moseley boasted of his Anglo-Saxon pedigree; his West Point class (1899) had only one Jew, who was soon eliminated. An Army War College graduate (in 1911), Moseley confirmed his Darwinism by waging racial warfare in the Philippines. In World War I, his courageous exploits were as legendary as his brilliance as a general; he twice won the Distinguished Service Cross. Serving as MacArthur's assistant chief of staff, he developed and implemented the emergency plan for forcing the Great Depression Bonus Marchers out of Washington, D.C., in 1932, with the assistance of his two protégés Eisenhower and Patton. In these years, he also proposed a eugenics program for reinvigorating U.S. manpower and a presidential emergency regime to suppress the political threat to the country posed by subversive, racially inferior minorities.

Moseley's eugenics caused a furor during the Jewish refugee crisis of 1938. Lecturing reserve officers on racial degeneracy and other social ills supposedly threatening the country's survival, he proposed sterilizing all Jewish refugees from Nazi Germany before admitting them to the United States. Top officers were forced to reprimand Moseley, but they remained privately loyal to him. Retiring later that year, the general campaigned against a Roosevelt administration he thought was leading the United States into a war to establish Jewish hegemony throughout the world.

His extremist congressional testimony in 1939 ended his brief presidential bid but not his crusade. Like Hitler's Germany, he argued, the United States had to combat Jewish communism while salvaging its race and government through selective breeding, sterilization, and elimination of the unfit. He also defended German expansion in Europe, stating that American boys should not die protecting Christ-killing Jewish communists. His decades-long correspondence and unpublished, multivolume memoir, *One-Soldier's Story,* embodied every variety of antisemitism, which he buttressed with scientific racial theories and elaborate historical and political allusions. For example, he contended that through inbreeding, Jews had evolved into a despised, animal-like race whose repulsive and dangerous hereditary traits had to be bred out of humanity. After the war, Moseley, still defending his country from Jewish subversion, maintained that the existence of the state of Israel proved that Jews now dominated the United States.

—*Joseph W. Bendersky*

See also Armed Forces of the United States; Eugenics; Judeo-Bolshevism; Lindbergh, Charles; *Passing of the Great Race;* Patton, Gen. George; Racism, Scientific; Social Darwinism

References

Bendersky, Joseph W. *The "Jewish Threat": Anti-Semitic Politics of the U.S. Army* (New York: Basic Books, 2000).

## Mosley, Oswald (1896–1980)

Sir Oswald Mosley, leader of the British Fascist movement in the 1930s, was born into privilege and was attracted to public service from an early age. As a returning war hero, he moved in the best circles and married the daughter of Lord Curzon; the royal family came to his wedding. For the first twenty years of his adult life, he showed few antidemocratic inclinations, and in the 1920s, he was elected to Parliament, first as a Conservative, then as an Independent, and finally as a Labourite.

How such a man could evolve into a defender and even an admirer of Nazi Germany remains puzzling. His early life was, in most regards, a perfect antithesis to Hitler's. Indeed, neither Mosley nor most of his lieutenants fit into familiar generalizations about Fascists being insecure men motivated by cranky resentments and drawn to demagogy. Even after he had embraced fascism, Mosley's intellectual sophistication was widely recognized; he was known for speeches that delved into complex economic issues, and throughout his career, he firmly denied harboring a racial hostility to Jews, terming antisemitism a repellent and "nonsensical" doctrine.

That denial depended, in part, on a rather narrow definition of antisemitism and a selective memory. But there seems little doubt that Mosley's move toward fascism in the early 1930s was driven not by a belief that Jews were an evil race but rather by his mounting frustrations with Britain's political elite, who, he decided, were unable to do anything effective to remedy the depression or reverse Britain's decline as a world power. His experiences at the front had shaken his confidence that Britain's liberal-democratic institutions could deal with the realities of the modern world, and the floundering of the established parties from 1929, when he served in a Labour ministry, powerfully revived his earlier doubts.

Throughout the 1920s, Mosley had little or nothing to say about Jews. He dismissed Benito Mussolini as a vulgar bully and a dangerous na-

British fascist leader Sir Oswald Mosley acknowledges the salute of his Blackshirt followers during a rally in Hyde Park. (Hulton-Deutsch Collection/Corbis)

tionalist when many other British politicians, most notably Winston Churchill, were singing the praises of Italian fascism. But by 1932, at the depth of the depression, Mosley visited Italy and concluded that Mussolini, so unlike the British political elite, had new ideas and was applying superior methods in dealing with unemployment. Soon afterward, he formed the British Union of Fascists (BUF). At this point, antisemitism was not a significant aspect of Italian fascism, and when Hitler took power in early 1933, Mosley declared that the anti-Jewish measures of the Nazi regime were "a great mistake." However, he also expressed admiration for that regime's dynamism, popular acclaim, and openness to new economic ideas.

Given the record of both the Italian Fascists and the German Nazis in destroying the Left in their countries, it was hardly surprising that Mosley's move toward fascism earned him pas-

sionate denunciations as a traitor. It was equally unsurprising, given Hitler's record, that Jews in Britain perceived Mosley and the British Fascists to be deadly enemies. For Mosley to insist that he harbored no antipathy to Jews as a race was, to say the least, too subtle a distinction to be given much credence at the time or since. Moreover, the BUF undoubtedly attracted antisemites of a more extreme sort; its members became especially notorious for clashes with the Jews of London's East End, each group claiming the other to be the aggressor but, in truth, both itching for a fight. In increasingly combative terms, often goaded by Jewish hecklers, Mosley attacked Jewish bankers, journalists, and leftist politicians—all, he claimed, were attempting to pull Britain in directions contrary to its national interests.

Mosley attracted much notoriety but few followers; the BUF's membership peaked at perhaps 40,000, about the same as the British Communist Party. As the 1930s progressed, Mosley adamantly opposed Britain's drift to war, and he drew closer to both Italian fascism and German Nazism. He seemed unable to recognize the full extent of the barbarism of Nazi rule and its encouragement of racial hatred; he professed to be more impressed with the dangers of war. He was interned at the outbreak of World War II but released in 1943. After the war, he attempted, with little success, to reorganize a neo-Fascist movement. His target at that point was immigrants of color; he avoided attacks on Jews, but he apparently never gained a genuine appreciation of the horrors of Nazi antisemitism.

—*Albert S. Lindemann*

See also Britain; British Union of Fascists; Mussolini, Benito; National Socialist German Workers' Party

**References**
Lebzelter, Gisela C. *Political Anti-Semitism in England, 1918–1939* (New York: Holmes and Meier, 1978).
Mandle, W. F. *Anti-Semitism and the British Union of Fascists* (London: Longmans, 1968).
Skidelsky, Robert. *Oswald Mosley* (New York: Holt, Rinehart and Winston, 1975).

## Müller-Guttenbrunn, Adam (1852–1923)

The "Don Quixote of Antisemitism," as Adam Müller-Guttenbrunn once described himself, rose from humble beginnings to prosperity as the author of *völkisch* (racist-nationalist) novels, many of which glorified the German Swabian enclave of his native south-central Hungary. He was a resident of Vienna from 1879, where his role as an antisemite was that of polemicist and then director of the world's first explicitly antisemitic theater. He also presided over a nationwide anti-Jewish writers' association. As early as 1887, he wrote in Viennese newspapers against the Jewish influence in German art, "a sickness which had to be fought." (Geehr 1973, 25–44). He subsequently collaborated with the notorious and fanatical Guido von List in a series of rancorous articles about the need for an antisemitic theater to combat alleged Jewish cultural influence. Müller-Guttenbrunn used this opportunity to campaign for the directorship of an Aryan the-

ater, the repertoire of which, he vowed, would embrace nationalism and antisemitism. In this effort, he was successful, becoming the theater's first director from 1898 to 1903.

From the outset, he was plagued by the interference of members of Karl Lueger's Christian Social Party over questions of repertoire, management, and especially profits. Only partially funded by the municipality and individual Christian Socialists, Müller-Guttenbrunn was forced to borrow at high interest rates and succeeded in securing the necessary support only by promising substantial profits to investors. When these failed to materialize, he resorted to a number of questionable business practices. The Aryan Theater steadily declined into debt.

Meanwhile, he had irritated influential Christian Socialists. Though some antisemitic plays were performed, Müller-Guttenbrunn was obliged to refute charges in Lueger's party press that he was failing to live up to the original ideological goals of the theater. He attempted to produce three blatantly racist antisemitic plays. When the censor forbade their performance, Müller-Guttenbrunn had the first two works published at his own expense and distributed in thousands of copies. But this move failed to satisfy the growing number of antisemitic critics who wanted to see their racial hatreds acted out on the municipal stage. Müller-Guttenbrunn's final production was a play that dramatized the failure of racial intermarriage and reminded one critic of the writings of Houston Stewart Chamberlain and Count Joseph Arthur de Gobineau. Although this play was doubtless intended as an expression of Müller-Guttenbrunn's own antisemitism, it was no more successful than earlier, less ideological plays; unable to avoid bankruptcy, he resigned his directorship in June 1903.

Later that autumn, under a pseudonym, he published a racist antisemitic novel that summed up his experience as a theater director. He had struggled to undo the baleful influence wielded by Jewry over Vienna's cultural life. But he had failed, and a stronger man was needed. In December 1938 in the Nazi Party paper *Völkischer Beobachter,* one of Müller-Guttenbrunn's sons celebrated the fortieth anniversary of the opening of the Aryan Theater. According to him, the recent annexation of Austria by Hitler's Germany had at last created the sociopolitical conditions that would allow a "truly German *Volk* stage" to flourish. His father's efforts had not been in vain.

—*Richard S. Geehr*

*See also* Aryan Theater; Austria; Chamberlain, Houston Stewart; Christian Social Party (Austria); Film Propaganda, Nazi; Gobineau, Joseph Arthur de; List, Guido von; Lueger, Karl

**References**

Geehr, Richard S. *Adam Müller-Guttenbrunn and the Aryan Theater of Vienna: 1898–1903* (Göppingen, Germany: Göppinger Arbeiten zur Germanistik, 1973).

# Multiculturalism

The complex and sometimes contradictory history of American multiculturalism, an ideal that promised pluralist democracy and respect for ethnic difference, paralleled much of the American Jewish acculturation process. Beginning the twentieth century as the nation's greatest proponents of multiculturalist thinking, Jewish intellectuals and social activists faced marginalization late in the century when many of their onetime political allies invoked antisemitic canards to discredit the Jewish communal commitment to tolerance and pluralism.

In 1908, the Jewish writer Israel Zangwill wrote the famous play *The Melting Pot,* which popularized the notion of an American nation committed to integrating its diverse immigrants. Zangwill pressed for immigrant assimilation as the most effective remedy for the challenges of ethnic diversity in the United States. Seven years later, Horace Kallen, a German-born American Jew, offered a reinterpretation of the traditional melting pot model of immigrant acculturation. Acculturation, he argued, should not be seen as a matter of adding a variety of ethnic ingredients to produce a common stock. Instead, in a bid to celebrate diversity, Kallen employed the metaphor of the symphony orchestra. According to this model, each minority group lent its own unique sound to a powerful and harmonious crescendo. "As in an orchestra," he explained, "every type of instrument has its specific timbre and tonality . . . so in society, each ethnic group may be the natural instrument." Respect for eth-

nic difference would forge "a multiplicity in a unity, an orchestration of mankind." Kallen's ideas helped establish "cultural pluralism" as the best alternative to the melting pot assimilation model (in Dollinger 2000, 41).

In the immediate post–World War II period, black and Jewish leaders attached these multicultural ideals to the burgeoning civil rights movement, arguing alternately for a melting pot nation committed to social and economic inclusion and a pluralist society willing to embrace distinctive cultural forms. Martin Luther King Jr., joined famously by Rabbi Abraham Joshua Heschel, imagined a nation that would offer the inclusiveness of Zangwill's melting pot and the respect for diversity championed by Kallen.

With the end of the civil rights movement in the late 1960s, a new generation of black civil rights activists pressed for ethnic nationalism, a separatist reformulation of the multicultural model. Jewish liberals faced exclusion from many national civil rights organizations, whereas the most extreme black nationalists mixed their rejection of accommodationism with strident antisemitism. In the minds of some ethnic nationalists, Jews had joined the white middle class in the United States and could neither appreciate nor support a version of multiculturalism committed to empowering the weakest and most persecuted Americans. By the end of the twentieth century, multiculturalism became synonymous with relativist calls for the wholesale reevaluation of the political, economic, and educational systems of the United States.

—*Marc Dollinger*

*See also* African American–Jewish Relations; Black Nationalism; New Left

**References**

Biale, David, Michael Galchinsky, and Susannah Heschel, eds. *Insider/Outsider: American Jews and Multiculturalism* (Berkeley: University of California Press, 1998).

Dollinger, Marc. *Quest for Inclusion: Jews and Liberalism in Modern America* (Princeton, NJ: Princeton University Press, 2000).

# Music, Nazi Purge of Jewish Influence in

Hitler conceived of his taking power in 1933 as a cultural revolution. As Richard Wagner might well have wished, music was to play a central role in the National Socialist state. The "most German of all the arts" and a direct expression of the racial soul, music bore the task of shaping Aryan man. Bach, Beethoven, and Wagner were elevated to representatives of the national essence and racial role models. To perform these lofty functions, German music needed to be cleansed of alien elements.

In the first years of the dictatorship, the battle against political opponents, especially socialists and communists, took precedence. Musicians, such as Otto Klemperer, Arnold Schoenberg, and Kurt Weill, were defamed as cultural Bolsheviks. Protests organized mainly by the Kampfbund für deutsche Kultur (Combat League for German Culture) were followed by legal actions against artists of Jewish descent. In April 1933, the purge of the civil service led to the dismissal of many "non-Aryan" musicians, musicologists, directors, and composers from their university positions, state-run opera houses, and orchestras. It was immaterial whether these non-Aryans were assimilated or not, whether they were religious Jews or Christian converts.

From around 1936, non-Aryans were excluded from the Reich Chamber of Music, essentially prohibiting them from practicing their profession. Politically inspired firings gave way to racially motivated purges, and the slogan cultural Bolshevism was supplanted by "cultural degeneration" (*Entartung*), which the Nazis declared to be the product of race mixing. Even though Wagner had written his antisemitic *Judaism in Music* in 1850 and Houston Stewart Chamberlain had later picked up Wagner's line of argument, European music had largely been spared a "racialist" analysis before 1933. Neither the requisite scientific interest nor a plausible methodology was available for such an undertaking. The Nazis, therefore, relied predominantly on dilettantes for this endeavor. Although their racist political-cultural writings were criticized by musical specialists, they were effective expressions of antisemitic defamation. Around 1938, academic musicologists took issue with the race question, but they did not dare challenge the National Socialist state's discriminatory policies.

In May 1938, Hans Severus Ziegler, the artistic director of the city of Weimar's theater, staged the Degenerate Music Exhibition in Düsseldorf during the Reich Music Days, which coincided with a conference of musicologists. He seized on Ernst Krenek's opera *Jonny spielt auf* (Jonny Strikes Up) as the symbol of the Weimar Republic's decadence and typical of its cultural miscegenation. As early as 1930, Ziegler had published a manifesto titled "Against Negro Culture" protesting what he insisted was the foreign domination of German music by jazz and American dance music. The Düsseldorf exhibit cited numerous examples of the inordinate Jewish influence on German musical life before 1933.

Ziegler's propaganda show, which traveled to Weimar and Vienna, became an object of contention even among Nazis, however. It made fine distinctions between "pure German" and "racially mixed" music that were not all that easy to discern and that, more important, had no bearing on the purge that was under way. The decisive criterion, as far as the regime's oppressive measures were concerned, was solely the ancestry of the musician. Non-Aryans could no longer belong to the Reich Chamber of Music, no matter that they played the works of Bach or Beethoven or composed in that style. An independent Jewish culture was far less dangerous than the assimilation of Jews to German culture; thus, Jews were systematically to be driven from the concert hall, the radio, and the recording industry, and their names were to be stricken from musical catalogs. They would thereafter dwell in the ghetto of the Jewish Cultural League (Kulturbund Deutscher Juden) and be forbidden to perform the works of German composers.

In their officially sanctioned *Lexikon der Juden in der Musik* (Lexikon of the Jews in Music) (1940), Theophil Stengel and Herbert Gerigk drew up the balance sheet of Nazi persecution. Some assimilated Jews—Schoenberg and Weill, for example—responded by returning to the practice of Judaism. Klemperer, Schnabel, Walter, Alfred Einstein, Fritz Kreisler, Paul Bekker, and Victor Ullmann, among many others, were undeterred in their steadfast adherence to Austrian-German musical culture. In defiance of the Nazis, persecuted musicians found new homes in the USSR, North and South America, Africa,

Asia, and Australia, where they became, regardless of their Jewishness, exponents of a world musical culture. No country benefited more from this exodus than the United States.

—*Albrecht Dümling*
*Richard S. Levy, translation*

**See also** Chamberlain, Houston Stewart; Degeneration; *Judaism in Music;* Musicology and National Socialism; Nazi Cultural Antisemitism; Nazi Legal Measures against Jews; Purge of the German Civil Service

**References**

Brinkmann, Reinhold, and Christoph Wolff, eds. *Driven into Paradise: The Musical Migration from Nazi Germany to the United States* (Berkeley: University of California Press, 1999).

Dümling, Albrecht. "The Target of Racial Purity: The 'Degenerate Music' Exhibition in Düsseldorf, 1938." In *Art, Culture and Media under the Third Reich.* Edited by Richard A. Etlin (Chicago: University of Chicago Press, 2002), 43–72.

## Musicology and National Socialism

Musicology, the study of music in its aesthetic, social, and historical contexts, was as seriously affected by the National Socialists' assumption of power in 1933 as every other academic discipline in Germany. The requisite purge of Jews from academic positions drove out several important scholars. Alfred Einstein, cousin of the physicist and longtime editor of the leading disciplinary journal *Zeitschrift für Musikwissenschaft* (Journal for Musicology), was one of the most prominent Jewish scholars to be removed. Einstein's colleague Johannes Wolf resigned from the journal's board in protest against the removal, but his example was not widely emulated within the profession.

German musicologists contributed to the war effort by producing what Pamela Potter has described as "*Lebensraum* [living space] propaganda." Such propaganda consisted largely of articles written for the popular press, designed to legitimize Nazi military advances in Europe either by establishing connections between conquered regions and German culture through supposed interrelationships between regional musical styles or (in the case of France) by showing that the conquered region had either no authentic musical identity or a severely degraded one and thus required German cultural management to set matters right.

Even before the establishment of the National Socialist state, there was a comparatively muted strain of antisemitism running through the writings of some German musicologists, particularly with respect to the work of such problematic Jewish composers as Gustav Mahler and Arnold Schoenberg (both converts to Christianity). With the encouragement of Hitler's propaganda minister, Joseph Goebbels, musicologists began to address the issue of the Jewish "race" and Jewish musicality with varying degrees of enthusiasm. Prominent figures, including the Bach and Beethoven specialist Arnold Schering (who engineered Alfred Einstein's dismissal) and the Wagner scholar Alfred Lorenz, vigorously endorsed racialist aesthetics, claiming that a composer's musical style derived, at least in part, from biologically determined characteristics. Lorenz wrote three or more articles on the subject, including one specifically entitled *Musikwissesnschaft und Judenfrage* (Musicology and the Jewish Question), which rehearsed the standard arguments of inherent Jewish noncreativity; he also offered a course on "music and race" at the University of Munich.

Friedrich Blume, the editor of the magisterial reference tool *Die Musik in Geschichte und Gegenwart* (Music in History and the Present) and one of the most important figures in the postwar reestablishment of the discipline, offers a particularly interesting case study. In spite of his own skepticism, Blume recognized that musical racialism as a field of study offered a path to professional advancement under the National Socialist regime. He took it on himself to claim a prominent position in the field, delivering the keynote address at the 1938 "Music and Race" conference of musicologists in Düsseldorf at Goebbels's invitation. He went on to publish a volume of his own and to edit a series of monographs devoted to the subject. His success was such that he was invited to contribute an article to a volume honoring Hitler's fiftieth birthday. Yet in his own discussion of the intersections between race and music, Blume avoided making specific mention of Jews and offered criticisms of the assumptions driving his colleagues' work that were veiled enough to escape the notice of his government sponsors. After the war, acknowledgment of these criticisms within the scholarly community helped Blume recover his international reputation. The postwar careers of other scholars were seriously tarnished when aspects of their involvement with National Socialism became public knowledge.

In some ways, the nature of musicological practice itself paved the way for the surrender to National Socialism. Beginning in the early nineteenth century, the initial development of historical perspectives on music was premised on the identification of differences among regional and national musical traditions. Largely dominated by German-speaking scholars, the field had developed a tendency to place the German tradition at the center of Western music, establishing a narrative that viewed music history as the story of advancing German hegemony. By the 1930s, however, German musical preeminence was being challenged from several directions; composers from Russia and France crowded their Austrian and German colleagues from opera stages and concert halls; the Second Viennese School composers Schoenberg, Alban Berg, and Anton Webern appeared to be doing their best to undermine the German tradition; and the growing enthusiasm in Europe for American popular music, with its strong African American influences, was threatening to render that tradition all but irrelevant. Together with the disastrous effect exercised on academia by World War I, the hyperinflation, and the Great Depression, as well as chronic anxiety within the field about its own social and cultural relevance, these factors left musicology as a discipline ready to place itself in the service of the National Socialist regime's propaganda machine. In the end, however, its usefulness proved rather more limited than some German musicologists had initially hoped.

—*David Isadore Lieberman*

***See also*** Music, Nazi Purge of Jewish Influence in; Nazi Cultural Antisemitism; Wagner, Richard

**References**

Kater, Michael. *The Twisted Muse: Musicians and Their Music in the Third Reich* (New York: Oxford University Press, 1997).

Levi, Erik. *Music in the Third Reich* (New York: St. Martin's Press, 1994).

Meyer, Michael. *The Politics of Music in the Third Reich* (New York: Peter Lang, 1991).

Potter, Pamela. *Most German of the Arts: Musicology and Society from the Weimar Republic to the End of Hitler's Reich* (New Haven, CT: Yale University Press, 1998).

# Muslim Brotherhood

Founded in Ismailiyya, Egypt, in 1928, the Society of Muslim Brethren (Jam 'iyyat al-Ikhwan al-Muslimin) was the pioneer, militant Islamic fundamentalist movement of the twentieth century. Its charismatic founder, Sheikh Hasan al-Banna, who assumed the title of the guide-general, preached a salvationist message and called for the establishment of an ideal Islamic social and political order, first in Egypt and thereafter for a united Muslim world. He attracted a mass following through cadres of missionaries, effective propaganda, and an extensive network of educational, social, and charitable institutions. In the 1930s, he also organized a clandestine military apparatus.

By the mid-1930s, the Muslim Brotherhood had taken up the cause of the Arabs in Palestine and began to cooperate closely with the Arab Higher Committee, led by the Mufti Hajj Amin al-Hussaini. Along with other militant groups, the brotherhood accused Egyptian Jews of being fifth columnists for Zionism, and in May 1936, it called for a boycott against them. In what was to become standard for later Islamist groups, the anti-Zionist and anti-Jewish propaganda in the militants' pamphlets, tracts, and speeches combined traditional Islamic images of the Jews as opponents of the Prophet and of Muslims with well-known stereotypes drawn from European antisemitism. The brotherhood's anti-Jewish rhetoric became increasingly violent. The president of the Tanta branch delivered a speech in 1944 in which he said it was necessary for Muslims to unite in a jihad, or holy war, to destroy the Jews like "dirty dogs." He referred to them as "the world's parasites" and even echoed the blood libel, saying that they "dip their matzah at Passover in the blood of Muslims and Christians." A year later, verbal attacks gave way to physical violence. On Balfour Day (November 2) in 1945, demonstrations in Cairo and Alexandria, organized by the brotherhood and other groups to protest British policies in Palestine, deteriorated into rioting that resulted in the pillaging of Jewish and foreign-owned businesses, the torching of the Ashkenazi synagogue of Cairo, and five Jewish deaths in Alexandria.

During the first Arab-Israeli war (1948 to 1949), members of the brotherhood volunteered to fight for the Palestinians. Following the war, the organization ran afoul of the authorities in Egypt, both under the monarchy and then under the regime of Gamal Abdel Nasser. After involvement in an attempt against Nasser's life in 1954, the brotherhood was brutally suppressed and driven underground. This period also produced the movement's great ideologue, Sayyid Qutb, who, while imprisoned from 1954 to 1964, wrote highly influential Islamicist works that were smuggled out and received wide circulation. The most important of these were his account of life in prison, *Ma'alim fi Tariq* (Milestones), with its programmatic call for the destruction of secular government and the establishment of an Islamic state, and his massive Koranic exegesis, *Fi Zill al-Qur'an* (In the Shade of the Koran). In both works, Jews appear as the embodiment of evil, a sinister force seeking world domination through Zionism. They take their place alongside the crusaders (Christian imperialists), communists, and secularists as the ultimate enemies of the Muslims.

Qutb was hanged in 1966 when the brotherhood underwent a new wave of suppression. The movement, however, lived on not only in Egypt but also in other Muslim countries, and Qutb's writings became the inspiration for many Islamist groups.

—*Norman A. Stillman*

**See also** Anti-Zionism; Arab Antisemitic Literature; Farhud; Hamas; Hussaini, Mufti Hajj Amin al-; Islam and the Jews; Islamic Diaspora; Islamic Fundamentalism; Khomeini, Ayatollah; Mohammed; Nasser, Gamal Abdel; Ritual Murder (Modern); Zionism

**References**

Kepel, Gilles. *Muslim Extremism in Egypt: The Prophet and Pharoah* (Berkeley and Los Angeles: University of California Press, 1986).

Krämer, Gudrun. *The Jews in Modern Egypt, 1914–1952* (Seattle: University of Washington Press, 1989).

Laskier, Michael M. *The Jews of Egypt, 1920–1970: In the Midst of Zionism, Anti-Semitism, and the Middle East Conflict* (New York and London: New York University Press, 1992).

Mitchell, Richard P. *The Society of the Muslim Brothers* (Oxford: Oxford University Press, 1969).

Nettler, Ronald L. *Past Trials and Present Tribulations: A Muslim Fundamentalist's View of the Jews* (Oxford: Pergamon Press, 1987).

## Mussolini, Benito (1883–1945)

Benito Mussolini has often been described as opportunistic, unsystematic, and unprincipled, defying categorization—an assessment that is in no instance more obviously true than in his attitudes toward antisemitism. In his early career, from the immediate pre–World War I years through the 1920s, he was first a Socialist and then a Fascist and established a number of political contacts, social acquaintances, and romantic liaisons with Jews; his affair with Margherita Sarfatti, a member of a prominent Jewish family and a close adviser to him, lasted for over a decade. During these years, he spoke out on many occasions and with seeming conviction against antisemitism and racism in general.

Mussolini was, above all, a supple and savvy politician, concerned with power and popularity; in his first decade as a Fascist leader, he obviously did not consider antisemitism to be an effective political device in Italy. He remarked that antisemitism was not only morally repellent but also foreign to the Italian people. As late as 1932, he observed to an Austrian political leader that even in Germany, "Hitler's antisemitism has brought him more enemies than is necessary" (in Michaelis 1978, 31). A number of Fascist leaders, Mussolini included, were known to make derogatory remarks about Hitler and to observe that Nazi racism and antisemitism were barbaric, Germanic vices, which they considered beneath the more civilized Latin people of Italy.

Jews, who constituted approximately 0.1 percent of the Italian population, played an important role in the early Fascist movement, especially in its leading ranks, as they had in the

Italian national unification movement more generally. Mussolini was well aware of that fact, but as early as 1919, when attempting to exploit the cause of anticommunism, he was nonetheless capable of denouncing "world Jewry" as supporting both Bolshevism and capitalism. Still, his attacks were often contradicted by more friendly pronouncements, and he explicitly disavowed his initial statements about what German antisemites were calling Judeo-Bolshevism. Similarly, Mussolini's remarks about Jews, even later in his career, tended to lack the fanatical and hate-filled virulence that characterized Nazi rhetoric, such as the description of Jews as vermin worthy of total destruction.

From mid-1936 on, Mussolini was increasingly pulled into Hitler's orbit. He blamed world Jewry for supporting the League of Nations in its arms embargo on Italy after his country invaded Ethiopia in 1935. Hitler's support for Fascist Italy in that ill-advised adventure was one of several factors that moved Mussolini from denigration to growing esteem for the German leader, culminating in the military Pact of Steel between Italy and Germany in 1939.

The Racial Laws that were put into effect in Italy in late 1938, removing Jews from government positions and forbidding intermarriage, were apparently initiated and partly composed by Mussolini himself. They did not reflect direct pressure from Nazi Germany, although they paralleled the September 1935 Nuremberg Laws in many regards and may be seen as part of a general trend by the Fascist government, from the mid-1930s to the end of the war, toward racism and xenophobia. There is little evidence, however, that a majority of Italians desired or supported the laws, and once Nazi Germany had occupied Italy, Italian Jews found that many ordinary Italians, Catholic clergy, and even some Fascist officials were willing to help them escape capture. The survival rate of Italian Jews during the Holocaust was one of the highest in Europe. For this outcome, however, one cannot give any credit to Mussolini. On his own, he probably would not have initiated a systematic program of mass murder, but he and Fascists of all ranks cooperated with their Nazi allies in that effort.

—*Albert S. Lindemann*

See also Hitler, Adolf; Judeo-Bolshevism; *Manifesto of the Racial Scientists;* Nuremberg Laws; October Roundup; Preziosi, Giovanni; Racial Laws

**References**

Felice, Renzo de. *The Jews in Fascist Italy.* Translated by Robert L. Miller (New York: Enigma Books, 2001).

Michaelis, Meir. *Mussolini and the Jews: German-Italian Relations and the Jewish Question in Italy, 1922–1945* (Oxford: Clarendon Press, 1978).

Zuccotti, Susan. *The Italians and the Holocaust: Persecution, Rescue, and Survival* (New York: Basic Books, 1987).

## Myth of the Twentieth Century, The (1930)

Even before arriving in Germany from his native Riga by way of Moscow in 1919, Alfred Rosenberg had constructed an eclectic worldview based on a decisive rejection of Bolshevism, Jewry, and established Christian religion. In Munich, he came into contact with the antisemite Dietrich Eckart, contributing several articles to his periodical *Auf gut Deutsch* (In Good German). During the early 1920s, he pumped out a steady stream of antisemitic, anti-Bolshevik, anti-Freemason, anti-Zionist, and anti-Christian essays and pamphlets. He introduced Hitler to Eckart and played a formative role in articulating Nazi ideology and framing the Nazi Party Program of 1920. Rosenberg's magnum opus appeared in 1930 as *Der Mythus des 20. Jahrhunderts* (The Myth of the Twentieth Century), with the subtitle *An Evaluation of the Spiritual-Intellectual Battles Shaping Our Era* (*eine Wertung der seelischgeistigen Gestaltenkämpfe unserer Zeit*). Freemasonry, modern art, the Jesuits, the Christian denominations, and especially the Jews were among the forces singled out for exposure and condemnation. More than 1.25 million copies had been printed by 1944, making it second only to *Mein Kampf* as a seminal text of National Socialism. Hitler reportedly called it the "most powerful work of its kind." But it is dubious that even the leaders of the party, including Hitler, ever actually read the book.

Houston Stewart Chamberlain's *Foundations of the Nineteenth Century* exercised the most palpable influence on Rosenberg, as evidenced by his allusive choice for the book's title and the numerous instances of ideological agreement found in the two works. *Myth,* the meditations of a dilettante, is arranged in three books: "Struggle for Values," "Essence of Germanic Art," and "Coming Reich." Each is divided and subdivided into several parts—the table of contents alone requires fifteen pages. Rosenberg, for whom myth and dream were essentially one, expected and feared a political collapse. An apocalyptic "catastrophe of the soul" would witness the German people's disappearance from history. But then, a new world would arise, for which Germanic traits of character would form the basis. The new myth, given shape and form in the twentieth century, would be stamped with the "age-old and eternally young" force and passion of the Nordic race soul, in its specifically Germanic format (*Mythus,* 601).

In the ponderous work's attempt at a universal Nordic history, Rosenberg ascribed all cultural achievements to Aryans, the progeny of an original Nordic people whose creative center had been Atlantis (25). Their cultural mission had been perpetuated by Indians, Persians, Romans, and Germans. The *Mythus* never arrived at an exact definition of race, relying instead on the writings of Chamberlain and Paul de Lagarde. Rosenberg did not argue from biology or anthropology or base his text on any sort of empirical data. Instead, the *Mythus* unfolded a conception of race that is best described as metaphysical, mystical, and, at times, wholly indecipherable. History consisted of a contest that pitted one spiritual value (*Seelenwert*) against another. The spirit or soul was to be seen as the inner essence of the race, whereas the race was but the outer shell of the spirit (2). The "system" set forth in the murkiest of language amounted to a religious racism.

In that antagonistic theology, Jews occupied the role of the "counter-race" (*Gegenrasse*) to the Germanic-Nordic, which, thanks to its divine blood and soul, mediated between God and humans. The Jew, by contrast, was the son of Satan-Nature (265). Jews were enjoined by their Talmud to practice a religion that legislated lies, cunning, theft, murder, and perjury. "Greedy for the goods of the earth, the Jew moves through the world, from city to city, country to country, seeking the place where his parasitism will meet the least resistance. Driven out, he returns. A generation is struck down, undeterred another begins the same old game" (265). Rosenberg assured his readers of the unchanging nature of Jewish evil. Nothing about the Jews had really changed in 2,500 years. Their destructive middleman function was a constant, no different in Joseph of Egypt and Rathenau of Germany (463): "The Old Testament, the Talmud, and Karl Marx transmit the very same views" (128).

Rosenberg embellished the idea of the "chosenness" of the Jews to spell out their "parasitical dream of world domination" (459–460) from which emanated an awesome—and purely destructive—force working for the decline of various Nordic high cultures. Jews did not engage in heroic battles for dominance. Instead, they sought only to convert the world into interest-bearing (*zinsbar*) matter. They lacked all genuine soul and artistic creative power because they were without a true religious impulse—a fact that, Rosenberg alleged, Jewish Marxism clearly demonstrated.

—*Matthias Brosch*
*Richard S. Levy, translation*

**See also** Chamberlain, Houston Stewart; Deutsche Christen; Freemasonry; Hitler, Adolf; Jesuit Order; Judeo-Bolshevism; Lagarde, Paul de; Nazi Party Program; *Protocols of the Elders of Zion;* Rosenberg, Alfred; *Völkisch* Movement and Ideology

**References**

Cecil, Robert. *The Myth of the Master Race: Alfred Rosenberg and Nazi Ideology* (New York: Dodd, Mead, 1972).

Smelser, Ronald M., and Rainer Zitelmann. *The Nazi Elite* (New York: New York University Press, 1993).

# N

## Nasser, Gamal Abdel (1918–1970)

President of the United Arab Republic of Egypt from 1956 until his sudden death in 1970, Col. Gamal Abdel Nasser was the leading voice of Pan-Arab nationalism and one the most influential Arab political leaders of the twentieth century. He was a key figure in the Free Officers' coup that overthrew the Egyptian monarchy in 1952, installing Gen. Mohammed Naguib as the provisional figurehead president and premier of the new republic. By 1954, Nasser took power openly, wresting first the office of premier and later the presidency from Naguib; he then proceeded to establish an authoritarian, socialist, one-party system headed by an all-powerful president. Under Nasser, the Jewish community of Egypt, which numbered almost 65,000 at the time of the revolution, dwindled to fewer than 1,000 by 1970.

Nasser does not seem to have held the virulent antisemitic notions espoused by some Pan-Arabist movements, such as Misr al-Fatat (Young Egypt) or by the Pan-Islamists, such as the Muslim Brotherhood, although many of the Free Officers had been pro-Axis during World War II and had been receptive to Nazi propaganda. Immediately after the coup, however, the regime went out of its way to ease the fears of Jews and other minorities. Even the trial of several young Egyptian Jews for espionage and sabotage on behalf of Israel between 1954 and 1955 did not bring about any markedly anti-Jewish reactions.

Nasser's attitude changed following the Anglo-French-Israeli campaign of October 1956. Nearly 900 Jews were arrested. Under military proclamation, the assets of at least 500 Jewish-owned businesses were sequestered and their bank accounts frozen; a further 800 enterprises with Jewish proprietors were blacklisted and had their assets frozen. Jewish employees were dismissed from non-Jewish firms, and Jewish professionals found themselves unable to practice medicine, law, and engineering. As part of the anti-Jewish crackdown, Jews who had previously acquired Egyptian citizenship were denaturalized by using vague technical clauses in the Egyptian Nationality Law of 1950, which was amended for that purpose by a decree promulgated by Nasser himself. By the end of November 1956, at least 500 Jews had been expelled from Egypt. The combined official and unofficial measures against Jews resulted in widespread panic: by the end of June 1957, over one-third of the Jewish population had fled the country. The policy of expelling or pressuring Jews to leave Egypt was, in part, guided by former Nazis who had found refuge in Egypt. Israeli intelligence, the World Jewish Congress, Simon Wiesenthal, and exiled leaders of the Egyptian Jewish community have claimed that a number of these Germans, who had adopted Arabic names, held important positions in Nasser's bureaucracy, including the Ministry of National Guidance and the National Committee for the Struggle against Zionism, which produced and disseminated blatantly antisemitic literature. Nasser himself publicly recommended the *Protocols of the Elders of Zion* as an exposé of the Jewish plot for world domination. In interviews and speeches, he also decried the global influence of Jewish capitalism.

Although only 2,500 to 3,000 Jews remained in Egypt at the outbreak of the June 1967 Six Days' War, the humiliation of Egypt's defeat brought Nasser's anti-Jewish policies to their zenith. The majority of the remaining Jewish males were imprisoned, some of them until three years after Nasser's death. Those not in prison could leave Egypt on renouncing their citizenship, forfeiting their assets, and pledging never to return. Only 600 Jews remained in the country.

Nasser was not a fanatical antisemite. His anti-Jewish policies evolved along with xenophobic and antiminority tendencies that led to the dissolution of Egypt's ancient Greek community as well. Those he perceived to be enemies were subject to draconian measures, as the brutal suppression of the Muslim Brotherhood demonstrated. Like many Arab leaders, Nasser claimed to Western listeners that he distinguished between Zionists and Jews, but for Arab and Third World audiences, he often made no such distinction.

—*Norman A. Stillman*

*See also* Anti-Zionism; Arab Antisemitic Literature; Arab Boycott; Muslim Brotherhood; Nuremberg Laws; *Protocols of the Elders of Zion*

**References**
Laskier, Michael M. *The Jews of Egypt, 1920–1970: In the Midst of Zionism, Anti-Semitism, and the Middle East Conflict* (New York and London: New York University Press, 1992).
Stillman, Norman A. *The Jews of Arab Lands in Modern Times* (Philadelphia: Jewish Publication Society, 1991).

# Nation of Islam

The Nation of Islam (NOI) emerged in the late twentieth century as a center of African American antisemitism. In a series of high-profile statements, its leaders have propagated myths of Jewish media control, usury, and racist behavior.

The NOI claims to descend from "the original members of the Tribe of Shabazz from the Lost Nation of Asia" (Tynetta Muhammad 1996). In 1933, Elijah Poole, who took the name Elijah Muhammed, became the group's first leader. Under his tutelage, Malcolm X rose to prominence in the organization. After the highly public split between Elijah Muhammed and Malcolm X in 1964, a decades-long power struggle ensued, leading to Louis Farrakhan's emergence as the undisputed head of the NOI.

As late as the 1950s, representatives of the organized Jewish community did not perceive the NOI as a threat to Jews. In a confidential memo written in response to a *Time* magazine article of August 10, 1959, stating that the NOI was antisemitic, Anti-Defamation League officer Arnold

Forster denied, "in no uncertain terms," that there was any solid evidence of a specific antisemitism in Elijah Muhammed's movement. The NOI's general hostility toward whites, of course, included Jews.

Forster's confidence proved short-lived. By the mid-1960s, NOI leader Malcolm X and others mixed vitriolic attacks on Jews into their larger critique of white America. As the Black Power movement gained strength, the antisemitic rhetoric of NOI speakers intensified. Malcolm X retreated from some of his antisemitic views following his pilgrimage to Mecca, but with his assassination in 1965 and the subsequent rise of Louis Farrakhan, the group's antisemitic orientation revived.

In the 1970s and 1980s, the NOI recruited a number of prominent speakers, including Khalid Muhammed, who created a national uproar when he used a college campus appearance to articulate his antisemitic views. The NOI moderated its public stance in the 1990s as it sought a broader base of support, culminating in 1995 with the Farrakhan-led Million Man March on Washington, D.C.

—*Marc Dollinger*

*See also* African American–Jewish Relations; American Jewish Committee and Antidefamation Efforts in the United States; Farrakhan, Louis

**References**
Friedman, Murray. *What Went Wrong? The Creation and Collapse of the Black-Jewish Alliance* (New York: Free Press, 1995).
Tynetta Muhammad. "A Brief History on the Origin of the Nation of Islam in America: A Nation of Peace and Beauty." International Symposium on Sufism, San Francisco, March 1996).
Van Deburg, William L., ed. *Modern Black Nationalism: From Marcus Garvey to Louis Farrakhan* (New York: New York University Press, 1997).

# National Democrats (Poland)

The National Democrats (Endeks or Endecja, from the initials ND) were right-wing Polish nationalists of various political groupings, including the National Democratic Party (1897–1919), all of which followed Roman Dmowski's ideology and program. The Endeks defined the Polish nation as consisting exclusively of Catholic Poles, with Jews as its principal enemies. Jewish influence was to be combated through propaganda, restrictive laws, economic boycotts, and their "voluntary" emigration.

The National Democratic Party was renamed the Popular National Union (ZLN) in 1919. With 37 percent of the popular vote in the 1919 elections, it became the largest single party in the Sejm (parliament), but the Center bloc held the balance of power and governed in shifting coalitions with the Left or Right. Soon, secessions reduced the ZLN's share of parliamentary seats to 25 percent. In an effort to broaden its base, the ZLN joined the Christian Democrats (Chadeks) in the Christian Alliance of National Unity but won only 29 percent of the vote in 1922. The following year, with German hyperinflation spilling over into Poland, a Center-Right coalition was formed under Endek Władysław Grabski, whose stringent economic measures brought inflation under control but caused recession and unemployment.

These conditions and the violent reaction to them by segments of the Polish population prompted an exodus of Jews to Palestine (the "Grabski *aliyah*"). The Grabski government fell in 1925, and in the following year, the former socialist Marshal Józef Piłsudski took power in a military coup. Dmowski responded to Piłsudski's coup by forming the Great Poland Camp (OWP); meant to unite the right-wing parties, the OWP soon developed into an extremist fringe group. Meanwhile, the ZLN's popular vote plummeted to 8 percent in 1928 elections. Reconstituted as the National Party (SN), it won 14 percent in 1930 despite electoral manipulation by Piłsudski. The OWP, in the meantime, continued as a fascist-style splinter group until it was banned in 1933. A section of the OWP youth then founded the National Radical Camp (ONR), which promptly splintered into the ONR-Falanga and the ONR-ABC. Modeling themselves on the Italian Fascists, the ONR groups proposed one-party rule and depriving Jews of civil rights. The ONR-Falanga gained only 1.2 percent of the popular vote in the last prewar elections in 1938, but it had considerable support at the universities and was briefly seconded to run the government party's youth wing

in 1938. The ONR organized violent anti-Jewish gangs and campaigned for the *numerus clausus* (maximum number on enrollments) and "ghetto benches" or segregated seating, as a step toward excluding Jewish students altogether.

After Piłsudski's death in 1935, the governing Sanacja adopted numerous National Democratic ideas, including tacit support for the economic boycott and ghetto benches, nationalization of industries in which Jews predominated, a law limiting ritual slaughter, and measures to encourage Jews to emigrate; it was also considering a version of the Nuremberg Laws when war broke out. Thus, even though the National Democrats had never ruled the country, their ideas were dominant by the late 1930s.

During the war, the OWP reemerged; together with the ONR, it formed an underground army called the National Armed Forces (NSZ), which fought against the Nazis but attacked Jewish partisans and Polish political opponents as well. In 1944, its own leader was murdered by a breakaway faction. The more moderate SN was one of the major parties represented in the Polish government-in-exile and in the underground Home Army. It opposed the formation of the Council to Aid Jews (Zegota) in 1942 and did not participate in it. It also opposed the return of Jews to Poland after the war and the restoration of Jewish property confiscated by the Nazis. After the war, right-wing diehards blamed the Jews for bringing Communist rule to Poland and carried out a campaign of terror in which hundreds of Jews were randomly shot. The Endeks went underground in 1945, but elements with similar tendencies have reemerged in the post-Communist era.

—*Steven Paulsson*

***See also*** Dmowski, Roman; Ghetto Benches; Kosher Slaughtering; Poland; Poland since 1989
***References***
Polonsky, Antony. *Politics in Independent Poland, 1921–1939* (Oxford: Clarendon Press, 1972).

# National Socialist German Workers' Party

The Nazi Party was founded in February 1919 as the Deutsche Arbeiterpartei (German Workers'

Party [DAP]), not by Adolf Hitler but by an all but forgotten Munich toolmaker by the name of Anton Drexler. Hitler joined the party in September 1919; less than two years later, he had pushed the hapless Drexler aside and become chairman, with virtually dictatorial powers. Under Hitler's leadership, the party (which had become the Nationalsozialistische Deutsche Arbeiterpartei or National Socialist German Workers' Party [NSDAP] in 1920) modeled itself on Benito Mussolini's Fascist Party. Like its Italian counterpart, the Nazi Party had both a political and a paramilitary wing. In the early years of its existence, the paramilitary wing, the Storm troopers (Sturmabteilung, or SA) was the more important of the two because Hitler, like Mussolini, intended to overthrow democracy by means of an armed coup. At the same time, Hitler used the political wing and his considerable oratorical skills to attract new members to both the party and the SA, although in this initial phase of hectic activity, the NSDAP was essentially still a Bavarian phenomenon.

The coup strategy failed ignominiously in the November 1923 Hitler Putsch, also known as the Beer Hall Putsch. The attempt to topple the Weimar Republic by force ended almost before it began. Along with a few of his associates, Hitler was subsequently arrested and tried for high treason, but the lenient judges sentenced him to only five years in prison. He was paroled after serving just nine months in quite comfortable surroundings at the fortress of Landsberg.

Although Hitler had originally intended to run things from jail, he soon realized this was impossible and had to look on as the party disintegrated into warring factions. When he was released from jail, he refused to identify with any of the feuding splinter groups, and for all practical purposes, he reorganized the party from the bottom up. To be sure, much about the "new" party was familiar. The name stayed the same, the swastika emblems did not change, and many of Hitler's associates from the old party quickly rallied to his cause again.

But there were important changes. Hitler recognized that overthrowing the Weimar Republic by force would not work. As a result, although the new NSDAP still had both a political and a paramilitary wing, the emphasis now shifted to the political side. Hitler was determined to turn the NSDAP into a nationwide organization that would become a formidable vote-getting machine. The SA's primary purpose was no longer to prepare a coup but to guard Nazi Party rallies and to engage in political violence against the party's political enemies.

The old NSDAP had shown no interest in elections, but the new party prioritized certain segments among the German voters. Before any political plan could be put into effect, however, Hitler had to deal with an internal revolt. Led by Otto and Gregor Strasser, a faction in the party challenged the leader's dictatorial power. Hitler eventually prevailed, and the NSDAP remained the "Hitler movement." Ironically, the confirmed Führer adopted much of the substantive program advocated by his critics. For the May 1928 Reichstag election campaign, the NSDAP concentrated on organizing the industrial areas of the country, notably the Ruhr, the ports of Hamburg and Bremen, and the national capital, Berlin. To gain a foothold in Berlin, Hitler sent his best propagandist, Joseph Goebbels, to become the party's regional leader (*Gauleiter*) in the capital. The thinking behind this so-called urban plan was to draw blue-collar workers away from Marxism and toward the NSDAP's antisemitic National Socialism.

This strategy was a dismal failure. The NSDAP gained only 2.6 percent of the popular vote in 1928, and few of these votes came from the targeted constituency of industrial workers. Germany's blue-collar workers did not respond to the Nazis' combination of antisemitism and anticapitalism. However, the party did well in some rural and small-town middle-class precincts, especially in Protestant areas. Hitler, in some ways a quintessential opportunist, readily shifted the NSDAP's organizing efforts to the constituencies that were attracted to the party. Instead of attacking the abuses of capitalism, the party now stressed that it stood for middle-class respectability, morality, and the right to property. Even the party's strident antisemitism was toned down. Above all, however, the NSDAP insisted that it and only it could save Germany from Bolshevism. Goebbels pushed the anti-

Communist theme during nonstop campaigning, while the SA engaged in unceasing and increasingly violent encounters with Communists and Social Democrats.

We will never know if the NSDAP's new tack might have succeeded under "normal" conditions because soon after the party adopted what came to be called its rural strategy, the times became extremely abnormal. Beginning in 1930, the Great Depression sent Germany's economy into a precipitous cycle of business failures and chronic, large-scale unemployment. A series of democratic and, later, authoritarian cabinets were unable to solve Germany's severe economic problems. The NSDAP moved to exploit the opportunity, becoming the country's first catchall party by promising relief to virtually every segment of German society. The solution to the nation's problems, the party argued, could only mean one thing: Adolf Hitler and the NSDAP had to be given dictatorial powers.

As a catchall party, the NSDAP had a unique structural profile, which was largely the work of Gregor Strasser, the party's Reich organizational leader. Strasser organized the NSDAP into three wings. The Political Organization undertook virtually incessant campaigning for national and state elections. For this purpose, Germany was divided into administrative units called *Gaus,* each corresponding to one of Germany's federal election districts. The second wing, the paramilitary organizations (notably the SA), presented the militant face of the NSDAP. The third wing comprised a network of affiliates designed to attract professional groups to the party. Ranging from the National Socialist Farmers' Organization to the National Socialist Association of Munich Coal Dealers, they served as means of attracting voters and members to the party.

In the last years of the Weimar Republic, the NSDAP was astoundingly successful. The party's national vote increased from 2.6 percent in 1928 to 18 percent in 1930 and 37 percent (the pinnacle of its popular success) in July 1932. Hitler also gained 37 percent of the vote when he ran (unsuccessfully) for president in April 1932. At the same time, the Storm troopers were responsible for unprecedented levels of political violence. Finally, the affiliates succeeded in gaining

control over a number of professional and social organizations, most especially those of farmers and university students.

By the middle of 1932, the NSDAP had become the most successful political party in German history. But it had not been able to win a majority of the national vote or gain power through the ballot box. Despite the party's numerous strong showings at the polls, all was not well: as Goebbels put it, "We are winning ourselves to death" (in Orlow 1969–1973, 307). This was not an exaggeration. At the end of 1932, the NSDAP was facing a crisis on several fronts. The Storm troopers were getting increasingly impatient, literally putting their lives on the line while waiting in vain for long-promised rewards. The party was deeply in debt, and most important, there were clear signs that the NSDAP's popularity had peaked. In the November 1932 national elections, the party's vote declined for the first time since 1930. Hitler and the Nazis rose to power in January 1933 not because they were elected but through a combination of personal intrigues and because Germany's conservative elite was willing to make a pact with them in order to destroy the hated Weimar Republic. Paradoxically, the party's role during the twelve years of the Third Reich was considerably less important than during the "years of struggle."

It is true that the party was instrumental in destroying Germany's political pluralism during the *Gleichschaltung* (coordination) phase in 1933 and 1934, and party members were responsible for much of the random terror during the early months of the regime. Further, most of the Gauleiter also became state administrators, and many SA leaders became municipal police chiefs. But the party did not succeed in carving out a long-term future for itself. There were a number of reasons for this development.

To begin with, Hitler refused to assign the party any specific role other than the vague task of indoctrinating the German people with the precepts of National Socialism. But leaders could not agree among themselves on the NSDAP's future role. One group—led by Rudolf Hess (the deputy führer for party operations after December 1933) and his chief of staff, Martin Bormann—envisioned a role for the party that was modeled on the position of the Communist Party in the Soviet Union, with the Nazi Political Organization forming the elite of the Third Reich. That approach failed, partly because Hitler did not endorse it but also because the party did not have the skilled personnel to run a modern society. In addition, important party leaders such as Goebbels and Hermann Göring chose to base their power in the Third Reich on state offices (the Propaganda Ministry for Goebbels and the Office of the Four Year Plan for Göring). Formally, Hitler was head of the SA, but the Storm troopers' chief of staff, Ernst Röhm, and his close associates were convinced that only they, as soldier-politicians, could bring National Socialism to Germany. That illusion ended in the bloody purge of the Storm trooper leadership in June 1934.

The purge was carried out by the SS execution squads; it signified the eclipse of the SA and allowed the SS—until then a small organization subordinated within the SA structure—to advance its own claim to elitism. According to its chief, Heinrich Himmler, the SS was entitled to elite status because it was the "racially purest" element of the entire Nazi movement. Up to a point, the SS was, indeed, the most successful of the Nazi organizations, and by the time the Third Reich came to an end, it controlled the Nazi terror apparatus, including the elements involved in implementing the Holocaust, the police, and, through Himmler, the armed forces reserves. Only once was the party permitted to play a leading role after 1933—during the infamous *Reichskristallnacht* pogrom of November 1938. The widespread burning of Germany's synagogues, the vandalism, and the physical assaults against individual Jews were largely the work of local party and SA members.

As an organization, the party receded further into the background after Hitler unleashed World War II. Reduced to mouthing increasingly meaningless propaganda slogans, the NSDAP acquired an even more sinister image once the death toll at the front mounted. One of the party's wartime duties was to deliver death notices to the relatives of soldiers who had died in battle. Attired in his party uniform, the local leader paid a condolence call on the stricken family. Because the party uniform was khaki brown with golden trim, these dreaded occasions became known as "visits by the golden pheasants." By the end of the war, the party was a moribund and useless organization. Most of the Gauleiter deserted their posts as the Allied armies closed in on their territories. Efforts by Martin Bormann and the Party Chancellery to have the Political Organization lead a *levée en masse* failed completely.

Ironically, the only party affiliation that retained any positive image in the eyes of most Germans was the Nationalsozialistische Volkswohlfahrtsorganisation (National Socialist Welfare Organization [NSV]), a unit that had been in the backwater among the party's groups for most of its existence. Founded in the early 1930s as a way of providing financial aid for Storm troopers injured in the brawls of the last Weimar years, the NSV was charged with providing aid to the victims of Allied bombings during the war. Because this was a task that became increasingly important as the conflict went on, it is understandable that for most Germans, only the NSV among all the NSDAP organizations seemed to be doing something useful.

After the Third Reich's unconditional surrender in May 1945, the Allies prohibited the NSDAP from organizing in any form, although the party had already disappeared from the political landscape by that point. In his last testament, Hitler had willed all of his material possessions to the party, but that directive was obviously meaningless. Instead, the beneficiary of both the party's assets and Hitler's personal possessions was the state of Bavaria. In the end, then, the NSDAP had come full circle. It had begun and ended in Bavaria.

—*Dietrich Orlow*

**See also** *Angriff, Der;* German National People's Party; Goebbels, Joseph; Göring, Hermann; Himmler, Heinrich; Hitler, Adolf; Hugenberg, Alfred; Mussolini, Benito; Nazi Cultural Antisemitism; Nazi Legal Measures against Jews; Night of Broken Glass (November 1938 Pogrom); Weimar

**References**

Kershaw, Ian. *Hitler: 1889–1936 Hubris* (New York: Norton, 1999).
———. *Hitler: 1936–1945 Nemesis* (New York: Norton, 2000).

Orlow, Dietrich. *The History of the Nazi Party: 1919–1945*. 2 vols. (Pittsburgh: University of Pittsburgh Press, 1969–1973).

Pätzold, Kurt, and Manfred Weissbecker. *Geschichte der NSDAP: 1920–1945* (Cologne, Germany: PapyRossa, 1998).

## Nazi Cultural Antisemitism

The elimination of Jewish influence over German artistic and cultural life was a central element of Nazi ideology, propaganda, and policy. During the years of the Weimar Republic, the Nazi movement held Jews responsible for alleged "degenerate" tendencies in music, theater, the visual arts, architecture, and related areas of creative endeavor. Once in power, the Nazis erected a wall of cultural separation between Jews and Aryans, purged Jews from German cultural life, censored works produced by Jews, mobilized German cultural production to reinforce a malevolent image of the Jews, and robbed Jews of their artistic possessions.

The demonization of the Jew as a cultural alien in Germany (and elsewhere in Europe) was not a Nazi innovation but had emerged as a prominent antisemitic theme in the nineteenth century, as emancipation allowed Jewish artists to move into the cultural mainstream. Among the more notorious antisemitic texts of that era was the essay *Judaism in Music* by the German composer Richard Wagner. Jews, wrote Wagner, could only produce inauthentic imitations of the aesthetic characteristics of their host cultures. The Jewish essence, he argued, prevented them from producing art that was truly German. Wagner's 1850 essay predated the emergence of a full-blown racial antisemitism, but it anticipated the cultural essentialism that would later characterize the *völkisch* (racist-nationalist) movement and Nazism.

This essentialism was clearly present in the early political statements of Hitler and the Nazi Party. Modernist tendencies in cultural life, such as Bauhaus architecture, atonal music, abstract expressionism, and jazz, were condemned as manifestations of a cultural Judeo-Bolshevism, the alleged intention of which was to undermine traditional Germanic values, weaken the national spirit, and render German society more susceptible to Jewish power. The writings and speeches of Hitler, Alfred Rosenberg, and other Nazi leaders resonated with such ideas, which also featured prominently in book-length works by scholars connected to the Nazi movement, such as Paul Schultze-Naumburg's *Kunst und Rasse* (Art and Race), published in 1928.

The Nazis advocated a national cultural policy that would eliminate Jewish influence. The Nazi Party Program of February 1920 demanded the "legal prosecution of all those tendencies in art and literature which corrupt our national life, and the suppression of cultural events which violate this demand." In *Mein Kampf,* Hitler observed that it is "the business of the state to prevent a people from being driven into the arms of spiritual madness" (258–259) and to assure the "the preservation of those original racial elements which bestow culture and create beauty" (391). Under the Weimar Republic, much of the right-wing activism on the cultural front was carried out by the Kampfbund für deutsche Kultur (Combat League for German Culture), a Nazi Party front organization headed up by Alfred Rosenberg.

Once in power, the Nazis moved quickly to translate their cultural principles into policy. Some artistically prominent Jews, such as the orchestra conductor Bruno Walter, were intimidated into stepping down from their positions; many others were hounded into exile. The Civil Service Law of April 1933 resulted in the dismissal of a significant number of Jewish musicians, theater people, art instructors, and others employed by publicly administered cultural institutions. In late 1933, the Nazi government created the Reich Chamber of Culture, which rapidly became the compulsory occupational organization for Germans working in the artistic and cultural fields. The chamber was actually an umbrella organization of seven "subchambers" set up for the fields of music, theater, the visual arts, literature, cinema, radio, and the press. These agencies operated under the supervision of Joseph Goebbels, the Reich minister for propaganda and public enlightenment as well as the Nazi *Gauleiter* (district leader) of Berlin, who was among the more fanatical antisemites in the Nazi leadership. Goebbels pushed the chambers to expel their Jewish members, a measure tanta-

Two men prepare to hang German Expressionist painter Max Beckmann's triptych *Temptation* at the twentieth-century German Art Exhibition at the New Burlington Galleries, London. The exhibition included work by all the German artists pilloried by Adolf Hitler in the Degenerate Art exhibition in Munich of 1937. (Photo by Topical Press Agency/Getty Images)

mount to banning them from activity in their occupations. The mass, systematic expulsion of Jews from the chambers occurred mainly in 1935. Although the chambers lacked an explicit "Aryan clause," article 10 of their founding charter provided for the expulsion of artists who were judged to be "unreliable and unfit" for participation in Germany's cultural life. Goebbels made it clear that Jews, by definition, fit into this category. The "*Mischlinge* of the First-Degree" (half-Jews) and Aryans who were married to Jews were also routinely expelled, even though exceptions were sometimes made for prominent artists. The victims of this cultural purge also included certain Communists, homosexuals, Gypsies, and others deemed unreliable and unfit, but in none of these categories was the purge as thorough and relentless as it was for Jews.

In some cases, Jewish artists and entertainers who were fired from their positions or expelled from the chambers were able to find work with the Jüdischer Kulturbund (Jewish Cultural League). This organization, founded in 1933 by Jewish communal leaders with permission from Nazi officials, was designed to enable German Jews to pursue a cultural existence segregated from the German mainstream. Under the auspices of the Kulturbund, Jewish artists were allowed to perform Jewish works before Jewish audiences. The Nazi regime claimed that this practice was consistent with its broader goal of encouraging the dissimilation of German Jews. Although "German" culture would be off-limits to Jews, Jews would be able to cultivate their own culture among themselves. The German official who supervised the Kulturbund was Hans Hinkel, a Nazi "old fighter" who had helped run the Nazi-affiliated Kampfbund für deutsche Kultur in the Weimar period and who had later co-ordinated the purge of Jews from state-supported cultural institutions in Prussia, Germany's largest state. The Kulturbund operated until September 1941, when the Gestapo dissolved it just prior to the beginning of the systematic deportation of German Jews to the East.

Simultaneously with the purge of Jewish artists, the Nazi regime erected a complex system of censorship that was intended to insulate German society from contamination by works created by Jews. Formal lists of prohibited works constituted only one element of this system. Equally important were the personnel policies of the Third Reich, which assured that the people in charge of German cultural institutions understood which forms of art and entertainment were acceptable and which were not. Although the position of the regime was ambiguous in certain cases (for example, in regard to the music of the non-Jewish Igor Stravinsky), the cultural production of Jews was proscribed without exception. The relevant definition of *Jew,* it should be emphasized, was a racial one, so the works of converts from Judaism, such as the composer Felix Mendelssohn, fell under the prohibition. The program of censorship included the removal from German museums and galleries of paintings by Jewish artists. In some cases, these works of art were destroyed, but in many instances, they were offered for sale for a fraction of their real or potential value.

In addition to the system of exclusion and censorship, the Nazis encouraged and sponsored culture with antisemitic content. The high-profile "Degenerate Art" Exhibition in 1937 included numerous objects by Jewish artists, as did the similar "Degenerate Music" Exhibition in 1938. Among the most notorious examples of Nazi antisemitism in the cultural sphere were two films of 1940, *Jud Süss* and *Der ewige Jude* (The Eternal Jew), in which the depictions of Jewish characters conformed to vicious stereotypes of sniveling, hook-nosed moneylenders, sexual predators, and animal torturers. The antisemitism of these two films was especially prominent because the vast majority of the feature films produced in Nazi Germany avoided overt propaganda for tactical reasons.

The Nazi regime despoiled Jews of works of art and other cultural property. Jews seeking to emigrate from Germany during the 1930s were often forced to leave many of their valuables behind, with only meager compensation from the German government or from the Aryan Germans who ultimately took possession of the property. The Reich Chamber of the Visual Arts, acting as the occupational representative of German painters and sculptors, participated in this systematic pillaging of Jewish property by providing expert appraisals of the value of artworks, for which the departing Jews had to pay a fee. Even this token pretense to fair compensation did not apply to German and other European Jews who were deported during the war and, in most cases, killed. In our own day, we are occasionally reminded of this sordid story by news reports about art museums that display the stolen property of murdered Jews.

—*Alan Steinweis*

***See also*** Aryan Paragraph; Book Burning; Degenerate Art; Emancipation; Film Industry, Nazi Purge of Jewish Influence in; Goebbels, Joseph; Hitler, Adolf; *Judaism in Music; Mein Kampf;* Music, Nazi Purge of Jewish Influence in; Musicology and National Socialism; *Myth of the Twentieth Century, The;* Nazi Party Program; Purge of the German Civil Service; Rosenberg, Alfred; *Verjudung; Völkisch* Movement and Ideology

***References***

Cuomo, Glenn R., ed. *National Socialist Cultural Policy* (New York: St. Martin's Press, 1995).

Dahm, Volker. "Kulturelles und geistiges Leben." In *Die Juden in Deutschland, 1933–1945: Leben unter nationalsozialistischer Herrschaft.* Edited by Wolfgang Benz (Munich, Germany: C. H. Beck, 1988), 75–267.

Steinweis, Alan E. *Art, Ideology, and Economics in Nazi Germany: The Reich Chambers of Music, Theater, and the Visual Arts* (Chapel Hill: University of North Carolina Press, 1993).

# Nazi Legal Measures against Jews (1933–1939)

During the prewar years of the Third Reich, discriminatory legislation was the platform for the Nazi assault on German Jewry. National Socialists called for purging Jews from the professions and the business world and, above all, stopping their biological intrusion, by way of marriage, into the superior Nordic bloodstream. The Nazis speedily enacted repressive laws to translate this ideology into action. The opening wave of anti-Jewish legislation in April 1933 was directed against Jews in the civil service and the professions of law and medicine. On April 7, Adolf Hitler promulgated the first of these laws—the Law for the Restoration of the Professional Civil Service. This legislation allowed the Nazis to expel political and racial undesirables from the civil service. A supplementary decree on April 11, called the Aryan Paragraph, established a way to define the racially undesirable "non-Aryan" (or Jew). Anyone "with one parent or one grandparent who adhered to the Jewish religion" was, by definition, labeled non-Aryan. This remained the standard definition applied in anti-Jewish legislation until the Nuremberg Laws of 1935.

On April 7, the same day the civil service law was promulgated, Hitler issued a law restricting the number of Jewish attorneys admitted to the bar. Jewish medical doctors became the target on April 24, when they were banned from participating in the government-sponsored health insurance panels. On April 25, the Law against the Overfilling of German Schools and Universities prescribed a reduction in the number of Jews entering these institutions and other professional fields, stipulating that their numbers not exceed the proportion of Jews in the population at large. The legal assault against the Jews, though not their persecution, stalled in the aftermath of the anti-Jewish legislation of April 1933. An exception was the Denaturalization Law of July 14, 1933, which allowed the government to revoke the citizenship of eastern European Jews (*Ostjuden*) who had entered Germany after World War I.

Until the Nuremberg Laws of 1935, the Nazis left untouched the problem of race mixing that was at the core of their racist ideology. Logic would have demanded they begin their legislative assault on the Jews with such a proscription, but political reality demanded otherwise. Nazi leaders waited more than two years to address this issue because they recognized the legal thicket they would be entering. Socially sensitive matters of divorce, parental responsibility (financial and otherwise), inheritance, and

the like were involved. All of these issues were regulated by a civil code deeply rooted in pre-Nazi social and legal practice.

Late in 1933 and throughout 1934, party radicals grew increasingly agitated about the issue of race mixing. Rank-and-file activists often harassed marriage officials, demanding that they refuse marriage licenses to mixed-race couples. If that effort failed, they frequently enlisted Storm trooper roughnecks to "counsel" the couples. By the summer of 1935, marriage registry offices were in chaos. This was the political and social backdrop for the Nuremberg Laws of September 15, 1935. The first law, aptly called the Law for the Protection of German Blood and German Honor, prohibited both marriages and extramarital relations between Germans and Jews. The second, the Reich Citizenship Law, revoked citizenship for Jews by reducing them to "State Subjects."

The Nuremberg legislation also established a new definition of the Jew, one less inclusive than that of the Aryan Paragraph of 1933. In 1933, a single Jewish grandparent had been sufficient to make one non-Aryan. The new definition, contained in a decree supplementary to the Citizenship Law, required that an individual have at least two Jewish grandparents in order to be classified a Jew. Even then, one could escape that classification by not practicing the Jewish religion or not being married to a Jew. In that case, one was labeled a *Mischling* (half-breed). Most Mischlinge eventually escaped the Final Solution. Anyone with three or four Jewish grandparents was deemed to be Jewish and fated to suffer the full force of Nazi persecution.

Nazi legislation aimed at driving Jews out of the German economy proved particularly difficult to implement. At first, the difficulties stemmed from the economic depression, during which any measures that disrupted economic activity were dangerous. Germany's foreign trade imbalance and its need to earn foreign exchange likewise protected, for a time at least, those Jewish firms engaged in commerce abroad. But there was the additional problem of defining with precision how a business could be identified as Jewish. Did its governing board need to be Jewish? Did a majority of its shares need to be owned by Jews? Was it sufficient if its management was Jewish?

Not until 1938 did the Nazis feel confident enough to launch an all-out, systematic assault against the economic position of Jews. On April 26, Hermann Göring ordered all Jews to register a complete inventory of their assets, an order that was the prelude to the seizure of those assets. The complicated legal definition of a Jewish business contained in the third supplementary decree to the Reich Citizenship Law served a similar purpose. Additional decrees excluded Jewish doctors, dentists, lawyers, and patent attorneys from practicing their professions; defined Jewish businesses so as to ensure their confiscation; and reduced pensions for retired Jewish civil servants.

Finally, on November 12, 1938, in the aftermath to the nationwide Night of Broken Glass (the November 1938 pogrom), Göring decreed the Elimination of Jews from German Economic Life. As of January 1, 1939, they were to be excluded from virtually every form of economic activity, be it owning retail or mail-order businesses, acting as vendors of goods or services at markets or fairs, or serving as managers of business enterprises. Even as employees, they were subject to dismissal without recourse. By September 1939, when Germany invaded Poland, there were few areas of Jewish life left untouched by discriminatory legislation. A final and by then totally irrelevant decree on July 7, 1943, detached the few surviving Jews in Germany from all possible protections under the law.

—*Karl A. Schleunes*

**See also** Aryan Paragraph; Aryanization; Boycott of Jewish Shops; Göring, Hermann; Hitler, Adolf; Night of Broken Glass (November 1938 Pogrom); Nuremberg Laws; *Ostjuden;* Purge of the German Civil Service

**References**
Miller, Richard Lawrence. *Nazi Justiz: Law of the Holocaust* (Westport, CT: Praeger, 1995).
Stolleis, Michael. *The Law under the Swastika: Studies on Legal History in Nazi Germany.* Translated by Thomas Dunlap (Chicago: University of Chicago Press, 1998).
Walk, Joseph, ed. *Das Sonderrecht für die Juden im NS-Staat: Eine Sammlung der gesetzlichen Massnahmen und Richtlinien—Inhalt und Bedeutung* (Heidelberg, Germany: C.F. Müller, 1981).

## Nazi Party Program

The Nazi Party Program, generally known as the Twenty-five Points, was adopted in February 1920 by what was then still called the Deutsche Arbeiterpartei (German Worker's Party [DAP]). It was initially intended to be a document of short duration, but in May 1925, Hitler, who faced demands from within the party to write a much more detailed document, proclaimed the 1920 program to be "unalterable." He was almost true to his word: only the seventeenth point was "interpreted" in April 1928. Originally, the party had demanded the expropriation of all landed estates, but now this proposed measure applied only to Jewish-owned estates.

The Nazi Party Program was not the work of one man, least of all Hitler himself. Instead, Hitler, Dietrich Eckart, Alfred Rosenberg, and Gottfried Feder all had a hand in formulating it. Each author contributed the points that were of particular interest to him. Hitler probably formulated the items dealing with foreign policy and government operations, Eckart and Rosenberg wrote the *völkisch* planks, and Feder contributed the economic and financial proposals. Scholars still debate how seriously the authors regarded the program as a set of guidelines for future legislation. Feder and Rosenberg probably saw the Twenty-five Points as a rudimentary blueprint for a future National Socialist society, but for Hitler, the vague and demagogic program was little more than a propaganda ploy.

The Twenty-five Points contained very little that was either original or well thought out. The characterization of the document as a compendium of "everything that was offered by reactionary thinking in the nineteenth and twentieth century" (Pätzold and Weissbecker 1998, 45) is not unfair. The authors certainly did not refrain from plagiarism; points 3 through 6, 14, 16, and 23 were essentially copied from Heinrich Class's pre–World War I brochure *If I Were the Kaiser.* Above all, many of the program's individual planks were designed to respond to the wishes and resentments of the DAP's primary target audience in 1920: skilled workers, lower-middle-class artisans, and civil servants.

The contents of the document can be divided into three broad categories: nationalist demands, völkisch and antisemitic sentiments, and social and economic proposals. By far the largest number of points (thirteen) dealt with economic and social issues. Like the program of the Pan-German League before World War I, the Twenty-five Points insisted on the inclusion of all ethnic Germans in a Great German Reich (point 1) and the need for more *Lebensraum* (living space). A diatribe against the Treaty of Versailles and a demand for the return of the German colonies comprised the second and third points.

The basic tenor of the völkisch and antisemitic points was to deprive Germany's Jews of their political rights and to eliminate their "excessive" power in public life. Specifically, Jews were to be divested of their citizenship and treated as resident aliens (points 4 and 5). All non-German immigration was to be stopped, and Jews who had moved to Germany after the beginning of World War I were to be deported (point 8). The demand that all editors of newspapers published in Germany had to be members of the "German race" came as no surprise; it was a long-standing myth in antisemitic circles that Jews controlled the press. The party also endorsed "positive Christianity." Point 24 promised to respect all religious denominations, provided their teachings did not offend the moral sensibilities of the German race. That requirement served to exclude the Jewish religion from any form of protection.

The most detailed section of the program dealt with social and economic policies. Here was the program that was to cure the problems plaguing Germany's post–World War I economy. National Socialism turned out to be a naive combination of state intervention and benefits to the lower middle class. The program demanded the death penalty for all usurers and profiteers (point 18), the confiscation of all war profits (point 12), the nationalization of trusts (point 13), and preferential treatment for small businesses in awarding government contracts (points 15 and 16). Gottfried Feder inserted his universal solution to all economic woes in point 11: interest charges would be abolished in the future National Socialist Reich. Finally, in case one did not own a small business, the Twenty-five Points called for increased old-age pensions (point 15) and profit sharing for employees of large-scale enterprises (point 14).

Remarkably, the longest and most detailed point (point 20) dealt with education. Reputed to have been written by Hitler, it certainly reflected his resentment of the traditional Austro-German educational system. In the future, the program called on the state to make it possible for every gifted child to have access to all levels of education. The DAP also demanded curriculum reforms that would instill love and respect for the German nation-state in the students.

Did the Nazis implement the program after they took power? The answer is, yes and no. On the one hand, it could of course be argued that the regime fulfilled much of the nationalist and antisemitic parts of the program. After all, Hitler did create the Greater German Reich, and the Holocaust went far beyond the discriminatory policies promised in 1920. On the other hand, the social and economic demands were ignored. The Third Reich did not abolish interest charges, trusts remained unscathed, and the regime generally favored large enterprises at the expense of small businesses.

—*Dietrich Orlow*

**See also** Austria; Capital: Useful versus Harmful; Hitler, Adolf; *If I Were the Kaiser;* "Jewish" Press; *Mein Kampf;* National Socialist German Workers' Party; Pan-German League; Rosenberg, Alfred; Versailles Treaty; *Völkisch* Movement and Ideology; Weimar

*References*

Lane, Barbara Miller, and Leila J. Rupp, eds. *Nazi Ideology before 1933: A Documentation* (Austin: University of Texas Press, 1978).

Noakes, Jeremy, and Geoffrey Pridham, eds. *Nazism, 1919–1945: A Documentary Reader.* 4 vols. (Exeter, UK: University of Exeter Press, 1994–1998).

Pätzold, Kurt, and Manfred Weissbecker. *Geschichte der NSDAP: 1920–1945* (Cologne, Germany: PapyRossa, 1998).

## Nazi Research on the Jewish Question

Consistent with its elevation of the Jewish Question to a leading position in its ideology and policies, the Nazi regime encouraged and sponsored scholarly research about Jews, Judaism, and Jewish-Christian relations. The research was carried out across a number of academic fields, including such humanistic areas of scholarship as theology and literary studies, as well as political economy, demographic sociology, and other social sciences and the "harder" scientific disciplines of physical anthropology, medicine, and human genetics. The work was carried out under the auspices of German universities, venerable government-supported research institutes, and new institutes created by the Nazi regime specifically for the purpose of studying Jews.

This field, which historians refer to as Nazi *Judenforschung* (research on the Jews), must be seen in the wider context of the historical evolution of antisemitism. The utility of a "rational" antisemitism of this sort had been recognized well before 1933. The writings of Wilhelm Marr, Eugen Dühring, and Theodor Fritsch, among other nineteenth-century publicists, had already attempted to shift the focus of Jew-hatred away from the tradition of emotional religious anti-Judaism and toward a more modern racist essentialism. Hitler, for his part, endorsed an "antisemitism of reason" in several early speeches and, most notably, in his letter to Adolf Gemlich of September 1919. During the 1920s, antisemitic writers associated with the Nazi movement produced a host of works attempting to demonstrate the innate, intractable, racial basis of Jewish behavior. The most prominent of these was Hans F. K. Günther, whose book *Rassenkunde des jüdischen Volkes* (Racial Characteristics of the Jewish People [1930]) offered a summary of the existing state of antisemitic racial anthropology. The Nazis rewarded him with a professorship at the University of Jena, after they had entered a coalition government in the German state of Thuringia.

During the Third Reich, Judenforschung constituted but one element of a complex strategy for legitimizing and reinforcing antisemitism in public opinion and official policy. The Nazi regime propagated antisemitism on several social and intellectual levels simultaneously. Different types of antisemitism were targeted at diverse constituencies in German society. These antisemitic discourses differed in their level of intellectual sophistication, their balance between appeal to emotion and appeal to reason, and the nature of their representations of Jews. Among the most familiar examples of Nazi antisemitic propaganda were the newspaper *Der Stürmer* and the film *Jud Süss,* whose grotesque Jewish caricatures reinforced familiar stereotypes of Jews as financial and sexual predators. Their intended audience was the low-brow masses, and the nature of their appeal was primarily irrational. Nazi Judenforschung, by contrast, was designed to legitimize antisemitism within the numerically much smaller but influential educated middle class (*Bildungsbürgertum*) and the German academic world. The appeal of Judenforschung, then, derived from its apparent respectability, which was perceived to depend on its ostensibly "scientific" methodology and apparatus; its emphasis on racial theory; its heavy utilization of Jewish sources; and its downplaying of medieval superstition, shocking caricature, and venomous name calling.

Professional historians played an especially prominent role in this enterprise. Among the most prolific was Walter Frank, who served as director of the Institute for the History of the New Germany, which the Nazi government founded in 1935. Frank himself published books on, among other subjects, the nineteenth-century antisemitic court chaplain Adolf Stoecker and the Dreyfus Affair. One of the institute's most active departments was devoted to research on the history of the Jewish Question and was headed by another historian, Wilhelm Grau, whose publications focused on Jewish-Christian relations in Reformation Germany. Grau's research department sponsored a series of annual symposia, the proceedings of which were published in the house journal, *Forschungen zur Judenfrage.* Grau also edited a newly established review section on the Jewish Question in the venerable *Historische Zeitschrift.* When Alfred Rosenberg decided to create the alternative and more ideologically strident Institute for the Study of the Jewish Question in 1939, he enlisted Grau as a key collaborator.

One of the most accomplished of the Nazi scholars working in this field was the political economist Peter-Heinz Seraphim. His most notable work was the formidable *Das Judentum im Osteuropäischen Raum* (Jewry in the Region of

Eastern Europe [1938]). In it, he focused on the social and occupational structure of east European Jewry, making extensive use of statistical data compiled by Jewish scholars, especially the Zionist sociologist Arthur Ruppin. Seraphim sought to use such Jewish sources, in addition to official data compiled by east European governments, to confirm the arguments of Werner Sombart, who had posited a unique Jewish predisposition for capitalism two decades earlier.

Research on Jewish racial origins and characteristics was conducted by a number of scholars working in physical anthropology, medicine, and human genetics. Eugen Fischer, the director of the Kaiser Wilhelm Institute for Anthropology, Human Heredity, and Eugenics, collaborated with the antisemitic theologian Gerhard Kittel on a study of the racial origins of ancient Jews. Another figure connected with this institute, Othmar von Verschuer, performed analyses on Jewish blood samples from Auschwitz in an attempt to identify the genetic characteristic that made Ashkenazic Jews less susceptible to tuberculosis than other Europeans. Jewish race research also created opportunities for graduate students seeking cutting-edge and politically relevant topics for their doctoral dissertations. One such student was Alexander Paul, whose ambitious dissertation, entitled "Jewish-German Blood Mixing," utilized the files of almost 2,000 "*Mischlinge* of the First-Degree" (half-Jews) placed at his disposal by the Reich Ministry of the Interior.

Several of the scholars who engaged in Judenforschung also served as functionaries or consultants to the Nazi Party and the government, thus helping to implement policy in a direct way. It would be very difficult, however, to demonstrate that any of these scholars exerted a decisive influence over policy. Their most important function lay in generating intellectual respectability for racist expropriation, exclusion, and ultimately mass murder.

—*Alan Steinweis*

**See also** Churches under Nazism; Dühring, Eugen; Fritsch, Theodor; Gemlich Letter; Hitler, Adolf; Hitler's Speeches (Early); Japan; Marr, Wilhelm; *Myth of the Twentieth Century, The;* Rosenberg, Alfred; Sombart, Werner; Stoecker, Adolf; *Stürmer, Der*

**References**
Papen, Patricia von. "'Scholarly' Antisemitism during the Third Reich: The Reichinstitut's Research on the Jewish Question, 1935–1945." Dissertation, Columbia University, 1999.
Steinweis, Alan E. "Antisemitic Scholarship in the Third Reich and the Case of Peter-Heinz Seraphim." In *The Impact of Nazism: New Perspectives on the Third Reich and Its Legacy.* Edited by Alan E. Steinweis and Daniel E. Rogers (Lincoln: University of Nebraska Press, 2003), 68–80.
Weinreich, Max. *Hitler's Professors: The Part of Scholarship in Germany's Crimes against the Jewish People.* Reprint ed. (New Haven, CT: Yale University Press, 1999).

## Nazi Rock

Since the early 1990s, the term *Nazi rock* has become widely used in reference to any kind of rock music that openly propagates messages of hate, violence, racism, antisemitism, and the glorification of National Socialism. The origins of Nazi rock can be traced back to the late 1970s and early 1980s, when it first emerged as a subculture of the British punk movement. Originally known as "Oi" music, it became particularly popular among British working-class skinheads and spawned a distinctive style of appearance, which is still a highly recognizable attribute of many right-wing youth groups today: shaved heads, steel-toe boots, bomber jackets, and other paraphernalia of this nature.

Gradually evolving since the mid-1980s, the Nazi rock music scene is now an international phenomenon with over 550 self-proclaimed right-wing rock bands active in more than thirty countries in 2001. By far the largest number of Nazi rock bands exist in the United States, Germany, and the United Kingdom. With names such as Final Solution (from the United States), Sturmtrupp (from Germany), or Zyklon B (from Poland), Nazi rock bands often make their political orientation unmistakably clear, and many of them are typically associated with right-wing extremist organizations, such as the White Power movement in the United States, the National Front in Britain, or various neo-Nazi groups in Germany and elsewhere.

Although it is a relatively small musical subculture, shunned by the mainstream music industry and therefore operating independently, Nazi rock has attracted a loyal and steadily growing following among right-wing youth groups, making it an increasingly profitable business. Thanks, in part, to free publicity and notoriety gained from often sensationalistic media coverage, some Nazi rock recordings have achieved sales of up to 10,000 copies, and many bands regularly draw average crowds of 200 or more to their concerts. In a few cases, ambiguously right-wing rock music has even crossed over into the pop music mainstream (for example, the music of the German band Rammstein). The Nazi rock fan community, composed primarily of skinheads, neo-Nazis, and militia groups, is well connected by a tightly knit, informal network of activists, publishing "fanzines" and maintaining Internet websites.

Nazi rock music is typically loud and fast—in many ways similar to punk music or heavy metal music—with pounding drums, distorted guitars, heavy bass, and screaming vocals. Songs are usually short and simple in structure, played with a kind of raw, aggressive energy that is meant to elicit a physical response from the listener. However, the main distinguishing feature of Nazi rock is in the lyrical content of the songs, which are usually performed in the bands' native languages. Some of the recurring themes in the vast majority of all Nazi rock include extreme nationalism and xenophobia, glorification of the Aryan race ("blood and honor"), Holocaust denial, militarism, criticism of specific politicians or government policies, general hatred of the Left, and fascist nostalgia. Many Nazi rock songs are intended as calls to action, and they have sometimes inspired their listeners to acts of violence or vandalism, soccer hooliganism, and attacks on foreigners.

—*Frederic M. Kopp*

**See also** Germany, Federal Republic of; Internet; Militia Movement; Neo-Nazism, German; White Power Movement
### References
Anti-Defamation League. "Bigots Who Rock: An ADL List of Hate Music Groups." Available at http://www.adl.org/extremism/intro.asp. Accessed on July 15, 2002.

Hazlehurst, Kayleen, and Cameron Hazlehurst. *Gangs and Youth Subcultures: International Explorations* (New Brunswick, NJ: Transaction Publishers, 1998).

## Neo-Nazism, German

Neo-Nazism can be defined as the attempt to keep Nazi ideology alive or to glorify the Nazi era and its way of life. Since 1945, neo-Nazism has waxed and waned as social, economic, and generational factors have made the ideology more or less appealing.

Under the Allied military government immediately after World War II, any expression of Nazi ideology in Germany was banned and punished. Nascent political parties serving as fronts for a revival of Nazism were prohibited. Although opinion polls showed that a strong current of appreciation for many of Hitler's achievements persisted among the broader populace, there were no public outlets to express such sentiments. When two German states were created in 1949, neo-Nazism flourished in the Federal Republic of Germany (West Germany), where open party politics and basic civil liberties were reestablished. The first major neo-Nazi organization to be established was the Socialist Reich Party, which won 11 percent of the vote in state elections in Lower Saxony in 1951. The party was banned in 1952 according to a provision in the West German Constitution prohibiting political parties that threaten the liberal democratic order.

During new economic uncertainties in the 1960s, the extreme right-wing National Democratic Party (NPD) had moderate successes in some local and regional elections. But it failed to gain representation in the federal parliament when it gathered only 4.3 percent of the vote in the 1969 elections. In the 1980s and 1990s, new parties such as the Republicans and the German People's Union (DVU) replicated the local and regional successes of the NPD. Publicly, these parties distanced themselves from the tyranny and genocide of the Nazi regime, but privately, they benefited from the support of Germans who understood their coded language.

Included in the ideology of neo-Nazi groups is one or more of the following elements: denial of the Holocaust or its full extent, hatred of foreigners, antisemitism (including allegations or intimations of a Jewish world conspiracy), racism, militarism, and celebration of the "sunny side" of the National Socialist years and of Germany's military prowess in World War II. Neo-Nazis often engage in "revisionist" historiography, denying Germany's responsibility for starting World War II and justifying Nazi antisemitic persecution based on supposedly hostile acts or statements by Jews before or during World War II.

After German unification, neo-Nazism thrived once again, especially in the economically depressed former East Germany. For decades, the Communist regime there had suppressed Nazi (or "fascist") sentiments, even as many old Nazis who were willing to change ideologies found jobs and positions of influence. After communism's collapse, foreigners bore the brunt of the neo-Nazi surge, but antisemitic graffiti and vandalism were also rampant. Neo-Nazis and right-wing extremists killed a number of foreigners in the 1990s. Such incidents were, however, always followed by massive counterdemonstrations, showing a vastly larger percentage of the populace to be repelled and frightened by the rise of the neo-Nazis. The German Office for the Protection of the Constitution estimates that there were approximately 2,000 Germans active in 150 or so neo-Nazi associations in the year 2000 (not including the more numerous but much less organized skinhead gangs and music groups). The widest neo-Nazi influence today may come from the Internet, where, in the second half of 2002, the agencies in charge of protecting the constitution counted 920 sites devoted to right-wing extremism and neo-Nazism in Germany.

—*Daniel Rogers*

**See also** German Democratic Republic; Germany, Federal Republic of; Holocaust Denial, Negationism, and Revisionism; Internet; Nazi Rock
**References**
Rogers, Daniel E. *Politics after Hitler: The Western Allies and the German Party System* (New York: New York University Press, 1995).

## Netherlands in the Twentieth Century
In 1878, a series of articles appeared in the Dutch Calvinist daily *De Standaard* (The Standard), en-titled "Liberalisten en Joden" (Liberals and Jews). For the author, Abraham Kuyper, the charismatic leader of the newborn Dutch Reformed Party, liberals and Jews were one and the same. Under the cover of liberalism, he asserted, Jews held absolute sway not only in the Netherlands but also in the whole of Europe, although it should have been obvious that, as "guests" of a Christian society, they should wield no political influence at all. Kuyper's views drew both outrage and approval. When he became prime minister (serving from 1901 to 1905), however, he did not seek to reverse the emancipation of 1796, which had made the Jews full citizens.

This episode is symbolic of the historical relationship between Jews and non-Jews in Holland. In differing historical contexts and to various degrees, new anti-Jewish stereotypes and prejudices attached themselves to the traditional ones: Jews were portrayed as Christ killers, cunning merchants, cowards, traitors, strangers, and conspirators and described as rich, greedy, arrogant, pushy, and materialistic. These prejudices fed religious, socioeconomic, and cultural antisemitism, but until 1936, they never became the program of a political party or achieved any institutionalized form.

From 1796, a slow, uneven, but ongoing process of Jewish integration and assimilation unfolded. A. C. Wertheim (1832–1897), a well-to-do banker and philanthropist and a high-ranking administrator of the Jewish Council, expressed a common attitude among Dutch Jews when he declared that they were *Israëlieten* (Israelites) in church but considered themselves undividedly and wholeheartedly "fellow-citizens" outside the realm of religion. H. Polak, the undisputed leader of the Dutch Diamond Workers Union, articulated a slightly different view of Dutch Jewish identity when he told an interviewer in 1928 that he considered himself to be a Dutchman among the Dutch but also a Jew among the Jews. In reality, the situation was not as ideal as either man wanted it to be. Social distance between Jews and non-Jews diminished only very gradually. Both Wertheim and Polak were confronted with prejudice and well-entrenched negative views about Jewish character and reliability.

During the1930s, under the influence of Nazi

Germany, economic depression, and the arrival of German Jewish refugees, the depiction of the Jew as the Other revived and grew more visible and venomous. The Protestant press and the Catholic press articulated ambivalent feelings toward Hitler's antisemitism. On the one hand, they severely denounced the systematic banishment of the Jews from German society and anti-Jewish violence and persecution. But on the other hand, the newspapers commonly stressed that Germany's Jews had brought misfortune on themselves because of their unbelief and their disproportionate presence in the press and in the economic and financial world. Jewish "overrepresentation" was an issue in Dutch politics as well. In Amsterdam around 1930, there were some 65,000 Jews, comprising nearly 60 percent of all the Jews in Holland and almost 9 percent of the city's population. In 1933, four out of six aldermen were Jews (three of them socialists), provoking some Catholic spokespeople to comment that this was "untactful" because the Jews were "a race apart." Amsterdam was the exception, however. There were few Jews to be found in high political or administrative posts elsewhere in Holland, and before World War II, there was not a single Jewish mayor in the country.

But despite tensions and lingering prejudice, evidence of radical antisemitism was uncommon in national life. Even in the party platform of the Nationaal-Socialistische Beweging (National-Socialist Movement [NSB]), founded in 1931, antisemitism was absent initially. Jews could become members, which they did in very small numbers. In the first elections in which the NSB participated, in 1935, it won a surprisingly high 8 percent of the vote. From that point on, the movement became ever more radical. It embraced antisemitism openly in 1936. Nevertheless, extreme antisemitism and, more generally, right-wing extremism proved to have little attraction for most of the Dutch. By 1939, the NSB had lost half of its supporters.

It is fair to say that antisemitism did not prosper in the Netherlands before the outbreak of World War II, although it definitely was a lurking presence in Dutch politics. The persecution of the Jews in Nazi Germany met with much public censure and led to protests, organized by Jews and left-leaning non-Jews. The Dutch government used the "latent" antisemitism of Dutch society as a pretext to restrict Jewish immigration. A consequence of the attention given the Jewish Question, both positive and negative, was the gradual and almost imperceptible increase in the distance between Dutch Jews and non-Jews.

The distancing that had begun in the late 1930s became the deliberate and systematic policy of the Nazis during their occupation of the Netherlands (from May 1940 to May 1945). Jews were isolated from their neighbors, step by step. Then, in May 1942, the deportations of Jews of foreign nationality began. Of the 140,000 Jews living in Holland in May 1940, 107,000 were deported. Approximately 5,500 returned from the camps. Nearly 24,000 Jews went into hiding, of whom 8,000 were discovered or betrayed; the remaining 16,000 were saved. Some Jews managed to escape to England or Switzerland. Most of those with Christian spouses were exempted from deportation, although not from discrimination and the ever-present possibility of death. The death toll for Jews in the Netherlands was 75 percent, a percentage comparable only to the mortality rates of eastern European countries.

How this could happen in a country proverbially tolerant of its Jews is an ongoing question, debated by scholars, journalists, and public figures. Several explanations have been advanced. That the occupying forces were controlled by the SS, which was much more ideologically motivated than the regular army (the Wehrmacht), accounts for some of the deadliness of the Final Solution in Holland. Further, the traditional law-abiding mentality of the Dutch, including the Dutch Jews, often played into the hands of the SS. Obedient civil servants carried out the tasks assigned to them without noticeable resistance. Then, too, the Netherlands was surrounded by other occupied countries; flight was difficult. Topographically, the country offered few hiding places or remote corners, making the sheltering of Jews a very risky enterprise. Finally, some observers point to the characteristic compartmentalization of Dutch society. Several social and religious groups coexisted but did not develop intimate relations with one another. Thus, Jews may have thought they were more integrated and accepted than they actually were, an illusion that accentuated their vulnerability.

The stress of the war years revealed that the acceptance of Jews as fellow human beings was, at least for some Dutch people, only a facade. Significantly, antisemitism increased during the German occupation, a development recorded at the time in the illegal press and documented by survivors, journalists, and historians soon after the country's liberation. From 1943, rumors began to circulate about nervous, cowardly, and stingy Jews in hiding, who hoarded their money and denounced their hosts, thus getting them sent to concentration camps. The old stereotypes of Judas and Shylock swiftly returned, adapted to a new historical situation. They continued to poison the atmosphere after the war, when it was alleged that Jews dug up their enormous hidden wealth and were soon driving about in luxury automobiles, taking the best jobs, and lording it over the gentiles. Some of this overt antisemitism was the product of emotionally charged property disputes occasioned when returning Jews sought to regain their assets. Jewish survivors were generally perceived as competitors with regard to jobs, housing, and money in a society in which there was a shortage of everything. Moreover, Jews who survived the camps and then returned home were living accusations of the Dutch failure to render them aid against the Germans.

As ugly as this hostility was, it should be stressed that Dutch postwar antisemitism was mainly of a social and verbal character; the few propositions put forward to institutionalize restrictions on Jews in Dutch law quickly died for want of support. Jews defended themselves against antisemitic slurs, and in their struggle, they found many non-Jewish allies in public life. The Dutch government, however, adopted the ambivalent, hypocritical stance of the prewar period, at once downplaying the importance of antisemitism and using "the feeling of the people" as an argument against measures on behalf of Jews.

After 1950, antisemitism in the Netherlands once again seemed on the point of being overcome. Occasional anti-Jewish incidents, usually emanating from the extreme Right, could expect to be met with indignant protests, often on a na-

tionwide scale. The state of Israel was embraced enthusiastically by the Dutch public. Gradually, however, this sympathy began to diminish, especially after the 1967 Six Days' War. Today, on the extreme Left and within certain youthful segments of the Arab immigrant communities, the rhetoric of anti-Zionism frequently crosses into overt antisemitism. Indeed, the line between valid criticism of Israel's policies and the demonization of Israelis and Jews sometimes disappears altogether.

—*Evelien Gans*

***See also*** Anti-Zionism; Emancipation; Holocaust; Islamic Diaspora; Nazi Legal Measures against Jews
***References***
Blom, J. C. H., R.G. Fuks-Mansfeld, and I. Schöffer., eds. *The History of the Jews in the Netherlands.* Translated by A. J. and E. Pomerans. (Oxford and Portland, OR: Littman Library of Jewish Civilization, 2002).
Gans, Evelien. *Gojse nijd & joods narcisme* [Goyish Envy and Jewish Narcisism]. (Amsterdam: Arena, 1994).
———. "De joodse almacht: Hedendaags antisemitisme" (Jewish Omnipotence: Current Anti-Semitism), *Vrij Nederland* (November 29, 2003).
Hondius, Dienke. *Return: Holocaust Survivors and Dutch Anti-Semitism* (Westport, CT: Greenwood Press, 2003).
Israel, Jonathan, and Reiner Salverda., eds. *Dutch Jewry. Its History and Secular Culture.* (Leiden, the Netherlands: Brill, 2002).

## Neustettin Pogrom (1881)

The anti-Jewish riots that broke out on July 17, 1881, in the Pomeranian provincial town of Neustettin (with 8,500 inhabitants, including approximately 400 Jews) and spread from there throughout Pomerania and West Prussia were the first violent excesses against Jews in Germany since the 1840s and were directly provoked by the new movement of antisemitism. In February 1881, the radical antisemitic agitator Ernst Henrici toured the region, collecting signatures for the Antisemites' Petition intended for Chancellor Otto von Bismarck. A few days after his appearance, the Neustettin synagogue went up in flames, and liberal public opinion in Germany linked the fire with his provocative speech.

Countering this, Henrici and the antisemitic press accused the Jews of setting the fire themselves, to cash in on a generous insurance policy and to damage the reputation of the antisemitic movement. Although this interpretation was based on transparent lies, rumors, and manipulated witness reports, the public prosecutor believed it was credible enough to commence proceedings against five Neustettin Jews for the crime of arson. It took two lengthy and costly trials to establish the absurdity of this accusation and to acquit the Jewish defendants.

In the highly charged atmosphere of spring 1881, relations between Christians and Jews in Neustettin rapidly deteriorated. Business and social contacts declined, Jewish shops were boycotted, and Jews were excluded from clubs and associations. To counter the antisemitic climate of opinion in the town fostered by the daily *Norddeutsche Presse,* the Jews of Neustettin launched a liberal local paper, the *Neustettiner Zeitung,* which was edited by the Cohn brothers. The accumulating tensions broke out into rioting in July 1881. A local antisemite, the building contractor Luttosch, insulted by an article in the *Neustettiner Zeitung,* attacked one of the Cohn's who was, however, able to repel the assault with the help of his brother. Bleeding from the head, Luttosch rushed around various taverns and called on those present to drive off the Jews and "beat them to death." Soon, some hundred people gathered and marched through the streets chanting "Hep-Hep!" and smashing Jewish shop windows. Following Luttosch's arrest, the situation continued to escalate over the next two days. The mob destroyed the editorial offices and printing machinery of the *Neustettiner Zeitung* and smashed the windows of Jewish shops and houses. After police reinforcements arrived, the situation calmed down on the third evening.

The Neustettin riots spread to other towns and villages in the region. They followed the same pattern almost everywhere, with mass rallies on the streets, "Hep-Hep" chants, and stone throwing. Unlike the Russian pogroms of the same year, physical attacks were by and large avoided. Actions were especially aimed at those Jews who had achieved some official status, public influence, or economic leadership. In some towns, the state authorities brought in the military. Still, it took them six weeks (until the beginning of September 1881) to end the attacks and restore order in the region.

—*Christhard Hoffmann*

*See also* Antisemites' Petition; Henrici, Ernst; Hep-Hep Riots; Konitz Ritual Murder; Pogroms
**References**
Hoffmann, Christhard. "Political Culture and Violence against Minorities: The Antisemitic Riots in Pomerania and West Prussia." In *Exclusionary Violence: Antisemitic Riots in Modern German History.* Edited by Christhard Hoffmann, Werner Bergmann, and Helmut Walser Smith (Ann Arbor: University of Michigan Press, 2002), 67–92.

# New Age

As a proper name, *New Age* (NA) refers to a mystical, evolution-based belief in a coming era of spiritual enlightenment, marked by religious conformity, world peace, and human advancement toward godhood. A necessary prerequisite for this coming era is the elimination of nationalism and other resistant ideologies dating from the "old" or outmoded age; such ideologies (together with their human carriers) are identified as "separatist" obstacles to worldwide Divine Oneness. NA often refers to both this utopian expectation and the frameworks in which it might be achieved, which go by many names in various contexts: Age of Aquarius (astrology), New World Order (politics), Benign Conspiracy (social activism), personal transformation (psychology), unity in diversity (anthropology), quantum leap or New Humanity (evolutionary theory), Gaia Hypothesis (ecology), spiritual humanism (philosophy), and the Plan of the Masters (occult religion). Even the most secularized variant presupposes a spiritual awakening in order to realize this New Age; therefore, any framework promoting NA should be considered religious at its base.

The term *New Age* and its precepts are credited by most scholars to the Theosophist Helena P. Blavatsky (1831–1891), whose work was further developed by the occultist Alice A. Bailey (1880–1949). However, proponents and critics agree that NA philosophy existed for millennia within older religions and esoteric systems, which freely borrowed from one another. Examples often cited are Gnosticism, Freemasonry, Tibetan Buddhism, Hinduism, and diverse ethnic religions (Egyptian, Norse, Mayan, and so on). Some date NA's origin even further back to ancient Babylonian religion, whereas many NA mystics credit it to Atlantis, an ancient, mythical, spiritually enlightened civilization that possessed spiritual enlightenment but met destruction in the great Flood of the Jewish-Christian tradition. Atlantean enlightenment, called "the Ancient [or Ageless] Wisdom" by devotees, is said to have been handed down by disembodied spirit beings ("Ascended Masters") to selected spokespeople ("channels" and "avatars", and further passed on through chosen teachers ("masters" and "guardians") to various levels of disciples ("initiates" and "adepts"). The teachings were kept secret from hostile audiences via encrypted stories and coded language ("blinds"), preserved for the day when humanity would again be ready to receive the Masters openly and return to the spiritual heights of Atlantis.

In the twentieth century, NA guardians received directives from the Masters to begin worldwide indoctrination in the Ageless Wisdom, paced incrementally according to public tolerance. These efforts were represented in innumerable organizations and projects under varying banners: the Human Potential Movement, the World Core Curriculum, World Servers, Lucis Trust, Planetary Initiative, Share International, the Findhorn Foundation, and State of the World Forum. Many observers consider 1975 a pivotal year for NA publicity and cite *The Aquarian Conspiracy* by Marilyn Ferguson (1980) as the first overt NA manifesto. Since then, apologists have become increasingly open about goals and methods, promoting their views in communications media, public education, and popular entertainment and on the Internet. As a result, esoteric NA terms have passed into everyday parlance, and classic texts once shielded from public scrutiny have become increasingly accessible.

As a movement, NA is largely unstructured, decentralized, and unsupervised, with an abundance of self-styled leaders claiming direct communication with divine beings. Certain common traits, however, characterize all devotees: (1) reverence for the Ascended Masters (a hierarchy of divine entities) and devotion to their "transmissions," especially "the Plan"; (2) participation in mystical experiences that awaken and develop higher consciousness, leading to interaction with "spirit guides"; (3) inconsistency in philosophy and conduct, the result of irrationalist beliefs, material reality, and objective moral standards; (4) belief in pantheism, an ageless collective consciousness ("Group Mind"), and humanity's potential godhood; (5) belief in the Hindu laws of karma, both personal and collective; (6) faith in a higher species of humans, which, according to Theosophy, will spring from the Aryan race and replace the present human race; (7) erasure of all religious dissent and "separatism," bringing victory to the Forces of Light; and (8) a united world ruled by the Masters, who will "overshadow," or possibly inhabit the bodies of human leaders.

The last three precepts require the prior elimination of groups and ideas that reject basic NA tenets. These groups and ideas are infected with the "virus of separatism," a cardinal sin holding back human evolution. Nature, understood as a divine entity, is expected to aid the elimination process by "purging" the earth of human carriers of separatism through disasters, epidemics, starvation, and "natural" extinction. Reincarnation, another core NA belief, interprets the prospect of millions of deaths as beneficial even to the victims because death is not the loss of life but rather promotion to the next life, where those unfit for the New Humanity can eventually become fit.

Although all religions are proclaimed acceptable—and indeed, many adherents try to live by that rule—seminal NA literature denounces one religion as totally unfit for inclusion: historical (erroneously termed "orthodox") Judaism. This rejection extends to any Jewish influence retained in its daughter religions, Christianity and Islam. The Jewish declaration of a universal morality, belief in a transcendent God, rejection of multiple deities (especially human deities), and serious interaction with the material world are all incompatible with NA philosophy, posing a serious challenge to its goals of religious uniformity. Zionism, which supports Jewish self-determination in the Jewish homeland, is doubly offensive in its blend of nationalism and Jewish identity, two forms of separatism. NA architects Blavatsky and Bailey, speaking for the Masters, particularly targeted the God of the Jews and the Jewish Bible as urgent priorities for elimination, believing them so perverted that they endangered human spiritual survival.

This visceral hostility toward Jewish religion and identity is supplemented with a benevolent rejection of the Jewish people "as a race." Of ancient alien origin and at one time spiritually advanced, the Jews are now seen as obsolete and deceived, tools of the "Dark Forces" possessing a mysterious cosmic energy that influences humanity to embrace the evils of separatism and materialism. This power is collectively wielded by the Jews as a race, a condition persisting over the ages and resulting in accumulated negative "racial karma" that pursues them through their generations and both necessitates and explains their unusually frequent and severe suffering.

Because of their innate spiritual and racial shortcomings, the Jews are considered unsuited for the New Age—and more important, they are seen to hinder its emergence. NA teachers vigorously deny any antisemitism in this conclusion: the Jews are not hated for their condition, any more than AIDS carriers are hated for being sick. However, the Jews constitute a "world problem" that must be solved so that the rest of humanity can enter the New Age. Only by abandoning all traces of Jewish identity can Jews hope to find their individual cure, which includes submitting to the karmic purification of suffering and death, in order to attain improved (non-Jewish) status in their next life.

It must be emphasized that many NA adherents are unaware of these foundational teachings, ostensibly vital components of the Divine Plan but apparently shared only among disciples considered ready for such sensitive information. Ample verification, however, can be found in the writings of Alice Bailey and Helena Blavatsky, two of the most oft-quoted sources in NA teaching.

—*Hannah Newman*

*See also* Aquarius, Age of; Bailey, Alice A.; Blavatsky, Helena P.; Freemasonry; Internet; Jewish Force; The Plan of the Hierarchy

**References**
Newman, Hannah. Jerusalem SearchLight. http://searchlight.iwarp.com. (Accessed February 28, 2005).

# New Left

The New Left, a loosely defined group of middle-class student activists organized after the June 1962 publication of Tom Hayden's *Port Huron Statement,* challenged the complacency of postwar American society and called for a more participatory form of democracy. Hayden's text celebrated a new generation, "bred in at least modest comfort, housed now in universities." He and his followers should have enjoyed material rewards but instead looked "uncomfortably to the world we inherit."

In its early years, Jews joined the New Left movement in disproportionate numbers. At a time when they represented just 3 percent of the U.S. population and 10 percent of those attending college, Jews constituted a majority of the New Left's most active members. Numerous social scientific studies pointed to strong Jewish influences in the nation's leading New Left groups. In rallies at the University of California–Berkeley, University of Wisconsin–Madison, and Brandeis University, Jewish New Leftists demanded free speech, racial equality, and, eventually, an end to the war in Vietnam.

But by the late 1960s, political divisions began to divide the New Left as anti-Israel, anti-Zionist, and antisemitic sentiments alienated most of its Jewish constituency. In the wake of Israel's victory in the 1967 Six Days' War, many non-Jewish New Leftists withdrew their support for the Jewish state, which they considered an imperialist and colonial oppressor of West Bank and Gaza Strip Palestinians. As Black Power leader Stokely Carmichael said at a 1968 convention of the Organization of American Students, "We have begun to see the evil of Zionism and we will fight to wipe it out wherever it exists, be it in the Ghetto of the United States or in the Middle East." Jewish New Leftists faced criticism for opposing the U.S. colonial presence in Southeast Asia while supporting government aid to Israel.

When African American activists organized around the Black Power movement, led in large measure by Oakland's Black Panther Party, Jewish New Leftists initially sought alliances with the Panthers; most eventually gave up on the effort. As Itzhak Epstein, a Jewish activist, explained, "Even if I were a superaltruistic liberal and campaigned among the Jews to support the Panthers' program, I would justifiably be tarred and feathered for giving aid and comfort to enemies of the Jews. I would rather it were not this way, but it was you who disowned us, not we who betrayed you" (in Jack Porter and Peter Dreier, *Jewish Radicalism: A Selected Anthology,* 1973, 70–71). In 1969, Eldridge Cleaver told a *New York Times* reporter that "the Black Panther Party in the United States fully supports Arab Guerillas in the Middle East."

By the 1970s, the New Left lost many of its most influential Jewish members just as a more violence-prone cadre of student activists emerged. The strength and internal cohesion once enjoyed by the New Left disintegrated in the wake of several high-profile and violent protests. Many of the movement's initial founders, including Tom Hayden, opted for more conventional political lives.

—*Marc Dollinger*

**See also** African American–Jewish Relations; Anti-Zionism; Black Nationalism; Student Nonviolent Coordinating Committee

**References**
Chertoff, Mordechai S., ed. *The New Left and the Jews* (New York: Pittman, 1971).
Isserman, Maurice. *If I Had a Hammer . . . The Death of the Old Left and the Birth of the New Left* (New York: Basic Books, 1987).
Rothman, Stanley, and Robert S. Lichter. *Roots of Radicalism: Jews, Christians, and the Left* (New Brunswick, NJ: Transaction, 1996).

# Nietzsche, Friedrich (1844–1900)

Friedrich Nietzsche's thinking on a great many subjects, including Jews and antisemitism, has been widely misunderstood, in large part because of the misrepresentation of his work by his sister during the years of his mental incapacity and after his death. His attitudes toward Jews were, in fact, rather fluid and subject to external influences. Chief among these was the extent to which his perspective was informed by the more compelling issues that engaged his imagination, particularly his implacable opposition to Christianity.

As a general rule, it would be fair to say that Nietzsche approved of Jews when he cast them as foils for contemporary Christians in general and German Christians in particular and disapproved of them when he chose to emphasize the roots of Christianity in Jewish schism and reaction against Roman subjugation. It also seems clear, however, that the changing perspective on Jews that emerged in his philosophical writings was affected, to some degree, by the progress of his stormy personal relationships. As a young man, Nietzsche evidently shared the reflexive antipathy toward Jews common to his time and place, an attitude that helped to smooth his entry into a close friendship with Richard and Cosima Wagner that lasted several years. That friendship deteriorated with the disaffection occasioned by Wagner's idiosyncratic embrace of Christian faith, manifested in *Parsifal,* and for their part, the Wagners' disenchantment with Nietzsche was only intensified by his friendship with Paul Rée, a philosopher of Jewish ancestry. The relationship with Rée soured, in turn, and Nietzsche was also deeply troubled by the marriage of his sister Elisabeth to the unstable antisemitic agitator Bernhard Förster. Yet whatever the state of his feelings toward Jews at a given moment, the mature, post-Wagnerian Nietzsche was as firm in his opposition to cultural and political antisemitism as he was in his opposition to Christianity itself.

In the immediate wake of Nietzsche's break with Wagner, references to Jews in his writings began to display the ambivalence noted earlier, with the ancient Jews of the Roman era being depicted in a negative light in contrast to a largely sympathetic portrait of modern Jews. This bifurcated perspective made an early appearance in *Human, All-Too-Human* (1878). In aphorism 114, in which the main point was to contrast Christian culture unfavorably with that of the ancient Greeks, Nietzsche referenced ancient Judaism as the source of Christianity's misanthropic view of humanity as essentially sinful; in aphorism 475, he credited modern Jews with having derived strength from a long history of suffering, while at the same time blasting the spirit of nationalism and the concomitant spread of antisemitism that were playing increasingly visible roles in European politics. The coupling of opposition to Christianity with an attack on its Jewish roots was not original with Nietzsche; Enlightenment-era rationalists had made comparable arguments a century earlier. Similarly, singling out the Jews of the early Christian era for particular opprobrium was a gesture as old as the New Testament itself. Nietzsche's exemption of contemporary Jews from this critique, however, distinguished his position both from the rationalists, who viewed Judaism as an archaic superstition and Jews as hopelessly backward, and from those Christians who viewed Jews as bearing hereditary responsibility for deicide.

In *Daybreak* (1881), *Beyond Good and Evil* (1886), and book five of *The Gay Science* (1887), Nietzsche emphasized the beneficial influence Jews had had on the development of European civilization. He suggested in *Daybreak* that their talents would eventually lead them to assume mastery of Europe (a development he anticipated with approval); in *Beyond Good and Evil*, he modified this claim—the Jews, "the strongest, toughest, and purest race now living in Europe," could well assume "mastery over Europe," and intensifying antisemitism might yet compel them to do so, but they did not seek such mastery of their own will. The core notion of a beneficial Jewish influence on European culture was, again, not new. Nietzsche may have been unique, however, in arguing in favor of Jewish "mastery" over Europeans, at least if one discounts the fantasies spun in the novels of Benjamin Disraeli.

Nietzsche's most extended and harshest criticism of Jews and Judaism appeared in *On the Genealogy of Morals* (1887), a work that coincided with the collapse of his friendship with Rée. Here, his attention was fixed almost exclusively on the Judaism of the prophets and of the early Christian era, and his argument rested on the contention that the Judaism of that era, thoroughly characterized by resentment against the superior strength of their conquerors, effected a decadent and pernicious inversion of values that privileged impotence, weakness, and suffering and held strength and vitality in contempt. This inverted "slave morality" was then exported to

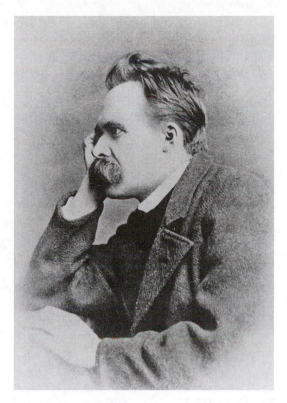

The German philosopher Friedrich Nietzsche (1844–1900). His legacy to modern antisemitism is still being debated. This quote suggests why: "Among my friends, I have no Jews … and, certainly, no antisemites." (Bettmann/Corbis)

Europe in the guise of Christianity. In *The Antichrist* (1895), he ameliorated this position somewhat, claiming that the apparent adoption of slave morality by the Jews during the generations of their subjugation was, in fact, an expression of their essential strength, a measure taken to ensure their survival in "impossible circumstances."

The intensity and consistency of his opposition to political antisemitism notwithstanding, at no time did Nietzsche challenge the generally accepted notion that behavioral differences between Jews and other European peoples reflected biological differences. Nor, as the outburst in *Genealogy of Morals* suggests, was he himself entirely free of the tendency to project conflict with an individual Jew onto the group. Nevertheless, it is clear that Nietzsche had great hopes for the continuing role Jews were to play in European culture in coming generations. The apparently still unshakable popular conviction that his ideas formed the foundation for the genocidal policies of National Socialism is perhaps the ghastliest of the many indignities that have been visited on his legacy.

—David Isadore Lieberman

*See also* Bauer, Bruno; *Coningsby;* Deicide; Dühring, Eugen; Förster, Bernhard; Förster-Nietzsche, Elisabeth; Misanthropy; Wagner, Cosima; Wagner, Richard

*References*
Duffy, Michael, and Willard Mittelman. "Nietzsche's Attitudes toward the Jews," *Journal of the History of Ideas* 49 (1988): 301–317.
Gilman, Sander L. "Nietzsche, Heine, and the Idea of the Jew: The Other and the Self." In *Inscribing the Other* (Lincoln: University of Nebraska Press, 1991).
Knodt, Eva M. "The Janus Face of Decadence: Nietzsche's Genealogy and the Rhetoric of Anti-Semitism," *German Quarterly* 66 (1993): 160–175.

# Night of Broken Glass (November 1938 Pogrom)

The German term for the pogrom of November 1938, *Kristallnacht,* highlights the expensive crystal and shop windows smashed during the night of November 9–10, all belonging to Jews. Yet this operation involved state-sanctioned violence that left 91 Jews dead, hundreds more beaten, 7,500 Jewish stores shattered, and several hundred synagogues destroyed by arsonists. Moreover, the rampage served as a prelude to the internment of thousands of Jewish men in Germany and Austria and accelerated the expropriation of the remaining businesses and wealth belonging to German Jews.

The Night of Broken Glass marked a sharp escalation in the antisemitic program Hitler had pursued since becoming chancellor. As he consolidated his power and revived his country's economy and military between 1933 and 1936, his regime disenfranchised its Jewish citizens, developed a legal definition of who was Jewish, and forced the sale of Jewish-owned companies to "Aryan" buyers. The intent behind these measures was to compel German Jews to emigrate.

The year 1936 was pivotal in restructuring the German government and articulating new economic and political priorities that laid the groundwork for the November pogrom. On the eve of the Winter Olympic Games in February, a Jewish medical student killed a Nazi Party official in Switzerland. The presence of foreign visitors at the Olympics precluded reprisals against the Jews, for they would damage public relations, but Hitler devoted part of his eulogy for his murdered comrade to blaming the Jews in general for instigating the slaying. In the summer, he appointed Heinrich Himmler to be chief of all German police forces, and around the same time, he enhanced Hermann Göring's power over the German economy. Both moves would be crucial for the unfolding of the pogrom and its aftermath.

The annexation of Austria in 1938 opened up opportunities for the Germans to experiment with more efficient means of driving Jews out of the economy and over the borders. The Storm troopers (SA) initially were encouraged to assault, humiliate, and intimidate Austrian Jews. After their brief reign of terror, a coercive system of expropriation was instituted, which confiscated the assets of richer Jews to assist poorer ones to emigrate. Nearly 5,000 Jews were expelled into neighboring countries. By August, the new Central Office of Jewish Emigration, headed by Adolf Eichmann, simplified the process for obtaining papers needed to leave Austria. In the next year, half of Austrian Jewry emigrated, compared to 30 percent of German Jews in the first six years of Nazi rule.

The success of the so-called Austrian model for the expatriation and impoverishment of Jews had immediate repercussions on anti-Jewish policies in the Old Reich. Jewish immigrants from the Soviet Union who had failed to return to the USSR as ordered in February were interned in concentration camps by May. The following month, the Gestapo arrested 1,500 German Jewish men designated as antisocials because they had prior criminal convictions.

The attempt to deport Polish Jews residing in Germany served as the immediate pretext for Kristallnacht. Polish Jews constituted the largest group of foreign Jews living in Germany. Fearing an influx of Polish refugees returning to their native land after the annexation of Austria, the Polish parliament passed a law to revoke the citizenship of Polish émigrés who did not meet certain qualifications. When it became evident that Germany might cite this law as a pretext to expel its Polish Jews, the Polish government responded with an order to cancel the passports of Poles living outside of Poland who did not submit them for certification by the end of October. On October 27 and 28, Himmler's police and SS transported approximately 17,000 Polish Jews to the Polish border town of Zbaszyn. Once there, Polish border guards refused them entry. The Jews huddled in makeshift camps in a no-man's-land between the two countries. Outraged by a letter from his sister describing the plight of their family in the camp, Herschel Grynszpan purchased a pistol in Paris and then shot the first secretary of the German diplomatic mission, Ernst vom Rath, on November 7, 1938. Vom Rath died two days later.

In the interim between the shooting of vom Rath and his death, spontaneous anti-Jewish riots had broken out in a few German cities. But the full-scale and nationwide attacks on Jews and their homes, stores, and places of worship that occurred after vom Rath died were orchestrated by the Nazi Party and approved by Hitler. The party and the controlled press called on readers to punish the Jews for inciting violence against German officials. On the evening of November 9, the party elite gathered in Munich to commemorate the anniversary of Hitler's 1923 Beer Hall Putsch. Hitler conferred there with Joseph Goebbels just before the propaganda minister announced the news of vom Rath's death to the assemblage. Goebbels clearly took the lead in unleashing the pogrom, perhaps hoping to carve out a larger role for himself in the formulation of anti-Jewish policy and to regain some of the favor Hitler had recently bestowed on his rivals, Himmler and Göring.

Goebbels whipped up the party faithful to engage in reprisals against the Jews without fear that the police would intervene. His speech was understood by party leaders as an order to stir up popular animosity toward the Jews and discreetly direct the riots, once they had initiated them. Goebbels's remarks were relayed via telegraph

A man clears away the broken glass from the Jewish Kaliski Bedding Establishment. The previous night, known as Kristallnacht, Hitler's Storm troopers murdered Jews, vandalized businesses, and burned hundreds of synagogues all over Germany. (Hulton-Deutsch Collection/Corbis)

and telephone to party *Gauleiter* (district party leaders) and SA members throughout the Reich. A command issued to an SA cell in Munich typified Goebbels's plan to undermine the basis for Jewish existence in Germany: all Jewish businesses were to be destroyed immediately by uniformed Storm troopers. After their destruction, SA guards were to be posted to ensure that no valuables were removed. Synagogues were to be burned at once, and neither the fire brigade nor the police were to be allowed to intervene. All Jews were to be disarmed.

The orgy of violence, arson, and vandalism that ensued surpassed Goebbels's expectations; it also immediately generated friction with Göring and Himmler, who felt their jurisdiction over anti-Jewish policy had been infringed on. In the aftermath of the pogrom, they went into action. The SS favored the orderly internment of Jews and the preservation of Jewish communal records. Himmler's subordinate, Reinhard Heydrich of the Reich Security Service, ordered his police to seize the archives housed in synagogues and Jewish communal agencies and to arrest wealthier Jewish males and hold them as hostages to speed up the pace of Jewish emigration. Approximately 30,000 Jewish men over the age of sixteen in Austria and Germany were arrested by the SS and interned in concentration camps. Although hundreds died from maltreatment, most were released in the coming months when their families obtained the visas required to leave the country.

On November 12, Nazi leaders met to discuss the impact of the pogrom on solving the Jewish Question in Germany. An irate Göring castigated his colleagues for destroying Jewish businesses rather than transferring them to Aryan owners, as envisioned in the Four Year Plan. He also expressed concern that German insurance companies would be bankrupted if they had to make good on all the claims of Jewish policyholders. To transform this blunder into an advantage, he proposed that German Jewry as a whole be held accountable for the murder of vom Rath and fined 1 billion marks to atone for their complicity. All insurance payments to Jews would be placed in a fund to pay the fine. Denied the means of making a living and with thousands of men languishing in camps, Jews were given the clear message to emigrate—or else. The Central Office of Jewish Emigration was established in Germany at the beginning of 1939 to reinforce the message.

The Security Police gathered intelligence suggesting that not many Germans had "spontaneously" participated in the pogrom and that many others disapproved of Kristallnacht. They were shocked by the wanton destruction of property and synagogues. Yet as one historian has noted, it was the violence rather than the removal of the Jews from the economy and the country that most Germans opposed. A few Christian ministers and priests condemned the pogrom, but no mainstream church issued a denunciation.

Though more strident, the foreign criticism of the Night of Broken Glass was not backed up with diplomatic action to enable German Jews to find refuge. Of the Americans responding to a Gallup Poll at the time, 94 percent disapproved of the German treatment of Jews and 72 percent approved of the temporary withdrawal of the U.S. ambassador to Germany as a protest. Yet 82 percent opposed changing U.S. immigration quotas. Soon afterward, Secretary of Labor Frances Perkins declared that President Franklin Roosevelt would not revise the immigration quotas.

In January 1939, Hitler addressed the Reichstag and "prophesied" the destruction of European Jewry if Germany were involved in a war he believed was being plotted by Jewish financiers and Bolsheviks. Few would have predicted then that Hitler's regime would order the mass murder of European Jewry two years later. Most thought that the zenith of Nazi antisemitism had been reached in the November pogrom. They failed to foresee that the methodical annihilation of an entire people would be accomplished not by riots but rather by systematic policies for expropriating, ghettoizing, transporting, and liquidating millions of innocent victims. Kristallnacht and the events that triggered it provided the precedents for confiscating Jewish wealth, incarcerating Jews, and deporting them. It is correctly seen as a major step toward the Final Solution.

—*Lawrence Baron*

**See also** Aryanization; Austria; Boycott of Jewish Shops; Eichmann, Adolf; Goebbels, Joseph; Göring, Hermann; Himmler, Heinrich; Hitler, Adolf; Hitler's "Prophecy"; Immigration and Naturalization Laws; National Socialist German Workers' Party; Nazi Legal Measures against Jews; Nuremberg Laws; *Ostjuden*

**References**

Friedländer, Saul. *Nazi Germany and the Jews: The Years of Persecution, 1933–1939* (New York: HarperCollins, 1997).

Pehle, Walter H., ed. *November 1938: From the "Reichskristallnacht" to Genocide* (New York: Berg, 1990).

Read, Anthony, and David Fisher. *Kristallnacht: Unleashing the Holocaust* (London: Joseph, 1989).

## Nilus, Sergei (1862–1929)

A Russian apocalyptic thinker and prolific religious writer of the early twentieth century, Sergei Nilus is best known as the publisher and commentator of the notorious antisemitic fabrication *Protocols of the Elders of Zion.* In the historical literature, the enigmatic Nilus appears in any number of guises: a professor, reputedly expert in Hebrew and Chaldean; a playboy; a priest or itinerant monk of the Russian Orthodox Church; even a "half-crazy pseudo-mystic." Some believe that Nilus was not his real name; others consider him the actual author of the *Protocols.* None of this is accurate. Recent research at last makes it possible to present a more precise and nuanced assessment of this controversial figure.

Born in Moscow, the son of a minor noble landowner, Nilus was descended on his father's side from Baltic German or Swedish forebears of Lutheran persuasion. Nilus's father was the first to be baptized in the Orthodox rite. His maternal ancestors were Russian landed nobility. Nilus studied law at the University of Moscow and briefly worked in the judicial system but then quit the state service. He withdrew to his estate in the Orel district, which he managed (ineffectively) in the old-fashioned, patriarchal way. Toward the end of the century, the religiously indifferent Nilus succumbed to the apocalyptic mood that was becoming ever more widespread in the country. He thus joined those victims of stepped-up modernization and secularization who identified the downfall of their own world with the end of the world in general. Nilus undertook pilgrimages and met the charismatic preacher and wonder-worker John of Kronstadt (1829–1908). Out of these experiences, he fashioned his own mystical-apocalyptic faith, based on miracles and signs.

Nilus became active as a writer, winning some acclaim for what he termed the "miraculous" discovery and deciphering of Nikolai Motovilov's manuscript detailing the latter's famous conversation with Serafim of Sarov, one of Russia's most popular saints, on the acquisition of the Holy Spirit. Nilus published this in 1903 in his devotional book *The Great in the Small: Notes of an Orthodox Believer.* In the second edition of this book, which came out at Tsarkoe Selo in December 1905 with a new subtitle, *The Antichrist as an Imminent Political Possibility,* Nilus took up the *Protocols of the Elders of Zion* for the first time. Later editions of his book, also containing the

The writer and religious mystic Sergei Nilus, here, is best known popularizing the fabricated *Protocols of the Elders of Zion.* The version of the forgery he included in a Russian book dating from 1903 was eventually translated into twenty languages and remains the most widely available in the world today. (Courtesy of Michael Hagemeister)

*Protocols,* appeared under varying titles in 1911 and 1912. The fourth edition was published in January 1917 by the famous Holy Trinity Monastery at Sergiev Posad and bore the menacing title *"It Is Near, Even at the Doors": Concerning That Which People Do Not Wish to Believe and Which Is So Near.* As to the origins of the *Protocols*—which Nilus certainly did not author but surely edited and revised—he gave differing accounts. At first, he described them as "secret documents" stolen from one of the most highly placed leaders of Freemasonry in France; later, he referred to the "Jewish plan for the conquest of the world" and said it had been presented at the First Zionist Congress in Basel (1897) by Theodor Herzl.

Nilus's commentary on the *Protocols* interpreted them within the framework of the apocalyptic worldview associated with Vladimir

Solov'ev (1853–1900) and John of Kronstadt. The *Protocols* according to Nilus unveiled the hidden strategy of the supernatural forces of darkness—and their worldly allies—in their unremitting struggle against the forces of light, a struggle that seemed to have entered its final stage at the turn of the twentieth century. Nilus was not a racist antisemite; rather, he shared the traditional conceptions of Christian anti-Judaism. Jews, according to his view, were part of the cosmic drama of Salvation, in which they played a villainous part: they were pathbreakers and agents of the Antichrist who contested with God for rule over the world. Ultimately, the divine plan of Salvation—after a brief reign of the Antichrist—included the collective conversion and redemption of Israel and, with that, an end to the Jewish Question. Nilus admonished his readers not to harbor enmity toward the Jewish people, who were, after all, simply blind and misguided.

Nilus spent several years near the monastery of Optina Pustyn, where he worked in the archives and conversed with the elder monks. It was in this period that he produced most of his written works, among them a diary entitled *On the Banks of God's River,* a kind of chronicle of the monastic life at Optina. Other works treated the lives of Egyptian anchorites and Russian hermits; meetings with monastic elders, miracle-workers, and "holy fools"; and reports of prophetic dreams, oracular pronouncements, and the activities of demonic powers.

To Nilus, the Russian Revolution of 1917 appeared to corroborate a number of the predictions contained in the *Protocols* and to usher in the eschatological reign of the Antichrist, the false messiah of the Jews. Nilus refused to leave Russia and joined the "Catacomb Church," the underground movement of Russian Orthodoxy that refused to compromise with the Bolsheviks. Together with his wife, he moved from place to place, mostly living in the Ukraine. Arrested several times, he was interrogated, and imprisoned but always let go, even though his identity was known to the authorities. Finally, utterly destitute, he found accommodation with a priest in the village of Krutets, about 75 miles northeast of Moscow. He died there of a heart attack in January 1929. His only son, Sergei (1883–1941), emigrated to Poland after the Russian Revolution of 1917. During the Bern trial in 1935, in which the *Protocols* was condemned as a fraud, Sergei acted as an expert witness by sending a report that vouched for the authenticity of the book.

In post-Soviet Russia, Nilus's works have been rediscovered. His writings appear in new and occasionally quite substantial editions. Conferences, lectures, the establishment of an annual Sergei Nilus Prize, and his presence in the press and on the Internet all testify to the esteem in which he is held in patriotic and church circles, as well as by antisemites.

—*Michael Hagemeister*
*Richard S. Levy, translation*

**See also** Antichrist; Freemasonry; Herzl, Theodor; Jewish Question; *Protocols of the Elders of Zion; Protocols of the Elders of Zion* on Trial; Russia, Imperial; Russia, Post-Soviet; Russian Orthodox Church; Zionism

**References**
Bagdasarov, Roman, and Sergei Fomin. *Neizvestnyi Nilus* (The Unknown Nilus). 2 vols. (Moscow: Pravoslavnyi Palomnik, 1995).
Hagemeister, Michael. "Wer war Sergej Nilus? Versuch einer bio-bibliographischen Skizze," *Ostkirchliche Studien* 40 (1991): 49–63.
———. "Sergej Nilus und die 'Protokolle der Weisen von Zion': Überlegungen zur Forschungslage," *Jahrbuch für Antisemitismusforschung* 5 (1996): 127–147.
———. "Vladimir Solov'ev and Sergej Nilus: Apocalypticism and Judeophobia." In *Vladimir Solov'ev: Reconciler and Polemicist.* Edited by Wil van den Bercken, Manon de Couten, and Evert van der Zweerde (Leuven, Belgium: Peeters, 2000), 287–296.
———. "Nilus, Sergej Aleksandrovic." In *Biographisch-Bibliographisches Kirchenlexikon,* vol. 21 (Nordhausen, Germany: Bautz, 2003), 1063–1067. http://www.bautz.de/bbkl/n/nilus_s_a.shtml. (Accessed February 28, 2005).

## Nordau, Max (1849–1923)

Nordau was the author of *Degeneration* (1892), which introduced the idea later popularized by the Nazis of modern art as "degenerate." He was also a leader of early Zionism.

Born Simon Maximilian Südfeld in Budapest in 1849, the son of a rabbi, Max Nordau was raised an Orthodox Jew, but gave up Jewish observance in his teens. In *The Conventional Lies of Civilization* (1883), he discussed organized religion as one of those "lies." Nordau moved to Paris in 1880 and enjoyed great success as a popularizing social philosopher and journalist who attacked the hypocrisies of modern society and preached the Darwinian idea of a morality based on natural human solidarity. His progressive and rationalist viewpoint led him to be severely critical of the "decadence" of "modern" art and literature, and he elaborated on this theme in *Degeneration* (1892). Trained as a physician, Nordau applied the medical concept of degeneration to the arts, to explain the opposition to bourgeois civilization of the most famous writers and artists of the age as a form of socially-induced insanity. He was thus central in the medicalization of cultural criticism, but he makes no connection in *Degeneration* to the Jewish Question; his one mention of antisemitism describes it as a German variety of degenerate disease, hysteria.

The effect of antisemitism was brought home to him in 1893, when he was hounded out of the resort of Borkum for being a Jew. This experience was the basis of his enthusiastic reception in 1895 of the Zionist ideas of Theodor Herzl. Nordau became Herzl's right-hand man in the Zionist movement and one of its main spokesmen.

He saw antisemitism as causing a moral crisis for Western European Jews that had the benefit, however, of forcing people such as himself to recognize their separate, Jewish national identity. These Western Zionists could then fulfill their Jewish *national* mission by founding a Jewish homeland as a refuge for the main victims of antisemitism, the desperate Jewish masses in Russia and Eastern Europe. Antisemitism was thus central to Nordau's Zionist argument, as the cause of the moral and material emergency of the Jewish people, which could be solved only by attaining Zionism's goal of a Jewish homeland.

Antisemitism was, for Nordau, morally pernicious, but it was also an inevitable result of human nature, as well as, in national terms, completely understandable. It was the result of the natural tendency of majorities in human societies to regard different, abnormal, minority groups as the enemy and hence as scapegoats for society's

problems. He was conscious of the many ways in which ruling elites had manipulated this basic instinct. As a Darwinian nationalist, though, Nordau accepted the antisemitic assertion that national societies should not accept "foreign" bodies that maintained their difference. Although he held out the prospect that individual "Jews of both worlds" could completely assimilate into their host societies, he thought that assimilation was a dead end and, moreover, morally questionable as a denial of Jews' true national identity. The continuation of Jews as an identifiable minority in other national societies guaranteed antisemitism's survival. The only proper solution would be to adopt the "either/or" logic of nationalism, so that Jews would have to choose between complete self-denial through assimilation, or assertion of their authentic identity by becoming Zionists and, ultimately, emigrating to the Jewish homeland.

—*Steven Beller*

**See also** Degenerate Art; Degeneration; Evolutionary Psychology; Herzl, Theodor; Jewish Question; *Ostjuden;* Social Darwinism; Zionism
**References**
Nordau, Max. *Zionistische Schriften.* Edited by the Zionistischer Aktionskomittee (Cologne: Jüdischer Verlag, 1909).

## Norris, Frank (1870–1902)

Frank Norris was an American novelist at the turn of the twentieth century whose best-known works depicted themes of major interest to muckraking journalists and the Populist movement. Because of the author's positive identification with early twentieth-century reform against trusts and monopolies, literary scholars and historians have overlooked the strenuous antisemitism in his most successful novels. Norris's derogation of Jews presented a more invasive and menacing image than either Henry Adams's elite and snobbish eastern intellectual antisemitism or Ignatius Donnelley's derisive populist sketch of a Jewish money broker in *Caesar's Column: A Story of the Twentieth Century* (1890). As villains in Norris's mug book, Zerko in *McTeague* (1899) and Behrman in *The Octopus* (1901) were toxic agents in nature itself, a death force brutalizing

Because of American novelist Frank Norris's positive identification with early twentieth-century reform against trusts and monopolies, literary scholars and historians have overlooked the strenuous antisemitism in his most successful novels. (National Archives)

California's urban and agrarian scene. These brute devils, lurking in the nature of everyman and prepared to corrupt Anglo-Saxon Christian civilization, transcended the conventional Jewish stereotypes of Shylock and Christ killers.

There is no evidence that Norris knew any Jews beyond those he ran into through chance encounters—for instance, while slumming as an apprentice writer on Polk Street in San Francisco, the lower-middle-class huckster's bazaar. Born in Chicago to a prosperous jewelry merchant and an actress, Norris moved with his family to San Francisco for reasons concerning his father's health, relocated to Paris for a year, and then returned to the Bay Area. Jews were visible in the jewelry trade, and it is possible Frank received early impressions of Jews from his father, who wanted his son to enter the business. Instead, Frank enrolled at the University of California but failed to pass the entrance examination in mathematics. Though he was unable to graduate first from Berkeley and later from Harvard, he took classes that introduced him to

literary romance and realism in the writings of Émile Zola, Rudyard Kipling, and Robert Louis Stevenson. Needing to make a living, he went to South Africa in 1895 to cover the Boer War for the *San Francisco Chronicle,* and in 1898, he moved to the reform-oriented *McClure's Magazine* to report on the Spanish-American War from Cuba. Norris first came to national prominence with the novel *McTeague* in 1899 and permanently established his reputation with the best-selling *The Octopus* in 1901, followed by *The Pit* in 1903.

Opposed to smiling Victorian gentility and family values in literary philosophy, Norris became a pioneer of naturalism. "I believe," he professed, "that the future of America lies in the direction of a return to the primitive elemental life, and an abandonment of 'elegant prose' and 'fine writing'" (in Norris 1899, 486). Advocating the superior virtue of Anglo-Saxon Christian commercial values, he was implicitly drawn to the vernacular *Jew* and *Jewing* as active pejorative verbs in American English. (In British English and continental languages, the word *Jew* functioned only as a noun—as did the names for all other nationalities in the United States.) Zerko's "clawing" prehensile fingers and Behrman's "crushing" vast stomach dominated the physical and psychological metaphors in Norris's melodramatic story lines. The character of the Jew in Norris's American West was a wild thing, uncanny and relentless in the consuming obsession with cornering wealth, including precious gold, productive property, and marketable commodities. In *McTeague*, archetypical greed perfected by the "Polish Jew," with his bloodless lips, shriveled body, and fiery-red hair, led to the destruction of well-meaning Anglos as well as Zerko's abused Mexican wife—later the basis for Eric von Stroheim's motion picture *Greed* (1924). In *The Octopus*, Norris modeled the manipulative and duplicitous banker–lawyer–railroad agent Behrman after a real California personality, Marcus Pollasky, an infamous Jewish financier. The repugnant Behrman, with his tremulous jowls, fat forehead, heavy breathing, gold chains, and pearl vest buttons, was not merely the front man for the railroad president. He also furnished the essential mechanism that directed the diabolical system against the honest, struggling farmers, largely to satiate his own appetite for monopolizing the wheat market. As a natural resource, wheat was life-giving; as malignant forces, both Zerko and Behrman brought only annihilation. Less significant and only mildly less unattractive depictions of Jews appear in Norris's posthumously published *The Pit* (1903) and *Vandover and the Brute* (1914).

After developing peritonitis following appendix surgery in 1902, Norris died at the age of thirty-two. By 1934, nearly 425,000 copies of his books had been sold. A century after his death, he remains best known both as a pioneer in experimental literary naturalism and as a muckraking novelist, his antisemitism remaining in the closet.

—*Burton Bledstein*

**See also** Adams, Henry Brooks; Capital: Useful versus Harmful; Caricature, Anti-Jewish (Modern); Deicide; English Literature of the Twentieth Century; *Passing of the Great Race;* Populist Movement; Shylock; United States

**References**
Forrey, Robert. "The 'Jew' in Norris' *The Octopus*," *Western States Jewish Historical Quarterly* 7, no. 3 (1975): 201–209.
Norris, Frank. "Aims and Autographs of Authors," *Book News, 17* (May 1899), 486.

## *Numerus Clausus* (Hungary)

The catastrophic defeat in World War I generated soaring unemployment and severe financial hardship throughout Hungary. To chauvinistic popular opinion, however, Jews remained immune to poverty because of their alleged dominance of finance, commerce, industry, and most professions, notably medicine and law. In September 1920, responding to pressure from the public, the government introduced the *numerus clausus,* the first significant antisemitic statute in postwar Europe: the numerus clausus restricted the number of Jews admitted to institutes of tertiary education to 6 percent of all matriculants—that is, the proportion of Jews in the population. According to the government, this measure would restore national prosperity, obviously at the Jews' expense. The numerus clausus was the first rupture in the constitutional equality granted Hungarian Jews in 1867.

In 1921 and 1925, when British and French Jewry petitioned the League of Nations to intervene on behalf of their Hungarian coreligionists, Hungary's Jewish leaders, conscious of the country's loathing for the Allies since the defeat of 1918, condemned any attempted international interference in Hungarian Jewry's internal affairs. It was traditional for Hungary's Jewish leadership to base the community's defense on conspicuous displays of patriotism and unquestioning loyalty to the "motherland."

Antisemites were not satisfied, however. The stipulations of the numerus clausus were often imperfectly realized. With the notable exception of the Military Academy, which attained *numerus nullius* (none at all) (in 1925), many Jews evaded the legislation by enrolling in foreign universities; moreover, many officials solicited "gratuities" (bribes) to ensure that quotas were administered haphazardly. A further undermining of the intent of the law occurred when the High Court questioned the act's legality in 1925. The moderate education minister responded to this opening by ordering the numerus clausus to be covertly disregarded. By 1932, the official 6 percent quota had expanded, practically speaking, to a de facto 14 percent. This figure represented half the prewar enrollment level of Jews but was still over twice that called for by the law.

Because strict enforcement of the act was a relatively brief phenomenon, the proportion of Jews in most professions declined only slightly, typically between 5 and 15 percent in the 1920s. But even though the spirit of the numerus clausus may have been circumvented, it nonetheless had at least one enduring and deleterious effect. It further radicalized Hungarian antisemitism, especially in institutions of higher education. With the endorsement of parliament, the numerus clausus revived and popularized the preemancipation notion that Jews were inherently alien and thus suitable targets of discrimination.

—*Tom Kramer*

**See also** Emancipation; Hungary; *Numerus Clausus* (United States)

**References**
Kramer, T. D. *From Emancipation to Catastrophe: The Rise and Holocaust of Hungarian Jewry* (Lanham, MD: University Press of America, 2000).
Mendelsohn, Ezra. *The Jews of East Central Europe between the World Wars* (Bloomington: Indiana University Press, 1983).
Patai, Raphael. *The Jews of Hungary: History, Culture, Psychology* (Detroit, MI: Wayne State University Press, 1996).

## *Numerus Clausus* (United States)

A *numerus clausus,* or quota, limiting Jewish students to a fixed percentage of college, university, and professional school enrollments developed in the United States during the 1910s and lasted over forty years. Beginning around the mid-1870s, however, native-born white, Protestant Americans reacted to the swelling immigration of eastern European Jews by excluding them from hotels, men's clubs, college fraternities, and residential neighborhoods. Then, from 1918 until World War II, Jewish students encountered covert quotas as a response to their enrollment in thirty leading colleges and universities, which peaked at 9.7 percent, or triple their percentage in the national population. From elite eastern liberal arts colleges, quotas rapidly spread to hundreds of private colleges, many state universities, and professional schools, although the institutional diversity of American higher education militated against an across-the-board quota system.

Academic administrators, particularly Harvard University president A. Lawrence Lowell, defended quotas. Believing that the personal and group characteristics of immigrant Jews in particular made them undesirable when they exceeded 15 percent of the student body, Lowell urged that "character" and proper social attributes be weighed along with academic criteria. To reduce Jewish enrollment, admissions officers used various devices, such as questions on religious affiliation and nationality, personal interviews, rejection of transfer students, required campus residency, and, at some institutions, chapel attendance. Elite universities also used "gentlemen's agreements" with secondary feeder schools to identify Jews and other immigrant applicants. Following the example of Columbia University, which cut Jewish enrollment from 40 to 20 percent by 1922, Harvard introduced a 10 to 12 percent Jewish quota. Yale (10 percent), Dartmouth (5 percent), and Princeton (3 percent) also reduced their undergraduate Jewish student bodies. The "Seven Sister" colleges—Barnard, Bryn Mawr, Mount Holyoke, Radcliffe, Smith, Vassar, and Wellesley—limited the admission of Jewish women from 6 to 12 percent. Some 700 other liberal arts colleges also adopted selective admissions policies, with the result that between 1935 and 1946, the percentage of Jews enrolled in men's colleges declined from 10.2 to 4.7 percent and in women's colleges from 11.8 to 8.4 percent.

State universities adopted geographic quotas limiting the admission of out-of-state students to prevent a feared influx of Jewish students from the East Coast. They also raised nonresident tuition fees and offered scholarships to non-Jewish students. Yet because they submitted multiple applications, Jews were usually able to find admittance to one or another college. Jewish applicants to western and southern universities experienced less discrimination, except for some private institutions (for example, Stanford University). West of the Appalachian Mountains, Jews were often among the first students at new colleges and universities and were usually accepted to the extent that they did not challenge southern prejudices against African Americans or western prejudices against Asians.

Jewish quotas existed in university graduate programs and at professional schools in medicine, dentistry, and law. Between 1935 and 1946, the percentage of Jewish professional students dropped from 8.8 to 7 percent, although their enrollment in higher educational institutions stayed at about 9 percent (192,476 out of 2,140,331 students). Medical schools were the first professional schools to resort to quotas. Columbia's College of Physicians and Surgeons cut its Jewish enrollment from over 50 percent to less than 20 percent between 1919 and 1924; by 1940, it had dropped to 6.4 percent. The Harvard and Yale medical schools had a 10 percent Jewish quota. Commonly limiting admissions of Jews to their percentage in the state's population or imposing geographic quotas, admissions officers required a higher academic average for Jewish applicants and assessed their social skills based on required interviews, personal statements, and confidential letters. Even though the Association of American Medical Colleges asked schools to administer the relatively objective Medical Aptitude Test to premedical students between 1930 and 1931, the association soon dropped the test because it eliminated few Jews. In 1933, when Jewish medical students numbered 912, the American Medical Association's Council on Medical Education recommended that medical enrollments be sharply decreased to boost physicians' incomes during the depression. By 1940, quotas had reduced the number of Jewish medical students almost 48 percent, to 477.

Quotas began to decline following the 1947 reports of President Harry Truman's Commission on Higher Education and the Committee on Civil Rights that attacked racial and religious discrimination. Pressured by state laws on fair educational practices and later by the 1964 Civil Rights Act, colleges and professional schools removed questions on nationality, race, and religion and admitted applicants with good scores on the Scholastic Aptitude Test (SAT) or on the new Medical College Admission Test. Jewish enrollments increased dramatically at the best universities.

—*Marcia G. Synnott*

*See also* American Jewish Committee and Antidefamation Efforts in the United States; *Ostjuden;* Restricted Public Accommodations, United States; Restrictive Covenants; United States
**References**
Borst, Charlotte G. "Choosing the Student Body: Masculinity, Culture, and the Crisis of Medical School Admissions, 1920–1950," *History of Education Quarterly* 42 (Summer 2002): 181–214.
Oren, Dan A. *Joining the Club: A History of Jews and Yale* (New Haven, CT: Yale University Press, 1985).
Synnott, Marcia G. "Anti-Semitism and American Universities: Did Quotas Follow the Jews?" In *Anti-Semitism and American History.* Edited by David A. Gerber (Urbana and Chicago: University of Illinois Press, 1986), 233–271.

## Nuremberg Laws (1935)

The Nuremberg Laws of September 15, 1935, promulgated at the site of the Nazi Party's annual rally, were the keystone of the Nazis' legislative assault on German Jews. Interior Minister Wilhelm Frick called them the "racial constitution" of the Third Reich. The first law, a Reich Citizenship Law, fulfilled the party's long-standing promise that "no Jew can be a citizen of the German nation." The measure stripped Jews of their citizenship and reduced them to the status of "State Subjects" (*Staatsangeh rige*). "Aryan" Germans, by contrast, were awarded the elevated status of "Reich Citizens" (*Reichsbürger*). A second edict, the Law for the Protection of German Blood and German Honor, commonly called the Blood Protection Law, prohibited marriages and extramarital sexual relations between Aryans and Jews. An additional provision barred German women under the age of forty-five from being employed as maids in Jewish households, for fear that they would be seduced by their male employers. This Blood Protection Law embodied one of the most basic of antisemitic demands, that there be no more so-called race mixing between Aryans and Jews. To racist antisemites, race mixing was a nightmare—one that Hitler described as the true original sin (*Ursünde*).

The initial drafters of these laws wanted to

limit their application to "full Jews." Hitler rejected this idea, however, without stipulating to whom the laws should then apply. Until the problem of definition was resolved, the laws were impossible to implement. In 1933, the Aryan Paragraph defined as "non-Aryan" anyone with at least one Jewish grandparent. However, that definition had been provisional, and radical Nazis found it far too lenient. Julius Streicher, the Jew-baiting publisher, was adamant that "one drop of Jewish blood" sufficed to make anyone a Jew. Gerhard Wagner, head of the National Socialist Physicians Association, pushed for the more inclusive "one-eighth principle," meaning that one Jewish *great*-grandparent was sufficient to make one Jewish. Bureaucrats in the Interior Ministry leaned toward a less inclusive definition. For many of them, even the Aryan Paragraph had gone too far. Some wanted to limit the concept to anyone with three or four Jewish grandparents. Others wanted to exclude the *Mischling,* or "half-Jew," with two Jewish grandparents.

It took eight weeks of protracted and rancorous debate between party radicals and bureaucrats before the issue was decided. Bernhard Lösener led the bureaucratic contingent and Gerhard Wagner the party radicals. Wagner and his colleagues had ideological purity on their side. They not only pushed for the one-eighth principle in defining the Jew but also demanded the annulment of already existing marriages between Jews and Germans, a measure the drafters had never considered. The latter demand would have opened a Pandora's box of legal entanglements and was easily dismissed. Wagner's position on defining the Jew, however, was not as easily rejected.

Lösener and his colleagues countered from a pragmatic rather than an ideological base. They pointed out that going beyond the Mischling (who was also half-German) invited the antagonism of people who had until then been loyal Germans. It would also bring down on the regime the enmity of the Aryan relatives of every half-Jew/German. The result would be an unnecessary upsurge of anti-Nazi feelings, which would, in turn, weaken the German economy and damage relations abroad. Lösener's most telling argument, however, was that a more inclusive definition of the Jew would exclude from military service the equivalent of two divisions of draft-age young men.

Hitler finally resolved the issue himself. In early November, he decided in favor of the bureaucrats, and on November 14, 1935, he approved the First Supplementary Decree to the Reich Citizenship Law. Paragraph 2 of this law defined as a "full Jew" someone with three or four Jewish grandparents. A person with two Jewish grandparents was considered Jewish only *if* he or she was also a member of a Jewish religious community or was married to someone defined as Jewish. If neither of those conditions applied, that person was defined as a Mischling of the first degree; someone with one Jewish grandparent was defined as a Mischling of the second degree. Those with Mischling status were, for the most part, spared the worst Nazi persecutions.

In the following years, the Nazis wrote decrees supplementing the Reich Citizenship Law and used them to remove Jews, step by step, from virtually every area of German life and culture.

—*Karl A. Schleunes*

**See also** Aryan Paragraph; Hitler, Adolf; National Socialist German Workers' Party; Streicher, Julius
**References**
Mommsen, Hans. "The Realization of the Unthinkable: The 'Final Solution' to the Jewish Question in the Third Reich." In *From Weimar to Auschwitz.* Translated by Philip O'Connor (Princeton, NJ: Princeton University Press, 1991), 24–53.
Noakes, Jeremy. "The Development of Nazi Policy towards the German-Jewish *Mischlinge,* 1933–1945," *Leo Baeck Institute Year Book* 34 (1989): 291–354.
Schleunes, Karl A., ed. *Legislating the Holocaust: The Bernhard Loesener Memoirs and Supporting Documents* (Boulder, CO: Westview Press, 2001).

# O

## Oberammergau Passion Play

A remote town nestled in the Bavarian Alps, Oberammergau is home to the world's most enduring Passion Play. According to local legend, the play's origins date to 1633, when plague ravaged the region. Seeking God's protection, Oberammergau's elders vowed that, should the town be spared, its people would stage a Passion Play, at regular intervals, into perpetuity. The first performance came the following spring; since that time, generation after generation has renewed the play every ten years or so. By the early nineteenth century, this homespun tradition had begun to attract outside attention, and enterprising locals started charging admission to their performances. In 1830, a new stage was built to accommodate the growing number of spectators, Protestant as well as Catholic, who flocked to the site. By 1900, the production had expanded to forty-seven performances, attended by some 174,000 pilgrims from Germany and abroad.

A new script was introduced in 1811 and revised by Oberammergau's parish priest in 1860; where earlier renditions had pitted Jesus against Lucifer and a host of lesser devils, the new version stressed the role of Jews as Christ killers. As the play moved toward a more naturalistic style, its melodramatic strategies relied increasingly on depictions of Jewish treachery and deceit. And its theatrical climax shifted to the crowd scene, taken from Matthew 27:25, in which hundreds of Jews cry out for Jesus' death: "His blood be upon us and upon our children!"

With its anti-Jewish stridency and blood-and-soil pedigree, the Oberammergau play proved a natural attraction to the Nazis. Adolf Hitler and Joseph Goebbels attended the 1930 production; four years later, the regime heavily promoted a special tercentennial version of the play. Critics and supporters alike noted the "Nazified" character of this 1934 performance, at which Hitler was warmly received; a high percentage of its cast members, including those playing Jesus, the Virgin Mary, and eight of the twelve apostles, joined the Nazi Party.

The Oberammergau tradition reemerged relatively unscathed after 1945. In 1949, Cardinal Michael Faulhaber blessed the town and its inhabitants, declaring their play consistent with church doctrine. Nor did Oberammergau's residents exhibit much repentance: the townsman they chose to play Jesus in the 1950 and 1960 productions, for example, had been convicted by de-Nazification courts as a Nazi follower in 1947. Only after 1965, when the Second Vatican Council repudiated the notion of Jewish guilt for the death of Jesus, did sustained protests begin to mount from Catholic, Protestant, and Jewish critics. A 1970 boycott caught the attention of Oberammergau's townspeople, though substantive changes in the play's text and performance were slow to arrive. The breakthrough came in 2000 as local reformers implemented wide-ranging changes, including the removal of the "blood curse" from the play and a new stress on the Jewishness of Jesus and his disciples. Although questions remain as to the ultimate extent and meaning of Passion Play reform, the play's new preface acknowledges that past productions contributed "to preparing the soil which eventually yielded the terrible harvest of the extermination of the Jews."

—*John Abbott*

*See also* Deicide; Goebbels, Joseph; Gospels; Passion Plays, Medieval; Vatican Council, Second
**References**
Shapiro, James. *Oberammergau: The Troubling Story of the World's Most Famous Passion Play* (New York: Vintage Books, 2000).

## October Roundup (Rome, 1943)

In the early hours of October 16, 1943, German forces started to comb Roman neighborhoods with the objective of identifying, arresting, and then deporting local Jews. To understand the significance of this operation, it is necessary to recall the condition of the "occupied ally" that materialized in Italy after September 8, 1943. The Italian government of Marshal Pietro Badoglio, established after Mussolini was brought down in July 1943, never repealed the Racial Laws promulgated in 1938, hoping to avoid additional conflicts with the Germans; nor did that short-lived government manage to retrieve from German control the Jewish lists compiled by the Fascist authorities, lists full of details and vital statistics. When the Germans restored Mussolini to power in September 1943, these lists provided crucial information for the October Roundup.

In the German-occupied territories, the Fascist regime's years of anti-Jewish propaganda, having given rise to suspicion and hatred toward the Jews on the part of the rest of the population, helped facilitate their active pursuit. Nonetheless, the sudden escalation of persecution came as a surprise. The antisemitic discrimination typical of the Fascist regime—which did not directly endanger people's lives—instilled a degree of frustrated passivity among Italian Jews, to the point of lowering their guard and rendering them highly vulnerable to the sudden move by the Germans.

The shocking decision to deport the Jewish population of the capital was the result of a typical dispute between the German army and the SS. It is noteworthy that the top military commanders did not favor inclusion of the Italian Jews in the Final Solution, partly out of concern for the Vatican's reaction. The SS leadership remained inflexible, however, and managed to obtain direct authorization from Berlin, in the form of a Führer order. A number of specialists, veterans of operations in northern Europe and later responsible for the extermination in Hungary, were employed for the deportations from Italy. An SS captain, Theodor Dannecker, was sent to Rome at the beginning of October with the order to "start" the arrest of the Italian Jews. In fact, a few operations targeting Jews had already occurred in northern Italy in the previous month; these should be seen within the larger context of deportation from the occupied territories. The operation in Rome resulted in the arrests of 1,259 people. From this number, a few non-Jews and people born of mixed marriages were later released. All those remaining were loaded onto eighteen freight cars and deported. The formal protest from the Vatican, feared by the German authorities, did not emerge. Bishop Alois Hudal of Rome lodged an *unofficial* request with German headquarters to stop the operation, evidently to allow Pope Pius XII to avoid taking a public stand. Pius XII's dilemma and the inaction of the Vatican hierarchy with regard to the October Roundup are the subjects of ongoing historical debate. Much clearer was the heroic intervention of ordinary clergy who, within the city of Rome, helped and sheltered in monasteries, convents, and churches more than 4,000 hunted Jews.

The Jewish deportation from Rome stands as the symbol of the Shoah in Italy. Commemoration, important moments of public mourning, and meditation on the racist past of Italian fascism and on the dangers of antisemitism are concentrated around the date of this event. But in reality, the October Roundup represented only the first step in the systematization of the Final Solution on Italian soil. A complex series of gradual steps followed. The first critical stage in the process came with the creation of confinement camps. The next was marked by the promulgation of the Verona Paper, issued by the resurrected Fascist Party in November 1943. The paper comprised an extensive set of rules that pointedly declared Italian Jews to be "national enemies." From that moment on, the regime actively collaborated with the Germans in the deportations, beginning with the order issued by the Fascist minister of internal affairs on November 30, 1943: all Jews were to be collected in concentration camps distributed in the provinces. Later, Jews were moved to larger holding camps, such as Fossoli, near Modena, and then Bolzano, there to await their last, tragic journey.

—*Simone Duranti*

**See also** *Manifesto of the Racial Scientists;*
Mussolini, Benito; Pius XII, Pope; Racial Laws

**References**
Michaelis, Meir. *Mussolini and the Jews: German-Italian Relations and the Jewish Question in Italy, 1922–1945* (New York: Clarendon Press, 1978).
Zuccotti, Susan. *The Italians and the Holocaust: Persecution, Rescue, and Survival* (New York: Basic Books, 1987).

## Odessa Pogroms

The Black Sea port of Odessa was the most pogrom-ridden city in the Russian Empire, with serious anti-Jewish riots occurring in 1821, 1859, 1871, and 1905 and smaller disturbances in 1849 and 1881.

A number of factors contributed to Odessa's proclivity for anti-Jewish violence. The city experienced explosive population growth, expanding from 2,350 persons (including 246 Jews) at the beginning of the nineteenth century to approximately 403,000 at its end (with about 138,000 Jews). The population was ethnically diverse and marked by intergroup hostility. In the last quarter of the century, the city was torn by social and political unrest, some of which resulted in attacks on Jews. Odessa also attracted large numbers of seasonal migrant workers, who joined the gangs of the indigent unemployed, "the barefoot brigade," in public disorders, including pogroms. Finally, the city was served by one of the most antisemitic newspapers in the empire, *Novorossiiskii telegraf* (New Russian Telegraph), which was widely accused of instigating pogroms in 1881.

Local officials dismissed the Odessa pogroms of 1821 and 1859 as the result of commercial rivalries and religious antipathies that divided the city's Greek and Jewish populations. But the pogrom of 1871, the first to be widely discussed in the Russian press, gave rise to explanations by journalists and government officials who asserted that violence against Jews was the response of the unsophisticated masses to "Jewish exploitation." After 1881, the "Odessa paradigm," with the additional charge that the Jews also promoted revolutionary unrest, was applied to subsequent pogroms in the city and elsewhere in the empire. The reaction of secular Jewish intellectuals to the Odessa violence was at first disillusionment and then expression in nascent forms of modern Jewish nationalism.

The pogroms between 1881 and 1882 did not assume major proportions in Odessa, in part because of extensive preventive measures taken by the police and military. The small disorders that did occur were answered by early forms of Jewish self-defense. They also inspired the proto-Zionist movement Hoveve Tsion (Lovers of Zion), which was based in Odessa and anticipated the movement of Theodor Herzl.

The Revolution of 1905 witnessed the worst pogrom in the history of Odessa. It grew out of clashes between patriotic right-wing demonstrators and left-wing elements celebrating the October Manifesto and calling for further reform. Amid a setting of revolutionary disorder and counterrevolutionary violence, at least 400 Jews were killed between October 18 and 22, 1905, and over 1,600 Jewish properties were ransacked or destroyed. The civil governor of the city, D. M. Neidhardt, and the commander of the Odessa military garrison, A. V. Kaulbars, were widely criticized for failing to coordinate their activities and for losing control of the situation. Odessa did not suffer pogroms during the Russian Civil War.

—*John D. Klier*

*See also* Black Hundreds; Herzl, Theodor; Kishinev Pogrom; Pale of Settlement; Pogroms; Russia, Imperial; Russia, Revolution of 1905; Russian Civil War; Zionism

**References**
Herlihy, Patricia. *Odessa: A History, 1794–1914* (Cambridge, MA: Harvard University Press, 1986).
Klier, John D., and Shlomo Lambroza, eds. *Pogroms: Anti-Jewish Violence in Modern Russian History* (Cambridge: Cambridge University Press, 1992).
Weinberg, Robert. *The Revolution of 1905 in Odessa: Blood on the Steps* (Bloomington: Indiana University Press, 1993).
Zipperstein, Steven J. *The Jews of Odessa: A Cultural History, 1794–1881* (Stanford, CA: Stanford University Press, 1985).

## On the Jews and Their Lies (1543)

Possibly the most notorious writing of Martin Luther, *On the Jews and Their Lies* appeared from the Wittenberg printing house of Hans Lufft, which issued some of the most important books of early Protestantism. Luther had once been sympathetic to the Jews, seeing their refusal to convert to Catholicism as evidence of the falseness of the Roman Church; later, however, saw the Jews' refusal to convert to the Evangelical faith as evidence of an inexcusable obstinacy. The foil and potential adherent of an expanding church became, after two decades, the foil and implacable enemy of a religious community under siege from all quarters.

Central to Luther's view of Jewry was his belief that the people's suffering since the first century was the result of their unbelief in the Christian atonement. The lack of faith was the product of an "earthly" interpretation of Scripture in which redemption was expected in historical experience. In believing that they continued to receive divine favor and protection, the Jews irritated God with their expressions of gratitude; Luther accordingly saw Jewish devotion as flagrant arrogance. The spiritual covenant inaugurated by Christ made Jewish claims to a continuing material covenant evidence only of pride. (The Catholic system of works received similar and often harsher denunciations.) For Luther, the continuation of the Davidic line required that the Christian covenant succeed the Jewish one.

Luther proceeded from his extended argument of theological anti-Judaism to an ethnic antisemitism, accusing the Jews of exploiting gentiles with their moneylending. He urged his Christian readers not to tolerate Jews in their own midst but rather to destroy their synagogues and houses, confiscate their books, forbid rabbis to teach, suspend protection of their property, and confiscate their earnings from moneylending. With such an aggressive repression of Jews, Christians would be able to demonstrate their own piety.

As an expression of frustration over the failure of the Reform to gain adherents from the original people of the book, Luther's denunciation helped perpetuate the marginalization of Jewish communities throughout Protestant Europe. Although no Lutheran pogroms were inspired by this book, it did leave a legacy in the form of an intensified anti-Judaism in many Lutheran communities. In the twentieth century, it achieved new prominence with the rise of the Deutsche Christen, thereby aligning Luther with the racial programs of the Nazi regime. In the post–World War II decades, Lutheran leaders and theologians distanced themselves from and even repudiated this part of Luther's work.

Luther's position suffered from one substantial weakness: the role of heredity in shaping identity. For Luther, the Jews' pride in their hierarchical order and relation to God were evidence of an obstinacy and blindness that guaranteed their damnation. Page after page, Luther denounced Jewish claims of inherited "nobility" and the privilege of circumcision, not recognizing that his own assertions of inherited guilt from original sin depended on a similar sense of succession, minus the awareness of inherited guilt.

—*Ralph Keen*

**See also** Churches under Nazism; Circumcision; Deutsche Christen; Ghetto; Luther, Martin; Melanchthon, Philipp; Reformation; Smith, Gerald L. K.; Stoecker, Adolf; Supersessionism; Usury
**References**
Edwards, Mark U., Jr. *Luther's Last Battles: Politics and Polemics, 1531–46* (Ithaca, NY: Cornell University Press, 1983), 115–142.

# Order Police

Ordnungspolizei (Order Police) were the Third Reich's uniformed police organizations, including the Schutzpolizei (precinct police), the gendarmerie, and the Gemeindepolizei (rural community police). Under the Weimar Republic, the individual state governments exercised control of the police forces within their borders. After the Nazis achieved power, Heinrich Himmler, Reich leader of the SS and chief of the German police, and Kurt Daluege, chief of the Order Police, pursued initiatives to centralize Germany's political and uniformed police forces and to transform them from civil servants into "political soldiers" and instruments of Nazi racial policy. Himmler and Daluege worked to instill in the Order Police a martial attitude and the SS military ethic. After the centralization of the individual state police forces under his command in June 1936, Himmler sought to fuse the organizations of the SS and the Order Police. The merger was, from the beginning, more than physical. It was designed to remold the policeman's worldview and to ensure his psychological subservience to National Socialist values. His absolute obedience to authority was to result from the carefully inculcated vision of a "higher purpose." Ultimately, the Order Police, together with the SS, acted as common guarantors of a brutal racial ideology, characterized by rabid expressions of antisemitism and anti-Bolshevism.

With the outbreak of war in 1939, the Order Police played a central role in the German administration of the occupied eastern territories by conducting a broad range of activities involving administrative, law enforcement, and security duties. The types of police forces operating in the East ranged from small groups in rural posts to battalion-sized units of several hundred men. In the case of the latter, the creation and employment of police battalions in the campaign in Poland set a new precedent for the use of police forces in direct combat operations and in the murderous activities of the Einsatzgruppen (mobile death squads). The invasion of the Soviet Union in June 1941 witnessed the emergence of the police battalions as effective and deadly instruments for the prosecution of National Socialist racial policy in the eastern territories. By the end of the war, approximately 100 police battalions had cut a bloody swath through these areas.

The Order Police routinely participated in direct combat actions across Europe and conducted so-called pacification operations against the full spectrum of Nazi enemies, including Jews, Bolshevists, Sinti, and Roma, as well as partisans throughout the occupied territories. In fact, the term *partisan* was employed to mask Nazi efforts to decimate the indigenous Slavic population and eliminate the Jews of eastern Europe. Himmler's Order Police played a key role in the prosecution of the Final Solution and in the racial war within the war.

—*Edward B. Westermann*

**See also** Einsatzgruppen; Himmler, Heinrich; Holocaust; National Socialist German Workers' Party

**References**

Browning, Christopher. *Ordinary Men: Reserve Police Battalion 101 and the Final Solution* (New York: HarperCollins, 1992).

Westermann, Edward B. "Shaping the Police Soldier as an Instrument for Annihilation." In *The Impact of Nazism: New Perspectives on the Third Reich and Its Legacy.* Edited by Alan E. Steinweis and Daniel E. Rogers (Lincoln: University of Nebraska Press, 2003).

## Origen (ca. 185–ca. 251 or 254)

Origen, one of the most important Christian theologians, had close relationships with different kinds of Hebrew- or Aramaic-speaking people. In Alexandria, he met the "Hebrews," who were members of a group of Jewish Christians living in that city; among them was Origen's "Hebrew master," who taught him Jewish and Jewish-Christian interpretations of the Bible. Origen also had knowledge of the Ebionites, a group of Palestinians who thought Jesus was the Messiah but not God's son. When he settled in Caesarea in 232, he met either Jews converted to Christianity or traditional Jews, one of whom he called "sage," that is to say, a rabbi. These Jews instructed Origen about the Bible's Hebrew text and perhaps its Greek transliteration, and they also imparted to him many rabbinic traditions.

In his discussions with Jews, Origen agreed to take into consideration only the biblical passages common to the Hebrew and Greek Bibles. He had a good knowledge of Philo's works. Occasionally in his voluminous writings, he stood up for the Jews and Judaism, as he did, for instance, against Celsus, a philosopher who attacked both Judaism and Christianity. But more often, he underscored Jewish unbelief. He considered the leaders of the Jews and the common people responsible for Jesus's death and also that of many prophets. However, he did not incriminate all Jews for having killed Jesus but only those who were "according to the flesh" and not "the spirit" (*kata sarka* as opposed to *kata pneuma,* in the biblical Greek). From the moment of the Crucifixion, Jews were abandoned by God. The destruction of Jerusalem and the Temple he considered a just punishment for Jesus' death and the refusal of the Jews to accept the testimony of the apostles.

According to Origen, Jewish observances had lost their justification, but they still possessed a symbolic and high significance. Israel, whom

Charles Kannengiesser and William L. Petersen (Notre Dame, IN: University of Notre Dame Press, 1988), 96–115.

Dorival, Gilles. "Un Groupe judéo-chrétien méconnu: Les Hébreux," *Apocrypha* 11 (2000): 7–36.

Origen of Alexandria, a Christian writer and teacher and one of the Greek Fathers of the church. Occasionally, he stood up for the Jews and Judaism in his writings, but more often, he underscored Jewish unbelief. (Mary Evans Picture Library)

God had called, had now fallen. The church had been called to supplant the repudiated synagogue. Thus, Christianity was true Judaism, and orthodox Christians were the real Jews: they authentically embodied in the spirit the practices Jews only performed in a material way. However, Origen proclaimed that Israel would be called a second time, when all the nations had entered the church. Then, as Paul says in Romans 11:25–26, "Israel will be saved."

—*Gilles Dorival*

**See also** Deicide; Iconography, Christian; Roman Empire; Supersessionism
**References**
Blowers, Paul. "Origen, the Rabbis and the Bible: Toward a Picture of Judaism and Christianity in Third-Century Caesarea." In *Origen of Alexandria: His World and His Legacy.* Edited by

## Ostjuden

The concept of the *Ostjude* (eastern European Jew), first used by Nathan Birnbaum, became popular at the turn of the twentieth century. Birnbaum, an early adherent of the Zionist movement, certainly attached no negative connotations to his neologism. But most of his contemporaries did. The Jews who immigrated to the West at that time, especially to Germany, were simply referred to as "foreigners," more specifically and dismissively as "Russian, Polish, or Galician" Jews, or even more negatively as "Pollacks" or "scroungers." In popular usage, the designation *Ostjude* combined two pejorative concepts, both with unambiguously antisemitic content: the East and the Jew. Both signaled the existence of boundaries thrown up to fend off and exclude. During World War I when the Germans occupied Russian Poland, the concept came into its own as an integrating, generic term, often in conjunction with other negatives, such as the *Ostjudengefahr* (eastern European Jewish danger) or *Ostjudenfrage* (eastern European Jewish Question).

The first verifiable settlements of Jews in Russia date from the ninth and tenth centuries, the result of migrations from the realm of the Khazars, the Byzantine Empire, the Caucasus, and Persia. The persecutions connected to the First and Second Crusades of 1096 and 1147 as well as the later expulsions from western Europe added considerably to the numbers of Jews in the East. Those emigrating to Russia from Germany maintained their cultural identity and Middle High German language, which, with the addition of Hebrew and Slavic words, lives on and continues to develop into the present as Yiddish. Up to the modern era, eastern Europe constituted the largest Jewish population center, with about 1.5 million Jews living there in the year 1800. By 1880, the Jewish population in the Russian Empire grew to nearly 4 million (70 percent of the world's Jews). By 1900, it numbered more than 7 million.

Eastern European Jews developed their own style of life, only marginally connected to the culture of the lands in which they lived. They retained their religious traditions and continued speaking Yiddish. Generally, they belonged to the middle or lower strata of society. From the eighteenth century, Jews in Russia were subject to special laws that eventually restricted their right of habitation to the so-called Pale of Settlement, in which the shtetl, or village, was the typical communal form. Access to educational institutions was severely controlled, limiting the number of Jewish students to their proportion of the total population. Elementary education for boys between four and six years of age took place in the *cheder* (religious schools run by the community) and represented the extent of formal schooling.

Special laws bearing on occupations permitted to the Jews of the Pale severely constricted economic opportunities. The overcrowding of the professions and in other means of making a living endangered the existence of many Jews, forcing them to become so-called *Luftmenschen* (men who lack substance, who live in and off the air), living from hand to mouth and with no rooted place in society. Amid the great majority of eastern European Jews, who were without property or means, stood a small group that had managed to acquire great wealth through trade or industry.

The political, economic, and social crisis that shook tsarist Russia unleashed a wave of pogroms in the 1880s that, in turn, engendered a mass migration of Jews. Their primary destination was the United States, with Germany as the most important transitional way station. Before 1914, almost 3 million Jews emigrated to United States, and 50,000 more went to Germany. This movement of people spawned an active hostility toward Jews, tolerated and sometimes fostered by governmental authorities, and led to bloody pogroms well into the twentieth century and even after the Holocaust. Such evidence of Jew-hatred fed Jewish nationalism and its political expression, Zionism.

Western European Jews, in the process of conscious assimilation, reacted ambivalently to the Jewish immigrants from the East and were often contemptuous and dismissive of those from another cultural tradition. Hasidism, for example, remained essentially incomprehensible to the westerners. They extended considerable philanthropic help but wanted the immigrants to move on to other countries as quickly as possible. In Germany, Ostjuden were considered dirty, loud, coarse, immoral, and culturally backward—representatives of the ghetto and the antithesis of the "modern," emancipated, acculturated German Jews. The mere term *Ostjude* evoked a complex of negative associations. Antisemites pointedly lumped Ostjuden and German Jews together to make the point that the Jewish citizens of Germany were essentially also Ostjuden—or their superficially assimilated descendants and relatives.

The German image of the Ostjude took shape in the mid-nineteenth century. Parallel to the movement toward Jewish emancipation, a popular discourse developed around a negative caricature of Jews that drew from and elaborated on the stereotyped prejudices of Christian tradition. In novels, the radiant Christian German heroes had their counterparts in sinister Jews—usurers, social climbers, heartless exploiters, and foreigners who spoke a debased German jargon (*mauschelnden Juden*). To this composite was added the Jewish revolutionary, the enemy of all that was good and a danger to civilization.

The influential nationalist historian Heinrich von Treitschke, writing in November 1879, warned against the prospect of an eastern European Jewish immigration and its attendant dangers. He feared this "horde of ambitious pants-peddling youths," pushing their way into Germany from the "inexhaustible Polish cradle," whose children and children's children would one day rule over the stock exchange and the press (in Levy 1991, 70). For Treitschke, the Ostjude was the Jew of the beard, sidelocks, yarmulka, caftan, and prayer shawl. These external traits embodied a national identity that many German Jews suppressed or denied in themselves. But antisemites chose to see only a variation of a single Jewish essence. Thus, when the prestigious Treitschke uttered his infamous slogan—"The Jews are our misfortune"—he gave the signal for modern, secular, racist antisemitism to launch an attack on *all* German Jews.

In the public discourse on the eastern European Jewish Question, three types of stereotypical prejudices emerged, based on national-economic, political, and cultural grounds. Between 1918 and 1923, in the turmoil of the lost war and the revolution that followed Germany's defeat, a radicalized antisemitism took shape. Ostjuden provided the catalytic agent. They were blamed for military defeat, economic depression, and political crises. Now, the term *Ostjude* became synonymous with *black marketeer, hoarder, speculator, usurer, gouger,* and *war profiteer.* Housing shortages in the big cities, growing unemployment, and high rates of inflation were the fault of the Ostjuden, according to the organizers of the antisemitic witch-hunt.

The Ostjuden presence in Germany was one of the dominant domestic political themes discussed in parliament and the broad public in the 1920s. Public opinion was clearly and systematically influenced by the militant agitation of German racist organizations. With a total lack of restraint, "the problem" was discussed in all strata of society, and many solutions to it were advanced. The anti-Jewish forces merged with antirepublican and antisocialist elements, mutually strengthening one another to the extent that they were able to force their antisemitic agenda into the political life of the republic. They demanded that the borders be closed to eastern European Jewish immigration, that citizenship or naturalization be withheld, and that Ostjuden be interned in concentration camps (already called by that name in 1920). An antisemitically inclined civil service was fundamental to this process. Within its ranks could be found the same collection of deeply rooted anti-Jewish prejudices as in the general public, which viewed the Ostjude as the epitome of the "un-German" individual.

At the high point of the immigration in 1925, Germany had 90,000 eastern European Jews, or one-fifth of the total Jewish population. Furthermore, Ostjuden did not constitute a monolithic group. During World War I and until 1922, approximately 150,000 Jewish workers went to Germany of their own free will or were forced to go there to boost the German war economy, although such immigration was illegal after 1918. Their numbers fluctuated, with some returning

to their homelands and others emigrating again. Most settled in the large cities of Germany, where they lived in their own neighborhoods, culturally and socially isolated from German Jewish life.

Even in its isolation, however, the many-faceted and highly nuanced culture of eastern European Jews exercised a positive influence, strengthening Jewish consciousness and enriching Jewish life. "Historical" eastern European Jewry may have perished, but its culture has outlived even the Holocaust to become a part of the world's cultural patrimony.

—*Ludger Heid*
*Richard S. Levy, translation*

**See also** Buenos Aires Pogroms; Caricature, Anti-Jewish (Modern); Crusades; *Debit and Credit;* France; German National People's Party; Immigration and Naturalization Laws; Judeo-Bolshevism; May Laws; Pale of Settlement; Pogroms; Pudor, Heinrich; Scheunenviertel Pogrom; Stavisky Affair; Treitschke, Heinrich von; Weimar; *Word about Our Jews, A;* Zionism

**References**

Aschheim, Steven E. *Brothers and Strangers: The East European Jews, 1880–1923* (Madison: University of Wisconsin Press, 1982).

Heid, Ludger. "East European Jewish Workers in the Ruhr, 1915–1922," *Leo Baeck Institute Year Book* 30 (1985): 141–168.

———. *Maloche—nicht Mildtätigkeit: Ostjüdische Arbeiter in Deutschland 1914–1923* (Hildesheim, Germany: Olms Verlag, 1995).

Levy, Richard S., ed. *Antisemitism in the Modern World: An Anthology of Texts* (Lexington, MA: D. C. Heath, 1991), 56–66.

Maurer, Trude. *Ostjuden in Deutschland, 1918–1933* (Hamburg, Germany: Hans Christians Verlag, 1986).

Wertheimer, Jack. *Unwelcome Strangers: East European Jews in Imperial Germany* (New York: Oxford University Press, 1987).

## Oswego Camp

The Oswego Camp, also known as the Fort Ontario Camp, was an emergency refugee shelter located on a former army base in Oswego, New York, and was established by the U.S. government in 1944. Originally proposed by the War Refugee Board's director, John Pehle, the idea of creating temporary refugee shelters in the United States was initially rejected by President Franklin Roosevelt. However, during his reelection campaign in 1944, Roosevelt agreed to the creation of one shelter. He explicitly stated that only 1,000 refugees would be admitted, that they would have no legal status, and that they would return to their countries of origin at the conclusion of the war. Roosevelt's decision did not indicate a significant liberalization of U.S. immigration policy. To maintain the restrictionist policies in force, these refugees were officially admitted only as "guests" and thus stood outside of the quota limit.

The refugees that were resettled in the United States came from an internment camp in Italy, not from Nazi-occupied territory. Over 3,000 applicants had applied for the 1,000 available slots. Roosevelt wanted those selected for Oswego to be representative of the countries oppressed by the Nazis and also to reflect the diversity of human victims. However, the overwhelming majority of the refugees chosen were Jewish, including 237 Austrians, 41 Czechs, 96 Germans, 146 Poles, and 369 Yugoslavs. All of them boarded the *Henry Gibbins* in Naples for transport to Oswego, arriving there in August 1944.

Once the refugees were admitted to the shelter, they were not allowed to leave for any reason. School and work activities were all confined to the camp. Although many of the refugees had friends and relatives living in the United States, they could not leave the camp even for weekend visits. Conflicts quickly developed, particularly among different nationalities. The refugees, pleased to be safe in United States, were nonetheless frustrated by their status as detainees. At the war's end, many had no desire to return to their country of origin, as outlined in Roosevelt's original policy. Although Congress wanted them sent back to Europe, President Harry Truman, in December 1945, granted legal immigrant status to any of the Oswego refugees who wanted to stay in the United States.

—*Melissa Jane Taylor*

**See also** Evian Conference; Holocaust; Immigration and Naturalization Laws; Long, Breckinridge; United States

*References*

Gruber, Ruth. *Haven: The Dramatic Story of 1000 World War II Refugees and How They Came to America* (New York: Random House, 2000).

Lowenstein, Sharon. *Token Refuge: The Story of the Jewish Refugee Shelter at Oswego, 1944–1946* (Bloomington: Indiana University Press, 1986).

## Our Demands on Modern Jewry

With his speech of September 19, 1879, *Our Demands on Modern Jewry*, Court Chaplain Adolf Stoecker put the antisemitic movement on the map in Germany. Others had preceded him in the political arena, but none possessed his moral authority or powerful friends, and few could match his oratorical gifts.

Rapid industrialization and the crash of 1873, followed by a long period of economic instability, created conditions in the national capital that begged for political exploitation. Alienated workers, who had only recently been peasants, flowed into the city to find industrial jobs, overwhelming the municipal infrastructure and sinking into misery. Stoecker founded the Christian Social Workers' Party in 1878 to win them back to "throne and altar" by means of a number of unoriginal social-economic reform ideas and a large dose of homiletics. Workers' ills, he insisted, were the result of a decadent, materialistic spirit and a falling away from Christianity.

Workers withstood the court chaplain's oratory. Nor could the Christian Socials make a dent in the electoral hegemony of the left-liberals in Berlin. But by 1879, Stoecker was speaking to a different constituency. His audience was now composed largely of lower-middle-class elements, "little people" who had also suffered from the economic downturn of the mid-1870s and who were angry. They enthusiastically applauded the court chaplain's denunciations and proved eager to blame German woes on the rise of the Jews.

Stoecker invited his listeners to compare the decline in their personal fortunes to the visible prospering of Jews since emancipation (in 1869). Jewish participation in the business, cultural, and educational life of the capital appeared to be insupportable arrogance on the part of a people traditionally thought inferior and despicable. Thus, his first demand, "pray, a little more modesty," echoed the feelings of many in his audience. The remaining "demands"—for more tolerance by Jews toward Germans and more equal treatment of them—exploited the perception that Jews had moved too far and too fast in the new German Empire, that they had, in fact, become a menace. Although Jews thought they were entitled to participate in political and cultural life as free and equal German citizens, many Germans did not accord them this right and instead saw them as aliens intruding where they did not belong.

Stoecker read these resentments and nurtured them adroitly. Although scornful of a superseded Judaism, he was careful in the speech to direct his barbs at "modern" (that is, acculturated) Jews, many of whom had distanced themselves from religion. The press, in particular, came in for his heartfelt condemnation. Although it was far from clear that only "Jewish" newspapers, reporters, and editors ridiculed his political efforts, Stoecker chose to deplore his critics as Jews and to level his most serious charges at the "Jewish" press, a malign force committed to destruction for its own sake.

The speech revealed Stoecker's political ambitions and also his enduring problems. He portrayed himself as a moderate on the Jewish Question. A man of the cloth and with the highest social and political connections, he could not afford to be too closely associated with the rowdy antisemitism (*Radauantisemitismus*) that was beginning to disturb public life and traditional authority. As a Christian, he also distanced himself from racial conceptions of the Jewish Question. Yet he worried aloud about the "cancer from which we suffer" and "Jewification (*Verjudung*) of the German spirit"—turns of speech any racist would be comfortable with. Most ominous in his rhetoric was the unsubtle allusion to the possibility of popular violence: "Here and there the summer lightning already flashes, heralding a distant storm" (in Levy 1991, 59). Were these pious warnings about the impending danger, in fact, a suggestion that violence might be warranted or at least forgivable, given the terrible wrongs being perpetrated on Germans by the Jews?

—*Richard S. Levy*

***See also*** Berlin Movement; Christian Social Party (Germany); Henrici, Ernst; "Jewish" Press; Stoecker, Adolf; *Verjudung*

***References***

Levy, Richard S., ed. *Antisemitism in the Modern World: An Anthology of Texts* (Lexington, MA: D. C. Heath, 1991), 56–66.

# P

## Pale of Settlement

The Pale of Settlement (*Cherta postoiannoi osed-losti Evreev*) was the name given to those regions of the Russian Empire where Jews were required to live. There were also restrictions within the Pale itself, including a ban on Jewish habitation in the countryside of the provinces of Belorussia, restrictions on residence close to international borders, and limited settlement in some cities, especially Kiev. The Pale did not include the provinces of the Kingdom of Poland, where different regulations prevailed, both before and after the limited emancipation in the kingdom in 1862. Free movement between the Pale and the kingdom was not permitted until 1868.

Certain categories of Jews were allowed temporary or permanent residence outside the Pale. These included first-guild merchants, some army veterans, professionals, and those with advanced degrees. Jews with specialized skills were also granted special rights. These Jews and their employees formed sizable Jewish communities in St. Petersburg and Moscow. In 1865, legislation permitted Jewish master craftsmen to leave the Pale, but bureaucratic obstacles prevented large numbers of them from availing themselves of the opportunity. Many Jews were illegally resident outside the Pale, dependent on and victimized by police capriciousness. The travails Jews experienced in attaining and keeping a *pravozhitel'stvo* (residence permit) was a recurrent theme in the Jewish fiction of the day.

The origins of the Pale can be traced to 1791, when the Russian Crown decreed that Jews had to reside in those territories that they inhabited when they first came under Russian rule in 1772. These arrangements were codified in the comprehensive law codes promulgated for the Jews in 1804 and 1835. The territory of the Pale included much of present-day Ukraine, Belarus, Moldova, and Lithuania. Throughout the nineteenth century, areas such as the Don Cossack Host were added or subtracted from the Pale.

The Pale was considered the single greatest legal restriction on the Jews of the Russian Empire, despite its considerable size (it was larger than France) and the inclusion of economically dynamic areas, such as Odessa. However, the fivefold increase of the empire's Jewish population in the course of the nineteenth century, the crowding of Jews into petty trade and artisan activities, and the absence of industrial growth sufficient to provide widespread employment exacerbated pauperization within the Pale.

Polemics on the Jewish Question in Russia focused on the Pale. Some Judeophobes urged its abolition so that "the burden of Jewish exploitation [would] be equitably shared" or "diluted like a drop of poison in the ocean" (in Klier 1995, 220). Other critics of the Jews, including many liberals, argued that the Jews had to be prevented from flooding into the Russian interior until the economic and intellectual level of the masses was sufficiently developed to enable the Russian peasantry to deal with Jewish competition. The central objective of liberal Jewish politics, however, was the attenuation or abolition of the Pale.

But the Pale endured almost to the end of the tsarist empire itself. In 1915, the government opened the Russian interior to Jewish war refugees evicted from the front lines by the Russian military, but their legal status was extremely ambiguous. One of the first acts of the Provisional Government in 1917 was to abolish all exceptional legislation pertaining to the Jews, including those that ruled the Pale.

—*John D. Klier*

**See also** Emancipation; Jewish Question; May Laws; Russia, Imperial; Zionism

**References**

Klier, John D. *Russia Gathers Her Jews: The Origins of the Jewish Question in Russia, 1772–1825* (DeKalb: Northern Illinois University Press, 1986).

———. *Imperial Russia's Jewish Question, 1855–1881* (Cambridge: Cambridge University Press, 1995).

Pipes, Richard. "Catherine II and the Jews," *Soviet Jewish Affairs* 5 (1975): 3–20.

Rogger, Hans. *Jewish Policies and Right-Wing Politics in Imperial Russia* (London: Macmillan, 1986).

# Pan-German League

The most radical of the many patriotic societies of imperial Germany, the Pan-German League advanced an ideological program that stressed the primacy of the nation and increasingly incorporated a discourse of scientific racism. Controversial during its time and since, the league has often been identified as the ideological forerunner of National Socialism, despite disagreements about style and the nature of authority.

Carl Peters founded the German General League (Allgemeiner Deutscher Verband) in April 1891, which then changed its name to the Pan-German League (Alldeutscher Verband) in 1894. The league foundered early and was on the verge of collapse in 1893. It was reorganized and revived under the chairmanship of Ernst Hasse and the management of its executive secretary, Adolf Lehr, in Berlin. The Pan-German League's stated objective was to promote German-National interests at home and abroad. Its claim to act as the authentic guardian of the nation brought it into conflict with the government on a host of issues, including support for Germans abroad, imperialist policy, the Polish Question, and antisemitism. By the first decade of the twentieth century, the league had consciously developed into a self-appointed national opposition.

The Pan-German League admitted Jews in theory, but there were antisemitic undercurrents detectable from its earliest days. Beyond a general certainty concerning Jewish "otherness," there was no consensus regarding the Jewish Question. At least initially, the league embraced a discourse of ethnicity that identified cultural rather than biological differences. Jews could, like other national minorities, assimilate into German society, a process that, for them, implied religious conversion in addition to cultural Germanization. The popularization of scientific racism in Germany at the turn of the twentieth century, however, transformed the league's approach to the Jewish Question. Although a younger, more radical generation of Pan-Germans, led by Heinrich Class, embraced racial antisemitism, the older leadership of the league, Hasse and Lehr, initially resisted these tendencies. Class's elevation to the position of the league's executive secretary in 1901 facilitated a reconsideration of the role of racial theory in the organization's ideology. Scientific racism and its corollary of racial antisemitism seemed to many Pan-Germans to offer scientific authority and legitimacy to the league's ideological program.

The Pan-German League increasingly became a vehicle for the spread of scientific racism and racial antisemitism, particularly after Class assumed the chairmanship in 1908 on the death of Hasse. The association's journal, the *Alldeutsche Blätter* (Pan-German Pages), featured articles on all aspects of racial theory from a wide assortment of racist authors, many of whom became frequent speakers at meetings of the league's local chapters. The league also strengthened its ties with other antisemitic organizations in Germany. Leading Pan-Germans, including Class and Paul Samassa, the editor of the league's journal, were active in Ludwig Schemann's Gobineau Society, which the league itself joined as a corporate member in 1902. The ties between the Pan-German League and Friedrich Lange's antisemitic German Union (Deutschbund) were also strengthened. Many leading figures were simultaneously members of the Deutschbund, and in 1913, almost two-thirds of the German Union's national directors were prominent Pan-Germans, including the executive secretary of the league, Leopold Freiherr von Vietinghoff-Scheel. The league also established ties to Theodor Fritsch's antisemitic movement and to the German eugenics groups.

Although the Pan-German League never formally incorporated racial antisemitism into its program, it was nonetheless clear that it had adopted the principles that biological race determined culture and that racial conflict was the dynamic of history. The Pan-German understanding of ethnicity was thereby transformed from a cultural into a biological category. Pan-Germans internalized Gobineau's and, later, Houston Stewart Chamberlain's belief that the Aryans stood at the pinnacle of the racial hierarchy and that, as the most pure (or least polluted) Aryans, Germans were the superior race. The league devoted itself to maintaining that racial purity against threats from lesser races, in particular from Jews, who embodied the worst threat of race mixing. That view led the league to call for the suppression of national minorities and especially Jews, who were to be stripped of their civil rights in the name of protecting German racial purity from alien pollutants. The league also called for racial hygiene laws, directed at the physically and mentally handicapped, and pronatalist policies, to strengthen the racial stock of Germans in both quality and quantity. Class took these ideas to a radical conclusion in his 1912 tract *If I Were the Kaiser,* in which he argued that Germany should conquer lands to the east, subordinating inferior Slavs and resettling the German population surplus on their evacuated lands.

After World War I, the Pan-German League found itself competing with a host of new groups claiming to speak for the nation, of which the most important was the National Socialist movement. Although the Nazis drew much of their ideological inspiration from the Pan-German League, the two groups remained at odds over questions of authority and style. Education, property, and culture conferred the authority to speak for the nation, and it was on these terms that the league claimed its role as guardian of the nation. Hitler and the Nazis, in contrast, viewed with disdain such "bourgeois respectability." For their part, the Pan-Germans viewed Hitler as base, uncivilized, and barbaric, even though they agreed with many of his ideas. As the Nazis adopted and then radicalized much of the league's ideological framework, the league itself lost relevance in the 1920s, largely because it remained a small bastion of the upper middle class,

failing to appreciate that the German-national public realm after World War I included a much broader segment of society.

—*Elizabeth A. Drummond*

**See also** Chamberlain, Houston Stewart; Class, Heinrich; Eugenics; Fritsch, Theodor; German Racial League for Defense and Defiance; Gobineau, Joseph Arthur de; Hitler, Adolf; *If I Were the Kaiser;* Jewish Question; Lange, Friedrich; National Socialist German Workers' Party; Racism, Scientific

**References**

Chickering, Roger. *We Men Who Feel Most German: A Cultural Study of the Pan-German League, 1886–1914* (Boston: Allen and Unwin, 1984).

Eley, Geoff. *Reshaping the German Right: Radical Nationalism and Political Change after Bismarck* (Ann Arbor: University of Michigan Press, 1990).

Peters, Michael. *Der Alldeutsche Verband am Vorabend des Ersten Weltkrieges (1908–1914): Ein Beitrag zur Geschichte des völkischen Nationalismus im spätwilhelminischen Deutschland* (Frankfurt am Main, Germany: Lang, 1996).

# Pan-Germans (Austria)

The term *Alldeutsche,* or Pan-German, denoted, in general, the radical *völkisch* (racist) wing of the German-National movement in the Habsburg Empire around 1900 and, more distinctively, Georg von Schönerer and his supporters, the Schönerianer. Ideologically, the Pan-Germans adhered to a concept of the nation defined by "blood" and "race," antisemitism, anti-Slavism, and anticlericalism, which, in the Austrian context, meant anti-Catholicism and could be summed up by the slogan *Los von Rom!* (Away from Rome). Their political ideal was the union of the "German" parts of the Habsburg Empire (including Bohemia) with the German Empire and the redefinition of Slav states as dependent satellites.

The Pan-Germans formed a minority—quite heterogeneous even among themselves—within the German-National movement. The authoritarian Schönerer was opposed by other would-be leaders such as Karl Hermann Wolf, parliamentary deputy and temporary chairman of the German-National Association (Deutschnationaler Verein). Given their inconsequential numbers, extreme views, and inner divisions, the Pan-Germans never had much of an impact on government policy. They were far more influential as representatives of an ideology and an ethos than as a political party.

The German-National Association, founded in 1882, was, from 1885 on, an instrument of a völkisch and antisemitic movement dominated by Schönerer. However, the Schönerianer did not succeed in becoming more than the ultra–right wing of the German-National movement. They obtained their best result in elections to the Reichsrat (parliament) in 1901 when the Pan-German Union won 21 seats out of 417, with 20 of them in Bohemia. By 1900, Bohemia and the Sudetenland had become the focus of Pan-Germanism. But soon, the Pan-German and radical wing of German-Nationalism split again into small, ineffectual rival groups.

With respect to racist antisemitism, the Pan-Germans were much more effective, materially contributing to its legitimization thanks to their strident and persistent political rhetoric. Utilizing newspapers such as the *Alldeutsches Tagblatt* (Pan-German Daily), the *Grazer Wochenblatt* (Graz Weekly), and the *Unverfälschte Deutsche Worte* (Genuine German Words) as well as the Alldeutsche Presse publishing house, they worked with a range of media that effectively spread their Jew-hatred. Jews were described as a parasitic nation, seeking dominance wherever they lived and bringing harm to every other people. "The struggle against Jewry," according to the *Pan-German ABC* handbook, "can succeed only through racial antisemitism." The conversion of a Jew to a Christian denomination did not erase the injurious qualities of the Semitic race, and baptism could not make the "Semite into an Aryan or Teuton."(Iro and Lischka 1911). Fear of "the extinguishing of Nordic blood" figured often in the Pan-German discourse, as did a more generalized xenophobia that warned against "the swelling of the non-Teutonic but German-speaking population in town and country: 'German' Jews, Gypsy offspring, Avar Slavs, and the like." Teutons and Slavs in Austria-Hungary were locked "in a battle to the end." The menacing "Black-Red-Gold (Catholic-Marxist-Jewish) International" had to be resisted at all costs. The modern metropolis— that cesspool of ethnic mixing and degeneracy— posed a deadly threat to the vitality and purity of the race.

The components of this ideology lived on after World War I, when the German Workers' Party of Bohemia, having seceded from the Pan-German movement, made contact with the emergent German Workers' Party, later renamed the National Socialist German Workers' Party. The Nazis eventually turned the murderous potential of Pan-Germanism into ghastly reality.

—*Werner Suppanz*

**See also** Austria; Linz Program; National Socialist German Workers' Party; Pan-German League; Schönerer, Georg von; *Völkisch* Movement and Ideology
**References**
Carsten, Francis L. *Fascist Movements in Austria: From Schönerer to Hitler* (London: Sage Publishing, 1977).
Iro, Karl, and Viktor Lischka, eds. *Alldeutsches ABC* (Vienna: Alldeutsche Presse, 1911).
Whiteside, Andrew G. *The Socialism of Fools: Georg Ritter von Schönerer and Austrian Pan-Germanism* (Berkeley: University of California Press, 1975).

## Papacy, Modern

When Napoleonic troops flooded into Italy at the end of the eighteenth century proclaiming liberty, equality, and fraternity, they released the Jews from the ghettos in which they were confined and granted them equal rights. It was, however, only a brief respite for those Jews most directly under papal authority, the Jews of the Papal States. At the time of the French invasion, under Pope Pius VI, the repressive measures connected with the sixteenth-century ghettoization of the Jews remained in effect. Jews could only live in a handful of cities where ghettos existed; they had to be locked in at night; they had to wear Jew badges so everyone would know of their reviled status; they could practice only menial occupations; and they were not to have any social contact with Christians. Jews were also regularly forced to hear sermons in churches by priests seeking to convince them of the evil of their religion.

On the restoration of papal authority in 1814, with the return of Pius VII to Rome, the pope reinstituted the ghettos and most of the old restrictions. The popes of the following years—Leo XII, Pius VIII, and Gregory XVI—all reiterated the evil of the Jews and the necessity of keeping them in a servile status and away from the larger Christian population. Jewish children were also subject to forced baptism, most notoriously in the Mortara case of 1858. When Pius IX took up the papacy in 1846, he briefly attempted ameliorative measures to relieve the miserable conditions in which the Jews lived. However, following the revolution of 1848 and 1849, during which the pope was driven out of Rome and the Jews were once again freed from their ghetto, Pius IX embraced a conservative agenda and reintroduced most of the old restrictions on the Jews.

As Jews were progressively emancipated in other parts of Italy and Europe, the popes of the nineteenth century vociferously protested, arguing that Jewish equality was a threat to Christian society. Change proved irresistible, however, even in the pope's temporal realm. With the crumbling of papal power in much of the Papal States in 1859 and 1860, Jews were liberated from their ghettos in such cities as Ferrara and Ancona, where they were given equal rights, including the right to choose where to live. The last ghetto under papal control fell in 1870 when Italian troops flooded into Rome, bringing an end to a millennium of papal secular rule. A year later, Pius IX shared his sentiments in an audience with a visiting women's group. In ancient times before Jesus, Pius IX told them, the Jews were "*children* in the House of God." But all this had changed, for "due to their obstinacy and their failure to believe, they have become *dogs*." Speaking just months after Italian forces had freed the Jews of Rome's ghetto, the pope bemoaned the result: "We have today in Rome unfortunately too many of these dogs, and we hear them barking in all the streets, and going around molesting people everywhere" (in Kertzer 2001, 130).

In reaction to the painful loss of the papacy's temporal power, both Pius IX and his successor, Leo XIII, lashed out against modernity, including, as Pius IX put it in the Syllabus of Errors (1866), the belief in freedom of religion and freedom of the press. The Vatican increasingly viewed the Jews—beneficiaries of the demise of the church's temporal rule—as part of the array of dangerous forces ranged against it. In 1880, with evident papal blessing, the journal *Civiltà Cattolica* kicked off a decades-long campaign against the Jews, accusing them of all the old sins and then many new ones, such as being responsible for both capitalism and communism, and of being disloyal to the countries in which they lived.

As modern political antisemitism began to gain force in the last two decades of the nineteenth century, the position taken by Pope Leo XIII varied, depending on the national context. In France, the Assumptionist fathers were a pillar of the budding antisemitic political movement; they published the largest-selling Catholic daily newspaper in the country, *La Croix*. Hopeful of developing amicable relations with the republican government, the pope became alarmed by the strident antigovernment tone of the Assumptionists. When their leadership of the drive against Capt. Alfred Dreyfus, the Jewish army officer framed for treason, turned into attacks on the government, the pope called for the Assumptionists to tone down their rhetoric. Even in this case, however, he never specifically criticized them for promulgating antisemitism. Austria was different, for there, the pope did everything he could to protect and back the virulently antisemitic Christian Social Party and its leader, Karl Lueger, the hero of the young Adolf Hitler.

Other churchmen sent pleas to the pope to do something about the spread of antisemitism, particularly that promulgated by the church itself. In England, especially, where Catholics themselves were a persecuted minority, there was great unease among the Catholic leadership about the Vatican's identification with renewed charges of Jewish ritual murder. Following the November 1899 publication of an article in the Vatican daily newspaper, *L'Osservatore Romano,* titled "Judaic Ritual Murder," the archbishop of Westminster wrote to the Vatican secretary of state. He called for an end to the ritual murder campaign, pointing out that in earlier centuries, popes had often defended Jews from such outrageous charges.

Leo XIII referred the matter to the Holy Office of the Inquisition for an opinion. In July 1900, the cardinals reached their conclusions, rejecting the archbishop's plea. A note accompanying the decision explained that "ritual murder is a historical certainty." It continued: "Such murder furthermore was charged and punished many times by lay courts." The conclusion was thus clear: "Given all this, the Holy See cannot issue the statement that has been requested, which, while it may please a few dupes in England, would trigger widespread protests and scandal elsewhere."

The first two decades of the twentieth century saw something of a thaw in papal relations with the Jews. Pius X, who became pope in 1903, had been friendly with a number of Jews from his earlier days as a bishop in northeastern Italy, and he continued these friendly contacts after assuming the papacy. However, in 1904, when he met with Theodore Herzl, leader of the Zionist movement, the pope—according to Herzl's account—espoused a traditional Catholic view of the Jews. "The Jewish faith was the foundation of our own," Pius X said, "but it has been superseded by the teachings of Christ, and we cannot admit that it still enjoys any validity" (in Kertzer 2001, 225).

Benedict XV, who became pope at the outbreak of World War I in 1914, was the first pontiff to abandon the antimodern line of his nineteenth- and early twentieth-century predecessors and so was much less close to the most antisemitic circles in the church. Concerned by reports that priests were involved in fomenting the pogroms that were spreading throughout Poland following the war, he sent secret instructions to his representative in Warsaw, Achille Ratti, to investigate the charges. Ratti, who would become Pope Pius XI on Benedict XV's death in 1922, undertook such an investigation but concluded that the anti-Jewish violence was likely the result of the Jews' own provocations. In these reports, the future pope described the Polish Jews as the "most evil" influence in the country. In 1928, a church organization, the Friends of Israel, founded two years earlier to work for the conversion of the Jews and counting many Catholic clergy as members, was dissolved on orders of the Holy Office of the Inquisition. Although the original goal of working for the Jews' conversion

was thoroughly orthodox, the Inquisitors—with the pope's blessing—faulted the organization for going too far in the direction of promoting brotherhood with the Jews.

As Nazi violence against Jews mushroomed in the mid-1930s, Pius XI began to have second thoughts about his attempts to come to terms with the Nazi regime. In September 1938, the physically ailing pontiff met with a group of visiting Belgians and, in accepting a prayer book they had given him, told them that "antisemitism is not compatible with the thinking and the sublime reality that is expressed in this text." Indeed, in reflecting on the Jews' plight, the pope was clearly moved, and tears began to well up in his eyes as he concluded, "Antisemitism is inadmissible. We are all spiritually Semites" (in Kertzer 2001, 280). Earlier that summer, he had called in an American Jesuit, John LaFarge, and asked him to draft an encyclical against racism and antisemitism. However—partially because of attempts by the superior general of the Jesuit order to undermine the effort—the pope did not receive the draft in time to issue such an encyclical before his death in early 1939. His successor, Pius XII, apparently was worried that such an encyclical would damage Vatican relations with the German government and thus took no action on it. Yet the draft encyclical itself was full of antisemitic language. What it opposed was not a negative view of the Jews as threats to Christian society but a racial view of the differences between Jews and Catholics, along with the notion that violence against Jews was acceptable.

Especially revealing is the fact that at the same time, in the fall of 1938, the Italian government in Rome issued its so-called Racial Laws, aimed against the Jews and barring them from schools, from public employment, and from scientific and literary organizations and prohibiting them from employing Christians in their homes. The pope voiced opposition only to one of the provisions of the racial laws, that which treated Catholic converts from Judaism as if they were Jews.

No subject has raised as much furor in the history of the popes' relations with the Jews as Pius XII's failure to speak out publicly against the slaughter of the Jews of Europe during World War II. As the Vatican's publication of eleven volumes of correspondence between the Holy See and the bishops throughout Europe makes clear, the pope was well aware of this mass murder by 1942. Yet in the years that followed, despite an avalanche of pleas from both Catholic and Jewish sources, he refused explicitly to condemn the Nazi murder of the Jews, much less to excommunicate Hitler or other nominally Catholic Nazi leaders.

It was only with the ascension to the papacy of John XXIII in 1958 that the rejection of antisemitism would become enshrined as church doctrine, set out in *Nostra Aetate* in 1965, following the pope's death. Promulgated by Paul VI, the encyclical explicitly condemned "any form of antisemitism as going against the spirit of Christianity." When John Paul II assumed the papacy in 1978, he sought to improve relations with the Jews further. In 1979, he visited the memorial at Auschwitz; in 1986, he visited the main synagogue of Rome; and in 2000, he paid a dramatic visit to Israel. Everywhere, he spoke against the evils of antisemitism. It was also under John Paul II, in 1993, that the Vatican finally established full diplomatic ties with Israel.

Yet the issue of the papacy's historical role in promulgating antisemitism remains an uncomfortable one in the church. The Vatican investigation of this issue, initiated by the pope himself, resulted in the release of "We Remember: A Reflection on the Shoah" in 1998. That report was criticized for failing to recognize the role played by the Vatican itself in the demonization of the Jews and for utilizing a historically untenable distinction between anti-Judaism (in which, the Vatican admitted, members of the church had been involved) and antisemitism (which was said to have derived entirely from sources that were antagonistic to the church) in order to distance itself from responsibility for the latter.

—*David I. Kertzer*

**See also** Christian Social Party (Austria); *Civiltà Cattolica;* Dreyfus Affair; Emancipation; Ghetto; Herzl, Theodor; Inquisition; Lueger, Karl; Mortara Affair; Pius XII, Pope; Racial Laws; Ritual Murder (Medieval); Ritual Murder (Modern); Supersessionism; Vatican Council, Second; Yellow Badge

**References**

Carroll, James. *Constantine's Sword* (Boston: Houghton Mifflin, 2001).

Kertzer, David I. *The Kidnapping of Edgardo Mortara* (New York: Knopf/Vintage, 1997).

———. *The Popes against the Jews* (New York: Knopf/Vintage, 2001).

Passelecq, Georges, and Bernard Suchecky. *The Hidden Encyclical of Pius XI.* Translated by Steven Rendall (New York: Harcourt, Brace, 1997).

Zuccotti, Susan. *Under His Very Window* (New Haven, CT: Yale University Press, 2000).

## Passing of the Great Race (1916)

Madison Grant's *Passing of the Great Race, or the Racial Basis of European History* makes the short list of the most influential twentieth-century racist diatribes in the United States on the subject of the mongrelization of superior Anglo-Saxons by inferior nationalities and races. In the wake of domestic hysteria following World War I, this best-seller became a bible for a nativist movement championing immigration restriction. Mainstream periodicals such as the *Saturday Evening Post,* the *American Historical Review,* the *Yale Review,* the *Nation,* and the *Literary Digest* reviewed the book approvingly. Only Franz Boas in the *New Republic* and Horace Kallen in the *Dial* dissented. Between 1916 and 1921, 16,000 copies were sold. By 1930, the work had been translated into German, French, and Norwegian and gone through thirteen editions. In 1925, J. F. Lehmann, the most important publisher of radical rightist and racist works, issued the book in the German translation that Hitler claimed to have read. Grant later boasted of having received a fan letter from Führer calling the book "his bible."

The reasons for the popular appeal of this philippic, especially among the eastern literary and cultural intelligentsia, were threefold. First, the argument was sweeping in its reach and boldly presented, exuding confidence. A declarative style devoid of circumlocutions and jargon highlighted memorable passages for the reader. Moreover, Grant covered an eclectic array of evidence with the patina of scientific truth. In the style of a grand Victorian synthesis, he deployed a pseudoanthropology, genetics, zoology, Darwinism, and history and succeeded in impressing amateurs in these disciplines.

Second, the euphemistic "*passing of the great race*" divulged a grievous insult—the supplanting of an older hegemonic leadership aristocracy in American cultural institutions, commerce, and politics. The argument asserted that the "great race" had been victimized by a "misguided sentimentalism" represented by the philanthropy of Christian humanitarianism, the democracy of the "melting pot," and the liberal gift of universal education. Values serving to dumb down the common denominator in civic society functioned to transfer power from superior Nordic peoples to inferior Mediterranean, Balkan, and eastern European breeds. According to Grant's operating laws of evolutionary progress, those of Nordic lineage had populated early America with their "splendid fighting and moral qualities" and endowed the antebellum slave-owning master class with its virtues. The dominant race was visibly identifiable by inherited physical features. Its exemplars were lean and muscular and fair of skin, with light hair, blue eyes, and straight noses. However, Grant warned, the swarthy and pug-shaped immigrant dregs of southern and eastern Europe saturating the industrial labor force were about to plunge modern America into the "racial abyss." The older aristocratic lineage faced inevitable mongrelization by promiscuous mixing with the human trash engrafting itself "on the stock of the nation." Accelerated by the "spread of socialism," vulgarization of the tone of American life became unavoidable as "the weak, the broken, and the mentally crippled of all races drawn from the lowest stratum" triumphed in society.

Third, with his Anglo-Nordic nerves rubbed raw, Grant turned his derisive resentment against a most hated and visible target, the hordes of a "wretched, submerged population of the Polish Ghetto" swarming over the streets of New York. Dwarflike in stature, ruthless in the pursuit of their self-interest, and crassly pushing the "old stock" out of its elite sanctuaries, Jews, no matter where they came, were a menace. For one thing, their reproductive potency was irrepressible: "The cross between a white man and an Indian is an Indian; the cross between a white man and a Negro is a Negro, the cross between a white man and a Hindu is a Hindu; and the cross between any of the three European races and a Jew is a Jew." Moreover, they wielded a malign cultural influence, made all the more dangerous by means of their cleverness and co-option. Although the Jews proceeded to assimilate the language of the native American, wear his clothes, take his names, and steal his women, seldom did they "adopt his religion or understand his ideals."

Reprints of the book, including the German edition, have continued to appear in the early twenty-first century. Its appeal for the mainstream, however, began declining in the 1930s with the hardship of the Great Depression, the surge in Nazi antisemitism, and the strenuous objections raised by an anthropology profession that complained of "dogmatic assumptions which cannot endure criticism" (Boas 1917, 305). If this is science, a philosopher sarcastically remarked, it is "so pure that it is altogether imperceptible" (Kallen 1917, 433).

—*Burton J. Bledstein*

*See also* Armed Forces of the United States; English Literature of the Twentieth Century; Eugenics; Evolutionary Psychology; Hitler, Adolf; Immigration and Naturalization Laws; Moseley, George van Horn; Racism, Scientific; Social Darwinism; United States

*References*

Alexander, Charles C. "Prophet of American Racism: Madison Grant and the Nordic Myth," *Phylon* 23 (1962): 73–90.

Boas, Franz. "Inventing a Great Race," *New Republic,* vol. 9 (January 13, 1917), 305.

Higham, John. *Strangers in the Land: Patterns of American Nativism, 1860–1925* (New York: Atheneum, 1963).

Kallen, H. M. "Racial Mythology," *Dial*, vol. 62 (May 17, 1917, 433).

Kühl, Stefan. *The Nazi Connection: Eugenics, American Racism, and German National Socialism* (Oxford: Oxford University Press, 1994).

## Passion Plays, Medieval

Passion Plays belonged to a large genre of spiritual dramas found throughout central Europe. They were based on the accounts of the four Evangelists of the New Testament, frequently supplemented by popular religious texts. In the fifteenth and sixteenth centuries, the plays developed into grandiose events lasting several days, often involving hundreds of lay actors and thousands of spectators. Theological instruction was not their paramount purpose. Rather, the plays sought to bring sacred history to life and to draw actors and onlookers into an emotionally bound community of Christian believers. The staging of the performance, documentary evidence of which has survived in various forms, was central to the experience.

The plays took place in great open spaces, without the accoutrements of the modern stage. Performance and spectator areas tended to be intermingled, except when a wooden barrier was erected to remind the public not to intervene in the action of the play, apparently a common occurrence. This kind of staging, without a meaningful separation of actors and the audience, engendered in the spectator a direct emotional involvement in the events of the Passion. The actors continually appealed directly to the audience, encouraging it to lend *compassio* (sympathy) and share grief. The sacred characters, consciously represented in the play as real and "human," spoke the same rough, earthy, everyday language as those watching the performance, helping to fuse the worldly experience of the audience and actors. The late medieval plays were purposefully produced to be living illustrations of sacred events. Intense scenes depicting violent confrontations, often with the obscene language familiar from contemporary life, were just as much a part of the experience as moments of sublime religious spirituality. The element of shared experience was enhanced by accompanying ritual: plays began in the morning with a communal mass followed by a procession to the performance space. The actual play lasted from midday until twilight. It could take place over a single or several days.

The Passion Play stood totally in the service of the Christian Gospels, building on the conflict between good and evil, heaven and hell, belief and unbelief. In most of the extant examples, Jews as a group embodied the evil counterworld. Often, they incarnated unbelief and blindness and were made to bear the guilt for the suffering and death of Jesus. They were to be considered—the point was hammered home again and again—the murderers of God. According to surviving directorial notations, actors portraying Jews were instructed to adopt a negative body language. Like the devil himself, these other deniers of God gestured grotesquely, made infernal noises, and danced wildly to the accompaniment of menacing songs, parading their vileness even during the scenes of the Crucifixion.

Among the most popular features of the plays was the exposure of the usurious Jew. The Judas scenes were particularly suitable for representing Jews as money-hungry and unscrupulous, catering to the familiar prejudices of the public; in some of the plays, the Jewish characters were even given the names of recognizable local money-lenders.

Especially in the scenes of the Crucifixion, which made unrelenting demands on the pity of the onlookers, Jews were presented as cruel torturers, merciless helpers of the executioner, and comrades of the devil. The emotional impact of such portrayals must have been powerful. Apparently, there was a constant danger that audience members, inflamed by what they had witnessed during the play, might band together to attack the Jewish quarter. Some surviving town ordinances make it clear that extra guards had to be posted to protect the Jews from the wrath of the mob. And in some towns, performances were forbidden because a particular play's depiction of Jews was thought to be too negative and provocative.

Like medieval texts and the graphic arts, the Passion Plays helped propagate a potent negative image of the Jew for mass consumption. By the end of the fifteenth century, the "evil Jew" had been established as stereotype and furnished with concrete physical attributes—he was grotesque in manner and physically ugly, and he spoke an eerie, bewildering language. This stereotypical Jew made his way into the new era and broke ground for modern antisemitism.

—Edith Wenzel
Richard S. Levy, translation

**See also** Deicide; Gospels; Iconography, Christian; Middle Ages, Late; Oberammergau Passion Play; Usury

**References**
Gilman, Sander L. *The Jew's Body* (New York: Routledge, 1991).

Mellinkoff, Ruth. *Outcasts: Signs of Otherness in Northern European Art of the Late Middle Ages*. 2 vols. (Berkeley: University of California Press, 1993).

Wenzel, Edith. *"Do worden die Judden alle geschant"—Rolle und Funktion der Juden in spätmittelalterlichen Spielen* (Munich, Germany: W. Fink, 1992).

## Patton, General George (1885–1945)

A brilliant military leader and revered national hero, George S. Patton Jr. also exemplified the antisemitism pervading the U.S. Army officer corps of his generation. At the very point of his great military triumphs over Nazi Germany, he repeatedly articulated views that, in their assumptions about inherent Jewish traits and in their vehemence of tone, mirrored the extremism of racial theorists.

Although born and raised in California, Patton was, from his earliest years, imbued with an intense consciousness of his heroic and aristocratic Virginia lineage—a self-image of an elite that perpetuated itself through good breeding culturally and selective marriage genetically. Inspired by the stature and exploits of his colonial and Confederate ancestors, reinforced by heroic military literature and history, the young Patton felt he, too, was destined for greatness as a military man. After a year at the Virginia Military Institute, he was appointed to West Point (class of 1909). Dedicated and ambitious, he developed into a skillful and insightful master of military history, strategy, tactics, and leadership. These abilities and his audacious personality account for his military successes in World War II.

Family background and a military education infused with racism also help explain his antisemitism. For most of his career, however, Patton's assignments kept him isolated from the Jewish Question that so concerned those officers, particularly in military intelligence, who engaged with it at home and abroad. But while he was commander in North Africa in 1942, his antisemitism surfaced, and he strongly opposed lifting Vichy-style restrictions on indigenous and refugee Jews in the region. After his historic victories in Europe, Patton became military governor of Bavaria (in 1945), the region that contained most of the Holocaust survivors in the U.S. occupation zone. Until his removal in September,

he interpreted events, problems, and people through a crude Darwinian political biology, delineating superior and inferior races. Lamenting the decline of the "great race" of Germans, he warned of the racial threat to Western civilization posed by "savage" Asiatic Russians. Patton displayed no sympathy for the Eastern European displaced persons (DPs) and Holocaust survivors whose immediate fate he determined. The DP was not a human being, he wrote, "and this applies particularly to the Jews, who are lower than animals" (in Bendersky 2002, 357). He attributed the lethargy and unsanitary habits of survivors not to their traumatizing genocidal camp existence but to their Jewish heredity. Jews were a "subhuman species" whose innate mental, moral, and physical traits reflected their long-standing racial degeneracy. Patton impeded de-Nazification and condemned efforts to improve conditions for Jewish survivors, especially taking resources and housing from Germans for this purpose. He also believed powerful American Jews conspired to undermine him, take "Semitic revenge" against the Germans, and communize Europe. It was not his antisemitism but his obstruction of de-Nazification that led to his removal. He died in an automobile accident in December 1945.

Although Patton's bombastic personality and outbursts made him unique, his postwar response to Jews typified the attitudes of other top and lower-level officers. When his antisemitism finally emerged, it significantly affected his leadership and policies, with dire consequences for Holocaust survivors.

—*Joseph W. Bendersky*

**See also** Armed Forces of the United States; General Orders No. 11; Jewish Question; Moseley, George van Horn; *Ostjuden;* United States; Vichy
**References**
Bendersky, Joseph W. *The "Jewish Threat": Anti-Semitic Politics of the U.S. Army* (New York: Basic Books, 2000).
Blumenson, Martin. *Patton: The Man behind the Legend, 1885–1945* (New York: Quill-William Morrow, 1985).

## Pauker, Ana (1893–1960)

Born to Orthodox Jewish parents on December 13, 1893, Ana Pauker (née Rabinsohn) worked as a Hebrew and Jewish religion teacher in Romania's capital, Bucharest. The rampant antisemitism of the country propelled her to the revolutionary Left. She entered the Romanian Social Democratic Party in 1915, joined the Communist movement after the Bolshevik Revolution of 1917, and gradually rose up through the ranks of the Communist International (Comintern) in Moscow. Emerging as the "Iron Lady" of Romania during the Soviet occupation of the country in 1944, Pauker served as the unofficial head of the Romanian Communist Party in 1944 and 1945 and remained its behind-the-scenes leader for several years thereafter. In November 1947, she was appointed foreign minister, the first Jew to serve as a government minister in Romania and the first woman in the modern world ever to hold such a post. In that capacity, she promoted the emigration of roughly 100,000 Romanian Jews to Israel between 1948 and 1952 and opposed the Kremlin-ordered show trial of Romanian Zionists in 1950 and 1952. The latter was an important factor in her abrupt removal from power in May 1952 and her arrest seven months later. Accused of espionage in the service of the United States and "Zionist Internationalism," she was slated to appear as the principal defendant in an antisemitic show trial. Stalin's death in March 1953, however, aborted the trial. Freed from prison but still in disgrace, Pauker resided with her family until her death from cancer on June 3, 1960.

Ana Pauker's story—and that of Jewish Communists generally—is an important part of the history of twentieth-century antisemitism. Throughout that period, Jews were continually castigated as "Judeo-Bolsheviks" and widely seen as being preeminent in the Communist movement. Although they did not lead the Soviet Union or the Communist International, Jews had been prominent in various Communist, Marxist, and Social Democratic parties. From the mid-nineteenth century, an increasing number had turned to revolutionary movements, whose universalism seemed the best weapon against discrimination. Indeed, Jews appeared to be the only revolutionaries who took universalism seriously: throughout Europe, they were the only true intra-European element on the Continent;

In November 1947, Ana Pauker was appointed foreign minister in the communist government of Romania. She was the first Jew and the first woman in the modern world to hold such a post. (Corbis)

in Russia, they were practically alone among their fellow radicals in embracing cosmopolitan, that is, universalist or internationalist, socialism.

But antisemitism remained a potent force even within the revolutionary movements. By the 1930s, Stalin began officially embracing "Great Russian Nationalism" as official state policy, and after World War II, he waged relentless campaigns against the "bourgeois nationalism" of ethnic minorities and the "rootless cosmopolitanism" of individual internationalists. Both campaigns targeted Jews and were coordinated with tactical moves to appease popular sentiment by waging antisemitic purges.

Animating popular antisemitism in the Soviet sphere was the fact that Jews were seen in positions of power for the first time. Although the majority of Jews did not adhere to communism, the trauma of fascism and Nazism led many to throw their support to the Communist regimes during the immediate postwar period. Often the only elements not tainted by fascism, these Jews were relied on to replace purged officials of the previous regimes. The sight of Jews in middle- or lower-level government posts triggered a pronounced antisemitic backlash among non-Jewish populations. As economic conditions worsened in the Soviet bloc and popular discontent mounted, the Kremlin opted to deflect popular hostility onto Jews it had conspicuously placed in the party leadership and bureaucracy. In this manner, by simulating a "nationalist" response to Jewish "domination," antisemitic purges such as Ana Pauker's were devised to provide a modicum of support for immensely unpopular Communist regimes.

—*Robert Levy*

**See also** Anti-Zionism in the USSR; Judeo-Bolshevism; Purges, Soviet; Romania; Slánský Trial; Socialists on Antisemitism; Stalinization of Eastern Europe

**References**

Levy, Robert. *Ana Pauker: The Rise and Fall of a Jewish Communist* (Berkeley: University of California Press, 2001).

Schatz, Jaff. *The Generation: The Rise and Fall of the Jewish Communists of Poland* (Berkeley: University of California Press, 1991), 11–19.

# Paul

Just as Paul created Christian theology, so did he create Christianity's attitudes toward Jews. These attitudes regularly are perceived through what Paul wrote in the Epistle to the Romans. Too rarely is a look cast at his other Epistles, especially Galatians and Corinthians.

Romans is the seat of Paul's central theological exposition: the inadequacy of man to achieve salvation through deeds. By this, Paul meant the failure of the commandments of the Torah to afford saving grace, and it has been said that he recreated Judaism and the Torah in propounding this doctrine. The new Torah was to be Christ, and the new Sabbath referred to the eternal repose Christ offered. Yet this concept of salvation was essentially not Jewish. A Jew observes commandments because they are God's law, to be followed out of simple obligation. Further, God will intervene to reward the righteous at the end of days; observance in this world ensures God's ongoing concern. But Paul was plagued with the idea that man is evil, from which anxiety he sought liberation and internal peace.

Had Paul only "reinvented" Judaism, he might have gone his own way, leaving Jews apart. However, he was deeply anchored in his Jewish roots, as he proclaimed in chapters 9, 10, and 11 in Romans: he was a Jew, and he worried for Jews, whom, he stressed, God had not rejected. They were a root to be grafted on, God's friends because of the Patriarchs, although now enemies because of the Gospel. In Romans, citing Genesis 25:23—"The elder shall serve the younger"—Paul wrote that the Jews were the older (son), who would serve the younger. Here, Paul inverted identities. In the Bible, the older son is Ishmael or Esau and the younger is Isaac or Jacob, the two sons of Abraham and Isaac, respectively, who were enemies. According to Genesis, Jacob = Israel (the name God gives Jacob after Jacob wrestles with an angel) is the Jews, and Ishmael signifies the Jews' enemies. For Paul, however, and for subsequent Christian exegesis, Jacob, the new and *Verus Israel* (True Israel), was Christianity and the Christians. This idea became central to Christian theology; it was the Christians who were now God's chosen. Yet at the end of days, the Jews would join Christianity, an event, furthermore, that would occur only when the Jews accepted Christ. Christianity thus became dependent on the Jews. In the meantime—these are the implications that would be drawn from Paul—Jews had to truly serve Christianity, realizing Paul's figure in fact, not in theory alone. Augustine, in the early fifth century, emphasized that Jews were *capsarii*, or slaves who bear the (younger) master's books. Later medieval canons ensured that this pecking order would not be disturbed, enacting a long series of restrictions on Jewish activity.

Romans was composed for gentile Christians in Rome (Paul called himself the apostle to the gentiles). But they were joined in one Christian conventicle with Jews who believed in Christ. These gentiles were troubled by Jewish Christian behavior. Putatively liberated from Judaism and Jewish observance, Rome's Jewish Christians maintained their Jewish practice; this was the case among Jewish Christians in Jerusalem, too, which also must have bothered Rome's gentile Christians. Paul tried to smooth this contradiction over in Romans, chapters 12 through 15, by saying that although each Christian was a limb of Christ's body, different limbs had different functions and needs and that Christians had to accept each other "as Christ accepted us" (Romans 12:4–6, 14:1–4, 15:7). The first eleven chapters of Romans seem to lead to this point. However, it is a point that centuries of scholars immersed in studying the theology of chapters 1 through 8 or the outlines of a program toward Jews in chapters 9 through 11 have overlooked.

The problem in Romans was more acute yet. Rome's gentile Christians had surely read Paul's earlier Epistles to the Galatians and Corinthians, wherein he confronted not Jews nor Jewish Christians but gentile converts to Christianity who were "Judaizing." The Christianity of such converts, as Paul saw it, perforce rested on unconditional faith. Jewish observance by them— Paul singled out circumcision—bespoke imperfect faith; it had to be excised. More, Paul forbade anyone who participated in alien ritual— especially idolatry but by implication Jewish practice, too (or so later generations understood Paul)—to partake of the table fellowship that united all Christians in the one body of Christ. Reading this, the gentiles in Rome must have questioned the practices of Rome's Jewish Christians. Romans, especially the later chapters (noted earlier), may have been a reply, distinguishing Jewish Christians, people who had observed Jewish ritual all their lives, from the new (gentile) converts Paul had chided for Judaizing in Galatians and Corinthians.

To underline the obligation to excise Jewish practice, Paul, in Galatians, invoked the same pair of opposing figures, Ishmael and Isaac, he would later invoke in Romans. Yet whereas in Romans, the pairing identified the True Israel, in Galatians, it was paradigmatic of proper and improper Christian behavior, which shunned the Judaizing identified with the servant woman's son Ishmael—who was to be expelled in favor of the faith of Isaac, the son of the free woman Sarah. Eventually, the Ishmael of Galatians was said to refer to the Jews themselves, enticing and endangering Christians through "overfamiliarity." Canon laws thus forbade domestic service to Jews and dining at a Jew's table. They also required Jews to wear special dress, lest they have sexual contact with Christians, which would invert the social pecking order of "Christians on top" and, even more, "pollute" and "contaminate" Christians themselves, making them unfit to accept the Eucharist. Beside the canons, these concepts also appeared in Christian Roman law and various theological tracts, such as those written by John Chrysostom and Agobard of Lyons. In the fourteenth century, to rid Christianity of Hagar's son became a (theoretical) legal pretext for expelling Jews. Avoiding *pericolosa familiarità* (dangerous proximity), especially in schools, was being advocated even at the end of the nineteenth century. All of this was thanks to the interpreters of Paul—but no less to the ambivalence of Paul himself. The concepts of Jewish friends and enemies (in Romans), linked to anxieties about Judaizing (in Galatians and I Corinthians), underlie all subsequent Christian teachings—and practice—on Jews.

—*Kenneth Stow*

**See also** Agobard; Augustine of Hippo; Chrysostom, John; Circumcision; Expulsions, High Middle Ages; Expulsions, Late Middle Ages; Gospels; Lateran Council, Fourth; Middle Ages, Early; Middle Ages, High; Supersessionism; Yellow Badge

**References**

Boyarin, Daniel. *A Radical Jew: Paul and the Politics of Identity* (Berkeley: University of California Press, 1997).

Davies, W. D. *Paul and Rabbinic Judaism: Some Rabbinic Aspects in Pauline Theology.* 4th ed. (Philadelphia: Fortress Press, 1980).

Gager, John. *Reinventing Paul* (New York: Oxford, 2000).

Stow, Kenneth. *Alienated Minority: The Jews of Medieval Latin Europe* (Cambridge, MA: Harvard University Press, 1994).

# Pavelić, Ante (1889–1959)

Ante Pavelić headed the Ustasha regime that governed the Independent State of Croatia between 1941 and 1945. Born in northern Herzegovina, he graduated from the university in Zagreb and practiced law there in 1918. He became politically active in the Croatian Party of State Rights (Hrvatska stranka prava [HSP]), entered the city council of Zagreb in 1921, and won election to the parliament in Belgrade in 1927. After the imposition of a royal dictatorship in Yugoslavia in January 1929, Pavelić fled the country. In 1932, with Italian help, he founded the Ustasha movement.

In his *Principles of the Ustasha Movement* (June 1933), Pavelić stated that the aim of the organization was Croatian independence, to be achieved by any effective means, including violence. He was directly engaged in the organization of the Velebit uprising against the royal dictatorship in 1932 and implicated in the assassination of King Alexander of Yugoslavia in Marseille in 1934. Bowing to international pressure, the Italians imprisoned him for two years but refused to surrender him for trial in France.

In his memorandum on the "Croatian Question," presented to the Ministry of Foreign Affairs of Nazi Germany in 1936, Pavelić designated the "Serbian government, international Freemasonry, Jewry and communism" as the enemies of Croatian liberation. After the German-Italian invasion of Yugoslavia in April 1941, he took the title of *Poglavnik* (leader) and also assumed the offices of prime minister and foreign minister. Pavelić was the main author and propagator of the Ustasha political program. He created a "New Order" based on the Italian-German fascist model that featured the cult of the nation, the state, and the leader. Racial laws similar to those in Nazi Germany were swiftly put in place. Under Pavelić's leadership, a system of concentration and death camps was established. Martial law was proclaimed, and the opposition was repressed; Serbs, Jews, and Gypsies were murdered. In May 1941, he promised that the "very serious" Jewish Question would be radically solved. He spoke openly of the need for a swift liquidation of Jews. Pavelić, together with members of his family, was among the first to pillage the Jewish villas in residential parts of Zagreb.

During the war, he loyally followed the lead of the Nazis, cooperating with them in the last deportations of the Jews from the Independent State of Croatia (in August 1942 and May 1943).

After the defeat of the Axis powers—and allegedly with looted property—Pavelić managed to escape to Austria, moved on to Italy, and then went to Argentina. After an attempt on his life was made in 1957, he lived under assumed names. He died two years later in Spain.

—*Ivo Goldstein*

*See also* Croatia; Croatia, Holocaust in; Holocaust; Ljotić, Dimitrije; Ustasha

**References**

Bogdan, Krizman. *Ante Pavelić i ustaše.* 2nd ed. (Zagreb: Globus, 1983).

Goldstein, Ivo. *Holokaust u Zagrebu* (Zagreb: Novi Liber and Židovska Općina, 2001).

## Pelley, William Dudley (1890–1965)

Leader of the Silver Shirt Legion of America, William Pelley was one of the best-known "American Führers" during the depression decade. His unique melding of spiritualism and antisemitism attracted a large following, until legal problems effectively silenced him.

Born into a religious family in Lynn, Massachusetts, Pelley worked as a reporter while still in his teens. He eventually became the editor of a series of unsuccessful New England newspapers before turning his attentions to writing fiction. By the late 1910s, he established himself as a prolific and well-regarded purveyor of genteel short stories, published in a variety of mainstream publications. He gained his first exposure to antisemitism while traveling in Russia under the auspices of the Young Men's Christian Association (YMCA) during the Bolshevik Revolution. In 1922, Pelley moved to Hollywood, where he spent the rest of the decade as an in-demand screenwriter. In 1928, having worked himself to exhaustion, he had an out-of-body experience that changed his life. Claiming to have visited souls on the "other side of the veil," Pelley developed his own religious system.

Two years later, he debuted his Liberation Doctrine, complete with a monthly magazine, several full-length monographs, and a correspondence school based in Asheville, North Carolina. This religious system, which mixed spiritualism, Theosophy, pyramidism, and millenarian Christianity, gave Pelley his initial following and served as the underpinning of his future public career. Disgruntled over his inability to establish a large national movement, which he attributed to Jewish machinations, Pelley created the paramilitary Silver Shirts in 1933. He maintained his Liberation theology but added a heavy layer of antisemitism to the organization's teachings. Claiming that Judaism was synonymous with communism and that the New Deal was part of the communist conspiracy to enslave gentiles, Pelley promoted the creation of his Christian Commonwealth as an alternative. The commonwealth would have established a corporate state that guaranteed housing, education, fair pay, and the creation of "Beth Haven" ghettos for American Jews. The Silver Shirts succeeded in attracting 15,000 members, primarily on the Pacific Coast and in the industrial Midwest.

His conviction for violating North Carolina security laws in 1934 hampered Silver Shirt expansion, but Pelley continued to operate his failing movement under the terms of a suspended sentence. After an abortive 1936 presidential bid on the Christian Party ticket, he tried to resuscitate the Silver Shirts. More legal entanglements stymied his efforts. He was sentenced to prison for violating the probation terms of his 1934 conviction, and while out on appeal in 1942, he was found guilty of sedition. Sentenced to fifteen years, Pelley was allowed out of prison to stand as a defendant in the 1944 mass sedition trial. He was paroled in 1950, but as a term of early release, he was enjoined from engaging in political affairs. He spent the 1950s reviving his religious career through his proto–New Age cult, Soulcraft. He died in obscurity in 1965 in Noblesville, Indiana.

—*Scott Beekman*

**See also** Judeo-Bolshevism; New Age; Theosophy; United States

**References**
Beekman, Scott. "Pelley: The Life and Times of William Dudley Pelley." Dissertation, Ohio University, 2002.
Ribuffo, Leo P. *The Old Christian Right: The Protestant Far Right from the Great Depression to the Cold War* (Philadelphia: Temple University Press, 1983).
Smith, Geoffrey S. *To Save a Nation: American Extremism, the New Deal, and the Coming of World War II* (Chicago: Elephant, 1992).

# Peter the Venerable (ca. 1092–1156)

Peter the Venerable, abbot of Cluny from 1122 to 1156, was an influential polemicist of the twelfth-century renaissance. Often described as a temperate protector of the church, guarding it against heterodoxy, he saw his task as refuting the church's enemies from within—the Petrobrusian heretics—and from without—Jews and Muslims. Whereas his book against the Saracens opens with an invitation to a discussion based on love, strong invective characterizes his *Adversus iudeorum inveteratam duritiem* (Against the Inveterate Obstinacy of the Jews). His book presents the theoretical side of his anti-Jewish polemic; the more practical aspects appear in his letters.

The first four chapters of *Adversus iudeorum* use traditional arguments to prove the truth of Christian doctrine: the Jewish inability to read the Bible properly, the result of deficient reasoning; the contrast between Christian hegemony and Jewish lack of sovereignty; and the question of the current validity of biblical precepts. Its fifth chapter, "De ridiculus et stutissimis fabulis Iudeorum" (On the Ridiculous and Stupid Jewish Legends), breaks new ground as the first full-fledged explicit invective against the Talmud. Peter the Venerable thought it a secret Jewish doctrine that blinded Jews to the verity of his treatise (5:30–40), and he viewed the talmudic legends, which he assumed the Jews accepted literally, as their alternative to the true *mysteria* (mysteries, in a religious sense). The Talmud was *intima sacramenta tua* (your inmost mysteries), a parallel to the Christian sacraments, and as such, it constituted the reason for obstinate Jewish refusal to convert (5:21–53).

Peter characterized the Talmud as "a vast sea of impiety" collected in great volumes for thousands of years (5:354). His main accusation against the work focused on its blasphemous nature, vested in its legends' anthropomorphic features. Evidently, he was familiar only with an anthology of legends and knew nothing of the Talmud's legal aspects. Among the passages singled out as blasphemous are the ones depicting God studying the Talmud in heaven (*Berakoth* 8a, *Abodah Zarah* 3b) and describing God as weeping daily (*Berakoth* 3a). For these and other instances, Peter's narrative is more elaborate than the actual talmudic versions; it therefore seems likely that he used a longer midrashic source. Of the fourteen legends attacked, five figured in the Disputation of Paris, which led to the burning of the Talmud in 1239. His angry outburst, "I would justly condemn it and its authors to eternal fire" (5:1444–1446), although not meant to be taken literally, exacerbated an already volatile situation. Peter further claims that the Talmud is immoral because it contains "evil and filthy stories." Citing the salacious tale of Sirach's mother's impregnation, not actually found in the Talmud (5:2004–2045), he implies that this story was just one of many similar obscenities.

Peter notes only one specifically anti-Christian example from the Talmud: a midrash in which Christians are being punished in hell (*Tosephta Sanhedrin* 13:5—again, not explicitly in the Talmud). Peter ascribes their damnation not to their failure to fulfill talmudic law but rather to their not "believing in the Talmud." This was apparently an embellishment on his part.

Peter's letters reflect another, less theoretical aspect of his anti-Jewish attitude, which targeted Jews for economic and social oppression. In his letter to King Louis VII in 1146, he advocates taxing Jews, not Christians, to finance the Second Crusade: "Let their lives be saved and their money taken away so that the blasphemous Jews' money would help the Christian to fight Saracens." Supporting this idea is the allegation that Jews became wealthy by selling stolen church vessels. This economic delegitimization is combined with allegations that Jews somehow injure the body of Christ through these transactions, a defamation not far removed from later accusations of host desecration.

Peter's theoretical treatise had a restricted readership, but his collected letters were more widely disseminated. Therefore, his practical portrayal of Jews as social parasites beyond the accepted social framework may have had a more destructive effect. Notwithstanding his denial of Jewish humanity and his virulent attacks both on the Jews and on talmudic legends, Peter did not overstep the bounds of the church's traditional policy: "Who would contain the hands of our people from your blood, but for the commandment of the Scripture" (5:603). He demanded

subjugation but also toleration. Peter's anti-Jewish hatred, more grounded in steadfast Jewish adherence to Judaism than in his aversion to the Talmud, did not deviate from this established principle. Nonetheless, his enmity toward Jews and Judaism influenced his own era and contributed to the growth of Jew-hatred through the Middle Ages.

—*Yvonne Friedman*

**See also** Crusades; *Entdecktes Judenthum;* Host Desecration; Middle Ages, High; Talmud; Talmud Trials

**References**

Friedman, Yvonne. "An Anatomy of Anti-Semitism: Peter the Venerable's Letter to Louis VII, King of France (1146)," *Bar-Ilan Studies in History* 1 (1978): 87–102.

———, ed. *Petri Venerabilis adversus iudeorum inveteratam duritiem, Corpus Christianorum, Continuatio Mediaevalis* 58 (Turnhout, Belgium: Brepols, 1985).

Langmuir, Gavin I. "Peter the Venerable: Defense against Doubts." In *Toward a Definition of Antisemitism* (Berkeley: University of California Press, 1990), 197–208.

# Petliura, Symon (1879–1926)

In the aftermath of the Bolshevik seizure of power in the Russian Empire in October 1917, the Central Rada, originally established as the representative of the Russian Provisional Government in Petrograd, declared national independence for Ukraine. Although the Central Rada signed a peace treaty with the Central Powers, it was replaced by a pro-German puppet government, the Hetmanate, in April 1918. German troops withdrew after the armistice of November 11, 1918, and the governing authority was assumed by the so-called Directory of the Ukrainian National Republic. Symon Petliura, a Ukrainian nationalist journalist, became prime minister of the directory and *Ataman,* or commander of its military forces, in February 1919. The forces of the directory were defeated by the Red Army in the course of the Russian Civil War, and Petliura and his government went into exile in Poland. The remnants of his army joined the Polish side in the inconclusive Soviet-Polish War of 1920, also choosing to remain in exile thereafter.

The forces of the directory were guilty of atrocities and pogroms against the Jewish population of Ukraine. Most of these acts were the result of simple banditry, rather than ideological antisemitism, and were carried out by local warlords. Other pogroms ostensibly had military objectives, such as those perpetrated by the notorious *Otaman* (commander) Semesenko in Proskuriv and Felshtin in February 1919, which left almost 1,500 Jews dead.

In 1921, the Revisionist Zionist leader Vladimir (Ze'ev) Jabotinsky entered into a controversial agreement with a representative of Petliura's government-in-exile, Maksym Slavinsky, for the creation of a Jewish militia to defend the Jewish population should Petliura's forces succeed in invading Soviet Ukraine.

On May 26, 1926, Petliura was assassinated on a Paris street by Shalom Schwartzbard, a Jewish émigré from eastern Europe. At his trial, the counsel for the defense turned Schwartzbard's act into an indictment of the directory and its leader, Petliura, holding them accountable for the pogroms that occurred under their authority. The trial attracted worldwide attention, and Schwartzbard was acquitted.

Those who condemn Petliura as a *pogromchik* (pogromist) emphasize his failure to control those troops under his command who carried out a wave of brutal pogroms in 1919. Defenders of Petliura note that he issued decrees that outlawed such violence in August 1919. They stress that for much of 1919 and in most places, Petliura and the directory did not exercise effective control over the forces that nominally fought in their name. The actions of Petliura as leader of the directory and the uncritical support given to his assassin by many Jewish organizations became issues that severely complicated Jewish-Ukrainian relations.

—*John D. Klier*

**See also** Judeo-Bolshevism; Pale of Settlement; Russia, Imperial; Russian Civil War; USSR; Zionism

**References**

Abramson, Henry. *A Prayer for the Government: Ukrainians and Jews in Revolutionary Times, 1917–1920* (Cambridge, MA: Harvard University Press, 1999).

Friedman, Saul S. *Pogromchik* (New York: Hart, 1976).

Hunczak, Taras. "A Reappraisal of Symon Petliura and Jewish-Ukrainian Relations, 1917–1921," *Jewish Social Studies* 31 (1969): 163–183.

Kleiner, Israel. *From Nationalism to Universalism: Vladimir (Ze'ev) Jabotinsky and the Ukrainian Question* (Edmonton and Toronto: Canadian Institute of Ukrainian Studies Press, 2000).

# Pfefferkorn, Johannes (1468/1469–1522)

Following his conversion from Judaism to Christianity (along with his wife, Anna, and son, Laurentius), Johannes Pfefferkorn became a missionary in 1504. From 1513, he was head of the hospital of St. Ursula and St. Revilien in Cologne. He was famous in his own day as the author of numerous anti-Jewish works.

Pfefferkorn's conversion involved him in the intense political and theological controversies that characterized the period leading up to the Reformation. As a convert, he was put under especially close scrutiny. Absolute devotion to the faith was expected of him, but since he was a renegade, not many wanted to trust his sincerity. He found sanctuary among the powerful Dominicans in Cologne and proceeded to accommodate himself to their anti-Jewish, antireformist agenda. The pressure of his mentors' expectations in this regard added to his anxieties and fanned his hatred. In his first work, *Judenspiegel* (The Jews' Mirror [1507]), he claimed to want to missionize the Jews. In reality, he wanted to force them to choose between baptism and repression. He called for the confiscation of their books, especially the Talmud, knowing full well that, deprived of their spiritual succor, Jews would feel compelled to emigrate. Supported by influential noblemen and the authority of the Holy Roman Emperor, he began an extensive campaign of book confiscations in Frankfurt am Main and in imperial cities along the Rhine, having prepared the way by arguing that Jewish books were responsible for the Jews' "unbelief" and that they were inherently dangerous and evil.

Pfefferkorn's calling into question the very humanity of the Jews contributed to the birth of modern antisemitism. But ironically, his denunciations and the excessiveness of his rhetoric returned to haunt him. In 1510, when the highly regarded jurist and humanist Johann Reuchlin responded to an imperial query with a defense of Jewish books, Pfefferkorn immediately and stridently attacked him in a number of pamphlets. He accused Reuchlin of being a "Judaizer" and a heretic and suggested that he ought to be drawn and quartered by the Inquisition. The Dominicans of Cologne also entered the fray, publishing tracts against Reuchlin's heresy and urging that he be brought up before the Inquisition. Reuchlin defended himself against these scurrilous and life-threatening charges and rallied to his cause leading humanists, including Erasmus of Rotterdam and Ulrich von Hutten, who proceeded to attack Pfefferkorn as a malicious Jew. Pfefferkorn also failed to deprive the Jews of their sacred books, which were returned to them.

The dramatic first steps of the Lutheran Reformation led to a sharp decline of public interest in the so-called Reuchlin affair. By that time, Pfefferkorn had been worn down by the disputations, and after a protracted illness, he died in Cologne in 1522.

—*Ellen Martin*
*Richard S. Levy, translation*

**See also** Dominican Order; Inquisition; Reformation; Reuchlin, Johann; Self-Hatred, Jewish; Talmud; Talmud Trials

**References**

Frey, W. "Der 'Juden Spiegel,' Johannes Pfefferkorn und die Volksfrömmigkeit." In *Volksreligionen im hohen und späten Mittelalter*. Edited by P. Dinzelbacher and D. R. Bauer (Paderborn, Germany: Schöningh, 1990), 177–193.

Martin, Ellen. *Die deutschen Schriften des Johannes Pfefferkorn: Zum Problem des Judenhasses und der Intoleranz in der Zeit der Vorreformation* (Göppingen, Germany: Kümmerle, 1994).

# Philosemitism

The hatred of Jews has long been shadowed by a contrary impulse toward fascination and idealization. The use of the term *philosemitism* to describe this phenomenon is, for some, controversial, as it can seem to suggest an unambiguously positive stance, whereas this is far from always the case. Philosemitism does not imply normaliza-tion. Alongside antisemitism, it is a form of "allosemitism": the view that Jews are, in some sense, radically different or exceptional. Nonetheless, positive attitudes toward Jews, even when heavily tinged with ambivalence, have played an important role in Jewish history and in Jewish-Christian relations at numerous junctures.

For the early church, the survival of the Jews as a dispersed minority was both meaningful and necessary. In Augustine of Hippo's classic formulation, the Jews, as a "witness people," preserved and transmitted crucial evidence for the truth of Christianity. Their suffering was also not to be permanent: the final completion of the church's mission would be signaled by the conversion of even these most obdurate enemies of Christ. As guardians of this mission, various medieval monarchs and in particular the papacy periodically asserted themselves as "protectors" of the Jews, a role reinforced in documents such as Pope Innocent III's *Constitutio Pro Judeis* (Edict in Favor of the Jews [1199]). Such "protection" was, of course, by no means incompatible with humiliation, and it also frequently overlapped with economic motives for promoting the presence of a vulnerable and readily taxable Jewish community. In the sixteenth and seventeenth centuries, the rise of Christian Hebraism intensified the intellectual dimension of the Christian fascination with Jews. In England, a powerful strain of philosemitic interest in Jews, fueled both by Hebraist scholarship and by conversionist zeal, played an important role in the readmission of Jews between 1655 and 1666.

In the eighteenth century, a discourse on the "improvement" of the Jews emerged. Although this was widely based on very negative assumptions about the nature of Judaism and Jewish life, it was also not infrequently inflected with an idealizing anticipation that, once freed from their exclusionary burdens, the Jews might rediscover the agricultural and military prowess of their biblical forebears. As early as 1714, the English Deist John Toland evoked the great prosperity and power that would ensue if the Jews were to resettle in Palestine. The exceptional theological status of the Jews made the prospect—and, in the nineteenth century, the reality—of their social transformation heavily overdetermined with meaning, in which admiration for the Jews' cultural or economic virtues were often closely intertwined with a more negative view of these same traits as being based on a conspiratorial or atavistic clannishness.

The German dramatist Gotthold Ephraim Lessing's play *Nathan the Wise* (1779), in which the Jew Nathan is presented as an idealized mouthpiece for the Enlightenment principles of toleration and human fellowship, remains a classic of modern philosemitism. As the most obvious beneficiaries of the establishment of civic rights in the wake of the Enlightenment, Jews were also closely associated with these values. Support for the Jewish cause in such incidents as the Damascus blood libel (1840) and the Mortara Affair (1858), as well as during the pogroms in Russia in 1881 and 1882 and later, was widespread among non-Jewish liberals, especially in the English-speaking world. A heightened sympathy for Jews among evangelical Christians contributed to support for these causes, as did an eagerness to condemn the intolerance of the Islamic, Catholic, or Slavic worlds: the fair treatment of Jews was, for many anglophone liberals, a key marker of the superiority of their own societies.

In the post-Holocaust era, philosemitism has become much more widely expressed. This is particularly the case in Germany, where, during the early postwar years in the West, an idealized enthusiasm for Jews and for expressions of Jewish culture emerged in public discourse and where Lessing's *Nathan the Wise* has risen to great popularity. This idealization, however, can often appear uncritical or fantastical. The religiosity, cultural traditionalism, or ethical nobility of the Jews of the philosemitic imagination often do not match the realities of contemporary Jewish existence. These philosemitic stereotypes also undoubtedly distort perceptions of the Israel/Palestine conflict. The strong attachment of many American evangelical Christians to Israel plays a significant role in contemporary U.S. politics. The Zionism of some of these groups, however, is based not only on a conversionist stance toward Jews but also on an eager anticipation of the unfolding in the Holy Land of apocalyptic biblical prophecies. Philosemitism could scarcely take a more double-edged form.

—*Adam Sutcliffe*

**See also** Augustine of Hippo; Damascus Blood Libel; Dohm, Christian Wilhelm von; Innocent III; Middle Ages, High; Middle Ages, Late; Mortara Affair; Pogroms; Zionism
**References**
Edelstein, Alan. *An Unacknowledged Harmony: Philo-Semitism and the Survival of European Jewry* (Westport, CT: Greenwood Press, 1982).
Katz, David S. *Philo-Semitism and the Readmission of the Jews to England* (Oxford: Oxford University Press, 1982).
Rubenstein, William D., and Hilary L. Rubenstein. *Philosemitism: Admiration and Support in the English-Speaking World for Jews, 1840–1939* (New York: St. Martin's Press, 1999).
Stern, Frank. *The Whitewashing of the Yellow Badge: Antisemitism and Philosemitism in Postwar Germany* (Oxford: Pergamon, 1992).

## Physics, "German" and "Jewish"

The anti-Jewish measures put into effect after the Nazis rose to power in 1933 had catastrophic consequences for physics research in Germany. Almost a quarter of the physicists were dismissed, 80 percent of whom emigrated. Among them were many Nobel Prize winners, including Albert Einstein, James Franck, and Max Born, as well as their numerous assistants and students. Physics in Germany suffered losses it has never made up.

The expulsion of Jewish physicists from German universities and research institutes was followed by an attack aimed at banishing their achievements from Germany. The struggle against "Jewish physics" waged by supporters of Nazism targeted the "Aryan" colleagues of the Jews who remained behind and who continued to practice modern theoretical physics, especially in regard to the theory of relativity and quantum theory. To combat the supposedly ever-growing and baleful influence of "Jewish physics," the weapon of "German physics" was called into being. Jewish physics was defined as the destructive adversary of German physics. Its origins considerably predated the Third Reich, however. During the 1920s, periodical literature in the field was already displaying racist political tendencies. The increasing importance given to the theory of relativity and the use of mathematical methods in modern research generated controversies that were later embraced by the German

Philipp Lenard receives congratulations from the rector of Heidelberg University, Dr. Paul Schmitthenner, for his honorary degree. (AIP Emilio Segre Visual Archives, Physics Today Collection)

physics assault. But only after 1933 did this trend assume crass and threatening forms.

Although the champions of German physics constituted a group of only about twenty-five individuals, the support they drew from the Nazi regime enhanced their power and influence. The phenomenon was limited to Germany and lasted just fifteen years or so. Its founders were the Nobelists and convinced Nazis Philipp Lenard (1862–1947) and Johannes Stark (1874–1957). Lenard set forth his views on the subject in a four-volume work, *German Physics* (1936), arguing that only the naive could believe that science was "international" rather than the product of blood and race. The physics of the Jews had gained enormous influence at the end of World War I, when, to his way of seeing things, Jewish power had become paramount in the Weimar Republic. Einstein sought nothing less than to revolutionize and dominate physics, but Jews lacked the Aryan's understanding and appreciation of truth: "Jewish physics is no more than an

illusion, the degenerate offspring of fundamental Aryan physics" (Lenard, *Deutsche Physik*, IX–XI).

Lenard made Nazi racism and antisemitism the unambiguous basis for German physics and placed the rejection of Einstein's theory of relativity at its core. However, his book did not make clear just how the work of German physics could be carried out. Nor did German physics ever produce a basic program. Certain "guidelines" could be culled from a collection of speeches on the opening of the Phillipp-Lenard Institute in Heidelberg (in 1935), in lectures on Jewish and German physics by Wilhelm Müller and Johannes Stark, and in articles printed in the *Zeitschrift für die gesamte Naturwissenschaft* (Journal for the Natural Sciences). German physics adhered to the universally recognized theories of matter—excluding quantum mechanics and relativity theory. Lenard's ideas concerning ether and Stark's model of the atom were meant to replace these essential elements of modern physics. The research of the German physicists was to be carried out in utter "harmony with nature" and to rely on exact observation and experiment. Mathematical tools were to be used as sparingly as possible, serving only as a means of clarifying experimental results.

It was, however, on the basis of the two rejected modern theories that Stark and his associates believed the opposition between Jewish and German physics could best be demonstrated. The two racially based physics stood for totally opposite values: on one side lucidity, on the other ambiguity. Order, clarity, law, and precision based on solid evidence supposedly distinguished German physics from the chaos, vagueness, license, and relativizing mental gymnastics of Jewish physics. Pitted against each other were the "deep-penetrating mind of the Aryan" and the surface-skimming formalism and "cold intellect" of Jewish physicists, who renounced all principle. As Stark formulated it, the "German pragmatic mind" contested the "Jewish dogmatic mind." There were two species of physics, but only one was legitimate. The polemic against the theory of relativity became increasingly shrill by the end of the 1930s, resorting to insult and censure. The "general relativity madness" was among the "trivial pet notions of mathematicians," the product of "conspiracy and mass suggestion," and finally no more than the "great world bluff of the Jews" (Stark and Müller, *Jüdische und deutsche Physik,* 1941).

Stark became increasingly strident, changing the thrust of his attack to include not only the Aryan physicists whom he accused of teaching Jewish physics but also younger scientists whose research, he proclaimed, breathed the same spirit as Einstein's. His main target was Werner Heisenberg at the University of Munich. In 1937, Stark gave his blessing to an article that appeared in the SS journal *Das Schwarze Korps,* entitled "White Jews in the Sciences" (*Weisse Juden in der Wissenschaft*). In it, Heisenberg was cited as a typical example of those who acted as proxies for Jewry in the intellectual life of Germany; they, just like the Jews, would have to vanish (*Das Schwarze Korps,* July 15, 1937). The fallout from this effort was that Heisenberg was unable to succeed to the chair held by the eminent Arnold Sommerfeld; instead, it was bestowed on the wholly unqualified aerodynamics specialist Wilhelm Müller, zealous party member and champion of German physics. With this victory, German physics achieved the high point of its influence and was emboldened to demand that a distinction be made between "responsible and irresponsible theory." Its supporters held six chairs in physics at the time.

The atmosphere of hostility and politicalization proved unbearable for the pursuit of modern theoretical physics in Germany. Matters came to a head when an attempt was made to bring exponents of German physics and other physicists together to arrive at some sort of compromise. On November 15, 1940, the ironically labeled Munich "religious disputation" sought to bring the German physics group to accept and acknowledge scientifically verifiable facts and tools, notably relativity and quantum theory, and to desist from conducting polemics in the guise of science. The Munich deliberations, followed by another meeting, resulted in a signed agreement by the German physics group. It acceded to the demands of modern theoretical physics, especially in regard to relativity and quantum theory, but shorn of their potential metaphysical or political ramifications. For example, the agreement solemnly rejected any connection between the theory of relativity and a universal philosophical relativism. Another face-saving gesture declared it desirable that physics move beyond mere formalism to gain a deeper understanding of the atom.

For most physicists, the agreement was doubtlessly a banal exercise, simply acknowledging what was obviously necessary for the pursuit of scientific research. It did, however, clear the air, allowing scientists to teach and elaborate modern theory without limitation and to base their own work on modern concepts. Most physicists held to the agreement. German physics, however, steadily lost influence. With the end of the Third Reich, the phenomenon of "German physics" and "Jewish physics" speedily disappeared.

—*Charlotte Schönbeck*
*Richard S. Levy, translation*

**See also** Degeneration; Nazi Cultural Antisemitism; Nazi Legal Measures against Jews; Psychoanalysis; *Schwarze Korps, Das;* Weimar

### References

Beyerchen, Alan D. *Scientists under Hitler: Politics and the Physics Community in the Third Reich* (New Haven, CT: Yale University Press, 1977).

Cassidy, David C. *Uncertainty: The Life and Science of Werner Heisenberg* (New York: W. H. Freeman, 1992).

Kleinert, Andreas, ed. *Johannes Stark: Erinnerungen eines deutschen Naturforschers* (Mannheim, Germany: Bionomica, 1987).

Richter, Steffen. "Die 'Deutsche Physik.'" In *Naturwissenschaft, Technik und NS-Ideologie.* Edited by Herbert Mehrtens and Steffen Richter (Frankfurt am Main, Germany: Suhrkamp Verlag, 1980), 116–141.

Schönbeck, Charlotte. *Albert Einstein und Philipp Lenard: Antipoden in Physik und Zeitgeschichte* (Berlin: Springer, 2000).

———. "Philipp Lenard und die 'Deutsche Physik.'" In *Philipp Lenard: Wissenschaftliche Abhandlungen,* vol. 4. Edited and commented on by Charlotte Schönbeck (Diepholz and Berlin: GNT, 2003), 11–22.

Pope Pius IX. Following the revolution of 1848 and 1849, Pius IX embraced a reactionary agenda and reintroduced most of the old restrictions on the Jews. (Library of Congress)

## Pius IX, Pope (1792–1878)

Pius IX was the pope responsible for convening the First Vatican Council, which opened in December 1869 and continued until permanently suspended in October 1870 in the wake of the fall of the Papal States. This council's most famous decree involved the definition of papal infallibility. Pius IX hoped that the council might instill new vigor into European Catholicism in particular, as it confronted the challenge of Enlightenment liberalism and the related attack on the Catholic Church's political power.

Pius IX had the second-longest tenure of any pope in history (1846–1878), and his papacy had a significant impact on the church worldwide. The shape he gave the church persisted in significant ways until the reforms undertaken by Pope John XXIII and the Second Vatican Council he convened, which largely reversed the generally hostile posture toward the secular order that prevailed during Pius IX's pontificate. The difference between Pius IX and John XXIII is especially stark on the question of the church's relationship to Jews and Judaism.

Pius IX impacted the Catholic-Jewish relationship in two significant ways. The first involved his strong attack on liberal modernism, which he regarded as the archenemy of the church and of a moral social order. Although he tended to associate primarily Protestants and secularists with such liberal modernism—or Freemasonry, as it was called in many circles—liberal Jews also felt the brunt of his attack directly or by implication.

In his confrontation with the liberal and socialist political movements that were transforming the face of Europe by insisting on human rights and religious freedom, ideas regarded as fundamentally pernicious by the popes of the nineteenth century, Pius IX struggled to maintain papal authority and influence over European states. At the beginning of his papacy, he was considered somewhat more moderate in his attitude toward liberalism than his immediate predecessors, who regarded notions of religious liberty as satanic in origin. But as the threat to the Vatican's continued sovereignty over the Papal States intensified, Pius IX grew ever more vocal in his condemnation of liberalism and its insistence on religious liberty. This papal attitude profoundly affected the situation of Jews, both religiously and in terms of civil rights, in countries where Catholicism was the dominant religion. This was especially the case in the Papal States at the moment when Pius IX's attack peaked in his famous Syllabus of Errors, issued in 1864, in which he described religious liberty as an "absurd principle."

In subsequent years, the church's attack on liberalism increasingly centered on the Jews, who were explicitly connected with Freemasonry in countries such as France and Poland. At the time of the rise of Nazism, the attack on Jews as Freemasons became a major source of antisemitism, which significantly muted the church's response to Hitler's mass murder of the Jews. Pius IX clearly laid the groundwork for a "new antisemitism" through the Syllabus of Errors and other writings.

The second situation involving Pius IX and the Jews had to do with the infamous kidnapping of Edgardo Mortara. Edgardo was secretly baptized as a child by a Catholic servant girl while he was ill. When this was discovered, the Catholic Inquisitor ordered the police to take Edgardo from his parents and send him to live in a Catholic institution in Rome; there, Edgardo was instructed in the Catholic faith. The incident became an international cause célèbre, with interventions made to Pius IX by Napoleon III and Sir Moses Montefiore. But the pope would not budge on the issue. The Jesuit newspaper *Civiltà Cattolica,* with close Vatican ties, launched a campaign against Edgardo's parents, arguing that they were motivated by hostility to the Catholic Church. Eventually, Edgardo was ordained a priest.

This case permanently tarred Pius IX and the Vatican. In Italy, it led to new legislation regarding parental rights that undercut the church's traditional control over all aspects of people's lives.

—*John T. Pawlikowski*

*See also* Alliance Israélite Universelle; Center Party; *Civiltà Cattolica;* Freemasonry; Mortara Affair; Papacy, Modern; Vatican Council, First; Vatican Council, Second

**References**

Flannery, Edward. *The Anguish of the Jews* (New York: Macmillan, 1965).

Kertzer, David I. *The Kidnapping of Edgardo Mortara* (New York: Knopf, 1997).

Perry, Marvin, and Frederick M. Schweitzer. *Antisemitism: Myth and Hate from Antiquity to the Present* (New York: Palgrave/Macmillan, 2002).

# Pius XII, Pope (1876–1958)

The response of Pius XII (r. 1939–1958) to the challenge of the Holocaust has been the subject of much controversy since the 1963 appearance of Rolf Hochhuth's play *The Deputy*. This discussion has often become polemical, as evidenced by John Cornwell's book *Hitler's Pope*. For some scholars, such as Peter Gumpel, S.J. (who has been officially examining the cause of Pius XII for possible canonization), there is little question that the pope responded with great courage and humanity to the plight of the Jews and other Nazi victims. He was responsible, according to Gumpel, for saving hundreds of thousands of Jews and therefore deserves eventual sainthood. Gumpel's view is reflected in the 1998 Vatican document on the Holocaust, *We Remember*.

Those arguing for a positive evaluation of Pius XII's response often cite statements by Jewish leaders such as Joseph Nathan of the Italian Hebrew Commission, A. Leo Kubowitzki of the World Jewish Congress, and Israeli prime minister Golda Meir, who, at the time of his death, praised the pope publicly for his efforts on behalf of Jews. Although these testimonials need to be included in any comprehensive assessment of his papacy, they do not represent the totality of thinking on Pius XII. Within the Jewish and Christian communities, there are trenchant critiques that also must be taken seriously in any overall assessment of Pius XII's record during the critical period of the Holocaust. It is unfounded to claim that criticism of this pope only began with the appearance of Hochhuth's play.

Pius XII's critics, both Christian and Jewish, argue that his public silence regarding Jews contributed to the staggering loss of Jewish lives under the Nazis. They seriously question the claim made by Gumpel and *We Remember* that he saved "hundreds of thousands" of Jews. Rather, they portray Pius XII as a rather cold and even callous person, a man with a deeply inward spirituality whose principal concern was preserving the institutional well-being of the church and consolidating papal power. As some of these critics would admit, Pius XII made a few efforts to save Jews, but their rescue never became a high priority for him.

An objective evaluation of the scholarly research thus far yields a very mixed picture of his papacy. Clearly, he made some important diplomatic interventions in Hungary, Italy, and Slovakia. He also let rescue efforts by convents of nuns and priests, as well as by certain papal nuncios, continue without interference. It seems that certain Catholic resistance groups, especially in France, understood his generic pleas for victims as applying specifically to the Jews.

But important questions remain. Did Pius XII wait too long to make any significant interventions, a point stressed by the late Gerhart Riegner of the World Jewish Congress? Did he use the tools at his disposal—for example, the diplomatic representatives of the Holy See (papal nuncios)—as effectively as he might? What about his positions right after the war toward the guilt of German Catholics and his attitude toward the Catholic efforts to help Nazis flee to South America? Such questions require additional research.

The case of Pius XII regarding the Holocaust is far from closed. New documents of significance continue to be found, such as one that indicates the papal secretary of state had delivered a rather strong, private letter to Ambassador Joseph Kennedy denouncing Nazism and its treatment of the Jews. From what we know at present, Pius XII was neither the great moral hero that some of his defenders make him out to be nor a man totally unconcerned about Jewish suffering and death under the Nazis, as many of his critics contend. What the final evaluation of his moral leadership will be remains an open question.

—*John T. Pawlikowski*

**See also** Holocaust; Hungary, Holocaust in; October Roundup; Papacy, Modern; Slovakia, Holocaust in; Ultramontanism

**References**
Blet, Pierre, S.J. *Pius XII and the Second World War: According to the Archives of the Vatican.* (New York/Mahwah, NJ: Paulist, 1999).
Phayer, Michael. *The Catholic Church and the Holocaust, 1930–1965* (Bloomington and Indianapolis: Indiana University Press, 2000).
Rittner, Carol, and John K. Roth, eds. *Pope Pius XII and the Holocaust* (London and New York: Leicester Press (Continuum), 2002).
Sanchez, Jose M. *Pius XII and the Holocaust: Understanding the Controversy* (Washington, DC: Catholic University of America Press, 2002).

## The Plan of the Hierarchy

The Plan of the Hierarchy, according to initiates, is the multistage program for establishing the New Age on earth. Its disciples regard "the Plan" as designed and directed by the "Hierarchy of Ascended Masters," a cadre of divine disembodied beings, evolved over many lifetimes, who offer their accumulated wisdom to guide humankind to divinity. According to Alice Bailey, the New Age spokesperson who first outlined the Plan in the 1930s (as dictated to her by Hierarchy member Djwhal Kuhl), this program is a nonnegotiable package to be embraced in its entirety by all who desire to enter the coming age.

The Plan's details appeared in Bailey's *Externalisation of the Hierarchy* (1957), a book restricted to an inner circle until 1975, when disciples received a Hierarchy directive to go public. Many New Age leaders have since expanded on Bailey's outline, but her version remains the authoritative blueprint. The Plan's centrality is emphasized in the introduction: "It is this revelation which lies behind all the activities which now engross the attention of the Hierarchy." Of prime interest for the subject of antisemitism is "the Plan for World Religion," which begins with two goals: (1) "the reorganization of world religions" to purge them of "ridiculous" beliefs, singling out "the churches" for this spiritual overhaul, and (2) "the gradual dissolution of the orthodox Jewish faith." Orthodox is defined here as all Jewish theology with a "separative emphasis" (monotheism), "hatred of the gentiles" (particularism), and "failure to recognize the Christ." Bailey noted repeatedly in her writings that this "Christ" is not the Jesus of Christianity but the New Age divinity known as Maitreya—a member of the Hierarchy's triune Logos, who, together with Sanat Kumara and Lucifer, will direct the Plan on earth.

Only after these two stages are accomplished will the third stage commence: "preparation for a revelation which will inaugurate the new era and set the note for the new world religion [and] the appearance of the Hierarchy on earth." Bailey predicted that by the time this "world religion" is implemented, "the old theological activities will have been completely broken; Judaism will be fast disappearing."

Elsewhere in *Externalisation,* Bailey described this plan to eliminate Judaism in the context of a cosmic war between "the Lords of Light" and "the Dark Forces," an ancient struggle in which the latter won the last round and defeated the New Age Hierarchy, forcing these entities to withdraw from the earth. The Plan, therefore, is a strategy enlisting human involvement in the Hierarchy's ongoing war, enabling them to return to earth and vanquish their Dark Foe, alternately identified by Bailey as the Jewish God, faith, and/or people.

—*Hannah Newman*

**See also** Aquarius, Age of; Bailey, Alice A.; Jewish Force; New Age

## Pobedonostsev, Konstantin (1827–1907)

Konstantin Pavlovich Pobedonostsev was born into an intelligentsia family of clerical–petty bureaucratic origins in Moscow. He was educated in the imperial School of Jurisprudence in St. Petersburg and embarked on a long career of state service in 1846. He served as an official in the Russian Senate, the supreme legal institution of the empire, and as a lecturer in law at Moscow University. He moved to St. Petersburg and served as tutor to the heir to the throne until the heir died in 1865, and then he tutored the future Emperor Alexander III. Pobedonostsev played an active role in the design of the reforms that transformed the Russian legal system in 1864. He was appointed a senator in 1868, and in 1880, he was made the director general of the Holy Synod, the bureaucratic governing body of the Russian Orthodox Church, a post he held until his forced retirement in 1905.

Pobedonostsev had a strong political influence on Emperor Alexander III and, to a lesser extent, on his son and successor, Nicholas II. This was of crucial importance because Pobedonostsev became increasingly conservative in the later years of the "Era of the Great Reforms." He was especially dismissive of popular democracy and constitutional government, which he famously branded as "the great lie of our time."

The high point of Pobedonostsev's influence came in the crisis period that followed the assassination of Emperor Alexander II in 1881. The Council of Ministers urged the new tsar to confirm an action that Alexander II had taken in the last hours of his life—a decision to create an elective, consultative assembly. Pobedonostsev was the lone dissenting voice, but he persuaded the new emperor to discard this quasi-constitutional experiment and safeguard his full autocratic powers. This decision launched the "Era of the Counter-Reforms."

The secondary literature has consistently depicted Pobedonostsev as a leading antisemite and a proponent of an aggressive campaign to convert Russian Jews to Christianity. Branded the "Grand Inquisitor of the Russian Orthodox Church," he is alleged to have said that the solution to the Jewish Question in Russia would come about when "a third [of Russia's Jews] will be converted, a third will emigrate, and a third will die of hunger."

In fact, Pobedonostsev was not a doctrinaire antisemite, although he came to see Jews as a symbol of change—which he detested—and used the pejorative word *Yid* as a synonym for *liberal* or *progressive*. In large part, he borrowed these attitudes from his social milieu, which included writers such as Fyodor Dostoevsky and the journalist Ivan Aksakov. They, in turn, acquired these sentiments from non-Russian sources, largely German antisemites. Pobedonostsev never encouraged the wholesale conversion of Russian Jews. Indeed, he considered many Jewish converts to be unprincipled renegades. He was more concerned with possible religious influences of Judaism on the peasant masses, fearful that it would promote religious sectarianism. Between 1881 and 1882, Pobedonostsev ordered Orthodox priests to deliver sermons denouncing the widespread pogroms.

—*John D. Klier*

**See also** Dostoevsky, Fyodor; Pogroms; Russia, Imperial; Russian Orthodox Church
**References**
Byrnes, Robert F. *Pobedonostsev: His Life and Thought* (Bloomington: Indiana University Press, 1968).
Klier, John D. *Imperial Russia's Jewish Question, 1855–1881* (Cambridge: Cambridge University Press, 1995).

## Pogroms (Russian, 1881)

The Russian term *pogrom,* etymologically related to words meaning "break," "smash," and "plunder," came into common usage in Russia and abroad as a result of the approximately 250 anti-Jewish incidents in the southwestern provinces of the Russian Empire from the spring of 1881 to the summer of 1882. The term replaced the usual bureaucratic terminology referring to "disorders" (*bezporiadki*) or "clashes between the Jews and the Christian population." In the early twentieth century, the meaning of the term expanded to include violence directed by right-wing groups, the so-called Black Hundreds, against Jews and other national minorities and liberal political elements. In the Soviet Union, the term became synonymous with *counterrevolutionary,* losing the anti-Jewish associations that it continues to retain in the West.

The 1881–1882 pogroms, which began with an outbreak in Elisavetgrad (Kirovgrad) on April 15, 1881, according to the Julian Calendar, were extremely diverse. They ranged from major urban riots (Elisavetgrad, Kiev, Smela, Balta), which were characterized by extremes of looting and destruction of property, to minor tavern brawls and petty vandalism. The military was often obliged to assist the suppression of the urban riots. Approximately twenty-five Jews were beaten to death in the course of the pogroms; about the same number of perpetrators, the *pogromchiki,* were killed by the armed forces. There were occasional rapes, but they were not the mass phenomenon of contemporary legend. The pogroms traveled in waves along communication arteries, such as railroads and rivers, spreading out from urban epicenters to peasant villages in the surrounding countryside. Pogrom mobs carefully differentiated their targets: only Jews and their property were victimized.

The pogroms generated a vigorous national debate in the Russian Empire. The government initially attributed the outbreak to the same revolutionaries who, a month earlier, had assassinated Emperor Alexander II. The conservative press and much of the liberal press attributed the violence to a popular protest against Jewish exploitation. Under Minister of Internal Affairs N. P. Ignatiev, the government eventually accepted this interpretation, which was reinforced by the reports of provincial commissions that were created by Ignatiev in 1881 to investigate Jewish–non-Jewish relations.

Some liberal publications and virtually all of the Jewish press attributed the violence to the restricted legal position of the Jews, especially in the Pale of Settlement. In the eyes of the unsophisticated peasant masses and the urban rabble, they argued, restrictions placed Jews outside the protection of the law and made them an inviting target for "the lovers of other people's property," as many official reports of the time referred to the rioters. Some members of the revolutionary movement welcomed the pogroms as a starting point for a wider social revolution. A manifesto, later repudiated by the revolutionary Narodnaia Volia (People's Will Party) as a whole, praised the masses for attacking the Jews, while urging them to move against other class enemies.

Ignatiev's acceptance of the "exploitation" theory of the pogroms induced a dramatic reversal of Russia's Jewish policies, which previously had involved a variety of strategies aimed at acculturation, integration, and assimilation. Ignatiev's so-called May Laws of 1882 were designed to segregate Jews by removing them from peasant villages and to reduce their economic power within the Pale.

Historians have seen the events of 1881 and 1882 as a major turning point in modern Jewish history in eastern Europe, as well. Jewish intellectuals, they affirm, moved away from liberal, integrationist ideals toward a modern Jewish politics characterized by political activism and a higher ethnic consciousness. This thrust was expressed in the proto-Zionist movement Hoveve Tsion (the Lovers of Zion) and the emergence of Jewish forms of socialism, especially the wing of the Social Democratic movement known as the Jewish Workers' Bund. Nonetheless, some Jewish liberals remained committed to reform rather than emigration or revolution.

The pogroms prompted a surge of Jewish emigration from eastern Europe and a debate as to whether the preferred destination should be Palestine or the United States. Approximately 30,000 refugees left the empire in the immediate aftermath of the violence. Despite the dramatic symbolism of the pogroms, however, after 1882 the absence of economic opportunities for a pauperized Jewish population remained the chief "push factor" promoting the extensive emigration.

The 1881–1882 pogroms gave rise to a mythology that endured well into the twentieth century. It was claimed that the outbursts were organized, possibly by a group of loyalist court officials known as the Holy Brotherhood or by the Jews' mercantile rivals in Moscow. Historians such as S. M. Dubnow asserted that the pogroms broke out simultaneously in far-flung areas and that they followed a common, three-day pattern. Provincial officials were accused of tolerating the pogroms, if not actually fomenting them, and there was allegedly a sustained press campaign that prepared the climate for the pogroms by accusing the Jews of having killed Tsar Alexander II.

The opening of the tsarist-era archives, briefly after 1917 and more widely after 1991, has led contemporary scholars to challenge the main elements of this myth. There is no archival evidence of advanced planning of the pogroms, nor any evidence that they were welcomed or tolerated by the national or local authorities. A thorough reading of the press failed to discover a press campaign blaming the Jews for regicide. There were, however, widespread rumors among the population that this was the reason the ruler had issued a decree to "beat the Jews." The origin and nature of these rumors remain unclear.

The pogroms of 1881 and 1882 were an exception to the generally peaceful relations between Jews and their Christian neighbors in eastern Europe. They were also an indication of growing interethnic tensions in the Russian Empire. In particular, they created a dangerous precedent and a model for future pogroms, which proved to be much more violent and deadly.

—*John D. Klier*

**See also** Black Hundreds; Kishinev Pogrom; May Laws; Pale of Settlement; Russia, Imperial; Socialists on Antisemitism; Zionism

**References**

Aronson, I. Michael. *Troubled Waters: The Origins of the 1881 Anti-Jewish Pogroms in Russia* (Pittsburgh, PA: University of Pittsburgh Press, 1990).

Dubnow, S. M. *History of the Jews in Russia and Poland.* 3 vols. (Philadelphia: Jewish Publication Society of America, 1916–1920).

Frankel, Jonathan. *Prophecy and Politics: Socialism, Nationalism, and the Russian Jews, 1862–1917* (Cambridge: Cambridge University Press, 1981).

Haberer, Erich E. *Jews and Revolution in Nineteenth-Century Russia* (Cambridge: Cambridge University Press, 1995).

Klier, John D., and Shlomo Lambroza, eds. *Pogroms: Anti-Jewish Violence in Modern Russian History* (Cambridge: Cambridge University Press, 1992).

Rogger, Hans. *Jewish Policies and Right-Wing Politics in Imperial Russia* (London: Macmillan, 1986).

# Poland (1918–1989)

## 1918–1939

Divided between Germany, Austria, and Russia for 123 years, Poland regained its independence on November 11, 1918. Much of eastern Europe was then in the grip of revolution, war, and civil war. Caught in the middle of numerous ethnic conflicts, Jews were the victims of thousands of pogroms, dozens of them in Poland. The American observer Henry Morgenthau estimated that the eight largest pogroms on Polish soil between 1918 and 1919 cost 230 lives.

Ethnic Poles made up 70 percent of the population of the reborn state, together with Ukrainians (14 percent), Jews (10 percent), Germans, Lithuanians, and Belorussians. The Jews, distinct not only by religion but also by culture and language (85 percent spoke Yiddish), were considered a national rather than a religious minority; numbering 3.3 million by 1939, they formed by far the largest Jewish community in Europe. Jews made up 30 percent of the population of Warsaw and some other large cities; in the smaller towns, or shtetls, of eastern Poland, they were often the majority.

Nearly all Polish political parties (the Jews had their own) agreed that the Jews were, in some sense, a problem for Poland, but they differed on the diagnosis and cure. For the parties of the Left, the problem was the Jews' "separateness," and the solution was assimilation on the Western pattern. The right-wing parties regarded the Jews as unas-

A demonstration against repression and antisemitism by Polish Jews at Lodz, Poland (1933). (Mary Evans Picture Library)

similable and a threat; they promoted discrimination and emigration, economic boycotts, and sometimes violence. Only a small group of liberals were prepared to accept Jews as they were, but this group included Józef Piłsudski, the dominant political figure of the interwar period. After taking power in a coup in 1926, Piłsudski formed a new political party that was ideologically amorphous and based on loyalty to the leader himself; it was nicknamed "the Sanacja" (sanitation) for its promise to clean up political life. The Sanacja stayed in power until the outbreak of war, but after Piłsudski's death in 1935, the more right-wing elements gained control of it. Although the Sanacja clamped down on the wave of anti-Jewish violence that broke out between 1935 and 1937, it allowed schools and universities to introduce anti-Jewish quotas (the *numerus clausus*), endorsed the right-wing National Party's eco-

nomic boycott of the Jews, nationalized some industries in which Jews were predominant, and limited ritual slaughter. In the international sphere, it proposed that Madagascar be made a Polish colony for the purpose of resettling Jews. When war broke out in 1939, the Polish government was actively considering its own version of the Nuremberg Laws.

Despite antisemitism and widespread poverty, the Jewish community in interwar Poland was the most vibrant and one of the freest in Europe. A wide range of Jewish political parties operated, and although they had little success nationally, they wielded some influence at the local level. An alliance of the Jewish Workers' Bund and the Polish Socialist Party was the dominant force in city politics in Warsaw and Lodz; Krakow elected a Jewish mayor. There was a thriving literature in Yiddish that included the work of the future

Nobel Prize winner Isaac Bashevis Singer, and many daily newspapers in Yiddish and Polish catered to a Jewish readership. A Yiddish-language theater and movie industry flourished, in which many leading figures in Hollywood and vaudeville got their start. There were Jewish sports and social clubs, as well as a scientific institute, the Jewish Research Institute (YIVO), in Vilna. A majority of Poland's doctors and lawyers were Jewish, and Jews predominated in many spheres of business. Though it was difficult for Jews to advance in the military and the civil service, Poland did have one Jewish general, Benjamin Mond. Julian Tuwim and Antoni Słonimski, both Jewish, are considered two of the finest poets in the Polish language; pianist Artur Rubinstein and violinists Bronisław Huberman and Henryk Szeryng enhanced Poland's reputation abroad.

## 1939–1945

Nazi Germany invaded Poland on September 1, 1939, launching World War II. On September 17, Soviet forces also invaded, under a secret agreement with the Nazis, and the two countries divided Poland between them. Eastern Poland fell under Soviet rule, western and northern areas were annexed to the German Reich, and central Poland became the German-administered General Gouvernement. Over 300,000 Jews fled from the German to the Soviet zone between 1939 and 1940 (and 50,000 went in the opposite direction). In the Soviet zone, all non-Communist political parties and social organizations were suppressed, and some 800,000 Poles and 200,000 Jews were deported to Siberia. In the German areas, Poles were rounded up for forced labor in Germany, killed in mass executions, and imprisoned in concentration camps. The camps at Auschwitz and Lublin (Majdanek) were first established in 1940 to house Polish prisoners. Eventually, more than 1.5 million Poles died under German occupation. Jews, in the meantime, were forced into ghettos, where starvation rations and overcrowding caused mass deaths from famine and disease. Jews were also forced to work in labor camps, where harsh conditions resulted in a high mortality rate. The Nazi-created Jewish Councils and the Jewish underground tried to alleviate the conditions in the ghettos,

but their resources were very limited. Half a million Polish Jews died in the ghettos and labor camps, but in some ghettos, underground cottage industries and large-scale smuggling brought in enough food and income, illegally, to keep the majority alive for a time.

In June 1941, Germany invaded the Soviet Union, and the Soviet-occupied areas of Poland came under Nazi control. Mobile killing units (Einsatzgruppen) operated behind the front lines, massacring Jewish men and then women and children as well. The Nazis also succeeded in inducing the local population to carry out pogroms in a few towns in Poland and elsewhere. Jews who survived the massacres and pogroms were forced into ghettos.

Experimental gassing of Soviet prisoners was carried out at Auschwitz in the fall of 1941, and the methodical killing of Jews began at the newly built extermination camp in Chelmno in December. Starting in the spring of 1942, new extermination camps at Bełzec, Sobibor, and Treblinka began implementing Project Reinhard, the complete destruction of the Jews of the General Gouvernement. Small gas chambers also went into operation at Auschwitz; large installations were added a year later. It is estimated that 150,000 Jews were killed at Chelmno, 1.1 million at Auschwitz, 1.6 million in the Project Reinhard camps, and 60,000 at Majdanek.

By the fall of 1943, the great majority of Polish Jews were dead. The Project Reinhard camps were razed; Jews remaining in labor camps in the Lublin district were massacred in the "Harvest Festival" action on November 3, 1943, and the last of the large ghettos in Lodz was liquidated in July 1944.

The Jews were kept in the dark, and the liquidation of the ghettos took place too quickly to give them much chance to respond, but when they could, they hid inside the ghettos, fled from them, or organized armed resistance. The Warsaw Ghetto uprising (in April and May 1943) is the best-known example of armed resistance, but there were dozens of smaller episodes, including prisoner revolts at Treblinka, Sobibor, and Auschwitz. Thousands of Jews also took to the woods and fought as partisans, and about 1,000 Jews fought in the Polish uprising in Warsaw in 1944.

About 350,000 Polish Jews survived the war, the great majority in the Soviet Union. Of those who had lived under German occupation, 40,000 survived in concentration and labor camps, 46,000 in hiding or passing as Aryans, and 13,000 as partisans or in "family camps." About 20,000 ended the war in western Europe and never returned to Poland. Thousands of Jewish children, adopted by Polish families, learned of their Jewish roots only years later, if ever.

Those who returned frequently encountered hostility. More than a thousand Jews were murdered in property disputes or by right-wing diehards who blamed them for bringing communism to Poland. Several pogroms broke out, most notoriously in Kielce on July 4, 1946, when as many as forty-two Jews were killed. When some of the perpetrators were tried and hanged by the Communist authorities, protest strikes and demonstrations took place all over Poland.

The Communists tried to reestablish Jewish life, founding Yiddish-speaking Jewish communities in territory gained from Germany, but the postwar violence induced most Jews to leave the country. Zionists organized the *bricha* (escape) movement, through which many Jews reached Palestine and (after 1948) Israel. By 1950, only 45,000 Jews remained in Poland, many of them active Communists.

De-Stalinization in 1956 brought the new, more nationalist regime of Władysław Gomułka to power and with it a purge of party apparatchiks, especially Jews, who became scapegoats for the "mistakes" of the Stalinist era. Thousands of Jews emigrated, but several thousand more returned to Poland in 1957 in the final wave of postwar repatriations from the Soviet Union.

Most of the remaining Jews emigrated as a result of the anti-Zionist campaign of 1968, when prodemocracy demonstrations in March, in which some Jews were prominent, led to a crackdown and a renewed search for scapegoats. The Warsaw Pact's alliance with the Arab states, recently defeated in the Six Days' War, provided the excuse for a campaign to root out "Zionist spies." Jews were forced out of government posts and pressured to emigrate; after the campaign, only 4,000 Jews remained in Poland, and Polish-Jewish relations became a forbidden subject.

The rise of the Solidarity movement in 1981 revived discussion of Polish-Jewish issues. Claude Lanzmann's 1984 documentary *Shoah*, which painted an unflattering picture of Poles, was shown on Polish television, and a vigorous debate followed. Subsequent conferences in Oxford (in 1984), at Brandeis University (in 1986), and in Jerusalem (in 1988) reestablished dialogue between Polish and Jewish academics, leading to the establishment of Jewish studies institutes at several Polish universities and a modest revival of Jewish life in Poland. In the final years of the Communist era, a dispute arose between Jews abroad and the Catholic Church over the construction of a convent 2 miles from the ruins of the gas chambers at Auschwitz. After long delays, the convent was finally moved in 1993.

—*Steven Paulsson*

**See also** Anti-Zionism; Anti-Zionism in the USSR; Boycott of 1912; Dmowski, Roman; Einsatzgruppen; Ghetto Benches; Holocaust; Jedwabne; Jewish Question; Judeo-Bolshevism; Kielce Pogrom; Kosher Slaughtering; National Democrats; Nuremberg Laws; Poland since 1989; Purge of 1968; Stalinization of Eastern Europe; Zionism

**References**

Davies, Norman. *God's Playground: A History of Poland.* Vol. 2, *1795 to the Present* (Oxford: Clarendon Press, 1981).

Gutman, Israel, and Shmuel Krakowski. *Unequal Victims: Poles and Jews during World War Two* (New York: Holocaust Library, 1986).

Leslie, R. F., ed. *The History of Poland since 1863* (Cambridge: Cambridge University Press, 1983).

Marcus, Joseph. *Social and Political History of the Jews in Poland, 1919–1939* (Berlin: Mouton, 1983).

Mendelsohn, Ezra. *The Jews of East Central Europe between the Two World Wars* (Bloomington: Indiana University Press, 1987).

Steinlauf, Michael C. *Bondage to the Dead: Poland and the Memory of the Holocaust* (Syracuse, NY: Syracuse University Press, 1997).

Tomaszewski, Jerzy, ed. *Najnowsze dzieje Żydów w Polsce w zarysie, do 1950 roku* (Sketch of the Modern History of the Jews in Poland, to 1950) (Warsaw: Wydawnictwo Naukowe PWN, 1993).

## Poland since 1989

Since the end of communism in Poland in 1989, a full range of tendencies has surfaced in political groupings, including parties modeled on the National Party (with its antisemitic ideology), supported by some elements in the Polish Catholic Church. Most notable is the openly antisemitic radio station Radio Maryja, headed by Father Tadeusz Rydzyk, which is opposed by the Catholic hierarchy but claims 4 million listeners. Most post-1989 governments have been liberal in their outlook, however, and many Polish intellectuals have faced up to the challenges of the past. Exemplary scholarly studies of the Kielce pogrom, the "anti-Zionist" campaign, and other issues have appeared, and Polish scholars now make a full contribution to Holocaust journals and conferences. Jewish concerns about the representation of the Holocaust at the Auschwitz State Museum and other issues connected with the camp site led to the appointment of a joint Polish-Jewish advisory committee, which, working with the government and museum staff, has resolved most of the problems. Warsaw has a long-established Jewish theater, which performs plays in Yiddish; there is a chief rabbi once again, a functioning synagogue in Warsaw, and a synagogue and yeshiva in Krakow, where a festival of Jewish culture is an annual event. The Museum of Jewish History is being built in Warsaw with government support. The Ronald Lauder Foundation helps to maintain Jewish memorial sites in Poland and to promote the revival of Jewish life.

Troubling issues continue to arise, however. The "battle of the crosses" at Auschwitz started with a well-meaning attempt by Polish high school students to memorialize the camp's victims by planting both crosses and Stars of David at the "field of ashes" near the crematoria. These were removed after Jewish protests. But in 1998, requests to remove a giant cross from a site near the camp prompted extremists to erect hundreds of crosses at the site. The government intervened, fining the organizer for spreading hatred and moving the additional crosses to a nearby monastery, but the main cross remains. Officials explain that it marks the spot where Pope John Paul II said mass on his 1979 visit, a highly significant moment in Polish history, and that it overlooks a part of the camp that was mainly occupied by Polish prisoners.

The publication in 2000 of Jan Tomasz Gross's book *Neighbors*, documenting the 1941 pogrom that destroyed the Jews of the small town of Jedwabne, sparked both an official inquiry, which substantially confirmed Gross's findings, and an unprecedented public debate in all Polish media. President Aleksander Kwaśniewski offered a symbolic apology on behalf of his nation, and the primate, Cardinal Józef Glemp, said a solemn commemorative mass. Glemp's remarks acknowledging the participation of Catholics in the massacre were highly qualified, however, and no church representative attended the sixtieth-anniversary ceremony in the town. The parish priest led the townspeople in a boycott of the ceremony, and the new plaque unveiled on that occasion does not mention the perpetrators.

The issue of property restitution is still unresolved. A law providing for the restitution of communal property was passed in 1997, but individual claims pursued through normal legal channels have been delayed or obstructed. A law that would have provided individual restitution or compensation only for current Polish citizens and residents, effectively excluding Jewish claimants, was passed by the Sejm (parliament) in 2001 but vetoed by Kwaśniewski after international protests.

—*Steven Paulsson*

**See also** Jedwabne; Judeo-Bolshevism; Kielce Pogrom; National Democrats; Poland; Stalinization of Eastern Europe

**References**

Steinlauf, Michael C. *Bondage to the Dead: Poland and the Memory of the Holocaust* (Syracuse, NY: Syracuse University Press, 1997).

## Polná Ritual Murder (1899)

In April 1899, Leopold Hilsner (1876–1928), a lowly Jewish shoemaker, was falsely accused of the "ritual murder" of the nineteen-year-old Christian girl Anežka Hrůzová in Polná, Czech Republic (then part of the Austro-Hungarian Empire). The "blood libel" case created a political sensation that was sometimes compared to the contemporaneous Dreyfus Affair. However, unlike Alfred Dreyfus, who was exonerated after a twelve-year investigation and reinstated in the army, Hilsner was never vindicated.

At his first trial in September 1899, Hilsner was convicted on indirect testimony and despite a lack of convincing forensic evidence. He was sentenced to death, a verdict immediately confirmed by the Supreme Court in Vienna. Hilsner's attorney, Zdenko Auředníček, and sociology professor Tomàš Garrigue Masaryk (eventually the first president of Czechoslovakia) succeeded in a call for a legal review. In October 1900, Hilsner was brought before a second court on the same charge and was convicted again. This time, an additional murder dating from 1898 was attributed to him, with the same key witnesses as in the first trial. This verdict, too, was swiftly confirmed by the Viennese Supreme Court. There were many protests from abroad, especially from France and Germany, by legal experts, journalists, and moral authorities. But within the Habsburg monarchy, only a few protested, notably Masaryk and Rabbi Joseph Samuel Bloch. Bowing to foreign opinion rather than domestic pressure, Kaiser Franz Joseph commuted the death sentence to life imprisonment in 1901. Thereafter, all subsequent pleas for rehabilitation were rejected.

The aftermath of the case is important. Not until March 1918, in a general amnesty granted to all hardened criminals, was Leopold Hilsner given his freedom. Later that year, he was the protagonist in a film called *Der Fall Hilsner* (The Hilsner Case). The film was censored immediately by the police, and its release in altered form was delayed for a year; once released, it was only shown in the Jewish district of Vienna. In 1922, earning his living as a traveling salesman, Hilsner changed his name to Heller in an attempt to escape his continuing notoriety. But even after his death in 1928, the case continued to be exploited. Adolf Hitler was familiar with it, and Julius Streicher made Polná part of a special ritual murder edition of *Der Stürmer,* an act he was later called to account for at the Nuremberg Trials of Major War Criminals.

During his life and after his death, Hilsner met with very little sympathy from Jews and non-Jews alike. The Prague Jewish community refused to help him find work after his release from prison, and the Jewish luminaries of his day remained silent about the injustices he had suffered. In the year 2000, the private initiatives to commemorate Hilsner and renovate his grave in Vienna brought only an indifferent response from the Austrian authorities. Even though the Czech minister of justice overturned the two verdicts of the lower courts regarding Hilsner's guilt (in 1998), the decisions of the Supreme Court in Vienna remain in force, and all pleas for their annulment in past years have been rejected.

—*Petr Vašíček*

**See also** Austria; Bloch, Joseph Samuel; Dreyfus Affair; Ritual Murder (Modern); Streicher, Julius; *Stürmer, Der*

**References**

Kieval, Hillel J. *Languages of Community: The Jewish Experience in the Czech Lands* (Berkeley: University of California Press, 2000).

Morini, Mario Umberto, and Petr Vašíček. "Hilsner—Masaryk Memorandum of 7 March, 2001 to the Presidents of Austria and the Czech Republic." Available at http://sicsa.huji.ac.il/hilsner.html or www.svu2000.org/issues/hilsner.htm. Accessed on November 15, 2002.

## Populist Movement

The history of the United States has had many populist movements. *The* Populist movement, however, was a short-lived rebellion of farmers and their allies during the 1890s. Officially organized in the People's Party, the Populists sought to deepen economic and political democracy by contesting corporate control of transportation, money, land, and the ballot box. They won several seats in Congress and also gained control over some state legislatures and governorships. The Populists' main strength was in the Great Plains and the South. Yet their national visibility, along with their radicalism, made them the most powerful third-party movement in the history of the United States.

The extent and nature of Populist antisemitism is one of the most contentious intellectual issues for those seeking to understand Jew-hating in the United States. Indeed, over the course of the last eleven decades, the *interpreta-*

*tion* of Populist antisemitism has become a historically and culturally important subject in its own right. Up through the New Deal, most scholars treated the Populists as staunchly democratic, part of the country's tolerant, progressive tradition of reform. With the ascendance of Joseph McCarthy in the 1950s, however, many intellectuals self-consciously turned against the masses who seemed to have inspired and certainly supported the bombastic demagogue.

The result was a full-scale rethinking of the Populists. Prominent historians from the Northeast, such as Harvard University's Oscar Handlin and Columbia University's Richard Hofstadter, wrote compelling indictments of the Populists' less attractive "soft side." In 1955, Hofstadter said, "The Greenback-Populist tradition activated most of what we have of modern popular anti-Semitism in the United States" (Hofstadter 1955, 80). Others went further, accusing the Populists not just of casual verbal antisemitism, as had Hofstadter, but also of laying the foundation for a homegrown tradition of American fascism.

With the restoration of confidence in the American radical tradition in the 1960s and 1970s, scholars reexamined populism and gave it a nearly clean bill of health. From the late 1950s, John Higham, Norman Pollack, Walter Nugent, and Lawrence Goodwyn began to recapture "the Tolerant Populists," which became the title of a book by Nugent. Pollack, following in the footsteps of the prestigious southern historian C. Vann Woodward, was particularly emphatic that the attack on the Populists went beyond what the archives supposedly revealed about the "myth of populist antisemitism" and was, in fact, part of a larger cultural battle between defenders and critics of popular democracy.

At the start of the twenty-first century, the pendulum has swung once again, and it is now possible to look at the issue of Populists and antisemitism in a less heated environment. The historical record is mixed and confused. Many Populists did engage in a search for the "Shylock" bankers who had come to control the global economy. Several prominent Populist authors blamed the House of Rothschild for agrarian misery, and still others told of scheming, devious, inbred commercial Jews. The fiery orator Mary E. Lease labeled President Grover Cleveland "the agent of Jewish bankers and British gold" (Hofstadter 1955, 79).

Such antisemitism—as significant as it was—seems pale in comparison to the upper-class Judeophobia of the national elite. The Populists never made antisemitism part of their formal political program. Ignatius Donnelly, one of the most prominent Populists, represents the ambivalence of the movement on the Jewish Question. He condemned the historical persecution of the Jews while deploying classic stereotypes in his popular writings.

In the end, the Populist moment of the 1890s bequeathed to its various successors a suspicion of elites and a taste for conspiratorial explanations that have, at times, nurtured antisemitism. Yet to point to the Populists as the exclusive or even a primary source of modern American antisemitism is itself an exercise in scapegoating.

—*Robert D. Johnston*

**See also** Agrarian League; Banker, Jewish; Ford, Henry; Norris, Frank; Rothschilds; Shylock; United States; Watson, Tom; Wharton, Edith

**References**

Handlin, Oscar. "How U.S. Anti-Semitism Really Began: Its Grass-Roots Source in the '90s," *Commentary* 11 (June 1951): 541–548.

Higham, John. "Anti-Semitism in the Gilded Age: A Reinterpretation," *Mississippi Valley Historical Review* 43 (March 1957): 559–578.

Hofstadter, Richard. *The Age of Reform: From Bryan to F.D.R.* (New York: Knopf, 1955).

Nugent, Walter T. K. *The Tolerant Populists: Kansas Populism and Nativism* (Chicago: University of Chicago Press, 1963).

Pollack, Norman. "The Myth of Populist Anti-Semitism," *American Historical Review* 68 (October 1962): 76–80.

## Pork

Although the understanding of Judaism in Christian popular culture is often rudimentary, it is evident that one of the few widely known facts about Jews is their religious avoidance of pork. Dietary prohibition of the flesh of the swine (Lev. 11:7–8) and distant recollection of the story of Eleazar (2 Macc. 6), who endures a terrible death by torture rather than submit to eating pork, lie behind the perverse antisemitic linkage of Jews

Eleazar Refuses Pork. A leading citizen of Jerusalem, Eleazar refuses to eat foods proscribed by the Jews' dietary laws and is killed by order of the king Antiochus IV. (Mary Evans Picture Library)

and pigs. At its most terrifying, the linkage manifests itself through the image of the *Judensau* (Jew's pig), but folkloric tales, proverbs, and antisemitic jests abound that play on the same connection (See illustration in Judensau). "Invite not a Jew to pig or pork," instructs a seventeenth-century English proverb, advice that is reiterated by the antiquary John Aubrey (1626–1697), who claims that "'twas always the Fashion for a [Christian] man to have a Gammon of Bacon, to shew himself to be no Jew" (*Remaines of Gentilisme and Judaisme,* ca. 1686). Bizarrely, Jews are often associated with that which they most abhor. In a tale that can also be traced back at least to the same period, the daughter of a convert to Judaism is born pig-faced, but when she eventually reverts to Christianity, her visage transforms to that of a beautiful young woman.

Representation of the Jews as porcine can be found on European cartoons and postcards from as recently as the first half of the twentieth century. Through several states in eighteenth-century Germany, road tolls were levied at turnpikes for Jews and pigs. Another tale that may have its origins as far back as the fifteenth century relates that after the death from natural causes of a Jewish merchant living abroad, his brother arranges for his body to be cut up and pickled before being shipped home for burial in a barrel marked "pork." En route, the ship is becalmed, and the hungry sailors pry open the barrel to consume its contents. An early nineteenth-century English caricature, *Pickled Pork* (1802; Rubens, no. 913, *The Jew as Other,* no. 45), captures this fictitious incident, which also survives as a contemporary street ballad (Ashton 1968, 170–172). Recollecting the treatment of Eleazar, an ultimate insult was to force-feed an observant Jew with pork, though conjoined with this was the conviction that once a Jew tasted swine's meat, he would

*Pickled Pork.* This early nineteenth-century English caricature tells the grisly tale of a man who arranges for his brother's body to be cut up and pickled before being shipped home for burial in a barrel marked "pork." (Jewish Theological Seminary)

recognize the error of his ways and become a good Christian. An English print of 1764, *The Conversion of Nathan* (Rubens, no. 866, *The Jew as Other*, no. 46), captures such an episode.

Although the Jews' taboo of pork was well known, it was often put out that their overt detestation concealed a secret desire for the forbidden meat. In Thomas Bridges's novel *The Adventures of a Bank-Note* (1770–1771), we witness "the ugliest dog of a Jew [falling on] the pork with such eagerness, that I expected he would not so much as leave the shank unswallowed." Charles Dickens probably had this notion in mind in *Oliver Twist* (1837–1839) when he depicted Fagin employing a devilish toasting-fork to turn the saveloys (pork sausages) that he is preparing to eat. Finally, in one of the most overtly antisemitic representations of the Jews' supposed hankering after pork, *Humors of Houndsditch* (1813; B.M. Cat, no. 12146; Rubens, no. 940), the caricaturist Thomas Rowlandson recaptured the grossness of the Judensau in depicting a plump Jewish woman gratifying her carnal impulses by embracing a young suckling pig.

In all these instances, the use of pork is intended to iterate fundamental differences between Christian and Jew. In modern Jewish humor, as Christie Davies reminds us, the prohibition is sometimes employed as a comic reminder of the bounds of one's faith in an age of religious laxity.

—*Frank Felsenstein*

*The Conversion of Nathan,* 1764. Although the Jews' taboo of pork was well known, it was often put out that their overt detestation concealed a secret desire for the forbidden meat. (Jewish Theological Seminary)

***See also*** Caricature, Anti-Jewish (Early); Caricature, Anti-Jewish (Modern); Dickens, Charles; Iconography, Christian; *Judensau;* Rowlandson, Thomas

**References**

Ashton, John. *Modern Street Ballads* (New York: Benjamin Blom, 1968; orig. 1888).

Davies, Christie. *Ethnic Humor around the World: A Comparative Analysis* (Bloomington: Indiana University Press, 1990).

Fabre-Vassas, Claudine. *The Singular Beast: Jews, Christians & the Pig* (New York: Columbia University Press, 1997).

Felsenstein, Frank. *Anti-Semitic Stereotypes: A Paradigm of Otherness in English Popular Culture, 1660–1830* (Baltimore, MD: Johns Hopkins University Press, 1995).

Felsenstein, Frank. *The Jew as Other: A Century of English Caricature, 1730–1830.* Exhibition catalog. (New York: Library of the Jewish Theological Seminary of America, 1995).

## Pound, Ezra (1885–1972)

After graduate study in Romance languages at the University of Pennsylvania, the American poet Ezra Pound moved to Europe in 1908. In London before and during World War I, he made himself the mentor of a group of writers who would soon become famous: teaching them, finding money for them, and badgering editors into publishing them. Just one of his accomplishments during that period was the shaping of an unsorted pile of verse fragments into the most influential poem in twentieth-century literature—T. S. Eliot's *The Waste Land.* To look at the facsimile of this manuscript is to understand that Pound was to literature what Sergei Diaghilev was to dance and music: the impresario who changed everything. It is impossible to overstate Pound's historical importance.

But World War I was cataclysmic for him. Though he did not serve himself, his closest friend, a brilliant young sculptor, was killed in the war, and the senseless loss left him searching his mind for an explanation. During the course of two more moves—to Paris in 1921 and then to Rapallo, Italy, near Venice, in 1924—he began writing what he called "a poem including history," *The Cantos.*

That work, which would occupy the rest of his life, is a vast lyric on the scale of an epic; it is longer than *Paradise Lost* and *Paradise Regained* together, organized not as a linear narrative but as an anthology of what Pound called "luminous moments," and written not just in English but in French and Italian, with passages in other languages ranging from Greek to Chinese to Egyptian hieroglyphics. Beginning with an episode translated from *The Odyssey* into a modern English version of Anglo-Saxon alliterative verse, *The Cantos* in its polyphonic language tells what Pound hoped would be the story of humanity itself—including humanity in its economic aspect. The son of an official in the Philadelphia mint, Pound had always been interested by the concepts of money and exchange. Now living in newly Fascist Italy, he sang to the world that it might heal itself of poverty, war, and debasement by casting off Jewish economics and the Jewish God. In his spare time, he also recovered the forgotten music of Antonio Vivaldi from the Venetian archives.

During World War II, without renouncing his U.S. citizenship, Pound made propaganda broadcasts to England and the United States from Fascist Rome. This activity, of course, constituted the capital offense of treason, for he was giving aid and comfort to the enemy while the United States was at war. Arrested by U.S. forces at the war's end, he was flown to Washington, found unfit to stand trial by reason of insanity, and committed to a mental hospital. There, for the next thirteen years, he added to *The Cantos;* translated Sophocles and Confucius; sent forth a stream of letters; and held court for visiting poets, scholars, students, Jew-haters, and eccentrics with "ideas about money." Released in 1958 at the urging of a group of the most distinguished writers in the United States, he returned to Italy, giving the Fascist salute as he stepped off the ship. At his death, *The Cantos* remained unfinished.

From the 1930s onward, a number of his fellow poets (notably Basil Bunting, Marianne Moore, and James Laughlin) tried to talk Pound out of his antisemitic obsessions, but on the subject of Jews, Pound was beyond reason. Indeed, hospital records and his recently published letters from the 1940s and 1950s make clear that his antisemitism was a mental illness. But even at its most acute, the antisemitism was nourished by the same culture that had brought forth Pound's great work of cultural synthesis. In fact, Pound's oeuvre is an exemplary case of the historical groundedness of antisemitism. How, then, are we to read it? The question remains unanswered, and an answer is required. Readers who wish to begin thinking about it may consult the references in the list that follows.

—*Jonathan Morse*

**See also** Eliot, T. S.; English Literature of the Twentieth Century; Mussolini, Benito
**References**
Casillo, Robert. *The Genealogy of Demons: Anti-Semitism, Fascism, and the Myths of Ezra Pound* (Evanston, IL: Northwestern University Press, 1988).
Eliot, T. S. *The Waste Land: A Facsimile and Transcript of the Original Drafts, Including the Annotations of Ezra Pound.* Edited by Valerie Eliot (New York: Harcourt, 1971).
Nadel, Ira, ed. *The Cambridge Companion to Ezra Pound* (Cambridge: Cambridge University Press, 1999).

# Prague Massacre (1389)

The first document mentioning Jews in Prague dates from the tenth century; the first evidence of a Jewish community comes from the end of the eleventh century. Many Jews in the city were murdered, robbed, or forced to convert during the Crusades. Nonetheless, a vibrant and important community developed in the city during the High and Late Middle Ages and in the early modern period, and a number of important scholars resided there.

The general insecurity of Jews throughout Europe in that era was made evident when many Jews in Prague were killed on Easter Sunday and one of the last days of Passover in the year 5149 of the Jewish calendar (April 18, 1389). The immediate cause was a charge of host desecration levied by a priest, who claimed that he and the host had been pelted by rocks thrown by Jews. The Prague events were recorded in various Jewish chronicles and described in a *selihah* (penitential prayer) written by the renowned Prague rabbi and Kabbalist Avigdor Kara (d. 1439):

Great dismay we had to bear,
Countless wounds drew our blood.
Yet no sufferings could tear
From our hearts the trust in God . . .
Yet the worst of our foe's crimes
Occurred in the year 5149,
When heavy fell our Lord's scorn
On Golden Prague, the city of beauty we
    mourn
Towards the end of the holy days
Of Passover blood stained our ways.
Without any reason they drew their knives
And slaughtered our men, children and
    wives.
Our homes, our precious homes, they
    burned,
Together with all our dear ones within.
Helpless and shuddering we learned,
What it is to lose one's home and kin.
Woe to the day that made us to suffer
When wild grew the mob, the drunkard,
    the duffer,
With axes and other weapons of dread
Our brothers' and sisters' blood was shed.

It is estimated that thousands of Jews were murdered during the devastation in Prague. Further, some took their own lives to escape their enemies, the synagogue was burned, holy books and scrolls were desecrated, and gravestones were overturned and destroyed. Despite the pressure for conversion mentioned in Kara's selihah, the few who converted to Christianity were probably older women and small children. Although the pope issued a bull on July 2, 1389, condemning the actions against the Jews and prohibiting forced conversions and efforts to keep them from their observances, the Jewish community of Prague had already been devastated, and Jews living in nearby communities were also being persecuted. The secular authorities, who, according to most accounts, were interested in appropriating Jewish possessions and resources, did little to assist them. In answer to the Jews' complaints, the Holy Roman emperor responded that they deserved the punishment they had received for leaving their homes on Easter, when they were forbidden to do so.

—Dean Phillip Bell

**See also** Crusades; Expulsions, Late Middle Ages; Host Desecration; Middle Ages, Early; Middle Ages, High; Ritual Murder (Medieval)
**References**
David, Abraham, ed. *A Hebrew Chronicle from Prague, c. 1615.* Translated by Leon J. Weinberger with Dena Ordan (Tuscaloosa and London: University of Alabama Press, 1993).
Graetz, Heinrich. *History of the Jews.* Vol. 4 (Philadelphia: Jewish Publication Society of America, 1956).
Maimon, Arye, Mordechai Breuer, and Yacov Guggenheim, eds. *Germania Judaica.* Vol. 3, *1350–1519,* Pt. 2 (Tübingen, Germany: J. C. B. Mohr, 1995).
Volavkova, Hana. *A Story of the Jewish Museum in Prague.* Translated by K. E. Lichtenecker (Prague: Artia, 1968).

## Pranaitis, Justinas (1861–1917)

Justinas Pranaitis was a Roman Catholic priest, Hebraist, and author of antisemitic tracts. Born to peasant parents in Panenupiai, Lithuania, he studied at the seminary of Sejny and the Roman Catholic Theological Academy in St. Petersburg; he graduated in 1887 with a master's degree and remained at the academy to teach Hebrew.

In 1892, he published *The Christian in the Talmud of the Jews, or The Secrets of the Rabbinical Teachings Concerning Christians,* a work based on his dissertation. By means of numerous citations in Hebrew and in Latin translations, he sought to demonstrate that the Talmud obliged Jews to injure Christians in multifarious ways and to work for their elimination. Pranaitis drew on the works of the German anti-Talmudists Jakob Ecker and August Rohling. The book received the imprimatur of the church and was published by the press of the Academy of Sciences. The Viennese priest Joseph Deckert produced a German edition in 1894, supplemented by quotations from the most recent antisemitic literature and reports of ritual murder trials. Pranaitis's work was translated into Lithuanian, Polish, Russian, Italian, Spanish, and English (as *The Talmud Unmasked*). Today, it is still being distributed by extreme right-wing and clerical circles and can be accessed from a number of antisemitic websites.

Pranaitis was active in the life of the Lithuanian community in St. Petersburg, where he gave religious instruction at several cadet schools. His special interest remained the "mysteries" of the Talmud, the Jewish religion, and their alleged close ties to Freemasonry. He published a series of articles in this vein, but they were criticized by contemporaries as slapdash and dilettantish, the work of a pseudoscholarly antisemite. From 1902, he lived in Tashkent, where he served the Roman Catholic community and did missionary work in Turkestan.

Pranaitis achieved dubious fame through his participation in the Kiev trial of Mendel Beilis, who was accused in 1911 of murdering a Christian boy for ritual purposes. In September 1912, as the trial gained worldwide attention, Pranaitis was commissioned as an expert witness for the prosecution because of his supposedly intimate knowledge of Judaism. Two months later, he laid before the court his "documentation," titled "The 'Secret of the Blood' among the Jews" (*Tajna krovi u evreev*). In it, he sought to prove that Jewish religious law prescribed the murder of Christians and the use of their blood for magic and ritual purposes. The Beilis case, he claimed, bore all the characteristic features of a typical ritual murder. At the jury trial in Kiev in October 1913, he appeared in person as an expert on the Talmud, but his competence was challenged by knowledgeable Jewish and Russian theologians, who rejected the charge of ritual murder. The members of the jury, however, even though they acquitted Beilis, confirmed the blood accusation and allowed antisemites to claim at least a partial victory.

Seriously ill, Pranaitis returned to St. Petersburg for medical treatment and died there in January 1917. But according to antisemites, as legend would have it, he was tortured and murdered by Jewish agents of the Soviet secret police (Cheka), following the October Revolution of 1917.

—*Michael Hagemeister*
*Richard S. Levy, translation*

**See also** Beilis Case; Freemasonry; Judeo-Bolshevism; Ritual Murder (Modern); Rohling, August; Russia, Imperial; Talmud; *Talmud Jew, The;* Talmud Trials

**References**

Hagemeister, Michael. "Pranaitis, Justinas (Justinus Bonaventura)." In *Biographisch-Bibliographisches Kirchenlexikon,* vol. 21 (Nordhausen, Germany: Bautz, 2003), 1221–1226. Available at http://www.bautz.de/bbkl/p/pranaitis_j.shtml.

Samuel, Maurice. *Blood Accusation: The Strange History of the Beiliss Case* (Philadelphia: Jewish Publication Society of America, 1966).

Tager, Alexander B. *The Decay of Czarism: The Beiliss Trial* (Philadelphia: Jewish Publication Society of America, 1935).

## Preziosi, Giovanni (1881–1945)

Considered one of the most important Italian antisemitic theorists and propagandists, Giovanni Preziosi directed journals specifically aimed toward creating and winning adherents for a political and cultural struggle against Jews. Thanks to his inspiration, the *Protocols of the Elders of Zion* was introduced and popularized in Italy.

Preziosi was born into a middle-class southern Italian family, studied philosophy, entered the priesthood, and became a strong supporter of conservative Catholicism. In 1911, he left the priesthood, although he retained a strong inclination toward the authoritarian moral positions of the Catholic Church.

He became a journalist and entered the debate about Italian emigration, founding *Vita italiana all'estero* (Italian Life Abroad), a magazine strictly dedicated to emigrants' problems; this, in turn, led to the establishment of his famous monthly *Vita italiana* (Italian Life). In July 1915, he urged Italian entry into World War I, violently criticizing as defeatist and anti-Italian all those who advocated nonintervention. After the humiliating defeat of the Italian army at Caporetto in 1917, he joined the Parliamentary Front for National Defense, one of the several nationalist and antidemocratic movements that would eventually merge into Italian fascism.

A Fascist militant and participant in Benito Mussolini's March on Rome in 1922, Preziosi distinguished himself as an aggressive crusader against socialism. However, it was in the struggle against the Jews that he exercised his greatest influence on Italian history. *Vita italiana* essentially became a journal for the organization and dissemination of antisemitic thought; belligerent racism and bullying rhetoric were its hallmarks. Interestingly, antisemitism had not been part of Preziosi's outlook before the defeat of Italian imperialist aspirations at the end of World War I. From that point on, however, the machinations of the Jews became his habitual explanation for all of Italy's woes, and antisemitism became the keystone of his entire outlook.

From 1919, *Vita italiana* grew increasingly shrill on the subject of the Jews. Their "double loyalties" and their sinister Zionism disqualified the thoroughly integrated and acculturated Jews from truly belonging to the Italian nation, as far as Preziosi was concerned. In this respect, the August 15, 1920, article titled "The Jewish International" can be seen as typical of his thinking; it also exemplified the several components that would come to characterize Fascist antisemitism generally—that is, the insidious and dangerous forces of plutocracy, Bolshevism, Freemasonry, democracy, and Judaism. Together, these evils constituted a gigantic international conspiracy that had denied Italy its fair share of the spoils of World War I and then continued to threaten the well-being of the nation. The many-sided threats to Italy and to all of Western civilization posed by international Jewry and its willing allies or hapless dupes remained constant concerns for Preziosi throughout the rest of his life.

His antisemitism, however, was not nurtured from Italian sources. Although not unknown in the nineteenth century, antisemitic literature did not have a great impact on Italian politics or society, with the exception of the entrenched anti-Judaism of the Catholic Church. Preziosi relied most heavily on *La Libre Parole* (The Free Word), the newspaper founded by Édouard Drumont, which had already injected the concept of a Judeo-Masonic conspiracy into French politics. Preziosi's infatuation with the *Protocols of the Elders of Zion* was fed by a series of articles published in 1920 by the *Morning Post* (London) and then as a book, *The Cause of World Unrest*. Henry Ford's more exhaustive treatment of the same themes in the *Dearborn Independent* also influenced him. Preziosi relied utterly on the fraud known as the *Protocols of the Elders of Zion* to substantiate his every claim about Jewish evil. He published the work in Italian in 1921 and

edited further editions in 1937, 1939, 1944, and 1945, always arguing for its "inner truthfulness," even after the document's falseness had been well demonstrated.

Through the 1920s, Preziosi aligned himself with the most radical antisemites in Europe, especially with the National Socialists in Germany. Never satisfied that his own Fascist regime took the Jewish Question as seriously as it should, he tirelessly hammered away, demonstrating how the prophecies of the *Protocols* were coming true. With the acceleration of the Fascist campaign on racism in the aftermath of the Ethiopian War and with the passage of the antisemitic Racial Laws of 1938, Preziosi at last came into his own, publishing his views not only in his own paper but in the national press as well. He reached out to Catholic readers by republishing anti-Jewish articles from the 1890s, in the hope that the pious would be persuaded by a language and an imagery more familiar and less exotic than that of the *Protocols*. Preziosi's influence filtered into the daily press, where young and ambitious Fascist writers emulated his style and extreme rhetoric.

Preziosi zealously served the regime as a propagandist on the Jewish Question, but he yearned for the power that would allow him actually to direct the war against the Jews. He was incensed by the numerous exceptions to the Racial Laws that the authorities granted to individual Jews. He ceaselessly condemned this softness and attacked the so-called pietists, people inside and outside the government who resisted a rigorously enforced antisemitism. He gained governmental power as a minister of state in 1942, but after the fall of Mussolini and his restoration as a German puppet in September 1943, Preziosi was transferred to Germany, where he played an important role as Hitler's expert informant on the Italian situation. His last attempt to obtain enough personal power to achieve the ultimate solution to the Jewish problem was successful. On March 15, 1944, on direct German instigation, he was named Inspector General for Race, finally having achieved control of a governmental agency that would allow him, he hoped, to exterminate the Jews in Italy. Although he proceeded to the work with enthusiasm, putting in place a legal system modeled on Germany's Nuremberg Laws of 1935, the progressive collapse of the German and Italian regimes limited the effectiveness of his work. While on the run with his wife and son, he committed suicide on April 26, 1945, and thus avoided having to answer for his crimes.

—Simone Duranti

**See also** Cause of World Unrest, The; Dearborn Independent and The International Jew; Drumont, Édouard; Ford, Henry; Gwynne, H. A.; Holocaust; Manifesto of the Racial Scientists; Mussolini, Benito; Nuremberg Laws; Protocols of the Elders of Zion; Racial Laws

**References**

Felice, Renzo de. The Jews in Fascist Italy: A History. Translated by Robert Miller (New York: Enigma Books, 2001).

Pichetto, Maria Teresa. Alle radici dell'odio: Preziosi e Benigni antisemiti (Milan, Italy: F. Angeli, 1983).

## Protocols of the Elders of Zion

The *Protocols of the Elders of Zion* is a faked document that purports to describe the secret plan of a Jewish world conspiracy to gain world domination through the destruction of Christian states. Manufactured around the turn of the twentieth century, the *Protocols* can claim to be the most famous and most widely distributed antisemitic work of all time.

The *Protocols* allegedly is the verbatim record of a speech by an unnamed Jewish leader, delivered at the meeting of the fictitious Elders of Zion in an undisclosed location on an unspecified date. The speech—it is meant to be taken as a surreptitiously overheard confession—minutely details the strategy by which the Jews have been carrying on their destructive work. That work, with the help of the Freemasons, will come to fruition in the near future. With cynicism and brutal candor, the chief elder sets forth how class conflicts, rebellions, wars, and revolutions grind down the nations, while the manipulation of gold brings them to economic ruin and rationalism, materialism, and atheism utterly demoralize them. On the ashes of the old order, a ruthlessly efficient police state will establish the world government of the Jews under a king from the House of David. This king will be said to possess charismatic powers; he will be honored and even deified by the people. Together with the Elders, who will designate themselves the benefactors of mankind, he will rule firmly over a peaceful, united, and ordered world whose inhabitants will live out their uneventful lives in satiated peace and quiet. Lurking behind this dull utopia, however, will stand a totalitarian regime manipulating the blind, spiritless mass of men and women by means of incessant propaganda, severe censorship, and an all-pervasive network of spies.

The first mention of the *Protocols* appeared in April 1902 in an article by the Russian journalist and notorious antisemite Mikhail Menshikov (1859–1918), who dismissed the work as a clumsy fake. The first documented publication occurred between August and September 1903 in Pavolaki Krushevan's St. Petersburg newspaper, *Znamia* (The Banner). It was entitled "Program for the Conquest of the World by the Jews." The text of the *Protocols* used at that time, according to Krushevan, was a Russian translation from the original French transcription of the meetings of the so-called World Union of Freemasons and Elders of Zion. In the years before World War I, more than a dozen editions were published in St. Petersburg, Moscow, and the provinces. The number of sections, or "protocols," varied between twenty-two and twenty-seven; their contents also varied considerably, as did the information concerning the origins of the book. A connection to Zionism was sometimes claimed and sometimes denied. The version that became world-famous, consisting of twenty-four protocols, appeared for the first time in Tsarskoe Selo in 1905 in a devotional book entitled *The Great in the Small*, by Sergei Nilus. A Russian religious writer, Nilus interpreted the text in the framework of his apocalyptic vision as an omen of the imminent coming of the Antichrist.

Before the Revolution of 1917, the book struck few sparks in Russia. Nor is there any convincing proof that the *Protocols* led directly to antisemitic violence. The upheavals of war, collapse of monarchies, world revolution as proclaimed by the Bolsheviks, and postwar economic and social crises created a dire need for simple explanations and the naming of those responsible for the chaos. The *Protocols* perfectly fulfilled this need.

This 1934 cover for "The Jewish Peril," one of the titles under which the *Protocols of the Elders of Zion* circulated in French-speaking lands, makes use of familiar graphic motifs: a spider (a vulture, serpent, octopus, or vampire were common variants) endowed with grotesquely caricatured Jewish features, sitting atop the globe. (Courtesy of Michael Hagemeister)

Carried to western Europe and the United States in 1918 and 1919 by Russian refugees, the work was quickly translated into all major languages and disseminated in successive new editions.

The *Protocols* made a powerful impression in England, where a part of the respectable press, including the *Times* (London), was inclined to accept it as authentic. In the United States, Henry Ford found it to be a mighty tool in the struggle against "International Jewry." In Germany, it immediately appealed to the *völkisch* (racist-nationalist) Right, including the Nazi ideologue Alfred Rosenberg and the "Nestor of German antisemitism" Theodor Fritsch, both of whom took

a large part in its dissemination. Hitler mentioned the *Protocols* in his early speeches and commented on it in *Mein Kampf.* Later, too, he expatiated on the Jewish world conspiracy but only rarely alluded expressly to the *Protocols.* Joseph Goebbels preached struggle against Jewish world domination and employed the image of the Jew as the "Antichrist of world history," but he, like Hitler, rarely mentioned the book. Only once in his voluminous diaries does he refer to the *Protocols,* leaving open the question of whether it was genuine. The Nazi propaganda machine, however, issued new editions throughout the 1930s. The question of authenticity was finessed with references to the "inner truth" of the text.

The end of the Nazi era did not bring the public career of the *Protocols* to an end. Rather, 100 years after its first appearance, it is being distributed more widely than ever today, thanks largely to the Internet. Since the Holocaust, a broad assortment of groups has adapted the book to suit whatever specific antisemitic agenda is being pursued. Christian fundamentalists, Black Nationalists, Islamic extremists, neo-Nazi pagans, Holocaust deniers, New Age zealots, and communists who would replace the "class enemy" with "Zionist world conspirators" have all found what they required in the *Protocols.* When, why, by whom, and to what purpose the *Protocols* was originally fabricated remain unanswered questions. The most frequent assertion is that the text was produced in the late 1890s, at the time of the Dreyfus Affair and the First Zionist Congress, by operatives of the tsarist secret police (Okhrana) working in France. Commonly identified perpetrators are Piotr Rachkovskii (1851–1910), head of the Okhrana abroad, and his collaborator Matvei Golovinskii (1865–1920). The alleged intention of the book was to counter the modernization policies of the tsar's finance minister, Sergei Witte, by portraying him as a tool of the Jews. There is, however, no concrete evidence for any part of this scenario. Recent research by Cesare De Michelis disputes the very existence of an original French manuscript as well as the actual involvement of the Okhrana or any other state agency. De Michelis has tried to demonstrate that the *Protocols,* as we know them today, are the result of a complex reworking of a text that must have been written in Russia between April 1902 and August 1903 by reactionary antisemitic publicists. Their aim was to discredit the Zionist movement.

Since 1921, there has been indisputable evidence that large segments of the *Protocols* were compiled from older texts that had nothing to do with one another. The unknown plagiarists relied most heavily on the work of the French lawyer Maurice Joly (1833–1878), titled *Dialogue in Hell between Machiavelli and Montesquieu, or the Politics of Machiavelli in the Nineteenth Century.* Published anonymously in Brussels in 1864, this work was a biting political satire aimed at the authoritarian regime of Napoleon III. It makes no mention of Jews at all. Comparative textual analysis shows that more than 160 passages in the *Protocols*—two-fifths of the work—and even the chapter divisions are lifted directly from Joly. Another of the plagiarists' sources was *The Rabbi's Speech,* composed from a chapter of Herrmann Goedsche's potboiler novel *Biarritz* (1868). Borrowings from French and Russian light entertainment literature as well as from Fyodor Dostoevsky's novels supplied the rest of what the fabricators needed. Without exception, everything came from fictional texts.

Hannah Arendt pointed out that, with its depictions of a police state, leadership cult, mass propaganda, denunciation, the power of organization, and striving after world conquest, the *Protocols of the Elders of Zion* anticipated the characteristic features of totalitarianism in the twentieth century. The *Protocols* can certainly be read as a malign dystopia. But it is the thematic emphasis on the notion of a world conspiracy that has made the book undyingly popular. It retains—for some audiences—the power to simplify a confusing reality and to render it wholly transparent but only after the reader accepts its essential fiction of a world controlled and manipulated by a "hidden hand." Beyond this, the *Protocols* offers a crystal-clear distinction between friend and foe—a Manichaean world that invites a community to band together *in* itself and *against* "the Other." Finally, it promises a future consolation. Once the unseen enemy and his terrible plan have been exposed and overcome, the time of suffering ends and redemption beckons.

—*Michael Hagemeister*
*Richard S. Levy, translation*

**See also** Antichrist; *Biarritz; Dearborn Independent* and *The International Jew;* Dostoevsky, Fyodor; Freemasonry; Fritsch, Theodor; Hitler's Speeches (Early); Internet; Judeo-Bolshevism; *Mein Kampf;* New Age; Nilus, Sergei; *Protocols of the Elders of Zion* on Trial; *Rabbi's Speech, The;* Rosenberg, Alfred; Russian Orthodox Church; Zionism

**References**
Cohn, Norman. *Warrant for Genocide: The Myth of the Jewish World Conspiracy and the "Protocols of the Elders of Zion."* New ed. (London: Serif, 1996).

De Michelis, Cesare G. *The Non-Existent Manuscript: A Study of the Protocols of the Sages of Zion* (Lincoln: University of Nebraska Press, 2004).

Hagemeister, Michael. "Die 'Protokolle der Weisen von Zion' und der Basler Zionistenkongress von 1897." In *Der Traum von Israel: Die Ursprünge des modernen Zionismus.* Edited by Heiko Haumann (Weinheim, German: Beltz Athenäum, 1998), 250–273.

———. "Der Mythos der 'Protokolle der Weisen von Zion.'" In *Verschwörungstheorien: Anthropologische Konstanten—Historische Varianten.* Edited by Ute Caumanns and Mathias Niendorf (Osnabrück, Germany: Fibre, 2001), 89–101.

Taguieff, Pierre-André. *Les Protocoles des Sages de Sion.* 2 vols. (Paris: Berg, 1992).

## *Protocols of the Elders of Zion* on Trial

The most extensive public inquiry into the nature of the *Protocols of the Elders of Zion* resulted from a suit brought by the Jewish community of Bern and the united Jewish communities of Switzerland against the Swiss National-Socialist League. The legal action was based on article 14 of the Bern cantonal law on offensive literature (defined as writings that might incite or teach someone to commit a crime, to endanger good morals, to violate gravely the feeling of decency, to exert a corrupting influence, or otherwise to arouse serious objections). The four individuals accused of distributing the *Protocols* included newspaper editor Theodor Fischer and Silvio Schnell, manager of the book department of the antisemitic Swiss National Front.

The trial began on November 16, 1933, lasted nearly two years, and involved three separate court sessions. At the start, the court decided that it would consider whether the *Protocols* was genuine; the trial judge asked each of the parties to select an expert on this issue, and he appointed his own expert as well. The second session, from October 29 to November 1, 1934, was devoted to presentation of documents and testimony by witnesses, most of whom appeared on behalf of the plaintiffs. The witnesses included several participants at the First Zionist Congress in Basel, most notably Chaim Weizmann; two distinguished Freemasons; and a group of Paris-based émigrés from Russia, Jews and non-Jews, including Vladimir Burtsev, Count Alexander du Chayla, and several others. The third session lasted from April 29 to May 14, 1935, with much of it spent on statements by the expert for the defendants—Ulrich Fleischhauer, a retired colonel and head of the antisemitic Weltdienst (World Service) propaganda organization in Nazi Germany.

The legal action had a wider purpose: to challenge publicly a major component of the propaganda distributed worldwide by the Hitler regime. The international circumstances made it possible to conduct an exceptional collaborative inquiry into the *Protocols*. Elias Tscherikower, head of the Historical Section of the Jewish Research Institute (YIVO), coordinated the research effort in Paris, commissioning several studies on various aspects of the document's Russian context; the lawyer Aleksandr Tager, author of a notable book on the Beilis Affair, coordinated a search for relevant documents in Soviet libraries and archives. The circumstances of the collaboration are yet to be clarified, and much of the material produced by Tscherikower and his associates remains unpublished.

In turn, the Weltdienst organization mobilized considerable resources in support of the defendants. A number of Russian émigrés with right-wing and Nazi connections participated in this endeavor.

On May 14, 1935, trial judge Walter Meyer ruled that the *Protocols* was a forgery based largely on Maurice Joly's *Dialogues* and that it was "liable to excite hatred against a part of the population and lead to agitation and violence" (*Times* [London], May 15, 1935). Defendants Fischer and Schnell had to assume a significant portion of the trial costs; the others were acquitted on technical grounds. Two years later, the Court of Appeal of Canton Bern set the verdict aside. In its judgment, although the *Protocols* constituted "writings of a very low class," it did not fall under the definition of the law on offensive literature (*Times* [London], November 5, 1937). Underscoring its view of the *Protocols* as "scurrilous" and "immoral," the appellate court did not award the defendants any damages. This legal "victory" on the appellate level has been used by defenders of the *Protocols* as "proof" of the book's authenticity.

—*Henryk Baran*

***See also*** Beilis Case; Freemasonry; National Socialist German Workers' Party; *Protocols of the Elders of Zion;* Rosenberg, Alfred
**References**
Ben-Itto, Hadassa. *Die Protokolle der Weisen von Zion: Anatomie einer Fälschung* (Berlin: Aufbau-Verlag, 1998).
Burtsev, Vladimir. *V pogone za provokatorami; "Protokoly sionskikh mudretsov"—Dokazannyi podlog* (Hunting Provocateurs; "Protocols of the Elders of Zion"—A Proven Fabrication). Introduction by Iu. V. Davydov and commentaries by L. G. Aronov (Moscow: Slovo, 1991), 295–345, 414–426. This is a reprint of two of Burtsev's books.
Cohn, Norman. *Warrant for Genocide: The Myth of the Jewish World Conspiracy and the "Protocols of the Elders of Zion."* New ed. (London: Serif, 1996).

# Proudhon, Pierre-Joseph (1809–1865)

Pierre-Joseph Proudhon, a journalist and early socialist political theorist, developed ideas that became the basis for many concepts in modern radical politics, especially international socialism, communism, and anarchism. Born into poverty in the Jura city of Besançon, Proudhon was self-taught and eventually became a printer. While practicing his craft, he became acquainted with the socialist theories of his day, especially those of the utopian socialist Charles Fourier, also from Besançon. Far more than Fourier, however, Proudhon attacked the Jews. He characterized them as parasitic forces of evil in the world, who had "made the European bourgeoisie, high and low, in his image," that is to say, the force behind the economic exploitation he saw as inherent in modern capitalism (in Poliakov 1974, 2: 207). In his writings, Proudhon sometimes used traditional anti-Jewish tropes, for example, calling the Jew "Satan," but at times, he also employed xenophobic, racial, and conspiratorial categories of a distinctly modern cast. His rhetorical style influenced late nineteenth-century French antisemitic theorists, many of whom acknowledged his work explicitly.

Proudhon is perhaps best known for his radical statement, "Property is theft," offered as an answer to the question he asked himself in his 1840 work *What Is Property?* Influential among workers, Proudhon described his system, which he called Mutualism, in his journal *Le Représentant du peuple* and in his most important works, *Economic Contradictions, or the Philosophy of Poverty* (1846), *The General Idea of the Revolution in the Nineteenth Century* (1851), and *The Principle of Federation* (1863). As opposed to Karl Marx, his longtime opponent, Proudhon envisioned a world society without national borders or centralized authority. The world federation would not have states or laws but rather free contracts between workers organized in small, local associations with communal institutions of credit to support them. The revolution, he believed, would come not through a centralized authority, political action, or violence but through the free economic actions of the workers themselves. A participant in the short-lived French republican government of 1848, Proudhon was imprisoned in 1849 because of his outspoken criticism of President Louis Napoleon, who became emperor of France in 1852. Released from prison in 1852, Proudhon continued to criticize the government and was forced to flee to Belgium, where he continued to publish radical works until his death in 1865. His theories have remained a source of inspiration for working-class activists, anarchists, and theorists of a decentralized, nonnational world order; one could even argue that his influence can still be seen today in the antiglobalization movement.

Proudhon's anti-Jewish statements were not systematically developed in comparison to those of the Fourierist Alphonse Toussenel, a contem-

Journalist and early socialist political theorist Pierre-Joseph Proudhon characterized Jews as parasitic forces of evil in the world. His rhetorical style influenced late nineteenth-century French antisemitic theorists, many of whom acknowledged his work. (Hulton-Deutsch Collection/Corbis)

porary. Proudhon was, however, outspoken in calling for the expulsion of Jews from France, identifying them as foreigners, polytheists, and obstinate enemies of Christ who had thus placed themselves "outside of the human species" (in Poliakov 1974, 2: 208). Proudhon's penchant for combining religious anti-Jewish stereotypes with decidedly new racial and economic prejudices makes him an important transitional figure in the history of antisemitism.

—*Lisa Moses Leff*

**See also** Fourier, Charles; France; Socialists on Antisemitism; Toussenel, Alphonse
***References***
Poliakov, Léon. *The History of Anti-Semitism.* Translated by Richard Howard. 2 vols. (New York: Schocken Books, 1974).
Woodcock, George. *Pierre-Joseph Proudhon: His Life and Work.* Reprint ed. (New York: Schocken Books, 1972).

# Psychoanalysis

Sigmund Freud (1856–1939), the founder of psychoanalysis, was born in Freiberg, Moravia, a rural backwater within the Austrian Empire. He was the son of a Jewish wool merchant and grew up in a family environment of secular Judaism. In search of better economic opportunities, the family moved to the Austrian capital of Vienna, where liberal reforms removed the last vestiges of legal discrimination against Jews by 1867. But a severe economic downturn beginning in 1873, the year Freud entered university to study medicine, led to a revival of antisemitism and a search for a scapegoat in the large Jewish community of Vienna. For Freud, this wave of prejudice recalled a story his father had told him of having his cap knocked off by a Christian in Freiberg and being told to walk in the muddy street instead of on the dry sidewalk. Freud vowed never to be so subservient, and his conception and development of psychoanalysis, though rigorously scientific in its ambition, was thus marked by considerable defiance of convention and authority, reflective of his position as an oft-maligned outsider in Christian civilization.

The eruption of racial antisemitism in the last decade of the nineteenth century all but ended liberal Jewish influence in the governance of Vienna and of Austria. The upheaval, along with the controversial nature of the theories he was developing on the unconscious sexual origins of neurotic behavior, played a role in stalling Freud's academic career. His quotation of the seventh book of Virgil's *Aeneid* as the epigraph for his seminal *Interpretation of Dreams* (1900) reflected both the disappointment and the defiance that helped prompt his exploration of the chaotic and unplumbed depths of the psyche: "If I cannot bend the higher powers, I will move the infernal regions."

The emphasis in psychoanalytic theory and practice on the sexual nature of human emotions and relationships from early childhood on was certainly objectionable to the strong Catholic and Protestant traditions in European society. But it was only after World War I that a widespread effort was made to associate Jews in particular with such "degenerate" ideas. The charge that psychoanalysis was an exercise in "pansexualism," for example, often arose from a common cultural stereotype that associated Jews with mental and physical illness and with sexual disorder. By the 1920s, Freud himself was, with some justification, ascribing much of the resistance to psychoanalysis to antisemitism. That most of the early members of the psychoanalytic movement were Jews only exacerbated the problem. This preponderance was largely a response to the less-than-friendly reception Jews found in the medical profession in Vienna, Berlin, and Budapest in particular, which prompted Jewish physicians to seek refuge within the psychoanalytic movement. Freud consequently worried that psychoanalysis would continue to be regarded as a "Jewish science," a major reason why he so warmly welcomed Carl G. Jung, the son of a Swiss pastor, into the ranks of psychoanalysts. Freud tapped Jung as his heir apparent, to promote psychoanalysis as a widespread and confessionally neutral science.

Jung disappointed Freud badly, first by breaking with central tenets of Freudian analysis and later by flirting with the "Aryanization" of psychoanalysis in Nazi Germany. Jung's apostasy was, moreover, one especially dramatic instance of the growth and diversification of psychotherapeutic theory and practice in Europe during the first half of the twentieth century. Particularly in Germany, university psychiatry continued to be dominated by a model of the mind that insisted all mental illness was a result of physical dysfunction. Psychoanalysts were the most visible and organized of those who argued that mental illness was mostly psychological in origin. Their position was strengthened when psychiatrists proved unable to do much about the phenomenon known as shell shock during World War I. Individual psychoanalysts and psychotherapists, however, claimed significant success in addressing the symptoms of shell shock by means of psychological methods of treatment. A variety of psychotherapeutic—that is, non-Freudian—theories and practices became organized in Europe after the war and were particularly common in Germany, where psychoanalysts established training institutes in Berlin and Vienna.

In 1933, antisemitic agitation against psychoanalysis became official policy under the Hitler dictatorship. For the Nazis, Freud's psychoanalysis was just another part of the Jewish conspiracy to undermine the Aryan race. In May 1933, Freud's books, along with those of many other Jewish and non-Jewish authors, were burned in the quadrangles of German universities. By the end of 1935, all Jewish members of the German Psychoanalytic Society had been forced to resign. The Berlin Psychoanalytic Institute was assimilated into the German Institute for Psychological Research and Psychotherapy, whose members sought to advance the professional fortunes of a properly "German" psychotherapy under the leadership of Matthias Göring, a cousin of Nazi bigwig Hermann Göring. It was the proclaimed task of the institute to unite the various schools of psychotherapy into a single theoretical and practical entity in service to the state and the nation. Along with this went systematic vilification of "Jewish psychoanalysis" as materialistic "dismemberment of the soul," even though non-Jewish psychoanalysts were allowed to train, teach, and practice at the institute.

In 1938, the annexation of Austria by Nazi Germany meant the end of the Vienna Psychoanalytic Institute. Freud was allowed to emigrate to England when the Nazis concluded that his international fame, advanced age, and infirmity precluded his arrest. Jung, his former heir, had been recruited in 1933 as president of the International General Medical Society for Psychotherapy by German psychotherapists eager to prove their "non-Freudian" (that is, non-Jewish) professional credentials to a Nazi regime still officially and dangerously suspicious of a field so closely identified with the Jew Freud. Jung took the opportunity to advance the interests of his own school of analytical psychology, which substituted an emphasis on the religious depths of the collective unconscious for Freudian concern with individual sexual conflict. In the first years of the Third Reich, Jung made public statements on fundamental differences between "Germanic and Jewish psychology" and praised the course of events in Italy and in Germany that had culminated in the emergence of strong leaders in accord with the collective soul of their peoples. In the later 1930s, Jung began to view Nazism and

fascism with a more critical eye, and after the war, he denied that he had said anything of an antisemitic nature.

Paradoxically, perhaps, antisemitism among psychotherapists in Nazi Germany became less important as both the institute and the nation turned to the task of mobilizing German resources in the struggle for hegemony in Europe. German psychotherapists and psychoanalysts argued that they had an important role to play in keeping Germans psychologically fit to meet their national responsibilities. This turn away from the ideological assault on "Jewish psychoanalysis" meant that the distant and vacillating Jung became irrelevant to the affairs of psychotherapy in Germany and, after the outbreak of World War II, in Nazi-occupied Europe as well. By this time, almost all of the Jewish psychoanalysts had fled the Continent, eventually providing much of the basis for the huge postwar psychoanalytic boom in the United States. Since there were no longer any Jewish therapists or (with a few partial exceptions) patients in Europe, psychotherapists and psychoanalysts there turned to the practice of their newly organized discipline, leaving the wartime culmination of Nazi racial antisemitism to a specialized hierarchy and bureaucracy of mass murder.

The Holocaust largely discredited antisemitism, but in Europe, Nazism had almost completely destroyed the practice of psychoanalysis by Jews, at least in the years immediately following the war. For these reasons, antisemitic accusations about so-called Jewish psychoanalysis lost credibility. Ironically, in Germany, the protected practice of psychoanalysis at the Göring Institute from 1936 to 1945 contributed to the reemergence of organized psychoanalysis in the postwar era. In the process of professional reestablishment, few questions were raised about the conduct of psychoanalytic practitioners under the Third Reich. It was only in the 1970s that younger members of the psychoanalytic community in West Germany began investigating the history of their professional elders. (In East Germany, psychoanalysis was officially suppressed, not so much because of a specific antisemitism but because of the Marxist conviction that Freud was representative of bourgeois capitalist values.) In a final irony, the enthusiasm for psychoanalysis among younger practitioners often stemmed, in part, from psychologically complex and even problematic identification with Jews who had been so hideously victimized by Germans in the recent past.

—*Geoffrey Cocks*

**See also** Austria; Billroth, Theodor; Book Burning; Freud, Sigmund; Homophobia; Jung, Carl Gustav; Nazi Cultural Antisemitism; Nazi Legal Measures against Jews

**References**

Cocks, Geoffrey. *Psychotherapy in the Third Reich: The Göring Institute* (New Brunswick, NJ: Transaction, 1997).

Gay, Peter. *Freud: A Life for Our Time* (New York: Norton, 1988).

## Pückler, Count Walter von (1860–1924)

Count Walter von Pückler was one of the strangest characters in the waxworks of antisemitic agitators in imperial Germany. From 1899 to 1907, he inherited Hermann Ahlwardt's mantle as Germany's most outrageous agitator. He by and large avoided the antisemitic political parties of his day and was also avoided by them. He made no contribution to antisemitic ideology and never published anything aside from leaflets replicating his numerous inflammatory speeches. He was eventually certified insane. Notwithstanding all these factors, it would be a mistake to dismiss the significance of Pückler or his radicalizing influence on antisemitic agitation. Julius Streicher's journal, *Der Stürmer,* lionized him in 1934 as a great National Socialist before National Socialism yet existed.

Born into a well-known and widely ramified Silesian aristocratic family, Pückler studied law and graduated from the University of Heidelberg in 1887 but then withdrew from the practice of law in 1891. Three years later, he acquired an estate in Klein-Tschirne, Lower Silesia. According to his own testimony, he became embroiled in a series of legal disputes in which he lost out to Jewish lawyers. This experience revealed to him that the Prussian state in general and the judiciary in particular were in the clutches of the Jews. He shared this new knowledge of overweening

Jewish control with local gatherings of agricultural organizations. The favorable reception he met with in this venue persuaded Pückler to present his antisemitic exposés in Berlin and its environs. There, he was taken up by Wilhelm Bruhn, editor of the unsavory and antisemitic *Staatsbürger-Zeitung* newspaper. Bruhn's unscrupulous promotional skills soon made Pückler Berlin's most prominent agitator, able to attract hundreds or even thousands to his rallies. Like no one before him in the relatively staid German Empire, Pückler openly urged the use of physical violence—including pogroms and mass murder—as the only solution to the Jewish Question. He also called on the burglars of Berlin to loot Jewish shops and homes. His picturesque, if brutal, language earned him the nickname "Dreschgraf" (scythe count).

Pückler repeated the attempt of Court Chaplain Adolf Stoecker to bring antisemitism to the working classes of the capital, hoping to undermine the influence of the "Jewified" Social Democratic Party. He called on workers to practice what he called "Berlin Socialism," that is, the peremptory expropriation of all Jewish property. But like Stoecker before him, Pückler failed to impress the proletariat. Instead, his rallies turned into circus performances that drew Berlin's sensation-hungry crowds of no particular class or politics.

Count Pückler was not a racist antisemite but rather a deranged religious fanatic who claimed that it was Jesus Christ himself who urged him to fight Jews and Jewry to the death. Apparently, there were enough like-minded individuals to organize a small but devoted circle of supporters into the Pückler Association (Pückler-Vereinigung). Six months of confinement in a fortress, three months of imprisonment, and numerous fines failed to stop him.

His lofty social standing and the influence of his family afforded him a degree of protection for quite some time. But when he finally extended his condemnations to the "Jewified" aristocracy, including the Hohenzollern dynasty, the judiciary, and the entire civil service—excepting only the army—the relative immunity he enjoyed when merely attacking Jews quickly evaporated. In 1908, he was judicially certified insane and institutionalized. His subsequent attempts to return to the political arena failed. Pückler died in obscurity in 1924.

—*Christoph Jahr*

**See also** Ahlwardt, Hermann; *Antisemitic Correspondence;* Antisemitic Political Parties; Stoecker, Adolf; *Stürmer, Der*

**References**

Goldhagen, Eric. "The Mad Count: A Forgotten Portent of the Holocaust," *Midstream* 22, no. 2 (1976).

## Pudor, Heinrich (1865–1943)

During the imperial era in Germany, Heinrich Pudor was but one of many activists on the antisemitic scene. In the early years of the Weimar Republic, however, he gained special notoriety by explicitly condoning violence. His fame was short-lived. Early in the 1920s, his obsessive dogmatism served to marginalize him; even fellow extremists on the Right thought him mad.

Born in Dresden, the son of a member of the famous Leipzig Gewandhaus Orchestra, Pudor experimented with the alternate lifestyle movement (*Lebensreform*) before World War I. Vegetarianism, anti-immunization, nudism, the "reform of clothing"—he neglected none of these trends of the moment. While engaged in such activities, he also became active, by 1890 at the latest, in antisemitic politics. He joined Theodor Fritsch's Organization of the German Middle Class (Deutsche Mittelstandsvereinigung) and the German Social Party (Deutschsoziale Partei) but became disillusioned as a result of the latter's lack of electoral success. Pudor confronted the failure of the antisemitic parties with publications calling for concrete measures against the Jews. In his "How to Get Them out of Here" (*Wie kriegen wir sie hinaus* [1913]), he, more categorically than many others, demanded the peremptory disenfranchisement of Jews.

His antisemitic writings were banned by the military censors during World War I, by which time his extremist antisemitism had begun to strain his loyalties to the German Empire. He ignored the political truce declared by all the parties at the outbreak of the war and became increasingly susceptible to violent solutions for the Jewish Question. After the Revolution of 1918, he was one of the first antisemites to go onto the offensive, far in advance of the still passive German National People's Party and its sympathizers on the Right. In a pamphlet published in August 1919, Pudor managed to inject his views into the heated discourse on antisemitic tactics. Under the headline "Culture-Antisemitism or Pogrom-Antisemitism?" he seriously recommended to his readers the value of the pogrom. He declared any means justified if it "frees us from the Jews" and that if the pogrom fulfilled this aim, there was "nothing to be said against it." Even Hitler felt compelled to enter the debate at that point, rejecting the pogrom (in the so-called Gemlich Letter of September 1919), while nonetheless advocating, somewhat enigmatically, the "general elimination [*Entfernung*] of the Jews."

Pudor isolated himself from the mainstream antisemites of the Weimar Republic. He remained skeptical about the Nazi Party and is not known ever to have been a member, although he occasionally penned articles for Hitler's newspaper, the *Völkischer Beobachter* (Racial Observer). He produced a host of lesser writings, including an autobiography, *My Life,* which contains interesting details about his prewar experiences but breaks off in 1914. In 1927, he was imprisoned for threatening the foreign minister of the republic, Gustav Stresemann. Not much is known about Pudor's life after 1933. He claimed to have received an honorary pension from Hitler's chancellery, but nonetheless, his publications were banned by the Nazis from 1940 forward.

—*Dirk Walter*
*Richard S. Levy, translation*

**See also** Antisemitic Political Parties; *Culture-Antisemitism or Pogrom-Antisemitism?;* Fritsch, Theodor; Gemlich Letter; German National People's Party; Hentschel, Willibald; Hitler, Adolf; Settlement *Heimland*

**References**

Mohler, Armin. *Die konservative Revolution in Deutschland, 1918–1932.* 3rd ed. (Darmstadt, Germany: Wissenschaftliche Buchgesellschaft, 1989).

Walter, Dirk. *Antisemitische Kriminalität und Gewalt: Judenfeindschaft in der Weimarer Republik* (Bonn, Germany: J. H. W. Dietz Verlag Nachf., 1999).

## Punch

The British humorous and satirical illustrated magazine *Punch, or the London Charivari* was founded in 1841 and continued to appear without interruption until 1992. It was revived briefly in 1996 but ceased publication in 2002.

Purporting to be the mouthpiece of Mr. Punch, a humpbacked figure with a protruding nose whose ancestry harked back to puppetry and also perhaps to traditions of sixteenth-century Italian *commedia del'arte,* the magazine projected itself, often with a strong strain of sardonic mockery, as the voice of the British people. Its attitude toward Jews, particularly in its earlier years, has been the subject of debate. Among its first contributors were a number of writers and illustrators, including the novelist William Makepeace Thackeray and the cartoonist John Leech, whose antisemitism pervaded their works. However, some scholars have questioned the significance of *Punch*'s putative antisemitism, contending that the objective of the magazine was no more than to poke innocent fun. In the view of Anne and Roger Cowen, "One could accuse *Punch* of being unsympathetic to the Jews but when coming out with its views *Punch* was honest and forthright and not anti-semitic" (Cowen and Cowen 1999, XXII). Their remarks echoed those of M. H. Spielmann, *Punch*'s nineteenth-century apologist, who had argued that some readers too easily "failed to appreciate *Punch*'s robust irony" and that its hatred of Jews "was really only skin-deep, or, at least, was directed against manners rather than against men" (Spielmann 1969, 104).

Despite its earlier negative stance, *Punch* did finally show lukewarm support for Jewish emancipation, which Parliament acceded to in 1858. But in upholding such a position, Mr. Punch was not necessarily showing a new warmth toward Jewish rights. More probably, he was echoing the fundamental liberal beliefs of the day concerning the rights of man that stemmed from the Enlightenment and from the abolition of the slave trade throughout the British Empire in 1833. In 1851, for instance, during the year of the Great Exhibition in London, *Punch* frequently pointed to the paradox of the United States as a land of liberty that would not free its black slaves. Yet in

**THE DEALER IN OLD CLOTHES**
TEACHING THE YOUNG IDEA HOW TO STEAL.

John Leech's cartoon, perhaps inspired by Charles Dickens's character Fagin, portrays the corruption of English youth by the Jews. (Punch, Ltd.)

the same year, the Jews were invariably represented as less than holy in their incessant wheeling and dealing and anything but worthy of being granted the full liberties of British citizenship. Leech's cartoon, "The Dealer in Old Clothes: Teaching the Young Idea How to Steal" (XX, 25, 1851), portrayed a Faginesque scoundrel bribing a young English boy, suggesting the deleterious influence of the Jews. Richard Altick was closer to the mark than the Cowens in recognizing that, although *Punch* may have endorsed "Jewish emancipation as a civil-rights principle," its liberalism was too frequently "qualified by the prejudices of its day" (Altick 1997, 265, 269). In a parallel study, L. Perry Curtis Jr. found similar ambivalences in *Punch*'s caricatural portrayal of Irishmen and noticed that during the early years of the journal, its "leading writers and artists . . . reveled in anti-Semitic gibes" (Curtis 1997, 117).

**DRESSING FOR A MASQUERADE.**

MR. D—SR—LI AS A GREAT PROTECTIONIST LEADER.

*Punch* reminded its readers, once again, of the celebrated Benjamin Disraeli's inescapable Jewish roots. (Punch, Ltd.)

Throughout that period, *Punch*'s depiction of Benjamin Disraeli, who had converted from Judaism at an early age, never allowed the celebrated writer and politician to shake off his ethnic and religious ancestry. As Altick pointed out, he was alternately portrayed as "a clothes horse past the peak of fashion, a tailor of the Moses sweatshop ilk, and an old clothes dealer, thus running the gamut of the sartorial as well as the Hebraic theme" (263). An example of this is "Dressing for a Masquerade. Mr. D-sr—li as a Great Protectionist Leader" (XX, 87), one of many prints that represent Disraeli as a dandy but also perhaps suggesting a kinship, however distant, to the dealer in rags and to the "pawnbroker within" that are camouflaged here by the masquerade of fashion. Little work has been done as of yet on *Punch*'s treatment of the Jews during the twentieth century.

—*Frank Felsenstein*

***See also*** Caricature, Anti-Jewish (Early); Caricature, Anti-Jewish (Modern); Dickens, Charles; Disraeli, Benjamin; Emancipation; English Literature from Chaucer to Wells; *Fliegende Blätter; Gartenlaube, Die; Kladderadatsch; Simplicissimus*

**References**

Altick, Richard D. *Punch: The Lively Youth of a British Institution, 1841–1851* (Columbus: Ohio State University Press, 1997).

Cowen, Anne, and Roger Cowen. *Victorian Jews through British Eyes* (Oxford: Littman Library, 1999).

Curtis, L. Perry, Jr. *Apes and Angels: The Irishman in Victorian Caricature.* Rev. ed. (Washington, DC, and London: Smithsonian Institute Press, 1997).

Felsenstein, Frank. "Mr. Punch at the Great Exhibition: Stereotypes of Yankee and Hebrew in 1851." In *The Jews and British Romanticism: Politics, Religion, Culture.* Edited by Sheila A. Spector (New York: Palgrave Macmillan, 2005).

Spielmann, M. H. *The History of "Punch"* (Detroit, MI: Gale Research, 1969; orig. ed. London: Cassell, 1895).

Wohl, Anthony S. "'Ben JuJu': Representations of Disraeli's Jewishness in the Victorian Political Cartoon." In *Disraeli's Jewishness.* Edited by Todd M. Endelman and Tony Kushner (London: Valentine Mitchell, 2002), 105–161.

## Pure Blood Laws

From the middle of the fifteenth century in Spain, Pure Blood Laws (*limpieza de sangre*), aimed at excluding those who could not prove Christian descent from posts in ecclesiastical, local, or state institutions; from certain professions; or, in isolated cases, from the right to settle in a village or town. In principle, the laws were also to apply to Muslim converts and their descendants. But in practice, these measures had the greatest impact on former Jews, called *conversos* (New Christians) or—more contemptuously—*marranos* (converts who continue to practice Judaism secretly).

Pure Blood Laws were introduced for the first time in 1449 in the city of Toledo, where, shortly before their imposition, a rebellion against royal prerogatives took place. Leaders of the rebellion objected to a forced war loan. Soon, they focused their opposition on the conversos, who, it was widely believed, had provided the initiative for the loan. The Pure Blood Laws, an act of retaliation, excluded converts from all secular and ecclesiastical functions in Toledo.

However, differentiating between Old and New Christians contradicted the principles underlying Christian missionizing efforts and undermined their effectiveness by denying the equality between all who had been baptized. Therefore, only a few months passed in 1449 before Pope Nicolas V moved to abolish the Toledan Pure Blood Laws; the Castilian king followed suit.

The next attempt to introduce the laws came in 1486. In this instance, the immediate cause was the discovery by the religious order of the Hieronymites of "Judaizing" monks within its ranks. This time, the archbishop of Toledo vetoed the implementation of the laws with the backing of King Ferdinand and Queen Isabella. In 1496, however, Pope Alexander VI sanctioned the Pure Blood Laws, making them the first such laws accepted by the church hierarchy. In the same year, the Dominican monastery of Ávila enacted similar statutes, as did the Colegio de San Antonio in Sigüenza in 1497.

In 1501, the laws were issued for the first time by the central royal authorities: no person found guilty of heresy and no son or grandson of such a person could exercise a public function without special permission. This formulation represented a somewhat more lenient version of the Pure Blood Laws, which normally excluded all converts, even if they had not been found guilty of heresy.

Slowly, the Pure Blood Laws spread throughout Spain. In 1515, they were introduced in the bishopric of Seville; in 1525 and 1531, respectively, they were adopted by the Spanish Franciscans and the Dominicans. In the secular world, the Colegio of San Ildefonso took the lead in 1519, with the Universities of Salamanca, Valladolid, and Toledo following in 1522. Emigration to the Americas also became subject to several decrees forbidding conversos the right to participate. Enabling the process of exclusion was the purpose behind the mid-sixteenth-century *Libro verde de Aragon* (Green Book of Aragon), which claimed to document Spanish noble families and members of the clergy whose ancestors had converted from Judaism in the previous cen-

tury. Later on, the work also included information about the developing Spanish bourgeoisie. Proving or disproving "purity of blood" was a complicated process, involving oral testimony and documentation covering great spans of time.

Pure Blood Laws never covered all of the Spanish state or society. Some institutions openly refused to introduce such regulations. The degree of enforcement always depended on personal relations or the possibility of bribery. Nevertheless, the laws hindered integration of the New Christians, identifying them as a group apart, and had a paralyzing effect on Spanish life. This was especially true in the higher reaches of the social scale because most of the converts were from the upper classes—the very classes that normally enjoyed the privileges revoked by the laws. In fact, the laws may be understood as a kind of plebeian revenge against noble prerogatives, aimed at the conversos because they were more vulnerable than the "Old Christian" upper classes. Several attempts to abolish the Pure Blood Laws, mainly in the seventeenth century, failed. They were finally abrogated only in 1865.

—*Bernd Rother*

See also Dominican Order; Franciscan Order; Inquisition; Nuremberg Laws; Torquemada, Tomás de

**References**
Friedman, Jerome. "Jewish Conversion, the Spanish Pure Blood Laws and Reformation: A Revisionist View of Racial and Religious Antisemitism," *Sixteenth Century Journal* 18 (1987): 3–29.

Sicroff, Albert. *Les controverses des statuts de pureté de sang en Espagne du XVe au XVIIe siècle* (Paris: Didier, 1960).

## Purge of 1968 (Poland)

The government of Władysław Gomułka took power as part of the de-Stalinization wave of 1956. Gomułka cleared out the Stalin-era apparatchiks to distance himself from Stalinism, to make room for his own supporters, and to reduce the number of Jews in the party apparatus, hoping thereby to counter the popular association of communism with Jews. Later, Poland, as part of the Warsaw Pact, found itself allied with the Arab states against Israel; anti-Israeli propaganda thus became a part of the party line. By the time of the

Six Days' War in 1967, the Gomułka regime's popularity had waned. Its early promise of reform had been sidetracked, and the humiliating Arab defeat was gleefully registered in the Polish street as a defeat for the regime as well. The secret police, monitoring public opinion, reported these attitudes, particularly among Jews. The events of 1968 unfolded against this background.

In January 1968, the authorities shut down a Warsaw production of Adam Mickiewicz's anti-Russian play *Forefather's Eve,* a classic of nineteenth-century Polish theater. This action provoked anger and frustration among students and intellectuals, culminated in demonstrations in favor of free speech, called the "March events," in which a few of the prominent leaders were Jews. The Gomułka regime responded with a ferocious campaign of denunciation, blaming "Zionists" for the unrest. Denunciation was soon followed by a purge.

Behind the scenes in the meantime, there was a power struggle within the party between Gomułka and the interior minister, Gen. Mieczysław Moczar, who had built a base of support among war veterans, called the "Partisan" faction. It was Moczar who engineered the anti-Zionist purge, hoping to install his Partisans in positions vacated by the Jews and to win support from a Kremlin already unhappy with Gomułka's failing liberalism. Gomułka outmaneuvered Moczar, however, by sending armed forces to help suppress the "Prague Spring" in Czechoslovakia and co-opting the anti-Jewish campaign.

Between March and July, local party meetings were held across the country, at which Jewish members were bullied into admitting to Zionist sympathies and then fired from their jobs and expelled from the party on grounds of disloyalty. It was then made clear to them that they would not be able to get other jobs in Poland. If they sought to emigrate, they were told that exit permits would be issued only to Israel and on the condition of renouncing their Polish citizenship. The subsequent exodus to Israel was taken as confirmation that the loyalties of those expelled had indeed lain with Israel rather than Poland.

More than 15,000 Jews emigrated from Poland as a result of the anti-Zionist campaign, reducing the number of Jews in Poland to a few thousand. Most of the emigrants settled in Israel, the United States, and Western Europe. After the campaign was over, Polish-Jewish relations became a taboo subject, and they remained so until the next round of liberalization, in 1981.

—Steven Paulsson

**See also** Anti-Zionism; Judeo-Bolshevism; Moczar, Mieczysław; Poland; Stalinization of Eastern Europe
**References**
Steinlauf, Michael C. *Bondage to the Dead: Poland and the Memory of the Holocaust* (Syracuse, NY: Syracuse University Press, 1997).
Stola, Dariusz. *Kampania antysyjonistyczna w Polsce, 1967–1968* (The Anti-Zionist Campaign in Poland, 1967–1968) (Warsaw: Instytut Studiów Politycznych Polskiej Akademii Nauk, 2000).

## Purge of the German Civil Service (1933)

On April 7, 1933, Hitler made his first use of the dictatorial powers granted him by the Enabling Act of March 23 to make Jewish policy. His Law for the Restoration of the Professional Civil Service was meant to give the Nazi regime the power to reshape the civil service into a reliable tool for administering its National Socialist revolution, so that, as the interior minister Wilhelm Frick, among other Nazis, explained Germans could once again be governed by Germans. This law was an essential step in what the Nazis called the *Gleichschaltung*, that is, the step-by-step expansion of their political control over all aspects of the state.

The word *restoration* in the law's title is instructive. The Nazis believed that the vaunted German civil service had been corrupted during the Weimar years by the infiltration of leftists, liberals, and Jews, all of whom were considered dangerously unreliable. Under the new law, these groups could now be purged. Paragraph 3 called for the dismissal of all civil servants of "non-Aryan descent" (Jews). There were exceptions. President Paul von Hindenburg insisted on exemptions for those who had been in service before August 1, 1914, had themselves served at the front during World War I, or had fathers or sons killed in that war. Paragraph 4 allowed the Nazis to discharge from service those with suspect political affiliations: liberals, democrats, socialists, and communists. In fact, the "infiltration" of Jews and the politically suspect into the civil service had, with certain exceptions, been minimal. In democratically governed Prussia during the 1920s, for example, Jews had for the first time found acceptance on a somewhat equal footing. And in some of the newer ministries, such as the Labor Ministry, union leaders and socialists had managed to make inroads. Overall, however, the civil service had remained an overwhelmingly conservative body.

The drafters of paragraph 3 failed to provide a clear definition of the concept "non-Aryan descent." Pending such a definition, the provision remained impossible to implement. A supplementary decree issued on April 11 supplied the definition that came to be known as the Aryan Paragraph. Henceforth, a "non-Aryan" was defined as anyone "who is descended from non-Aryan, especially Jewish, parents or grandparents." To be classified as such, one parent *or grandparent* sufficed to make one non-Aryan. The Aryan Paragraph provided the official Nazi definition of the Jew and was appended to every piece of racial legislation until September 1935, when it was revised in the Nuremberg Laws.

The precise effects of the civil service law and the Aryan Paragraph are difficult to measure. The number of people expelled from the German civil service can only be estimated, for official records have been lost or destroyed. An unusually well-informed U.S. consular official in Berlin, Raymond Geist, estimated that as of July 1934, some 17,000 Jewish civil servants had been dismissed. The most immediately measurable effect was the requirement that all civil servants provide documentary evidence—in the form of marriage records and baptismal certificates—to verify their Aryan ancestry.

—*Karl A. Schleunes*

**See also** Nazi Legal Measures against Jews; Nuremberg Laws; Weimar

**References**

Caplan, Jane. *Government without Administration: State and Civil Service in Weimar and Nazi Germany* (Oxford: Clarendon Press, 1988).

Mommsen, Hans. *Beamtentum im Dritten Reich: Mit ausgewählten Quellen zur nationalsozialistischen Beamtenpolitik* (Stuttgart, Germany: Deutsche Verlags-Anstalt, 1966).

# Purges, Soviet

According to the original statutes of the Communist Party of the Soviet Union (from 1919), a "cleansing" or "purge" was a process whereby members were to be scrutinized at irregular intervals and, if necessary, expelled for activities deemed harmful to the party; if the infractions were grave enough, a member in question might be criminally prosecuted. The first purge occurred in 1921 and led to the expulsion of a quarter of the party membership. In this early phase, antisemitism played no role. In fact, at the time, there was a sizable jump in the number of Jewish members of the party and within its apparatus of repression.

The term *purge* is most often associated with the show trials and the massive persecutions that accompanied them from 1935 to 1938 and again from 1948 to 1953. The first set of purges served to fortify Joseph Stalin's rule. Almost the entire old party elite was arrested; accused of participating in a Trotskyist, anti-Soviet conspiracy; and then executed. Many of the prominent veteran Bolsheviks were Jews, a fact made abundantly clear in the show trials. From exile, Leon Trotsky spoke out against the antisemitic character of the spectacle. The chief prosecutor referred to him as "Judas" Trotsky. But Jews were neither the only nor the major victims of the purge. Stalin's goal was to build a wall of terror around himself and to eliminate real and potential opposition to his rule from within the party. By 1938, party membership had declined by almost half to 1.9 million. Of those associated with the Central Committee of the party, nearly 100 (70 percent) were murdered.

The second great wave of purges, from 1948 to 1953, were meant to solidify the position of the party in the USSR and the satellite states of Eastern Europe and to remove national obstacles in the way of socialism. Suspicion fell particularly hard on those persons who had once had relationships to other socialist parties or movements, those who had fought in resistance movements not controlled by Stalinists, and/or those who survived exile during World War II in the West instead of in the USSR. The prominent main defendants, however, were almost exclusively loyal Stalinists who, in part, had helped prepare the show trials before succumbing to them.

This wave of purges was antisemitic in two respects. In the first place, it coincided with the appearance of anti-Zionism as an essential element of Soviet ideology. Primarily Jewish communists were accused of Zionism, that is, participation in a worldwide, Zionist-fascist-imperialist conspiracy against the socialist camp. The accusation was absolutely central to the Slánský trial (in 1952) and the so-called Doctors' Plot (in 1953). The purges affected all social spheres. Thus, for example, almost all the Jewish officers in the Red Army, including sixty-three generals, were cashiered. Although Jews were disproportionately victimized by the purges, non-Jews suffered more in terms of absolute numbers.

The second antisemitic aspect of the purges, covered again by the accusation of Zionism, concerned the destruction of all attempts to preserve the cultural identity of Eastern European Jewry. These efforts had revived after the persecutions of the 1930s ended. The Jewish Anti-Fascist Committee, founded during the war as a Jewish umbrella organization, was abolished in 1948; its leading representatives were arrested and murdered. The committee's *Black Book,* detailing Nazi crimes against Jews on Soviet territory, was never published in the USSR. With the dissolution of the committee began a wave of persecution targeting the cultural elite of Soviet Jewry, especially its Yiddish-language writers; many were arrested, and many were murdered. After 1953, organized Yiddish-language cultural life virtually came to an end. The number of synagogues steadily dwindled until, in 1962, there were only sixty-two left in the entire country. Although Jews as individuals could remain party members (there were 260,000 in 1982) and pursue professional careers in a number of areas, the resuscitation of a corporate Jewish cultural life was prevented, even in the post-Stalin thaw following the Twentieth Party Congress of 1956.

—*Klaus Holz*
*Richard S. Levy, translation*

**See also** Anti-Zionism in the USSR; Doctors' Plot; Jewish Anti-Fascist Committee; *Ostjuden;* Purge of 1968; Slánský Trial; Stalin, Joseph; Stalinization of Eastern Europe; USSR

**References**

Hodos, Georg Hermann. *Schauprozesse: Stalinistische Säuberungen in Osteuropa, 1948–54* (Zurich, Switzerland: Verlag NZZ, 1988).

Levin, Nora. *The Jews in the Soviet Union since 1917.* 2 vols. (New York: New York University Press, 1988).

Weber, Hermann, and Dietrich Staritz, eds. *Kommunisten verfolgen Kommunisten: Stalinistischer Terror und "Säuberungen" in den kommunistischen Parteien Europas seit den dreißiger Jahren* (Berlin: Akademie Verlag, 1993).

## Purishkevich, Vladimir Mitrofanovich (1879–1920)

A prominent right-wing political activist in late imperial Russia, noted for his virulent antisemitism, and a leading participant in the murder of imperial favorite Gregori Rasputin, Vladimir Purishkevich was born to a wealthy landowning family in Kishinev, Bessarabia Province (present-day Chisinau, Moldova). After attending Novorossiisk University in Odessa, he participated in the work of the district and provincial *zemstvos,* the organs of local self-government in the Russian Empire. In 1900, he entered the civil service in St. Petersburg, pursuing a short-lived career in the Ministry of Internal Affairs.

Purishkevich was an active member of the Russian Assembly (Russkoe Sobranie), an upper-class body that was initially devoted to supporting Russian culture before evolving into a right-wing political organization. The Russian Assembly regarded the autocracy and the Russian Orthodox Church as the safeguards of national integrity. "Troublesome" national minorities, especially the Jews, met with that body's hostility.

After the Revolution of 1905, Purishkevich helped A. I. Dubrovin found the militantly right-wing Union of the Russian People (Soiuz Russkogo Naroda [SRN]), a political party known for its attempt to build a broader rightist political coalition. He served as deputy chairman of the SRN's council and contributed to its paper, the *Russian Banner* (*Russkoe znamia*).

Purishkevich was elected to the Second, Third, and Fourth State Dumas, the Russian parliament, where he was an articulate critic of the Left and Center and a gadfly to the government over such issues as Prime Minister Peter Stolypin's effort to extend the zemstvo system to the western provinces, which had a large Polish population. He was also a frequent critic of alleged Jewish influence in the Russian universities. Purishkevich broke with Dubrovin and the SRN in 1908, founding his own Union of the Archangel Michael, which also included antisemitism as one of its ideological props. These and similar bodies constituted the so-called Black Hundreds, some of whose adepts were responsible for street violence and political terrorism against the Center and Left.

At the outbreak of World War I, Purishkevich was a leading organizer of civilian efforts in support of the army. Soon, however, he became disenchanted at the incompetence and malfeasance that he encountered. In a celebrated Duma speech in 1916, he blamed the failures of Russia's war effort on "dark forces" surrounding the throne. Purishkevich played a major role in organizing and carrying out the removal of one such force in the assassination of Rasputin on the night of December 16, 1916.

Purishkevich was imprisoned by the Bolsheviks after the 1917 October Revolution. Released under an amnesty, he made his way to the south, where he joined the White, anti-Bolshevik movement in the Russian Civil War. He died of typhus in February 1920 in Rostov-on-Don.

Purishkevich's brand of antisemitism was typical of the political Right in fin-de-siècle Russia, depicting the Jews as a corrupting force undermining the foundations of Christian Europe. His special contribution was to play on the insecurities of Russia's landed elite by developing the motif of a Jewish plot to gain control of Russia's landed wealth. This plot was exemplified by the land-redistribution policies advocated by centrist parties, such as the Constitutional Democrats, which also advocated full and equal rights for Jews. Like his associate Pavolaki Krushevan, Purishkevich was a "man of the borderlands," using Russian superpatriotism to compensate for his own non-Russian origins.

—*John D. Klier*

**See also** Black Hundreds; Kishinev Pogrom; Krushevan, Pavolaki; Russia, Imperial; Russia, Revolution of 1905; Russian Civil War; Russian Orthodox Church

*References*

Rawson, Don C. *Russian Rightists and the Revolution of 1905* (Cambridge: Cambridge University Press, 1995).

Rogger, Hans. *Jewish Policies and Right-Wing Politics in Imperial Russia* (London: Macmillan, 1986).

# R

## Raabe, Wilhelm (1831–1910)

The history of Wilhelm Raabe's reputation is one of the more peculiar in the annals of German letters. After achieving a *succès d'estime* with his first novel, *Die Chronik der Sperlingsgasse* (The Chronicle of Sparrow Alley [1856]), he pursued three not fully congruent goals over the rest of his life: to remain faithful to a thematically and stylistically idiosyncratic voice and vision, to be recognized as a preceptor to his nation, and to make a living exclusively from fiction writing. In the 1860s, he attempted to force a breakthrough with ambitious novels. One of these, *Der Hungerpastor* (The Hunger Pastor [1863–1864]), parallels the career of Hans Unwirrsch, whose German virtues of moral introspection and selfless idealism led to a life of humble service, with that of Moses Freudenstein, who, with "Semitic" heartlessness, becomes a Frenchified intellectual renamed Théophile Stein, a violator of women, and a government spy. The novel was indifferently received at first, but as Raabe increasingly escaped readers' horizons with subtle narrative experiments, the public returned to it until it became his best-known and most enduring work.

He attracted a petty-bourgeois coterie that admired him less as a literary artist than as a wise man and nationalist icon. After his death, the group constituted itself as the Society of the Friends of Wilhelm Raabe, the second-largest literary society in Germany. The largest such group was the Goethe Society, which, when Nazified, celebrated *The Hunger Pastor* as an antisemitic masterpiece. This imputation burdened Raabe's reputation after World War II until, beginning in the 1960s, he was wrested from his "friends" by scholars who emphasized his variety of narrative perspective, generating a critical renaissance. Nevertheless, the shadow of antisemitism persisted among less specialized observers.

It is plausible that Raabe modeled his novel on Gustav Freytag's best-seller, *Debit and Credit.* Raabe did not admire Freytag or his novel and likely thought that, if that was what the public wanted, he could do it better. In this, he was correct. Especially his Jewish antagonist is more capable, dangerous, and suavely captivating than Freytag's scruffy Veitel Itzig, to whom the hero is never attracted. However, in the long run, Raabe's tactic was an error in judgment. There are parallels to Charles Dickens's situation in the wake of *Oliver Twist.* Raabe, too, replied defensively to a sorrowful reproach from a Jewish lady, and he, too, compensated with positive Jewish figures, among them the tragic dancer Jemima from the Prague ghetto in *Holunderblüte* (Elder Blossom [1863]) and the wise, brave Jewish banker's widow in *Frau Salome* (Madame Salome [1875]).

As with Freytag, there is no indication of antisemitic attitudes in Raabe's personal life. He had normal relationships with Jewish friends and acquaintances and attracted numerous Jewish admirers. For many years, a literary historian of Jewish origin was vice-president of the Raabe Society and president of the Berlin chapter until he was expelled in 1933. Nevertheless, today's understandable desire to liberate Raabe from the burden of his reception history sometimes fails to acknowledge his responsibility for a novel too easily assimilable to malevolent purposes.

—*Jeffrey L. Sammons*

**See also** *Biarritz;* Dahn, Felix; *Debit and Credit;* Dickens, Charles; Emancipation; Freytag, Gustav; Jewish Question; Nazi Cultural Antisemitism; Riehl, Wilhelm Heinrich

**References**

Sammons, Jeffrey L. "Raabe and the Jews: The Case of the *The Hunger Pastor.*" In *Wilhelm Raabe: The Fiction of the Alternative Community* (Princeton, NJ: Princeton University Press, 1987), 73–87.

———. *The Shifting Fortunes of Wilhelm Raabe: A History of Criticism as a Cautionary Tale* (Columbia, SC: Camden House, 1992).

## Rabbi's Speech, The

Touted by antisemites as "proof" of a Jewish world conspiracy, *The Rabbi's Speech* derives from the chapter "In the Jewish Cemetery in Prague" in the multipart novel *Biarritz* (1868) by the minor German writer Herrmann Goedsche (whose pseudonym was Sir John Retcliffe). The chapter features a clandestine meeting held in 1860 by the heads of the twelve tribes of Israel, where each man, speaking in Chaldean (in Prague!), outlines his past activities and future plans aimed at suborning and enslaving the gentiles. These proceedings, in which the conspirators worship the Golden Calf, are secretly observed by a German and a baptized Jew, who commit themselves to unmasking the conspiracy.

*Biarritz* was translated into several languages, including Russian (under the title *To Sedan!*), and as a result, the "Jewish Cemetery" chapter took on a life of its own and became a link in the chain of spurious documents leading to the *Protocols of the Elders of Zion*. In 1872, the chapter was published in Russia in the form of an anonymous brochure, *The Jewish Cemetery in Prague and the Council of Representatives of the 12 Tribes of Israel*. In 1876 and again in 1880, the brochure appeared under a title that explicitly identified it as an excerpt from "Retcliffe's" novel. Sometime during the 1880s, a new text arose, in which the separate statements of the participants in the cemetery merged into a single speech, supposedly given by a famous rabbi to a gathering of his coreligionists in 1880 (in some versions, 1869). The identity of the person responsible for this reworked document has not been established. By the 1900s, *The Rabbi's Speech* (appearing under varying titles), by then regarded as the record of a real event, had appeared in several languages. The author of the *Protocols* was clearly familiar with it; parallels between the two works have been noted by scholars. Conversely, since the first appearance of the *Protocols,* those who insist that work is genuine—for example, Georgii Butmi in his 1906 edition—have pointed to this similarity as evidence of their claim.

Throughout the twentieth century, both the original chapter from "Retcliffe's" novel and its reworking continued to appear. As recently as February 2002, a version of *The Rabbi's Speech* was published in the Russian extremist newspaper *Kazachii krug* (Cossack Circle), which led to the newspaper receiving an official warning from the Press Ministry.

—*Henryk Baran*

**See also** *Biarritz*; *Protocols of the Elders of Zion*; Russia, Imperial

**References**

Cohn, Norman. *Warrant for Genocide: The Myth of the Jewish World Conspiracy and the "Protocols of the Elders of Zion."* New ed. (London: Serif, 1996).

Neuhaus, Volker. *Der zeitgeschichtliche Sensationsroman in Deutschland, 1855–1878: "Sir John Retcliffe" und seine Schule* (Berlin: Schmidt, 1980), 110–118; 191–196.

## Racial Laws (Italy)

With the collection of Racial Laws passed in September 1938, the Fascist government officially launched systematic antisemitic politics in Italy. New laws appeared serially, following the general trend from a gradual loss of rights to complete the disenfranchisement of the Jewish population. A vital preparatory step to the introduction and the successive application of the racial measures was the census of August 22, 1938, the importance of which cannot be overestimated. The updated census of 1942 provided the basis for Jewish forced labor; that of 1943 provided an essential tool enabling the German occupiers to extend the Final Solution to Italy. The principal legislative dispositions were based on the census of 1938 and were drawn up between the beginning of September and November of that year. These laws profoundly impacted the civil and then the human rights of Italian Jews. By design, the first measures sought to separate Jews from the rest of the population. For example, the law of September 5, 1938, initiated by Minister of National Education Giuseppe Bottai for *la difesa della razza nella scuola fascista* (the defense of the race in the Fascist schools), essentially expelled Jewish students from public schools and universities. Simultaneously, the issuance of the first articles restricting the rights of Jews necessitated creation within the Ministry of the Interior of the Office of Demography and Race, known as the Demorazza. This body functioned as the administrative and bureaucratic nerve center and carried out Fascist anti-Jewish policy; it issued many directives, usually in the form of circular letters, ranging from the pettily vexatious to the seriously immiserating. During these years, the Jewish birthrate declined, even as the suicide rate rose.

Aside from the initial ban on school attendance, most of the laws focused on eliminating Jewish economic activities, another process made easier by the essential Census of 1938. Jews were driven from the professions and prohibited from working in banking or insurance, owning property beyond a fixed value, marrying non-Jews, or employing them. They could no longer serve in the military or civil administration.

Traditional historiography has attempted to portray the Racial Laws and other measures leading up to the deportation and murder of Italian Jews as forced on Benito Mussolini by the Germans; antisemitism, the argument runs, was not really intrinsic to Italian fascism. Yet there is no historical evidence to support the contention that the Racial Laws were inspired or dictated by the Nazis or that they can be understood as anything other than voluntary. True, the deportations did not begin until the fall of Mussolini and his return as a German puppet in the Italian Social Republic (in September 1943). But well before that moment, his regime had categorized Jews as "enemy aliens" or Bolshevik agents. A press campaign aimed at Jewish anti-Fascists, equating them with Zionists, appeared in Fascist journals in 1934. In 1938, the press campaign spread from known antisemitic vehicles into the national press in general, focusing on foreign Jews and scapegoating them for high food prices and unemployment. No dissenting voices about the uselessness, the harmfulness, and the worthlessness of Jews were heard. Fi-

nally, the *Manifesto of the Race* (July 1938) provided a "scientific" basis for the Racial Laws, declaring that Jews did not belong to the pure Aryan Italian race.

Although these interventions by the Fascist state did not directly threaten the lives of Jews, they prepared the climate and laid the foundation on which the persecution ultimately rested. Although hunted Jews often received the help of neighbors and strangers, the example of the corruption of the regime was bound to spread to the people. Individuals and groups readily took advantage of the elimination of Jewish competitors or enriched themselves with the expropriation of their property. In the economic crisis of the war years, it was not unusual to petition the government to take occupancy of a house previously owned by Jews. Some went so far as to become bounty hunters, earning paltry sums by betraying Jews to the Fascist and German authorities.

—*Simone Duranti*

See also Holocaust; *Manifesto of the Racial Scientists;* Mussolini, Benito; October Roundup; Papacy, Modern; Preziosi, Giovanni

**References**

Michaelis, Meir. *Mussolini and the Jews: German-Italian Relations and the Jewish Question in Italy, 1922–1945* (Oxford: Clarendon Press, 1978).

Sarfatti, Michele. *Mussolini contro gli ebrei: Cronaca dell'elaborazione delle leggi del 1938* (Turin, Italy: S. Zamorani Editore, 1994).


# Racism, Scientific

Scientific racism (or biological racism) was an ideology with roots in the Enlightenment that became especially prominent in late nineteenth- and early twentieth-century Western culture. It alleged that biological differences between races were considerable, not only in their physical and mental traits but also in their moral characters. Scientific racists assiduously gathered empirical evidence about the anatomy, intellectual abilities, and moral character of humans from all over the world, believing it would support their racial in-egalitarianism. They were zealous about measuring body parts, especially cranial capacities and facial features, by which to compare different races. Though claiming the authority of science, proponents ignored contrary evidence and sys-

The anatomist Robert Knox played a key role in spreading scientific racism (and antisemitism) in the United Kingdom through his book, *The Races of Men* (1850). (National Library of Medicine)

tematically interpreted all evidence in light of their racial prejudices.

Scientific racism thus reinforced Europeans' overblown opinions of their cultural and biological superiority and provided justification for European oppression of other races. Most scientific racists constructed racial hierarchies with Europeans (and their descendants) at the top of the scale. They wrongly assumed that since Europeans, on the average, had larger cranial capacities than people of other races, they must also have greater intellectual powers. They believed this accounted for the technological and cultural superiority of the Europeans, which they generally assumed.

From the University of Edinburgh medical school, the anatomist Robert Knox played a key role in spreading scientific racism (and antisemitism) in Britain through his book *The Races of Men* (1850), wherein he wrote, "Race is everything: literature, science, art—in a word, civi-

lization depends on it" (7). James Hunt, first president and leading figure of the London Anthropological Society in the 1860s, likewise portrayed race as the most influential factor in history and culture, and he strongly opposed racial egalitarianism and universal human rights. Comte Joseph Arthur de Gobineau's *Essay on the Inequality of Human Races* (1853–1855) was highly influential in spreading biological racism on the Continent, although it enjoyed greater popularity in Germany than it ever did in his native France.

The introduction and growth of Darwinism in the late nineteenth century gave impetus to scientific racism by emphasizing biological inequality. Like many of his contemporaries, Charles Darwin thought non-European races were inferior intellectually and morally, and this belief provided him and his followers a powerful argument for human evolution, since biological evolution required variation within species. Thus, many Darwinists believed that black Africans, American Indians, Australian Aborigines, and other non-Europeans were less advanced members of the human species. Some Darwinists went even further in emphasizing human variation by classifying different human races as distinct species. The leading Darwinian biologist in Germany, Ernst Haeckel, was intensely racist, not only separating humans into twelve distinct species and four genera but also claiming that the intellectual difference between the highest humans and the lowest humans was greater than that between the lowest humans and dogs or elephants.

Although scientific racism was not always antisemitic—often categorizing the black and yellow races even lower than Jews on the hierarchy—it nonetheless played an important role in perpetuating and bolstering antisemitism among secular intellectuals from the late nineteenth century onward. The rise of religious toleration in nineteenth-century Europe and the United States benefited Jews, but the replacement of religious bigotry with scientific racism ultimately resulted in even greater discrimination against Jews. When the famous German pathologist and anthropologist Rudolf Virchow carried out a scientific study of racial features among schoolchildren in Germany in the 1870s, he clearly distinguished between German and Jewish "racial types" in his study. Though he was not antisemitic in his personal disposition, his study taught Germans to differentiate between Germans and Jews as separate races. Ironically, some Jewish scientists and physicians embraced scientific racism in one form or another in the late nineteenth and early twentieth centuries. Even though they often did so in order to use racial theory to combat the antisemitism rampant among scientific racists, they nonetheless unwittingly contributed to an ideology that would later underpin the Holocaust.

From the late nineteenth century, scientific racism provided secular antisemites with a rationale for perpetuating many of the prejudices inherited from Christian tradition. In Germany, Wilhelm Marr and Eugen Dühring began promoting a biological racist form of antisemitism in the late 1870s, and later, Theodor Fritsch and his Hammer movement disseminated antisemitism as an integral part of the Darwinian racial struggle. Madison Grant's influential book *Passing of the Great Race* warned Americans that the Anglo-Saxon racial stock was being "driven off the streets of New York City by the swarms of Polish Jews" (1916, 91). At the beginning of the twentieth century, some antisemitic racial theorists, such as the extremely influential Houston Stewart Chamberlain, blended scientific racism with elements of mysticism. Jörg Lanz von Liebenfels, a Viennese occult race theorist emphasizing Aryan supremacy, also synthesized mystical and scientific racism in his journal *Ostara,* which Hitler may have read as a young man in Vienna.

These antisemites argued that stereotypes commonly attributed to Jews—greed, deceit, materialism, sexual depravity, and numerous other vices—were biological traits fixed in the Jewish racial constitution. Thus, they construed these immoral characteristics as unchanging, inherent features of the Jewish personality. If Jews could not alter their moral character, as this biological determinist vision of human nature implied, then assimilation was ultimately impossible. Neither baptism nor education could alter the biological character of the Jew. The "logic" of this thinking suggested that the only way to combat the purportedly pernicious Jewish influence was to eliminate the Jews, either by segregation, expulsion, or yet harsher means.

Scientific racism was influential throughout Western culture. It was rampant in the German and Austrian press in the early twentieth century and was especially pronounced among eugenicists and in Pan-German circles, where Hitler imbibed it. Hitler's worldview was impregnated with scientific racism, as is apparent in his speeches and in *Mein Kampf.* He defined the Jews as a biological race, not a religion (even though the Nazis found it impossible to use this definition when they actually formulated antisemitic policy).

In Western culture, scientific racism declined after the 1920s, except in Germany, where its precipitous decline dated instead from the collapse of the Nazi regime. Most scientists and other scholars in the mid- to late twentieth century recognized that racial differences were not as prominent or as provable as scientific racists had imagined. Many rejected biological determinism altogether, especially when it purported to explain human behavior, and even when biological determinism was revitalized in the late twentieth century by sociobiology and evolutionary psychology, most sociobiologists denied that their views were racist.

—*Richard Weikart*

**See also** Austria; Chamberlain, Houston Stewart; Dühring, Eugen; Eugenics; Evolutionary Psychology; Fritsch, Theodor; Gobineau, Joseph Arthur de; Hitler, Adolf; Imperial Hammer League; Lanz von Liebenfels, Jörg; Marr, Wilhelm; Pan-German League; *Passing of the Great Race;* Social Darwinism

**References**

Efron, John F. *Defenders of the Race: Jewish Doctors and Race Science in Fin-de-Siècle Europe* (New Haven, CT: Yale University Press, 1994).

Tucker, William H. *The Science and Politics of Racial Research* (Urbana: University of Illinois Press, 1994).

Weikart, Richard. "Progress through Racial Extermination: Social Darwinism, Eugenics, and Pacifism in Germany, 1860–1918," *German Studies Review* 26 (2003): 273–294.

———. *From Darwin to Hitler: Evolutionary Ethics, Eugenics and Racism in Germany* (New York: Palgrave Macmillan, 2004).

## Rathenau, Walther (1867–1922)

The German industrialist, intellectual, and public servant Walther Rathenau was the son of Emil Rathenau, the founder of the German General Electric Company (AEG). Despite his artistic and literary inclinations, the young man took a doctorate in physics in 1889. He served his requisite one year of military duty in the elite cavalry guards in Berlin, but Prussian proscriptions against Jewish officers dashed his hopes of an army career. Rathenau worked as an engineer before joining the AEG as a director in 1899, becoming chairman of the board in 1907. While also serving as a director or board member of over 100 German and foreign firms, he built the AEG into the largest electric conglomerate in Europe. As his prominence grew in Germany, Rathenau became the target of antisemites, who viewed him as the symbol of supposed Jewish dominance. He was denounced in the antisemitic press as one of the so-called Three Hundred Elders of Zion, who were accused of secretly manipulating the fate of Germany and the world.

Rathenau remained an eclectic intellectual and social critic throughout his life. He supported the arts and was close to several leading European artists and intellectuals. At home both with high society and the avant-garde, he won acclaim as a provocative essayist writing on social, economic, and cultural issues of the day. His major books include *Zur Kritik der Zeit* (Criticism of the Age [1912]) and his best-selling *Von Kommenden Dingen* (In Days to Come [1917]). Following World War I, he addressed the new situation in Germany in widely read pamphlets on the economy, state, and society.

Rathenau's nature abounded in self-contradiction. He was a monarchist who yearned for a peoples' democracy; a capitalist who was greatly disturbed by the problems of wealth, urging a rationalized planned economy and heavy, progressive taxation; and a connoisseur who decried luxury. Throughout his life, there was a tension between the pragmatic and the romantic and a tendency to self-dramatize. His relationship to Judaism exemplified the man's complexity.

Rathenau strove for assimilation, and in opposition to the Zionists, he refused to see Jews as a separate people. "My people are the Ger-

Industrialist, organizer of the German war effort, and first foreign minister of the Weimar Republic, Walther Rathenau was assassinated in 1922 by rightwing extremists who claimed he was one of the so-called Three Hundred Elders of Zion. (Library of Congress)

mans, nothing else," he stated, arguing that it was culture rather than religion that defined a people. Although he rejected Judaism as a religion, he remained conscious of his Jewish background. Disdaining opportunism, he refused baptism despite the social advantages it entailed and also rejected it as a solution to the so-called Jewish problem. His lifelong preoccupation with the role of Jews in German society expressed itself in major works on the subject, *Höre, Israel* (Hear, Israel [1897]) and *Staat und Judentum* (The State and Judaism [1911]).

Rathenau's direct involvement in politics began in World War I with his leadership of the War Materials Department. In 1918, he advocated sweeping democratic reforms and a *levée en masse* (mass national rising) to sustain the war effort. He ghostwrote the German notes to President Woodrow Wilson in preparing the way for the Armistice of 1918 and served as a government expert at the Paris Peace Conference in 1919 and at subsequent economic conferences. His views about economic reconstruction, voiced in the German Socialization Commission, won him the enmity of his fellow industrialists. Although a vehement opponent of the Versailles Treaty, he accepted the position of reconstruction minister in the government of Joseph Wirth. Together, they backed the policy of fulfillment, which sought to revise the Versailles Treaty by demonstrating its unworkability. With reluctance, Rathenau also took the position of foreign minister in January 1922. Continuing to work for revision of the Paris Peace Settlement, he sought the intervention of the United States and cooperation within Europe. The lack of progress in these efforts led him to sign the Treaty of Rapallo, establishing equal relations with the Soviet Union during the Genoa conference on European reconstruction.

The spread and radicalization of antisemitism following the war greatly disturbed Rathenau. Already embattled with the extreme nationalists over his fulfillment strategy and as the most prominent Jew in German politics, he experienced numerous threats on his life. The Rapallo Treaty served to confirm the worst suspicions of the antisemitic Right—that Rathenau was in league with the Bolsheviks. On June 24, 1922, he was murdered by young nationalist and antisemitic officers, proud that they had struck a blow against the Weimar Republic and the Jews.

—*Mark Swartzburg*

**See also** Fritsch, Theodor; German National People's Party; Germanic Order; Jew Census; *Protocols of the Elders of Zion;* Self-Hatred, Jewish; "Three Hundred," The; Versailles Treaty; Weimar; Zionism

**References**

Felix, David. *Walther Rathenau and the Weimar Republic: The Politics of Reparations* (Baltimore, MD: Johns Hopkins University Press, 1971).

Kessler, Harry Graf. *Walther Rathenau: His Life and Work* (New York: Harcourt, Brace, 1930).

Pogge von Strandmann, Hartmut, ed. *Walther Rathenau: Industrialist Banker, Intellectual, and Politician: Notes and Diaries, 1907–1922* (Oxford: Clarendon Press, 1985).

## Ratzinger, Georg (1844–1899)

Georg Ratzinger, a Catholic social critic and publicist, devoted most of his career to addressing the plight of the German peasantry, for which he held Jews uniquely responsible. A peasant's son raised near Deggendorf in Lower Bavaria, he was able, through church support, to gain a higher education, first at preparatory school in Passau and then at the University of Munich, where he received a doctorate in theology in 1868.

For the following two decades, he juggled a prolific journalistic career with various clerical offices, until he finally left the priesthood in 1888 to devote himself fully to political activism. An early influence was the Catholic notable Count Ludwig von Arco-Zinneberg, whose *Weekly for the Catholic Nation* Ratzinger edited between 1868 and 1870. On Arco's death, Ratzinger transformed his mentor's reform proposals into *The Preservation of the Peasant Estate* (1883), a book that gained widespread discussion in the Catholic and Bavarian press.

In this work, Ratzinger sounded the themes that defined his subsequent career: the scourge of usury and the ways in which increasingly liberalized real estate markets were allegedly fragmenting landed property, family farms in particular, into small and unproductive parcels. Both evils Ratzinger blamed on the stereotypical "big capital" of the Catholic social imagination, in which Jewish banking and speculative interests supposedly dominated. His proposed solutions to these problems grew more ambitious over the years; his early writings focused chiefly on social insurance schemes, but by 1893, he was promoting legislation to create closed "economic communities" in the countryside, mandatory corporative bodies that would control all economic transactions and thus keep outside creditors and real estate brokers at bay. What remained consistent in his vision was his abiding pessimism about peasants' abilities to manage their own affairs. Credit, he insisted, would inevitably lead most peasant producers to ruination; as for cooperatives, he deemed them a noble but unrealizable idea, given the lack of "the right men" from among the peasantry to run them. In idealizing the peasant past, Ratzinger largely replicated the hierarchical assumptions of his aristocratic mentors. His attitudes toward the real peasantry of his day were unabashedly paternalistic, and his fussy moralizing earned him the disdain of many peasant leaders of the 1890s.

In 1893, Ratzinger won a Bavarian Diet mandate as a candidate for the insurgent Bavarian Peasants League. His relations with the movement's more populist factions proved tempestuous, however, and he departed acrimoniously in 1894; his corporative schemes, in particular, rankled peasant audiences more interested in extending their property rights than surrendering them. His influence remained substantial in the Bavarian Diet, where aspects of his corporative program were adopted by those politicians, mainly Catholic or Conservative, who also identified "the Jew" as a mortal threat to a struggling peasantry. In 1898, he added a Reichstag mandate to his Diet seat, holding both until his death from stomach cancer in the following year. Among his other works are *Peasants, Unite Yourselves!* (1897) and two overtly antisemitic tracts written under other names: *Jewish Occupational Life: Sketches from Today's Social Life* (as "Robert Waldhausen" [1892]) and *Jewry in Bavaria: Sketches from the Past and Proposals for the Future* (as "Gottfried Wolf" [1897]).

—*John Abbott*

See also Agrarian League; Antisemitic Political Parties; German Peasant League; Memminger, Anton; Riehl, Wilhelm Heinrich; Usury
**Reference**
John Abbott. "Peasants in the Rural Public: The Bavarian *Bauernbund,* 1893–1933." Dissertation, University of Illinois at Chicago, 2000.

# Raymund of Peñafort (1175/1180?–1275)

The Dominican jurist, moral theologian, and master general of the Order of Preachers, Raymund of Peñafort retired from administrative work in 1240 to devote the last decades of his life to the conversion of Jews and Muslims to Christianity.

Raymund was born at Peñafort, in Villafranca del Penedes, near Barcelona, between 1175 and 1180 and began his academic studies in Barcelona, where he also taught. He studied canon law at Bologna from 1210 to 1218, returned to Barcelona, and joined the Dominican order (Order of Preachers) in the early 1220s. In 1229, he was called to the papal curia by Gregory IX and charged with compiling Gregory's proposed collection of canon law. Raymund's work, the *Liber Extra,* was published in five books in 1234 and officially dispatched by the pope to the law school of Bologna and to the University of Paris. It remained part of the canon law of the Catholic Church until 1917. Shortly after 1234, Raymund published the second edition of his "summa" on penance, a handbook for confessors in which he included his revision of an earlier treatise on matrimony.

Involved in the establishment of the papal inquisitorial office in Aragon in 1232, Raymund returned to Catalonia in 1236 and was elected master general of the Dominican Order in 1238. His revision of the Dominican constitutions remained in force until 1924. In 1240, Raymund resigned as master general and spent the remaining thirty-five years of his life converting Spain's Jews and Muslims to Christianity; he also established Dominican schools in Murcia and Tunis that taught Arabic and Hebrew to missionaries and religious disputants. Among his disciples were Pablo Christiani and Raymund Martini, both of whom would later become influential disputants.

In 1259, Raymund urged his fellow Dominican Thomas Aquinas to prepare a statement of Christian doctrine that could be used by preachers to convert Muslims and Jews. Aquinas responded with the *Summa contra gentiles,* a defense of Christian doctrine allegedly based on human reason alone. In the work of Aquinas, the *Liber Extra,* the language schools, and his disciples, Raymund exerted enormous influence on Jewish-Christian relations in the later thirteenth and fourteenth centuries. In 1601, Raymund of Peña, who had died in 1275, was canonized.

—*Edward Peters*

See also Dominican Order; Inquisition; Middle Ages, High
**References**
Chazan, Robert. *Church, State and Jew in the Middle Ages* (New York: Behrman House, 1980), 37–42.

Cohen, Jeremy. *The Friars and the Jews: The Evolution of Medieval Anti-Judaism* (Ithaca, NY: Cornell University Press, 1982), 104–108.

Hinnebusch, William A. *The History of the Dominican Order: Intellectual and Cultural Life to 1500.* Vol. 2 (New York: Alba House, 1973), 248–252.

## Rebatet, Lucien (1903–1972)

Born in a French village of the Drôme region, Lucien Rebatet had an undistinguished scholarly career, abandoning studies in religion, law, and philosophy. In 1929, he began contributing to the Catholic royalist *Revue de l'Action Française* and served briefly as personal secretary to its founder, Charles Maurras. When Rebatet's views grew more radical, he turned to the fascist paper *Je suis partout* (I Am Everywhere), for which he organized two special issues on Jews (in 1938 and 1939). With virulent harangues and assertions that Alfred Dreyfus was, indeed, guilty, Rebatet's antisemitism harked back to the era of Édouard Drumont. After the 1940 armistice with the Germans, Rebatet worked briefly for Vichy radio and the fascist collaborator Jacques Doriot's *Le cri du peuple* (*The People's Cry*). Under the pseudonym François Vinneuil, Rebatet published *Les tribus du cinéma et du théâtre* (*The Tribes of Cinema and Theater* [1941]), which attributed a corrupting hegemony to Jews in these arts. His increasingly aggressive stance also led him to castigate the traditional Right: Philippe Pétain (for not collaborating thoroughly enough with Nazi Germany), the Catholic Church (for having in his eyes succumbed to the influence of the Jews), and his former idol Maurras (for being a Germanophobe and obstinately against taking action). Rebatet's breakthrough came in 1942 with the publication of *Les décombres* (*The Ruins*). An insult-laden diatribe that is one of the most extreme expressions of French fascism and antisemitism ever published, it became the Occupation's best-selling work, with demand far exceeding the rationed paper available for new editions. At a time when France's deportation of Jews was already under way, the book was rife with ominous threats much in the vein of Louis-Ferdinand Céline: "Jewry offers the sole example in the history of humanity of a race for whom collective punishment is the only just recourse" (Carroll 1995, 212). By the end of the war, Rebatet was one of the most extreme supporters of French collaboration, extolling the virtues of a fascist Europe.

In August 1944, while fellow fascist authors Robert Brasillach and Pierre Drieu la Rochelle chose to stay behind, Rebatet fled with the Vichy government to Sigmaringen, Germany. Flight doubtless saved his life. He was eventually arrested and sentenced to death, but after Brasillach's execution in February 1945 provoked disapproval in some quarters, Rebatet gained a reprieve in late 1946. (Arguably, a reversal of roles would have been just as equitable.) He left prison in 1952 with a completed manuscript, the 1,312-page novel *Les deux étendards* (*The Two Banners*). Although Rebatet is still almost universally reviled as an individual, this work about a love triangle has nonetheless won begrudging praise from a few contemporary critics.

In 1976, Jean-Jacques Pauvert brought out a posthumous edition of Rebatet's *Les mémoires d'un fasciste* (*Memoirs of a Fascist*), an autobiography that included a version of *Les décombres* that elided 135 of the book's most offensive pages. Because there was no editorial indication of these crucial deletions, the public received a thoroughly misleading view of Rebatet's prior public pronouncements.

—Ralph W. Schoolcraft III

**See also** *Action Française*; Brasillach, Robert; Céline, Louis-Ferdinand; Dreyfus Affair; Drumont, Édouard; France; Maurras, Charles; Vichy

**Reference**

Carroll, David. *French Literary Fascism: Nationalism, Anti-Semitism, and the Ideology of Culture* (Princeton, NJ: Princeton University Press, 1995).

## Reformation (1517–1648)

The term *Reformation* denotes the Christian movement that replaced the illusory medieval vision of united belief and administration in Western Christendom with the diverse beliefs and denominations that characterize modern Christianity. Church groups that stem from this break with the Roman Catholic Church are termed Protestant. The movement's origins lay in the intensification of piety after 1400, complaints about financial and administrative abuses within the church, and Renaissance humanism. The Reformation was influential in England, France, the Netherlands, German-speaking areas, and North America. The hallmark of the Reformation is the belief that humans are justified by divine grace and not through their own works. But the Reformers attacked many other aspects of traditional piety, particularly the church's ritual and magical components. Reformers supported retranslation of the Bible into vernacular languages, in order to correct errors in the Vulgate, provide broader access to Scripture, and narrow the relationship between doctrine and biblical teachings.

The Reformation began during an expulsion of Jews from western Europe (under way by the 1480s) that shifted the population center of European Jewry to Poland by 1550, where it remained until the Chmielnicki massacres. The Reformation did not cause the persecution of Jews, however; Christian hostility toward Judaism based on supersessionism—the idea that Jesus' resurrection abrogated God's covenant with Abraham's progeny, replacing his descendants with the church as the "new Israel"—was established at Christianity's origins. Since the 1980s, scholarly consensus has called this belief anti-Judaism rather than antisemitism because Jews could often convert to Christianity to avoid persecution. The Reformation also coincided with a peak in the persecution of Jews based on fantasies that they ritually murdered Christian children, used their blood to make matzah, or tortured the consecrated host, which Christians of the time believed had been transubstantiated into the body of Christ during Holy Communion. It is possible that Reformation attacks on transubstantiation and the Eucharistic piety so focused on blood imagery contributed to the decline in ritual murder accusations after about 1550. The Reformer Andreas Osiander published works denying ritual murder allegations. Scholars also argue that antisemitism in its nineteenth- and twentieth-century forms (the wish to expel or exterminate Jews based on racial or social Darwinist views) did not exist during the Reformation, since race thinking emerged in Europe only later. Reformation theological writing

on the Jews, it has been argued, suggests that Jewishness was not an indelible characteristic.

Moreover, with their focus on Bible translation, Reformers inaugurated a widespread Christian interest in original Hebrew texts and Jewish commentaries, an intellectual trend called Christian Hebraism. Johann Reuchlin, Philipp Melanchthon, Ambrosius Blaurer, Konrad Pellikan, and others introduced Hebrew language as a compulsory topic in theological and liberal arts education. Reformers were typically instructed in Hebrew by converts from Judaism. Jewish commentaries were frequently consulted in Martin Luther's definitive 1534 German Bible translation. At the same time, as the Pfefferkorn affair and the uproar surrounding it suggest, the willingness to profit from the Jewish intellectual tradition disturbed contemporary intellectuals. Protestant authorities were not more hostile toward Jewish texts than Catholics, however; incidents of Talmud burning or suppression typically occurred under Catholic (often Inquisition) auspices. Indeed, some Reformers (Wolfgang Capito, Osiander, Sebastian Münster, Paul Fagius) conducted extensive exchanges and conversations with Jews. These exchanges always included attempts at mission, however, and without exception, the most notable mainstream Reformers (Luther, Melanchthon, Ulrich Zwingli, Martin Bucer, John Calvin) can be considered supersessionists. Only Reformers on the margins, such as the notorious Michael Servetus, maintained a positive attitude toward Jews and Judaism. Catholics and Protestants agreed that Servetus's views on the Trinity were heretical, and he was burned at the stake in Geneva in 1553 shortly after evading the Inquisition, which would have executed him as well had he not escaped from its prison.

Given the dispersion caused by the persecution of Jews in territories affected by the Reformation (in the sixteenth century, there were no Jews in England and very few in Germany), most Reformers had contact with Jewish ideas rather than Jewish individuals. Perhaps because of this state of affairs, initial Reformation attitudes toward Jews were less condemning than those of the Catholic tradition. Luther's writing was both influential and typical in this regard. An early sympathy expressed in his 1523 pamphlet *That Jesus Christ Was Born a Jew* caused Jews to be hopeful about what the consequences of the Reformation might mean for their toleration in Europe. But Luther's disappointment with the Jews' failure to convert marked his last years and was expressed in works such as *Against the Sabbatarians* and *On the Jews and Their Lies*—writings that urged forced conversion, expulsion, compulsory labor, and the suppression of Jewish books in order to convince the Jews of their errors. Contemporaries found this work extreme; Jews in such as Strasbourg successfully petitioned to have *On the Jews and Their Lies* suppressed or not reprinted. Because of the complex administrative arrangements that governed Jewish communities in Germany, city governments could not always expel Jews granted residence by territorial lords or the Holy Roman emperor. Still, it is often clear from Christian dealings with Jewish communities that Jews were tolerated as long as the city thought that conversion would be possible; this religious form of pressure to assimilate presaged similar expectations placed on Jews during the German Enlightenment.

Although it has been questioned, the distinction between anti-Judaism and antisemitism is preferable to the ahistorical presentation of the Reformation in recent works, which conflate at least three variants of anti-Jewish sentiment. Nonetheless, it is difficult to know where to draw the line. Mark Edwards noted that the language of antisemitism and that of anti-Judaism are similar because nineteenth-century antisemites drew on imagery from the earlier anti-Jewish tradition. Particularly considering the importance of scholarship as a component in Jewish culture, as Andrew Gow noted, it is difficult to see the desire to eliminate Jewish beliefs and teachings as anything less than the desire to eradicate Jewish life as such. In sixteenth-century preaching, Protestants did not distinguish between Old Testament Israelites, New Testament Jews, and contemporary Jews; this sloppy characterization, which equated "Israel" and "Jews" with sinful humanity, introduced the suggestion of an indelible taint of sin to be associated with Jews and may have foreshadowed the concept of the Jews' irremediable character. Removed from its religious roots, the idea of an incorrigible Jewish essence was later advanced through the rhetoric of race.

Because of the cultural weight of the Reformation, its reception by subsequent scholars is also significant. Reformation historiographers Johannes Mathesius, Cyriakus Spangenberg, and Johannes Sleidan recounted anti-Jewish superstitions, but Johann Andreas Eisenmenger cited them in the eighteenth century to add authority to very different works. Similarly, German National Socialists, drawing on Luther's role as a hero of German nationalism as it developed after the nineteenth century, reprinted *On the Jews and Their Lies* in support of their political goals. In the Anglo-American world, the Reformation has often been cited as a cause of German totalitarianism and the Holocaust, in that Protestantism stressed obedience to secular authority and allegedly failed to develop a theory of political resistance to the unjust sovereign. Although Reformation historians refute this claim, troubling questions about the connection between the Reformation and the subsequent persecution of European Jews have yet to be resolved.

—*Susan R. Boettcher*

**See also** Chmielnicki Massacres; Churches under Nazism; *Entdecktes Judenthum;* Erasmus; Expulsions, Late Middle Ages; Host Desecration; Inquisition; Lavater, Johann Kaspar; Luther, Martin; Melanchthon, Philipp; Michaelis, Johann David; *On the Jews and Their Lies;* Pfefferkorn, Johannes; Ritual Murder (Medieval); Stoecker, Adolf; Supersessionism; Sweden; Talmud Trials

**References**

Bell, Dean Philip. *Sacred Communities: Jewish and Christian Identities in Fifteenth-Century Germany* (Leiden, the Netherlands: Brill, 2001).

Boettcher, Susan R. "Preliminary Considerations on the Rhetorical Construction of Jews in Lutheran Preaching at Mid-Sixteenth Century." In *Reformierter Protestantismus und Judentum im Europa des 16. und 17. Jahrhunderts.* Edited by Achim Detmers (Wuppertal, Germany: Foedus, 2004).

Israel, Jonathan. *European Jewry in the Age of Mercantilism, 1550–1750* (Oxford: Clarendon Press, 1985).

Oberman, Heiko. *The Roots of Anti-Semitism in the Age of Renaissance and Reformation* (Philadelphia: Fortress, 1984).

Ruether, Rosemary Radford. *Faith and Fratricide: The Theological Roots of Anti-Semitism* (New York: Seabury Press, 1974).

## Régis, Max (1873–1950)

A charismatic leader of the anti-Jewish movement in late nineteenth-century French Algeria, Max Régis helped establish antisemitism as a key component of settler political culture in Algeria. Born Massimiliano Milano to parents of Italian origin, Max Régis, as he was called, grew up in a comfortable, middle-class, and Frenchified milieu near the capital city of Algiers. At the time, the settler-dominated civil territories of Algeria were official parts of France and governed by many of the same legal and political institutions as the metropole. Régis became active in settler politics in his early twenties as economic depression and the Dreyfus Affair hit Algeria in the 1890s. He joined with autonomists, socialists, and antisemites in their campaigns for increased independence from France and limits on the rights of Jews. As a law student, Régis, together with his brother Louis, organized student protests against the appointment of a Jewish professor. In 1897, veteran antisemites installed him as president of the Anti-Jewish League of Algiers, from which they built a broadly based settler political movement. They led petition drives, mass demonstrations, and attacks against Jews and French government officials. In May 1898, Régis's league helped elect four anti-Jewish deputies, including Édouard Drumont, to the French National Assembly.

After Régis's brief stint as mayor of Algiers in late 1898, his political power went into decline as the French government quelled anti-Jewish activities and appeased moderate autonomist settler elites. His support dwindled to a small but fiercely antimetropolitan faction from lower-class Spanish neighborhoods. His youth groups were banned and favorite meeting places closed; he often holed up in his "Villa Antijuive" or lived as a fugitive in Spain. In 1901, he made a last stand in an Algiers café in a bar brawl with an old rival. This event, along with the conclusion of the Dreyfus Affair, precipitated the end of the anti-Jewish crisis in Algeria and issued in a general discrediting of Régis and his anti-Jewish movement. He disappeared from the historical record after 1905, although numerous legends describe his life in later decades.

Even though Régis's public career was brief, it signaled an important shift in the dynamics of European antisemitism. Not simply an intellectual current or wave of extralegal violence, antisemitism in Algeria—or *antijudaisme,* as it was called there, to distinguish the Jews from Semitic Arabs—had become a mainstream social movement that used the tools of popular democracy to challenge the supremacy of central state power. This situation made Régis's movement appealing to the Left in the late nineteenth century and to right-wing organizations in the twentieth. According to Hannah Arendt, the crisis in Algiers in 1890 was a harbinger of the formidable antisemitic regime that waged war in Europe in the 1940s. Régis's career also reflected the troublesome relationship that persisted between hardcore Algerian settlers and French Republican governments in Paris until the end of French rule in Algeria in 1962.

—*Lizabeth Zack*

*See also* Algeria; Dreyfus Affair; Drumont, Édouard; France

**References**

Dermenjian, Geneviève. *La Crise Antijuive oranaise, 1895–1905* (Paris: Editions L'Harmattan, 1986).
Hebey, Pierre. *Alger, 1898: La Grande vague antijuive* (Paris: NiL Editions, 1996).

## Renan, Ernest (1822–1893)

Ernest Renan was one of the towering intellectual figures in French society during the nineteenth century. A man of exceptional breadth and knowledge, he had a profound interest in many of the overriding cultural concerns of his day—religion, language, science, nationhood, and government—and wrote extensively on all of them. Many of his books and essays became classics of the era, most notably *The Life of Jesus* (1863), *Intellectual and Moral Reform* (1871), and the famous lecture *What Is a Nation?* (1882). His interest in Jews, Judaism, and Palestine figured prominently and resulted in his five-volume *History of the People of Israel,* completed toward the end of his life. Renan's arguments on the nature of Christianity and Judaism intensively engaged a circle of Jewish writers and thinkers who rejected his characterization of Judaism as an inferior religion.

French philosopher, philologist, and historian, Joseph Ernest Renan (1822–1893). Renan's interest in Jews, Judaism, and Palestine resulted in his five-volume *History of the People of Israel*. (Hulton-Deutsch Collection/Corbis)

Reared for the priesthood, Renan left his theological training in 1845 and turned to philosophy and history, retaining his attachment to Christianity, which he counted as one of the great creations of the human spirit. A positivist, he accepted its Judaic source but concluded that Jesus succeeded in creating a wholly new entity, freed from a narrow-minded, formalistic, ritualistic, and extremist Judaism. According to Renan, the Pharisees had recognized Christ's rupture with Judaism and responded vehemently, calling for his crucifixion. Though Renan questioned the religious tradition of Christianity, arousing, in turn, angry opposition among French clerical figures, he did not absolve the Jewish nation of responsibility for the Crucifixion. Furthermore, he attributed Christianity's manifestations of intolerance to its Jewish origins.

But Renan, who reappraised his opinions on the relationship between Judaism and Christianity on many occasions, did not see Judaism as a mere fossil following the appearance of Christianity; he was fascinated by its staying power and highly regarded its contribution to civilization. Yet his philological studies and his inquiry into the study of the origin of language brought him to see an intrinsic connection between religion, race, and language. Though the Jews were not considered pure Semites, he argued, their identification with this "inferior race" was distinct and the source of their innate deficiencies. In his comparative historical analysis of the Semitic languages (1855), Renan characterized the Semitic race as lacking mythology, science, fiction, plastic arts, abstract thinking, and other basic qualities that were intrinsic to the Indo-Europeans.

Nonetheless, he did not turn his adherence to racial theories into support for antisemitic legislation or suppression of the Jews. Not only did Renan acknowledge that contemporary Jews had distanced themselves considerably from the "fanatical" Pharisaic tradition, he also rejected antisemitic manifestations during his lifetime, supported Jewish emancipation and integration in France, and gradually accepted the tenets of democratic rule.

—*Richard I. Cohen*

**See also** Antisemitism, Etymology of; Deicide; Devi, Savitri; Drumont, Édouard; France; Supersessionism

**References**

Almog, Shmuel. "The Racial Motif in Renan's Attitude to Jews and Judaism." In *Antisemitism through the Ages*. Translated by Nathan H. Reisner (Oxford: Pergamon Press, 1988), 255–278.

Graetz, Michael. *The Jews in Nineteenth-Century France: From the French Revolution to the "Alliance Israélite Universelle."* Translated by Jane Marie Todd (Stanford, CA: Stanford University Press, 1996).

Olender, Maurice. *The Languages of Paradise: Race, Religion, and Philology in the Nineteenth Century.* Translated by Arthur Goldhammer (Cambridge, MA: Harvard University Press, 1992).

## Restitution (Switzerland)

In 1995, the question of what became of Swiss bank accounts belonging to Jewish victims of

Nazism surfaced and prompted a reexamination of Switzerland's role in World War II. The banking scandal also occasioned a new wave of antisemitic discourse.

In 1934, Switzerland had passed a law guaranteeing bank secrecy that attracted many banking customers from all over Europe, including Jews in German-controlled territories. Beginning in 1945, World War II survivors began to appear in Switzerland in search of accounts opened before the war. Most were told either that their documentation was insufficient to prove they owned the accounts or that the accounts had been closed (at the behest of Nazi agents working under cover). The great majority of victims gave up and moved on.

In May 1946, the Washington Accords were signed between Switzerland and the Allies, calling for the Swiss to pay an indemnity of some 250 million Swiss francs for the Nazi gold the country had stored during the war. Switzerland also agreed to consider "with sympathy" the question of the unclaimed bank accounts of victims of Nazism.

The Swiss Banking Association (SBA) foiled governmental attempts at implementing a policy of transparency, even though a federal mandate to deal with "the property in Switzerland of foreigners or stateless persons persecuted on religious, racial, or political grounds" went into effect in December 1962, requiring Swiss banks to locate dormant accounts and match these to owners. The sum of 9.5 million francs suddenly appeared, 75 percent of which found legitimate owners. However, of the approximately 7,000 people listed, only 1,000 claimed funds.

In early 1995, Israeli media criticized the SBA's action. The bankers' association denied that "billions" might still be stored in Switzerland. Nonetheless, under pressure from the World Jewish Congress and with the involvement of U.S. senator Al D'Amato, the first of several commissions to deal with the banking scandal was formed and reached an early agreement, in 1996, to investigate the matter of dormant accounts and restitution. Such measures were insufficient, however, as "new" evidence (actually available in academic publications since the 1970s) came to light regarding Swiss economic cooperation with Nazi Germany. World media scrutiny of Swiss behavior in World War II fostered a sense of encirclement in Swiss political and banking milieus.

Unfortunately, many members of the Swiss elite, seeking to defend the nation, issued oral and written statements that smacked of old religious and political antisemitism. The Swiss ambassador to United States, Carlo Jagmetti, was forced to resign in early 1997 following his descriptions of a "war with organized Jewry" in a confidential report. The former president of Switzerland Jean-Pascal Delamuraz also made inflammatory comments, for which he later apologized. Even as several funds were being set up privately and nationally in early 1997 to deal with the need for restitution, the scandals continued—for example, the Zurich bank guard Christoph Meili reported that his employer was destroying archival material pertaining to World War II. This and other accusations soon prompted more barbs, many of them characterized by a mix of antisemitism, anti-Americanism, and nationalistic isolationism, particularly among some conservative groups.

In October 1997, the head of the Swiss Federation of Jewish Communities and director of the Swiss Fund for Victims of the Holocaust issued the first check, to a Holocaust survivor from Latvia. The SBA's noncooperative attitude had elicited multiple lawsuits, but most were dropped when Swiss banks reached an agreement with plaintiffs' lawyers on damages in March 1998. In August, the World Jewish Congress, the U.S. government, and the SBA signed an agreement calling for banks to pay out between $1.2 and $1.9 billion. The special fund of 273 million francs begun in 1997 was expended, having paid nearly 110,000 Holocaust victims.

The crisis of the Swiss banks and Jewish dormant accounts opened the doors to the questioning of neutral countries' behavior in World War II. In the Swiss case, it also raised anew the specter of antisemitism, prompted a reexamination of Swiss identity, and called into question the country's humanitarian tradition. This debate continues, in both public and academic circles.

—*Guillaume de Syon*

**See also** Aryanization; J Stamp; Switzerland
**References**
Barkan, Elazar. *The Guilt of Nations* (New York: Norton, 2000).
Independent Committee of Eminent Persons. *Report on Dormant Accounts of Victims of Nazi Persecution in Swiss Banks* (Bern: Staempfli Publishers, 1999).
Rickman, Gregg J. *Swiss Banks and Jewish Souls* (New Brunswick, NJ: Transaction Books, 1999).

## Restricted Public Accommodations, United States

Groucho Marx, offered membership in a restricted country club on the condition that his family not use the swimming pool, reportedly quipped in response, "My daughter's only half-Jewish—can she wade in up to her knees?"

Social discrimination against Jews in hotels, resorts, and clubs was, at least as a widespread and thorough phenomenon, a creation of the late nineteenth century. Before the famous Seligman-Hilton controversy of 1877, Jews were occasionally denied access to such establishments. But by the 1880s, many elite venues excluded Jews, and by the early twentieth century, a systematic pattern of exclusion had solidified. The pattern's exact configuration changed over time. In the 1920s, hotel and resort discrimination weakened as the automobile made travel a mass experience and thereby expanded the leisure market. But early twentieth-century suburbanization also popularized country clubs, many of which were built by real estate developers to enhance the elite reputation of their home offerings. As an extension of the elite resorts' leisure lifestyle, most country clubs employed rigid barriers against Jews of any economic station.

Just as Jews had established their own hotels and resorts in response to discrimination, Jews established their own country clubs—more than fifty of them by 1925. Initially, the clubs catered to German American Jews, many of whom hoped to demonstrate their assimilation of gentile values, tastes, and behaviors and to distance themselves from newer east European immigrants. During the depression, when many country clubs of all kinds closed under financial pressure, upwardly mobile east Europeans began to be admitted.

In 1865, Massachusetts had banned racial discrimination in public conveyances, accommodations, and places of entertainment, and New York State did so in 1875. By 1900, similar laws existed in eighteen states, including those where most Jews lived. But enforcement was lax, and courts interpreted these laws narrowly. Jewish organizations, especially the American Jewish Committee (founded in 1906) and the Anti-Defamation League (founded in 1913), were active in efforts to expand state protections against discrimination in public accommodations. (Federal civil rights laws were not yet applicable to individual actions.)

Ethnic restrictions in country clubs persisted long after other areas of American social life opened up; restrictions on Jews were common through the 1950s. By the 1980s, more clubs opened up in response to pressure from prominent members and golf associations (racially restricted clubs cannot host Professional Golf Association tournaments) and as courts tightened the definition of "private" establishments exempt from new federal civil rights laws. In the meantime, Jewish country clubs helped integrate German and east European Jews in the creation of new patterns of Jewish philanthropy and defense activism.

—*Amy Hill Shevitz*

**See also** American Jewish Committee and Antidefamation Efforts in the United States; *Ostjuden;* Restrictive Covenants; Seligman-Hilton Affair; United States
**References**
Higham, John. *Send These to Me: Immigrants in Urban America* (Baltimore, MD: Johns Hopkins University Press, 1984).
Konvitz, Milton R. *A Century of Civil Rights* (New York: Columbia University Press, 1961).
Levine, Peter. "The *American Hebrew* Looks at 'Our Crowd': The Jewish Country Club in the 1920s," *American Jewish History* 83 (March 1995): 27–49.

## Restrictive Covenants

Restrictive covenants are provisions of deeds that restrict the activities of the deed holders. Since the nineteenth century, they have been used by developers and homeowners' associations in the

United States and Canada to prescribe standards for residential developments, ranging from materials used in construction to minimum sales prices for homes. Within the United States and Canada, they have also been used to restrict the rights of owners to sell, lease, or otherwise make their properties available for occupancy by members of racial, religious, and ethnic groups deemed undesirable.

The primary group targeted in both the United States and Canada was African Americans. However, individuals of Asian, Hispanic, and Jewish ancestry were also victims of covenant campaigns. Identified by racial ("Semite," "non-Aryan," "Hebrew") and religious ("non-Christian") rubrics, Jews were banned by such agreements from establishing residence in areas of Boston, Denver, Miami, Minneapolis, St. Paul, Montreal, and other cities, as well as suburbs including those outside Chicago, Los Angeles, New York City, Phoenix, San Diego, and Washington, D.C. One study observed that in central Canada in the mid-twentieth century, Jews were the primary targets of covenants. Concurrently, Jews also participated in covenant campaigns against African Americans and other groups.

The primary period of covenant use ran from the 1910s through the 1940s. Enforcement efforts varied greatly because of the cost of litigation, the energy devoted by advocacy organizations to challenge covenants in court, and the reluctance of some judges to enforce them. Only one state, Minnesota, banned their use through statute (in 1919)—on the basis of religious, not racial, classifications. By the 1940s, liberal sentiment against discrimination, documented by organizations such as local chapters of the Anti-Defamation League (ADL) and human relations commissions, led to additional attempts to ban their use. One key success was the Ontario Supreme Court's ruling in *Drummond v. Wren* (1945) that racial and religious covenants were unconstitutional.

The ideals of racial and ethnic tolerance that emerged with the Allied defeat of Hitler's Germany in 1945 accelerated movements in the United States and Canada to ban racial or religious covenants through judicial challenges nationally. These culminated in the U.S. Supreme Court's *Shelley v. Kraemer* decision in 1948, ruling that public (that is, judicial) enforcement of the private agreements was unconstitutional, thus deeming them unenforceable. Although the cases heard in *Shelley v. Kraemer* involved restrictions against African Americans, organizations such as the American Jewish Committee, the American Jewish Congress, and the ADL submitted "friend of the court" briefs against the restrictions (this was the first such brief for the ADL). The *American Jewish Year Book* also kept readers abreast of the case. A footnote in the U.S. Supreme Court's decision referred to the use of such agreements against Jews and included them in the ban on enforcement. Then, in the 1950 case *Noble and Wolf v. Alley,* the Canadian Supreme Court ruled that the restriction against Jewish purchase and occupancy of a home in an Ontario resort area was unlawful. The Canadian Jewish Congress took a leading role in the case.

Racial and religious restrictive covenants continued to be included in real estate contracts, although to a far lesser extent, after these decisions. A 1958 report by the ADL described their use against Jews in sections of Colorado, Maryland, suburban Washington, D.C., and Florida. Battles were fought with title companies that refused to issue clear titles to Jewish families trying to buy restricted properties, even though the restrictions could no longer be enforced. In the 1960s and thereafter, public figures such as Richard Nixon and Supreme Court Justice William H. Rehnquist were forced to dissociate themselves from the covenants for properties they owned, and others, such as Estes Kefauver, took additional steps to have covenants removed from the deeds.

The use of restrictive covenants was only one of many private strategies to prevent Jews and other groups from settling in certain areas across both the United States and Canada, before and after they were judicially outlawed. From the late nineteenth century on in sections of many cities, owners and landlords frequently refused to deal with Jewish buyers and renters, and "No Jews" signs were common. Unwritten "gentlemen's agreements" to withhold residential property from Jews were even more common. A popular novel of the post–World War II era, Laura Hobson's *Gentleman's Agreement,* publicized their existence in 1947. When local, state, and federal fair housing laws (including the 1968 Fair Housing Act in the United States) banned most private housing discrimination, real estate firms and community members developed more subtle tactics. Cooperatives and other housing developments required "board approval" or club membership as a condition of occupancy. Realtors established secret codes to indicate when homes were not available to Jews or members of other groups.

Over time, discriminatory attempts often succumbed to economic, social, and political pressures for integration. For example, La Jolla, California, had to forgo its discriminatory tactics against Jews in order to attract the new campus of the University of California, which had a large number of Jews on its faculty. And many formerly restricted places, such as Delray Beach in Florida and Northbrook and Highland Park on Chicago's North Shore, eventually became known for their large Jewish communities.

Clearly, restrictive covenants and gentlemen's agreements reveal a past in which Jewish housing choices were circumscribed externally, but it is likely that residential discrimination against Jews has diminished greatly in the United States and Canada, although it has not entirely disappeared.

—*Wendy Plotkin*

**See also** American Jewish Committee and Antidefamation Efforts in the United States; Canada; Hollywood, Treatment of Antisemitism in; Restricted Public Accommodations, United States; Seligman-Hilton Affair; United States

**References**
Belth, N. C., ed. *Barriers: Patterns of Discrimination against Jews* (New York: Friendly House Publishers, 1958).
Epstein, Benjamin R., and Arnold Forster. *"Some of my best friends . . ."* (New York: Farrar, Straus, and Cudahy, 1962).
Hobson, Laura Z. *Gentleman's Agreement* (New York: Simon and Schuster, 1947).
Stratthaus, Mary Ellen. "Flaw in the Jewel: Housing Discrimination against Jews in La Jolla," *American Jewish History* 84 (1996): 189–219.
Walker, James W. St. G. *"Race," Rights and the Law in the Supreme Court of Canada: Historical Case Studies* (Waterloo: Osgoode Society for Canadian Legal History and Wilfred Laurier University Press, 1997).

# Reuchlin, Johann (1455–1522)

A Christian humanist and advocate of Judaic study, Johann Reuchlin was born in Pforzheim, Germany, and educated first at Freiburg, then in Paris, and finally in Basel, where he received his B.A. (in 1475) and M.A. (in 1477) and began the study of Greek: he was one of the first Germans to learn that language. In 1480, he received a law degree at Poitiers and then practiced and taught law at Tübingen and Heidelberg, becoming counselor to secular rulers. But humanistic interests continued to draw him to the study of languages and ancient literature. Reuchlin's interest in Hebraic studies led him to Bologna, where he studied Hebrew language and Talmud with Rabbi Obadiah Sforno, one of the more prominent exegetes of his time.

As a Christian humanist who sought a synthesis of classical, Jewish, and Christian traditions, Reuchlin was drawn to the Kabbalah and published *On the Miraculous Word* and *On the Kabbalistic Art,* as well as a Hebrew grammar that remained a standard for decades. Significant as these were for introducing Jewish thought to the Christian West, they are eclipsed by one of the defining episodes in the history of Christian attitudes toward Judaism in the early modern period. The Pfefferkorn Affair, involving a Jewish convert to Christianity who embarked on an ambitious mission of proselytizing among the Jews of the major Rhineland cities, concerned the utility of censorship and banning of Jewish books. Johannes Pfefferkorn had advocated the collection and destruction of the traditional books of Jewish learning and had staged several spectacular book burnings. Reuchlin countered Pfefferkorn with a defense of Jewish literature, insisting that only those works plainly disagreeable to Christian sensibilities should be suppressed.

The pamphlet war that ensued was an early demonstration of the power of the printing press, as Reuchlin's allies and opponents all entered the fray with letters and defenses both serious and satirical. The conflict pitted a number of parties against each other but did not, in any real sense, oppose Jews and Christians themselves, as no unconverted Jews entered the dispute. The importance of the conflict lay in its ramifications for Christian attitudes toward the study of Judaism, and in that, Reuchlin's role was unambiguously supportive of the study of Hebrew and the close reading of the Hebrew Scripture and its interpreters.

It seems evident that there were two aspects to Reuchlin's interest in Hebraic studies. On the one side was his desire to gain and maintain the goodwill of the Jews for the sake of converting them to Christianity. On the other was the humanistic desire to probe more deeply into the biblical text with the aid of Jewish exegesis and learning. The difficulty of determining whether these two were related is symbolic of one of the more perplexing enigmas in our understanding of humanism, especially the more pious tradition that flourished in the northern Europe.

Reuchlin lamented the outbreak of the Reformation and entered the priesthood shortly before his death in 1522.

—*Ralph Keen*

*See also* Dominican Order; Franciscan Order; Middle Ages, Late; Pfefferkorn, Johannes; Philosemitism; Reformation; Talmud Trials
**References**
Peterse, Hans. *Jacobus Hoogstraeten gegen Johannes Reuchlin: Ein Beitrag zur Geschichte des Antijudaismus im 16. Jahrhundert* (Mainz, Germany: Zabern, 1995).
Rummel, Erika. *The Case against Johann Reuchlin: Religious and Social Controversy in Sixteenth-Century Germany* (Toronto, Canada: University of Toronto Press, 2002).

## Reventlow, Ernst zu (1869–1943)

Born of a noble Schleswig-Holstein family in 1869, Ernst zu Reventlow served in the German navy from 1888 to 1899 and then turned to a career in journalism and politics. He gained notoriety by his unsparing criticism of the official fleet-building policies of the Imperial Naval Office. His call for a more aggressive naval and foreign policy brought him into close contact with many organizations, newspapers, and lobbying groups on the German Right, including the chauvinistic Pan-German League. Reventlow's books, *Kaiser Wilhelm und die Byzantiner* (Kaiser Wilhelm and the Byzantines [1906]) and *Der Kaiser und die Monarchisten* (The Kaiser and the Monarchists [1913]), were highly critical of the

policy and governing style of Wilhelm II. His journalistic activities, together with his "unsuitable" marriage to a French woman, led to a break with his family. In 1907, he went before a military court of honor because of his disparagement of the Officer Corps. But Reventlow's disregard for class and position and his reputation as a maverick won him popularity with the new and more active populist Right in Germany.

Following World War I and the Revolution of 1918, he became a vehement critic of the Weimar Republic. He had been close to the antisemitic parties before the war; now, he became even more emphatically antisemitic and racist (*völkisch*) in outlook. In 1920, he founded the journal *Der Reichswart* (Reich Guardian), which adopted an increasingly social revolutionary tendency. Reventlow became one of the most vigorous propagators of the *Protocols of the Elders of Zion* in Germany, although he clearly was aware of the manuscript's fraudulence. Abandoning the German National People's Party, he became a leader of the breakaway völkisch German Racial Freedom Party in 1922. In 1924, he won a seat in the Reichstag and then, together with a greater part of the north German racists, transferred his political loyalties once again, this time to the Nazi Party (in 1927). He served as a Nazi deputy in the Reichstag until his death in 1943, first as a follower of the socially minded Strasser faction and then as a steadfast supporter of Hitler.

A key figure in what George Mosse called the "interlocking directorate of the Right," Reventlow contributed greatly to Nazi success by bringing north German nationalists and racists into the National Socialist German Workers' Party (NSDAP), thereby expanding its base at a critical juncture. In the 1930s, his interests shifted to religious matters; he became a leader of the German faith movement, dedicated to the formulation of a German Christianity cleansed of its Jewish origins.

—*Mark Swartzburg*

*See also* Antisemitic Political Parties; *Deutsche Christen*; German National People's Party; Hugenberg, Alfred; Ludendorff, Mathilde; Pan-German League; *Protocols of the Elders of Zion*; *Völkisch* Movement and Ideology; Weimar

**Reference**

Puschner, Uwe, Walter Schmitz, and Justus H. Ulbricht, eds. *Handbuch zur "Völkischen Bewegung," 1871–1918* (Munich, Germany: K. G. Saur, 1999).

## Riehl, Wilhelm Heinrich (1823–1897)

In the genealogy of German antisemitism, Wilhelm Heinrich Riehl occupies a singular place. A near contemporary of Karl Marx, Riehl focused his attention on the ways modern class society was destroying the cultural and social integrity of Germany's old estate (*Stände*) system. In so doing, he developed an antiurban, agrarian-romantic critique of modernity that proved highly serviceable to subsequent generations of German *völkisch* (racist-nationalist) ideologues, up to and including the National Socialists.

Born into a lower-middle-class family in the Rhineland, the young Riehl aspired to a clerical career; while pursuing his theology degree at Bonn, he came under the influence of Ernst Moritz Arndt, whose stirring history lectures impelled Riehl onto the more engaged path of journalism. Over the 1840s, Riehl developed his journalistic approach, a kind of intuitive ethnography that sought its story at the intersection where natural landscape, social custom, and folklore met. This journalism would serve as the foundation for Riehl's magnum opus, the multivolume *Natural History of the German People* (1851–1855).

The *Natural History* made his reputation and led to his appointment as Munich University professor. More important, it provided the foundation text for the emerging discipline of *Volkskunde,* a distinctly German approach to ethnography that, in its retrieval of fading customs and folklore, combined empiricist rigor with frequently hazy speculations about landscape, race, and culture. Writing in the soured aftermath of Germany's failed 1848 revolution, Riehl idealized the rural order for its authenticity and traditional ways, presenting it as the chief social bulwark against the destructive "proletariat" he saw haunting Europe. Among these proletarians, he considered "the Jewish intellectual proletariat" especially destructive, motivated as it was by its "hatred of society and the state." Riehl also

found in Jewry "the true priesthood of the modern cult of wealth," (Riehl 1907, 336–337) and his account of rural society included pungent descriptions of Jewish rural peddlers and "hucksters" and their corrosive function (Diephouse 1990, 84).

Small wonder, then, that later *völkisch* thinkers frequently identified Riehl as the spiritual forerunner to their own views. Riehl's forest reveries, his rejection of urban cosmopolitanism, and his idealization of an antique peasantry provided a language congenial to antisemites in particular, and there is much to support Klaus Bergmann's contention that in Germany, "antiurbanism and the romantic cult of the countryside have always been variations on a theme by Wilhelm Heinrich Riehl" (Bergmann 1970, 38). The National Socialists were also quick to embrace Riehl: his *Natural History* enjoyed four new editions under the Third Reich, with a special 1944 edition issued expressly for Wehrmacht consumption. In 1934, Germany's leading *Volkskunde* scholars established a new Wilhelm Heinrich Riehl Prize, to be awarded only to regime loyalists of "Aryan, German descent"; over the following years, the *Volkskunde* discipline would be enlisted wholesale into serving the agendas of Nazi "racial science."

None of this necessarily argues that Riehl should be viewed as a proto-Nazi, and his public stance regarding Jews was, in fact, ambiguous. His brief against Jewish intellectuals in the *Natural History* specifies those who "have abandoned true Judaism without converting to Christianity," and his criticism of Christian-Jewish marriage targets only those unions that neglect religious tradition, whether Christian or Jewish. His portraits of the countryside mention the "shameful persecution of Jews in many southern communities" and so on. It seems that for Riehl the antimodern polemicist, "the Jews" were, at least in part, a metaphorical device that he, like many others, found useful as a weapon of moral condemnation. Yet for Riehl the would-be social scientist, the Jews were also an empirical proposition, and he was honest enough to recognize that there could be a contradiction between the two. Indeed, in later editions of the *Natural History,* he regretted that certain of his earlier lines might be "construed as anti-Jewish agitation, something I despise from the bottom of my heart and would also have despised at the time I wrote them if such calumniation had even been conceivable in Germany in those days" (Diephouse 1990, addendum). Yet even as Riehl thus distanced himself, his celebration of the German peasantry's "naive instinct and tradition" continued to provide intellectual legitimation for those *völkisch* thinkers who saw in Germany's rural antisemitic traditions a vital wellspring for racial purification and national renewal. However selectively they might have appropriated Riehl, his contributions to Germany's *völkisch* movement were genuine enough.

—*John Abbott*

**See also** Arndt, Ernst Moritz; Bauer, Bruno; Böckel, Otto; Dahn, Felix; 1848; *Judaism as an Alien Phenomenon;* Marx, Karl; *Völkisch* Movement and Ideology
**References**
Bergmann, Klaus. *Agrarromantik und Grossstadt-feindschaft* (Meisenheim am Glan, Germany: Hain, 1970).
Mosse, George. *The Crisis of German Ideology* (New York: Schocken, 1981).
Riehl, Wilhelm Heinrich. *Die bürgerliche Gesellschaft* (Stuttgart, Germany: Cotta, 1907; orig. 1851).
———, *The Natural History of the German People.* Translated and abridged by David J. Diephouse (Lewiston, NY: E. Mellen Press, 1990).

## Rindfleisch Massacre (1298)

In the immediate context of circulating accusations of ritual murder (in Mainz, Munich, and Oberwesel in the 1280s) and host desecration (in Paris in 1290), Jews in the Franconian city of Röttingen were accused of host desecration shortly after Easter 1298. Twenty-one Jews were attacked and murdered by a mob led by a knight named Rindfleisch (although some scholars have contended that his name perhaps alluded to his possible profession as a butcher). In the following months, widespread pogroms erupted in 146 different communities or settlements scattered throughout Franconia, Upper Palatinate, Swabia, Hesse, and Thuringia, claiming between 3,500 and 5,000 lives. In brutality and number of victims, these pogroms far exceeded the violence

against Jews in that area during the First Crusade in 1096.

The Rindfleisch massacre of 1298 resulted in the murder of many Jews in smaller towns and greater numbers in the larger south German population centers: 470 in Rothenburg ob der Tauber, over 700 in Nuremberg, and over 800 in Würzburg. To escape death, many fled to far distant communities. Among the Jews killed were some of the most prominent rabbinic scholars of the era, such as Jechiel ben Menachem haKohen and Mordechai ben Hillel in Nuremberg.

In most cases, the mobs responsible for the violence came from the lower and middling urban classes, although often with the tacit approval, if not the outright assistance, of the ruling strata of various locales. In some places, clergymen attempted to stop the mobs, but only in Augsburg and Regensburg were the Jews successfully protected from the violence. The first wave of murders ended with the ascension of the Habsburg Albrecht I in September 1298, but a number of subsequent massacres occurred during the early years of the fourteenth century.

According to one historian, the Rindfleisch massacres marked a new and deadly tendency in violence perpetrated against medieval Jews. Accusations such as host profanation, originally lodged against individual Jews, could no longer be confined to the locales where they first appeared. Massacres radiated outward from these places to engulf whole regions.

—*Dean Phillip Bell*

**See also** Crusades; Host Desecration; Middle Ages, High; Ritual Murder (Medieval)
**References**
Lotter, Friedrich. "Die Judenverfolgungen des 'König Rintfleisch,' in Franken um 1298: Die endgültige Wende in den christlich-jüdischen Beziehungen im Deutschen Reiches des Mittel-alters." *Zeitschrift für historische Forschung* 15 (1988): 385–422.
Poliakov, Leon. *History of Anti-Semitism: From the Time of Christ to the Court Jews* (New York: Vanguard Press, 1972).

## Ritual Murder (Medieval)

The ritual murder accusation, first recorded in England in the case of William of Norwich (d.

An early depiction of a ritual murder in which Jews were said to kill Christian children in order to use their blood for religious rituals. The first such charge occurred in England in 1144. (Hulton-Deutsch Collection/Corbis)

1144) around the time of the Second Crusade, is often distinguished from that of the blood libel. The first recorded accusation involving the blood libel occurred in Fulda, Germany, in 1235, when Jews were accused of collecting blood and body parts for secret rituals; they allegedly used the blood to make Passover matzah, for medicinal reasons, or for some magical purpose. The terms *blood libel* and *ritual murder,* however, were coined only in the modern era. The medieval accusation, which dates to the twelfth century, seems to have been less specific. The basic elements of the charge were that Jews were obligated to kill or torment a Christian youth (almost always a young boy); that they participated as a group either in the killing, the alleged ritual, or the cover-up; and that they did so in mockery of Christ and as a form of reenactment or punishment for the claim made in the Gospel of Matthew that Christ's "blood be upon us and our children."

In the early cases, accusations of ritual murder were not always distinguished from other claims of malicious murder made against Jews, with or without the mention of blood or crucifixion. The discovery of a Christian corpse found in a well or river could prompt the charge based on proximity to Jewish homes or alleged markings on the body that seemed to resemble Hebrew. By the later Middle Ages, the belief was so commonplace that Jews were the first to be blamed when a child went missing or suffered an accidental death.

Jewish law prohibits the consumption of blood, and no case of ritual murder has ever been proved. But the libel has continued for nearly a millennium despite frequent investigations and denunciations by popes, emperors, and kings. Ritual murder was at once secular (homicide) and religious (deicide). It was the forerunner of accusations of host desecration, which charged

Jews with abusing the communion wafer used in Christian masses. It may be that ritual murder, a felony prosecuted by the state, mutated into the blood libel and then into the charge of host desecration, through which, it was claimed, Jews tortured the actual body of Christ in its eucharistic form on the holy altar. Desecration of the host, a charge more serious even than murder, was also easier to prove in a court of law.

The origins of the ritual murder accusation have yet to be determined. It occurred outside Christian communities only in the modern period, which suggests that the idea derived, in part, from Christian theology or popular culture, not merely as a misunderstanding of some actual Jewish ritual, as was thought in the nineteenth century. Jews caught up in the events frequently expressed bewilderment about the myth. Under torture, some confessed their "guilt" but maintained that they did not understand the crimes that they had supposedly committed.

Some scholars speculate that the accusations of ritual murder or blood libel were psychological projections of Christians who were wrestling with their own understanding of the central ritual of the mass, in which the body and blood of Christ are consumed. Others point to Jewish practices, such as the rite of circumcision, in which observers saw Jewish leaders holding a knife near a child, drawing blood, and sucking the wound to staunch the flow. The dietary laws that require Jews to drain an animal of blood thoroughly before cooking it may also have contributed to ideas of the blood libel. More recently and far more controversially, it has been suggested that accounts of Jewish ritualized martyrdom during the First Crusade in 1096, echoing accounts of the Temple sacrifice, may have prompted subsequent Christian ideas about Jewish blood vengeance. None of these explanations has unqualified support, and there is no agreement whether the ritual murder accusation began in popular culture and folk beliefs or in scholarly and elite circles of theologians and church officials.

Some rulers who gave little credence to the charge nevertheless seized on it as a convenient excuse to expropriate Jewish property and increase their own political and religious authority. Scholars continue to debate whether the charge

was created in England or imported from Germany, where the discovery of a Christian corpse during crusade preparations in 1147 provoked attacks on Jews. The accusation had a longer and more malignant history in the German Empire. The few cases in England were widely reported, but those recording the accusations were often skeptical. It remains to be proven, however, that the accusation was substantially different in England and on the Continent in the thirteenth century—a notion that gained acceptance in the English-speaking world in the early twentieth century.

The ritual murder accusation flourished during the High Middle Ages. The most famous cases were those of St. William of Norwich, St. Hugh of Lincoln (1255), and St. Simon of Trent (1475). Other early cases were those of Harold of Gloucester (1168), the unnamed child of Blois (1171), Richard of Pontoise (1179), St. Robert of Bury (1181), a case in Winchester (1192), five children in Fulda (1235), and a young girl in Valreas (1247). Only the Blois case appears in Jewish sources of the twelfth century. The bodies of other purported victims, such as the Holy Infant of LaGuardia made famous by Lope de Vega, St. Andreas of Rinn (1462), and St. Werner of Oberwesel (1287), became objects of pilgrimage, with the relics of the holy martyrs said to produce miracles. Cases proliferated in Spain, Germany, Switzerland, Austria, and northern Italy: Lewis of Ravensburg (1249), Dominic of Val (1250), Troyes (1288), Rudolph of Berne (1294), Conrad of Weissensee (1303), and Lorenzino Sossio (1485). However, many of the elaborate "medieval" tales of ritual murder are, in fact, literary creations of later times. Of the 52 cases produced in the eighteenth century for the canonization of Andreas of Rinn and frequently cited in modern studies, many cannot be substantiated from medieval sources. Nonetheless, it was widely believed in the medieval period and beyond that Jews committed or were capable of committing ritual murder, even if knowledge of specific cases was lacking.

In later years, the ritual murder myth took on a more secular character, serving both as the excuse for civil attacks on Jews and the pretext for levying huge fines on them, expropriating their lands, and eventually expelling them. In many alleged cases, no body was ever found; rumors alone produced the desired result. In others, elaborate show trials took place. In 1235, when Emperor Friedrich II undertook one of the rare investigations, he created a panel of Jewish converts to Christianity and wrote to other countries to learn about this accusation. As a result of his findings, he denounced the charge. But his investigation seems merely to have advertised the idea, for it soon spread elsewhere.

Stories of medieval ritual murder persisted in the popular imagination long after Jews were expelled from England and France and the number of trials and investigations diminished on the Continent. The stories lived on in ballads, in Marian miracle tales, and in secular literature. Shakespeare's Shylock demanded a "pound of flesh," an allusion to the blood vengeance of the Jews. The legend was spread most viciously by itinerant Franciscan and Dominican preachers such as Bernadino da Feltre, who promulgated the cause of St. Simon of Trent, and the Praemonstratensians, who maintained a long list of alleged ritual murders. The ritual murder accusation retained its power because it addressed basic fears about blood and the vulnerabilities of children.

The ritual murder fantasy resulted in the deaths of thousands of Jews in the Middle Ages. Some were killed after judicial inquiries and the use of torture (Blois, Lincoln, Troyes, Trent); many more perished in riots after word of their "heinous deeds" spread through the town. There is now a conscious effort among many church officials to quash the ritual murder accusation. For more than a generation, the cathedral at Lincoln has had a prayer for victims of prejudice at the site of Hugh's shrine; the cathedral at Norwich has a similar prayer near the altar once dedicated to William. Simon of Trent was removed from the Roman Catholic calendar of saints in 1965, and the Bishop of Innsbruck ordered the suppression of the cult of Andreas in 1984.

—*Emily Rose*

**See also** Circumcision; Dietary Laws; Dominican Order; *Entdecktes Judenthum;* Expulsions, High Middle Ages; Franciscan Order; Host Desecration; Hugh of Lincoln; Iconography, Christian; Kosher Slaughtering; Passion Plays, Medieval; Ritual Murder (Modern); Simon of Trent; Sorcery/Magic; William of Norwich

**References**
Dundes, Alan, ed. *The Blood Libel Legend: A Casebook in Anti-Semitic Folklore* (Madison: University of Wisconsin Press, 1991).
Hillaby, Joe. "The Ritual-Child-Murder Accusation: Its Dissemination and Harold of Gloucester," *Jewish Historical Studies* 34 (1997): 69–110.
Hsia, R. Po-Chia. *The Myth of Ritual Murder* (New Haven, CT: Yale University Press, 1989).
Langmuir, Gavin I. *Toward a Definition of Antisemitism* (Berkeley: University of California Press, 1990).

## Ritual Murder (Modern)

During the last two decades of the nineteenth century and the first decade and a half of the twentieth—following a hiatus of close to 300 years—accusations against Jews for the crime of ritual murder (the killing of Christian children or adults for the purpose of employing the victim's blood in religious ritual) proliferated throughout central Europe and as far east as the Russian Empire. This is not to say that the medieval blood libel had disappeared from the Christian imagination after the Reformation; rather, it was increasingly relegated to the margins of serious political and legal discourse, considered by most state officials to constitute superstition or discredited knowledge. Although narratives of Jewish ritual murder continued to circulate within popular culture and even emanate from local church pulpits, they failed, for the most part, to move police officials and magistrates during the seventeenth, eighteenth, and most of the nineteenth centuries to conduct criminal investigations or trials against Jews on that account. The major exception to this rule was found in Poland-Lithuania, which, though it did not have a medieval tradition of ritual murder accusations against Jews, produced scores of such accusations (some leading to formal criminal proceedings) from the Counter-Reformation to the end of the eighteenth century.

The Damascus Affair of 1840 bore characteristics of both the medieval and the modern blood libel. As in premodern times, confessions were

This photograph is reprinted from the *Westdeutscher Beobachter* of Cologne, an area of Germany in which the ritual murder accusation had been popular for centuries. (Bettmann/Corbis)

extracted from suspects through the use of torture (some of those arrested died as a result), and local authorities, including the French consul, appeared to accept the traditional blood accusation at face value; at the same time, the imperial protector of the Jews, the Ottoman sultan, responded in the traditional manner, issuing a *firman* (edict) condemning the charge. The case's modern dimensions included the dissemination of purportedly "neutral" coverage of the ritual murder accusation in mass-circulation newspapers in England, France, and Germany (including the *Times* of London); the implication of the affair in nineteenth-century international diplomacy; and the political mobilization of Jewish communities across Europe to achieve justice for

their coreligionists. Finally and obviously, the Damascus Affair occurred not in Europe but in the Ottoman Empire.

In Europe itself, the modern transformation of the ritual murder accusation would not take place for another forty years. When it did reemerge on the political and cultural horizon, however, it did so with great vitality. One turn-of-the-twentieth-century observer, combing largely through German and Austrian newspapers, detailed no fewer than 128 public accusations of Jewish ritual murder between 1881 and 1900. He also claimed to have uncovered only 44 blood libels during the preceding six centuries. The spate of modern accusations actually increased as the nineteenth century drew to a close.

According to a Jewish defense organization based in Berlin, at least 79 "bona fide" ritual murder accusations were leveled against Jews from 1891 to 1900—primarily in Austria-Hungary, Germany, and Bulgaria. The majority of the late nineteenth- and early twentieth-century claims of Jewish ritual murder may never have gone beyond rumormongering or sensational reporting in the mass media. It is equally conceivable that dozens of accusations were followed up by criminal investigations of varying duration and intensity. Four central and east European states—Germany, Austria, Hungary, and Russia—chose to prosecute Jewish defendants at six public trials between 1879 and 1913, thereby breaking with a long-standing tradition of skeptical neutrality.

The trials in question took place in Kutaisi (Russian Georgia, 1879), Tiszaeszlar (Hungary, 1882–1883), Xanten (Germany, 1891–1892), Polná (Austrian Bohemia, 1899–1900), Konitz (Germany/West Prussia, 1900–1901), and Kiev (Russian Ukraine, 1911–1913). Each of the trials received extensive coverage and publicity both at home and abroad, but three appear to have generated the most discussion in the foreign press: (1) Tiszaeszlar because it was the first modern prosecution in central Europe and, as such, elicited widespread questioning of the compatibility of ritual murder discourse and modern culture; (2) Polná because it coincided with the Dreyfus Affair in France and was implicated in the heated national controversy between Germans and Czechs and because it featured a dramatic intervention on the Jewish defendant's behalf by Tomáš Masaryk, a leader of the progressive wing of the Czech national movement who would go on to become the first president of independent Czechoslovakia; and (3) Kiev—the Beilis case—because it seemed to epitomize to the Western world both the backwardness of imperial Russia and the hopelessness of its oppressed Jewish population.

It would be mistaken, however, to view the ritual murder trials of modern Europe as a return to medieval superstition. In each of the states in question, prosecutors and ministry officials who made the decision to conduct formal criminal investigations and, eventually, to prosecute the Jewish defendants in open trial did so while trying to maintain their identity as scientifically trained, bureaucratic rationalists. Their cases also relied, to a large extent, on the opinions of a variety of expert witnesses—including physicians, forensic scientists, criminologists, theologians, and academic scholars of Judaism—whose testimony appeared to provide the modern ritual murder accusation an aura of scientific respectability. Far from being a throwback to the Middle Ages, the modern ritual murder trial was, in fact, a product of post-Enlightenment politics, fears, and conventional wisdoms. It succeeded for as long as it did because it was articulated through the idioms of scientific discourse and rationality.

Eventually, the very sources of authority on which the modern proceedings rested began to undermine the credibility of the ritual murder accusation. A case in point is the Polná affair, in which Leopold Hilsner stood accused of the murder of Anežka Hrůzová, a nineteen-year-old peasant woman from a neighboring village. The prosecution had built its case on what it claimed was a foundation of forensic evidence: a sweep of the crime scene, blood on the trousers of the defendant, and a medical autopsy of the victim's corpse. At the same time, it left open the question of motive—a void quickly filled by local rumor, the daily press, and the attorney who represented the victim's family in court. Yet when the medical faculty at the Czech University in Prague redid the forensic examinations and publicized their results, which were highly critical of the original findings, the high court in Vienna ordered a retrial for the defendant. That Hilsner was also convicted of murder at his second trial and sentenced once more to death indicates the depth both of public antipathy toward him as an individual and of societal suspicions of Jews as a whole. But the ritual murder accusation in its modern form—and the willingness of state agents to prosecute trials on its basis—was to have a finite lifespan. Outside the realm of Nazi rhetoric, the ritual murder accusation would not survive as a viable object of social knowledge beyond World War I.

In light of this history, what were the political and cultural meanings of the modern ritual murder accusation? What was it saying about the world in which one lived? Why was it an attractive or compelling belief to those people who held it? A partial answer is that the modern accusation of Jewish ritual murder functioned politically as a rhetorical assault on the recently completed emancipation of the Jews of central Europe and on the liberal state that acknowledged the legal equality of the Jewish religion. Proponents of the accusation claimed to have discovered precisely in the religious culture of the Jews the code that determined their unsociability and, hence, their disqualification from the political category of citizen and the social category of neighbor. The cultural meanings of the accusation were bleaker still. It articulated a new sense of danger stemming from the social effects of modern life, located in the secret proclivities of the recently emancipated Jews, and inscribed on the mutilated bodies of their victims.

—*Hillel J. Kieval*

See also *Alliance Israélite Universelle*; Beilis Case; Damascus Blood Libel; Emancipation; Konitz Ritual Murder; Lithuania; Liutostanskii, Ippolit; Poland; Polná Ritual Murder; Pranaitis, Justinas; Ritual Murder (Medieval); Tiszaeszlar Ritual Murder; Xanten Ritual Murder

*References*
Erb, Rainer, ed. *Die Legende vom Ritualmord: Zur Geschichte der Blutbeschuldigung gegen Juden* (Berlin: Metropol-Verlag, 1993).
Frankel, Jonathan. *The Damascus Affair: "Ritual Murder," Politics, and the Jews in 1840* (Cambridge: Cambridge University Press, 1997).
Kieval, Hillel J. "Representation and Knowledge in Medieval and Modern Accounts of Jewish Ritual Murder," *Jewish Social Studies: History, Culture, Society*, n.s., 1 (1994–1995): 52–72.
Smith, Helmut Walser. *The Butcher's Tale: Murder and Anti-Semitism in a German Town* (New York: W. W. Norton, 2002).

# Rockwell, George Lincoln (1918–1967)

George Lincoln Rockwell, a leading figure in the neo-Nazi revival, established the strategic foundation that facilitated the transition from Hitlerian National Socialism to a form of the Nazi ideology that was more politically viable in the United States in the late twentieth century.

To gain a political foothold in the United States, Rockwell knew he would have to appeal to a constituency broader than "pure Aryans" of Anglo-Saxon heritage and Protestant beliefs. Such narrow parameters would have confined American Nazism to too small a base. So, in one bold stroke, Rockwell redefined a "white" as anyone who was not born black or a Jew, thus opening his movement to a vast pool of potential members. To attract them, he coined the slogan "White Power," an attempt to tap into the white middle class's growing resentment of the contemporaneous Black Power movement.

Rockwell also understood that Nazism needed to resonate with cherished American values if it was to flourish and that fundamentalist religion could serve him as the necessary tool of mobilization. Seizing on the obscure Christian Identity sect, Rockwell placed several of his most trusted lieutenants within its ministry and began the process by which its congregations became active neo-Nazi political cells. He did not live to see the full implementation of the strategy that has become a mainstay of the neo-Nazi movement.

Rockwell devised yet another strategy he hoped would make Nazism work in the United States. He helped launch the trend of Holocaust denial in an attempt to soften the future generation's historical memory of Hitler and his era, making possible the reemergence of Nazism as a force in world politics. His plan was to challenge the very existence of the Holocaust, not for the generation that witnessed it but for the next generation, thereby sowing the doubts that would make the claim that the Holocaust had never occurred a legitimately debatable matter. Although documentary evidence does not exist to detail with certainty the specific roles Rockwell and his associate Willis Carto played in devising the Holocaust denial strategy in the mid-1960s, it is clear that Rockwell took the lead in popularizing the myth that there had been no Holocaust.

In practical terms, however, George Lincoln Rockwell was a failure. A tall, handsome, intelligent, and charismatic student with considerable skill as both a public speaker and an artist, he left Brown University to join the U.S. Navy during World War II. After distinguishing himself as a navy pilot and rising to the rank of lieutenant commander, he left active duty and drifted into a series of unsuccessful business ventures and extremist political crusades. For reasons that have never been adequately explained, he embraced Adolf Hitler and Nazism in 1959 and founded the American Nazi Party (ANP). Thanks to his flamboyance and showmanship, the ANP briefly won great public attention. Even so, the party never gained a national following and never moved from the fringe into mainstream politics.

Rockwell was murdered in Arlington, Virginia, on August 25, 1967, by John Patler, a member of the ANP, a captain in its Storm troopers, and a young man whom Rockwell looked on as a son.

—*Frederick J. Simonelli*

**See also** American Nazi Party; Carto, Willis; Christian Identity Movement; Holocaust Denial, Negationism, and Revisionism; Ku Klux Klan; Militia Movement; White Power Movement
**Reference**
Simonelli, Frederick J. *American Fuehrer: George Lincoln Rockwell and the American Nazi Party* (Champaign: University of Illinois Press, 1999).

## Rohling, August (1839–1931)

Educated in Rheine and Münster, August Rohling started advanced studies at the Theological Academy of Münster in 1858. Five years later, he was ordained as a priest and then served as a private tutor in Paris and Brussels. Back in Germany, he was appointed curate at Rheinberg/Moers. In 1865, having submitted an Old Testament study on Moses' remarks on the immortality of the soul, he received the theological licentiate qualifying him as a university lecturer for Old and New Testament in Münster. One year later, Rohling also became a *Privatdozent* (unsalaried lecturer) at the Academy of Münster.

In search of a better-paying appointment—he had been offered only an associate professorship in exegesis at the Academy of Münster—Rohling went to the seminary in Milwaukee, Wisconsin, in 1874 and taught moral theology there. The next year, he returned to Europe, traveling first to Italy and Great Britain and then to Austria. Finally, he was offered a full professorship in Old Testament exegesis at the German University of Prague. When his 1897 study on the *Zukunftsstaat* (state of the future) was forbidden by church authorities, Rohling gave up his position and moved to Salzburg, where he was active as a scholar and publicist.

Rohling's early publications show an old-fashioned but highly competent knowledge of the Old Testament and its interpretations. But it was his writing of anti-Jewish books that truly engaged his energies. Although he had never studied the Talmud and the Jewish tradition of its interpretation, Rohling, by that time a fanatical Ultramontanist, wrote an exposé that fully distorted the work. To prove that the Talmud commanded Jews to commit sins and practice vice, he manipulated pieces of the text and forged evidence. His most significant contribution to anti-talmudic literature was *Der Talmudjude* (The Talmud Jew), first published in 1871 and reprinted a total of twenty-two times. The book was distributed widely by the Boniface Society for Catholic Germany.

*Der Talmudjude* reflected the traditional anti-Judaism of the Catholic Church but was also influenced by the new social, economic, and cultural arguments of the developing secular antisemitic movement. This collection of false and corrupted quotations from the Talmud, based on Johann Andreas Eisenmenger's *Entdecktes Judenthum* (Judaism Exposed [1711]), accused Jews of ritual murders and triggered fierce controversies. Rohling himself instituted proceedings against his critics but finally had to withdraw his action. He was suspended from his chair in 1885 but nevertheless continued to write and publish anti-Jewish works.

—*Carsten Kretschmann*

**See also** Austria; Bloch, Joseph Samuel; Boniface Society for Catholic Germany; Drumont, Édouard; *Entdecktes Judenthum;* Talmud; *Talmud Jew, The;* Talmud Trials; Ultramontanism
**References**
Noack, Hannelore. *Unbelehrbar? Antijüdische Agitation mit entstellten Talmudzitaten: Antisemitische Aufwiegelung durch Verteufelung der Juden* (Paderborn, Germany: University Press, 2001), 421–442.
Schmitt, Christoph. "Rohling, August." In *Biographisch-Bibliographisches Kirchenlexikon.* Edited by Friedrich Wilhelm Bautz and Traugott Bautz. 18 vols. (Herzberg, Germany: Bautz, 1994), 8:577–583.

## Roman Empire

Around the time of the birth of Christ, 5 to 6 million Jews dwelled under the Roman state, which stretched from the British Isles to the Euphrates River and from Germany to Africa. They constituted approximately 10 percent of the population, with their main centers in Palestine and Syria, Egypt, and its metropolis Alexandria, Mesopotamia, and Asia Minor. From the second century BCE, however, new Jewish communities arose in the western parts of the Mediterranean, especially in Rome. In the aftermath of the Jewish-Roman wars that began in the first century BCE, greater numbers of Jews moved westward to Italy, Spain, and Gaul, either of their own free will or under compulsion. The sources (Josephus, Philo, Strabo) tell us that there was hardly a town to be found in the Imperium Romanum in which Jews had not formed a strong community. Beyond these generalities, however, little can be said about the size of these settlements. An estimated 30,000 Jews lived in Rome; in Alexandria, the number was several times larger. In most cases, Jewish social status was low. Jews usually worked in the skilled trades and in agriculture. In Rome, they were often beggars, a fact that subjected them to the scorn and anger of contemporaries. In late antiquity, many owners and traders of slaves were Jewish.

The Roman Empire underwent three major transformations affecting all its subjects.

The Roman Republic gave way to the monarchical form of government—the Principate—in 27 BCE. In 218 CE, the Emperor Caracalla conferred civil rights on all the empire's inhabitants (*constitutio Antoniniana*). Under Diocletian, the Principate was reformed; this work continued under Constantine, who moved the capital from Rome to Constantinople and began the process of Christianization in the early fourth century CE. The end of the antique Roman Empire is marked by the reign of Justinian, who ruled from Constantinople between 527 and 565 CE.

The policy of the Roman state toward the Jews varied in response to multiple factors and was neither consistent nor uniform. Generally, Jewish existence was protected throughout the history of the empire. The practice of the Jewish religion was permitted and safeguarded by privileges. However, the increasing importance of the idea that the empire's parts should be better integrated and, at the same time, conflicts over the status of the Jewish Diaspora settlements brought about a change for the worse in the relationship between Jews and the Roman state.

The Roman Republic encouraged the Jews in the fight waged by the Maccabeans against the Seleucidian state, signing at least six treaties with them between 161 and 104 BCE. But during the same period, Jews were expelled from Rome (in 139 BCE) because of fears regarding the negative influence of eastern cults on the traditional agrarian character of Roman society. Nevertheless, their infiltration, along with other foreign elements, could not be effectively hindered. The Emperors Tiberius (in 19 CE) and Claudius (in 41 and 49 CE) tried in vain to strengthen the hold of Roman customs (*mos maiorum*) by expelling the Jews. The granting of civil rights to them in 218 CE put an end to these temporary measures.

After the capture of Jerusalem by Pompey in 63 BCE, Judea lost its independence; after the reign of the vassal King Herod (37–4 BCE), it became a Roman province in 6 CE. This integration into the Roman Empire, which both Rome and the Jews had advocated, turned out to be a complete failure. The powerful insurgent movements that erupted in the heartland of Judea around Jerusalem testify to this fact. Between 66 and 74 CE, the Jewish War ended with the demolition of the Temple. The defeat of the Bar Kochba Revolt (131–135 CE) transformed Jerusalem into a Roman colony. The consequences of these uprisings were severe. From 70 CE, Jews had to pay a special tax to Rome (*fiscus Iudaicus*), which was rigorously enforced starting with the reign of Domitian (81–96 CE); after 135 CE, Jews were forbidden to enter Jerusalem. Romans increasingly thought of Jews as innately rebellious. They were also regarded as irreparably eccentric, impossible to integrate, and practitioners of an outlandish religion. Roman policies designed to coerce Jewish integration in the Diaspora settlements also led to conflict, especially in Alexandria, where long-standing enmity between the Greek and Jewish populations led to a great pogrom in 38 CE. In the reign of Trajan, the whole eastern part of the empire was engulfed by the Diaspora Revolt (115–117 CE), during which Jews and the local gentile populations came to blows. Over the next two centuries, the historical record indicates incidental anti-Jewish measures and further Jewish revolts, but it seems as though an acceptable modus vivendi had been arrived at by both sides. Although the evidence for this period is quite sparse, the uneasy peace may have been the result of the increasing influence of the Jewish patriarch of Jerusalem, who was able to act as an effective mediator between the Jews and Rome. Gamaliel, the last incumbent of this office, died at the beginning of the fifth century.

The general situation of the Jews in the Roman Empire was determined by the principle *Iudaeorum sectam nulla lege prohibitam satis constat* (the Jewish religion is not forbidden by any law, as everybody knows). The constitutional character of the Roman state did not permit a prohibition of Judaism, whose practitioners could cite legally binding privileges and guarantees (*religio licita*) valid since the time of Caesar and Augustus. The Jews had their own (limited) judicial and financial institutions, and they were exempted from military service, performance of public duties on the Sabbath, and participation in the municipal councils. When threatened with violence by their non-Jewish neighbors, they could usually depend on the physical protection of the state. All Roman emperors were bound to recognize these privileges, even though they ran counter to their desires to reduce the empire's regional and ethnic particularities. The Jews experienced the greatest pressure to conform to Roman ways under the Emperors Caligula, Nero, Domitian, Hadrian, Septimius Severus, and Diocletian, who were most serious about subordinating the disparate parts of the empire under one Hellenistic-Roman aegis.

The policy of the Roman state toward the Jews did not materially change with the Christianization of the empire during the reign of Constantine (306–337 CE). But the rivalry between Jews and Christians, by no means new or one-sided, became more severe. Christians staged assaults on synagogues and individual Jews in a number of locales. In Menorca, compulsory conversions were carried out. Such acts were regarded as infringements on the power of the state and were, for this reason, severely punished.

In the last stages of late antiquity, the pressure on Jews to give up their special status and privileges became more intense. The situation in the towns (*civitates*) became desperate as the financial exactions to support the administration of the empire grew more and more onerous; at the same time, the central authority found itself unable to protect the borders from a variety of invaders and marauders. The impact of these conditions on the Jews is recorded in the corpus of the Roman law, especially the Theodosian Code of 439 and the Justinian Code of 534. The freedom of worship was preserved, and persons and property were still protected. But Jews were drafted for services in the towns (as members of the curiae) and the country, functions they had hitherto been spared on religious grounds. This change was now possible because, with the triumph of Christianity, all sorts of religiously based or "heathen" exemptions from such duties had vanished. In the fifth and sixth centuries, the pressure on a distinct Jewish identity continued to build, even as the weakness of the Roman state became more pronounced. The Emperor Justinian, in a last desperate bid to unify the empire, decreed its complete Christianization. He did not dare to interdict Judaism, but he removed Jews from their offices in the administration and burdened them with the performance of all public functions, without conferring the usual honors that went with them. With his reign, the empire of late antiquity reached new levels of compulsion.

In late antiquity, the Roman state's pressure on Jews to conform had further and far-reaching consequences for Jewish life, culminating in Justinian's *Corpus Iuris Civilis* (Justinian Code). Pope Gregory the Great (r. 590–604) "interpreted" these Roman laws for the Jews and created a tolerant legislation, even though its basic aim was to convert them to Christianity. His policy, which recognized the right to live as a Jew, formed part of ecclesiastical law and constituted the basis of medieval European legislation governing Jewish life. In contrast, the eastern Roman Empire moved toward the prohibition of Judaism altogether.

—*Ernst Baltrusch and Dagmar Beate Baltrusch*

**See also** Alexandrian Pogrom; Arch of Titus; Bar Kochba Revolt; Chrysostom, John; Claudius; Constantine, Emperor; Diaspora Revolt; Gregory the Great, Pope; Justinian Code; Middle Ages, Early; Roman Literature; Slave Trade and the Jews; Theodosian Code

**References**

Baltrusch, Ernst. "Die Christianisierung des Römischen Reiches: Eine Zäsur in der Geschichte des Judentums?" *Historische Zeitschrift* 266 (1998): 23–46.

————. *Die Juden und das Römische Reich: Geschichte einer konfliktreichen Beziehung* (Darmstadt, Germany: Wissenschaftliche Buchgesellschaft, 2002).

Feldman, Louis. *Jew and Gentile in the Ancient World: Attitudes and Interactions from Alexander to Justinian* (Princeton, NJ: Princeton University Press, 1993).

Schwartz, Seth. *Imperialism and Jewish Society, 200 B.C.E. to 640 C.E.* (Princeton, NJ, and Oxford: Princeton University Press, 2001).

Smallwood, E. Mary. *The Jews under Roman Rule: From Pompey to Diocletian.* 2nd ed. (Leiden, the Netherlands: Brill, 1981).

## Roman Literature

There are no traces of the Jewish people to be found in Roman literature before Cicero, despite the quite intensive relationship that had existed between the Hasmonean state and Rome since 161 BCE and the expulsion of the Jews from Rome in 139 BCE. After Pompey seized Jerusalem in 63 BCE and turned Judea into a client kingdom, however, the interest in the Jews and their religion grew. The first commentary and judgments of Roman writers about the Jews appeared in the first century BCE. In his didactic poem "*De rerum natura*" (On the Nature of Things), the Epicurean Lucretius spoke exclusively about the strange character of the Dead Sea. Somewhat earlier, Marcus Tullius Cicero and the polymath Marcus Terentius Varro dealt with the religion and the habits of these new Roman subjects. From that time until the end of the sixth century CE, special Jewish topics were treated repeatedly in the heathen Latin literature.

The following Latin terms were used for the Jewish land and people: *Judaea* and sometimes *Idumaea* (the name of the Jewish province until 135 CE), *Syria Palaestina* (the name of the province from 135 onward), and *Judaei* and *Hebraei* (for the Jews themselves). The latter term was common in the Greek language area but was used in Latin only from the end of the first century CE (with the poet Statius being the first to employ it). The work *De Iudaeis* (On Jews) by a certain Antonius Silvanus of the first century has not survived. Frequently, detailed discussions of the Jews can be found in geographic, scientific, or historical works.

For the growing interest of the Romans in Jewish affairs, three factors were decisive: first, the Roman wars against the insurgent Jews in the first and second centuries CE; second, the growing Jewish community in Rome; and third, the rise of Christianity, which, from the second century onward, was considered threatening enough to warrant greater literary attention to the Jewish mother religion. Sources of information were personal contacts with Jews as well as Greek and Roman writings but, strangely enough, not Jewish works, although these were fully accessible in Greek translations. Quintilian spoke about *primus Iudaicae superstitionis auctor* (the founder of the Jewish superstition) without naming Moses, who was known to him; further, many Jewish rites and customs were described wrongly (for example, it was commonly believed that observance of the Sabbath required fasting). Only from the second century are there signs that the Bible was known to Latin writers. One of the last heathen authors with strongly antisemitic tendencies was Rutilius Namatianus (in the fifth century), who delivered tirades about a Jewish fishpond owner in his poem *De reditu suo* (On His Return).

The image of the Jews in Latin literature was determined by interest in the land and people as well as their religion. Although the natural history of the area was presented rather neutrally, the history and culture of the Jews were treated, for the most part, disapprovingly, angrily, and contemptuously. Literary accounts dealt with the environment around the Dead Sea and its characteristics, mineral resources, and useful plants. Judea was especially famous for the extraction of asphalt, according to Pliny the Elder's *Naturalis Historia* (Natural History).

Historical treatments, especially concerning

the Jewish-Roman wars in the time of Pompey, mainly emphasized his capture of Jerusalem in 63 BCE and its reconquest by Titus in 70 CE. The point of view in these histories was exclusively Roman and was intended to furnish proof of the rebellious character of the Jewish people. Although Greek literature was concerned with the more distant era of the Exodus and the kings of biblical times, these topics were of less interest to Latin authors.

The religion of the Jews appeared throughout as *superstitio* (superstition), the characteristics of which were monotheism and the noncorporeal conception of God. Following Livy, the poet Lucan called the Jewish God *incertus deus* (uncertain god); others considered the Jews worshipers of heaven (Juvenal, Florus) and proverbial for their credulity (Horace, *Sermones* 1, 100). The only positive judgment about the nonfigurativeness of God in heathen Latin literature is found in Varro, who compared Jahwe with Jupiter and believed that humans would honor God more if He were not represented pictorially.

The Jewish way of life was thought outlandish, especially because of the minute religious regulations that pervaded the Jews' everyday existence and differentiated them conspicuously from the Romans. The meaning of Jewish rituals such as keeping the Sabbath and other holy days and of practices such as circumcision and the dietary laws were more often ridiculed than discussed. Tibull, Horace, and other writers used Jewish motifs metaphorically, usually with satirical or derogatory intent.

Jews, as a large minority in Rome, shared a very bad reputation with other alien elements who came from the eastern parts of the empire. Juvenal said about Rome in 100 CE: "Oh fellow-citizens, I cannot abide a Rome of Greeks; and what fraction of our dregs comes from Greece?" (Juvenal 3, 60–62). The numbers, coherence, law-abidingness, or inclination toward unrest of foreigners determined the degree of Roman xenophobia. By these standards, the Jews were judged most negatively. They attracted attention with their observance of the Sabbath and were identifiable as they crowded the streets carrying baskets lined with hay (in which they kept food warm without lighting a fire). The worst stench Martial knew was that of Jewish women "fasting on the Sabbath" (*Sabbatariae* 4, 7). The day of rest was declared to be a celebration of indolence of both the people and their God, even though the Roman calendar also numbered a great many feast days. This interpretation of Jewish slothfulness was confirmed by the low social position of most Jews. Large numbers of Jews could be found loitering around the gates of Rome, begging alms and molesting passersby (Juvenal, Seneca). Romans, of course, never needed to resort to begging because they had a right to state-financed maintenance. Another misinterpreted rite, that of circumcision, became part of the literature on love and sex. Circumcision, it was thought, was responsible for the excessive sex drive of the Jews and also gave them an unfair advantage with Roman women. They were described by Tacitus and Rutilius Namatianus as an *obscena gens* (an obscene people).

The biggest source of concern, however, was political in nature. Romans feared the lack of self-control, inability to assimilate, and innate rebelliousness of the Jews. Eerily prefiguring the claims of later antisemites was the judgment of Rutilius Namatinus: "And it is their own conquerors that a conquered race keeps down" (*De reditu suo* 1, 398). Seneca echoed this dread of alien conquest. Many Romans had all but pathological fears not only of riots, infiltration by foreign elements, and proselytism (Horace, Martial, Tacitus) but also of the appeal of Jewish feasts and rites for high-ranking Roman women. Bishops such John Chrysostom preached vigorously against the lure of the Jewish religion. Specifically in this regard, the Jewish *gens* (people) was characterized throughout much of Latin literature as *impia* (impious), *fera* (fierce), or *perniciosa* (a curse to others).

These prejudicial views of Jews and Judaism, generalized in the culture of Rome, were refined by the classic authors of Roman literature and transmitted through the ages to the entire civilized world.

Marcus Tullius Cicero (106–43 BCE), the most prolific speaker and prose writer of the Latin language and one of the most distinguished politicians of the Roman Republic, was the first Latin author whose comments about the Jews have been preserved. His literary work comprised philosophical and theoretical treatises on statecraft, speeches, and letters to friends and politicians. He mentioned Jews only twice: in the year 59 BCE in a speech defending Flaccus (*Pro Flacco*), who was the governor of the Roman province of Asia, and in the year 56 BCE when Cicero pleaded in a speech *de provinciis consularibus* (on the provinces administrated by ex-consuls) for removal of the governor of Syria. Both texts are seminal in the formation of Roman hostility toward Jews. Centuries later, Cicero's judgments made their way into numerous antisemitic anthologies.

Although his words must be seen in the context of his defense counsel and prosecutorial functions, Cicero expressed the fundamental Roman antagonism toward people who essentially wished nothing more than to retain their identity. In the speech *Pro Flacco*, he castigated the Jews as a shadowy, quasi-conspiratorial community that illegitimately—they were not citizens—sought to influence political decisions in Rome. Cicero insinuated an undefined danger emanating from the Jews. They had gathered into a mob near the site of court; thus, he claimed, he had better talk in a low voice. In order to clear Flaccus of the charge that he had lined his pockets with money from the Jewish Temple, thus angering the Jews, Cicero branded the Jewish religion as barbaric superstition and the Jewish community as untrustworthy, perfidious, and contrary to Romans and their customs. The most important sentence in his defense of Flaccus read:

> Each state . . . has its own religious scruples, we have ours. Even while Jerusalem was standing and the Jews were at peace with us, the practice of their sacred rites was at variance with the glory of our empire, the dignity of our name, the customs of our ancestors. But now it is even more so, when that nation by its armed resistance has shown what it thinks of our rule; how dear it was to the immortal gods is shown by the fact that it has been conquered, let out for taxes, made a slave. (*Pro Flacco,* 69)

Cicero went on to make an issue of Jewish status in the Roman Republic. There should, he said, be less tolerance shown toward foreign religions in general. The liberality of Pompey toward the Jews was mistaken because they were completely unable to assimilate to any other human community; they were also subversive and rebellious and had weapons in hand. True, defeat and diaspora caused them to suffer, but such was a just, divine punishment for their contrariness.

In his second speech, *De provinciis consularibus,* Cicero added one further element to his characterization of the Jews. In 56 BCE, he represented the interests of the equestrian leaseholders of taxes against the governor of Syria Aulus Gabinius who, he charged, "led [the leaseholders] into slavery to the Jews and Syrians, themselves born for slavery." Since Aristotle, the association between barbarian people and slavery had been axiomatic. Cicero's term *servituti nati* (born to be slaves) for the Jews and Syrians simply expressed the general Roman contempt for these peoples.

Horace (Q. Horatius Flaccus, 63–8 BCE), the son of a freed slave from Venusia, began his literary career in the time of the civil war in the thirties of the first century BCE. He was supported by Maecenas, who recommended him to Octavian/Augustus. In his wide-ranging work, he spoke three times about the Jews. Horace, unlike Cicero, did not have any political office or function; neither did he have to consider the political implications of the Jewish religion or have occasion to use anti-Jewish arguments in courts of law. Rather, he observed Jewish practices and commented on them in passing in his poems, especially in his *sermones* or satires, which he published between 41 and 30 BCE. These contained criticism of everyday life and manners and included a number of Jewish subjects. Clearly, Horace was familiar with Jewish mores and largely unsympathetic toward them. The missionary activity of the Jews (*Sermones* 1, 4, 143), their deep religiosity (*Sermones,* 1, 5, 100), and the rigorous observance of the Sabbath (*Sermones* 1, 9, 69f) he equated with obsessiveness, stubbornness, credulity, and narrow-mindedness. He helped establish the Roman notion that Jews were irrational and superstitious. The assertion that frankincense would melt without fire was a joke for Horace, about which Jewish believers were unable to laugh. Only the "circumcised Jew" could believe such nonsense, he said.

Horace had no agenda with regard to the Jews, nor did he draw a coherent picture of them, but his depictions defined them as unmistakably Jewish to his contemporary and posthumous readers. His literary stature was such that the traits he ascribed to Jews came to be regarded as synonymous with being Jewish. Other authors of the Augustan age, such as Tibull and Ovid, worked in a similar fashion. However, later poets, including Martial, Juvenal, and Rutilius Namatianus, expressed their prejudices much more radically and forcefully.

Seneca the Younger (1–65 CE) was born in Cordoba, Spain, the son of a famous orator of the equestrian order. He gained considerable political influence in Rome by educating and advising Emperor Nero, until he was forced to commit suicide after having participated in a conspiracy against his former pupil in 65 CE. His literary work was extensive and comprised philosophical treatises, tragedies, satires, and speeches. Along with Lucan, Martial, and Quintilian, he represents the Spanish sector of Latin literature; its attitude toward the Jews can be classified as antisemitic in a broad sense, combining the love of Roman traditions with the rejection of pernicious eastern influences. Seneca praised Jews for the earnest conduct of life, but this rare positive assessment was lost amid his more extensive and detailed criticism of them.

Seneca's work contained the first philosophical discussion of Judaism to be preserved, although the religion of the Jews always remained essentially alien to him. In his early years, he had been a vegetarian under Pythagorean influence, but he once again began to eat meat later in life, when he held dietary laws to be un-Roman (*alienigena sacra*). Presumably, the abstinence from pork and other meats by the Jews was what was he meant by "un-Roman rites." Seneca, showing his total ignorance of the meaning of Jewish ritual, also disapproved of lighting Sabbath candles because "gods do not need any lamps" (*Epistulae morales* 95, 47). In his lost treatise *De superstitione*, he expressed his opinion on the Jews in a most aggressive way; Augustine still knew and quoted it in the fifth century (*Civitas*

*Dei* 6, 11). Of all Jewish rites, Seneca most deplored the Sabbath, which he called a useless institution. One day of rest in every seven was a waste of time; Jews lost nearly a seventh part of their lives, he calculated. Apparently unaware of any contradiction, he praised those legislators of the Greek and Roman past who had arranged feast days for recreation. Presumably, it was not merely the frequency of the Sabbath but also the eccentric way the Jews spent the day that annoyed him. Romans partook in entertainments and games on their holidays. The Jews did not.

*De superstitione* passed harsh judgments on the Jews and found them a disturbing people. They were a *sceleratissima gens* (accursed race) whose customs had spread through all the world: "The vanquished have given their rules to their victors" (*Civitas Dei* 6, 11). Seneca never deepened his knowledge or understanding of Jewish writings—at least there are no traces of his having done so. His works were widely read in antiquity and during the Middle Ages. His formative influence on the image of the Jews can hardly be overrated.

Cornelius Tacitus (55–120 CE) was a Roman senator and high-ranking politician from Forum Iulium. After the death in 96 CE of the Emperor Domitian, whose tyranny he despised, he began to work as a writer, earning fame in his own day and down to the present as a prolific historian. In addition to several works of smaller scope (*Germania, Agricola, Dialogus de oratoribus*), he wrote two large-scale histories of Rome in the first century CE. The *Annals,* which covered the time of the dynasty of the Julio-Claudians (14–68 CE), and the *Historiae,* which recorded the rule of the Flavian dynasty (68–96 CE), have both survived in their original, complete forms. Tacitus was a severe critic of his times. The principate did not meet his expectations of political order, and the individual emperors, with the exception of Vespasian, also fell short of his standards.

In his two major works, he very often referred to the Jews, mostly reporting events. However, an excursus at the beginning of the fifth book of his *Historiae* (5, 1–13) in connection with the Jewish War of 66–74 CE obliged him to explain what made the Jews enemies of the Roman Empire, and in the process, he revealed his prejudices. Attempting a thorough treatment of the subject, he relied on several unnamed sources (but not on the Bible) for his depiction of the inimical Jews. His topics were: Roman authority in Judea at the beginning of the year 69 (1), legends of the origins of the Jews (2), the Exodus and Moses (3–4), rites (5), the land and its towns (6–7), pre-Roman history (8), Rome and the Jews since Pompey (9), the beginning of the Jewish War (10), and the beginning of the siege of Jerusalem (11–13). Long before the Romans knew them, the Jews, according to Tacitus, were driven out of Egypt by the pharaoh as a people odious to the gods. Under the leadership of Moses, they marched through the desert and *six* days later, after the expulsion of the indigenous population, they founded Jerusalem and its Temple. Moses promulgated laws that isolated the Jews from all other peoples; he made them venerate the head of an ass in the Temple because this animal had helped them to cross the desert. He installed the Sabbath as a feast day in memory of their troubles and added the sabbatical year as a comfort for them; he forced them to abstain from pork because this animal was leprous and allowed them to eat only unleavened bread. Because of the innate reprehensibility of this people, further measures had to be instituted, which, however, only made them worse. These laws and customs produced a "hostile hatred against all other people" (*adversus omnes alios hostile odium*). Circumcision was the outward sign of their difference; a strong sex drive, ritual human sacrifices, xenophobia, and self-love were but some of the negative traits ascribed to Jews by Tacitus.

Tacitus's historical treatment of the Jews occasionally seemed to be neutral, but, in fact, it was loaded with insults. He was less censorious about the Jews' incorporeal concept of God, but he was offended by their refusal to venerate the Roman emperor. Contrary to others, he refrained from comparing the cult of Dionysus with that of the Jews. The first was joyous and festive, the latter preposterous and mean. The topography of Judea and the world of its plants were gloomy, which again explained the character of the people. Classified among the Assyrians, Medes, and Persians, the Jews were the most contemptible of these subject peoples (*despectissima pars servien-*

*tium*). He praised Antiochus IV because he had tried to abolish Jewish superstition and to introduce Greek civilization. He scolded the Jewish kings because, under the mask of religion, "they banished citizens, destroyed towns, killed brothers, wives and parents, and dared essay every other kind of royal crime" (*Historiae* 5, 8).

Although Tacitus admitted to errors in Roman policies leading to the outbreak of the Jewish War, Jewish resistance was characterized as stubborn and suicidal. His text pretended to be objective, based on exact research and knowledge of (undisclosed) sources. But prejudice was clearly at work. The excursus differed both literarily and historically from Tacitus's criticism of other foreign peoples, such as the Germans or Britains. In order to glorify the generals Vespasian and Titus, the opposing Jews had to be shown in a very bad light indeed. The rebel Jews, although long a part of the Roman Empire, nonetheless refused to assimilate and give up their identity. With this trope, Tacitus sounded a theme repeated by antisemites of every succeeding age.

Juvenal (Decimus Junius Juvenalis, 67–140 CE) was born in Campania in Italy. He was the most distinguished poet of satires at the time of Emperor Hadrian, who fought against the Jews in the Bar Kochba insurrection. Juvenal disseminated his negative picture of the Jews in five of his sixteen satires. Unlike Tacitus, he was especially critical of the infiltration of foreign elements into the Roman capital. Juvenal decried the Jews as beggars and condemned the incestuous relationship between the Jewish king Agrippa II and his sister Berenice. Otherwise, he repeated the by then familiar accusations that the Jewish religion was mere superstition and that Jews were narrow-minded and unable to abandon their self-imposed isolation. Like other Roman authors, Juvenal did not probe the meaning of Judaism, satisfied to show instead how Jewish customs and rites adversely impacted Roman life. In his satire on Rome, a certain Umbricius leaves the capital filled with revulsion, for he has been accosted at the *porta Capena* by Jewish beggars who have driven away the Muses and given the whole wood over to begging (*Satura* 3, 16). Their synagogues are the beggars' sitting rooms (3,

290–296). Equally annoying are Jewish female soothsayers who offer to interpret dreams at knock-down prices. Juvenal's satire on Roman matrons (6) rebuked them for being enamored of Egyptian and Jewish superstition.

In his satire on education (14), he expressed with great thoroughness his views on the deleterious influence of Jews. He listed the main elements that Romans identified with the Jews as the Sabbath, the immaterial character of God, the prohibition against pork, circumcision, disobedience to Roman laws in favor of Jewish laws, the menacing secrecy of the occult Mosaic law, and their insularity and refusal to communicate with strangers. Juvenal worried that these uniformly negative traits—negative because they were specifically Jewish—were affecting Roman behavior. He blamed fathers for miseducating their children, passing these bad Jewish habits on to succeeding generations.

—*Ernst Baltrusch and Dagmar Beate Baltrusch*

**See also** Augustine of Hippo; Bar Kochba Revolt; Chrysostom, John; Circumcision; *Handbook of the Jewish Question;* Kosher Slaughtering; Marr, Wilhelm; Misanthropy; Paul; Pork; Ritual Murder (Medieval); Roman Empire

**References**

Baltrusch, E. "Bewunderung, Duldung, Ablehnung: Das Urteil über die Juden in der griechisch-römischen Literatur," *Klio* 80 (1998): 403–421, and 81 (1999): 218.

Gager, John. *The Origins of Anti-Semitism: Attitudes toward Judaism in Pagan and Christian Antiquity* (New York and Oxford: Oxford University Press, 1983).

Schäfer, P. *Judeophobia: Attitudes toward the Jews in the Ancient World* (Cambridge, MA: Harvard University Press, 1997).

Yavetz, Z. "Latin Authors on Jews and Dacians," *Historia* 49 (1998): 1–22.

## Romania (1878–1920)

The unification of the Danube principalities of Moldavia and Wallachia in 1859 marked the birth of modern Romania. The winning of independence from the Ottoman Empire moved the unresolved question of the Jewish minority's legal status onto the center stage of European politics. At the Congress of Berlin (in 1878), the assembled European Great Powers pressured Romania to amend article 7 of its constitution, which restricted citizenship to Christians. The demand that Romania honor the principle of equality of status for all its people unleashed a stormy debate and a wave of antisemitic violence, after which the government acceded to the pressure and changed the law. Even then, however, only 883 of more than 135,000 Jews actually gained full rights of citizenship.

Early in the country's history, intellectuals and politicians spoke out against the political and social emancipation of Jews, whom they generally regarded as unassimilable aliens. Influenced by foreign antisemites, writers such as Vasile Alecsandri (d. 1890) produced a series of works describing Jews as parasites and exploiters. The press denounced the Jews' lust for profit without labor and blamed them for many economic problems. "Despised by all nations," they were called usurers, purveyors of adulterated alcohol, spies, and bloodsuckers. Instead of the neutral word *evreu* (Jew), the derogatory *jidan* (Yid) gained currency.

"Wandering Jewry has flooded into Romania's towns infecting our people with its moral and physical decadence," wrote the national poet Mihai Eminescu in 1881. One of the Romanian pioneers of a Christian, economic, and *völkisch* (racial) antisemitism, Eminescu demanded that Jews be put to productive "muscle" work and warned ominously that in the defense of the Romanian race and soil, all means were justified (Eminescu, *Opere* 12: 359, 367, 373). The philosopher Vasile Conte pleaded for an ethnically homogenous national state based on unity of race and religion. He saw no room for non-Orthodox Christians. Nae Ionescu later expressed this notion in the form of an equation that became one of the ideological cornerstones of Romanian fascism: Romanian = Orthodox Christian. Conte was also the proponent of the theory of a Jewish world conspiracy that claimed Jews schemed to transform Romania into "their Palestine."

The militant antisemites A. C. Cuza and Nicolae Paulescu helped transform a largely literary anti-Jewish ideology into a common denominator of party politics. Cuza, whose theories rested on biological arguments and owed much to the writings of Houston Stewart Chamberlain, was also an aggressive politician. Paulescu preferred French models, especially the works of Joseph Arthur de Gobineau. Both men integrated the traditional anti-Judaism of the Romanian Orthodox Church into their outlooks. Paulescu wrote increasingly paranoid works exposing the satanic dangers posed by the Talmud, Freemasonry, liberalism, socialism, and communism. These forerunners of Romanian fascism, although differing on details, were united in their opposition to the Jewish presence in the land—a danger to the "Romanian national essence."

The antisemitic movement also produced new institutions to combat the so-called Jewish danger. The International Antisemitic World Alliance was founded in Bucharest in 1886. In 1895, Cuza and the historian Nicolae Iorga helped establish the Romanian Antisemitic Alliance. Iorga published the ultranationalist newspaper *Neamul romanesc* (Romanian Community of the Race), which was one of the most important platforms for antisemitic agitation prior to World War I.

In 1907, what has been called the last great peasant uprising in Europe swept over Romania, the result of a structural crisis in the agricultural economy. Agitators blamed the suffering of the rural population on "exploitative" Jewish leaseholders, many of whom lost their lives in the ensuing bloody revolts. In the wake of the disturbances, Cuza and Iorga founded the Democratic Party (in 1910) on the basis of an unambiguously antisemitic program. Later, Cuza and Paulescu brought out the antisemitic newspaper *The National Defense,* using it as a tool of indoctrination among the radical rightist university students who ultimately formed the core membership of various fascist organizations.

The peace treaties that ended World War I added new territories to Moldavia and Wallachia, forming Greater Romania and giving rise to a nationalistic euphoria with pronounced racist underpinnings. These territorial acquisitions made the country much more of a multi-ethnic entity, with nearly a third of the population now consisting of non-Romanians, including a larger Jewish minority (778,100, or 4.9 percent). In the immediate postwar years, university students engaged in wild antisemitic acts as well as attacks on the forces of order. Nostalgia for the war, hostility toward minorities, and fear of "bolshevism" spawned, in 1920, the Guardian of National Consciousness. The organization advocated a peculiarly Romanian blend of biological and Christian antisemitism and claimed to represent "national, Christian, and antisemitic socialism." One of its members was Corneliu Zelea Codreanu, who founded Romania's most important fascist organization a few years later—the Legion of the Archangel Michael, also known as the Iron Guard.

—*William Totok*
*Richard S. Levy, translation*

**See also** Chamberlain, Houston Stewart; Codreanu, Corneliu Zelea; Cuza, A. C.; Emancipation; Gobineau, Joseph Arthur de; Iron Guard; Judeo-Bolshevism; Usury

**References**

Hausleitner, Mariana. *Die Rumänisierung der Bukowina: Die Durchsetzung des national-staatlichen Anspruchs Großrumäniens, 1918–1944* (Munich, Germany: Oldenbourg Verlag, 2001).

Volovici, Leon. *Nationalist ideology and Antisemitism: The Case of Romanian Intellectuals in the 1930s* (London: Pergamon Press, 1994).

## Romania, Holocaust in

Before World War I, Romania was ethnically relatively homogenous, with a minority population of under 5 percent. As a result of the peace treaties ending the war, the country experienced an enormous increase in the non-Romanian population with the addition to its territory of Transylvania, Bukovina, and Bessarabia. In the 1920s and 1930s, at least in part because of these changes, numerous antisemitic and fascist organizations became politically active. LANC–National Christian Defense League founded in 1923 and Corneliu Codreanu's Legion of the Archangel Michael founded in 1927, renamed the Iron Guard in 1930, were the most significant.

In 1937, the government of Octavian Goga, the leader of the rightist National Christian Party, introduced a series of anti-Jewish laws that marked the beginning of the juridical disenfranchisement and isolation of Romania's Jews. A quarter million Jews (36.7 percent of the Jewish population) lost their citizenship by 1939. Mixed marriage was outlawed in 1940, and prohibitions on public school teaching and army and civil service careers followed. Jews excluded from the military had to pay a special tax and do compulsory labor. From the summer of 1941, the Moldau and Bukovina districts mandated the wearing of the yellow star.

Following the abdication of King Carol in September 1940, Gen. Ion Antonescu became leader of the National Legionnaire state, ruling with members of the fascist Iron Guard, as well as nonpartisan experts, and initiating a more methodical persecution of the Jews. "Romanianization" of the economy, administered by a special office, expropriated Jewish businesses and nationalized agricultural and forest lands owned by Jews.

Shortly after the invasion of the USSR, in which the Romanian army participated, a deadly pogrom took place (on June 29, 1941). Military officials spread the rumor that the Jewish population was supporting Soviet troops. Antonescu ordered retribution for an alleged attack on German soldiers. Jews were taken into custody, amid plundering and murder. Several thousand were herded onto the grounds at police stations, whereon they were shot by Romanian and German soldiers. Survivors were loaded onto sealed cattle cars and left without food, water, or sanitation while the trains traveled around the countryside. The number of victims in this pogrom is estimated at anywhere from 3,000 to 10,000.

As a reward for its military aid in the Soviet campaign, Romania received the right to administer Transnistria, formerly a part of the Ukraine, on August 31, 1941. Gheorghe Alexianu, the newly installed governor, proceeded to erect ghettos and concentration camps. Between September 1941 and the end of 1942, 150,000 Jews from Bukovina, Bessarabia, and the Dorohoi region were deported to Transnistria. They suffered great deprivation and succumbed to disease, forced labor, and arbitrary executions. Only a third of them survived beyond 1943. This was a purely Romanian enterprise, carried out by the military and the gendarmerie, without the participation of German units.

In October 1941, a bomb that killed several Romanian officers stationed in Odessa prompted Antonescu to order the arrest of 20,000 Jews, who were then driven to the outskirts of the city and shot. Only the intervention of the mayor stopped the reprisals. But two months later, Antonescu ordered the deportation of the 65,000 surviving Odessa Jews to the Golta region of Transnistria, where most of them perished.

In July 1942, a census of the remaining Jews was conducted, and other preparations were made in concert with German officials to deport them to the death camps in occupied Poland. However, military defeats and strong domestic and foreign pressure led the authorities to abandon the deportation plans. Further pressures from international organizations and large sums of money persuaded Romanian officials to allow approximately 10,000 deportees to depart Transnistria, leaving the majority to languish there. In the summer of 1944, after protracted negotiations, 3,000 Jewish orphans were allowed to leave for Palestine. Finally, the Red Army liberated Transnistria in March 1944, and the ghettos and concentration camps were emptied.

Estimates of Romanian Jewish mortality in the Holocaust vary according to which population groups are counted. They range from 250,000 to 400,000, when the Odessa mass murders are included. Ion Antonescu and Gheorghe Alexianu stood trial for war crimes in 1946. Both were condemned to death.

—*Brigitte Mihok*
*Richard S. Levy, translation*

**See also** Antonescu, Ion; Codreanu, Corneliu Zelea; Iron Guard; Romania; Yellow Star
**References**
Braham, Randolph L., ed. *The Destruction of Romanian and Ukrainian Jews during the Antonescu Era* (New York: Columbia University Press, 1997).
Hausleitner, Mariana, Brigitte Mihok, and Juliane Wetzel, eds. *Rumänien und der Holocaust: Zu den Massenverbrechen in Transnistrien, 1941–1945* (Berlin: Metropol, 2001).
Ioanid, Radu. *The Holocaust in Romania: The Destruction of Jews and Gypsies under the Antonescu Regime, 1940–1944* (Chicago: Ivan Dee, 2000).

# Romania, Post-Soviet

The fall of the regime of Nicolae Ceausescu in December 1989 signified the disappearance of the communist state but the survival and revival of some unsavory nationalist traditions. Romania's nationally tinged communism was an unoriginal amalgam of Stalinist and prewar radical rightist elements. From the beginning of his reign in 1965, Ceausescu oversaw the state's monopolization of prewar nationalism and chauvinism, which necessitated the relaxation of official antifascist policy. He more or less laid fascist and nationalist antisemitism to rest but then reactivated many of its features for his antiliberal national communism.

When Ion Antonescu, Hitler's loyal partner, was executed as a war criminal in 1946, he was reviled as the epitome of the anticommunist fascist. In the Ceausescu era, his image underwent a gradual modification in a positive direction. Soon after Ceausescu was murdered in 1989, Antonescu, the antisemitic politician and "heroic anticommunist," a man of "complex personality" and a "great patriot," was transformed into a figure of national integration. The forces that carried out this rewriting of history made little or no mention of his antisemitic policies, their Jewish victims, or the country's role in the Holocaust.

Postcommunist antisemitism in Romania was inextricably bound up in the Antonescu revival and the atmosphere of general insecurity that followed the fall of communism. Antonescu's ghost, newly cleansed of all blemishes—especially his direct responsibility for the deaths of tens of thousands Jews—rose up to answer the need for a postcommunist national icon. The arguments for his rehabilitation advanced in 1990 and then embellished in the following years were first voiced by Radu Campeanu, chairman of the new National Liberal Party, who claimed that Antonescu was a great Romanian, deserving honorable commemoration. He described the Antonescu dictatorship as more moderate than many others and certainly not responsible for extremist antisemitism—in fact, Campeanu said, Antonescu had attempted to protect the Jews from annihilation and from the Hungarians who were actually responsible for the deportations. Finally, Campeanu denounced the "historical untruth" that 400,000 Romanian Jews had been killed.

The context for such arguments was provided by the radical transformation of the early 1990s, which was accompanied by the return to an exaggerated nationalism and pronounced hostility toward Jews, Hungarians, Roma, and Slavs. The antisemitic component of reborn Romanian nationalism found expression in a few prominent postcommunist publications and made its home in several political parties whose right-wing extremism could draw, at least in part, on prewar fascist and nationalist traditions. Among the most blatant of the antisemitic gazettes, *Europa* asserted in 1991 that Romania had fallen victim to a Zionist world conspiracy and that Jewish agents wanted to turn the country into "Israel's colony" (*Europa*, no. 24, 1991). Anti-Romanianism, *Europa* and like-minded papers thundered, had to be punished. The student leader Marian Munteanu's Movement for Romania, before it was forcibly dissolved, appealed directly to the legacy of the fascist Iron Guard and its founder, the Orthodox Christian and nationalist Corneliu Codreanu.

Between 1992 and 1996, however, a nonpartisan nationalism asserted itself in Romanian politics, initiating a period of liberal middle-class rule (from 1996 to 2000). In response to the international outcry, the government rescinded Antonescu's officially proclaimed rehabilitation and, as a consequence, renewed the debate about him and about Romania's role in the Holocaust. Ion Coja, leader of the League for Combating Anti-Romanianism, explained away the bestial murder of Jews in Bucharest in 1941—many were hung up on meat hooks in slaughterhouses—as an invention of irresponsible publicists. He also denied that there was any proof thousands of Jews were murdered in the ghettos and camps of Transnistria during the war.

In the spring of 2002, the radical Right's massive circulation of antisemitic literature, including Hitler's *Mein Kampf,* and the continued flourishing of the Antonescu cult prompted the government to promulgate an emergency decree banning the establishment of fascist, racist, or xenophobic organizations. Membership in such organizations, as well as the distribution, possession, or display of their symbols, was punishable with imprisonment. Public denial of the

Holocaust or its effects could bring up to five years in prison.

—*William Totok*
*Richard S. Levy, translation*

**See also** Antonescu, Ion; Codreanu, Corneliu Zelea; Holocaust Denial, Negationism, and Revisionism; Iron Guard; Romania; Romania, Holocaust in

**References**

Shafir, Michael. "Between Denial and 'Comparative Trivialization': Holocaust Negationism in Post-Communist East Central Europe." In *Acta: Analysis of Current Trends in Antisemitism.* Vol. 19. Edited by Leon Volovici. (Jerusalem: Vidal Sassoon International Center for the Study of Antisemitism, 2002).

Totok, William. "Der revisionistische Diskurs." In *Sanduhr aus Steinen: Jüdische Zwangsarbeiter in Rumänien, 1940–1944* (Konstanz, Germany: Hartung-Gorre Verlag, 2000).

Volovici, Leon. "Antisemitism in Post-Communist Eastern Europe: A Marginal or Central Issue?" In *Acta Occasional Papers* 5 (Jerusalem: Vidal Sassoon International Center for the Study of Antisemitism, 1994).

# Rosenberg, Alfred (1893–1946)

An eminent scholar of the Third Reich has called Alfred Rosenberg "the single person most responsible for what happened to the Jews in Europe under Nazi domination." Although this claim may "unfairly" slight some of Rosenberg's more active and influential colleagues, such as Heinrich Himmler and Joseph Goebbels, it is more than sheer exaggeration, for Rosenberg relentlessly—and with great effectiveness—disseminated an intense brand of racist antisemitism. He blamed Jews for the major ills of Western culture, for the "dirty flood of the Jewish press," and for "Jewish international capitalism" and accordingly treated them as a "counter race" (*Gegenrasse*) and as *the* most pressing threat to the health of the German *Volk* (people). Rosenberg's most famous book, *The Myth of the Twentieth Century* (1930), sold approximately 1 million copies.

During the Weimar Republic and the Third Reich, Rosenberg was able to spread his scurrilities through a whole array of periodicals. He wrote, edited, or served as publisher for the Nazi Party's newspaper, *Völkischer Beobachter* (Racial Observer), from 1921 onward, and he edited the *National Socialist Monthly,* the party's theoretical journal. In addition, he occupied crucial political offices and was able to translate horrific theory directly into horrific practice.

Even before Hitler took power, Rosenberg had installed himself as head of the Nazis' shadow foreign affairs office. In this capacity, he lobbied for an invasion of the East and later helped govern the eastern occupied territories, which is where the mass murder of Jews was carried out. Rosenberg also served from 1934 on as Hitler's "commissioner for the supervision of the entire intellectual and philosophical schooling and training of the National Socialist German Workers' Party." To use the modern expression, Rosenberg was the Nazis' ideology tsar.

He was born to solidly middle-class parents on January 12, 1893, in Reval, which was then part of imperial Russia but had a significant community of "ethnic Germans," or *Volksdeutsche*. Orphaned early, he was raised by two paternal aunts. According to his own accounts, he began his reading of Arthur Schopenhauer, Indian philosophy, and Houston Stewart Chamberlain at an early age. Later, he stylized himself as the philosopher of Nazism. First, however, he studied architecture at the Technical University of Riga, which was evacuated to Moscow during World War I. There, Rosenberg is thought to have begun working on *The Myth of the Twentieth Century*. He also may have encountered the *Protocols of the Elders of Zion* for the first time. He maintained a lifelong attachment to that text, reediting and commenting on it in a widely circulated and often reprinted version of 1923. He also introduced it to colleagues and friends, possibly including Hitler.

Like most early members of the party, Rosenberg experienced Germany's defeat in World War I as a terrible shock and trauma, explicable only as the result of betrayal. Indeed, even before he relocated to Germany, he began to hold the Jews responsible for Germany's military collapse. Rosenberg made his way to Munich, where, in 1919, he joined the German Workers' Party, slightly after Hitler and even before it was renamed the National Socialist German Workers' Party in 1920. When Hitler was imprisoned after the failed putsch attempt of 1923, he entrusted one of his earliest intimates, Rosenberg, with stewardship of the outlawed party, now operating under a new name.

During this period, Rosenberg fell out of favor with Hitler, perhaps because of his poorly disguised ambition to exercise independent power within the movement or perhaps because he did such a bad job of holding the party together. On leaving prison, Hitler ostracized Rosenberg from his most intimate circle, the place from which all power flowed. Hardly a formidable personality, Rosenberg thereafter tended to come out on the losing end of clashes with Hitler's chief henchmen, especially Goebbels, his longtime rival for control over Nazi propaganda. Rosenberg not only lacked vital direct access to Hitler but was also unable to counter Goebbels's political savvy, tactical finesse, and complete lack of scruple. A true believer, Rosenberg seems never to have doubted any of his obscure ideological principles, although others in the party, including Hitler, found him a ludicrous blowhard. His rhetoric, though at times useful, was often clumsy and inappropriate to the political situation.

Rosenberg remained on the periphery, but he continued to accumulate titles, establish prominent organizations, and exercise control over the lives and especially the property of Europe's Jews. Found guilty at Nuremberg, he was executed on November 16, 1946.

—*Paul Reitter*

See also Chamberlain, Houston Stewart; Goebbels, Joseph; Himmler, Heinrich; *Myth of the Twentieth Century, The;* National Socialist German Workers' Party; Nazi Research on the Jewish Question; *Protocols of the Elders of Zion;* Thule Society

**References**

Cecil, Robert. *"The Myth of the Master Race": Alfred Rosenberg and Nazi Ideology* (London: Willmer Brothers, 1972).

Weinreich, Max. *Hitler's Professors: The Part of Scholarship in Germany's Crimes against the Jewish People* (New York: YIVO, 1946).

## Rosenberg Trial

On July 17, 1950, the Federal Bureau of Investigation's director, J. Edgar Hoover, announced the arrest of Julius Rosenberg, an electrical engineer who lived in New York City with his wife and two young sons. Rosenberg was accused of being a central organizer of a spy ring that was planning to pass vital U.S. atomic secrets to the Soviet Union. On August 11, his wife, Ethel, was also arrested and charged with conspiracy to commit espionage. When the Rosenbergs' trial began in March 1951, the prosecution requested that the couple receive the death penalty if convicted, even though it did not make the same demand for a third codefendant, Morton Sobell.

To a remarkable degree, not much commented on at the time, the conspiracy trial of the Rosenbergs was a Jewish affair. Rosenberg himself was a second-generation Jew from an immigrant Orthodox background. Ethel Rosenberg also came from an East European Jewish family. The federal judge, Irving R. Kaufman, was Jewish, and so, too, were the district attorney and counsel for the defense. The district attorney's special assistant, Roy M. Cohn, of German Jewish heritage, would soon achieve national prominence as chief counsel in the McCarthy hearings. Additional key figures in the trial were also Jews. Notably, David Greenglass, who confessed that he had been a spy for the Russians and whose testimony for the government helped convict the couple, was Ethel's younger brother. And David's wife, Ruth, charged as a coconspirator, also provided crucial testimony against her sister-in-law.

Also not commented on at the time was that the jury was composed entirely of non-Jews. The Rosenberg trial thus became a kind of political show trial performed by Jews for the morbid fascination of a wider and gentile American audience. Relevant, as well, is that the indictment, trial, and conviction of the Rosenbergs occurred exactly as the Cold War approached its zenith. Julius was arrested only months after Sen. Joseph McCarthy began his national campaign to ferret out communist infiltrators in the State Department and other important government posts. The Korean War had begun only a month before the arrest. By the time that war was over and the televised Army-McCarthy hearings had concluded—and the Cold War had passed its peak—the Rosenbergs were dead.

It had not taken long to convict them. Less than a month after their trial began, the couple was found guilty of conspiracy to commit espionage. In April 1951, Judge Kaufman sentenced them to death. Despite an international campaign that sought to have the death sentence commuted, President Dwight D. Eisenhower denied a final clemency plea, and the Rosenbergs were executed in the electric chair on the evening of June 19, 1953.

It is difficult to say with certainty what role antisemitism played in the trial of Julius and Ethel Rosenberg. Certainly, they (and Ethel in particular) frequently described the charges against them as evidence that the United States had succumbed to fascism. Soviet bloc countries such as East Germany orchestrated mass demonstrations that hailed the Rosenbergs as martyrs and accused the U.S. government of antisemitism. A small remnant of pro-Stalinist American Jews made comparable accusations, arguing that in the Cold War era, the United States employed antisemitic tactics reminiscent of Nazi Germany.

No leading American Jewish group dared to suggest that antisemitism played a role in the espionage trial. To the contrary, prominent Jewish organizations (such as the American Jewish Committee) energetically drew the opposite conclusion, namely, that the Rosenbergs were cynical opportunists who now harped on their own Jewish identities merely because it might help save their own lives. Prominent Jewish commentators forcefully condemned every inference made by the couple's supporters that antisemitism had a part in the trial or the convictions. These Jewish spokespersons advised the Jewish community to turn a deaf ear to the couple. To a great degree, this advice was heeded.

The Rosenbergs did not die because the organized Jewish community failed to come to their defense. But the Rosenberg case provides a most painful example of the tragic limitations of postwar American Jewish liberalism. Hostile to the possibility that antisemitism may have been a factor in the Rosenberg trial, fearful of being tainted themselves by the antisemitic slur that associated Jewishness with communism, American Jewish organizations sought to dampen hostility against Jews in general through an active embrace of the Cold War anticommunist consensus. Iron-

ically and tragically and despite the chance that the Rosenbergs may have been scapegoated in part because they were Jews, this meant that open debate about this possibility was placed completely off-limits. The topic remains embittering for many American Jews to this day.

—*Michael E. Staub*

**See also** American Jewish Committee and Antidefamation Efforts in the United States; Judeo-Bolshevism; United States

**References**

Garber, Marjorie, and Rebecca L. Walkowitz, eds. *Secret Agents: The Rosenberg Case, McCarthyism, and Fifties America* (New York: Routledge, 1995).

Moore, Deborah Dash. "Reconsidering the Rosenbergs: Symbol and Substance in Second Generation American Jewish Consciousness," *Journal of American Ethnic History* 8 (1988): 21–37.

Staub, Michael E. *Torn at the Roots: The Crisis of Jewish Liberalism in Postwar America* (New York: Columbia University Press, 2002).

## Roth, Alfred (1879–1940)

Alfred Roth, active in Theodor Fritsch's Imperial Hammer League (Reichshammerbund) before the war, became better known by the alias Otto Arnim, author of the popular antisemitic pamphlet *Die Juden im Heere* (*The Jews in the Army*). Roth served as an officer in the German army, and it was probably this position that allowed him to gain access to some of the statistics collected for the military's Jew Census of November 1916. The 1919 publication of his book caused a sensation, adding more force to the gathering wave of antisemitism that had begun flooding a defeated Germany. For those Germans who already believed Jews were responsible for Germany's military collapse and the subsequent Revolution in 1918, Roth's statistical study provided a thin veneer of "scientific" respectability to their baseless antisemitic accusations.

Alfred Roth maintained, without citing any relevant statistics, that most Jews involved in World War I were spies, smugglers, or profiteers. He thus provided an agreeable explanation as to why the German army failed on the battlefield. Most German soldiers, he wrote, were "Jewified" by their officers (this despite the very small number of Jews allowed to serve in the officer corps). Even before the battle was joined, Jews had succeeded in infusing Germany with a decadent "shopkeeper spirit" and overwhelming the traditionally heroic German spirit. Roth concluded that it was this defeat of German values prior to the war that led ineluctably to Germany's military humiliation. In *The Jews in the Army,* he traced the history of Jewish military cowardice by reciting old accusations about Jews performing badly in the Russian military during the Russo-Japanese War (1904–1905). After citing such bogus historical precedents, Roth delivered his version of the Jew Census, the centerpiece of the book. Most scholars agree that he was fed Prussian War Ministry correspondence related to the census, including some of the raw numbers provided by the military commands; the information was, in all likelihood, leaked by sympathetic officers. Roth combined antisemitic invective with impressive-looking but essentially meaningless statistical data. Compared to most of the antisemitic pamphlets that circulated after the end of the war, however, *The Jews in the Army* appeared polished and rigorous. It discussed Jews in every branch of service, in the occupation authorities, at the front, in industry, in the volunteer forces, and in civilian positions. In each chapter, it delineated how Jews supposedly undermined the war effort, while exploiting the national struggle for survival to enrich themselves and inflate their own importance.

Roth claimed that *The Jews in the Army* was the official result of the Jew Census conducted in November 1916. The Prussian War Ministry never released the results, he further stated, because unnamed powerful Jews prevented publication. Roth considered himself a hero and the publication of his book a service to the German nation. He remained active in radical rightist politics during the Weimar Republic, serving as leader of the Deutschvölkischer Schutz- und Trutz-Bund (German Racial League for Defense and Defiance) and, briefly in 1924, as a member of the Reichstag, sitting for the right-wing German National People's Party.

—*Brian Crim*

**See also** Fritsch, Theodor; German National People's Party; German Racial League for Defense

and Defiance; Imperial Hammer League; Jew Census; Masculinity

*Reference*
Zechlin, Egmont. *Die Deutsche Politik und die Juden im Ersten Weltkrieg* (Göttingen, Germany: Vandenhoeck and Ruprecht, 1969).

## Rothschilds

The founder of the Rothschild dynasty, Mayer Amschel (1743–1812), was the descendant of undistinguished merchants and money changers in the Jewish ghetto of Frankfurt. He took his first major steps, especially during the Napoleonic period, in amassing a legendary fortune by serving as the financial agent for a German count (Landgraf) of Hesse-Kassel. His descendants branched out into the major cities in Europe, most notably London, Paris, Vienna, and Naples; before long, the name Rothschild became associated with fabulous capitalist opulence, charitable causes, and support for the arts, as well as horse racing and other activities previously dominated by the nobility and royalty. In Sholem Aleichem's original Yiddish text, Tevye's celebrated soliloquy "If I were a rich man" is *"Ven ikh bin Rothschild"* ("If I were Rothschild").

For nineteenth-century antisemites, the Rothschilds loomed as a symbol of the rising power of the Jews under modern capitalism. It became a commonplace, even among those without particular hostility toward the Jews, that the Rothschilds were becoming the "kings" of an age when money was the ultimate source of power. Jewish leftists were perhaps even more ardent than left-wing gentiles in denouncing the Rothschild family as the epitome of destructive capitalist greed and corruption. Traditional Jews often shared with gentiles a sense of unease about these astonishing nouveaux riches, but in the Jewish case, that fear was often mixed with hopes and fantasies about the Rothschilds as modern protectors of the Jews who—with their great wealth—could effectively intervene behind the scenes among the gentile powerful.

Typically caricatured as many-tentacled octopi, reaching everywhere and strangling the common people, the Rothschilds as a symbol were prominent in the blending of anticapitalism, antimodernism, and antisemitism in the nineteenth century. However, much of the favorable commentary about Jews, especially in Britain, also concentrated on the Rothschilds. In particular, Lionel Rothschild (1808–1879), a friend of Benjami Disraeli and a recognized leader in the struggle for Jewish emancipation in Britain, enjoyed remarkable esteem, both among the gentile common people and the ruling elites. He assumed a seat as the first Jewish member of Parliament in 1858. The powerful and admirable character Sidonia in Disraeli's influential novel *Coningsby* was widely believed to have been modeled after Lionel. Nathaniel Mayer Rothschild (1840–1915) became the first Jewish peer of the realm in 1885.

Favorable attitudes were not uncommon among the royalty and nobility on the Continent, as well. In the course of the nineteenth century, titles of nobility were granted to the Rothschilds, and by the end of the century, there were even a number of intermarriages between branches of the family and European nobility, including a few minor members of the royalty. Early in the century, such conservatives as Prince Klemens von Metternich established friendly contacts with the founding members of the family—as well as negotiating loans from them. For antisemitic observers, such connections revived memories of the court Jews, believed to be evil and corrupt advisers to the reigning princes of earlier centuries. But even on the Continent, positive and negative imagery often blended; some, in particular those of social Darwinist bent, saw the material success and the alleged manipulation of the modern economy and politics by Jews (with the Rothschilds as prime examples) to be indications of racial superiority, a theme much emphasized by Disraeli and, in related ways, perpetuated by figures as different as Beatrice Webb, Winston Churchill, and Lord Balfour. Those who respected success, as long as they were not particularly threatened by it, tended to esteem the Rothschilds. Lord Granville, for example, advised Queen Victoria that it was highly desirable to "attach them to the aristocracy rather than drive them into the democratic camp" (in Ferguson 1999, 2: 253).

Given the fears and the hopes that their wealth and prominence awakened, the Roth-

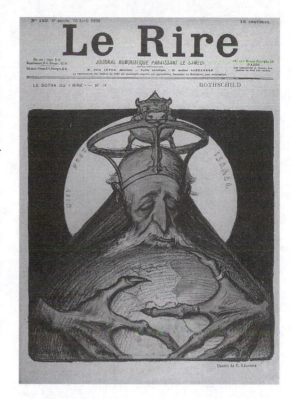

A caricature of Alphonse de Rothschild, crowned by the Golden Calf and whose talonlike hands have France in their grasp. (Mary Evans Picture Library)

schilds inevitably became entangled in extravagant charges made not only by antisemites but also by the many factions of the Jewish communities of Europe. Theodor Herzl saw them as a "national misfortune" for the Jews when they expressed serious reservations about his Zionist program—a particular irony given the charges by antisemites that the Rothschilds were a major power behind Zionism. Bitterness and resentment within the Jewish community toward the Rothschilds also arose because of some of the family members' supercilious attitudes concerning Jews from eastern Europe, the hesitations and reservations some of them expressed in regard to immigrants and refugees (whether in the late nineteenth century or in the Nazi period), and their tendency to blame antisemitism on the actions of the Jews themselves.

Although the Rothschilds were well known during much of the nineteenth century for secretiveness, clannishness (especially in their hostility toward intermarriage), and a concern to keep their wealth within the family, a number of family members not only married Christians by the end of the century but also distanced themselves from Jewish causes and attitudes. Their failure to establish a solid outpost in the United States has been seen as one of several reasons for their relative financial decline in the twentieth century; that failure also helps explain why the Rothschilds played a relatively less prominent role in anticapitalist symbolism in the United States. By the second half of the twentieth century, the image of the Rothschild family had distinctly diminished in the rhetoric of antisemites.

—*Albert S. Lindemann*

**See also** Caricature, Anti-Jewish (Modern); *Coningsby;* Court Jews; Disraeli, Benjamin; Emancipation; Herzl, Theodor; Webb, Beatrice; Zionism

**References**

Davis, R. W. "Disraeli, the Rothschilds, and Anti-semitism." In *Disraeli's Jewishness.* Edited by Todd Endelman and Tony Kushner (London: Vallentine Mitchell, 2002).

Ferguson, Niall. *The House of Rothschild: The World's Banker.* Vol. 1, *Money's Prophets, 1798–1848,* and vol. 2, *The World's Banker* (New York: Viking, 1999).

In the print, *Raising the Wind,* Thomas Rowlandson shows two evil-looking Jewish moneylenders purchasing the title deeds of an estate from an inebriated young English aristocrat. (Jewish Theological Seminary)

## Rowlandson, Thomas (1756–1827)

Although comparatively little attention has been devoted to his depiction of Jews, Thomas Rowlandson, the English illustrator and engraver, has long been acknowledged, along with James Gillray, as one of the two most influential graphic satirists in England in the era after William Hogarth. Whereas Gillray's powerful cartoons are primarily political and, in their occasional depiction of Jews, not particularly antisemitic, Rowlandson's drawings and prints are far more evidently social and, in their recurrent representation of Jews, often derogatory. Perhaps because he lodged for much of his career in their vicinity near the street market of Rag Fair in Houndsditch, he took delight in sketching and etching London's Jewish poor. At least sixty graphic works (as well as a large number of drawings and watercolors) by Rowlandson contain Jewish fig-

ures, as against scarcely more than two by Hogarth earlier in the eighteenth century.

Many of these works contain antisemitic themes. Rowlandson's Jews are almost invariably grasping moneylenders, stockjobbers, old-clothes men, sexual predators, or deviants from their avowed religious practice. In a print of 1812, entitled *Raising the Wind* (1; B.M., no. 10486; Rubens, no. 939; Grego, 3: 234; *The Jew as Other,* no. 5), he shows two evil-looking Jewish moneylenders purchasing the title deeds of his estate from an inebriated young English aristocrat. The paintings on the wall, portraying gambling and horse-racing scenes, mark the means of the aristocrat's downfall. Rowlandson imputes here (and elsewhere) that scheming Jews were unscrupulously buying up the patrimony of the English landed gentry. Another print, *A Jew Broker* (1801; Rubens, no. 905), shows a latter-day Shylock bearing a bond in his pocket, and,

An example of Thomas Rowlandson's representation of old clothes men is *Trafic*. Here, two rascally old clothes dealers bargain with a maid servant over the price of a torn pair of breeches. (Jewish Theological Seminary)

as Joseph Grego describes him, "musing . . . over a chance lost, a bargain missed, a gain which has slipped through his prehensile fingers" (1880, 2: 24). An example of Rowlandson's representation of old-clothes men is *Trafic* (1785; Rubens, no. 1125; Grego, 2: 289 and 324; *The Jew as Other*, no. 14), produced in collaboration with Henry Wigstead, an amateur artist. Here, two rascally old-clothes dealers bargain with a maid servant at the door over the price of a torn pair of breeches. The caption reads: *Vat you say: Twopence / By Got Almighty / Thay are not worth a penny / Are they Moses [?]*. The guttural English of the dealer picks up the dialectal mimicry commonly employed on stage when representing a Jew and often so performed in the late eighteenth century by Rowlandson's close friend the actor Jack Bannister (1760–1836). In *Introduction or Moses with a Good Bargain* (Rubens, no.

919), we see a young English girl being introduced by a procuress to an overblown Jew whose sexual arousal is denoted by his standing on tiptoe and by the erect state of his beard. Finally, in *Jews at a Luncheon, or a Peep into Duke's Place* (1794; B.M., no. 8536; Rubens, no. 888; Grego, 2: 324–25), we witness three grotesque Jews drooling over a sucking pig, reflecting the anti-semitic belief that even in the environs of their place of worship—Duke Street was the site of London's Great Synagogue—Jews would secretly indulge in their love of pork. Alfred Rubens (1959) notes that Rowlandson also produced an aquatint from the life of the Great Synagogue for Rudolph Ackermann's *Microcosm of London* (1809) and remarks that this "is one of the rare instances of Rowlandson exercising restraint in his Jewish characterisation" (13).

—*Frank Felsenstein*

*See also* Agrarian League; Caricature, Anti-Jewish (Early); Caricature, Anti-Jewish (Modern); Hogarth, William; Pork; Shylock

**References**
Grego, Joseph. *Rowlandson the Caricaturist*. 2 vols. (London: Chatto and Windus, 1880).
Paulson, Ronald. *Rowlandson: A New Interpretation* (London: Studio Vista, 1972).
Rubens, Alfred. *Portrait of Anglo-Jewry, 1656–1836* (London: Jewish Historical Society of England, 1959; reprinted from *Transactions of the Jewish Historical Society of England,* vol. 19).
———. *A Jewish Iconography.* Rev. ed. (London: Nonpareil Publishing, 1981).
Stephens, F. G., and M. Dorothy George. *Catalogue of Political and Personal Satires Preserved in the Department of Prints and Drawings in the British Museum.* 11 vols. (in 12) (London: British Museum, 1870–1954) = B.M. Cat.
*The Jew as Other: A Century of English Caricature, 1730–1830.* Exhibition catalog. (New York: Library of the Jewish Theological Seminary of America, 1995).

## Rozanov, Vasilii (1856–1919)

A Russian writer, religious thinker, and philosopher whose controversial ideas played an important role in the Beilis case and influenced many Russian writers and literary critics, Vasilii Rozanov developed a strange love-hate relationship with the Jewish people.

His early book *Judaism* (1903) presented Judaism as a religion of sacred eroticism, sexual joy, and familial relations and opposed it to Christianity. He interpreted the Jewish ceremonial practices—circumcision, ritual baths, and celebration of the Sabbath—as elements in the religion that were, in many ways, identical with the archaic fertility cults and phallus worship of the ancient Middle Eastern religions. Rozanov attributed the vitality and potency of the Jewish people to the sexual nature of their religion and pitted it against a sterile and abstract Christianity. The revitalization of Aryan people, he claimed, required the adoption of the life-affirming attitudes and sexual aspects of Judaism. Commonly interpreted as Judeophilic, the book actually argues that Jewish vitality and sexuality thwart the development of creative genius typical of the Aryans.

In 1913, Rozanov wrote *The Olfactory and Tactile Relationship of the Jews to Blood,* a work that stirred up wide public debate in imperial Russia. In it, he reaffirmed his thesis about the sensual and materialistic character of the Jewish religion, but this time, he attributed to it a special interest in blood and the elements of sadistic ritual cruelty, dwelling at length on circumcision and kosher slaughtering and claiming that Old Judaism incorporated human sacrifice. In the famous ritual murder trial of 1913 known as the Beilis case, Rozanov suggested that—although the accused Mendel Beilis was not necessarily guilty—the murderer was likely driven by some tendencies inherent to Judaism and perhaps belonged to a cruel and secretive Jewish sect.

Rozanov devoted several other notable articles to the Jewish topic. In "Angel of Jehovah," he construed the ritual of circumcision in Judaism as an indication of phallic worship. In "Judean Cryptography," he focused on the special nature of Hebrew writing, which, he said, was secretive and obscure and contrasted to the openness of Christian writing. This distinction corresponded to the general tendency of the two religions: Judaism was the religion of concealment (*sokroveniie*), whereas Christianity was the religion of revelation (*otkrovenie*). Most of Rozanov's other works offered observations about Jews or at least some passing remarks about their character. Among the most prominent motifs were ideas about the feminine character of Jews and their constant attempts to take advantage of the gullible and vulnerable Russians, a theme common to the works of Rozanov's spiritual father, Fyodor Dostoevsky.

In his last work, *The Apocalypse of Our Times* (1918), Rozanov declared his intention to convert to Judaism, and a few days before his death in 1919, he dictated two letters—"My Last Testament" and "To the Jews"—in which he asked them for forgiveness and expressed his love and respect for the Jewish people. He also left a written request to burn his books relating to the Beilis case.

Many of Rozanov's ideas were clearly influenced by Fr. Pavel Florensky, the Russian Orthodox philosopher and theologian; some of his writing was, in fact, attributed to Florensky. It is also remarkable that Rozanov shared the themes and views of the well-known contemporary Austrian and German writers Otto Rank, Richard von Krafft-Ebing, and Otto Weininger. Rozanov's influence survived his death, finding an outlet in the ideology of some militant Russian and international antisemitic groups. In post-Soviet Russia, he became one the most popular Russian philosophers of the so-called Silver Age, to a great extent because of his colorful language and exquisite literary style.

—*Vadim Rossman*

**See also** Beilis Case; Circumcision; Dostoevsky, Fyodor; Masculinity; Ritual Murder (Modern); Russia, Imperial; Russia, Post-Soviet; Russian Orthodox Church; Weininger, Otto

**References**

Engelstein, L. *The Keys to Happiness: Sex and the Search for Modernity in Fin-de-Siècle Russia* (Ithaca, NY: Cornell University Press, 1992).

Glauberman, E. "Vasilii Rozanov: The Anti-Semitism of a Russian Judeophile," *Jewish Social Studies* 38 (1976): 120–133.

Khanin D. "Beauty and the Beast: Vasily Rozanov's Aesthetic and Moral Ideal," *Russian Review* 71 (1998): 72–86.

## Russia, Imperial

Just as in western Europe, the Jewish Question had a prominent place in political, social, and cultural discourse in fin-de-siècle Russia. The thriving, daily, semiofficial newspaper, *Novoe vremia* (New Times), in which journalists baited Jews and denounced nefarious "Jewish influence" for over two decades before the end of tsarism is evidence of this fact. At the same time, Jews gained prestigious positions in the press, law, education, creative writing, the plastic arts, and philosophy in an environment that was often hostile.

In Russia, the so-called Jewish Question emerged from the attitude of the tsars toward Jews. Although considered divinely anointed to govern Russians and stand at the head of the Russian church, the tsars were not always certain about what to do with the minorities of their multinational empire—the Poles, Finns, Ukrainians, Belorussians, Tatars, and many others, absorbed during the imperial expansion of the eighteenth and nineteenth centuries. Among these aliens were Jews, over 5 million of them by the end of the nineteenth century.

Under Alexander I and especially his successor, Nicholas I, the goal was to foster integration both by force and with inducements. During his reign (1825–1855), Nicholas I recruited Jews into the army (even boys younger than twelve years old) in numbers that exceeded their percentages in the population, while creating special state Jewish schools. Both methods were intended to transform "religious fanatics" into "useful" members of society. Alexander II took a different tack during his reign (1855–1881), offering privileges to Jews who successfully integrated into Russia. Alexander III (r. 1881–1894) thought his father's mild liberalism and reforms had only encouraged the radicals and led to his murder. Under the influence of Konstantin Pobedonostsev, the head of the Holy Synod, Alexander III clamped down on all expressions of independence in society. He held Jews in particular disdain, believing them to be behind the revolutionary movement in the country. Nicholas II (r. 1894–1918) continued his father's repressive policies, making concessions to the national minorities only when forced to do so by political pressure. Despite the differences in the approach to Jews from each of these autocrats, a single thread unites all their policies: the issue of what to do with this large group of subjects that was educated and ambitious but also "foreign" and dangerous. It was clear that they could not be easily assimilated. Jews had a different religion, they spoke Yiddish and not a Slavic language, and they seemed content to keep to themselves. Moreover, it was believed that they exploited the local population, kept the peasants indebted and intoxicated, controlled the banks and the press, and were responsible for anti-Russian attitudes in western Europe. Over the preceding two centuries, the Romanovs felt that Jews had to be kept down lest they ascend to positions of wealth and power.

What is most striking about the period from the pogroms of 1881 to the October Revolution of 1917 was the reversal in the attitude of the state. Before 1881, the tsarist government had pressed Jews to integrate and "cohere" with their neighbors. The May Laws of 1882, actually a temporary decree passed by the Ministry of Interior and signed by the tsar, imposed a number of new liabilities on Jews, designed to separate them from the non-Jewish population. These restrictions, among other things, forbade new Jewish habitation in the countryside and curtailed Jewish ownership of taverns and other forms of livelihood.

In the early 1880s, Alexander III instructed the Pahlen Commission to examine legislation regarding Jews. Although the commission voted in 1887 to expand their rights, the tsar ignored the advice, initiating instead a policy of severe quotas on Jewish student admissions to most of the country's schools and universities. The rule limited the Jewish student body to 10 percent of total enrollment in the Pale of Settlement, 5 percent in the regional capitals, and 3 percent in St. Petersburg and Moscow. In 1891, the government "cleansed" Moscow of its Jewish population, forcing over 20,000 people from their homes and subjecting countless families to economic ruin. In this period of worsening conditions for Jews, two important blood libel trials took place (the Blondes and the Beilis cases of 1902 and 1911–1913, respectively), and the Russian secret police commissioned the fabrication of the *Protocols of the Elders of Zion*. Although scholars have shown that it was not the St. Petersburg government that organized the periodic pogroms, local officials often failed to defend Jews. Moreover, Jews who suffered from the government's blatantly antisemitic policies firmly believed that the authorities colluded in the violence visited on them.

Although many Jews emigrated from Russia between 1881 and 1914, the two and a half decades of Alexander II's reign had left a deep and positive imprint on Russia's Jews, helping to counter the negative experience of antisemitism. By the 1870s, the Russian Jews seemed prepared to enter modern times; they made vigorous efforts to modernize, "Russify," and assimilate. Economic development, one historian confidently wrote, would lead to integration, welding the Jews onto the body of the Russian people. A broad and ambitious Russian Jewish intelligentsia formed, and ironically, it was just at this moment, at the end of a short and limited period of progress, that this group began to express its vision for Russian Jewry. Instead of a politics of *shtadlanut*—the Jewish leaders' diffident intercession with the government—the intelligentsia began demanding human rights, legal equality, and the benefits of citizenship.

Much of the development of educated Russian Jews in these years can be understood as a reaction to Russian antisemitism. A crucial first step was the creation of a press able to express the goals of a more confident Jewish intelligentsia. In 1880, three Russian-language Jewish weekly newspapers were published in St. Petersburg alone. The Hebrew-language *Ha-Meliz* and the *Yidisches Folksblat* were also published in the capital. Jewish readers were now eager for information about politics, culture, and Russian life and were able to get it in periodicals as broad in scope as the famous Russian "thick" journals.

Jews in the cultural elite reacted to the change in outlook and expectations by advocating such new political ideologies as Zionism, diaspora nationalism, and political radicalism. The historian Simon Dubnow and the Zionists Moses Lillienblum, Leo Pinsker, and Ahad Ha'am (Asher Hirsch Ginsberg) turned their efforts exclusively to national goals. Nationalists wanted to create schools in which students learned Hebrew and Jewish history and religion and cultural institutions devoted to the cultivation of Jewish identity. Zionists in particular envisioned emigration to Palestine, although they understood the need for political organization within Russia itself to achieve this end. Socialists led by Alexander Medem created the General Jewish Workers' Union in Lithuania, Poland, and Russia, commonly known as the Bund. This organization encouraged the Jewish proletariat to fight for social and economic gains while retaining their identity as Jews.

Other talented Jews could become active agents of Russian culture. The symbolist Akim Volynsky (Flekser) and the philosophers Lev Shestov, Semyon Frank, and Mikhail Gershenzon moved in the rarified circles of Russian, not Jewish, cultural life. Another group of intellectuals, Menashe Morgulis, Alfred Landau, Henry Sliozberg, and Maxim Vinaver, sought a compromise, retaining hope in the ultimate victory of liberalism. They believed a transformation to a democratic form of government would give Jews equal rights, permit full acculturation, and put an end to antisemitism.

The twenty-six-year period from 1881 to 1917 can perhaps best be divided into two parts: the pessimism of the 1880s and the striving toward Jewish autonomy from the mid-1890s to 1917. Unmistakably, political reaction had a powerful influence on literary life. Because of the government's treatment, no self-respecting Jew could collaborate with the state. On the contrary, every group, including Russia's richest Jews, realized that change could only come from within, from the Jews themselves, and in alliances with Russian opposition groups. The huge participation of Jewish voters in the first elections to the state parliament (the Duma) in 1906 reflected the intense politicization of Jews in the previous decade. Jewish representatives were winners in every party to the left of the conservative Octobrists. The first Duma, which lasted only three months, counted twelve Jewish legislators from such parties as the Constitutional Democrats (Kadets), the Zionists, and the Social Democrats.

Jewish communal life in the last years of tsarist rule took on a distinctly national tone and reached new levels of sophistication. In 1907, the Jewish Literary Society was established in St. Petersburg and in a number of provincial towns and cities. In addition, local initiatives brought remarkable results in the establishment of local organizations devoted to aiding students, teachers, orphans, mothers, workers, and the poor. These institutions, many of which had had a shadowy existence previously, were instrumental in taking responsibility for communal welfare from religious institutions and putting it in the hands of political leaders.

Jewish literature made impressive progress during this time. The appearance of Sholem Aleichem showed that Yiddish literature had risen to the level of other European literatures. His Die Yiddishe Folksbibliotek (Popular Jewish Library) marketed Yiddish works in accessible and affordable editions. Meanwhile, avant-garde authors David Bergelson and Der Nister attracted a reading public that was nourished on the latest fashions. The Hebrew language experienced a revival, fashioned into a modern literary medium in the hands of Chaim Bialik and Saul Tchernichowsky. In addition, Jewish literature in Russian also showed a growing maturity in works by Semyon Yushkevich, Semyon Ansky, and David Aizman, who found a venue for their work in the left-leaning Russian press.

In the plastic arts, Jews also flourished. From the school of Yehuda Pen in Vitebsk emerged artists eager to paint images of the shtetl with the latest avant-garde techniques. Marc Chagall, Solomon Yudovin, Natan Altman, and El Lissitzky were especially effective in creating a new kind of Jewish modernism in Russia.

Amid this blossoming of Jewish culture, historical writing represented a particular and profound achievement. The Jewish Historical-Ethnographic Society, the brainchild of Simon Dubnow, was created in St. Petersburg in 1908. Its quarterly, *Evreiskaia starina* (Jewish Antiquity), became a major intellectual force during the years before World War I. In addition, the ethnographic expeditions of Semyon Ansky into the Pale of Settlement to collect the remnants of traditional Jewish life inspired many intellectuals to regard their roots with nostalgia and pride. Finally, the sixteen-volume *Evreiskaia entsiklopediia: Svod informatsii o russkikh evreiakh* (Jewish Encyclopedia: A Collection of Information on Russian Jews [1907–1913]), was a major intellectual accomplishment and a monument to a highly developed Jewish culture.

Despite or perhaps because of legal restrictions, many Jewish intellectuals sought integration into the larger society with even greater intensity at this time. One area where Jews found acceptance was the Russian press, which, in its left-leaning sector, considered it shameful to support the government's prejudicial treatment of the national minorities. Nevertheless, conflicts between Jews and Russians did take place. The famous Chirikov affair of 1907 is emblematic. At a reading by the non-Jewish Evgenii Chirikov of his play *The Jews,* the Yiddish writer Sholem Asch asked by what right Chirikov dared treat the internal life of Russia's Jews. Asch's views were picked up in a number of newspapers, setting off a string of articles by several famous Russian writers, who, in turn, asked how it was that Jewish writers could write about Russians but object when Russians wrote about Jews.

The acquittal of Menahem Beilis in the blood

libel trial in 1913 revealed the conflicting attitudes toward Jews that could be found among educated Russians. For some, it served as a stinging public condemnation of the government's antisemitic policies. Despite government collusion in trying to convict Beilis on the flimsiest of evidence, several major Russian philosophers identified themselves with the official Russian Orthodox Church's anti-Jewish stance during these years. The harmful statements of Pavel Florensky and Vasilii Rozanov, however, were countered by the tolerance of such liberal priests as Sergei Bulgakov and Lev Karsavin and the Christian intellectual Nikolai Berdiaev. The Jewish Question posed significant problems for neo-Slavophilism, influencing the legacies of the anti-Jewish Fyodor Dostoevsky and the deeply tolerant Vladimir Solov'ev. What attitude one took on the Jewish Question mattered and was seen as a marker of one's political orientation.

The outbreak of World War I had an especially damaging effect on the Jews, who found themselves literally caught between contending armies. The decision of the Russian armed forces to evacuate untrustworthy Jews to prevent espionage led to untold horrors; the aged and sick were forced from their homes and made to wander to areas more fully under Russian control. Many Jews were killed as a result of atrocities on both sides, despite the fact that both armies had many thousands of Jews in uniform. As the German and Austrian troops pushed into Ukraine and Belorussia, Russian enforcement of the Pale of Settlement became impossible; thus ended a policy of discrimination dating back to Catherine the Great, a wholly unintended "benefit" of the war.

The March 16, 1917, declaration of the Provisional Government giving equal rights to all the national minorities was seen by Russia's Jews as a reward for enduring decades of suffering. The fact is that many Jews—like many Russians—welcomed the Bolshevik regime. To the Jews, it promised, at last, complete legal equality, permanent abolition of the Pale, access to education, and support for Yiddish culture. But as became obvious only too quickly, there were severe drawbacks, as well. The communists showed no tolerance for the Jewish religion, Hebrew literature,

or Zionism. Jews, like all Russians, suffered from general restrictions on their liberty.

—*Brian Horowitz*

***See also*** Beilis Case; Black Hundreds; Dostoevsky, Fyodor; Judeo-Bolshevism; Kishinev Pogrom; May Laws; Odessa Pogroms; Pale of Settlement; Pobedonostev, Konstanin; Pogroms; Pranaitis, Justinas; Russian Orthodox Church; Socialists on Antisemitism; Twain, Mark

***References***

Dawidowicz, Lucy. *The Golden Tradition: Jewish Life and Thought of Eastern Europe* (New York: Holt, Rinehart and Winston, 1967).

Frankel, Jonathan. *Prophecy and Politics: Socialism, Nationalism, and the Russian Jews, 1862–1917* (Cambridge: Cambridge University Press, 1981).

Rogger, Hans. *Jewish Policies and Right-Wing Politics in Imperial Russia* (London: Macmillan, 1986).

Stanislawski, Michael. *For Whom Do I Toil?: Judah Leib Gordon and the Crisis of Russian Jewry* (New York: Oxford University Press, 1988).

Zipperstein, Steven. *Elusive Prophet: Ahad Ha'am and the Origins of Zionism* (Berkeley: University of California Press, 1992).

## Russia, Post-Soviet

Post-Communist antisemitism emerged in the aftermath of perestroika, to a large extent in response to the failure of liberal political and economic reforms. This new phenomenon had many elements of continuity with the old state-sponsored antisemitism of the Communist period. But it also entailed new practices and new lines of argument. The new ideologists developed and articulated many doctrines that could not be openly discussed in the Soviet period: ideas of ethnic superiority, blood libel, religiously inspired anti-Judaism, and concepts based on geopolitics and race. The classics of antisemitism were rediscovered and widely disseminated, including the *Protocols of the Elders of Zion* and Hitler's *Mein Kampf.* Native Russian contributions, such as the diaries of Fyodor Dostoevsky and articles and books by Vasilii Rozanov, fed into the reservoir of hate literature.

In the late 1980s, the movement was dominated by the national-patriotic group Pamyat, led by Dmitry Vasiliev. Previously marginal parties became conspicuous in later years, including Russian National Unity, the Black Hundreds, the Russian Party, the Party of Russian Nationalists, the Right Radical Party, among many others. Antisemitic ideas also found their way into several mainstream political organizations, such as the Liberal-Democratic Party of Vladimir Zhirinovsky and the Communist Party of the Russian Federation. According to one estimate, Russia had 157 antisemitic periodicals by 1994.

One can distinguish five groups in Russian post-Communist antisemitism, based on their specific targets, interests, and political orientation: the neo-Slavophiles, the national communists, the Russian Orthodox nationalists, the Russian ideologists of race, and the Eurasian geopolitical ideologists.

Neo-Slavophiles, among them many village prose writers and literary critics, originally united around the magazine *Nash sovremennik* (Our Contemporary). The central concern of this group was and is the decline of the Russian peasantry, the backbone of Russian culture and society. Neo-Slavophiles believe that the Bolshevik Revolution was provoked by the Jews and that communism destroyed all authentically Russian manifestations of culture, morality, and tradition. They dwell on the atrocities committed by Leon Trotsky and other Bolsheviks of Jewish origin, including the murder of the Romanovs. Many neo-Slavophiles see Stalinism as the practical application of the principles of Trotsky and ultimately as the political extension of the cruel principles of the Old Testament.

The other key concern of neo-Slavophiles is the purity of Russian language and literature and its freedom from alien influences. The literary critics from this group introduced a distinction between "Russian" and "Russian-speaking" writers; by the latter, they meant the Russian writers of Jewish origin, who supposedly corrupted Russian culture and literature by smuggling their own values into it. Aleksandr Solzhenitsyn's recent book *Two Thousand Years Together* plays into some of the ideas of neo-Slavophiles, although his approach is much more subtle and qualified.

The second group, the nationalist communists, follow the old Soviet line of antisemitism expressed in the anti-Zionist campaigns. Some important members of the two Russian communist parties draw on Karl Marx's essay *On the Jewish Question* (1844) to place Jews at the heart of Russia's economic misery. The process of economic reforms, they see as the looting of Russia by International Jewry, led by prominent Jewish financiers. In many accounts, Russian individuals of Jewish origins—specifically the so-called oligarchs—are often singled out as the culprits behind criminal privatization and fraudulent business practices. All Russian nouveaux riches are branded as "Jews." Some ideologists of this trend contrive an artificial Jewish genealogy for the creation of capitalism in the tradition of Werner Sombart.

Nationalists claiming the Russian Orthodox faith as their inspiration constitute the third important grouping hostile to Jews. Some of those aligned with this tendency accept the notion of an eternal war of Christianity and Judaism and proceed on that basis to deny the common historical roots of Christianity and Judaism.

Two more recent and related post-Communist groups include the Russian ideologists of race and the Eurasian geopolitical ideologists. Although the ideologists of racist antisemitism repeat and freely borrow the old stereotypes of Nazi Judeophobia, the Eurasians introduced a new ideology and a special variant that might best be described as "geopolitical antisemitism." Drawing on the ideas of German geopoliticians and the émigré Russians of the 1920s, the present-day proponents introduced a distinction between continental Eurasian and maritime Atlanticist civilizations. According to Aleksandr Dugin, the leader of this group and an adviser to State Duma speaker Gennadii Seleznev since 1998, the Eurasian ethnicities—primarily German, Russian, and Asiatic peoples—share the common values that derive from their continental lifestyles. This ethos is opposed to the crass commercial values of Great Britain and the United States, the two main Atlanticist civilizations. Dugin portrayed the Jews as the natural allies of Atlanticism and mondialism and traitors to Eurasian and specifically Russian values. Dugin also suggested that Muslim civilizations and Islamic fundamentalism were the natural allies in Russia's struggle against Atlanticism and the Jews.

The other prominent Eurasianist, Lev Gumilev, introduced before his death in 1992 several potent historical myths and developed a pseudoscientific ethnological theory that essentially disqualified Jews from membership in the grand Eurasian family. Gumilev suggested that Russian history was, in fact, the history of opposition between the union of Russian people and the nomads of Eurasia, on the one hand, and the cosmopolitan Jews, on the other. Although Russians and the nomads shared the heroic ethos and were attached to their native land, the Jews displayed a different code of behavior, characterized by perfidy, commercialism, and the lack of attachment to their own land and the countries where they lived. Gumilev's speculations about Khazaria—foregrounding the sadistic cruelty, religious intolerance, and racist nature of the Khazarian Jews and Judaism—have been used by many Russian antisemites as the historical foundation of their ideologies. His ideas influenced the thinking of many prominent antisemitic ideologues of the recent past and present, such as Metropolitan Ioann, Vadim Kozhinov, and Yurii Borodai.

Since the collapse of the USSR, Russian antisemitism has undergone a vigorous development and has not been confined to the fringes of society. Many people responsible for systematic antisemitic statements and incitement occupy powerful positions in contemporary Russian life, including the governors of two important regions, the metropolitan of St. Petersburg and Ladoga, prominent members of the second-largest political party, academicians, and an army general.

—*Vadim Rossman*

*See also* Anti-Zionism in the USSR; Dostoevsky, Fyodor; Islamic Fundamentalism; Judeo-Bolshevism; Marx, Karl; *Protocols of the Elders of Zion;* Russian Orthodox Church; Solzhenitsyn, Aleksandr; Sombart, Werner; USSR

**References**
Allensworth, Wayne. *The Russian Question: Nationalism, Modern, and Post-Communist Russia* (Lanham, MD: Rowman and Littlefield, 1998).
Midford, P. "Pamyat's Political Platform: Myth and Reality," *Nationalities Papers* 19, no. 2 (1991).
Rossman, Vadim. *Russian Intellectual Antisemitism in the Post-Communist Era* (Lincoln: University of Nebraska Press, 2003).
Thom, F. "Eurasianism: A New Russian Foreign Policy." *Uncaptive Minds* 7, no. 2 (1994).

# Russia, Revolution of 1905

The Revolution of 1905 grew out of an ongoing economic, political, and social crisis in the Russian Empire. At the beginning of the year, the cumulative effects of agrarian disorders, labor unrest, political terrorism, and growing discontent within Russian society was exacerbated by the failure of Russian arms in the Russo-Japanese War. On January 9, 1905, troops outside the Winter Palace in St. Petersburg fired on workers who sought to present a petition to Tsar Nicholas II. The outcry surrounding "Bloody Sunday" helped to persuade Nicholas to announce plans for a consultative assembly to review all imperial legislation. Unrest continued to grow, further encouraged by the restrictive electoral guidelines for the assembly announced on August 6, 1905. At the beginning of October, a general strike was organized in St. Petersburg by the Soviet of Workers' Deputies, which then spread to the entire country. Forced to choose between repression and concession, Nicholas issued the October Manifesto (of October 17, 1905), which promised an elected parliamentary system. The manifesto was followed by the "October Days," marked by violent clashes between right-wing defenders of the autocracy and those on the Left who demanded further concessions. On December 9, 1905, Moscow was the scene of an armed rebellion. The following year saw the implementation of the State Duma (the Russian parliament), which was elected against a background of continuing violence and massive military repression.

A widespread feature of the period of revolutionary unrest, especially during and after the October Days, was the outbreak of pogroms carried out by groups known generically as the Black Hundreds. In general, the violence was directed against all groups perceived to be enemies of the regime, such as liberals, radical workers, or students. Because Jews were viewed by the Right as the instigators of the revolutionary movement, they became the single most common target of violence. There were an estimated 57 pogroms between February and October, the most serious occurring in Zhitomir (in April), Kiev (in July), and Bialystok (in August). By the end of the year, over 690 attacks, claiming almost 900 Jewish victims, had been recorded.

An aged man labeled "Russian Jew" carrying a large bundle labeled "Oppression" on his back; hanging from the bundle are weights labeled "Autocracy," "Robbery," "Cruelty," "Assassination," "Deception," and "Murder." (Ben and Beatrice Goldstein Foundation Collection, Library of Congress)

Following the issuing of the October Manifesto, there were severe pogroms in Kiev, Odessa, Rostov-on-Don, and Minsk.

The identity of the rioters, the *pogromchiki*, remains a contested issue. Although some of the participants may have been true "patriots," there was clearly a large criminal element involved. The stereotypical pogromchik was a right-wing thug who saw all Jews as revolutionaries. There is copious evidence that the local police authorities took no measures to prevent or repress pogroms in many areas. Although Prime Minister Count Sergei Witte strongly opposed pogrom violence, rogue elements in the Central Department of Police encouraged them as a demonstration of popular loyalty. Tsar Nicholas II clearly saw them in this light, writing to his mother that "the impertinence of the Socialists and revolutionaries has angered the people once more; and because nine-tenths of the troublemakers are Jews, the people's anger turns against them. That's how the pogroms happened."

Jewish self-defense, though common, was largely ineffective. Especially when organized by radical political groups, such as the Jewish Workers' Bund, it gave the police and military an excuse to join in the attacks on Jewish areas. Despite the promises of the October Manifesto, the large body of law restricting Russia's Jewish population, especially the Pale of Settlement, was not significantly relaxed by the Duma.

—*John D. Klier*

**See also** Black Hundreds; Krushevan, Pavolaki; Odessa Pogroms; Pale of Settlement; Purishkevich, Vladimir Mitrofanovich; Russia, Imperial

**References**
Ascher, Abraham. *The Revolution of 1905*. 2 vols. (Stanford, CA: Stanford University Press, 1988–1992).
Klier, John D., and Shlomo Lambroza, eds. *Pogroms: Anti-Jewish Violence in Modern Russian History* (Cambridge: Cambridge University Press, 1992).
Rawson, Don C. *Russian Rightists and the Revolution of 1905* (Cambridge: Cambridge University Press, 1995).
Rogger, Hans: *Jewish Policies and Right-Wing Politics in Imperial Russia* (London: Macmillan, 1986).

# Russian Civil War

The Russian Civil War was a military struggle for control of the former Russian Empire, fought between October 1917 and November 1920. The participants were extremely variegated. They included the Bolshevik revolutionaries who had seized power in October 1917 (the Communists, or the "Reds"); their political rivals on the Left (the Socialist-Revolutionaries) and on the Right (diverse counterrevolutionary military forces throughout the empire, known collectively as the "Whites"); military units of the Central Powers (Germany, Austria-Hungary, and Turkey); the pro-Allied Czechoslovakian Legion; interventionist Allied forces from the United States, Britain, France, and Japan; an array of nationalist movements, especially in the Ukraine (which failed, however, to mobilize effectively on a military basis); anarchist peasant movements, such as that led by Nestor Makhno in the Ukraine (the "Greens"); and gangs of freebooters and bandits. In the midst of the Civil War, the Communist regime also fought a war with the newly independent Polish state between April and October 1920. The Whites drew much of their strength from the remnants of the Russian Imperial Army; the Communist fighting force depended on the newly created and supposedly "proletarian" Red Army, organized by Lev Trotsky, which, however, also utilized former imperial officers and peasant levies. Both Reds and Whites recruited large numbers of irregular forces—who were not reluctant to change sides at opportune moments.

One of the main centers of conflict was the Ukraine, where the forces of the new Ukrainian government were no match for the occupying Central Powers or, after 1918, the contending Red and White armies. The main White unit in southern Russia was the so-called Volunteer Army, commanded by Gen. Anton Denikin and composed mainly of Don and Kuban Cossacks. In 1919 and 1920, now reorganized as the Armed Forces of South Russia (AFSR), it fought major engagements in the Ukraine until its ultimate defeat by the Red Army.

The southwestern theater of the Russian Civil War encompassed precisely those areas of the Pale of Settlement where the vast majority of the Jewish population of the Russian Empire lived. Anti-Jewish pogroms became a common feature of the war in this area. All the military forces in the Ukraine carried out pogroms, but only troops of the Red Army were held accountable for them. The AFSR was the major perpetrator of violence against Jews. Although Denikin himself was no antisemite, his officer corps was steeped in the antisemitism of the prewar Russian army—as was already evident from its treatment of Jewish civilians during World War I—and convinced that the Communist movement was a Jewish plot to subvert Russia. The notorious antisemitic forgery known as the *Protocols of the Elders of Zion* was widely disseminated among the officers and men of the AFSR. Their most infamous pogrom was inflicted on the Jews of Fastov in September 1919; it claimed approximately 1,500 victims. These atrocities drove many Jews to support the Red Army, thus making the antisemitism of the Whites a self-fulfilling prophecy.

Although troops of the AFSR probably killed the largest number of Jewish pogrom victims, the forces of the Ukrainian army nominally loyal to the so-called Directory headed by Symon Petliura earned a reputation for the scale and cruelty of their pogroms, most notably in Berdichev, Zhitomir, Proskuriv, and Felshtin. As opposed to the ideological antisemitism of the AFSR actions, many other pogroms were acts of banditry and rapine carried out by undisciplined irregular forces. The inability of the Petliura government to control its followers or to prevent pogroms—which it formally repudiated—cost it much support abroad. Petliura himself was assassinated in exile in Paris in 1926 by Shalom Schwartzbard, a Jew who claimed to be avenging the pogroms.

The number of Jewish pogrom casualties in the Russian Civil War is notoriously difficult to ascertain. One reliable estimate puts it as high as 60,000. In any event, the pogroms led many Jews to support the new Communist regime, whose conquest of the Ukraine put an end to the pogroms.

—*John D. Klier*

**See also** Judeo-Bolshevism; Pale of Settlement; Petliura, Symon; *Protocols of the Elders of Zion*; Russia, Imperial; USSR

### References

Abramson, Henry. *A Prayer for the Government: Ukrainians and Jews in Revolutionary Times, 1917–1920* (Cambridge, MA: Harvard University Press, 1999).

Kenez, Peter. *Civil War in South Russia, 1919–1920: The Defeat of the Whites* (Berkeley: University of California Press, 1977).

Klier, John D., and Shlomo Lambroza, eds. *Pogroms: Anti-Jewish Violence in Modern Russian History* (Cambridge: Cambridge University Press, 1992).

## Russian Orthodox Church (ROC)

Russian Orthodoxy shares most centuries-old ideas of Christian antisemitism with other Christian denominations. However, several unique features provide a special coloration to Orthodox antisemitism and its theological attitude toward Jewish matters. The Russian Orthodox Church (ROC) puts special emphasis on the works of the church fathers, who drew a sharp distinction between Christianity and Judaism and published many bitter anti-Judaic statements. The theological tradition of Byzantium, where the polemical anti-Judaic treatise became the most popular genre, greatly influenced Russia. The anti-Judaic treatise "Sermon on Law and Grace" by Metropolitan Hillarion of Kiev (in the eleventh century), a classic of ancient Russian literature, became the first Russian theological work.

The Russian Orthodox Church is also distinguished by a special interest in apocalyptic topics and demonology. Many old Orthodox works identify the coming Antichrist as a Judean prince. It was suggested that the Jews, having rejected Jesus, are especially vulnerable to demonic forces and hence will play an important role as the supporters of the Antichrist in the eschatological period. The special interest in the "theology of replacement" is also important. In the Middle Ages, some Orthodox monks conceived of Moscow as both the "Third Rome" and the "Second Jerusalem," taking over the missions of both the great imperial and religious centers. The status of the sole custodian of the true faith in the world of apostasy made the ROC the only legitimate claimant to the title of the "New Israel."

Following the collapse of the Soviet Union, the dark antisemitic legacy of the Orthodox Church rose to the surface again. Although some leaders of the church condemned antisemitism, it remains a strong presence. Many senior officials in the hierarchy have formed political alliances with hate groups, made antisemitic remarks in public, and published antisemitic writings without reprimand from the patriarch. Several groups within the ROC—the Orthodox-Monarchist Alliance, the Union of Orthodox Brotherhoods, and the revived Black Hundreds—have been especially active in the propaganda of antisemitism. Even after his death in 1996, the late Metropolitan Ioann of St. Petersburg and Ladoga retains, through his writings, an influential voice for antisemitism within the church. Both Ioann and Bishop Varnava of the ROC Abroad collaborated with Pamyat, the oldest antisemitic nationalist group in Russia. The bishops of several important regions (Ekateringburg, Voronezh, Nizhnii Novgorod) openly maintained ties with the neo-Nazi organization Russian National Unity. In many parts of Russia, local ROC newspapers carry antisemitic articles and proclamations by extremists. Some clerics have revived and supported the ideas of the notorious *Protocols of the Elders of Zion,* and the dioceses of Ykaterinburg, Kemerovo, and Kaluga have published and distributed this forgery. Finally, sociological research suggests a positive correlation between antisemitic beliefs and membership in the church.

Several post-Communist Russian Orthodox clerics cast Judaism in the most negative light. Metropolitan Ioann's popular history of Russia is governed by the idea of a "two-thousand-year war" between Christianity and Judaism. Ioann claims that the Jews worship a "Jewish" God, who is, in reality, a demon. In his narratives, Jews are often referred to as the "God-killer people." Judaism is the "religion of hate" and is frequently described as racist.

The Judaizing heresy has been another important target for the ideologists of Orthodox antisemitism. A religious movement in fifteenth-century Russia that ran parallel in many ways to the Protestant Reformation, Judaizing is viewed as a source of the most destructive religious and social movements and ideologies: iconoclasm, rationalist interpretations of the Bible, replacement of Old Slavonic with the vernacular, and liberal attitude toward church ritual. The modern interpretation of the heresy by the Orthodox hardliners is much broader, however. Both Protestantism and Catholicism are seen as manifestations of Judaizing. Protestantism sometimes appears as no more than a branch of Judaism, whereas Catholicism is condemned for its too conciliatory resolutions regarding Christian-Jewish conflicts. Judaizing is attributed to the "subversive" activity of ROC priests of Jewish origins. Orthodox clerics expressed special concern about the activities and spiritual influence of Fr. Alexander Menn, a charismatic Orthodox priest and writer of Jewish origin who converted many members of Russian intelligentsia to Orthodoxy and whose murder in 1990 remains unsolved.

The other conspicuous component of contemporary antisemitic ideology grounded in Orthodox tradition is the belief in ritual murder. Vladimir Osipov, the head of the Union of Christian Rebirth, cochairs the Organizational Committee of Russian Orthodox Forces, which calls for "the unmasking of the talmudic conspiracy against Russia" and "Hassidic and satanic sects" that practice "ritual murder." In post-Communist Russia, one can find both simplistic revivals of the blood libel as well as more politically sophisticated allegations. The example of the so-called ritual murder of the Romanov family will suffice to illustrate the point. In the mid-1990s, a polemical exchange took place in Russian periodicals about the sainthood of the last Russian emperor, Nicolas II, who was murdered, along with his family, by the Bolsheviks. Orthodox antisemites took an active part in the debate, singling out the Jews among the persecutors—especially Yakov Yurovsky—and portraying the execution as a ritual murder, not simply an execution; the act was meant to humiliate Russia and mock the Orthodox Church. That the tsar was tormented by Jews, according to some clerics, makes him similar to Christ and by itself qualifies him for sainthood. Yet other clerics go even further to suggest that Russian history has replicated Christ's life. The Bolshevik Revolution, with its Jewish executioners, recapitulates the moment of Russia's crucifixion.

The collapse of the Soviet Union and the end of the millennium produced an environment especially ripe for apocalyptic speculations and anxieties. Many Russian Orthodox narratives present real or imagined Jews as the new Antichrist, working to bring about the world's end. In the 1990s, the popular candidates for this title included Mikhail Gorbachev—he appears wearing a yarmulke in many ultranationalist newspapers—and George Romanov, the heir of the Romanov dynasty living in Germany, who counts several Jews among his ancestors, at least according to some Orthodox genealogists.

—*Vadim Rossman*

***See also*** Antichrist; Black Hundreds; Chrysostom, John; Church Fathers; Deicide; Judeo-Bolshevism; Nilus, Sergei; *Protocols of the Elders of Zion;* Reformation; Ritual Murder (Medieval); Russia, Imperial; Russia, Post-Soviet; Talmud

**References**
Dunlop, John B. *The Faces of Contemporary Russian Nationalism* (Princeton, NJ: Princeton University Press, 1983).
Hagemeister, Michael. "Eine Apokalypse unserer Zeit: Die Prophezeiungen des heiligen Serafim von Sarov über das Kommen des Antichrist und das Ende der Welt." In *Finis mundi: Endzeiten und Weltenden im östlichen Europa.* Edited by Joachim Hösler and Wolfgang Kessler. (Stuttgart, Germany: F. Steiner Verlag, 1998).
Rossman, Vadim. *Russian Intellectual Antisemitism in the Post-Communist Era* (Lincoln: University of Nebraska Press, 2003).

# S

## Sartre, Jean-Paul (1905–1980)

Born in Paris on June 21, 1905, Jean-Paul Sartre lost his father when he was only fifteen months old. He was reared by a doting mother and by his grandfather, a published author of German-language educational works. He completed his education at two elite preparatory schools in Paris, the Lycées Henri IV and Louis-le-Grand, and then entered the École Normale Supérieure in 1924 along with three other famous writers of his generation, Raymond Aron, Paul Nizan, and his lifelong companion, Simone de Beauvoir. Graduating at the top of his class, he became a high school professor and began publishing philosophical treatises. He spent 1933 in Germany, just as Hitler rose to power. There, he worked on his modernist masterpiece, *La Nausée* (Nausea [1938]), and steeped himself in Martin Heidegger's philosophy. In 1937, he wrote *La Transcendence de l'ego* (Transcendence of the Ego), a criticism of Edmund Husserl's conception of consciousness.

He returned to a France increasingly polarized by fascism and antisemitism, leading to his first overt work of political *engagement* in the form of his novella *L'Enfance d'un chef* (Childhood of a Leader [1938]). The story is forcefully ironic and deeply critical of the Action Française shock troops, the Camelots du Roi,, and, by extension, the politics of the extreme Right that defined Frenchness against the abject image of "the Jew."

Sartre spent the war years as a "writer who resisted, not a resister who wrote," engaged in various organizations opposing Vichy and Nazi propaganda, while publishing his magnum opus, *L'être et le néant* (Being and Nothingness [1943]), and overseeing the performance of his first plays, during the Nazi Occupation. By the end of the war, he had gained intellectual celebrity. In the years that followed, he became possibly the most famous thinker in the world, revered as the high priest of existentialism, the philosophical principles of which he was able to articulate compellingly in a variety of genres.

Amid the general silence about the Holocaust, Sartre published *Réflexions sur la question juive* (Anti-Semite and Jew [1946]). Insisting that the French take responsibility for their part in the Final Solution, he presented an innovative analysis that influenced the entire postwar intellectual debate about Jewish identity, its relation to anti-semitism, and the politics of (Jewish) emancipation. He described the inherent dilemmas of the Jewish struggle for authenticity based on the antiessentialist and antifoundationalist premise that "the Jew is a man that other men consider a Jew," thus posing the question of Jewish identity in terms of the antisemite's gaze. He maintained that antisemitism did not rest on economic, historical, religious, or political foundations but demanded an existential analysis of the self-identity of the antisemite and "the Jew." Radically, he also castigated the "politics of assimilation"—the Enlightenment and liberal tradition that defined Franco-Judaism and Jewish emancipation—contending that it ultimately eliminated Jewishness because its universal and abstract principles did not recognize Jewish difference. Seeking to solve the problem of antisemitism, the contradictions of liberalism, and the antinomies of Jewish existence in one fell swoop, he offered a socialist revolution as the only viable solution to the Jewish Question.

This analysis became the basis of Sartre's antiracist interventions in support of decolonization and helped to spur his existential-Marxist critique of the mediating links between systems of social oppression. He was a lifelong supporter of the state of Israel, which he saw as the culmination of the national liberation struggle of the Jews. After the Six Days' War, he identified with socialist and peace-oriented elements within the Zionist camp, always insisting on Israel's right to exist, while acknowledging the Palestinian struggle as an equally legitimate national liberation movement. Sartre's *Anti-Semite and Jew* not only defined the terms of the debate on the Jewish Question in postwar France but also formed a central leitmotif in his existential analysis of the human condition, providing a key to understanding his philosophy as a whole.

—*Jonathan Judaken*

**See also** *Action Française; Camelots du Roi;* France; Socialists on Antisemitism; Vichy

**References**

Holier, Denis, ed. *Anti-Semite and Jew.* (Cambridge, MA: MIT Press, 1999).

Judaken, Jonathan. "Jean-Paul Sartre and 'the Jewish Question': The Politics of Engagement and the Image of the 'the Jew' in Sartre's Thought, 1930–1980." Dissertation, University of California–Irvine, 1997.

## Schemann, Ludwig (1852–1938)

One of the most important racial theorists of imperial and Weimar Germany, Ludwig Schemann is best known for his translation and popularization of the works of the French racial theorist Comte Joseph Arthur de Gobineau and for his own publications in the field of scientific racism.

After studying history at Bonn, Schemann worked as a bibliographer at the university library in Göttingen. He was first introduced to the ideas of Gobineau by Richard Wagner, who had met Gobineau in 1876 and who encouraged Schemann to study scientific racism. After retiring to Freiburg, Schemann devoted himself to the translation, publication, and popularization of Gobineau's theories. With other Wagner disciples, he founded the Gobineau Society in 1894. The society raised money to support the translation and publication of Gobineau's famous *Essay on the Inequality of the Human Races,* which had originally been published in French between 1853 and 1855, without attracting much attention in Germany. Schemann worked on the translation himself, publishing it in three vol-

umes as *Versuch über die Ungleichheit der Menschenrassen* (1897–1900) and distributing it through the society.

After completing the translation, he turned to winning acceptance for its theories in Germany. He downplayed Gobineau's pessimism and injected ideas drawn from Darwinian notions of natural selection. Where Gobineau argued that the historical inevitability of racial mixing would result in the degeneration of society, Schemann argued that, because the Germans were the least degenerate race according to Gobineau's racial hierarchy, the Germans could make conscious decisions to safeguard their race and thus save Western culture. Racial breeding was the means by which to halt the damage of race mixing and to effect cultural and physical regeneration. In the ensuing and unavoidable struggle for survival with inferior races, the superior Germanic race would triumph. In Schemann's system, Jews figured as the primary racial enemy.

Schemann's dissemination of Gobineau's theories greatly influenced academic, scientific, and political circles in Germany. In person and in thought, he served as an important link between various centers of German racism and antisemitism, including the eugenics movement, the school of sociobiology, the Pan-German League, Friedrich Lange's antisemitic German Union (Deutschbund), and Theodor Fritsch's many antisemitic initiatives. Schemann continued his work after World War I, most notably with the publication of his three-volume *Race in the Humanities: Studies on the History of Racial Thought* (1928–1931). His writings were acknowledged by the leading ideologists of the Nazi regime, and he was awarded the Goethe Medal by the Third Reich "for services to the nation and the race," a fitting honor from a regime that would take Schemann's beliefs to their most radical end.

—*Elizabeth A. Drummond*

**See also** Bayreuth Circle; Eugenics; Evolutionary Psychology; Fritsch, Theodor; Gobineau, Joseph Arthur de; Lange, Friedrich; Pan-German League; Racism, Scientific; Rosenberg, Alfred; Social Darwinism; Wagner, Richard

**References**

Chickering, Roger. *We Men Who Feel Most German: A Cultural Study of the Pan-German*

League, 1886–1914 (Boston: Allen and Unwin, 1984).

Kennedy, Paul M., and Anthony J. Nicholls, eds. *Nationalist and Racialist Movements in Britain and Germany before 1914* (London: Macmillan, 1981).

## Scheunenviertel Pogrom (1923)

The pogrom that took place in the Scheunenviertel, a working-class neighborhood near the center of Berlin, between November 5 and 6, 1923, targeted primarily *Ostjuden* (east European Jews) and marked the highest level of anti-Jewish violence during the Weimar Republic era. The democratic press described the event as an ignominious breach of civilization. "Berlin has had its pogrom," read the lead article in the Social Democratic newspaper *Vorwärts,* and "Berlin has been defiled."

The riot began outside an employment office on the morning of November 5. Much of what actually happened and what set it off is still uncertain. According to contemporary police records, eastern European Jewish dealers triggered events by attempting to buy welfare vouchers distributed to unemployed workers at below their legally set value. However, the antisemitic slant to these reports makes them less than reliable. Newspapers loyal to the republic, by contrast, reported that right-wing agitators had premeditatedly incited a crowd of angry unemployed workers against the Jews. The accuracy of this theory of efficient demagogic manipulation is also by no means certain. A more modern view suggests that the violence should be seen in the context of riots provoked by rising prices that occurred in many cities during the hyperinflationary years of the Weimar era. Because the Scheunenviertel had a particularly high number of businesses owned by Jews, it was almost automatic that the violence would be directed primarily against them. According to a police report, 55 clothing and shoe stores and 152 grocery stores were pillaged in the Scheunenviertel and neighboring areas of the city. Sixty-one of the owners were Jewish, 146 were Christians. Nevertheless, there can be no doubt about the antisemitic tendency of the riots. Several store owners, for example, attempted to avert plundering with placards in their windows reading "Christian business." The brutality of individual rioters was horrifying. Individual Jews, according to newspaper reports, had the shirts ripped off their backs and were nearly beaten to death. Only because the police took several victims into protective custody at the nearby Alexanderplatz barracks were there no deaths recorded. Nevertheless, the literature on the pogrom constantly reproduces tales of numerous deaths; these are in all likelihood false. There were certainly several dozen injured and at least one non-Jewish death, probably a bystander in a nearby dwelling who was hit by a misdirected warning shot.

Another salient antisemitic feature of the pogrom centered not on the mob but on the police mistreatment of a delegation from the League of Jewish War Veterans who had rushed to the Scheunenviertel to defend Jews. Armed and wearing their war medals, they were recognized and attacked by a mob of about a hundred men. Brought to a police barracks for their own protection, the veterans were insulted by policemen and beaten with gun butts. It should be said on behalf of the often defamed "weak" Weimar Republic that the main perpetrators in this episode were tried, found guilty, and dismissed from the police force.

In consequence of the Scheunenviertel pogrom and the Munich Beer Hall Putsch a few days later, there was a vocal, although short-lived, backlash against antisemitism in the German public. The German Social Democrats took the most substantial countermeasure by forming the republican defense organization, the Reichsbanner Black-Red-Gold. Its founding call to arms made explicit mention of the need to fight antisemitism.

—*Dirk Walter*
*Richard S. Levy, translation*

**See also** *Ostjuden;* Pudor, Heinrich; Social Democratic Party (Germany); Weimar

**References**

Geisel, Eike. *Im Scheunenviertel: Bilder, Texte und Dokumente* (Berlin: Severin and Siedler, 1981).

Walter, Dirk. *Antisemitische Kriminalität und Gewalt: Judenfeindschaft in der Weimarer Republik* (Bonn: J. H. W. Dietz Verlag Nachf., 1999).

## Schnitzler, Arthur (1862–1931)

Viennese novelist, playwright, and physician, Arthur Schnitzler, in his private life, is best remembered as being neither an enthusiastic supporter nor a public advocate of any political or social movement of his time. Like many of his assimilated Jewish contemporaries, he remained cynical about the successive trends passing over Vienna, yet he could not escape the effects of these currents or their turbulence. In his later years, he alleged that the Austrian antisemitism of the 1870s was not at all dangerous, yet his diary entries from those days reveal him to have been both anxious and bitter about the gathering assault on humane values. By 1900, what once appeared innocuous began to take a more menacing turn. As the antisemitic outbursts became more frequent and more impossible to ignore, Schnitzler's literary work began to focus increasingly on Jewish topics and themes.

Of all the great works of Viennese luminaries, writers, and artists of the fin de siècle, Arthur Schnitzler's oeuvre stands out as perhaps the most connected to the pulse of the imperial city. Trained as a medical doctor, and a contemporary of Sigmund Freud, Schnitzler created figures in his plays and novels whose lives reflected the psychological, political, and social turmoil of Vienna's bourgeois culture. Two of his most celebrated works that deal with matters of Jewishness and antisemitism are the novel *The Road into the Open* (*Der Weg ins Freie*) published in 1908 and his play *Professor Bernhardi* from 1912.

In *The Road into the Open* Schnitzler presents a wide-ranging and in-depth view of the problems Jews experienced in Vienna. Schnitzler provides a rich cross section of Jewish characters, from the nouveau riche Ehrenberg family to the communist-minded Therese Golowski and her Zionist brother Leo. Each of the roughly twelve Jewish figures that populate the novel struggle with their own personal sense of what being Jewish means. The novel, hence, has less to do with the social phenomenon of antisemitism in Vienna, but more with individual responses of what constitutes being Jewish during the final decade of the Austro-Hungarian monarchy. The psychological strains that each of the Jewish characters reveals, however, is no doubt a clear—though sometimes unconscious—response to the mounting hostilities against Vienna's Jewish population. The only solution to the disgust, anger, and despair reflected by Schnitzler's Jewish characters in the novel (which mirrors Schnitzler's personal view) is spoken by Heinrich Berman: "It's up to each person to find his own inner way."

Schnitzler's play *Professor Bernhardi*, in a slightly different fashion, places the Jewish question and antisemitism in the forefront, although the basis for this play was more immediately personal, prompted by problems Schnitzler's father experienced in his medical practice. The Jewish doctor Bernhardi, by refusing to allow a priest to administer the last sacrament to a young patient on humanitarian grounds, is accused of offending the Catholic Church and the clinic. Bernhardi is ultimately forced to stand trial and resign his position. The powerful social commentary that Schnitzler captures in this play is not centered exclusively on Bernhardi himself, but rather the political intrigue and intense antisemitic sentiments that this case unleashes in the press, in the parliament, and in the larger Viennese society.

—Istvan Varkonyi

**See also** Aryan Theater; Austria; Degeneration; Herzl, Theodor; Lueger, Karl; Self-Hatred, Jewish; Weininger, Otto; Zionism

**References**
Gay, Peter. *Schnitzler's Century: The Making of Middle-Class Culture 1815–1914* (New York: W. W. Norton, 2002).
Thompson, Bruce. *Schnitzler's Vienna: Image of a Society* (London: Routledge, 1990).

## Schönerer, Georg von (1842–1921)

Georg Ritter von Schönerer exerted a major influence on the German-National movement in Austria, transforming its once dominant liberal nationalism to an extreme form of *völkisch* (ethnically based) and racist nationalism.

At the outset of his career, Schönerer gained renown as a left liberal and social reformer who sought to improve the lot of the peasants on his estate. In 1873, he was elected to the Austrian Reichsrat (parliament) and associated himself with the German Progressive club. From the end of the 1870s, when the conservative government of Count Taaffe began relying mainly on ethnically Slav, rather than German, parties, Schönerer responded by trying to form a broadly based German-National party. He founded the Deutschnationaler Verein (German-National Association) based on the Linz Program of 1882 and temporarily gained the cooperation of reform-minded politicians such as the Christian Social Karl Lueger and the Social Democrats Viktor Adler and Engelbert Pernerstorfer.

In the following years, Schönerer radicalized the German-National movement, taking it in an anti-Slav, antisemitic, and increasingly anti-Habsburg direction. His primary goals were the establishment of German supremacy in Cisleithania (Austria proper, Bohemia, Moravia, Austrian Silesia, Slovenia, and Austrian Poland) and a close alliance with the German Reich. In 1885, he demanded the removal of Jewish influence from all fields of public life in a "twelfth article" of the Linz Program, effectively ending cooperation with most of his allies from other political movements.

Prone to arrogance and physical violence, he drew support mostly from the small-town middle class and the German-National student fraternities (Burschenschaften), whose members formed his bodyguard. Schönerer's aggressive antisemitism became public knowledge in 1888, when he and a group of his supporters vandalized the offices of the Neues Wiener Tagblatt, a newspaper he considered a typical example of the "Jewish" press. The consequences for such lawlessness were severe. Schönerer was sentenced to four months of imprisonment, loss of his titles as Ritter (knight) and military officer, and removal from his seat in the parliament for five years. In 1897 and 1901, he again won election to the Reichsrat. But by that time, his influence on Austrian politics had already crested. He spent the last years of his political career in a fruitless competition with the Christian Socials, the Social Democrats, and rivals from within the German-National movement.

Characteristic of Schönerer's ideology and demagogy was the combination of radical German nationalism with antisemitism and anti-Slavism. His antisemitic rhetoric was explicitly racial: "We must thus insist unconditionally on the separating out of Jewish children and on the complete exclusion of Jewish instructors, whether baptized or not, from the schools of our race. . . . Instead, we wish our youth to receive instruction and education according to Christian-Aryan principles," he declared in a speech in Vienna on February 24, 1888. Calling for the protection of "German blood" from that of the inferior Jewish race was a permanent feature of his rhetoric. His influence on the German-National movement in Austria was enduring, and its significance should not be underestimated, even though he never managed to fashion a powerful party. From the 1880s on, Schönerer cleared the way for racial antisemitism to become a part of Austrian political culture. It is no exaggeration to label him a precursor of Nazism and Hitler, who admired his ideas.

—*Werner Suppanz*

**See also** Aryan Paragraph; Austria; Burschenschaften; Christian Social Party (Austria); Hitler, Adolf; "Jewish" Press; Linz Program; Lueger, Karl; Pan-Germans (Austria); *Völkisch* Movement and Ideology
**References**
Carsten, Francis L. *Fascist Movements in Austria: From Schönerer to Hitler* (London: Sage Publishing, 1977).
Whiteside, Andrew G. *The Socialism of Fools: Georg Ritter von Schönerer and Austrian Pan-Germanism* (Berkeley: University of California Press, 1975).

## Schopenhauer, Arthur (1788–1860)

Arthur Schopenhauer is considered the founder of the philosophy of the "Will to Life," influenced by the ideas of Immanuel Kant and characterized by pessimism and the ethics of compassion. Early in his life, he taught at the University of Berlin but could not compete for attention with the lectures of G. W. F. Hegel. Independently wealthy, Schopenhauer never attained a full professorship. A philosopher of compassion for all creatures, he nevertheless harbored a wealth of burning resentments, including resentment of Jews. His hostility toward them was threefold. First, he was subject to rather baffling antisemitic hatreds of a cultural rather than a biological sort. Second, he was a bitter opponent of Jewish emancipation. And, third, he was moved by explicitly anti-Judaic ethical and philosophical considerations.

Schopenhauer firmly believed that the biblically based image of the world, which he correctly described as Jewish, had deeply influenced European thinking. The epitome of this conception, in his opinion, was represented by the complete separation between humans and animals, a separation that ran counter to his own ethics of compassion. He reviled this view of the world with a derogatory topos from antiquity: the *foetor judaicus* (Jewish stench; in German, *Judengestank*). This phrase surfaces repeatedly in his varied writings. His hostility went well beyond this dismissive formula, however. He embraced the entire tradition of pagan Judeophobia, starting with Manetho the Egyptian (as mediated by Josephus). He subscribed to the inverted version of the Exodus story that the Jews had not left Egypt of their own free will; rather, the Pharaoh had had them deported in ships to the Arabian coast because they were a leprous people. Schopenhauer objected to the way Jews wore their beards and called on the police to ban the practice.

Schopenhauer's antipathies had political significance. In the aftermath of the failure of the revolutions of 1848 in Germany, Jewish emancipation, granted and then rescinded in many places, was still being talked about. Schopenhauer's *Parerga und Paralipoma*, which contained many derisive comments about Jews, appeared in 1851. He expressed a visceral opposition to the idea of Jewish equality. Monotheism for the Jews was not a matter of belief but a nationality trait. It was a mistake, he argued, to see Judaism as an authentic religious confession, deserving of equal status with the other denominations. Jews, as a result of centuries of persecution, lacked delicacy of feeling and even a sense of connection to their own people. Conversion to Christianity, as some demanded, was not at all a sensible solution to the problem of assimilation. And, true to his convictions, Schopenhauer adamantly opposed not only emancipation but mixed marriage, as well. Jews, he said, even if granted civil equality, would still remain Jews (*Parerga*, para. 133).

These political statements were the expression of Schopenhauer's system of ethics, which he conceived of as being in the same relationship as the New to the Old Testament. All ethics in antiquity were beholden to a despotic theism, whereas his ethics of compassion renounced the idea of laws and commandments. The genealogy of his system can be traced to parts of the New Testament—the Jewishness of which he disputed—and also to the ethics of Hindu religion. In 1813 and 1814, he had read the Upanishads, then only available in French translation, and wrote: "Everything here breathes the air of India and of an original existence close to nature. And, how one's spirit is washed clean of all the Jewish superstition drummed into one at an early age" (in Safranski 1990, 302).

Schopenhauer's philosophy and his desire to free Christianity from its Jewish roots led logically to the notion of an "Aryan" Christ, like the one Richard Wagner presented later in his opera *Parsifal*. Writing in her diary, Cosima Wagner attributed to her husband the comment, "Yes, Schopenhauer and others have already spoken about the misfortune that Christianity was propped up on Judaism" (July 26, 1878). In fact, Wagner had long ago been converted to Schopenhauer's world-denying pessimism. In 1855, he reproached Judaism for being filled with a callous and shallow optimism.

—*Micha Brumlik*
*Richard S. Levy, translation*

**See also** Christian State; 1848; Emancipation; Hegel, G. W. F.; Kant, Immanuel; Manetho; Roman Literature; Wagner, Cosima; Wagner, Richard

**References**

Brumlik, Micha. "Das Judentum in der Philosophie Schopenhauers." In *Israel und Kirche heute: Beiträge zum christlich-jüdischen Dialog*. Edited by Ernst Ludwig Ehrlich, Marcel Marcus, Ekkehard Stegemann, and Erich Zenger (Freiburg im Breisgau, Germany: Herder, 1991), 256–272.

Poliakov, Léon. *The Aryan Myth: A History of Racist and Nationalist Ideas in Europe*. Translated by Edmund Howard (New York: Barnes and Noble, 1996; orig. 1971).

Safranski, Rüdiger. *Schopenhauer and the Wild Years of Philosophy*. Translated by Ewald Osers (Cambridge, MA: Harvard University Press, 1990).

## Schwarze Korps, Das

*Das Schwarze Korps* (The Black Corps) was a weekly magazine that served as the official mouthpiece of the SS. Heinrich Himmler and other SS leaders used its pages as a means of policing all aspects of German life under National Socialist rule and presenting the SS as an organization of the pure Aryan elite. Its writers emphatically promoted the extreme pseudobiological agenda of Himmler, which included ridding the country of its Jews. Under the editorship of Gunter d'Alquen, *Das Schwarze Korps* became one of the most virulent antisemitic publications of the period.

Soon after the SS participated in the 1934 purge of Ernst Röhm's Storm troopers (SA) Himmler began to consolidate the position of the police force within the party. As with other party institutions, Himmler felt that the SS needed a coherent and prominent outlet for its views. Latching on to the twenty-five-year-old Nazi journalist and SS member d'Alquen, Himmler assigned him the task of producing *Das Schwarze Korps*. The first issue appeared in February 1935 with a run of 80,000. Within the year, this circulation doubled, and by the outbreak of war in September 1939, it reached a peak of 750,000, with the vast majority of readers coming from the various arms of the SS. The last issue came out on April 12, 1945.

The expansion and the popularity of *Das Schwarze Korps* resulted not only from the growing influence of the SS in the Nazi state but also from the diversity and extremism of its articles. Ranging widely in its coverage, the weekly addressed such topics as antisemitism, the struggle against the Christian churches, and issues surrounding the "race question." In aggressive, sometimes vituperative prose, authors attacked universities, businesses, rival press organs, and other institutions in German life for falling short of what they considered the appropriate goals of the Nazi state. The consistency of its racist rhetoric, as well as its exhortations to SS men about the potential uses of their biological superiority, set the extremist standard against which other National Socialist publications ought to be judged.

With the coming of war, as well as the stepped up involvement of the SS in genocide, *Das Schwarze Korps* became a major venue for justifying the antisemitic agenda of the regime, often finding itself out in front of even the official policies of the moment. During the war, Himmler wrote articles for it proclaiming the necessity of reoccupying the eastern territories that had supposedly once been part of the great Teutonic past. In general, the journal's writers conceived of German expansionism in the East as intimately tied to the necessity of racial purification, that is, the ethnic cleansing of the inferior Jews and Slavs. *Das Schwarze Korps* maintained its popularity through the last month of the war. Bound by and attuned to the unremitting antisemitism of the state and the SS, it had become the emblematic journal of a terrifying new Germany.

—*Paul B. Jaskot*

**See also** Himmler, Heinrich; Holocaust; Racism, Scientific

**References**

Augustinovic, Werner, and Martin Moll. "Gunter d'Alquen: Propagandist des SS-Staates." In *Die SS: Elite unter dem Totenkopf*. Edited by Ronald Smelser and Enrico Syring (Paderborn, Germany: Ferdinand Schöningh, 2000), 100–118.

Combs, William L. *The Voice of the SS: A History of the SS Journal "Das Schwarze Korps"* (New York: Peter Lang, 1986).

## Secret Doctrine, The (1888)

An esoteric two-volume work by Helena P. Blavatsky, founder of the Theosophical Society, *The Secret Doctrine* is revered by many adherents of New Age religion as a prime reference source. Also regarded as her greatest work, the treatise revealed its aim in the subtitle: *The Synthesis of Science, Religion and Philosophy.* To achieve that synthesis the work required rejection of the Jewish religion, particularly its concept of God.

Blavatsky characterized the "God of Abram, Isaac and Jacob" as "spiteful and revengeful." In volume two of the book, she recognized him as both Creator of man and the God of Moses but further identified him as a gnostic "Demiurgos" (minor deity) named Ilda-Baoth, who rebelled against his mother Sophia in order to create the physical universe. His creation of man was a failure, resulting in a soulless creature blocked from spiritual ascension because the demiurge deliberately left him ignorant of good and evil.

In contrast, Blavatsky identified the head of the holy Logos as Satan, the oldest and highest of the angelic gods who also bears the names Lucifer and Kumara. The creative fiasco of Ilda-Baoth prompted a rebellion by Lucifer and one-third of the angelic host, who decided to approach mankind with the enlightenment his creator withheld. Therefore, Blavatsky credits "Satan, the Serpent of Genesis, as the real creator and benefactor, the Father of Spiritual mankind." Predictably, Judaism was seen as a reflection of its deity: "a religion of hate and malice toward everyone and everything outside itself." When Blavatsky nevertheless borrowed from the despised Jewish religion for certain arguments, she attributed any spiritual wisdom shown by the Jews as something learned "from the Chaldeans and Egyptians." In a footnote, she equated "solar angels" with "fallen angels," a uniquely Jewish-Christian concept derived from the Hebrew *Nefilim* described in Genesis 6:4. In a discussion of Satan, she cited the "Rabbins" (*sic*) and the Talmud to support her case but concluded that "Jehovah (mankind, or 'Jahhovah') and Satan (therefore the tempting Serpent) are one and the same in every particular." Blavatsky's translation of the word *Jehovah* here is symptomatic of her arbitrary approach to biblical Hebrew, which she declared to be a dead language understood by no one and dating from no earlier than the fourth century CE.

Blavatsky credited the entire contents of *The Secret Doctrine* to direct transmissions from one of the "Ascended Masters" (the disembodied spirit guides of the New Age), namely, "the Tibetan," or "Djwhal Khul." This is the same entity credited in the writings of Alice A. Bailey, who later expanded on Blavatsky's teaching.

—*Hannah Newman*

**See also** Bailey, Alice A.; Blavatsky, Helena P.

**References**

Blavatsky, Helena P. *An Abridgement of The Secret Doctrine.* Edited by Elizabeth Preston and Christmas Humphreys. (London: Theosophical Publishing House, 1966).

Washington, Peter. *Madame Blavatsky's Baboon: A History of the Mystics, Mediums, and Misfits Who Brought Spiritualism to America* (New York: Schocken Books, 1995).

## Secret Relationship between Blacks and Jews, The

*The Secret Relationship between Blacks and Jews* (1991), written by anonymous members of the Nation of Islam's Historical Research Department, purports to document an array of historic injustices committed against blacks by Jews. In a volume that totals 334 pages and includes over 1,200 footnotes, the authors surveyed a wide spectrum of Jewish historical literature to win credibility for numerous antisemitic claims.

The book contends that Jews played a pivotal role in the African slave trade. "The most prominent of the Jewish pilgrim fathers," it argues, "used kidnapped Black Africans disproportionately more than any other ethnic or religious group in New World history" (vii). Few Jews joined the abolitionist movement, they contend, and those who did "were scorned and rebuked most harshly by their own brethren in the synagogue" (2) Faced with evidence that Jews opposed slavery in eighteenth- and nineteenth-century America, the authors concluded that economic self-interest motivated Jewish "altruism."

*The Secret Relationship between Blacks and Jews* employs a variety of antisemitic strategies that go well beyond the exaggerated claims of responsibility. The authors indulge in guilt by association by charging that "Jews have been conclusively linked to the greatest criminal endeavor ever undertaken against an entire race of people . . . the Black African Holocaust" (vii). They see Jewish sufferings as no more than just: "the Jews' participation in the slave trade, particularly their trafficking in non-Jewish slaves, incited the moral indignation of Europe's gentile population" and resulted in either anti-Jewish taxes or outright expulsion (10). Other chapters argued that Jews were the original authors of Christian-based biblical justifications for slavery, that the Spanish Inquisitors were fully justified in their persecution of Jews, and that Jewish law permitted the economic exploitation of non-Jews.

By relying almost exclusively on a tendentious reading of Jewish sources, *The Secret Relationship* distorts the historical record and ignores both context and historical causation. One example of the book's methodology illustrates this point. Southern Jewish historian Bertram Korn thoroughly detailed an antisemitic newspaper account that depicted Jewish involvement in the slave trade. *The Secret Relationship* authors selected only the offensive newspaper quotations, omitted Korn's criticism of the article's version of reality, and thereby implied that "the Jewish writer" Korn had found evidence of Jewish complicity in slavery. He had not. As historian David Brion Davis reflected, "A selective search for Jewish slave traders becomes inherently antisemitic unless one keeps in view the larger context and the very marginal place of Jews in the history of the overall system" (Davis 1994, 14–16). In another example, the book's authors state incongruously that—thirty years prior to their arrival in colonial North America—Jews initiated the slave trade there.

In 1994, *The Secret Relationship between Blacks and Jews* entered its fourth printing. Although promoters of the book contend that it enjoyed great support on college campuses in the United States, there is no evidence to back their claim.

—*Marc Dollinger*

*See also* African American–Jewish Relations; Black Nationalism; Farrakhan, Louis; Nation of Islam; Slave Trade and the Jews; Talmud; United States

**References**

Davis, David Brion. "The Slave Trade and the Jews," *New York Review of Books,* 41, (December 22, 1994): 14–16.

Dinnerstein, Leonard. *Anti-Semitism in America* (New York: Oxford University Press, 1994).

Friedman, Murray. *What Went Wrong? The Creation and Collapse of the Black-Jewish Alliance* (New York: Free Press, 1995).

## Self-Hatred, Jewish

For many reasons, including connotations of betrayal and an attendant emotional charge, Jewish self-hatred has prompted vigorous debate. Yet the many critics who have discussed it agree on a fundamental point: the actual phenomenon of Jewish self-hatred occurs when Jews have internalized antisemitic attitudes. If that is so, then Jewish self-hatred would be as difficult to define precisely as antisemitism itself. Put another way, a precise definition of Jewish self-hatred would require a precise definition of antisemitism.

Students of Jewish self-hatred must also reckon with difficulties particular to their subject. "Self-hating Jews" seldom practice violence against their fellow Jews or engage in antisemitic political activities. In contrast to non-Jewish antisemites, Jewish self-haters have left almost exclusively verbal evidence of their anti-Jewish sentiments. Such evidence is often semantically complicated and very open to interpretation—generally more so than acts of physical brutality. Moreover, self-hating Jews have tended to avoid explicitly racist antisemitism. This, too, makes the antisemitism of the most notorious self-hating Jews seem less dogmatic and more ambiguous than the antisemitism of their non-Jewish analogs.

What some readers understand to be verbalized self-loathing others can view as provocatively worded, ultimately salutary self-criticism. For example, the satirical journalist Karl Kraus (1874–1936) has been called both "the most glaring instance of self-hatred" and "a great Jew." And some scholars have even made efforts to rehabilitate Kraus's fellow Viennese Otto Weininger. Long a focal point in the study of Jewish antisemitism, Weininger freighted his main work, *Geschlecht und Charakter* (Sex and Character [1903]), with invective against Jews and Judaism. In fact, Hitler is said to have lauded Weininger's "honest" assessment of the Jewish Question. Here is a sample of Weininger's antisemitism: "For all eternity, real Jews will lack: true existence, the grace of God, the oak tree, the trumpet, Siegfried's motif, self-authorship, the words, 'I am.'" This assessment is quite literally annihilating, for Weininger denied Jews a "true existence." But because he insisted that Judaism is a cultural "principle" rather than a racial category—a principle that non-Jews can exhibit just as much as ethnic Jews—Weininger can be and has been read as a thinker who tried to counter flatly racist notions of Jewish identity. However, Weininger acted out his antisemitic beliefs, violently. He killed himself in 1903.

There are further complexities. The concept of Jewish self-hatred has a troubled history that encumbers its application. Although the phrase *Jewish self-hatred* gained currency in late Wilhelmine Germany, a myth to the effect that Jews are the worst antisemites—that Jews invented

Jew-hatred—goes back much further. This tradition of emphasizing Jewish antisemitism is itself antisemitic. More specifically, anti-Jewish thinkers have cited the antisemitic works of self-haters in order to bolster their own attacks on Jews, their presupposition being that antisemitism uttered by Jews possesses a special authority. Hence, for example, the popularity among latter-day antisemites of Johannes Pfefferkorn (1469–1522), a converted Jew who vilified Judaism.

The antisemitic myth of Jewish self-hatred also has functioned by doubling the Jews' status as scapegoats. Not only have Jews been held responsible for various social ills, they have also been held responsible for having been held responsible. Witness the very persistent sense that Hitler *must* have been Jewish.

It is certainly no coincidence that the first monograph-length study of Jewish self-hatred, *Der jüdische Selbsthass* (Jewish Self-Hatred [1930]), was written by a Jewish author who had himself expressed antisemitic beliefs, Theodor Lessing. To be sure, Lessing presented himself as a recovered self-hater, as someone sufficiently familiar with that psychic abyss to help others climb out of it. But Lessing also treated the subjects of his six case studies, none of whom was ever formally associated with an antisemitic organization or qualified as a racist antisemite, as though each of them had decisively influenced anti-Jewish ideology. In doing so, he reinforced the notion of Jewish responsibility for antisemitism.

Lessing made dubious use of the concept of Jewish self-hatred in other ways. For example, by labeling Kraus a pathological self-hater, he tried to discredit his critical voice and to suggest that self-doubt stifled his creativity. He asserted that Kraus could not conceive of himself, a Jew, as a great artist and therefore squandered his talent, producing only a huge "pile of newspapers" whose value was wholly ephemeral. Given the intensity of Kraus's anti-Jewish rhetoric—he spoke of the "world-destroying power of Jewish capitalism"—it is certainly reasonable to associate him with Jewish self-hatred. But demolishing Kraus's literary accomplishments in the process seems highly overdetermined. Lessing was neither the first nor the last to succumb to the temptation of deploying Jewish self-hatred as a polemical tool.

It was not only the concept of self-hatred that Jewish writers appropriated strategically. In quite a few cases, their use of antisemitic discourse extended well beyond a brute articulation of antisemitic beliefs. Unfortunately, recent critics have relentlessly overlooked this tendency. Consider the case of Kraus's essay on Heinrich Heine, "Heine and the Consequences" (1910). Referring to the poet's alleged syphilitic condition, Kraus labeled Heine's writing effete because "the German language only sings and thinks for someone who can give her children." But Kraus went on from this crude insult to dismantle precisely such ideas. Later in the text, he characterized linguistic creativity as a gentle process of "gathering" words. Then, he explicitly rejected the sort of patriarchal theories of linguistic mastery that he advanced at the beginning of his essay and that played such an important role in antisemitic broadsides against Jewish writers. He also praised Heine's late poetry, which abounds with Jewish motifs.

Sander Gilman, the most prominent theorist of Jewish self-hatred, argued that Kraus's "Heine and the Consequences" sets up a strict dichotomy between "good" German and the "bad language" of Heine and the Jews. As Gilman himself put it, "This attack on Heine using the rhetoric of the anti-Semitic views on the nature of the Jews' language is meant by Kraus to be a defense of 'good' language . . . and an attack on the 'bad' language attributed by Kraus . . . to the Jew" (Gilman 1986, 240–241). Gilman's simplification resulted from a narrow, monocausal understanding of antisemitic discourse in writings by Jews, from the premise that it is the expression of internalized stereotypes. This theory cannot, however, explain why Kraus would pour antisemitic scorn on Heine's "bad language" and then proceed to celebrate his late poetry. A more flexible theory of Jewish self-hatred, one that can account for appropriations of antisemitic discourse as ironic and as self-subverting as Kraus's "Heine and the Consequences," would seem to be in order.

Yet Gilman was certainly right to insist that in nineteenth- and early twentieth-century Germany and Austria, many Jews did "accept" antisemitic ideas about Jewish cultural inferiority. Strikingly, the most precocious Jewish intellects very often articulated doubts about the ability of Jews to be truly creative. And they frequently did so in candid settings, such as diaries, and without any willfully obfuscatory self-stylization. Rahel Varnhagen, Sigmund Freud, Walther Rathenau, Ludwig Wittgenstein, and Arthur Schnitzler all speculated on what Theodor Gomperz, a respected classicist, called the "limits of the Jewish intellectual gift."

In addition, there was the more everyday self-hatred that Schnitzler's literary works chronicled so well. Through characters such as Oskar Ehrenberg of *The Road into the Open* (1908), Schnitzler showed how nonintellectual Jews tried to assimilate into the realms of German culture—in part by adopting and eventually accepting the antisemitism of the culture by which they wanted to be accepted. Schnitzler also suggested that class and gender identity helped determine the particular coloration of such Jewish self-hatred. Unlike the high-profile figures Gilman treated, the kind of Jews whose antisemitism Schnitzler represented generally left no readily accessible record of their self-hatred. This part of the phenomenon certainly merits further study; perhaps that will alter our conception of the problem.

—*Paul Reitter*

*See also* Freud, Sigmund; Heine, Heinrich; Jewish Question; Kraus, Karl; Rathenau, Walther; Schnitzler, Arthur; Weininger, Otto

**References**

Gilman, Sander. *Jewish Self-Hatred: Anti-Semitism and the Secret Language of the Jews* (Baltimore, MD: Johns Hopkins University Press, 1986).

Mayer, Hans. *Outsiders: A Study in Life and Letters.* Translated by Denis Sweet (Cambridge, MA: MIT University Press, 1982).

Mendes-Flohr, Paul. *Divided Passions: Jewish Intellectuals and the Experience of Modernity* (Detroit, MI: Wayne State University Press, 1991).

# Seligman-Hilton Affair (1877)

The story made headlines. Joseph Seligman, one of New York City's leading citizens, Union financier in the Civil War, personal friend of President Ulysses S. Grant, and exemplar of the German Jewish immigrants' stunning rise to the upper class, arrived with his family at the Grand Union Hotel in the resort city of Saratoga, New York. A longtime patron, he was, on this occasion, unceremoniously turned away on instruction from the hotel's new owner, Judge Henry Hilton: no Jews were to stay at the Grand Union. Decent Christian folk were tired of putting up with these uncouth Jewish Johnny-come-latelies, Hilton proclaimed publicly; he wished to protect his desirable clientele from mingling with undesirables. With this June 1877 event, American antisemitism came of age.

The protagonists' personal histories and the larger social context shaped the Seligman-Hilton affair. Seligman had served on an important city commission that quashed the corrupt Tweed Ring, in which Hilton was a major operative, and he belonged to the prestigious Union League club, which had rejected Hilton's membership bid. In 1876, Hilton became the executor of the estate of a close friend, department store magnate A. T. Stewart, who also had reasons to dislike Seligman. Hilton's acquisitions of Stewart's holdings put him in a position to strike at Seligman. Also, the Grand Union was losing prestige as Saratoga was abandoned by the gentry and adopted by a new economic aristocracy of merchants, financiers, and industrialists. Other hotels already restricted their clientele in order to cultivate an elite image.

The event became a cause célèbre when the irate Seligman spoke out angrily in the press. Invective flew back and forth, condemning and commending both sides. As the controversy grew nastier, Seligman canceled a public protest meeting; Hilton, probably worried for his business, pledged $1,000 to Jewish charities. Ultimately, a Jewish boycott of the Stewart wholesale operation helped bankrupt it.

Yet Hilton was definitely on to something bigger than his personal animosity. This affair was by no means the first instance of social antisemitism in the United States, but soon, the phenomenon was widespread. Although blatantly anti-Jewish actions shocked some, it also released much latent antisemitism. Negative stereotypes of Jews as venal and crude, which had deep roots in the gentile distrust of Jewish economic practice, were extremely useful tools in the wars of social status that marked the Gilded Age. For every voice applauding the Jews' "manly" response to Hilton, as did the weekly *Puck,* there were others that interpreted it as "pushy." Social-climbing non-Jews felt free to condemn the social "excesses" of the Jewish nouveaux riches, while ignoring their own extravagances. In John Higham's words, "Discrimination was an instrument of social ambition" (Higham 1984, 129). In this environment, Seligman may have, by publicizing antisemitism, unwittingly helped make it socially acceptable. Soon, elite hotels, schools, and clubs began to exclude Jews explicitly. In 1881, Seligman's nephew was even refused membership in the Union League. Still playing by the same rules of the game, German Jewish Americans founded their own clubs and developed their own resorts, creating and sheltering a Jewish society that was defensive, insular, and cautious.

—*Amy Hill Shevitz*

**See also** Restricted Public Accommodations, United States; Restrictive Covenants; United States; Wharton, Edith

**References**

Birmingham, Stephen. *Our Crowd: The Great Jewish Families of New York* (New York: Harper and Row, 1967).

Higham, John. "Antisemitism in the Gilded Age: A Reinterpretation," *Mississippi Valley Historical Review* 43 (1957): 559–578.

———, *Send These to Me: Immigrants in Urban America* (Baltimore: Johns Hopkins University Press, 1984).

Livney, Lee. "Let Us Now Praise Self-Made Men: A Reexamination of the Hilton-Seligman Affair," *New York History* 75 (January 1994): 66–98.

## Settlement *Heimland*

Settlement *Heimland,* considered the first race-based (*völkisch*) commune in Germany, came into existence in 1909. The enterprise was the brainchild of the well-known Leipzig antisemite Theodor Fritsch. In the previous decade, he had written *Two Fundamental Evils: Land-Profiteering and the Stock Market* (1894) and *City of the Future* (1896), books that called for "new communities" to be built far from the corrupting metropolis and to be organized as rural cooperatives. The premise of these schemes lay in the conviction that the German race was threatened with extinction by the forces of Semitism and Americanism. The healthy remnant of the race could be saved only through creation of living conditions that answered the needs of the German essence. For Fritsch, such conditions included eliminating economic competition, socializing agriculture, working the soil, and following Germanic customs. His experiment failed but provided the impetus for further race-based communes following World War I.

Fritsch's own plans were given new life in the decade before the war by the more or less successful founding of the vegetarian, life-reforming, fruit-growing colony Eden, which provided the immediate model for Settlement *Heimland.* The establishment of the German Renewal Community (in 1904), which propagated land reform and the cultivation of a stronger, healthier Germanic type, was also influential. Answering an advertisement in Fritsch's *Hammer: Journal of the German Way* in the spring of 1908, sixty people "fed up with urban life" declared themselves ready to settle in the countryside, according to Fritsch's principles. In October 1908, the Settlement Society *Heimland* was formed with Fritsch as chairman of the supervisory board and his illegitimate son, Walther Kramer, as its manager. In July 1909, the society acquired 450 acres of land in the vicinity of Rheinsberg, about 60 miles northwest of Berlin.

The land was divided into two concentric circles. The inner circle was given over to communal farming carried out by young, unmarried men and women who lived in existing habitations. The outer circle consisted of approximately fifty parcels of land on which settler families practiced horticulture. Before the outbreak of war, Jorg Brücke, a young architect and later a famous painter as well, designed homes for eleven of the farmsteads. The communal farmers grew a variety of crops and raised livestock on a modest basis. From 1910 to 1914, between ten and fifteen communal farmers lived in the settlement, some of them for only a few months at a time. Visits from youth groups and other ideological sympathizers were frequent enough to warrant the building of a guest house in 1910.

Prominently displayed on the Settlement *Heimland* barn stood a swastika. The communal farmers, after completing a probation period, received Germanic first names, such as Eckhart, Siegbert, or Roland, by which they were then addressed. Alcohol was banned. The *Hammer* and several other *völkisch* and life-reforming journals reported regularly on the progress of the experiment, as well as on the annual conference of the Settlement Society. Until the war, Fritsch placed great political store in the spread of new, planned settlements. However, weighty voices from within the *völkisch* movement criticized the isolationist aspect of the undertaking; others complained that such separatism would weaken the antisemitic propaganda effort. But Fritsch found supporters as well, especially among those who urged the young to return to the land.

World War I dealt the settlement a serious setback, when most of the young men went into the army. By that time, it had also become clear that the land was short of water and the climate unsuitable for horticulture. The attempt to revive the community after the war foundered on these problems and was also undermined by the beginning of the inflationary spiral. In the spring of 1919, a German children's home was established at the settlement, with the avowed purpose of saving a number of "racially valuable" youngsters from the "degenerate world." This project, as well as a school to train *völkisch* farmers, struggled and then failed. In stages between 1926 and 1936, the enterprise went into irreversible decline, divestiture, and finally liquidation.

—*Christoph Knüppel*
*Richard S. Levy, translation*

**See also** Förster, Bernhard; Förster-Nietzsche, Elisabeth; Fritsch, Theodor; Imperial Hammer League; *Völkisch* Movement and Ideology

**References**
Knüppel, Christoph, ed. *Dokumente zur Geschichte der völkischen Siedlung Heimland bei Rheinsberg* (Herford, Germany: Knüppel, 2002).
Linse, Ulrich. "Völkisch-rassische Siedlungen der Lebensreform." In *Handbuch zur "Völkischen Bewegung," 1871–1918.* Edited by Uwe Puschner, Walter Schmitz, and Justus H. Ulbricht. (Munich, Germany: K. G. Saur, 1996), 397–410.

# Shabbetai Zevi

Shabbetai Zevi, born in 1626 in Smyrna, was at the center of an important messianic movement within Judaism that was named after him. Steeped in traditional rabbinic learning, he emerged, after a period of semiseclusion between 1642 and 1648, as a self-proclaimed messiah. He was then swept up by the publicity campaign of Nathan Ashkenazi of Gaza (1644–1680). In 1665, Nathan fell into a trance during a religious service and made a number of utterances, including reference to an acquaintance, Shabbetai Zevi; after coming out of the trance, he claimed that he was chosen by God as a prophet and that Shabbetai Zevi was the Messiah. In May 1665, Shabbetai Zevi accepted this announcement and proclaimed the seventeenth day of the Hebrew month of Tammuz (traditionally a fast day) as a feast day.

The reaction to Shabbetai Zevi was extremely mixed and at times very intense. Expelled from Jerusalem, his movement spread throughout the Islamic countries and Europe accompanied by tales of miraculous deeds. Shabbetai Zevi was forced to move a great deal between cities in the Balkans, in Egypt, and throughout the Middle East because of his numerous transgressions of Jewish religious law. He gathered a large number of fervent believers in Aleppo, Smyrna, and Constantinople, although a significant portion of wealthy and rabbinic leaders in his native Smyrna continued to oppose him. More guardedly enthusiastic believers lent him important support in Gaza, Hebron, and Safed, and he found backing among segments of the Jewish populations of Amsterdam, Hamburg, Ancona, Venice, and perhaps also Frankfurt, Prague, and Vienna. Poland, Bohemia-Moravia, Hungary, France, and most parts of Germany showed less zeal for him.

In early 1666, he sailed from Smyrna to Constantinople, with the expectation that he would remove the crown from the sultan and assume rule over the Ottoman Empire, ushering in a messianic age. Instead, his ship was intercepted, and he was taken ashore in chains. Not wishing to create a martyr, the sultan imprisoned him and offered a choice between immediate death or conversion to Islam. Shabbetai Zevi converted, and although the conversion destroyed the faith of many followers, the allure of his personality sustained the movement for a very long time afterward.

Scholars have explored the reasons for the widespread reception of the movement, citing popular belief in the Messiah, Christian millenarian concepts and contemporary enthusiasm, the expectations of *marranos* returned to Judaism, the general political instability of the age (reflected in the 1648–1649 massacres in Poland), and the general climate of political and religious crisis in the seventeenth century. Some scholars have emphasized Shabbetai Zevi's apparent psychological instability and his secondary role in the emergence and organization of the movement (behind Nathan of Gaza); others have picked up on internal Jewish communal tensions or the growth of interest in kabbalistic and messianic ideas of the period.

The movement was significant in the context of anti-Judaism primarily because its failure encouraged some to convert from Judaism and because it afforded Christian polemicists the opening to argue that the Jews were dangerous, that they would take the first opportunity for open revolt, and that they were both gullible and blind in following the "false messiah." Jews, according to this line of thought, were not capable of discerning the true Messiah, as was proved by the conversion of Shabbetai Zevi. Friar Michel Feyre, who presented a book of recollections of his stay in the Ottoman Empire to the lord general inquisitor of Milan in 1680, drew this conclusion from the events:

Then the Mulla, or Preacher of the Gran Signor, named Vanli Affendi, said that before embracing Islam it was necessary that he believe in Christ, son of the Virgin Mary, and that he recognize him as a Great Prophet and as the true Messiah sent by God. Shabbatai Zevi readily agreed to this and added that the Jews were greatly mistaken and blind to accept any other faith. . . . He was then ordered by the Gran Signor expressly not to get involved in any way with the Jews, otherwise he would be executed. He promised to respect this punctually, all the more so, he added, as he saw in the Jews an abominable nation, hated by God and by Men. (in Saban 1993, 115)

—*Dean Phillip Bell*

**See also** Chmielnicki Massacres; Inquisition
**References**
Carlebach, Elisheva. "Sabbatianism and the Jewish-Christian Polemic." In *Proceedings of the Tenth World Congress of Jewish Studies, Jerusalem, August 16–24, 1989.* Division C: Jewish Thought and Literature (Jerusalem: World Union of Jewish Studies, 1990): 1–7.
Popkin, Richard H. "Three English Tellings of the Sabbatai Zevi Story," *Jewish History* 8, nos. 1–2 (1994): 43–54.
Saban, Giacomo. "Sabbatai Sevi as Seen by a Contemporary Traveller," *Jewish History* 7, no. 2 (1993): 105–118.
Scholem, Gershom. *Sabbatai Sevi: The Mystical Messiah, 1626–1676* (Princeton, NJ: Princeton University Press, 1973).
Van Wijk, Jetteke. "The Rise and Fall of Shabbatai Zevi as Reflected in Contemporary Press Reports," *Studia Rosenthalia* 33, no. 1 (1999): 7–27.

## Shakespeare, William (1564–1616)

Was Shakespeare an antisemite? His treatment of the character Shylock is not sufficient proof that he was, especially in the absence of personal statements from the author himself. Nevertheless, some have inferred on this basis alone that he was, indeed, an antisemite. A more productive question, however, is whether *The Merchant of Venice* is an antisemitic play or whether it has been misinterpreted and misused in the course of its reception in order to enlist Shakespeare as an antisemitic propagandist.

*The Merchant of Venice* is primarily a comedy about love and friendship, with Shylock a subordinate part of the subplot. This character has gained its immense importance only in the history of the piece's reception, with the consequence that it has been read and produced, in turn, as a tragicomedy, a tragedy, or a problem play. The work was probably written between 1596 and 1598, when anti-Jewish feelings in London were still inflamed by the trial and 1594 execution of the Jewish Portuguese Rodrigo

López, who, as Queen Elizabeth's personal physician, was accused of having tried to poison her. Jews had been expelled from England in 1290, and although a few still lived there in Shakespeare's day, they were mostly known from medieval legends and religious plays, in which they were represented as malicious monsters.

In Shakespeare's source, a novella by Giovanni Fiorentino (1558), the old story of a Jew lending money on security of a pound of flesh had been merged with a love story into a crude tale of sex and money. In Shakespeare's hands, this Jew is given a name and comprehensible motives and is presented as the humiliated and despised victim of Christian hatred and contempt. Shylock, a usurer, and Antonio, a merchant, despise each other: Shylock hates Antonio because he is a Christian and because he lends out money gratis, thus lowering the rates of interest Shylock himself can charge; Antonio hates Shylock because he is a Jew and a usurer. Queen Elizabeth declared loaning money at interest was lawful in 1571, but usury had not, in theory, been permitted for Christians because it was considered an offense against Christian charity and a perversion to make money increase like livestock. There were Christian usurers in England, mostly Puritans in the absence of Jews, who were also treated with hatred and contempt. Thus, the subplot can be interpreted as dealing with usury and usurers and not specifically with Jews. Shylock and Antonio also represent two different attitudes about commerce and the uses of money. Antonio spends his money freely among his friends and invests his fortune in risky sea expeditions, trusting in the "hand of heaven." Shylock, in contrast, relies on economic shrewdness for increasing his fortune. This points to an important debate in Shakespeare's time about the right use of money—either as something to be spent liberally in order to establish a happy society of mutual love and friendship or as a commodity to be hoarded and increased as an end in itself.

Shylock's offer involving a pound of flesh is ambiguous: it can be taken for a joke or a trap. His hatred of Antonio and the Venetian aristocrats, the result of long-endured humiliation, flares up into blind thirst for revenge only after Jessica's elopement with her father's ducats and jewels. His fa-

Henry Irving, as Shylock. Irving's Shylock was received enthusiastically by Victorian audiences, who prided themselves on their tolerance and integration of other races, cultures, and religions, provided they conformed to Victorian norms. (Time Life Pictures/Getty Images)

mous monologue (3.1), so often quoted as a plea for accepting Jews as fellow creatures, ends with him defending his claim for revenge.

With the confrontation of Shylock and Portia in the climactic courtroom scene (4.1) the theme of justice and mercy is introduced in the play, with Shylock insisting on the literal fulfillment of his bond and Portia, in her famous monologue, pleading the necessity of mercy. This led to a reading of the play as a debate about justice and mercy or even as an allegory: the Christian (Antonio) threatened by the devil (Shylock) is saved by grace (Portia). But the trick by which Shylock's claim is rejected is legally most questionable. It was perhaps only to Elizabethan audiences that the Jew's final punishment, by saving both his life and soul, may have appeared both just and merciful.

The history of the play has been determined

not only by ambivalence in the presentation of its characters but also by the changing attitudes of European societies toward Jews. The play does not seem to have been very popular until it was revived in 1701 in a crude but successful adaptation by George Granville (*The Jew of Venice*), which presented Shylock as a low-comedy figure. In 1741, the great actor Charles Macklin restored Shakespeare's text and played Shylock with great success as a cunning, ferocious, and vengeful villain. This interpretation was superseded by Edmund Kean in 1814, at the time when Jewish status was improving. Kean, divesting Shylock of all his repulsive traits, presented him as a tragic figure driven to catastrophe by long-suffered humiliations. But the most famous and influential Shylock, created by Henry Irving in 1879, was the one received enthusiastically by Victorian audiences, who prided themselves on their tolerance and integration of other races, cultures, and religions, provided they conformed to Victorian norms. Irving's Shylock was a proud aristocrat of an ancient race and religion, breaking out in scorn only when goaded by contempt.

In the last century, Shylock was presented in a greater range of interpretation than ever before: as a comic figure, as a sinister and repulsive villain confirming the worst prejudices of audiences, as a dignified victim, as an outsider trying in vain to integrate himself in a Christian society, or as a businessman gradually becoming aware of his Jewish identity. The play generated several offshoots, such as Arnold Wesker's *The Merchant* (1976) or Charles Marowitz's *Variations on the Merchant of Venice* (1978), which attempted to rewrite this supposedly antisemitic text from the Jewish point of view or in the light of modern Jewish history, without surpassing Shakespeare's original, however.

In creating Shylock, Shakespeare amalgamated traditional Christian prejudices with some traits of the stage Jew, of the Vice figure, and of the Machiavellian villain. At the same time, however, he supplied Shylock with humanly comprehensible motives and presented his hatred and thirst for revenge as the result of the hatred and contempt he was exposed to in a Christian society. Thus, the Jew was both perpetrator and victim, and he appeared both comic and tragic, both villainous and pitiable. Shylock turned the comedy into a play about antisemitism in action, which lends itself to being read and performed as both an antisemitic play and a plea for tolerance.

—*Wolfgang Weiss*

**See also** Capital: Useful vs. Harmful; Caricature, Anti-Jewish (Early); English Literature from Chaucer to Wells; Jew Bill; *Jew of Malta, The;* Misanthropy; Passion Plays, Medieval; Shylock; Usury

**References**

Gross, John J. *Shylock: Four Hundred Years in the Life of a Legend* (London: Chatto and Windus, 1992).

Mahon, J. W., and E. M. Mahon, eds. *"The Merchant of Venice": Critical Essays* (London: Routledge, 2002).

Shapiro, J. *Shakespeare and the Jews* (New York: Columbia University Press, 1996).

Yaffe, M. D. *Shylock and the Jewish Question* (Baltimore, MD, and London: Johns Hopkins University Press, 1997).

# Shylock

Along with Judas and the Wandering Jew, Shylock is one of the preeminent antisemitic images in Western culture. His name is a byword for the Jewish usurer, banker, loan shark, pawnbroker, slumlord, and businessman, driven by greed, misanthropy, and a pathological lust for revenge.

In both his theatrical and literary existence, Shylock evokes long-standing themes in the history of Christian antisemitism. Although the name is not biblical (or even Jewish, for that matter), the character was based, in part, on Christopher Marlowe's Barabas (*The Jew of Malta*), himself the namesake of the Gospel criminal spared crucifixion by the Jewish mob that demanded Christ's (Matt. 27:15–33). In eighteenth-century performances of Shakespeare's *Merchant of Venice,* moreover, Shylock appeared with red beard and hair, as well as an enormous nose, evoking images of Judas and the devil derived from medieval Passion plays. Even hoary Christian theological disputes with Judaism resound in the play. In its climactic trial scene, Shakespeare's text juxtaposes Pauline grace with the Jew's carnal attachment to the letter of the law. Against Shylock's demand for retribution, Portia (disguised as the judge) reminds the audience that "in the course of justice, none of us should see salvation"(act 4, scene 1: 199–200) Shylock's reply, "My deeds upon my head! I crave the law," recalls Matthew 27:25 ("His blood upon us and upon our children"), among the most fateful New Testament lines for the subsequent history of antisemitism.

Given this complex of negative associations, the Shylock image was often employed for anti-Jewish propaganda purposes outside of its original dramatic context. This occurred, for instance, in the controversy over the 1753 Jew Bill, a law designed to enable wealthy foreign-born Jews to acquire the status of British subjects. Its passage unleashed a torrent of anti-Jewish invective, which accomplished its hasty repeal; the words *Shylock* and *Jew* were employed interchangeably by the bill's opponents to connote the subversive usurer. The pamphlet "The Prophesies of Shylock," for example, depicted God granting England to the Jews as their eternal possession, "ripe for Destruction." Such propaganda played on widespread fears of a conspiracy to "Judaize" England through infiltration of the country's leading economic and political institutions.

The popularity of Shakespeare's play, translated into twenty languages by the mid-nineteenth century, accorded the Shylock image immense cultural prominence. In the United States between 1870 and 1940, *The Merchant of Venice* was, along with *Julius Caesar,* the most widely studied of Shakespeare's works in the high school classroom, prompting a campaign by the Anti-Defamation League to curtail its use. Shylock exerted a nearly archetypal influence on subsequent literary depictions of Jews, such as Dickens's Fagin and Balzac's Nuncingen and Gobseck. This influence, however, also extended to philosemitic images that attempted to invert the ugly stereotype, such as Gotthold Ephraim Lessing's *Nathan the Wise* and Walter Scott's Isaac of York. Efforts to reclaim Shylock as a sympathetic Jewish hero—one who exposes Christian hypocrisy while rendering the Jew both formidable and complex—are likewise to be found in William Hazlitt's essays, the writings of Heinrich Heine, and the drama criticism of Yiddish essayist Shlomo Bickel, to cite but a few examples.

This partial neutralization of Shylock is also a function of his increasing banality. In the United States, Shylock has entered the vocabulary of hard-boiled crime literature, spelled with a small *s* or deployed as a verb: to shylock, according to the *Oxford English Dictionary,* is to force repayment of a loan through extortion or violence. This transformation of Shylock into slang underworld jargon for loan shark suggests a near-complete severance from the name's anti-Jewish origins.

—*Jonathan Karp*

***See also*** Balzac, Honoré; Banker, Jewish; Deicide; Dickens, Charles; Gospels; Heine, Heinrich; Jew Bill; *Jew of Malta, The;* Misanthropy; Passion Plays, Medieval; Shakespeare, William; Usury; *Verjudung;* Wandering Jew

***References***

Felsenstein, Frank. *Anti-Semitic Stereotypes: A Paradigm of Otherness in English Popular Culture, 1660–1830* (Baltimore, MD: Johns Hopkins University Press, 1995).

Gross, John J. *Shylock: Four Hundred Years in the Life of a Legend* (London: Chatto and Windus, 1992).

Penslar, Derek. *Shylock's Children: Jewish Economics and Identity in Modern Europe* (Berkeley: University of California Press, 2002).

## Simon of Trent

St. Simon of Trent is one of the most famous purported victims of Jewish ritual murder. His cult lasted longer than that of any of the boy martyrs whom the Jews were accused of murdering in mockery of Christ. His death occurred in 1475 at a time of social and economic tension in the northern Italian town of Trent, a prince-bishopric where secular and ecclesiastical powers were concentrated in the hands of one man. Unlike many earlier accusations of ritual murder, this charge was fully investigated, and records of the proceedings survive in Latin and Italian.

The itinerant Franciscan preacher Bernardino da Feltre had stirred up much of Italy with horrific accusations against Jews. He arrived in the Tyrol and incited the community there with vitriolic antisemitic sermons at Lent, predicting that something evil would happen, just before Simon, age two and a half, disappeared on the evening of Maundy Thursday in Easter week. In 1475, this coincided with the Jewish celebration of Passover 5235. The boy's father, Andreas, immediately blamed the Jews because he had heard that they

German illustration of the martyrdom of Saint Simon of Trent after a woodcut by Michael Wohlgemuth. Jews are identifiable by circular badges on their clothing, their names, and their heinous deeds. (Stapleton Collection/Corbis)

kidnapped and killed Christian boys, and he demanded that their houses be searched.

The boy's body washed up in the River Adige and floated into the water cellar in the house of the leading Jew in town. Inconsistent and contradictory testimony from neighboring Christians and converts who had heard a child crying confirmed the prejudices of the investigators, and seventeen Jews were tortured into confessing. The interrogations were held in German, with questions and answers translated into Italian and copied down in Latin. Bishop Hinderbach investigated and prosecuted. The Jews of the area protested and gained a new trial before Guidici of Ventimiglia, who upheld the guilty verdict. Further Jewish protests brought the case to the attention of Pope Sixtus IV, who commissioned a famous law professor, assisted by six cardinals, to investigate again. They, too, confirmed the sentence, and the seventeen Jews were burned at the stake. Immediately afterward, miracles were attributed to Simon, and his cult quickly spread throughout Italy and Germany.

Pope Gregory XIII canonized Bernardino da Feltre as a prophet and Simon as a martyr. Pope Sixtus V recognized Simon's cult in 1588; it was confirmed in 1770, remained vital throughout the seventeenth century, and was reinvigorated at the beginning of the twentieth. Only in 1965, after the Second Vatican Council, was Simon of Trent removed from the Roman Martyrology, his veneration no longer approved by the Catholic Church.

Because the accusation took place at the dawn of printing and involved such a shocking tale, gruesome images of the alleged murder were widely distributed. Itinerant preachers spread Simon's tale throughout Italy, and mobs attacked Jews in Veneto, Lombardy, and the Tyrol. Humanist poets and Italian doctors joined in celebrating Simon, whose fame also spread with visitors to the Council of Trent (in 1545).

The most famous image, a terrifying illustration in Hartmann Schedel's *Nuremberg Chronicle* (*Buch der Chroniken*) of 1493, is still often reproduced. It shows nine Jews (men and women) surrounding Simon, holding him in the position of a crucifixion on a table, piercing his genitals, and collecting his blood. The evil Jews are identified by Jewish badges, moneybags, and identifying labels with Jewish names. This image and many other portrayals spread the story of Simon.

—*Emily Rose*

**See also** Franciscan Order; Middle Ages, Late; Ritual Murder (Medieval); Sorcery/Magic; Vatican Council, Second; William of Norwich; Yellow Badge
**Reference**
Hsia, R. Po-chia. *Trent 1475: Stories of a Ritual Murder Trial* (New Haven, CT: Yale University Press in cooperation with Yeshiva University Library, 1992).

## Simplicissimus

The satirical illustrated weekly *Simplicissimus* took its name from the Latin word meaning "most stupid" or "simple-minded," an allusion to the famous seventeenth-century novel *The Adventurous Simplicissimus* by Grimmelshausen that described his simpleton hero's experiences during the Thirty Years' War. The first issue appeared in 1896 in Munich, published by Albert Langen and Th.(omas) Th.(eodor) Heine, a graphic artist baptized at birth by his parents who made no secret of his Jewish extraction. In 1906, at the height of the journal's popularity, with close to 90,000 issues sold each week, ownership of *Simplicissimus* passed into the hands of a cooperative of its main artists and contributors, led by Heine.

The years before World War I were, from an artistic point of view, the heyday of *Simplicissimus*, which rapidly made a name for itself on the basis of its irreverent attitude toward most of the sacred cows of Wilhelmine Germany: church, autocracy, militarism, chauvinism, and the high aristocracy. Its fame also had something to do with its frequent, well-publicized clashes with the authorities, its prominent featuring of semiclad female figures, and—for the times—its open treatment of sexuality. A specially printed, expensive edition was produced for collectors, who cherished the full-page artistic illustrations in *Jugendstil*, the German equivalent of *art noveau*.

The social milieu of *Simplicissimus* readership may be construed as the politically and socially more progressive-minded elements of the *Bildungsbürgertum* (academically educated bourgeoisie), in particular those with broader intellectual and artistic interests and pretensions of sophistication. In this milieu, both narrow-minded German patriotism and political antisemitism were mocked. The number of items devoted to "Jewish" subjects was minuscule, between half a dozen to a dozen and a half per annum. Jewish jokes (*Judenwitze*), utilizing stock figures such as *der kleine Isidor* (Little Isidor) or *der kleine Moritz* (Little Moritz) were popular fare, as were those of the boastful, greedy *Kommerzienrat* (the title often granted to wealthy philanthropists) with a Jewish-sounding name or of his snobbish, status-conscious wife. Other staples were nimble-witted *Ostjuden* (eastern European Jews).

The popularity of such humor indicates the extent to which these jokes were acceptable to significant parts of German society. Sigmund Freud made frequent use of such material in his book on the joke and its connection to the unconscious. The ambiguity of the material, however, makes it difficult to arrive at clear-cut conclusions concerning the existence, prevalence, or dangerousness of antisemitism. The jokes and graphic material may just constitute evidence of a high level of tolerance and acquaintance with subjects Jewish, at least among educated Germans.

During World War I, Jewish jokes and caricatures practically vanished from *Simplicissimus,* which felt itself called on to support the political truce and national unity demanded by the perilous times. During the Weimar Republic, *Simplicissimus* gradually lost almost two-thirds of its original readership, the cost, perhaps, for its turn toward more innocuous editorial and artistic policies. It continued to mock antisemitism, racist nationalism, and Nazism, but *Judenwitze* also kept on appearing, some of them in poor taste and quality.

Paradoxically, *Simplicissimus,* which had often been attacked by conservatives, antisemites, and Nazis as having been contaminated through and through by Jews (*verjudet*) and for spouting cosmopolitanism and modernism, survived into the Third Reich with most of its original staff intact. (Heine emigrated to Sweden.) Its literary standards suffered more than its artistic ones, but graphic and nongraphic antisemitic material of *Der Stürmer* type was, as in the past, generally avoided.

—*Henry Wassermann*

**See also** *Angriff, Der;* Caricature, Anti-Jewish (Modern); *Fliegende Blätter; Gartenlaube, Die; Kladderadatsch; Stürmer, Der; Verjudung*
**References**
Allen, Ann Taylor. *Satire and Society in Wilhelmine Germany: "Kladderadatsch" and "Simplicissimus," 1890–1914* (Lexington: University Press of Kentucky, 1984).
Wassermann, Henry. "Jews in *Jugendstil*—The *Simplicissimus,* 1896–1914," *Leo Baeck Institute Year Book* 31 (1986): 71–104.

## Sin against the Blood (1917)

The prolific Artur Dinter, a familiar figure on the *völkisch* (racist-nationalist) Right before and after World War I, suffered numerous setbacks in his literary career—which he blamed on Jews and the general decadence of the times—before writing a sensational best-seller. His trilogy *Sins of the Age* (1917–1922) included *Sin against the Spirit: A Period Novel Concerning the Teachings of the Spirit and Spiritual Christianity Based on Personal Experience* and *Sin against Love: A Period Novel Concerning Contemporary Social and Religious Questions, with Extensive Religio-Historical and Philosophical Elucidations.* But the book that made him famous was the first in the series, *Sin against the Blood: A Period Novel Concerning the Jewish Question and the Race Question,* a lurid outpouring of Dinter's racist antisemitism, religious mysticism, and sexual obsessions.

The novel's hero, the Aryan Hermann Kämpfer, is married to the half-Jewish Elisabeth, daughter of a wealthy, money-grubbing, and thoroughly despicable Jew, a man who maintains relations with young girls in bordellos all over Germany. Hermann and Elisabeth's marriage is sickly, the result of the Jewish blood that has endowed her with an insatiable sexual appetite and robbed her of any interest in "higher" things. Before the marriage founders, she dies of a heart attack, after hearing of her father's pending trial for statutory rape. Elisabeth and Hermann's child is a liar and a precocious usurer who gouges his school pals. Fortunately, he drowns. Hermann marries again, this time an Aryan hospital nurse. The son they have together—shockingly—bears the "mark of Cain," the "frizzy black hair and dark eyes of a genuine Jew-child" (262). The mother's blood had been poisoned because, when a girl, she had been seduced, impregnated, and abandoned by a baptized Jewish officer, in consequence of which, according to Dinter's elaborate theories, she could bear only Jewish children in the future. She kills herself and the child. The surviving Hermann now sees his life's mission as the emancipation of Aryan man from the Jewish devil race. He kills his wife's seducer, fully prepared for martyrdom. But the court sets him free to follow his true vocation, the preaching of salvation through an Aryan religion that follows Christian ideals of chastity, forsakes earthly happiness, and particularly spurns all sexual fulfillment.

DIE SÜNDE WIDER DAS BLUT

EIN ZEITROMAN
VON Dr. ARTUR DINTER
Matthes & Thost Verlag Leipzig

Poster advertising the hugely popular racist and anti-semitic novel, *Sin against the Blood*, by Artur Dinter (1917). (Eduard Fuchs, *Die Juden in der Karikatur* [Munich, 1921], plate 303, p. 39)

Aside from titillating its readers—numbering an estimated 1.5 million—*Sin against the Blood* "educated" them concerning the ineluctable calamities of miscegenation. Dinter, a celebrity, was at first highly prized by the Nazis but eventually alienated Hitler with his bizarre religious projects. During the Third Reich, he was actively persecuted. In 1945, his de-Nazification trial resulted in a fine of 1,000 reichsmarks because his novels were deemed an inspiration for the antimiscegenation Nuremberg Laws of 1935.

—*Matthias Brosch*
*Richard S. Levy, translation*

**See also** Degeneration; Dinter, Artur; Hentschel, Willibald; Nuremberg Laws; Weimar
**Reference**
Hartung, Günter. "Artur Dinter: A Successful Fas-cist Author in Pre-Fascist Germany." In *The Attractions of Fascism.* Edited by John Milfull (New York: Berg, 1990), 103–123.

## Slánský Trial

The trial of Rudolf Slánský, secretary-general of the Czechoslovakian Communist Party and the vice–prime minister, along with other high party and state functionaries, took place in Prague at the end of 1952. Most of the accused were longtime party members; some of them had connections with the Soviet special forces. Most were also of Jewish descent. All were charged with antistate activity. The indictments based on fabricated evidence charged the defendants with plotting a coup, acts of espionage, contacts with Zionist organizations, and illegal relations with representatives of the Jewish state. Of the fourteen accused, eleven, including Slánský, were sentenced to death, the others received long prison terms.

The Slánský trial was prepared by Soviet advisers to tighten Joseph Stalin's grip on Eastern Europe. It served multiple purposes: to solidify Soviet control over its satellites, prepare for possible armed conflict with the West in case the Cold War turned hot, and identify scapegoats on whom responsibility for political and economic setbacks could be fastened. The Slánský trial also sounded a warning to other Eastern European communist leaders about the risks they would run should they decide to follow Tito's independent path in Yugoslavia.

The Slánský trial also inaugurated the use of antisemitism and anti-Zionism as overt tools of Stalinist repression. Within the USSR, an ominous campaign against "cosmopolitans," a buzzword for Jewish citizens and party members, gathered strength. The Jewish Anti-Fascist Committee—an important part of the wartime propaganda offensive against Nazism—was liquidated, and several of its leading members were imprisoned and executed. The Soviet Ministry of State Security underwent a purge. The (Jewish) Doctors' Plot against the lives of top Soviet leaders was allegedly uncovered and might well have developed into a campaign specifically targeting Jews had Stalin not died before it progressed too far. Zionism and Zionist organizations were pronounced inimical to communism, preparatory to a breaking off of relations between the USSR and the state of Israel.

Many of these themes surfaced first during the Slánský trial. The controlled press made a point of the Jewish origins of the accused. Their suspected relations with Zionist organizations and agents of the state of Israel—now seen as a pawn of the capitalist West—were decried as treason. The Jewish ethnicity of the traitors, it seemed, had proved stronger than their commitment to the workers' state. The trial made a concerted appeal to the public's anti-Jewish prejudices, exploiting the still common belief that Jews were inveterate schemers and aliens who would sell out the country for personal gain. The rhetoric of the judicial authorities and of the press drew extensively from such historical antisemitic stereotypes.

The Slánský trial marked an ominous deterioration of the position of Jews in Stalinist Eastern Europe. With the prompting of Moscow, other regimes inaugurated show trials of their own in which Jews were often the prime victims. Under the guise of anti-Zionism, antisemitism once again performed the same demagogic and manipulative functions in the region as in the days before the arrival of the "liberating" Red Army.

During the "Prague Spring" of 1968, a commission within the Central Committee of the Czech Communist Party was appointed to clarify the circumstances of the political trials during the Stalinist period. Its findings would have led to a rehabilitation of the accused, but the Soviet military intervention in August 1968 prevented publication of the report.

—*Bożena Szaynok*

**See also** Anti-Zionism in the USSR; Bulgaria, Holocaust in; Croatia; Doctors' Plot; Jewish Anti-Fascist Committee; Purges, Soviet; Stalin, Joseph; Stalinization of Eastern Europe; USSR

**References**
Cotic, Meir. *The Prague Trial: The First Anti-Zionist Show Trial in the Communistic Bloc* (New York: Herzl Press, 1987).
Hodos, George H. *Show Trials: Stalinist Purges in Eastern Europe, 1948–1954* (New York: Praeger, 2001).

## Slave Trade and the Jews

In the wake of the Holocaust, a new canard against Jews has gained currency. First suggested by Jamaica-bred nationalist Marcus Garvey in the 1920s, it has been given new life since the mid 1990s by black militants such as Louis Farrakhan and Leonard Jeffries. In essence, the charge holds that Jews not only introduced chattel slavery into European society but also dominated the trade in the Old World, in Latin America, and in the Caribbean. Jewish merchants from Newport to Charleston supposedly were responsible for deracinating more than 100 million Africans between 1430 and 1880. The proof is offered in *The Secret Relationship between Blacks and Jews,* published by the Historical Research Department of the Nation of Islam in 1991.

The accusation will not withstand scrutiny of the historical record, but there is just enough evidence to give pause. Historians such as Henri Pirenne, Robert Reynolds, Robert Latouche, Pierre Dockes, and Houston Stewart Chamberlain noted the prominence of Jewish slavers along the Rhine in the High Middle Ages. The Historical Research Department of the Nation of Islam, listed as the author of *Secret Relationship,* cited anecdotal comments from Jewish historians that seemed to support their contention (and deliberately misquoted other sources when they did not). The same editors were scrupulous to a fault in recounting Jewish activity in the slave trade in Brazil, Surinam, and Curaçao, indicting the Monsanto family and Judah Benjamin of New Orleans, the Mendes family in Bordeaux, Aaron Lopez and the de Wolfes in Rhode Island, Jacob Cohen of Charleston, and the Nuñez family of Savannah.

The notion that one small group of people—especially the Jews—could dominate a critical aspect of mercantilism cannot be supported by the facts. A pariah people reviled for their religion, economic skills, and alleged blood lust, Jews enjoyed little security after the destruction of their ancestral homeland. Poets mused about periods of prosperity in Sura, Cordoba, and Cracow. But these "golden eras" usually ended with tragedy. Jews who could trace their lineage in Spain long before the arrival of the Visigoths were given less than ninety days to leave by Ferdinand following his success against the Moors in 1492. Those who tried to outwit the bigoted Spanish monarch and his bride were hounded out of Portugal. Jews were barred from living anywhere in the British Isles for nearly 400 years after 1290, and only a handful of Sephardic merchants were permitted to reside in France until 1789. No Jew is listed among the many nobles who held the *asiento* (monopoly on bringing slaves to the New World) after 1595. Jewish converts to Christianity are listed among the *conversos* (New Christians) or *marranos* (converts who continue to practice Judaism secretly) hounded by the Inquisition between 1497 and 1820. Perhaps 1,000 Jews enjoyed a temporary respite in Brazil when the Dutch controlled that region between 1630 and 1654.

The historical record has something to say about the extent of Jewish involvement in slavery. According to Arnold Wiznitzer, Jews operated 10 of 166 sugar mills in Brazil. Those Jews who trekked to Surinam at the end of the seventeenth century owned 10 percent of the slaves in the colony. According to a census taken in 1764, Jews accounted for 50 percent of the white population of the island of Curaçao—and owned 15 percent of the slaves on the island. Charts compiled by Johannes Postma suggest Jews may have commanded 9 of 500 Dutch slave ships to the New World. The Code Noir made it virtually impossible for Jews to remain in French Martinique, Santo Domingo, or Louisiana. After examining ninety-one volumes of records of the East India, Royal Africa, South Seas, and Guinea Companies of England, Bertram Korn found virtually no Jewish slavers based in Liverpool, Bristol, and London. According to W. E. B. DuBois, none of the illegal slavers operating off the coast of Cuba after slavery was declared illegal in 1808 were Jews. Jews played no role in the importation of more than 1 million African slaves to Brazil in the nineteenth century.

Much the same may be said for North America. Jews had been warned out of Boston at the start of the eighteenth century. The first U.S. census in 1790 indicated Jews owned a total of 21 slaves, or 0.5 percent of all the slaves in the six New England states. According to Jay Coughtry,

the family of Aaron Lopez and Jacob Rivera owned 25 (2 percent) of 934 slave ships that operated out of Rhode Island between 1709 and 1807. Elizabeth Donnan noted that 33 (5 percent) of 760 ships that entered New York between 1715 and 1760 were owned by Jews.

Proof of Jewish domination of the slave trade in the antebellum South should have been found in Charleston, South Carolina, the nation's major slave port. By 1820, Charleston was, coincidentally, the center of the largest Jewish population (800 persons) in the United States. British naval records and ships registries on file with the South Carolina Historical Society reveal that of 789 vessels registered with authorities in the eighteenth century, only 8, or less than 1 percent, were owned by Jews. In the decade for which records are most complete (1757–1767), 183 of 17,815 slaves, or approximately 1.5 percent, entered Charleston aboard two Jewish-owned ships.

At no time were Jews among the major planters or factors in what was to become the United States. Solomon Polock of Philadelphia was the only Jew known to have served as overseer on a plantation (near Mobile, Alabama). As Frederick Bancroft has pointed out, 4 of the top 44 slave traders in Charleston in the nineteenth century were Jews, 1 of 12 in Memphis, and 3 of 70 in Richmond. It was the same among plantation magnates. The microfilm Alphabetic Index to Bills of Sale in Columbia lists every slave transaction in South Carolina between 1773 and 1873. The Levi clan, consisting of 48 persons, bought or sold 150 slaves in that period. By way of contrast, Gen. James Hamilton, a member of Charleston's aristocracy, purchased 173 on a single day, May 2, 1837. Catherine Verdier, a Christian woman of some repute, disposed of 161 slaves on April 26, 1855. Outside South Carolina, the story was the same. None of the major slaveholders listed in the African-American Family History project in Atlanta were Jews. Karl Menn's index of the 5,000 largest slaveholders in Louisiana, Texas, North Carolina, Mississippi, and Alabama names hundreds of women, twenty Christian ministers, and even some Native Americans and African American slaveowners—but no Jews.

The overwhelming majority of Jews in the

nineteenth century were innocent and ignorant of African slavery and its horrors.

—*Saul S. Friedman*

**See also** African American–Jewish Relations; Chamberlain, Houston Stewart; Colonial America; Farrakhan, Louis; Inquisition; Nation of Islam; *Secret Relationship between Blacks and Jews, The*

**References**

Coughtry, Jay. *The Notorious Triangle: Rhode Island and the African Slave Trade, 1700–1807* (Philadelphia: Temple University Press, 1981).

Friedman, Saul S. *Jews and the American Slave Trade* (New Brunswick, NJ: Transaction Publishers, 1998).

Korn, Bertram W. *Jews and Negro Slavery in the Old South, 1789–1865* (Elkins Park, PA: Reform Congregation Keneseth Israel, 1961).

Postma, Johannes. *The Dutch in the Atlantic Slave Trade, 1600–1815* (Cambridge: Cambridge University Press, 1990).

Wiznitzer, Arnold. *Jews in Colonial Brazil* (New York: Columbia University Press, 1960).

## Slovakia, Holocaust in

Slovakia as an independent state came into being on March 14, 1939, and from the beginning had close relations to Nazi Germany, based on various agreements. Since the autumn of 1938, that is, after the federalization of Czechoslovakia, the most important political party in Slovakia was Andrej Hlinka's Slovak People's Party (HSPP). All other parties, aside from those of the German and Hungarian minorities, were either dissolved or fused with the HSPP. The party's ideology was strongly nationalist, authoritarian, and anti-Jewish.

In 1939, the Jewish minority in Slovakia numbered about 90,000 people, or 5 percent of the population. From the end of the nineteenth century onward, the Slovak national movement and later the HSPP were convinced that Jews had helped themselves in an unjust way to Slovak property. Therefore, soon after taking power, the government in Brataslava enacted antisemitic legislation. Laws defined who was to be regarded a Jew and restricted access to the universities and liberal professions, other schools, media, and state bureaucracy. Wages and pensions were cut, and Jewish property began to be "Aryanized" in 1940. Further measures were aimed at excluding Jews from society. The rapidly expanding antisemitic legislation was brought together in September 1941 under the Jewish Codex. The codex departed from traditional anti-Jewish legislation by adopting the racial basis of the Nazis' Nuremberg Laws, even surpassing them in severity in some areas. Dieter Wisliceny, Adolf Eichmann's deputy in Slovakia, had great influence on these and other matters related to the Jewish Question.

The measures taken by the Slovak government led to the pauperization of the Jewish population, a problem that, from Bratislava's point of view, could be solved by forced labor. The government started setting up camps in Sered, Nováky, and Vyhne, and officials toured German camps in Upper Silesia to see how such installations were handled there. When Berlin asked for workers in 1942, Bratislava sent Jewish laborers without hesitation. Between March and October 1942, about 58,000 Jews from Slovakia were deported to the death camps in German-occupied Poland, mostly to Auschwitz and Lublin; only about 300 of them survived. When the deportations stopped in the autumn of 1942, they were meant to be restarted in the spring of the following year. But although there was some German pressure to resume in 1943, no further transports left the country up to the suppression of the Slovak national uprising in the autumn of 1944. The explanation for this is manifold. After the catastrophe at Stalingrad, a German victory became more and more unlikely. Apart from this, by 1943, all Jews in Slovakia either were in forced labor camps or had "papers of exemption" as "economically important Jews." Moreover, public opinion in Slovakia about the deportations had changed, at least partly because the churches had voiced criticism.

How many Jewish victims were claimed by the forced labor, deportations, and the suppression of the national uprising can only be estimated. Counts after the war showed only 20,000 Jews living on the territory of Slovakia, suggesting that 70,000 perished during the Holocaust.

—*Tatjana Tönsmeyer*

**See also** Aryanization; Bulgaria, Holocaust in; Croatia, Holocaust in; Hlinka Guard; Hungary, Holocaust in; Nuremberg Laws; Tiso, Jozef

**References**

Kamenec, Ivan. *Po stopách tragédie* (Bratislava: Archa, 1991).

Lipscher, Ladislav. "The Jews of Slovakia, 1939–1945." In *The Jews of Czechoslovakia: Historical Studies and Surveys.* 3 vols. (Philadelphia and New York: Jewish Publication Society, 1984), 3:165–261.

Tönsmeyer, Tatjana. *Das Dritte Reich und die Slowakei, 1939–1945: Politischer Alltag zwischen Kooperation und Eigensinn* (Paderborn, Germany: Schöningh, 2003).

## Smith, Gerald L. K. (1898–1976)

Gerald Lyman Kenneth Smith was born on February 27, 1898, in Pardeeville, Wisconsin. He graduated from Valparaiso University in Indiana in 1917. Smith did not take up the antisemitic banner until fairly late in life, after World War II.

A Disciples of Christ minister, he revitalized several Midwestern churches, married his lifelong supporter, Elna Sorenson, and relocated to Shreveport, Louisiana, in 1929. In 1934, he became an organizer for Sen. Huey Long's Share-Our-Wealth Society. After Long's assassination in September 1935, he attached himself to Francis E. Townsend's Old Age Revolving Pension Plan, a depression nostrum, and fused Townsend's movement with the followers of radio priest Charles E. Coughlin. Together, they promoted William Lemke as the Union Party presidential candidate in 1936.

Shrill in his criticism of President Franklin D. Roosevelt, Smith organized the Committee of One Million in 1937 to save Christian America from communism. Isolationist members of Congress asked him to testify in both the House and Senate against the Lend-Lease bill in 1941. Sometime during the war, Smith's bigotry toward Jews and blacks began to define his life. He credited Henry Ford's *The International Jew* with opening his eyes to the link between Jews and communism. In 1942, he founded *The Cross and the Flag* magazine and ran for the U.S. Senate in Michigan on a platform promoting Christian nationalism. Defeated in the Republican primary, Smith blamed the Jews. He ran for the presidency three times. After establishing his America First Party, he challenged Roosevelt in 1944, when he demanded that the "Jewish Problem" in the United States be dealt with "honestly, realistically, and courageously." In 1948 and 1952, he ran under the banner of the Christian Nationalist Party. Smith called for the deportation of blacks and Zionist Jews and ghettos for Jews remaining in the United States.

Smith's antisemitism grew ever more far-reaching after 1944 when he described the Anti-Defamation League as a "Gestapo organization" and insisted "extreme" Jewish groups and the "Jew Walter Winchell" promoted more antisemitism "than all the Jew baiters combined" (in Ribuffo 1983, 172). In August 1945, at the San Francisco UN conference, he insisted the "Jew-nited Nations" was an international conspiracy. To combat these and other enemies, he established the Nationalist News Service, providing free copies of its bulletin to 200 right-wing publications. In January 1946, he testified before the House Committee on Un-American Activities that Jews in Hollywood used movies to spread communism.

By the 1950s, with headquarters now in Tulsa and Los Angeles, Smith had earned his reputation as the country's leading antisemite. Jews, he contended, were behind the French Revolution, Freemasonry, liberalism, communism, modernism, abstract art, and war. The Rothschilds, he proclaimed, were responsible for the assassination of President Abraham Lincoln. He denied the Holocaust and reprinted Martin Luther's tract *Against the Jews and Their Lies,* papal statements against Jews, and the *Protocols of the Elders of Zion.* Roosevelt, Smith asserted, had not died but had been sequestered by Jews in a mental hospital until he could be installed as president of the world. In 1952, he denounced Dwight Eisenhower as a "Swedish Jew." After the 1952 elections, Smith claimed that the Jewish financier and presidential adviser Bernard Baruch had become the "dictator of America" and that he planned to repeal U.S. immigration laws "so 20 million Jews and colored will be dumped on American shores" (in Roy 1953, 24). In 1964, Smith moved to Eureka Springs, Arkansas, and began a series of "sacred projects" that revitalized the town and attracted national attention. Most famously, in 1968, he built an amphitheater to host a Passion Play modeled on Oberammergau.

It soon became the largest pageant performed in the United States, but like its German counterpart, it generated charges of antisemitism.

Notwithstanding his extremism, Smith gained impressive financial support in the last two decades of his life. In 1967, donations to his Christian Nationalist Crusade amounted to $325,000, up from $209,000 in 1959. Smith's last public crusade was in defense of President Richard Nixon, who, he insisted, had fallen victim to the Zionists and been forced to resign because he had made overtures to Arab nations. Smith's movement evaporated after his death on April 15, 1976.

—*Peter R. D'Agostino*

*See also* American Jewish Committee and Antidefamation Efforts in the United States; Anti-Zionism; Coughlin, Charles E.; *Cross and the Flag, The; Dearborn Independent* and *The International Jew;* Ford, Henry; Freemasonry; Hollywood, Treatment of Antisemitism in; Holocaust Denial, Negationism, and Revisionism; Immigration and Naturalization Laws; Judeo-Bolshevism; Luther, Martin; Oberammergau Passion Play; *Protocols of the Elders of Zion;* Rothschilds; United States

**References**

Jeansonne, Glen. *Gerald L. K. Smith: Minister of Hate.* Reprint ed. (Baton Rouge: Louisiana State University Press, 1997).

Ribuffo, Leo P. *The Old Christian Right: The Protestant Far Right from the Great Depression to the Cold War* (Philadelphia: Temple University Press, 1983).

Roy, Ralph Lord. *Apostles of Discord: A Study of Organized Bigotry and Disruption on the Fringes of Protestantism* (Boston: Beacon Press, 1953).

## Social Darwinism

The central tenet of social Darwinism, an ideology that emerged in the late nineteenth century, was the belief that humans are subject to biological laws, including those governing the Darwinian struggle for existence. In constructing his biological theory of evolution, Charles Darwin relied on social and economic ideas, especially Thomas Malthus's population theory. Malthus argued that, just as with other organisms, the human population tends to expand faster than the food supply. Darwin explained that this oversupply of offspring leads to competition for scarce resources among organisms, especially those within the same species.

In applying Darwinism to human society, some social Darwinists emphasized the struggle between individuals within society, whereas others stressed the collective competition between nations and races. Many believed that both forms of the human struggle for existence occurred simultaneously. Social Darwinism did not necessarily entail a specific political position. Some social Darwinists justified the capitalist system; others claimed that capitalism unfairly influenced the outcome of the struggle for existence by giving an advantage to individuals with money, whatever their individual biological prowess. Also, some social Darwinists argued that the economic struggle for existence among individuals should be subdued to make society stronger in the national and racial struggle for existence.

Darwinism radicalized late nineteenth-century scientific racism by stressing the struggle for existence between races. Darwin wrote in *The Descent of Man,* "At some future period, not very distant as measured by centuries, the civilised races of man will almost certainly exterminate and replace throughout the world the savage races." Ernst Haeckel, the leading Darwinian biologist in Germany, likewise taught that the Darwinian struggle for existence would eventually eliminate "inferior" races. Ludwig Gumplowicz, a Jewish sociologist at the University of Graz in Austria, relied on Darwin's theory to develop his idea of "racial struggle," the title of his 1884 book. Though Gumplowicz defined races by social rather than biological criteria, most later Darwinian race theorists embraced biological racism.

Not all social Darwinists were antisemitic, nor did they all apply the racial struggle for existence to Jews. However, some did, justifying racial persecution as a natural and inevitable part of the universal struggle for existence. A leading social Darwinist thinker in Austria, Gustav Ratzenhofer, whom his mentor Gumplowicz called a genius, came under the spell of Aryan racism and antisemitism after 1900, largely through the influence of Houston Stewart Chamberlain. The French social Darwinist Georges Vacher de Lapouge, who wanted to replace the French Revolutionary slogan of "Liberty, Equality, Fraternity" with "Determinism, Inequality, Selection," believed that the "Aryan" race would ultimately annihilate all the inferior races, and he counted the Jews among those who would be destroyed.

By the early twentieth century, social Darwinist racism became extremely prominent in antisemitic circles, especially in Germany and Austria. Though social Darwinism, scientific racism, and eugenics were not necessarily antisemitic, many antisemites adopted these increasingly influential ideologies. The antisemitic leader of the Pan-German movement in Austria, Georg von Schönerer, embraced social Darwinist racism in the 1880s. In Vienna and Munich, Adolf Hitler encountered social Darwinist racism through the press and through his Pan-German contacts. Hitler's speeches and writings are littered with social Darwinist concepts, which served as a major justification for the Nazi persecution of the Jews. Social Darwinism declined in influence after World War II, although sociobiology and evolutionary psychology in the late twentieth century showed some similarity with earlier social Darwinist ideology.

—Richard Weikart

See also Chamberlain, Houston Stewart; Eugenics; Evolutionary Psychology; Hitler, Adolf; Racism, Scientific; Schönerer, Georg von

References
Hawkins, Mike. *Social Darwinism in European and American Thought, 1860–1945: Nature as Model and Nature as Threat* (Cambridge: Cambridge University Press, 1997).
Weikart, Richard. "The Origins of Social Darwinism in Germany, 1859–1895," *Journal of the History of Ideas* 54 (1993): 469–488.
———. *From Darwin to Hitler: Evolutionary Ethics, Eugenics and Racism in Germany* (New York: Palgrave Macmillan, 2004).

# Social Democratic Party (Germany, 1875–1933)

The Social Democratic Party of Germany (Sozialdemokratische Partei Deutschlands [SPD]), established in 1875 as the Socialist Labor Party of Germany and renamed in 1890, combined Marxist theory with a program of democratic social and economic reform. The largest political party in Germany from 1912 to 1932, it worked to change the autocratic political structures of the German Empire until 1918 and defended the democratic Weimar Republic thereafter. It was ambivalent about Jews, most of whom were opposed to socialism, but that did not prevent the SPD from combating antisemitism as dangerous to the interests of workers.

The SPD's earliest confrontation with political antisemitism in the years between 1878 and 1885 involved Court Chaplain Adolf Stoecker's Christian Social Party, which appealed to the workers' grievances by holding the Jews responsible for the abuses of capitalism. The SPD successfully kept its members in line with a vigorous campaign that accused Stoecker of plotting to distract the workers from their true enemy, the capitalist system as a whole. This oversimplified view of antisemitism as a diversionary weapon of the ruling class continued to influence the SPD, but it was temporarily overshadowed a few years later by Marxist theories that had become more influential in the party as a result of persecution under Otto von Bismarck's Anti-Socialist Laws during the 1880s. The Marxists considered antisemitism an immature form of anticapitalist revolt that would eventually awaken some individuals to the true nature of their plight and lead them to socialism. As a product of capitalism, the argument continued, Judeophobia would disappear with the triumph of socialism. When a new wave of political antisemitism in the 1890s stirred up the peasants and lower middle classes, the SPD brushed it aside. Hence, before World War I, German socialists reacted to antisemitism with a mixture of opposition and apathy.

On one hand, the SPD resented Jewish support for capitalism, but on the other, it sympathized with Jews as victims of persecution by conservative institutions. Karl Marx had attacked his fellow Jews as incorrigible capitalists, and his followers in Germany, noting that most Jews had supported the Anti-Socialist Laws, saw no reason to view them as friends of the workers. Such resentments rarely led to outright antisemitism, but they generated a few unflattering portrayals of greedy and selfish Jews in popular working-class literature. At the same time, the SPD took an uncompromising stand against all forms of discrimination against the Jews. It also welcomed Jews as members, appointed them to party posts, and nominated them as candidates for public offices.

The intensification of antisemitism in Germany after World War I prompted the SPD to return to the more confrontational tactics that had characterized its crusade against Stoecker. With Germany's new Weimar Republic, founded with strong support from the Social Democrats, being castigated as the "Jew Republic" for its liberal democracy and its recognition of Jewish rights, the SPD revived the "plot theory" that viewed antisemitism as a diversionary tool of the old ruling class to combat socialism and undermine political liberty. In so doing, it bound working-class interests to the fight against Judeophobia. Party propaganda heaped abuse on charges that Jews were behind Germany's woes and on racist notions in general. SPD public officials steadfastly upheld Jewish rights. When the Nazis suppressed the party in 1933, Germany lost its strongest political bulwark against racial antisemitism.

Although the Social Democrats had left no doubt about their opposition to antisemitism, they had not given it a central role in their campaign against Nazism. They remained ambivalent about Jews, and they did not want to lend credence to charges that they were philosemites. Moreover, evidence that the Nazis were inconsistent and opportunistic in their antisemitism further encouraged the Social Democrats to underestimate the issue. Having interpreted Nazi Judeophobia as an instrument to manipulate the voters and bring Hitler to power, rather than as an end in itself, the SPD contributed to the belief, widespread in Germany at the time, that Jews faced little prospect of serious harm at the hands of a Nazi government.

—*Donald L. Niewyk*

**See also** Berlin Movement; Marx, Karl; Mehring, Franz; National Socialist German Workers' Party; Socialists on Antisemitism; Stoecker, Adolf; Weimar
**References**
Massing, Paul W. *Rehearsal for Destruction: A Study of Political Anti-Semitism in Imperial Germany* (New York: Harper and Brothers, 1949).
Mosse, George L. "German Socialists and the Jewish Question in the Weimar Republic," *Leo Baeck Institute Year Book* 16 (1971): 123–150.
Niewyk, Donald L. *Socialist, Anti-Semite, and Jew* (Baton Rouge: Louisiana State University Press, 1971).

## Socialists on Antisemitism

The history of the socialist movement is full of internal splits and vigorous debates. Socialists have not adopted a unified approach toward what has come to be known as the Jewish Question anymore than they have done on many other issues. In the countries with significant socialist parties surveyed in this essay—France, Germany, and Russia—socialists manifested a variety of attitudes toward Jews and Jewry. Individuals associated with socialist movements used antisemitic rhetoric at various times and for various reasons. Yet the most prominent representatives of the chief social democratic parties at the end of the nineteenth century and throughout the first decades of the twentieth century, generally tended to distance themselves from explicitly antisemitic stances.

Neither Henri de Saint-Simon nor Louis Auguste Blanqui, two early French socialists, displayed any particular interest in contemporary Jewry. Their compatriot Charles Fourier, however, found Jews distasteful and associated them with thievery. He suggested that the political emancipation of Jewry in France had been overly rapid, that Jews should be prohibited from living in border areas (in which smuggling took place), that they should be excluded from trade, and that they should be compelled to engage in "productive labor."

The leadership of the Marxist movement in France, which first emerged in that country in the 1880s, never endorsed such positions. In an article entitled "The Jewish Question" (1892), Jules Guesde, head of the Parti Ouvrier Français (French Workers' Party), underscored that capitalists, not Jews, were the enemy of the working class and that those who focused attention on Jewish financiers were misleading workers. Paul Lafargue, the other leading figure among the Guesdists, was also wholly unsympathetic to political antisemitism. To be sure, Guesde was no more philosemitic than he was antisemitic. He insisted, for example, that the Dreyfus Affair was ultimately a disagreement among wings of the bourgeoisie and thus not a dispute in which socialists should participate. Jean Jaurès, who was not committed to the more moderate doctrines of the French Socialist Party (which he led up to World War I), took a more active role than the orthodox Marxists in combating the anti-Dreyfusards. He condemned antisemitism as a "capitalist fake" intended to deceive French workers as to the true state of their condition.

Jaurès's friend Léon Blum, who was a Jew, became a leader of the French socialists between the two world wars and headed the 1936–1937 Popular Front government. He was sympathetic to the Zionist movement, deliberately proclaimed his Jewish identity in public contexts in the face of attacks by French antisemites, and delivered a symbolically significant address to the International League against Antisemitism (Ligue Internationale contre l'Antisémitisme) in 1938.

A comparable range of positions existed among German socialists. Ferdinand Lassalle, who founded the General Union of German Workingmen a year before his death, was of Jewish origin but distanced himself from Judaism from an early age. He published no works during his mature years on the Jewish Question or on antisemitism. He did, however, reveal, in a private letter to a young lady he was trying to impress, that he detested Jews and believed them to have taken on slavish characteristics. Antisemitic phrases appeared in the official newspaper of the General Union in the early 1870s, especially in attacks on German socialists who were not Lassalleans, and they were also used in speeches by Lassallean agitators such as Wilhelm Hasselmann. But antisemitism never played an important role in the program of the Lassalleans. After 1873, in fact, traces of antisemitism in the party's paper generally diminished.

Antisemitism was absolutely never a central plank in the program of the Social Democratic Party of Germany (SPD)—the largest and most important socialist party in Germany—which was formed in 1875 as a result of a merger between the Lassalleans and a Marxist party. The (partially) Marxist roots of the SPD should not be taken to mean that its position on anti-

semitism was that of Karl Marx. In truth, the party's stance tended to have more in common with the late pronouncements of Friedrich Engels than with any statements ever made by Marx himself.

Although Marx, in the 1840s, advocated political emancipation for the Jewish community, he never publicly and explicitly attacked political antisemitism per se. Engels, however, did. In his *Anti-Dühring*, which first appeared between 1877 and 1878, Engels specifically linked antisemitism with medievalism. In a letter published in the socialist press in 1890, he stressed that antisemitism was nothing other than a reactionary movement of decaying, retrograde social groups against modern society. It served only reactionary purposes underneath its socialistic disguise, Engels added, and ought to be shunned.

August Bebel, a key leader of the SPD from its formation until his death on the eve of World War I, first became aware of Engels's letter of 1890 in the summer of 1892 and promptly drafted a resolution on antisemitism that was similar to the piece by Engels in both spirit and tone. Antisemitism, it said, was the result of dissonance within bourgeois society and had to be struggled against by Social Democrats because it was contrary to the natural development of society. Bebel's resolution was passed by a large majority at the SPD's party congress in 1892 and again the following year, that time by acclamation.

In the first decades of the twentieth century, the leading ideologists along the entire spectrum of German Social Democracy—Rosa Luxemburg, Eduard Bernstein, and Karl Kautsky—differed sharply from one another in their writings on various aspects of the Jewish Question (for example, in their approaches to Zionism), but none of them ever endorsed political antisemitism in any way, shape, or form. Although not without some deviation—there were a few anti-Jewish slurs by significant German Social Democrats— the SPD in general stood as a bulwark of "antiantisemitism" from the late Wilhelmine era into the Weimar Republic.

The SPD stood by its anti-antisemitism even during the years of the Nazi rise to power, when it might have been politically advantageous to back off. Leading Jewish members of the SPD were, with one exception, never pressured to accept less visible positions within the party than they had had before the emergence of the Nazi threat. The SPD's record of consistent opposition to Nazism compares favorably to that of all other important political parties in Germany, including the occasionally opportunistic Communist Party.

Antisemitic sentiment was widespread in the Russian populist movement at certain key points, as, for example, during the pogroms of the 1880s. In August 1881, the Executive Committee of the Narodnaia Volia (People's Will Party) issued a proclamation that declared the Jews were the greatest exploiters of the people of the Ukraine and that encouraged the peasantry to "rebel" against "the Jews." The Marxist-oriented Russian Social Democratic Workers' Party (RSDRP), which came into being in 1898, opposed political antisemitism. Vladimir Lenin was sharply critical of the national program of the (anti-Zionist) Jewish Workers' Bund, as well as that of the Zionist movement. His criticisms of the Bund and of Zionism, however, were not motivated by either personal or political antisemitism but rather by the conviction that Jewry did not constitute an authentic nationality. Lenin condemned the 1906 pogrom in Bialystok as a maneuver instigated by the government, supported draft legislation against antisemitic discrimination in 1914, and gave a speech in March 1919 in which he declared that only the most ignorant and downtrodden people could believe the lies spread about the Jews.

The various factions of the RSDRP did not disagree on this point. Neither Georgii Valentinovich Plekhanov, often thought of as the father of Russian Marxism, nor those who eventually formed the leadership of the Menshevik faction of the party can fairly be accused of antisemitism. Plekhanov's approach to the Dreyfus Affair was similar to that of Guesde. To be sure, Russian Marxists did not always consider the struggle against antisemitism to be their primary task. When, in April 1903, Bundists accused some prominent Russian socialists of fighting harder against Zionism than against antisemitism, L. Martov, a leading Russian Social Democrat who was himself of Jewish origin, replied that this was not only true but was as it ought to be. He insisted that Zionism had to be fought even more vigorously than antisemitism because Zionists wooed members of the Jewish proletariat (who might otherwise become class-conscious members of the RSDRP), whereas the antisemites lured only backward and undesirable elements. Martov, however, only wished to make a point about political priorities and most definitively did not mean to endorse antisemitism. Pavel Axelrod, who was Jewish, and who, like Martov, eventually became a prominent anti-Leninist Russian Marxist, was troubled by the Beilis blood libel trial of 1913. He publicly condemned antisemitism in forthright language in 1917 (and also expressed sympathy for Zionist goals).

The tradition of consistent opposition to antisemitism manifest in the RSDRP, however, was not carried over into the Communist Party of the Soviet Union, which engaged in anti-Jewish actions, particularly during the Stalin era.

In conclusion, a few broad generalizations can be made concerning the complex question of the relationship of socialists to antisemitism. Specific non-Marxist socialists, including French utopian socialists, Lassalleans, and Russian populists, were open to the exploitation of antisemitic rhetoric. The foremost Marxist-influenced social democratic parties, as distinguished from communist parties, although by no means wholly immune to the use of anti-Jewish slogans, were usually hostile to the political and social movements that employed antisemitism. Even though individual Marxists—including Marx and Engels—indulged in anti-Jewish slurs, the most important social democratic parties opposed political antisemitism, which they perceived as reactionary.

—*Jack Jacobs*

*See also* Alsace; Beilis Case; Dreyfus Affair; Dühring, Eugen; Emancipation; Fourier, Charles; France; LICA—International League against Antisemitism; Marx, Karl; Mehring, Franz; Pogroms; Russia, Imperial; Social Democratic Party; Stalin, Joseph; USSR; Zionism

**References**

Jacobs, Jack. *On Socialists and "the Jewish Question" after Marx* (New York: New York University Press, 1992).
Traverso, Enzo. *The Marxists and the Jewish Question: The History of a Debate, 1843–1943* (At-

lantic Highlands, NJ: Humanities Press, 1994).

Wistrich, Robert S. *Revolutionary Jews from Marx to Trotsky* (London: Harrap, 1976).

## Solzhenitsyn, Aleksandr (1918– )

A survivor of Stalin's prison camps, Aleksandr Isaevich Solzhenitsyn gained world renown in the 1960s and 1970s for his exposés of the Soviet gulag in *One Day in the Life of Ivan Denisovich, The First Circle,* and *The Gulag Archipelago.* During that period, Solzhenitsyn's courage in confronting the Soviet authorities made him a leader among the dissidents; however, unlike the physicist Andrei Sakharov, he saw Russia's future not in Western-style democracy but in a return to its native religious (Orthodox Christian) and cultural traditions. His second major subject as a writer became Russia's road to the Bolshevik takeover. In several novels that comprise the cycle *The Red Wheel* and beginning with *August 1914,* he identified the fatal errors made by both the Russian state and Russian society during World War I and the revolutionary year 1917. Awarded the Nobel Prize for Literature in 1970, he was expelled from the Soviet Union in 1974 and returned triumphantly to a new Russia in 1994.

The issue of Solzhenitsyn's antisemitism was debated in the 1970s, with Soviet Jewish émigrés and Western critics taking positions on both sides of the issue. The polemic was fueled, in part, by the documentary novel *Lenin in Zurich* (a selection of chapters from *The Red Wheel*), in which the author described the Marxist revolutionary Alexander Lazarevich Helphand (a pseudonym for Parvus) as a malevolent, physically repulsive figure dedicated to Russia's downfall. No less controversial was a section in *August 1914* dealing with the 1911 assassination of Prime Minister Peter Stolypin by the double agent Dmitri Bogrov, described by means of several traditional anti-Jewish stereotypes. Although the assassin came from an assimilated family with connections to both Lutheranism and Russian Orthodoxy, Solzhenitsyn attributed his motivation for the killing to a deep-seated desire to remove a political figure whose actions would prevent the "unbelievably talented" Jewish people from achieving their full potential—a depiction for which there is no reliable evidence.

Following the appearance in 2001 and 2002 of the two-part *Dvesti let vmeste (1795–1995)* (Two Hundred Years Together, 1795–1995), the controversy concerning Solzhenitsyn's position on the Jewish Question flared up again. This major work, covering the history of relations between the Russian and Jewish peoples, is prefaced by the author's call for mutual understanding and admission of wrongs done each to the other and an expression of hope that his study would serve the cause of reconciliation. This has not occurred, principally because Solzhenitsyn, however good his intentions, forced the story of Russia's Jews into an overarching historiosophic conception of the causes of modern Russia's tragedy, in the process frequently distorting the historical record. In Part One, he claimed that the condition of the Jewish community under tsarism was often far better than many historians have admitted, that resistance by the communal authorities frustrated many attempts by the government to improve the lot of the Jews, and that, whatever the faults of official policy, liberal and radical Jews committed an error of historical magnitude when they actively contributed to the collapse of the Russian state. In Part Two, Solzhenitsyn showed how Russia's Jews participated to a disproportionate degree in both the February and October 1917 revolutions; he also condemned their active support of and profiting from the Soviet regime during the 1920s and 1930s. He then traced the fate of Soviet Jews through World War II and the Holocaust, Stalin's antisemitic campaign, his successors' "struggle against Zionism," and the resultant struggle for freedom to emigrate.

Notwithstanding some generally favorable reviews of Part One, the celebrated author's work has been extensively criticized in both Russia and the West. Most scholarly responses thus far have dealt with this part, though some of the points raised are also applicable to Part Two. Reviewers have questioned Solzhenitsyn's reliance on a few largely outdated sources, his selective and often improper handling of quotations, and the absence of Russian sources that do not fit his historical interpretation, as well as many important Western studies on the subject. They have pointed out his readiness to absolve the tsarist government for anti-Jewish excesses and to place the responsibility on others—including the Jews themselves. Even more significantly, they have condemned his apparent embrace of anti-Jewish stereotypes: Jews as unproductive, exploitative, conspiratorial, and destructive. As a result of these and other major problems, stated historian Yochanan Petrovsky-Shtern, Solzhenitsyn's book will become a "masterpiece of Russian antisemitica."

—*Henryk Baran*

*See also* Anti-Zionism in the USSR; Judeo-Bolshevism; Pale of Settlement; Russia, Imperial; Russia, Post-Soviet; Russian Orthodox Church; USSR

**References**
Klier, John. "Review of *Dvesti let vmeste1795–1995*, Vol. 1." *History Today* 52 (November 2002), 60.
Petrovsky-Shtern, Yochanan. "Sud'ba srednei linii" (The Fate of the Middle Line), *Neprikosnovennyi zapas* (Moscow), 2001, no. 4 (18).
Pipes, Richard. "Solzhenitsyn and the Jews, Revisited: Alone Together," *New Republic* 25 (November 2002), 26.
Thomas, D. M. *Alexander Solzhenitsyn: A Century in His Life* (New York: St. Martin's Press, 1998), 489–496.

## Sombart, Werner (1863–1941)

Born in Ermsleben near Merseburg, Germany, Werner Sombart was educated at Göttingen and earned his Ph.D. in Berlin under Gustav Schmoller and Adolph Wagner (a leading Christian Social). He began his academic career as a Marxist, which greatly hindered his professional advancement although he ultimately replaced Wagner at the University of Berlin in 1917. Sombart was considered one of the foremost economists in his day (second only to Schmoller), as well as an important figure in sociology (second only to Max Weber). His ideas changed markedly during his long career, as did his political loyalties, for he began as a Marxist and ended up a National Socialist.

Sombart was an archetypal "public" intellectual. He was the author of many influential books and articles, the most important being his multivolume *Der moderne Kapitalismus* (Modern Capitalism) in 1902, which he revised significantly in subsequent editions throughout his life. He also edited the preeminent journal in sociology, the *Archiv für Sozialwissenschaft und Sozialpolitik* (Archive for Social Science and Social Policy); was prominent in the professional associations for sociology and economics; and gave frequent public lectures.

His contribution to German antisemitism was twofold, and it is difficult to ascertain which aspect was the more pernicious. Sombart was deeply influenced by Weber's work on the spirit of capitalism. Unlike Weber, however, he saw Jews rather than Calvinists as the creators of modern capitalism. One of the major chapters in his *Modern Capitalism* was entitled "The Significance of the Jewish Religion in Economic Life." His *The Jew and Modern Capitalism* (1911) contended that the "spirit of capitalism" entered into northern Europe with the Jews fleeing the Inquisition. They carried with them, he contended, a new morality, a new conception of legal relations, and a "genius for commercial enterprise." The scholarship of these works has been proven to be based on insufficient knowledge, caricature, and outright prejudice, although it, surprisingly, still finds the occasional defender. Recently, Sombart has come back into vogue as some economic historians have sought cultural causes for the Industrial Revolution and the growth of European capitalism.

Sombart was also influential when he argued for the validity of "race" as a "working hypothesis" in the social sciences. The practical impact of his writings, despite their nuance and their change over time, was to validate race as an objective criterion and to define the so-called Jewish race as particularly bonded with industrial capitalism. His embrace of antisemitism was dangerous because of his high public profile, respected professorial status, and the fact that he avoided association with the disreputable antisemites of the prewar era. In the Weimar years, his highly visible change of politics from Social Democracy to National Socialism struck many contemporaries as sheer fickleness, but it also served to validate the career paths of other antisemites and opportunists, who could claim him as a model of fearless intellectual honesty while climbing onto the Nazi bandwagon.

—*George Vascik*

*See also* Capital: Useful vs. Harmful; Christian Social Party (Germany); Fritsch, Theodor; Social Democratic Party; Socialists on Antisemitism; Weimar

**References**

Lenger, Friedrich. *Werner Sombart, 1863–1941: Eine Biographie* (Munich, Germany: C. H. Beck, 1994).

Stehr, Nico, and Reiner Grundmann, eds. *Economic Life in the Modern Era* (New Brunswick, NJ: Transaction Books, 2001).

## Sorcery/Magic

Throughout history, sorcery was (and remains for some) a real and terrifying phenomenon. Premodern people inherited a tradition regarding belief in Jewish sorcery from the ancient world. An ignorance of the Jewish religion and Jewish customs and a meager acquaintance with the Hebrew language, on the one hand, and the powerless minority status of the Jews, on the other, worked together to make Jews mysterious and suspicious in the eyes of non-Jews. Jewish practices such as washing hands on return from the cemetery or searching out leaven on the eve of Passover only confirmed for medieval Christians that Jews were magicians and allied with Satan, the ultimate source of all magic. Jewish ritual objects sometimes became objects of suspicion, as happened at the end of the fourteenth century when the bishop of Salzburg is reputed to have asked a Jew for a mezuzah to attach to the gate of his castle because of its magical qualities. (It was not provided.)

Jews were accused of a variety of magical practices and punished as sorcerers. In 1066, the Jews of Treves were accused of fashioning a waxen image of Bishop Eberhard, having it baptized by a priest, and burning it on their Sabbath, resulting in the death of the bishop. Interestingly, belief in the magic of the Jews circulated within both Jewish and non-Jewish circles. Throughout the Middle Ages, Jewish physicians were thought to have special healing—and harming—powers, making them sought out by princes and kings even at times when the Jews of their territories were being marginalized or expelled; such visions of Jewish power, however, were used as excuses for expulsions when, for example, Jews were suspected of

*The Witches* woodcut by Hans Baldung Grien, 1510. Witches, one seemingly on a cloud and the other on the back of a goat (which is surely a devil in disguise). (Charles Walker/Topfoto/The Image Works)

poisoning their royal patients. Charles the Bald, according to popular belief, was supposedly poisoned by his Jewish physicians in 877. In 1267, concern was so high that church councils at Breslau and Vienna forbade Christians to purchase foodstuffs from Jews because of fear that the provisions had been poisoned.

Such concerns over Jewish magical practices were well reflected in a variety of both learned and popular visual and written sources. These works provided a deadly accompaniment to the increasingly frequent accusations of well poisoning (especially in the fourteenth century), host desecration, and ritual murder. The martyred Simon of Trent, it was said, had been murdered by the Jews in 1475 so they could knead his blood into their Passover matzah. Matthew of Paris reported the "crucifixion" of Hugh of Lincoln by the Jews in 1255, noting that they intended to use the boy's bowels for purposes of divination.

—Dean Phillip Bell

**See also** Doctors' Plot; *Entdecktes Judenthum;* Host Desecration; Hugh of Lincoln; Iconography, Christian; Ritual Murder (Medieval); Simon of Trent; Well Poisoning

**References**

Idel, Moshe. *Golem: Jewish Magic and Mystical Tradition on the Artificial Anthropoid* (Albany: State University of New York Press, 1990).

Patai, Raphael. *The Jewish Alchemists: A History and Source Book* (Princeton, NJ: Princeton University Press, 1994).

Trachtenberg, Joshua. *The Devil and the Jews: The Medieval Conception of the Jew and Its Relation to Modern Anti-Semitism* (Philadelphia: Jewish Publication Society, 2002; orig. 1943).

Zimmels, H. J. *Magicians, Theologians and Doctors: Studies in Folk Medicine and Folklore as Reflected in the Rabbinic Responsa* (New York: Jason Aronson, 1997; orig. 1952).

## South Africa

Prior to the 1930s in South Africa, antisemitism was limited to negative cultural and literary stereotyping: Jewish knavery, financial machinations (exemplified in Hoggenheimer, a vulgar cartoon caricature), military "shirking," "Bolshevik" subversion, and "unassimilability." Calls to curtail the influx of eastern European Jews, made from the turn of the century, culminated in the Quota Act of 1930.

The 1930s and early 1940s witnessed a popular surge of antisemitism, ensuring a prominent position for the Jewish Question on the public agenda. Antisemitism formed an important and influential component of the Afrikaner nationalist worldview. It was particularly evident in the rhetoric and actions of the Greyshirts, an extreme Right movement inspired by Nazi forms and racist, or *völkisch,* discourse. In 1934, the Greyshirts disclosed "proof" of a world Jewish conspiracy. Evidence was allegedly based on a document stolen from a synagogue in Port Elizabeth, purportedly signed by the Reverend Abraham Levy, spiritual leader of the congregation. The document was modeled on the notorious forgery known as the *Protocols of the Elders of Zion.* Since the Reverend Levy was implicated by name, he was successfully able to sue for libel.

The groundswell of anti-Jewish feeling, especially demands for actions and threats against the existing Jewish community, prompted the ruling United Party to introduce stiffer educational and financial requirements for purposes of immigration. These were to take effect on November 1, 1936, and they resulted in an interim increase in German Jewish immigration. By the end of October, well-attended meetings, led by a group of Stellenbosch University professors, protested the arrival of the *Stuttgart,* carrying 537 German Jewish immigrants.

In an obvious response to flourishing antisemitism, coupled with a private bill introduced by the leader of the opposition, D. F. Malan, to restrict Jewish immigration and stiffen naturalization laws, the United Party introduced the Aliens Act of 1937, which prevented large-scale German Jewish immigration. Without specifying Jews, immigrants were to be permitted entry by a selection board on the grounds of good character and the likelihood of assimilation into the European population. Whereas 3,615 German Jewish refugees had entered South Africa between 1933 and 1936, fewer than 1,900 entered between 1937 and 1940.

Antisemitism was given further impetus following the South African parliament's very narrow decision to support the Commonwealth war effort to resist Germany in 1939. A powerful antiwar movement was orchestrated by the *Ossewabrandwag* (Ox-Wagon Sentinel) and the New Order, in which the appeal of fascism and, with it, the rhetoric of antisemitism was strong. A range of major National Party (NP) publications issued in the early 1940s demonstrated the formative influence of Benito Mussolini and Adolf Hitler on the exclusive nature of an insurgent Afrikaner nationalism in which Jews had no place. However, the struggle against Hitler gradually eroded the warm reception accorded to Nazi and fascist ideas. By 1942, mainstream National Party leaders were unequivocally rejecting National Socialism as an alien import into South Africa. Nonetheless, as late as 1944, an investigation into antisemitism demonstrated a wide-ranging hostility toward Jews.

Antisemitism declined rapidly after 1945, although Prime Minister Jan Smuts opposed large-scale Jewish immigration. The Greyshirts and New Order disbanded, and in 1951, the ban on Jewish membership in the Transvaal NP (the NP was structured along federal lines) was lifted. Nonetheless, the NP, in power after 1948, resented disproportionate Jewish involvement in liberal and communist activities and Israel's support for the African bloc at the United Nations in the early 1960s. Issues of Jewish dual loyalty were short-lived, as South Africa and Israel developed close ties in the 1970s. The relationship promoted favorable attitudes toward the Jews on the part of the white population, although anti-semitic outbursts, including expressions of Holocaust denial, were not unusual among elements of the white ultra-Right. The majority black population felt betrayed by Israel's close relations with South Africa and sympathized with the Palestinian cause. Although black leaders clearly distinguished between anti-Zionism and anti-semitism, there were indications of some anti-Jewish attitudes among black elites.

Since the "normalization" of South African politics following the country's first democratic elections in 1994, antisemitic incidents have been relatively isolated and largely confined to the Far Right and Islamist groups. Muslim anti-Zionist marches often exhibit anti-Jewish rhetoric and motifs. Holocaust denial has also crept into Muslim hostility. One should not, however, view the Muslim community, which comprises about 2 percent of the total population, as a monolith. Various intellectual discourses operate and compete. Some are innovative and progressive, with an emphasis on Islamic humanism, universalism, and interfaith cooperation; others are conservative, at odds with religious pluralism and ecumenism. For example, Khomeinism and some of the more radical schools of Islamic thought heavily influence Qibla and the Islamic Unity Convention. Common to both strands, however, is a hostile critique of Zionism. In some cases, this hostility is separated from antisemitism; in others, Zionism and Judaism are conflated into a combination that incorporates notions of international Jewish finance, manipulation, and imperialism.

—*Milton Shain*

*See also* Anti-Zionism; Caricature, Anti-Jewish (Modern); Holocaust Denial, Negationism, and Revisionism; Immigration and Naturalization Laws; Islam and the Jews; Islamic Fundamentalism; Jewish Question; Judeo-Bolshevism; Khomeini, Ayatollah; *Ostjuden; Protocols of the Elders of Zion; Völkisch* Movement and Ideology

**References**
Furlong, Patrick J. *Between Crown and Swastika: The Impact of the Radical Right on the Afrikaner Nationalist Movement in the Fascist Era* (Middletown, CT, and Johannesburg: Wesleyan University Press and Witwatersrand University Press, 1991).

Shain, Milton. *The Roots of Antisemtism in South Africa* (Charlottesville, VA, London, and Johannesburg: University of Virginia Press and Witwatersrand University Press, 1994).

———. "'If it was so good why was it so bad?': The Memories and Realities of Antisemitism in South Africa, Past and Present." In *Memories, Realities and Dreams: Aspects of the South African Jewish Experience.* Edited by Milton Shain and Richard Mendelsohn (Johannesburg: Jonathan Ball, 2002).

## Spain, Riots of 1391

In the year 1391, the Iberian Peninsula witnessed anti-Jewish riots surpassing any of those from the past. They took their starting point from the sermons of Archdeacon Fernando Martínez of Seville, who had demanded for years that the synagogues be destroyed and the Jews be placed in ghettos. The chance to realize his plans came when King John I of Castile and Leon died in October 1390, leaving a minor on the throne to succeed him. Martínez, now the acting archbishop of Seville, took advantage of this political vacuum to propagate his ideas. Freed from all restraint, he at once launched a violent "crusade" against the Jews, ordering the destruction of their synagogues.

From March 1391, anti-Jewish riots went on for weeks in the Andalusian capital. After a short period of calm, they once again erupted on June 6, 1391, with an attack on the Jewish quarter, followed by similar actions in neighboring locales. In response to the assaults, it is clear, there were many more conversions to Christianity than Jewish martyrdoms.

The pogroms crossed political borders,

spreading far beyond the Seville region. In some cases, the emissaries of Martínez provoked the attacks, in others, local forces took the initiative. Everywhere, the overwhelming majority of the populace stood behind them. The Jewish community of Ciudad Real perished; in Madrid, apparently all Jews chose conversion over death. In Toledo, with its centuries-old Jewish tradition, one of the two Jewish quarters vanished. In Burgos in northern Spain, the most important representatives of the community converted to Christianity. There is no record of any Jewish resistance.

The riots spread to other kingdoms. In the beginning of July 1391, the Jewish quarter of Valencia was destroyed despite increased vigilance, which the city authorities had ordered after receiving the news of the violence in Andalusia. In the wake of these events, nearly all Jewish communities of Valencia converted. In Mallorca, too, the authorities took protective measures but also failed to prevent riots. On August 2, the Jewish quarter was attacked, and 300 people were killed. Many survivors converted. The last wave of pogroms took place in Barcelona and the rest of Catalonia. There, the riots started in early August and took a more social character, without losing their religious impetus and rationale. In the Catalonian capital, 400 Jews were killed, and many converted. Barcelona's Jewish community essentially ceased to exist. Subsequently, Girona, Tortosa, Lleida, and other Catalonian towns were visited by the anti-Jewish fury. Only Aragon's Jewish quarters remained untouched.

Thus, within less than a year, the most important Jewish communities in Spain were decimated, sometimes even totally destroyed. What is striking, apart from the relentless proceeding of the Christian aggressors (supplied mostly from the lower clergy and ordinary people), is the high number of converts compared with anti-Jewish riots in other parts of medieval Europe. It was not long, however, before most Christian authorities began to see the remaining observant Jews as an even greater danger than before. They might, it was feared, seduce the New Christians to return to Judaism. "Backsliding," from a Christian point of view, was absolutely intolerable, no matter that baptism had been accepted under threat of death, not as a result of free will.

—*Bernd Rother*

**See also** Ferrer, Vincente; Ghetto; Inquisition; Torquemada, Tomás de

**References**

Fernández, Emilio Mitre. *Los judíos de Castilla en tiempo de Enrique III: El pogrom de 1391* (Valladolid, Spain: Universidad de Valladolid, 1994).

Wolff, Philippe. "The 1391 Pogrom in Spain: Social Crisis or Not?" *Past and Present* 50 (1971): 4–18.

## Spain under Franco (1938–1975)

Spain has had a troubled historical relationship with its Jewish population, resulting, in part, from the Spanish Inquisition, which sought to purge all non-Catholics from the country and its colonies. It was not until 1834 that the Inquisition was finally abolished, yet antisemitic sentiments still prevailed throughout the country. On the basis of such a history, it was unlikely that the fascist dictator Francisco Franco (1892–1975) would strive to protect or liberate Jews during World War II or seek to aid them in their conflicts with Arab governments after the war. Yet Spain's attitudes toward Jews and governmental policies regarding them were not without their inconsistencies. Theory and practice often diverged.

There was a period of reconciliation during the early nineteenth century, with several attempts by Spanish governmental leaders to welcome Jewish immigration. In 1924, under the military dictatorship of General Primo de Rivera, a law was passed, which, loosely read, would have permitted Jews of Spanish ancestry to acquire Spanish citizenship. This law applied mainly to Sephardic Jews. At the time of its passage, Franco, a supporter of the legislation, was fighting in the Moroccan conflict to protect Spain's interests and the lives of Spaniards residing there, including Jews. The law was initially drafted to be in force for six years, but it was used long afterward to extend citizenship to Jews and would play a significant role during the Holocaust. Its meaning and actual purpose have been much debated by Jewish scholars.

During the Spanish Civil War (1936–1939), Jews living outside Spain were mostly supporters of the Republican side, condemning the ruthless tactics of Franco; Jews living inside Spain, however, clearly backed Franco's nationalist movement, perhaps because of his previously demonstrated sympathies. But with the establishment of Franco's regime, most of the religious freedoms afforded by the Second Republic were abolished. Synagogues closed, and the Jewish community disintegrated, as evidenced by a growing number of conversions. Those who continued to practice their faith did so clandestinely. The growth and spread of antisemitic propaganda at the onset of World War II caused Spanish Jews to fear their expulsion from the country. Isolated incidents of violence did not, however, become systematic or widespread.

Throughout the war, Franco rescued many Jews, despite his close cooperation with Nazi Germany during the civil war years. Whether it was through the adjudication of the Primo de Rivera law (mentioned previously) or through other official channels, the Spanish government was able to protect many Sephardic Jews and their families, as well as other Jews in Hungary, Romania, Bulgaria, Czechoslovakia, and Austria. Thousands of French Jews were granted transit visas to cross Spain into Portugal to escape the Nazis' Final Solution. During the first stages of the war, such transit visas were readily available, but the regime soon began adding restrictions that forced many refugees to cross Spain illegally. The treacherous crossing through the Pyrenees, under the control of typically lenient border guards, sometimes failed, leading to imprisonment. Deportation and expulsion, however, were rarities. Once in Spain, some refugees were detained in prison camps that could be harsh, but they survived there in conditions comparable to those of average Spaniards suffering poverty and its attendant deprivations.

A classic example of the inconsistency in Franco's policy toward the Jewish population is illustrated by the case of the Sephardic Jewish community in Salonika, Greece, during the war. Jews with Spanish nationality were trapped in a bureaucratic battle between Germany and Spain. Franco vacillated for months over admitting them into Spain; meanwhile, German authorities held them in an interim concentration camp. Eventually, they were claimed by Spain, even as the great majority of Salonika's Jews perished in Auschwitz. After World War II, the Spanish government helped Jews being persecuted in Morocco to flee to Israel, despite Israel's repeated condemnations of the close relations that had existed between Spain and Nazi Germany.

Just how many Jews were saved by Franco's government during World War II is a matter of historical controversy. Franco has been credited with saving anywhere from approximately 30,000 to 60,000 Jews; the most reliable estimates suggest 45,000 is the likely figure. Why Franco chose to save any Jews at all is also a cause of considerable speculation. His government followed no clear-cut and consistent policy for handling the Jewish situation. There was no obvious motivation for Franco's assistance. Possible explanations range from theories about his own ancestry to effective pressure applied by the Allies to gratitude he might have felt toward Jews for past assistance. Regardless of the stimulus or justification, it cannot be denied that Franco's government was pivotal in the protection and rescue of numerous Jewish lives.

—*Gema A. Junco*

**See also** *Auto-da-fé;* Holocaust; Inquisition; Jewish Question; Pure Blood Laws; Spain, Riots of 1391
**References**
Avni, Haim. *Spain, the Jews, and Franco* (Philadelphia: Jewish Publication Society of America, 1982).
Lipschitz, Chaim U. *Franco, Spain, the Jews, and the Holocaust* (New York: Ktav Publishing House, 1984).
Payne, Stanley. *A History of Fascism, 1914–1945* (Madison: University of Wisconsin Press, 1995).

## Stahl, Friedrich Julius (1802–1861)

Born to a Jewish family in Würzburg, Bavaria, Friedrich Julius Stahl converted to Lutheran Christianity in 1819. After having taught jurisprudence in Munich, Erlangen, and Nuremberg, he was invited by Friedrich Wilhelm IV of Prussia to teach public law at the University of Berlin, where he became one of the leading scholars of the era and the chief representative of conservative political thought. In his masterly *Philosophy of Law* (1830–1837), he endorsed the principle of divine-right monarchy, arguing that the law of God—not the will of the people—was sovereign. But he did not advocate theocracy. According to him, private and public morality had to be strengthened by forming the political community into a moral realm (*sittliches Reich*). He postulated a strong monarchic executive but also a democratic representation of the people, thus attempting to reconcile political tradition with the demands of modernity. He was instrumental in forming the Prussian Conservative Party and its influential newspaper, the *Kreuz-Zeitung,* and he led the "High Conservatives" in the Prussian Parliament.

Stahl is often associated with the concept of the so-called Christian State, exploited by later Christian conservatives as an argument against granting legal equality to German Jews. But he made it clear in his pamphlet *On the Attitude of the Jews toward the Christian States* (1833) that he was not averse to the gradual granting of rights, at least to "useful" Jews, although the poorer masses of the Jewish population were to remain merely tolerated subjects.

During Stahl's lifetime, his Jewish roots were not much commented on. But nearly seventy-five years after his death, he became the subject of an extreme—some would say bizarre—antisemitic attack by Carl Schmitt, one of the leading experts on public law in the Weimar Republic and Third Reich. Schmitt made Stahl personally responsible for the degradation of German political culture and blamed Friedrich Wilhelm IV for having installed "a freshly assimilated Jew from the south German ghetto in order to have him combat the philosophy of Hegel" (*Deutsche Rechtswissenschaft 1939,* 117). Stahl's conversion, which was apparently heartfelt, was seen by Schmitt as no more than a means to allow him to meddle destructively in church and state, leading to a "spiritual paralysis." Although it was common on the German Right to ascribe liberal democracy and Marxism to "Jewish character," exposing the "Jewish roots of conservatism" was a much rarer occurrence. Stahl proved a convenient foil for the jaundiced

and opportunistic Schmitt. With the advent of the Third Reich, he could now demonstrate that whatever was "destructive" in the history of German political thought was the work of alien Jews.

—*Johann Baptist Müller*

*See also* Bauer, Bruno; Christian State; Emancipation; Jewish Question; Stoecker, Adolf; Vogelsang, Karl von; Wagener, Hermann
**References**
Füssl, Wilhelm. *Professor in der Politik: Friedrich Julius Stahl* (Göttingen, Germany: Vandenhoeck and Ruprecht, 1988).
Müller, Johann Baptist. *Die Staatslehre Friedrich Julius Stahls* (Munich, Germany, 1999).

## Stalin, Joseph (1879–1953)

Joseph Stalin, born Josif Vissarionovich Djugashvili in Georgia in 1879, was the first Soviet commissar of national affairs and assumed the position of general secretary of the Communist Party of the Soviet Union in 1922. Following the death of Vladimir Lenin in 1924, Stalin was involved in a struggle of succession, in which he used his powerful administrative position to eliminate his rivals and assume dictatorial power. From 1929 until his death in 1953, he was the unchallenged leader of both the Soviet Union and its Communist Party.

Prior to the revolution, Stalin emerged as a leading Bolshevik theoretician of national issues, famously arguing that the Jews did not constitute a nation because they lacked a territorial homeland. Stalin's theoretical opposition to Jewish nationhood has often been interpreted as early evidence of his antisemitism. It is contended that within prerevolutionary Communist circles, he scorned the many Jews with whom he associated. Sporadic comments ascribed to Stalin on the basis of secondhand reports also suggest he was prone to antisemitic rhetoric in private. Whatever the credibility of such evidence, it was not until after World War II that he began acting on unmistakably antisemitic motives.

As commissar of national affairs, Stalin was responsible for the party's treatment of national minorities, including Jews, within the Soviet Union. Before the war, he treated Jews in much the same manner as the other minorities; he granted them the right to use the Yiddish language and oversaw the establishment of the Jewish Section of the Communist Party and the Jewish Committee of the Commissariat of National Affairs to administer over them. He declared antisemitism to be a punishable offense and a phenomenon hostile to the Soviet government. His own government's record of punishing these crimes, however, was mixed.

In 1936, Stalin unleashed the Great Terror, in which millions of Soviet citizens were terrorized, arrested, and executed. Many of those imprisoned were Jews, including the most prominent Old Bolsheviks, who were executed after public show trials. Antisemitic rhetoric was not a part of the trials or a major factor in the Terror as a whole, but it did affect Jews in disproportionate numbers because they were disproportionately represented in the urban elites targeted by the Terror.

In the aftermath of World War II, Stalin started to single out Jews deliberately and aggressively. In the fall of 1946, he sanctioned a campaign against "bourgeois nationalism," in which Jewish writers were singled out for displaying expressions of national sentiment. Following the November 1947 UN vote on the partition of Palestine and foundation of Israel, which Stalin supported, he became particularly hostile to the voicing of Jewish national sentiment. In January 1948, the prominent actor and public activist Solomon Mikhoels was murdered on Stalin's direct order. The murder was followed by the arrests of dozens of leading Jewish political, cultural, and intellectual personalities. In late 1948 and early 1949, the most important Jewish institutions in the Soviet Union, including the Jewish Anti-Fascist Committee, the Yiddish printing press, and the Moscow State Yiddish Theater, were closed down. During the same period, dozens of prominent Jews were arrested; there followed a long-term campaign of persecution against Jewish journalists, academicians, artists, politicians, students, military personnel, and ordinary citizens. The officially controlled press used antisemitic rhetoric to disparage the victims.

Over the summer of 1952, Stalin intensified these antisemitic campaigns. On August 12, thirteen of the most well known, previously arrested Jewish intellectuals were executed in what came to be known as the Night of the Murdered Poets. The executions were followed by the arrest of several Jewish doctors, who, in January 1953, were publicly accused of collaborating with Jewish organizations abroad to poison leading Kremlin officials. Rumors circulated that Stalin was also overseeing the preparation of a massive roundup of Soviet Jews to be sent to labor camps.

In March 1953, Stalin died suddenly, leaving his plans unfulfilled. Following his death, the doctors were released, and in the years since, many of his victims have been posthumously rehabilitated.

—*Jeffrey Veidlinger*

**See also** Anti-Zionism in the USSR; Doctors' Plot; Jewish Anti-Fascist Committee; Pauker, Ana; Purges, Soviet; Slánský Trial; Stalinization of Eastern Europe; USSR

**References**
Vaksberg, Arkady. *Stalin against the Jews* (New York: Alfred A. Knopf, 1994).
Kostyrchenko, Gennadii. *Out of the Red Shadows: Anti-Semitism in Stalin's Russia* (Amherst, NY: Prometheus Books, 1995).

## Stalinization of Eastern Europe

The USSR subordinated the countries of east-central Europe (Poland, Czechoslovakia, Hungary, Romania, Bulgaria, Albania, and Yugoslavia) politically, economically, and militarily after World War II. The defeat of the Axis powers led to the direct occupation of most of these countries by the Red Army. Once present, the USSR showed itself to be unyieldingly ruthless in establishing its influence. Crucial to the erection of its hegemony was the conciliatory stance toward the demands of the USSR on the part of Great Britain and the United States, which readily accepted a division of spheres of influence at Yalta in February 1945. Subordination to the USSR took many forms: direct incorporation (Lithuania, Latvia, Estonia); infiltration by agents to carry out the USSR's agenda, often with the aid of the Red Army, Soviet organs of repression, and native communist parties (Poland, Czechoslovakia, Romania, Hungary, Bulgaria, and East Germany); and the empowerment of strong local communist parties (Yugoslavia, Albania).

The assumption of power by the communists proceeded with the step-by-step isolation and liquidation of the opposition. A favored pretext for attacking opponents was the "struggle against fascism," even though the victims frequently had not in any way collaborated with the Germans or the Italians during the war. Election results were falsified. Communists were placed into key government ministries, especially those responsible for the military and special (security) services. Propaganda promoted reconstruction and substituted "people's democracy" for "communism," a term that had strongly negative connotations for most East Europeans. Similarly, the unpopular communist parties were concealed behind more appealing "fronts," and "national" (or "people's" or "democratic") blocs. Attempts were made to tie various social strata to the system with the promise of opportunities for personal advancement. The reform of agriculture and the nationalization of industry strengthened the communist authorities, disposing of or weakening the material basis of various social groups. The lack of decisive opposition on the part of the Western powers, as well as the pro-Soviet sympathies to be found among certain sectors of Western societies, facilitated this complex process of subjugation.

Change in the international situation during the years 1947 and 1948—the emergence of the Cold War and the defection of Yugoslavia—inaugurated a new stage in Stalin's policy toward the countries of Eastern Europe. A signal of this change was the September 1947 creation of the Cominform (Communist Information Bureau), an innocuous-sounding designation for the Soviet-dominated, ideologically subordinated organization of the region's nine communist parties.

The entrenchment of the communists in a particular country made it possible to transform all aspects of social, political, and economic life according to the Soviet model. In the political realm, the most important changes included bringing the national communist parties under the firm control of Moscow. In each country, the domination of a single communist party became absolute in all state decisionmaking; surviving socialist parties were forced to fuse with the communists; universal terror liquidated all

remaining opposition; and the cult of the personality was instituted.

In economic life, the new stage was characterized by the accommodation to Soviet forms, calling for centrally directed, ideologically driven planning that entailed the domination of heavy and defense industries and the organization of all production according to five-year plans (often based on wholly unrealistic projections). The private sector was, of course, liquidated. Soviet "advisers" were omnipresent. Attempts to raise the level of production included the exploitation of prison labor and campaigns of labor competition that were based on ludicrously exaggerated and inhumane norms. In agriculture, collectivization began in June 1948. In January 1949, the Council of Mutual Economic Assistance was established to further the economic integration of its member states.

The introduction of political and economic changes was meant to be the foundation of a new social policy, the goal of which was the transformation of society in the spirit of communism. An important element of this policy was the isolation of particular sectors of society, particularly the strongly influential religious establishments of the various countries. Communist indoctrination at all levels of society sought to undermine the prestige and the power of the Catholic, Uniate, and Orthodox hierarchies; the state intervened in all the realms where the churches had once exerted great influence—culture, family life, and education. Clergy were arrested and put on trial, religious institutions were closed down, and popular participation in religious life was officially frowned on. The state sanctioned only the religious organizations clearly dependent on its authority.

Within the bloc of communist states, a significant measure of subordination to Moscow was the formal acceptance of ties with the USSR, the bilateral pacts of "friendship and cooperation." Yugoslavia, however, pursued a different path. Its leader, Marshal Tito, took a rather independent stand in relation to Stalin. In effect, Yugoslavia was removed from the Cominform, and Tito was denounced as a traitor. The case of Yugoslavia and the increasing tension of the international situation initiated a new stage of repression, characterized by a series of show trials of communist leaders, including Koçi Xoxe in Albania, László Rajk in Hungary, Traicho Kostov in Bulgaria, Rudolf Slánský in Czechoslovakia, and Ana Pauker in Romania, as well as the arrest of Władysław Gomułka in Poland. The death of Stalin on March 5, 1953, ended this phase of Soviet domination and, in fact, marked the apogee of Soviet power in east-central Europe.

After World War II, Soviet policy with regard to the Jewish populations of the region followed the pattern described earlier. Until 1948, Jews enjoyed a modicum of independence, in which the local characteristics of the communities predominated. From 1948 and 1949, a succession of the anti-Jewish, anti-Zionist, and anti-Israel policies emanating from Moscow altered this situation dramatically.

From 1945 to 1949, the authorities allowed attempts to rebuild Jewish life on the ruins of the Holocaust and sanctioned legal (and tolerated illegal) emigration, mostly to Palestine. In these years, activities of various nonrightist Jewish parties—communist, socialist, religious, Zionist—were still permitted. Jews formed their own representative institutions and social, educational, and cultural organizations. Religious organizations were active. Jewish schools functioned, some run by Zionists with Hebrew as the language of instruction as well as some run by religious bodies.

Antisemitism was rife in this early period, in part the product of traditional animosities and in part the result of encroaching Soviet power. Hatred found expression in antisemitic propaganda, harassment of the Jewish population, sometimes violent property disputes, assaults, robberies, and pogroms. Another theme of more recent vintage also entered into antisemitic propaganda at this time—the myth of Judeo-Bolshevism. The popular resonance of this charge stemmed from the visible presence of Jews in positions of authority in the state and communist apparatus of repression and propaganda. The new charges of Jewish betrayal blended easily with older views of Jewish conspiracy and hatred of Christians.

Whatever favor the Jews of east-central and eastern Europe enjoyed in the early years of Stal-inization disappeared by the end of 1948, replaced by increasingly oppressive conditions mirroring the developments within the USSR. The pretext for change was a dispute with the Zionist movement and its connections to the newly founded Jewish state. Zionists, it was claimed, posed a threat to communist states. As in the USSR, anti-Jewish activity began appearing in several guises. State authority permitted anti-Jewish, anti-Zionist, and anti-Israel propaganda. Orders were given to Jewish communities to break off contact with international Jewish organizations such as the World Jewish Congress and the Joint Distribution Committee. Representatives of these agencies were expelled from Czechoslovakia and Hungary, and their offices were closed. Zionist and Jewish socialist parties were abolished. A variety of other Jewish institutions, including those whose connection with the Zionist movement was solely an invention of the authorities were also banned. "Zionist" activists in Czechoslovakia and Hungary were arrested. The term *Zionist* had become a code word and was understood to include all Jews, no matter their allegiances or affiliations.

The repression was also present in the political conflicts of the Cold War, the Yugoslav affair, and the pro-Western policy of the Jewish state. Hunts for allegedly Zionist conspirators and the framing of Zionism as a grave threat to the "people's democracies" added a note of hysteria. In September 1949, the political trial of László Rajk, the first in Eastern Europe carried out according to the Soviet model, featured an attempt to link Zionism to U.S. intelligence agencies. This strategy was especially pronounced during the political show trial of the vice-premier and secretary-general of the Communist Party of Czechoslovakia, Rudolf Slánský, in November 1952, which ended with eleven death sentences. The antisemitism in Slánský's trial became unmistakable because of the emphasis put on the Jewish origins of eleven of the thirteen accused. Prosecutors alleged cooperation with foreign intelligence, Zionist organizations, and representatives of the Israeli government. Manifestations of an anti-Israel policy were also very clear. Accusations were leveled against Israeli diplomats; Israeli diplomats were declared personae non gratae in

Czechoslovakia and Poland. Hungary prohibited emigration to Israel, and other countries limited it radically. The anti-Zionist campaign culminated in the drastic curtailment of commercial trade with Israel and the severing of all diplomatic relations with Israel by the USSR in February 1953.

Slánský's trial was followed by many others like it in other eastern bloc countries, as part of a pattern of intimidation of the Jewish population. A wave of arrests of Jewish activists and the announcement in the USSR of the Jewish Doctors' Plot (in January 1953) led many to believe that a new purge was in the offing, one that would mainly target Jews. The death of Stalin, however, eased the policy of repression and improved relations with the state of Israel, including the resumption of diplomatic relations. Emigration to Israel became possible again, and in Poland, some Jewish institutions were allowed to reestablish themselves (from 1955 to 1957). Nonetheless, an important precedent had been established. The Jews of Eastern Europe were suspect, especially in their supposed loyalties to the state of Israel. This situation made possible a repetition of officially sanctioned antisemitism by the Communist Party in Poland in 1967 and 1968 and by the eastern bloc in general in June 1967, when the Warsaw Pact countries (except for Romania) broke off diplomatic relations with Israel once more.

—*Bożena Szaynok*
*John Kulczycki, translation*

**See also** Anti-Zionism in the USSR; Bulgaria, Holocaust in; Doctors' Plot; German Democratic Republic; Hungary, Pogroms in; Judeo-Bolshevism; Kielce Pogrom; Pauker, Ana; Poland; Purges, Soviet; Slánský Trial; Stalin, Joseph; USSR

**References**

Cohen, Stephen F. *Social Dimensions of De-Stalinization, 1953–64: Final Report to the National Council for Soviet and East European Research* (Washington, DC: National Council for Soviet and East European Research, 1983).

Held, Joseph. *The Columbia History of Eastern Europe in the Twentieth Century* (New York: Columbia University Press, 1992).

Muller, Jerry Z. "Communism, Anti-Semitism & the Jews," *Commentary* 86 (August 1988): 28–39.

## State-within-a-State

A common antisemitic slogan in the nineteenth and twentieth centuries, the phrase *state-within-a-state* was not originally used in reference to Jews. The term originated in eighteenth-century discussions about state sovereignty. For Enlightenment political theorists interested in increasingly centralized forms of state authority, the state's power was conceived to be absolute, linked to rights and privileges that, by definition, could not be shared with institutions such as the church, merchant and craft guilds, corporations, estates, and religious orders. Baron Jakob de Bielfeld, employed in the service of Frederick II of Prussia, used the term in this sense in his *Institutions politiques* (Political Institutions [1760]), making an explicit connection between this slogan and the state's claim to sovereignty. Like many others, de Bielfeld used the Latin version of the term—*status in statu*—lending this slogan the authority of classical legal discourse. In the eighteenth century, the term was used against an extremely diverse set of groups whose power was perceived to be at odds with that of the state. It was used against Jesuits, the Huguenots, Freemasons, craft guilds, nobility, and other corporations and religious orders that were under the protection of the state and perceived to limit individual freedom.

Before the emancipation of the Jews in the aftermath of the French Revolution, it would have made little sense to use this term against Jews. Jews were a religious-political minority existing at the margins of the state, not a state-within-a-state, and to use the term against them would have been an argument for granting them the rights and privileges of citizens. It was only when the Revolution abolished the rights and privileges of the estates and corporations and began moving toward granting Jews rights that the term began to be used in this context. In his often cited speech to the French National Assembly in December 1789, Count Stanislas de Clermont-Tonnerre argued that "everything should be denied to the Jews as a nation; everything should be granted to them as individuals. . . . It is impossible for them to be a nation within a nation" (in Mendes-Flohr and Reinharz 1995, 115). In his defense of the principles of the French Revolution, the German philosopher Johann Gottlieb Fichte prominently used this slogan in a distinctly antisemitic sense, to argue against Jewish emancipation. Fichte characterized the Jews as an example of a state-within-a-state whose alleged clannishness, misanthropy, and economic power were anathema to the ideals of human rights, legal equality, and human freedom. In the prolonged debates over Jewish emancipation in Germany and elsewhere, the term took on a life of its own, where it was frequently invoked as an argument against granting rights to Jews.

By the early nineteenth century, the term spread throughout Europe, primarily in relation to Jews, often without any reference to its original meaning. Jews followed—so went the logic— their own legal system and would never submit to the authority of the state. As a tightly knit social group with distinctive religious practices and disproportionate economic influence, Jews constituted a power base threatening state authority and the interests of the Christian majority. In Germany, the term appeared in the antisemitic writings of Karl Grattenauer, E. M. Arndt, Heinrich Paulus, Adolf Stoecker, and many others. Alphonse Toussenel and Édouard Drumont popularized it in France. It gained popularity in Romania, Hungary, and Russia, too, where Fyodor Dostoevsky cast the Jews as a state-within-a-state to argue against their emancipation.

—*Jonathan M. Hess*

*See also* Dohm, Christian Wilhelm von; Dostoevsky, Fyodor; Drumont, Édouard; Emancipation; Fichte, J. G.; Hungary; Romania; Russia, Imperial; Stoecker, Adolf; Toussenel, Alphonse

**References**

Katz, Jacob. "A State within a State, the History of an Anti-Semitic Slogan." In *Emancipation and Assimilation: Studies in Modern Jewish History* (Farnborough, UK: Gregg, 1972), 47–76.

La Vopa, Anthony. *Fichte: The Self and the Calling of Philosophy, 1762–1799* (Cambridge: Cambridge University Press, 2001).

Mendes-Flohr, Paul, and Jehuda Reinharz, eds. *The Jew in the Modern World* (New York: Oxford University Press, 1995), 115.

## Stauff, Philipp (1876–1923)

Although of the humblest social origins, Georg Philipp Stauff enjoyed unwonted authority on all the important questions of German life, at least among his closest friends and admirers in the *völkisch* (racist-nationalist) movement. The child of a blacksmith and a domestic servant, Stauff was born in Bavaria in 1876. He became a schoolteacher but gained public notoriety as a prolific writer of racist, nationalist, and antisemitic tracts, neglecting scarcely any of the topics of the day and publishing his views in a great variety of *völkisch* newspapers and journals. A tireless organizer on the German Right, he remained close to the successful antisemitic publisher Theodor Fritsch and wrote for his *Hammer* journal until his death in 1923.

Taking the antisemitic ideologue Eugen Dühring as his inspiration, Stauff conceived of Jewry as the most dangerous enemy of the German nation and the reason for Germany's multifaceted decline and fall. It was particularly in the realm of art and culture that Stauff detected the pernicious influence of the dominating Jews. To rescue German literature, theater, art, and journalism from certain destruction at their hands, he joined with Adolf Bartels in 1910 to establish a *völkisch* writers' association. Stauff's personal contribution to this effort was the *Semi-Kürschner,* a lexicon that identified the Jews in art, literature, politics, and the professions in order to provide incontrovertible proof to the German people that the aliens had achieved enormous power over them. Proceeding from these convictions, he wrote in a special 1912 issue of *Der Kunstwart* (The Guardian of Art) that all Jewish organizations were working in concert toward a common goal, the subjection of Germany. Stauff became captive to ever more elaborate conspiracy theories, prompting him to launch a campaign for the introduction of an "Aryan certificate" (*Ariernachweis*) for all *völkisch*, nationalist, and conservative organizations. Whoever refused to go along with this plan, he threatened with all-out war.

After publishing his *German Defense Book* (*Deutsches Wehrbuch*), a guide to all the radical nationalist organizations, Stauff joined with Bartels and the writer Wilhelm Schäfer in 1913 to organize a highly publicized meeting of Germany's most important *völkisch* groupings. The gathering resulted in the creation of an umbrella organization and a manifesto delivered to the German princes, calling on them to emancipate the German *Volk* from the Jews.

Stauff was a leading activist in the antisemitic Germanic Order and editor of its journal. He represented the order, closely linked to Fritsch's Imperial Hammer League, at the negotiations that led to the formation of the German Racial League for Defense and Defiance (in 1919), the most significant ultrarightist organization of the early postwar years. But by that time, Stauff had already begun to lose his influence in the *völkisch* movement. His obsessive dedication to the Ariosophy of Guido von List—he was president of the Guido von List Society until his death—went too far, even for those who normally had a high tolerance for *völkisch* mysticism. Health reasons also contributed to his withdrawal from politics after 1920. His death in Berlin was scarcely noticed.

—*Gregor Hufenreuter*
*Richard S. Levy, translation*

**See also** Bartels, Adolf; Dühring, Eugen; Fritsch, Theodor; German Racial League for Defense and Defiance; Germanic Order; Imperial Hammer League; List, Guido von; *Völkisch* Movement and Ideology

**Reference**
Hufenreuter, Gregor. "Philipp Stauff (1876–1923): Leben und Wirken eines völkischen Funktionärs." Master's dissertation, Free University of Berlin, 2003.

## Stavisky Affair (1933–1934)

The scandal associated with the name Stavisky was the most important political *affaire* in interwar France, resulting in the resignation of Camille Chautemps and his cabinet in January 1934, the removal of the Paris prefect of police, and riots on the Place de la Concorde (on February 6, 1934) that led to the formation of the Popular Front to fight the rise of fascism in France. For those who opposed the liberal political system, Stavisky was a symbol of the corruption and inefficacy of key institutions in the republic, including the highest levels of government, the police, the judiciary, and the financial system. The case thus marks a significant moment in the demise of the Third Republic.

Sacha Stavisky was born in the Ukraine in 1886 and emigrated to France with his middle-class, Jewish family in 1889. His father set up a dental practice, and the family was naturalized by 1900. At a young age, Stavisky was drawn to the underworld of the theater, gambling, and nightclubs, cheating clients with a number of scams and trading on and then betraying their confidence in him. After serving a couple of short stints in jail, he refined his craft, which he plied under the name of Serge Alexandre, taking advantage of precisely those social classes that buttressed the Radical (left-liberal) government in power. Between 1927 and 1933, a case against him for fraud was postponed nineteen times, and he was the subject of forty-five police investigations, without ever being arrested.

Manipulating political and press connections, Stavisky engineered his most profitable scheme by first serving as an agent for bonds floated through *crédits municipaux* (pawnshops), and then urging workers to invest their social insurance funds in them by claiming that they were backed by the state, whereon he turned the bonds into cash by placing them with insurance companies and banks. First launched in Orléans in 1928, the fraud reached its grandest scale in Bayonne, where the operation led to the issuing of over 200 million francs' worth of valueless bonds, abetted by the city's mayor and its representative in the National Assembly. Several other prominent politicians had connections with the bank, and all suspects were supporters of the party in power, the Radicals, as was Stavisky's lawyer and the Paris public prosecutor responsible for delaying his case, who also happened to be the brother-in-law of the prime minister, Chautemps. On January 8, 1934, after two weeks of political uproar, Stavisky was found dead in the Alpine ski resort of Chamonix.

Newspapers on the Left and Right all claimed his suicide was, in fact, a political assassination intended to silence his revelations about the corruption at the heart of the "republic of virtue." Xenophobia mixed with antisemitism as the case became an *affaire* whose political reverberations depended on Stavisky's symbolic status. At the trial that was supposed to be the denouement of the scandal, at least one witness made a special

Sacha Stavisky at his trial with his confidential secretary, Gilbert Romgins, and his attorney, Maitre Zevals (1935). (Hulton-Deutsch Collection/Corbis)

point of the defendant's Jewishness, referring to him as one "who became French" and who had come "to us from . . . between the Urals and the Volga." Stavisky, the Jew, became a sign of the corruption of the state, the impotence of political liberalism, and the parasitism of financial exploitation. Thus, the right-wing leagues agitated for change, the Left denounced fascism, and the climate of civil war deepened in France.

—*Jonathan Judaken*

*See also* Darquier de Pellepoix, Louis; Fascist Intellectuals; France

*Reference*
Jankowski, Paul F. *Stavisky: A Confidence Man in the Republic of Virtue* (Ithaca, NY, and London: Cornell University Press, 2002).

## Steiner, Rudolf (1861–1925)

Rudolf Steiner was born in Styria in 1861 and grew up in rural Austria. He attended primary and secondary school near Vienna and contin-

ued his studies at the Technical University of Vienna. Despite a strong interest in metaphysics and human spiritual development, Steiner worked in various academic occupations between 1884 and 1904, including a seven-year stint in the Goethe archives in the city of Weimar as editor for Goethe's scientific writings, and as a teacher at the Berlin Worker's School of Education.

Although he was familiar with the Theosophical teachings of Helena Blavatsky since the 1880s, it was not until around 1900 that Steiner became active in the German branch of the Theosophical Society. In 1913, he broke with the Theosophists to found the Anthroposophical Society. Whereas Theosophy relied heavily on Eastern mysticism and emphasized transcendence of the material world into the spiritual realm, Anthroposophy stressed the importance of the Western humanist tradition and recognized the significance of the material world as the counterpart to the spiritual. According to Steiner, humanity stood between these two realms and thus held a special position in the divine plan of the universe.

For the last twelve years of his life, Steiner dedicated himself to the Anthroposophical movement, constructing a new headquarters for the society in Switzerland and lecturing extensively throughout Europe on social renewal, which he believed would occur through cooperation between the cultural, political, and economic spheres—a view that bears some resemblance to late twentieth-century American libertarianism. In 1919, Steiner founded the first Waldorf School in Stuttgart. Steiner's pedagogical system is alive and well today throughout the Western world and is seen by many as an alternative to traditional methods of education. Steiner died in 1925, leaving behind a literary legacy of 350 titles.

Despite charges of antisemitism by some late twentieth-century scholars and critics, there is no evidence that Steiner subscribed to such views. Apart from a brief period of rabid anti-British patriotism during World War I, Steiner was a vehement opponent of any sort of rigid nationalism because he felt it hindered acceptance of the idea that all people shared in the spiritual brotherhood of man. As a staunch proponent of human rights, he spoke out against antisemitism in his writings, including an article in favor of Alfred Dreyfus and several articles for the Berlin League against Antisemitism (Abwehr-Verein). Such activities earned him the enmity of the National Socialists, who began their first campaign against Steiner in the early 1920s, denouncing his movement as a corruption of the human spirit through its Jewish methodology.

Critiques of Steiner come, in part, because of his anti-Zionist position, which had more to do with his distaste for nationalistic movements than any distaste for Jews. Complaints have also been levied against him because of the actions of certain prominent right-wing, post–World War II Anthroposophists, such as Werner Haverbeck, a rabid nationalist and environmentalist, and Baldur Springmann, a founder of the German Green Movement, who have used Steiner's copious and often conflicted writings for their own political agendas.

—*Keith R. Green*

*See also* Anti-Zionism; Blavatsky, Helena P.; Dreyfus Affair; League against Antisemitism; Theosophy

**References**

Bierl, Peter. *Wurzelrassen, Erzengel und Volksgeister* (Hamburg, Germany: Konkret Literatur Verlag, 1999).

Washington, Peter. *Madame Blavatsky's Baboon: A History of the Mystics, Mediums, and Misfits Who Brought Spiritualism to America* (New York: Schocken Books, 1995).

## Stoecker, Adolf (1835–1909)

A controversial Lutheran minister, founder and charismatic leader of the Christian Social Party and the Berlin Movement, conservative agitator, and "tribune of the people," Adolf Stoecker played a crucial role in the early history of political antisemitism in Germany. Born in Magdeburg in humble circumstances, he studied theology at Halle and Berlin and then worked as a private tutor for aristocratic families and as a country parson. In 1871, after the German victory over France, his patriotic sermons so impressed Kaiser Wilhelm I that he was appointed court and cathedral chaplain in Berlin in 1874. As leader of the City Mission from 1877, Stoecker confronted two related problems: the social misery of the lower classes in the heavily industrialized German capital and the rapidly continuing secularization of Protestants that was clearly evident in the low rates of baptism (65.8 percent) and church weddings (27.3 percent). To win the workers back to the church (and the monarchy), Stoecker concluded that it was necessary to resolve the social question through reforms and to confront the materialistic socialist party directly and politically. To this end, he established the Christian Social Worker's Party in 1878. Its founding in Berlin, however, turned into a fiasco for Stoecker when socialist workers outvoted the assembly and passed an anti-Stoecker and prosocialist resolution. Stoecker never succeeded in winning over Berlin's well-organized and ideologically steadfast working class to his Christian Conservative agenda.

Instead, small shopkeepers, artisans, officials, and traders, feeling the consequences of economic change, found Stoecker's message attractive. After Stoecker added antisemitism to the ideological mix, he soon began to draw a mass audience. Antisemitism offered a clear foe to the lower middle class in their economic struggle against liberal economic legislation and the competition of big capital and modern industry. Like other antisemites active at the time, Stoecker considered the Jewish Question to be the key to all political, social, and cultural ills of modern life. His "enemy" was no longer the religious Jew but the modern secular Jew, whom he represented as arrogant, intolerant, and "un-German." To present his movement as moderate and law-abiding, Stoecker distanced himself from the rowdy antisemitism (*Radauantisemitismus*) that was taking root in the capital and the provinces. But his anti-Jewish rhetoric was moderate only in comparison to that of the rowdies. Stoecker was not averse to using racist clichés, such as Jewish "parasitism" and the "poisoning of German blood."

Despite his oratorical ability and his appeal to the masses, he achieved only limited success as a politician. It is true that his Christian Social movement was instrumental in increasing the conservative share of votes in Berlin during the early 1880s and in integrating the lower middle class into the conservative camp, but it did not dislodge the dominant Left-liberals and socialists in the German capital. Stoecker sat in the Prussian parliament (from 1879 to 1898) and the Reichstag (from 1881 to 1893 and 1898 to 1909) but was elected in the Westphalian backwaters rather than in Berlin. Otto von Bismarck found him a problematic ally: he tolerated him as long as he seemed a useful foil in the political fight against Left-liberalism, but when the Berlin Movement turned out to be a failure, Bismarck immediately withdrew his support. Stoecker's involvement in an ultraconservative plot against the chancellor resulted in his forced suspension from political activities. After being dismissed as court chaplain in 1890, he made a short-lived comeback as a party politician. He succeeded in pressuring the German Conservative Party to adopt an antisemitic clause in its Tivoli Program of 1892. Nevertheless, his power was waning. During the 1890s, he increasingly lost control over the political movements he had founded. Within the antisemitic movement, radicals such as Otto Böckel set the tone. In the Christian Social move-

ment, his position was challenged by young liberals, including Friedrich Naumann, who advocated genuine reforms and renounced antisemitism. Meanwhile the reactionary big landowners in the German Conservative Party found Stoecker's reform ideas unacceptable for another reason. His program was too "socialistic." The Conservatives broke off the alliance with the Christian Social Party in 1896. After that, Stoecker, largely isolated, never recovered his political influence.

His significance in the history of antisemitism was not limited to party politics, however. With his reputation as court chaplain and the apparent moderation of his anti-Jewish agenda, he was instrumental in making antisemitism respectable for the middle class and within the Protestant Church. He transformed the tradition of Christian Judeophobia into a modern ideology by combining it with antiliberalism, anticapitalism, antimodernism, and chauvinist nationalism.

—*Christhard Hoffmann*

**See also** Antisemitic Political Parties; Berlin Movement; Böckel, Otto; Christian Social Party (Germany); Henrici, Ernst; Liebermann von Sonnenberg, Max; Marr, Wilhelm; *Our Demands on Modern Jewry;* Tivoli Program
**References**
Massing, Paul W. *Rehearsal for Destruction: A Study of Political Anti-Semitism in Imperial Germany* (New York: Harper and Brothers, 1949).
Pulzer, Peter. *The Rise of Political Anti-Semitism in Germany and Austria.* Rev. ed. (London: P. Halban, 1988).

## Streicher, Julius (1885–1946)

Julius Streicher was the most notorious, though not the most deadly, Nazi antisemite. He is best known as the founder and editor of *Der Stürmer* (The Stormer, published in Nuremberg from 1923 to1945). Streicher was born in Fleinhausen, a rural village near Augsburg, the ninth child of the village schoolmaster. He attended a teacher training institute and after several teaching jobs was hired by the Nuremberg school system in 1909. He served with distinction in World War I and returned to Nuremberg in 1918 to find the structure of his world in ruins.

He began looking for reasons. He had had

some antisemitic contacts before the war, but he now attended meetings of antisemitic organizations and read books such as Theodor Fritsch's *Handbook of the Jewish Question.* After finding the antisemitic organizations insufficiently radical, he took his personal following of about 5,000 into Adolf Hitler's Nazi Party in October 1922. Hitler never forgot Streicher's early loyalty, which gave him a critical boost. Streicher became *Gauleiter* (regional Nazi leader) of Franconia and was elected to the Bavarian parliament on the Nazi ticket in 1928 and to the Reichstag in 1932.

In May 1923, he published the first issue of *Der Stürmer,* primarily as a way to carry out his personal political battles. It quickly became a crude Jew-baiting weekly, which carried the wildest antisemitic charges and particularly featured reports on Jews accused of sexual crimes.

After 1933, Streicher had the blessing of Adolf Hitler to expand his antisemitic publishing empire. The circulation of *Der Stürmer* rose to about 500,000. He published a variety of antisemitic books, including some particularly vicious illustrated children's books. He also spoke to mass meetings throughout Germany and took pleasure in being called "World Jew-Baiter #1" or the "biggest bigot in the world" by the foreign press. Nuremberg was the site of the annual national rally of the Nazi Party, which added to Streicher's influence and visibility.

His extremism made him enemies even among many Nazis, but Hitler protected him. When a major financial scandal in Nuremberg, resulting from the expropriation of Jewish property after the 1938 pogroms, forced Streicher's removal as Gauleiter, Hitler personally guaranteed that Streicher could retire to his country estate and that he would have the resources to continue publishing his newspaper.

Captured by the Americans in 1945, Streicher was tried as one of the major war criminals at the Nuremberg trials. He claimed that his calls for annihilation (for example, his statement that "the causes of the world's misfortunes will be forever removed only when Jewry in its entirety is annihilated") (in Bytwerk 2001, 169) were simply rhetorical responses to Jewish attacks on Germany and that he had not known about the Holocaust. The tribunal sentenced him to death by hanging. There was some controversy about the sentence, since Streicher was convicted not of any particular act of violence but rather for propaganda that "poisoned the minds of a nation." Nonetheless, it is clear that even if Streicher may not have been responsible for any specific death, his twenty-five years of passionate antisemitism contributed to the increasing radicalization of Nazi antisemitism.

—*Randall L. Bytwerk*

*See also* Aryanization; Fritsch, Theodor; *Handbook of the Jewish Question;* Hitler, Adolf; Holocaust; National Socialist German Workers' Party; Night of Broken Glass (November 1938 Pogrom); *Stürmer, Der*

**References**

Bytwerk, Randall L. *Julius Streicher* (New York: Cooper Square Press, 2001).

Showalter, Dennis E. *Little Man, What Now?: "Der Stürmer" in the Weimar Republic* (Hamden, CT: Archon Books, 1982).

## Student Nonviolent Coordinating Committee (SNCC)

The Student Nonviolent Coordinating Committee (SNCC), founded in 1960 by leaders of the lunch-counter sit-in movement, spearheaded many of the direct-action protests of the civil rights era in the United States. In its early years, SNCC enjoyed widespread Jewish support, especially during the "Freedom Summer" of 1964 when hundreds of northern Jewish college students journeyed to the South in an impressive interracial movement for civil equality.

By the mid-1960s, growing frustration with the pace of civil rights reform led to a schism between accommodationist civil rights leaders such as Martin Luther King Jr. and a group of younger, nationalist-minded African American activists. In a bitterly contested 1966 vote, the nationalists, under the leadership of Black Power advocate Stokely Carmichael, took control of SNCC and distanced themselves from the nonviolent strategies of King. Eventually adopting a new name that replaced the word *nonviolent,* the Student National Coordinating Committee purged whites and Jews from leadership positions and joined a larger leftist movement for social revolution. As SNCC's "Position Paper on

Black Power" stated, "If we are to proceed toward true liberation, we must cut ourselves off from white people."

In the wake of Israel's victory in the 1967 Six Days' War, SNCC launched an anti-Zionist campaign loaded with antisemitic imagery, wild claims, and threatening slogans, issuing from the highest leadership circles of the organization. Tensions with the leadership of Jewish organizations peaked when SNCC newsletter illustrator Kofi Bailey drew a picture of an Israeli firing squad shooting a group of Arabs. The caption read, "This is the Gaza Strip, Palestine, not Dachau, Germany" (Dollinger 2000, 200–202). Although some SNCC officers distanced themselves from the article and illustration, the pieces galvanized SNCC's pro-Palestinian position and hastened the end of any meaningful Jewish organizational support.

In the late 1960s, SNCC leaders traveled the world, adopting an internationalist platform that strove to connect the struggle of African Americans to revolutionary regimes in Cuba, North Vietnam, and Moscow. On the domestic front, SNCC allied itself with the emerging Black Panther Party in Oakland, California. Its policy of racial separation intensified, especially after the 1968 assassination of Martin Luther King Jr. By 1970, decimated by police crackdowns on its violent behavior as well as by political infighting, SNCC ceased to function as a meaningful national organization.

—*Marc Dollinger*

*See also* African American–Jewish Relations; Anti-Zionism; Black Nationalism

**References**

Carson, Clayborne. *In Struggle: SNCC and the Black Reawakening of the 1960s* (Cambridge, MA: Harvard University Press, 1995).

Dollinger, Marc. *Quest for Inclusion: Jews and Liberalism in Modern America* (Princeton, NJ: Princeton University Press, 2000).

Van Deburg, William L., ed. *Modern Black Nationalism: From Marcus Garvey to Louis Farrakhan* (New York: New York University Press, 1997).

## Stürmer, Der

*Der Stürmer* (The Stormer), an antisemitic weekly published by Julius Streicher from 1923 to 1945, was the most notorious newspaper ever published. Adolf Hitler himself claimed to read it faithfully, and it provided a virtual gathering place for the most energetic of Nazi antisemites. Streicher began the newspaper in 1923 as part of his personal political battles. It quickly developed into a weekly devoted almost entirely to rousing hatred against the Jews. Despite frequent legal difficulties, it reached a modest circulation of about 25,000 by the time Hitler took power in 1933. But then, with the full support of Hitler, *Der Stürmer*'s circulation rose to about 500,000 by 1935. Special editions on such topics as Jewish sexual crimes or ritual murder had print runs as high as 2 million. Loyal readers built thousands of showcases throughout Germany to display each new issue.

*Der Stürmer* intentionally pandered to the crudest in the antisemitic movement. Filled with stories of sexual crimes, financial corruption, and misdeeds of every imaginable kind, each issue presented Jews as, literally, the devil in human form. The newspaper's banner motto on the cover of nearly every issue was "The Jews are our misfortune." Caricatures by Streicher's cartoonist Fips (Philipp Rupprecht) were a striking element of each issue. Fips presented Jews as ugly, fat, dirty, sex-obsessed, and evil individuals.

*Der Stürmer* had a relatively small staff. Much material came from readers, who denounced not only many Jews but also their non-Jewish acquaintances for such offenses as being courteous to a Jew, attending the funeral of a Jewish neighbor, or buying from a Jewish shop. At least 6,500 non-Jews were attacked by name for being "traitors to the German race." Articles of this type had an intimidating effect on other Germans, who chose to avoid Jews rather than risk being pilloried by *Der Stürmer*.

The paper favored increasingly radical solutions to the Jewish Question. When the 1935 Nuremberg Laws met *Der Stürmer*'s demands to outlaw sexual relations between Jews and non-Jews, the paper began calling for the death penalty in cases of miscegenation. In the 1930s, it joined in calls to deport all Jews to Madagascar or a similar remote location, but by the early war years, it was regularly calling for the annihilation of the Jews. Although *Der Stürmer* appealed to the most rabid antisemites in Hitler's Germany, it also provided an alibi for those who were less passionate, as they could and did pride themselves on being more moderate antisemites than the people who read *Der Stürmer*. The final issue of the paper appeared in February 1945.

—*Randall L. Bytwerk*

**See also** Caricature, Anti-Jewish (Modern); Hitler, Adolf; National Socialist German Workers' Party; Nuremberg Laws; Streicher, Julius; Weimar
**References**
Bytwerk, Randall L. *Julius Streicher* (New York: Cooper Square Press, 2001).
———, ed. German Propaganda Archive. Available at http://www.calvin.edu/academic/cas/gpa/ww2era.htm. Accessed on November 15, 2002.
Showalter, Dennis E. *Little Man, What Now?: "Der Stürmer" in the Weimar Republic* (Hamden, CT: Archon Books, 1982).

## Stuyvesant, Peter (1592–1672)

Petrus (Peter) Stuyvesant served as director-general of the Dutch West India Company's colony in North America from 1647 until the English seized it to create the colony of New York in 1664. Stuyvesant opposed the idea of allowing Jews to settle in New Netherland—and he also objected to the presence of Lutherans and Quakers. Religious zealotry was not the director-general's sole motive for wishing to deny them entrance, for Stuyvesant wrote that "to give liberty to the Jews will be very detrimental there because Christians there will not be able at the same time to do business" (in Marcus 1970, 1121). The twenty-three Jews who fled the Portuguese in Brazil and arrived in New Amsterdam in 1654 were ordered out by Stuyvesant. They petitioned the company's directors, promising that they would add to the well-being of the fledgling colony and to its economic health, as well. The directors took them at their word, and when influential Jewish merchants brought pressure to bear on the company back home in Amsterdam, Stuyvesant was ordered to allow the refugees to remain as long as they did not receive any poor relief. The directors indicated that the Jews were to be allowed to trade freely and acquire land, although they restricted their economic activities in other ways, and ruled that

they were to settle in their own community and worship in private. Stuyvesant, on his own authority, decided further that the Jews would not be allowed to trade with the Indians or to conduct business on the Hudson River.

Stuyvesant and the provincial council ignored the company's official position and continued to harass the newcomers. A merchant named Abraham De Lucena was arrested in March 1655 for retailing and for opening his store during a Sunday sermon. He was fined a sum many times greater than a Christian would have faced for a similar offense, although he was apparently never forced to pay it. Another merchant, named David Ferera, was arrested for insulting a bailiff, and he, too, was heavily fined and faced a public flogging and banishment. In the end, the fine was substantially reduced, and he remained in town unharmed. New Amsterdam's leaders long refused to allow Jews to establish their own cemetery, finally giving in but setting aside land outside the town's boundaries. Stuyvesant would not allow Jews to serve in the militia but taxed them for its support instead. By 1656, the Dutch West India Company had sent stern enough reprimands to make Stuyvesant back off to a certain extent. Jews could at last trade freely and own land, although both Stuyvesant and the company remained adamant that Jews (and all other non-Calvinists) be forbidden to worship in public.

—*Kim M. Gruenwald*

**See also** Colonial America; Emancipation; Slave Trade and the Jews
**References**
Faber, Eli. *A Time for Planting: The First Migration, 1654–1820* (Baltimore, MD: Johns Hopkins University Press, 1992).
Marcus, Jacob R. *The Colonial American Jew, 1492–1776.* 3 vols. (Detroit, MI: Wayne State University Press, 1970).

## Sudeten Germans

With the end of World War I, about 3.2 million Germans from the Bohemian lands found themselves reduced from a leading political and social group in the Habsburg monarchy to a minority in the new state of Czechoslovakia. Some of their prominent politicians wanted to better the situation of the minority by cooperating with the Czechoslovak authorities and joined the government coalition in 1926. The German National Socialist Workers' Party (DNSAP) rejected this approach and remained determinedly hostile toward the new situation.

In the 1930s, the Great Depression increased German-Czech tensions. Reacting to divisive and aggressive Nazi propaganda, the government banned the most ardent followers of Nazism, including the DNSAP. Konrad Henlein, the leader of a Sudeten German gymnastics organization, responded by founding the Home Front; renamed the Sudeten German Party (SGP) in 1935, it won two-thirds of the German votes in the elections held that year. Complete separation from Czechoslovakia was high on its agenda only after Henlein had been instructed by Hitler in November 1937 to make "impossible" demands on the Prague government. The ensuing crisis led to the Munich Pact of September 1938. Germany annexed the Sudetenland and appointed Henlein district leader (*Gauleiter* and *Reichsstatthalter*).

During the crisis in 1938, latent antisemitism turned violent: shops were demolished, towns were declared "Free of Jews," and "wild Aryanizations" took place. In late 1938 and early 1939, these expropriations were legalized retroactively, but further unauthorized steps were prohibited in favor of more systematic spoliation. The largest share of the booty went to principal banks and big businesses in the Old Reich, but Sudeten Germans also profited, accumulating an estimated 12 percent of Jewish assets (valued at 48 million of the 400 million reichsmarks total). The elimination of competition from Jewish handicraft and retail businesses was an added benefit. Other and related anti-Jewish policies enacted locally in the Sudeten district followed the national pattern: generally, the Jewish population was to be pressured to emigrate while leaving the remnants of its property behind. This goal was achieved quickly in the Sudeten district. In 1930, 27,000 Jews had lived in the area; by May 1939, the number had dwindled to 2,300.

Recent research suggests a degree of ambivalence concerning the attitude of the Sudeten Germans toward the Third Reich. The Security Service reported complaints regarding second-class treatment and neglect. Some Sudeten Germans had hoped for autonomy but instead witnessed the "coordination" of their region into the Reich. Others had urged the expulsion of the large Czech minority but were vetoed because Berlin did not want to disturb military production in the Protectorate. Yet the Sudeten district was one of the strongest in terms of membership in the Nazi Party. Although an overwhelming majority of the population voiced its approval with being part of the Reich in a plebiscite in December 1938, discontent with Berlin's control of the district, but not with Nazism per se, continued.

—*Tatjana Tönsmeyer*

*See also* Aryanization; Göring, Hermann; Hitler, Adolf; Nazi Legal Measures against Jews; Versailles Treaty

*References*

Smelser, Ronald M. *The Sudeten Problem, 1933–1938: Volkstumspolitik and the Formulation of Nazi Foreign Policy* (Middletown, CT: Wesleyan University Press, 1975).

Ziegler, Dieter, Harald Wixforth, and Jörg Osterloh. "Aryanization in Central Europe, 1933–1939: A Preliminary Account for Germany (the 'Altreich'), Austria and the 'Sudeten' Area." In *Business and Politics in Europe, 1900–1970*. Edited by Terry Gourvish (Cambridge: Cambridge University Press, 2003), 187–214.

## Supersessionism

The term *supersessionism* refers to any of a variety of Christian theological traditions claiming the Christian church has superseded the people Israel in the divine covenant (*b'rith* in Hebrew) made with Abraham and his descendants—initially described in Genesis 12:1–3 and expanded and reiterated in Genesis 13:14–17, 15:4–5, 17, and 22:15–19. The covenant enjoined Abraham to obey God's commandments and promised a reward for doing so; Christians claim that Jesus fulfilled the commandments. Some Christian churches teach "exclusivism" or "substitution": that the Christian church entirely replaced the people Israel with a new covenant (or "testament"—the Greek *diatheke*) announced during the Last Supper (Matthew 26:28; Mark 14:24; Luke 22:20; 1 Corinthians 11:25) and fulfilled in Jesus' death and resurrection. Others believe that Christianity represents a new covenant grafted onto but superseding the original covenant; this strand may include beliefs that the covenant with Abraham was legitimate in itself or that the covenant of Abraham was always intended to be superseded by the new covenant in Jesus. Still other churches teach that God's covenant with the Christian church is an additional, complementary covenant operating parallel to the covenant of Genesis (sometimes called "two-covenant theology"). In his Epistle to the Romans (especially chapters 9 to 11), the apostle Paul ponders the failure of Jews to accept Jesus as the Messiah, naming Christians as the spiritual heirs to the covenant of the Israelites as twigs are grafted to a root (Romans 11:17–21). Paul emphasized that God had not broken his covenant with Israel and that Israel, if presently excluded from salvation, would be regrafted to the root of salvation if it did not persist in unbelief. Exclusivism permeates the Gospels (which mainstream biblical scholarship suggests postdate the Pauline epistles) but is particularly strong in Matthew 1–2, in which messianic prophecies drawn from Isaiah and other prophets were interpreted to apply to Jesus. Traditionally, Pauline regrafting is supported via beliefs about the conversion of the Jews before the end of time as described in Revelation.

Though the relationship of the church to the people Israel is ambiguous in the New Testament, exclusivist supersessionism was characteristic of orthodox forms of Christianity from 325 CE until relatively recently. Supersessionism in the early church was concretized through the Christian assumption of the Hebrew Scriptures, or *Tanakh,* into its scriptural canon as the Old Testament. Church fathers including Augustine and John Chrysostom wrote about it. In the Middle Ages, supersessionism contributed to typology, a theological practice that interpreted the Bible based on symbolic prefiguration of certain events of the New Testament in the *Tanakh* (for example, "the Fall" into sin prefigured Jesus' crucifixion). Supersessionism was symbolized in medieval and Renaissance art through the contrasting figures of Synagoga (usually portrayed with a blindfold to symbolize the refusal of the Jews to acknowledge the new covenant) and Ecclesia (See

illustration in Caricature, Anti-Jewish (Early). Though scholarship emphasizes distinctions between anti-Judaism based on supersession and racial or cultural antisemitism, supersessionism resulted in persecutions of the Jews. Protestant Reformers such as John Calvin and Martin Luther embraced it. Early anti-Trinitarian opposition to supersessionism was quickly suppressed as heretical by both Catholic and Protestant authorities. John Wesley introduced supersessionism into modern Protestantism. This tradition led Christians to speak of themselves as "the new Israel," a trope with variations saturating Christian literature and culture that includes a rhetorical equation between Israelites, sinners, and Christianity.

Christian rejection of supersessionism was rare before the twentieth century. Two modern motivations for its rejection are dispensationalism and post-Holocaust theology. After the Shoah, numerous Christian theologians recognized the destructive consequences of supersessionism. Several major church bodies under the aegis of the World Council of Churches have issued statements validating the divine covenant with Israel and asserting that Jews can find salvation through the Abrahamic covenant. Statements of the Roman Catholic Church since 1965 have retracted anti-Jewish teachings but have recently withdrawn from rejecting the need for mission to the Jews.

Dispensationalists, in contrast, though insisting that belief in Jesus is necessary for salvation, teach that the Christian covenant is temporary, to last until the Jews recognize Jesus during the Great Tribulation. After time ends, in this view, a further covenant will apply. Dispensationalist sentiment frequently creates modern evangelical support in America for Israel. Many church bodies, including the Eastern Orthodox churches as well as some evangelical and fundamentalist groups, however, continue to teach exclusivist supersessionism and support missions to the Jews. Both exclusivists and dispensationalists support messianic Judaism, a movement that seeks to bring observant Jews to a complementary belief in Jesus. All major Jewish groups today reject supersessionism.

—*Susan R. Boettcher*

**See also** Augustine of Hippo; Chrysostom, John; Gospels; Iconography, Christian; Luther, Martin; Paul; Vatican Council, Second

"ET MAINTENANT DORS, MA MIGNONNE!"

Svengali mesmerizes Trilby. Svengali, the unsavory hypnotist, personified antisemitic fears of the secret infiltration of Jewish power. (Mary Evans Picture Library)

### References

Brockway, Allan, ed. *The Theology of the Churches and the Jewish People: Statements by the World Council of Churches and Its Member Churches* (Geneva, Switzerland: World Council of Churches Publications, 1988).

Littell, Franklin. *The Crucifixion of the Jews.* 3rd ed. (Macon, GA: Mercer University Press, 1996).

Wright, N. T. *The New Testament and the People of God* (Minneapolis, MN: Fortress Press, 1992).

## Svengali

Svengali is the sinister and fascinating Jewish villain at the center of *Trilby* (1894) by the popular Anglo-French novelist and illustrator George Du Maurier. The story concerns three British artists living the bohemian life in Paris—Taffy, a Welshman; the Laird, a Scotsman; and Little Billee, an Englishman. All are struck by the beauty of the working-class artists' model Trilby O'Ferrall and hope to reform and elevate her. Instead of being saved by the British, however, Trilby falls under the spell of Svengali, a ghetto-born Jewish musician, who seeks power over women and gentiles. Little Billee's love for Trilby is thwarted by his family, who persuade her to forsake him to preserve his respectability. Five years later, he has risen to a brilliant but empty career as a society painter, and Trilby, once tone-deaf, is transformed by Svengali's hypnotism into the greatest opera singer in Europe. During a concert in London, Svengali dies and Trilby's talent disappears. She has no memory of her life as a singer and pines away, momentarily reviving at the sight of a photograph of Svengali.

Svengali is the nightmare of fin-de-siècle Europe, "a sticky, haunting, long, lean, uncanny, black spider-cat, if there is such an animal outside a bad dream." Apart from his redeeming musical genius, he is thoroughly villainous: "Svengali walking up and down the earth seeking whom he might cheat, betray, exploit, borrow money from, make brutal fun of, bully if he dared, cringe to if he must—man, woman, child, or dog—was about as bad as they make 'em." Motivated by a vengeful lust for domination, he is finally driven to a furious and fatal frenzy by Taffy pulling his nose in public to humiliate him. Svengali the hypnotist, with his "bold, brilliant black eyes" and "long heavy lids," is also a personification of antisemitic fears of the secret infiltration of Jewish power.

The runaway best-selling novel perhaps drew on popular representations during the 1870s of Prime Minister Benjamin Disraeli, who was frequently portrayed as an oriental wizard holding the nation in his thrall. Disraeli himself had claimed in *Coningsby* (1844) that Jews possessed a unique genius for music. Svengali's charisma recalls the sinister influence over women held by Dickens's Fagin, a Jew (*Oliver Twist*, [1838]), and Jasper Bud, a musician (*The Mystery of Edwin Drood* [1870]). Also circulating in the novel's representation of Svengali is the charge by Richard Wagner that Jews could only ever be parasites, profiting from music but never creating it. The greedy, predatory, and gross-mannered Svengali, however, is both the agent of sublime transformation and its antithesis.

Yet the novel blurs the boundaries between Jew and non-Jew, especially in its suggestion that one requirement for artistic genius is "that strong, sturdy, irrepressible, indomitable, indelible [Jewish] blood which is of such priceless value in diluted homeopathic doses."

—*Nadia Valman*

*See also* Caricature, Anti-Jewish (Early); Disraeli, Benjamin; Dracula; English Literature from Chaucer to Wells; *Judaism in Music; Ostjuden;* Wagner, Richard

**References**
Pick, Daniel. *Svengali's Web: The Alien Enchanter in Modern Culture* (New Haven, CT: Yale University Press, 2000).
Rosenberg, Edgar. *From Shylock to Svengali: Jewish Stereotypes in English Fiction* (Stanford, CA: Stanford University Press, 1960).

# Sweden

Scattered Jewish settlements in Sweden date from as early as the sixteenth century, and a number of anti-Jewish laws and decrees were issued then and in the following century. Organized Jewish immigration on a somewhat larger scale started with the settlement of the engraver Aron Isaac and his family in Stockholm in 1774. Aron Isaac was allowed to settle there under a royal protective decree, which was expanded in 1775 to include other Jewish families "of use to the crown and country." The growth of Jewish immigration to Sweden by the late eighteenth century produced strong antisemitic sentiments in the populace, despite the fact that the Jewish minority was very small; in 1787, the Jewish population in the whole country was less than 150 people, and in 1815, the official number stood at only 785. Moreover, the conditions for settlement were highly regulated. Antisemitic propaganda in that era was particularly strong among the bourgeoisie and the Lutheran clergy, and it was often intertwined with anti-Catholic writings.

In 1815, Jewish immigration to Sweden came to a virtual halt. The reason for this was allegedly to solve the problem of "beggar Jews," illegal immigrants who had arrived in Sweden in the wake of the Napoleonic Wars and who lived as peddlers. These strict immigration laws remained in place until 1870, when Swedish Jews were granted full citizenship and Jewish immigration resumed.

The Jewish minority in Sweden has always been small and, since the latter part of the nineteenth century, well assimilated. Despite this, the extent and content of antisemitism in Sweden closely parallels that of continental Europe, with one exception. The depression that hit most of Europe in the 1870s and resulted in a wave of antisemitic propaganda did not hit as hard in Sweden, which may help to explain the relative lack of antisemitic propaganda in the 1870s and 1880s. Clearly articulated economic antisemitism, however, started to emerge in the last decade of the nineteenth century within the various retail trade organizations. Again, the issue was the "unlawful competition from Jewish pedlars," and the argument was, for the most part, centered around what can be described as "the Shylock stereotype" and therefore was contained within a primarily economic context initially. However, by the turn of the twentieth century, antisemitism in Sweden began to register the influence of *völkisch* (racist-nationalist) ideology and literature coming out of Germany, especially the writings and ideas of Houston Stewart Chamberlain and Julius Langbehn.

The first antisemitic association in Sweden, the Svenska Antisemitiska Förbundet (Swedish Antisemitic League), was founded in Stockholm in 1889. This organization was followed by numerous other clubs and societies until the 1930s. The general founding myth of organized antisemitism was the notion of a threatening Jewish world conspiracy, a myth that was also present within some of the trade organizations. One particular feature of Swedish antisemitism in the first decades of the twentieth century was its strong affinity with "racial science" and physical anthropology, areas of study that had a strong standing in Sweden at the time.

Organized antisemitism never became very successful in Sweden, but antisemitic rhetoric and symbolism was nevertheless widely known and tolerated. Evidence of this can be found, for instance, in the widespread popular comic press, which, during the first three decades of the twentieth century, was more or less laden with antisemitic stereotypes. Antisemitic trends are also discernible in the public debate on immigration and the enforcement of strict immigration regulations until the early 1940s. These attitudes had serious consequences. Despite a temporary relaxation of the immigration policies in the autumn of 1938, following the November pogrom (Night of Broken Glass), for instance, almost 50 percent of the 1,748 applications for residence permits from German citizens, almost all Jews, were denied by the Swedish government.

The most significant antisemitic organization in interwar Sweden was the Swedish Antisemitic Association, which was founded in Gothenburg in 1923 by the newspaper editor Barthold Lundén, who was also its main driving force. The association, which peaked at about 1,500 members, dissolved in 1931 because of Lundén's ill health and a lack of popular support for the organization. It was the first Swedish organization that used the swastika, and among its members were some of the future leaders of Swedish Nazism. Its most prominent member, however, was Hermann Göring, who belonged during his Swedish exile in the 1920s. Among the association's demands were a halt on Jewish immigration (and repatriation of newly immigrated Jews), occupational regulations, restrictions on "Jewish capital," and the enforcement of laws against intermarriage.

Antisemitism was present within all forms of fascism in Sweden during the 1930s. However, the most aggressive and far-reaching antisemitic propaganda was voiced not from within a national socialist framework but by politically independent individuals such as Elof Eriksson and Einar Åberg. Within Swedish Nazism, antisemitism was perceived as a predominantly racial issue rather than a cultural or religious one, and the notion of the Jewish world conspiracy was relatively muted in native Nazi propaganda. The Nazi movement in Sweden thus differed somewhat from its German counterpart, even if it is clear that antisemitism was a fundamental element for Swedish Nazism as well.

The revelations of the Final Solution that accompanied the end of World War II placed a strong taboo on expressing antisemitic sentiments in public in Sweden. During the last phase of the war when it became obvious that Nazi Germany would be defeated, the country had opened its borders to Jews and other refugees, starting with the reception of the Danish Jews in October 1943. The postwar period has thus been dominated by an anti-antisemitic consensus, which recently expessed itself, to name but one example, in the organization of the Stockholm International Forum on the Holocaust in the year 2000.

Antisemitism has, however, survived in a more virulent form within the plethora of ultranationalist, fascist, and White Power groups. As a less virulent and "semiconscious" cultural phenomenon, it has also occasionally surfaced in the broader public sphere, especially in relation to the debate on Israel and the Palestinians; as such, it has often been intertwined with anti-Zionist sentiments.

—Lena Berggren

**See also** Anti-Zionism; Chamberlain, Houston Stewart; Court Jews; Göring, Hermann; Night of Broken Glass (November 1938 Pogrom); Racism, Scientific; Reformation; Shylock; *Völkisch* Movement and Ideology

**References**
Berggren, Lena. *Nationell upplysning: Drag i den svenska antisemitismens idéhistoria* (National Enlightenment. Traits in the History of Swedish Antisemitism) (Stockholm: Carlsson Bokförlag, 1999).
———. "Elof Eriksson (1883–1965): A Case-Study of Antisemitism in Sweden," *Patterns of Prejudice* 34 (January 2000): 39–48.

## Switzerland

Jewish life in Switzerland predates the foundation of the Swiss Confederation in 1291. Swiss persecutions of Jews, ranging from expulsions to burnings, match the waves of maltreatment that swept central and western Europe, in particular during the Black Plague of the fourteenth century. However, local edicts sometimes collided with those of the Federal Diet, which made careful distinctions. In one case in 1658, the parliament rejected a town's request to expel Jews, banning the expulsion of people who had initially received refuge but also forbidding Jewish residents from taking in coreligionists other than their children. Several cantons also agreed to extend temporary, though renewable, letters of protection allowing Jewish residency and trade in certain areas. Yet further restrictions on residency and land purchase meant that by the eighteenth century, Jews could only reside in Lengnau and Oberendingen, communities of eastern Switzerland (canton Aargau).

The French Revolution and the invasion of Switzerland by Napoleonic forces changed this state of affairs. Special taxes were canceled by petition in 1798, and the following year, Jews gained the status of foreigners living in the republic, with freedom of movement and trade, although without civic equality. New communities began to thrive, especially in canton Aargau, but this caused considerable resentment among the local population. In 1802, after the French occupation ended, a local conflict led to the sacking of two Jewish villages there. This and other incidents prompted political discussions in the Diet, which conferred on each canton the right to decide on the status of its Jews. In the case of Aargau, the law of May 5, 1809, actually reduced the Jew's status from citizen to protected subject.

During the nineteenth century, as cantons slowly moved to emancipate Jews, federal authorities, who oversaw the establishment of a new constitution in 1848, faced pressure from abroad to enforce equality among Swiss citizens and to revise articles 41 (on the freedom to reside) and 44 (on freedom of religion) to include Jews and Judaism. These revisions became law only in the 1874 constitution, and it was not until five years later that the Jews of Aargau gained full equality. In 1893, however, the federal constitution was amended to ban kosher slaughtering, which many saw as a retreat from full equality and some Jews regarded as an attack on the free practice of their religion.

The presence of radical leftist refugees and a large number of eastern European Jews (55 percent of all Jews in Switzerland were foreigners) began adversely affecting Swiss opinion during World War I. Swiss antisemitism in the 1920s remained mostly a mix of religious and xenophobic regionalism, although Henry Ford's *The International Jew,* as well as the *Protocols of the Elders of Zion,* enjoyed some popularity. Still, antisemitic tendencies remained relatively marginal.

Things changed radically in the 1930s, with the advent of the *Frontenfrühling* (the spring of the fronts), whose members, referred to as Frontists, targeted foreigners, left-wingers, and Jews, playing on popular fears of communism. When Frontists distributed copies of the *Protocols* in 1933, their agitation led to a court challenge the following year. The world economic depression, as well as various incidents involving Nazi groups in Switzerland, fed antisemitic rancor. For example, the assassination of Nazi official Wilhelm

Gustloff in Switzerland by a Jewish student in February 1936 prompted heavy Nazi and Frontist propaganda claiming a conspiracy. Overall, however, dislike of Nazi Germany among the Swiss was a powerful factor working to contain antisemitic propaganda in the country.

Nevertheless, the ambient presence of antisemitic feelings succeeded in permeating much of the public. The tone of Swiss antisemitism, as reflected in the literature and movies of the time, was less crass than that of contemporary France or Germany. Switzerland's bourgeois social mores militated against open association with rowdy populist antisemites and encouraged polite, if distant, dealings with educated Jews, who were generally seen as contributing to the cultural life of the nation. Yet such ambivalence in the social sphere gave way to a hard line when it came to politics.

In the late 1930s, the penetration of antisemitism into government circles doubtless contributed to associating any refugee problems with Jews seeking to leave German-controlled territories. The fear of *Verjudung* (Jewification) led to the imposition of the J Stamp in 1938 and also to the closing of the nation's borders in August 1942—after the fact of the Holocaust had become known. By spring 1942, the Swiss consul in Cologne had obtained photographs of Jewish massacres; despite this intelligence, the authorities stood by their original decision to close the borders. Switzerland took in some Jewish refugees, some of whom later recalled being subjected to antisemitic measures by the officers and soldiers in charge of refugee camps. The head-in-the-sand attitude of the Swiss government concerning knowledge of the Holocaust and its callous refusal to alter its policies overshadowed the actions of a few Swiss who sought to circumvent the law in favor of humanity. Many such rescuers suffered legal consequences and were not rehabilitated until the late 1990s.

After World War II, antisemitism generally diminished, as reflected, in part, in a sentiment of small-state kinship for Israel that carried into the 1970s. But the Palestinian-Israeli conflicts of the late 1980s and 1990s and the eruption of the Swiss banking scandal in 1995 reinvigorated old stereotypes and misperceptions. Even though seemingly fully integrated, Swiss Jews are still considered by many to form a separate group. Antisemitic feelings in Switzerland are similar to those found in the rest of Western Europe but are both more ambiguous in their expression and more pervasive historically, reflecting a general discomfort with outsiders rather than a specific anti-Jewishness. Political events, such as those of the late twentieth century, can summon up such feelings with seeming ease.

The national reexamination of Switzerland's role in World War II, however, has led to some hopeful signs of change; innovative educational efforts and tolerance campaigns may help diminish some traditional antisemitic attitudes, although they will probably not overcome them entirely. Evidence of a new orientation is an amendment to the constitution that went into effect in 1995; it includes sanctions for denying crimes against humanity and inciting racial, ethnic, or religious hatred.

—*Guillaume de Syon*

**See also** *Dearborn Independent* and *The International Jew;* Emancipation; Expulsions, Late Middle Ages; J Stamp; Kosher Slaughtering; *Protocols of the Elders of Zion* on Trial; Restitution; *Verjudung*

**References**
Independent Commission of Experts. "Switzerland Second World War." Available at http://www.uek.ch. (Accessed March 2, 2005).
Mattioli, Aram. *Antisemitismus in der Schweiz, 1848–1960* (Zurich, Switzerland: Orell Füssli, 1998).
Piccard, Jacques. *La Suisse et les juifs, 1933–1945* (Lausanne, Switzerland: Editions d'en Bas, 2000).

## Szalasi, Ferenc (1897–1946)

Commissioned a Hungarian army officer in 1915, Ferenc Szalasi was elevated to the General Staff in 1925 and promoted to major in 1933. Szalasi was an extreme nationalist and xenophobe, fervent Christian and antisemite, and rabid anticommunist and irredentist, and in the early 1930s, he began to advocate the conversion of Hungary into a fascist state, the Great Fatherland of Carpatho-Danubia.

Szalasi resigned his commission in 1935 and

quickly established his first political vehicle, the Party of National Will (PNW), a group that appealed mainly to alienated elements and the lower echelons of Hungarian society. In April 1937, the government, increasingly anxious at the ultra-Right's growing power, dissolved the PNW and sentenced Szalasi to three months in prison, a counterproductive move that elevated his profile and influence throughout Hungary. Taking advantage of his enhanced stature, he united the PNW with several rival groups to form the Hungarian National Socialist Party in October 1937. Shortly thereafter, the government banned the party and placed him, together with seventy other ultrarightists, under surveillance. These measures were undermined by Hitler's foreign policy triumphs, which boosted the prestige of the radical Right in Hungary. Antisemitic legislation of increasing severity was the government's response to its waning popularity, an unsuccessful attempt to curry favor with Hungarians moving ever further to the Right. The (anti-) Jewish Laws of 1938, 1939, and 1941 were predictably dismissed by the ultras as inadequate.

In August 1938, Szalasi was charged with sedition, convicted, and sentenced to three years of hard labor. In late 1939, while he was still in jail, his party was once again banned because of its bombing of Budapest's ornate Dohany Street synagogue, the largest in Europe. By the time of Szalasi's release in September 1940, the party had grown, notwithstanding his absence, to approximately 110,000 members, up from 8,000 in 1935. Although he was genuinely popular in Hungary, he lacked the charisma of the dictators of Germany, Italy, and Spain. He also did not possess the skill and vision to overcome the country's numerous, continually squabbling ultra-Right parties. A deep schism separated Hungarist (xenophobic) hegemonists, who admired the Nazis but feared Germany's territorial ambitions, and the "Aryan" supremacists, who idealized the Third Reich, idolized Hitler, and believed in a Hungarian-German common destiny. Despite political and ideological divisions and often bitter clashes among rival leaders, the ultra-Right eventually settled into two broad groupings: one largely made up of businesspeople and professionals engaged in fierce competition with their Jewish counterparts and the other composed of lower-class and dispossessed individuals who advocated a comprehensive socioeconomic and political restructuring of Hungary. Extreme antisemitism and irredentism were the integrating factors that helped to gloss over some of these conflicts.

The sudden and unexpected German occupation of Hungary in March 1944 caused a political upheaval. Nazi interference in Hungarian affairs grew ever more blatant. Outraged by Miklós Horthy's attempted armistice with the USSR on October 15, 1944, the Germans implemented their political option of last resort. Horthy was overthrown, and Ferenc Szalasi and his cohorts in the Nyilas (Arrow Cross) Party (a generic term for the ultra-Right) were put into power. Throughout Szalasi's brief but slavishly pro-Nazi regime, Budapest's Jews were subjected to unprecedented, systematic terror. A large "common" ghetto and a noncontiguous "international" ghetto for protective passport (*Schutzpass*) holders were established. The infamous death marches to Austria began. In the six chaotic weeks before the ghettos' liberation by Soviet forces in mid-January 1945, roaming bands of bloodthirsty Arrow Cross brigands slaughtered 10,000 to 15,000 Budapest Jews in cold blood. During the Nyilas regime, possibly 100,000 Hungarian Jews lost their lives.

Szalasi and his junta were captured by U.S. forces in Germany. On their return to Hungary, they were charged with war crimes, tried, convicted, sentenced to death, and executed in 1946.

—*Tom Kramer*

**See also** Horthy, Miklós; Hungary; Hungary, Holocaust in; Kallay, Miklós

**References**

Braham, Randolph L. *The Politics of Genocide: The Holocaust in Hungary*. 2 vols. (New York: Columbia University Press, 1994).

Deak, Istvan. "The Peculiarities of Hungarian Fascism." In *The Holocaust in Hungary: Forty Years Later*. Edited by Randolph L. Braham and Bela Vago. (New York: Columbia University Press, 1985), 43–51.

Kramer, T. D. *From Emancipation to Catastrophe: The Rise and Holocaust of Hungarian Jewry* (Lanham, MD: University Press of America, 2000).

# T

## Tacuara

Movimiento Nacionalista Tacuara, widely known for its struggle against the Jews, was a nationalist and neo-Nazi group that emerged in Argentina in the early 1960s. Its members were young men in their late teens and early twenties, many of them sons of nationalists of the 1930s and 1940s. Tacuara—the name signifies the traditional gaucho's lance—was responsible for violence against Jews after the abduction of Adolf Eichmann in Buenos Aires and his trial and execution in Israel. Early on, its members expressed deep admiration for German Nazism, Italian Fascism, and Spanish Falangism. It was a militant Catholic organization, and in the mid-1950s, its eventual founders had protested the anticlericalism of Juan Perón, the Argentine president (from 1946 to 1955 and 1973 to 1974).

Tacuara's spiritual leader was Fr. Julio Meinvielle, a prolific author and defender of the Catholic faith who passionately crusaded against the Jews. His book *El judio* (The Jew [1936]) was revised in 1959 and republished repeatedly as *El judio en el misterio de la historia* (The Jew in the Mystery of History). Meinvielle saw the Jews as responsible for both capitalism and socialism, ideologies antagonistic to Christians—"capitalism to rob Christians of what they have, and socialism to poison the have-nots, and thus establish a struggle of classes" (in Mirelman 1975, 209). True Christians had the right to resort to the sword to defend against the hypocritical tactics of the Jews, he argued, adding that Argentina was dominated by communist agents with Jewish links, including U.S. petroleum concerns, Jewish financial super-capitalism, and the U.S. State Department.

Almost immediately, splinter groups formed as a result of conflicting ideologies within Tacuara.

The most important was Guardia Restauradora Nacionalista (Nationalist Guard of the Restoration), which emerged in October 1960 after its advocates argued that Tacuara had become infiltrated by Marxists, Trotskyites, Fidelists, and atheists. Another faction moved to the Left, abandoning part of the original right-wing posture though retaining a fierce nationalism. This sector formed the Movimiento Nacionalista Revolucionario Tacuara (Revolutionary Nationalist Movement) in 1964 and a year later became known as Juventud Perónista de Buenos Aires (Perónist Youth of Buenos Aires), a belligerent leftist organization bolstered by a paramilitary arm and guerrilla-like training camps. It retained potent anti-Jewish, especially anti-Zionist, leanings.

Tacuara was responsible for the kidnapping of Gabriela Sirota, a Jewish student, and for tattooing swastikas on her breasts in 1962, as well as the killing of Raul Alterman, a Jewish activist in the Communist Party, in 1964. Throughout the 1960s and early 1970s, a large number of violent acts against Jews and Jewish institutions were committed by members of Tacuara, its splinter organizations, and other such groups. Police forces brought criminal accusations against some of them. The organized Jewish community repeatedly denounced Tacuara's activities and appealed to governmental authorities and the rest of the nation for justice.

—*Victor A. Mirelman*

**See also** Anti-Zionism; Argentina; Eichmann Trial
**References**
Avni, Haim. "Antisemitism in Argentina: The Dimensions of Danger." In *Approaches to Antisemitism: Context and Curriculum.* Edited by Michael Brown (New York: American Jewish Committee, 1994), 57–77.

Deutsch, Sandra McGee. "The Argentine Right and the Jews," *Journal of Latin American Studies* 18 (May 1986): 113–134.

Mirelman, Victor A. "Attitudes toward Jews in Argentina," *Jewish Social Studies* 37 (1975): 205–220.

## Talmud

Literally meaning "learning," *Talmud* is the Hebrew name given to two sets of ancient rabbinic discussions of Jewish law, thought, and folklore. The more popular is the 2.5-million-word Babylonian Talmud, which was compiled in the fifth century; a smaller and slightly older Jerusalem Talmud also exists. Unspecified references to the Talmud are generally to the Babylonian version.

Since the twelfth century, the Talmud has been used by a variety of groups attempting to ridicule or demonize Jews and Judaism. In the Middle Ages, these groups were primarily Christian. They called attention to Jewish legends recorded in the Talmud, some of which contain anthropomorphic elements, claiming that these legends demonstrate the irrationality and parochialism of Judaism; they were also offended by the Talmud's insistence on the centrality of rabbis in the interpretation of the religion. Later generations of Christian polemicists found talmudic material that was discriminatory, blasphemous, or disrespectful to Christianity or that—in a manner similar to the way Christians reinterpreted biblical passages—actually proved the truth of Christianity. A few scholars have argued that in attacking the Talmud, some medieval Christians were attempting to show that Jews had developed a religion that differed greatly from ancient biblical Judaism and that they thereby forfeited the toleration afforded them by the Augustinian doctrine that Jews served as witnesses to the surpassed truth of the Old Testament.

Debates over talmudic passages became an integral component of the famous disputations between Jews and Christians in the High Middle Ages. The Paris Disputation of 1240 should actually be considered a trial of the Talmud, with Nicholas Donin, a Jewish convert to Christianity, serving as prosecutor and Rabbi Yehiel ben Joseph of Paris in the role of defense counsel. Despite the efforts of the latter, the Talmud was

*When God Created his World*, from the Talmud, collected discussions of Jewish law and lore, Germany early 1300s. From the twelfth century to the present day, the Talmud has been used by a variety of groups attempting to ridicule or demonize Jews and Judaism. (The Art Archive/Bodleian Library Oxford/The Bodleian Library.Arch Selden A 5 folio 2v)

condemned by papal authorities and burned. Through the later Middle Ages and early modern period, the Talmud and other Jewish books were often confiscated, destroyed, banned, and censored by church authorities.

In modern times, the Talmud has continued to attract antisemites. Some are radical Christians who cannot give up the struggle against Judaism, even though the broader Christian world appears to have done so. Talmudically inspired attacks on Jews also come from a variety of non-Christian groups, including radical Muslims, anti-Zionists, white supremacists, and Holocaust deniers. One tool at their disposal is the Internet, which has allowed the survival, reproduction, and dissemination of previously obscure anti-Talmud tracts.

Antisemites who use the Talmud as the basis for their attacks on Jews tend to focus on several themes. They attempt to show that Judaism espouses hatred for non-Jews and that Jewish law discriminates against them, even encouraging violence. They claim that Judaism promotes obscenity, sexual perversion, and other immoral behavior on the part of contemporary Jews. Some go so far as to claim that a "talmudic mind-set" inspired Jews to create movements and revolutions throughout history that were damaging to non-Jews—with Marxism the most commonly proffered example.

Although they sometimes try to present themselves as disinterested scholars or as defenders of non-Jews against Jewish depredations, the antisemites who attack the Talmud reveal themselves in their methods and tactics. They almost always quote the Talmud out of context, both in relation to the surrounding passages and to Jewish law as elaborated on elsewhere in the Talmud. Some purportedly talmudic laws that are cited by antisemites are simply fabricated. Even where they cite the Talmud accurately, however, they refuse to make good-faith consultations with rabbis or Jewish scholars to understand how the passages have been interpreted by contemporary Jews. When Jews object to their interpretations or seek to explain how the talmudic passages have been modulated by normative Jewish practice in the sixteen centuries since the work's composition, antisemites dismiss these efforts as "hairsplitting" or as dishonest attempts to portray Judaism in a favorable light. From their methods, it is clear that those who attack the Talmud in this way are seeking ammunition against Jews rather than honest understanding of contemporary Judaism, its holy writings, and historical development. Some examples of distortions of the Talmud include:

- A statement by Rabbi Simeon b. Yohai in the Jerusalem Talmud (Kiddushin 4:11) that "the best of the non-Jews should be killed," which antisemites cite as "proof" that a non-Jew should suspect his or her Jewish neighbor of secretly plotting murder. But Jewish tradition has always understood this statement as referring to

opponents on the battlefield; R. Simeon, who lived during the Hadrianic persecutions of the second century CE and participated in the Bar Kochba Revolt against Rome, was urging his followers to not take the status of a non-Jewish opponent into account, for war cannot be fought with half measures. In fact, every subsequent citation of this statement in Jewish legal literature has appended the words *at the hour of battle* to R. Simeon's statement.

- Based on a statement in the Babylonian Talmud (Ketubot 11b), antisemites allege that Judaism encourages men to molest young girls. The statement reads, "If an adult has sex with a girl under the age of three, it is ignored." Far from encouraging pedophilia, however, the Talmud was discussing the laws of the *ketubah*—a sort of reverse dowry that a woman may collect from her husband's estate in the event of his death or their divorce. In normal circumstances, a woman who was a virgin at the time of marriage could claim a higher ketubah. The statement in question was simply establishing that if a girl has been raped under the age of three, she does not forfeit the higher ketubah when she eventually marries. Elsewhere, the Talmud states explicitly (Yevamoth 33b) that any adult who has sex with a minor is guilty of rape.

- The Talmud records the text of a formula to be recited by one who has made a vow that he or she regrets. By saying the formula under proper conditions, the oath-taker may be freed of the vow by talmudic law; a variant of this formula is included by many Jewish congregations in a prayer called Kol Nidrei, which is recited on the Jewish Day of Atonement. Antisemites cite the prayer as proof that one should not trust the promise of a Jew and that Jews are a deceitful people looking to take advantage of non-Jews. But the normative code of Jewish law clearly states (Shulhan Aruh Y.D. 211:4) that the Kol Nidrei prayer is merely a way of releasing oneself from ill-considered vows to undertake extra religious obligations. It does not annul interpersonal oaths, promises, or affirmations that a Jew may make; Jewish law only releases an individual from such a commitment with the approval of the other interested party.

—*Aryeh Tuchman*

**See also** Anti-Zionism; Augustine of Hippo; Bar Kochba Revolt; Bloch, Joseph Samuel; *Entdecktes Judenthum;* Holocaust Denial, Negationism, and Revisionism; Judeo-Bolshevism; Liutostanskii, Ippolit; Peter the Venerable; Pranaitis, Justinas; Rohling, August; Supersessionism; *Talmud Jew, The;* Talmud Trials

### References
Anti-Defamation League. *The Talmud in Anti-Semitic Polemics* (New York: ADL, 2003). http://www.adl.org/presrele/asus_12/the_talmud.pdf. (Accessed March 2, 2005).

Maccoby, Hyam. *Judaism on Trial: Jewish-Christian Disputations in the Middle Ages* (London: Littman Library, 1982).

## Talmud Jew, The

First published in 1871 by the radical Ultramontane priest August Rohling, *Der Talmudjude* (*The Talmud Jew*) was an annotated collection of false and distorted quotations from the Talmud. It swiftly became a classic of modern antisemitism. Although he had never studied the Talmud or the complex commentary pertaining to it, Rohling adapted Johann Andreas Eisenmenger's *Entdecktes Judenthum* (1711) in order to misrepresent its meaning and spirit intentionally. Anti-talmudic literature was not his innovation. But Rohling was able to trade on his position as a professor at the German University of Prague to present his forgeries, plagiarism, and distortions as a work of high "science." To most contemporaries, unable (like Rohling) to read the original, his book may well have seemed a plausible interpretation, even an unassailable one.

Readers of *The Talmud Jew* supposedly learned that Jews were permitted to practice all sorts of sins and vices: falsehood and chicanery, usury and theft, murder and adultery. According to Rohling, all were sanctioned by the Talmud, at least when dealing with Christians. But he went beyond the traditional theological framework of this genre to warn his audience of the increasing influence of Jews in modern societies. Incorporating the themes of a developing secular antisemitism, he presented Jews as involved in a worldwide conspiracy to achieve dominance over the Christian world. The book triggered fierce controversies and became infamous through the Tiszaeszlar blood libel trial (in 1882), when Rohling, an expert witness, testified that Jews were commanded by the Talmud to use Christian blood for their rites. In 1883, Joseph Samuel Bloch, a Viennese rabbi and member of parliament, published a series of articles under the title "An Offer to Commit Perjury," in which he branded Rohling a liar and forger. To save his reputation, Rohling was forced to institute proceedings against Bloch. In 1885, even before the trial opened, Bloch built a watertight case, having gathered testimony from respected scholars such as Franz Delitzsch and the well-known Orientalist Paul de Lagarde, an antisemite in his own right. Rohling lost the case, had to pay the costs of the trial, and was suspended from his university chair.

The exposure of its author as a fraud did not put an end to *The Talmud Jew*. It continued to appear and reappear in successive editions, twenty-two in all. It was translated into English (in the 1970s), French (by Édouard Drumont), Hungarian, and Russian. The book's extraordinarily successful reception cannot be adequately explained on the basis of its author's standing within the Catholic milieu. The thoroughgoing transformation of German society, the effects of liberalism and capitalism, and the struggle to define the new Germany brought in their train an abrupt and disorienting decline of traditional values. Thus, Rohling's absurd interpretation of Jewish influence fell on fertile ground, especially in the Catholic middle class that found itself particularly threatened by modernity. The founding of the German Empire, which coincided with Jewish emancipation, appeared suspicious to many, and it was not difficult to portray Jews as the prime agents of social decomposition. Their allegiance to political liberalism was another black mark against them, especially since the organized attack on German Catholicism, the *Kulturkampf* (struggle for civilization) of the 1870s, relied on liberal votes and voices. The church, through the Boniface Society for Catholic Germany, did not hesitate to cater to these fears and resentments, distributing 38,000 free copies of the sixth edition of *The Talmud Jew*.

Holding Jews responsible for the radical and upsetting changes of the late nineteenth century, the *Talmudjude* can be read as a simplistic response to a confused situation that forced Catholics onto the defensive. But Rohling's work also had more far-reaching consequences as an early attack on the human rights of Jews, one that the Nazis were later able to make full use of in their own propaganda.

—*Carsten Kretschmann*

**See also** Bloch, Joseph Samuel; Boniface Society for Catholic Germany; Drumont, Édouard; *Entdecktes Judenthum;* Kulturkampf; Lagarde, Paul de; Rohling, August; Talmud; Tiszaeszlar Ritual Murder; Ultramontanism
**References**
Noack, Hannelore. *Unbelehrbar? Antijüdische Agitation mit entstellten Talmudzitaten: Antisemitische Aufwiegelung durch Verteufelung der Juden* (Paderborn, Germany: University Press, 2001).
Tal, Uriel. *Christians and Jews in Germany: Religion, Politics, and Ideology in the Second Reich, 1870–1914* (London: Cornell University Press, 1975).

# Talmud Trials

Between 1240 and the later sixteenth century, Latin Christian authorities engaged in a series of disputations, trials, condemnations, acts of censorship, and burnings of the Talmud. Neither the Babylonian (*Bavli*) nor the Jerusalem (*Yerushalmi*) Talmud was widely known to western European Christians before the late twelfth and early thirteenth centuries, although the sharp criticism of the texts in the works of two Christian polemicists of the early twelfth century—Petrus Alfonsi (a convert from Judaism) and Peter the Venerable, the abbot of Cluny—were notable exceptions. Substantial Christian legislation concerning Jews in the letters of Pope Innocent III, the canons of the Fourth Lateran Council of 1215, and the 1324

canon law collection of Pope Gregory IX (r. 1227–1241) made no mention of it.

Around 1225, Nicholas Donin of La Rochelle, a Jew who had rejected the Talmud, was excommunicated by the Jewish community. He converted to Christianity around 1235 and around 1236 went to Rome, where he presented a list of charges against the Talmud to Gregory IX. In 1239, Gregory wrote to the prelates and rulers of Europe condemning the Talmud and appending thirty-five articles prepared by Donin and probably other apostates from Judaism, urging them to confiscate the books of the Jews, burn those that contained errors, and hand the rest over to appropriate clerical authorities for examination. Donin carried the letter to Paris. In May and June 1240, the Talmud became the subject of a trial at Vincennes under the presidency of Queen Mother Blanche of Castile, with several bishops as judges and Donin apparently as accuser; Rabbi Yehiel b. Joseph of Paris handled the defense. This proceeding was the first Talmud trial. Although no formal condemnation is recorded, perhaps twenty cartloads of books in Hebrew, around 10,000 volumes, were publicly burned in Paris in 1242. Donin later compiled a treatise of excerpts from the Talmud allegedly containing expressions of hostility toward Christianity.

Jewish authorities in France appealed to Pope Innocent IV (r. 1243–1254), who in 1247 charged Odo of Chateauroux to form a commission of inquiry composed of forty-one Paris theologians, including Albertus Magnus, as well as Donin. The report of Odo's committee condemned the Talmud for errors, abuses, and blasphemies, and Innocent IV concluded, in addition, that the Talmud was heretical in terms of biblical Judaism. Attacks on the Talmud continued in force until the 1320s, when they appear to have temporarily ended before resuming briefly but intensively in the mid-sixteenth century.

—*Edward Peters*

**See also** *Entdecktes Judenthum;* Innocent III; Lateran Council, Fourth; Middle Ages, High; Peter the Venerable; Rohling, August; Talmud; *Talmud Jew, The*
**References**
Cohen, Jeremy. *Living Letters of the Law: Ideas of*

the Jew in Medieval Christianity (Berkeley: University of California Press, 1999), 317–334.

Rembaum, Joel E. "The Talmud and the Popes: Reflections on the Talmud Trials of the 1240s," Viator 13 (1982): 203–223.

Resnick, Irven. "Talmud, Talmudisti, and Albert the Great," Viator 33 (2002): 69–86.

Simonsohn, Schlomo. The Apostolic See and the Jews. Vol. 1, Documents, 492–1404 (Toronto, Canada: Pontifical Institute of Mediaeval Studies, 1988), 171–174; discussed in vol. 7, History, 297–307.

## Theater, Nazi Purge of Jewish Influence in

In the realm of cultural policy and propaganda, the Nazis put special emphasis on the theater because they ascribed to it an extraordinary capacity to influence human consciousness. Joseph Goebbels, who pursued German studies under the guidance of the Jewish historian of literature Friedrich Gundolf and who had also tried writing theater pieces, saw in both theater and the plastic arts the same creative and shaping power at work. Intent on placing the stage in the service of their völkisch ideology, the Nazis thought that the German theater could be restored to health by making it once again "nationalistic." Meanwhile, the creative, taboo-breaking, and challenging stage productions of the democratic Weimar Republic were subjected to their hate-filled attacks. In 1925, Adolf Hitler thundered against a theater that had sunk to depths so low that German youth needed to be protected from it. "How inflamed Schiller would be, how outraged Goethe! . . . For it is characteristic of this era that it not only produces mere filth but that it besmirches what was truly great in the past" (Mein Kampf, 259).

In the 1920s, the Nazis exploited the animosities already being deployed against the urbane, big-city theater by conservatives and rightists who depicted it as a product of the "Marxist-liberal-Jewish conspiracy." They also played to the resentments, evident for decades, of the educated bourgeoisie and its lower-middle-class imitators with regard to the avant-garde. This rebellion against modernity was waged with the slogan of a German theater "contaminated by the Jews." "The truth," proclaimed Hans Severus Ziegler, "is that since the turn of the century we have had a German theater of the Jewish nation. It is obvious therefore that this stage cannot and does not mirror German national culture but rather the Jewish spirit of the times." An inflammatory piece written during this era by Elisabeth Frenzel—and blithely published again after 1945—stated that 80 percent of the theater directors in Berlin were Jews and that in the year 1925, 95 of the 260 premiers were by Jewish authors. She remained silent, however, about the historical reasons for this Jewish presence in the arts.

To drain the "Jewish theater swamp" and "cleanse the temple of German art" became the task of the boundlessly cynical Goebbels and his rival Alfred Rosenberg, the man responsible for the "total spiritual and ideological schooling and education of the Nazi Party." Together, they recruited a phalanx of inquisitors who went about demanding proof of Aryan ancestry. Of course, there were exceptions. For example, the Jewish descent of Franz Lehar could be overlooked because Hitler was a fan of the composer's Merry Widow. Corrupt and self-serving, full of blackmail and chicanery, a campaign of annihilation was conducted against the "Jewish element" in the German theater. Its consequences were exile, suicide, deportation, and murder.

The criminals of the National Socialist regime found their accomplices among characterless academic humanists, theater critics, and so-called Aryan authors. Thomas Mann described their mentality as an amalgam of ideologically tainted linguistics, romantic Germanism, and Nordic religion. They traded in an idiom of mystical philistinism and extraordinary tastelessness, drumming their "heroic," "racial," "völkisch" clichés into the German public. Non-Jewish theater people behaved maliciously, indifferently, or simply looked the other way, as did, for example, Gustav Gründgens, one of the most popular film and theater personalities in the Weimar Republic, under the Nazis, and again in the Federal Republic of Germany.

Jews, as members of an inferior race, were stigmatized. However, the word Jewish was employed to defame all who did not conform to Nazi canons of art and culture. "Jewish looks" could also awaken mistrust. Thus, Rosenberg's office objected that Otto Laubinger, the first president of the Reich Theater Chamber (part of whose job was the expulsion of non-Aryan artists), did not "look German enough." The physical appearance of the beloved film comedian Theo Lingen was also cause for concern; it might lead the German people to believe that the de-Jewification of German cultural life had made no progress at all (Drewniak 1983).

The cultural exodus from Germany after 1933 comprised approximately 4,000 well-known actors, actresses, film and theater directors, script writers, dancers, choreographers, cabaret artists, and music and theater critics. They were considered Jewish in one way or another, either by descent or in spirit or both. Jews by descent included Max Reinhardt, Leopold Jessner, Fritz Kortner, and Elisabeth Bergner. Albert Bassermann left Germany because his Jewish wife could no longer perform. Joachim Gottschalk, one of the most popular young actors and star of several Ufa films, committed suicide along with his wife, who would have had to leave the country because she was Jewish. Before they died, they killed their son. When he had previously been pressured by an official in the Propaganda Ministry to divorce his wife, he asked what would become of her and his child. "Who cares what happens to a Jewess?" was the answer. Almost all the Jewish theater people who could not or would not flee Germany were killed in concentration or death camps. Among them were Otto Bernstein, Willy Buschoff, Kurt Gerron, Fritz Grünbaum, and Otto Walburg.

In summary, it can be said that a great number of those who had raised German theater in the 1920s to preeminence in the world and who broke new ground, either by bold and original stagings or impressive acting achievements, fled Germany or were killed. "The hardest man is for the iron future still not hard enough," intoned Rosenberg (Rosenberg 1941). Perhaps a more telling epigram was the one uttered by the visionary Franz Grillparzer in 1848: in Germany, "the path of modern culture leads from humanity through nationality to bestiality."

—*Hermann Glaser*
*Richard S. Levy, translation*

**See also** Degenerate Art; Goebbels, Joseph; Hitler, Adolf; Music, Nazi Purge of Jewish Influence in; Nazi Cultural Antisemitism; Rosenberg, Alfred
**References**
Drewniak, Boguslaw. *Das Theater im NS-Staat: Szenarium deutscher Zeitgeschichte 1933–1945* (Düsseldorf, Germany: Droste, 1983).
Liebe, Ulrich. *Verehrt, verfolgt, vergessen: Schauspieler als Naziopfer* (Weinheim/Berlin: Beltz Quadriga, 1992).
Möller, Horst. *Exodus der Kultur: Schriftsteller, Wissenschaftler und Künstler in der Emigration nach 1933* (Munich, Germany: C. H. Beck, 1984).
Rosenberg, Alfred. 1941. *Blut und Ehre. Ein Kampf für die deutsche Wiedergeburt. Reden und Aufsätz von 1919–1933* (Munich: Zentralverlag der N.S.D.A.P., 1941).
Wulf, Joseph. *Theater und Film im Dritten Reich: Eine Dokumentation* (Frankfurt am Main, Germany: Ullstein, 1983).

## Theodosian Code

Under Theodosius II (r. 408–450), Roman emperor of the East, an official collection of the statutes of the Christian emperors, called the *Codex Theodosianus* (Theodosian Code, hereafter C. Th.), was compiled. In 438, for the first time, the special laws regarding the Jews were systematically and conveniently brought together in one collection. Book 16 deals specifically with religious matters, and chapters 8 and 9 of this book are dedicated specifically to the legislation on the Jews and Samaritans. However, other parts of the code also contain laws regarding the Jews, sorted according to their context. A valuable historical source, the code can tell us much about the declining position of the Jews in the late Roman Empire.

The section of the code discussing "Jews living according to Roman and Common law" still classified them as Roman citizens (C. Th. 2.1.10). But the code also reveals that they had gradually come under special limitations, especially in their religious practices and in the sorts of relationships they could have with Christians. For example, they were prohibited from circumcising their Christian slaves and were threatened with exile and the death penalty if found to have done so (C. Th. 16.8.26). At first, the Christian emperors did not alter the privileges granted to the patriarch, whose ancient position they recognized (C. Th. 16.8.13, 15, and 17), but the patriarch's position suffered substantially from serious restrictions in an important law (the "Constitution" found in C. Th. 2.1.10). This law defined Jewish judicial autonomy: the constitution allowed for the Jews to appear before Jewish tribunals on various religious matters, but on civil matters, the jurisdiction was reserved to the state courts exclusively. The law permitted the appearance before Jewish tribunals provided that both parties consented, in which case, the Jewish tribunals functioned as arbitrators. C. Th. 15.5.5 prohibited all gatherings—explicitly Jewish gatherings—from being held on a Sunday. A list of other Christian festivals, during which no gatherings were allowed, was later added. The Christian emperors affirmed the prohibition on Jews taking part in public or private transactions on the day of the Jewish Sabbath and during other Jewish festivals (C. Th. 16.8.20; 2.8.26; 8.8.8). In the year 408, the Emperors Honorius and Theodosius issued a decree (C. Th. 16.8.18) banning certain kinds of expressive conduct, specifically during the Festival of Purim, which might be interpreted as being contemptuous of Christians. In 425, Theodosius II and Valentinianus enacted the law prohibiting a Jewish father from disowning his Jewish child or grandchild who converted to Christianity.

The Christian emperors' policy of unification—their attempt to bring the disparate elements of the empire under one system of law—was bound to erode the tolerance that had once allowed Jews, de facto, to govern their personal lives according to Jewish law and custom. C. Th. 16.8.6 barred Jewish men from taking Christian or pagan women out of the *gynaeceum* (the emperor's textile industry) to be their spouses. This rule was then extended more generally to apply to all Christian women. Typically, this limitation imposed on Jewish conduct had a variety of motives, including the fear of economic competition from the Jewish textile industry and religious-moral objections—marriage between a Jew and Christian was likened to adultery (C. Th. 3.7.2).

Over time, the Christian emperors grew especially concerned when the property rights of Jews impacted Christians. For example, when the laws governing the owning of Christian slaves were established, only the circumcision of the slaves was prohibited, reaffirming the decrees of the Emperors Antoninus and Severus (C. Th. 16.9.1). Later, the acquisition of a Christian slave was altogether prohibited, whether purchased or acquired as a gift. However, it was permitted to inherit such slaves and to continue using them, provided that their freedom of religion was safeguarded (C. Th. 16.9.2–5).

On January 31, 438, Theodosius II and Valentinian barred Jews from holding any state employment or administrative office (N. Th.3). This *novella* (new law) represented a dramatic further weakening of the position of the Jews.

—*Alfredo Mordechai Rabello*

**See also** Church Fathers; Circumcision; Constantine, Emperor; Gregory the Great, Pope; Justinian Code; Roman Empire

**References**

Linder, Amnon. *The Jews in Roman Imperial Legislation* (Detroit, MI: Wayne State University Press, 1987).

Rabello, A. M. "The Legal Conditions of the Jews in the Roman Empire." In *Aufstieg und Niedergang der Römischen Welt*. Vol. 13 (Berlin: Walter de Gruyter, 1980), 662–762.

———. *The Jews in the Roman Empire: Legal Problems—From Herod to Justinian*. Variorum Collected Studies series (Aldershot, UK: Ashgate, 2000).

## Theosophy

The Theosophical Society was founded in New York City on September 13, 1875, by Col. Henry Olcott and Helena Petrovna Blavatsky (1831–1891). Part religion, part philosophical movement, Theosophy—literally meaning "wisdom of the gods" or "divine wisdom"—had a threefold purpose: to study comparative religions within an essentialist methodological framework, to explore paranormal phenomena and the occult faculties of humans, and to help bring about a universal brotherhood of peoples through humane means.

These complex and often conflicting goals reflect the conflicted nature of its founders' thinking, especially that of Blavatsky, whose *Isis Unveiled* (1875) and *The Secret Doctrine* (1888) still exist as classic Theosophical texts. Her works stand also as monumental testaments to autodidacticism and plagiarism. Often without acknowledging her sources, Blavatsky freely borrowed ideas from Eastern and Western esoteric texts, various mythologies, and even the fiction of the nineteenth-century English novelist Edward Bulwer Lytton in order to produce an extensive, if inconsistent, treatment of world religions, cosmology, and human evolution. She disagreed with Charles Darwin's theory of evolution, preferring to believe that human beings were descended from spiritual aliens. The appeal of Theosophy, however, owed less to the eccentric ideas of Blavatsky than to its own strong emphasis on Buddhist and Hindu mysticism, which had become very popular in fin-de-siècle European and American society.

This Eastern emphasis, which, despite Theosophy's stated goal of studying comparative religions, existed largely at the expense of the monotheistic religions, became all the more pronounced when the society moved its headquarters from New York to Adyar, outside of Madras in India in 1878. By the mid-1880s, the society had 121 lodges worldwide and a varied and distinguished membership, including William Butler Yeats, Alfred Russell Wallace, and Thomas Edison. Exact membership numbers are difficult to determine, but it appears that by 1907, Theosophy had at least 100,000 official members throughout the world and probably a much larger unofficial membership. By the 1930s, in the face of the harsh realities of an imminent world war, Theosophy began to decline in popularity. The society still exists today, but 1998 estimates place its official membership at approximately only 36,000.

Especially in its formative years, Theosophical thought was a grab-bag of ideas that attracted a diverse group of people, not all of them emotionally stable or well intentioned. Some, such as Franz Hartmann (1838–1912) and the antisemitic Ariosophists in early twentieth-century Germany and Austria, found Theosophy's disinterest in the Western monotheistic faiths and its stress on the superiority of Aryan spiritual ideals an ideal venue through which they could more legitimately separate their culture from Judeo-Christian tradition and promote an antisemitic

agenda. Still, if there is little in Theosophy that actively encouraged such a program, there is also little that discouraged it. The eclectic nature of the movement and the confusing writings of early Theosophists have left the door open for individual Theosophists, if so inclined, to make a variety of unsavory claims.

—*Keith R. Green*

*See also* Blavatsky, Helena P.; Lanz von Liebenfels, Jörg; List, Guido von; New Age; Pelley, William Dudley; Steiner, Rudolph
**References**
Mosse, George L. "The Mystical Origins of National Socialism." *Journal of the History of Ideas* 22 (1961): 81–96.
Washington, Peter. *Madame Blavatsky's Baboon: A History of the Mystics, Mediums, and Misfits Who Brought Spiritualism to America* (New York: Schocken Books, 1995).

## "Three Hundred," The

The myth of the "Three Hundred" originated in the published comments of Walther Rathenau that appeared in the 1909 Christmas edition of Vienna's *Neue Freie Presse* (New Free Press). "Three hundred men, all of whom know one another, guide the economic destinies of the Continent and seek their successors from within their own environment." Rathenau actually deplored the oligarchic nature of this "truth" and nowhere suggested that the Three Hundred ruled over the heads of governments or that they were Jews. But by 1912, the words took on a life of their own. Theodor Fritsch characterized them as an "open confession of indubitable Jewish hegemony" and Rathenau as "really the secret Kaiser of Germany" (in Levy 1991, 197). The myth served as absolute proof of a Jewish conspiracy and that a secret Jewish world government already existed.

After the spurious *Protocols of the Elders of Zion* was published in Germany in 1920, the myth of the Three Hundred spread dramatically. Propagated by antisemitic organizations such as the German Racial League for Defense and Defiance and by prominent leaders such as Erich Ludendorff, the myth morphed into the "Three Hundred Elders of Zion" and assumed a near-religious truth for the racist Right. That Rathenau was one of the Elders could not be doubted, since he obviously knew their exact number.

Rathenau addressed the swelling of this myth in a 1921 letter to an old school friend, stating that the "Three Hundred" he referred to were not meant as Jews but rather as the leaders of the international business world. The insidious story turned deadly in June 1922 when Rathenau was assassinated by young radicals associated with extremist organizations and nurtured on this and related antisemitic myths. At the murder trial, one of the defendants explicitly cited Rathenau's membership in the Three Hundred Elders of Zion as his reason for committing the deed. Whether this was merely a propaganda ploy, as some have suggested, or an accurate description of the perpetrator's motives, it is clear that the myth provided an ideological legitimation for political murder.

In response to Rathenau's murder, the Reichstag passed the tough Law for the Protection of the Republic that made it possible to prosecute publicists who propagated the myth. However, the Nazis continued to make frequent use of it in their propaganda throughout the 1920s and 1930s. Variations are still being used by the radical Right today.

—*Mark Swartzburg*

**See also** Fritsch, Theodor; German Racial League for Defense and Defiance; Germanic Order; Ludendorff, Erich; *Protocols of the Elders of Zion;* Rathenau, Walther; Weimar

**References**

Cohn, Norman. *Warrant for Genocide: The Myth of the Jewish World Conspiracy and the "Protocols of the Elders of Zion."* New ed. (London: Serif, 1996).

Levy, Richard S., ed. *Antisemitism in the Modern World: An Anthology of Texts* (Lexington, MA: D. C. Heath, 1991).

## Thule Society

Founded in Munich by Rudolf von Sebottendorf on August 17, 1918, the Thule Society was originally a cover organization for the racist Germanic Order (Germanen-Orden) in Bavaria. One of a welter of fringe groups on the radical Right, the Thule Society was small but briefly important. Its approximately 1,500 members participated in the revolutionary upheavals of 1918 and 1919 and helped give birth to the Nazi Party. The society, with a strong affinity for the occult, served as a collection point for right-wing radicals and reactionaries; its chief activities were the diffusion of antisemitic propaganda and the hatching of conspiracies. Sebottendorf acquired the newspaper *Münchener Beobachter* (Munich Observer) to publish the group's propaganda. This newspaper eventually became the *Völkischer Beobachter* (Racist Observer), the organ of the Nazi Party.

The Thule Society was especially active in the fight to overthrow the Bavarian Soviet republic following the 1918 November revolution. It made several attempts to assassinate Kurt Eisner, the Bavarian Independent Socialist prime minister. Eisner was eventually murdered by a young officer, Count Anton von Arco-Valley, allegedly after he had been turned away from the Thule Society because of his Jewish background. Following the communist takeover in Munich, the Thule Society engaged in arms smuggling and espionage and founded the Freikorps (vigilante mercentaries) group Oberland in April 1919. The communists raided Thule Society headquarters, taking seven prominent members hostage; these individuals were subsequently shot, providing martyrs for the radical Right and a rationale for bloody repressive measures by counterrevolutionary forces.

The Thule Society counted several early Nazis as members or associates, including Rudolph Hess, Gottfried Feder, Alfred Rosenberg, Dietrich Eckart, Hans Frank, and Anton Drexler. Hitler, apparently, was never a member. The Thulists provided support and ideological direction for Drexler's German Worker's Party, the direct antecedent of the Nazi Party, and also passed along their swastika symbol. The Thule Society's influence faded with the rise of the Nazi Party. Sebottendorf tried to revive it after 1933, and in his book *Bevor Hitler Kam* (Before Hitler Came), he claimed it had been the vanguard of the Nazi movement. The Nazis, tolerating no competition, suppressed both the book and the society. Sebottendorf was forced to leave the country.

—*Mark Swartzburg*

*See also* Blavatsky, Helena P.; Hitler, Adolf; Judeo-Bolshevism; List, Guido von; National Socialist German Workers' Party; Rosenberg, Alfred; Weimar

**References**

Goodrick-Clarke, Nicholas. *The Occult Roots of Nazism* (New York: New York University Press, 1992).

Phelps, Reginald H. "Before Hitler Came: Thule Society and Germanen Orden." *Journal of Modern History* 35 (1963): 245–261.

## Tiso, Jozef (1887–1947)

Jozef Tiso, the president of the Slovak state from 1939 to 1945, was born October 13, 1887, in Bytča in northern Slovakia. After leaving school, he studied theology in Vienna and graduated in 1911, having been consecrated a priest the year before. As long as Slovakia belonged to Hungary, Tiso seems not to have been politically active. But in 1918, he joined the Slovak People's Party (SPP), later to be renamed the Hlinka Slovak People's Party (HSPP). This party drew supporters mostly from rural central and northern Slovakia. Nationalist and strongly conservative to begin with, it later developed authoritarian and anti-Jewish tendencies, as well.

From 1925 onward, Tiso was elected a member of the Czechoslovak parliament. In 1927, when the SPP first joined a government coalition, he became minister of health. But two years later, after Vojtech Tuka, a leading member of the SPP had been charged with treason, the SPP went back into opposition. During the 1930s, Tiso developed into one of the leading politicians of this party. His accession to power came after Hlinka's death and following the Munich Pact of September 29, 1938. The HSPP was now the single ruling party in the "autonomous country of Slovakia." Since Hitler's ambitions for the region had not been satisfied at Munich, he wanted the HSPP to help him undermine Czechoslovakia from within by demanding autonomous statehood for Slovakia. After talks in Berlin, Tiso arranged for a session of the Slovak parliament, and on March 14, 1939, Slovakia declared its independence. Tiso became the country's first president, and from 1942, he took the title *vodca* (leader).

Although Tiso would have preferred real independence, Slovakia was bound to Nazi Germany by various agreements, and as head of state, he was politically responsible for Slovak collaboration with the Third Reich. This cooperation required Slovakia's participation in Germany's war effort against Poland and the Soviet Union; it also included collaboration in the Final Solution. In 1942, about 58,000 Jews were deported from Slovakia to the German death camps. Although Tiso's followers even today claim that he had nothing to do with the transports, this contention stands on weak ground. In August 1942, as the transports were under way, Tiso, in his infamous speech in Holič, declared the Jews to be the enemies of the Slovaks and asked his fellow citizens to get rid of them. Tiso issued fewer so-called exemptions from deportation than did the other ministers of the Slovak government.

Even protests from the Vatican, voiced by the chargé d'affaires, Giuseppe Burzio, failed to move him. In his politically tainted trial, which began in 1946, he showed no remorse about the deportations, sticking to his belief that Slovakia had needed to "solve the Jewish Question." On April 15, 1947, the Czechoslovak People's Court sentenced Tiso to death; three days later, the judgement was executed.

—*Tatjana Tönsmeyer*

*See also* Croatia; Hlinka Guard; Holocaust; Hungary, Holocaust in; Pius XII; Slovakia, Holocaust in

**References**

Felak, James Ramon. *"At the price of the Republic": Hlinka's Slovak People's Party, 1929–1938* (Pittsburgh, PA: University of Pittsburgh Press, 1994).

Jelinek, Yeshayahu A. *The Parish Republic: Hlinka's Slovak People's Party, 1939–1945* (Boulder, CO: East European Monographs, 1976).

Kamenec, Ivan. *Dr. Jozef Tiso, 1887–1947* (Bratislava: Archa, 1998).

## Tiszaeszlar Ritual Murder (1882)

In the semifeudal, largely impoverished provinces of nineteenth-century Hungary, anti-Jewish prejudice rested on ingrained medieval beliefs regarding the "avaricious, satanic, Christ-killer" Jews. Deep suspicions were thus aroused when, on April 1, 1882, a fourteen-year-old domestic servant, Eszter Solymosi, disappeared from Tiszaeszlar, a village in northeastern Hungary. Because she vanished just three days before the Jewish Passover festival and was last seen near the local synagogue, a small group of parliamentary antisemites, including the representative for Tiszaeszlar, alleged that Jews had murdered the girl to use her blood for baking matzah, the unleavened bread eaten by Jews during Passover.

The extended investigation and subsequent trial, exploited by antisemites and broadcast by the sensational press, both secular and religious, turned the Tiszaeszlar case into one of the most famous "ritual murder" affairs of modern times. In scope and passion and in the damage done to political discourse in Hungary, Tiszaeszlar resembled the later Dreyfus Affair in France.

Supervised by officials already hostile toward the local Jewish community, the investigators used subterfuge and physical brutality to coerce a fourteen-year-old local Jewish youth, Moric Scharf, into confessing that he had witnessed his father and a group of Jews murder Eszter Solymosi in the synagogue and then drain her blood into a container. The acrimonious trial, accompanied by the widest possible publicity, demonstrations of public furor, and frenzied debates in parliament, ended on August 3, 1883, with the acquittal of all fifteen defendants. The outcome was inevitable, following the prosecutor's acknowledgment that the defendants were, in fact, innocent.

Judicial dismissal of the blood libel did not quell the antisemitic agitation. Demonstrations swept the country, with pogroms erupting in several places, even "sophisticated, cosmopolitan" Budapest (between August 5 and 12). The acquittal was upheld by both the Court of Appeal (in December 1883) and the Supreme Court (in April 1884), but neither ruling silenced the antisemites. Their propaganda continued to denounce the verdict, attributing it to the nefarious influence of the Jews on the Hungarian judiciary.

The extended furor engendered by Tiszaeszlar proved a decisive crossroads in the history of Hungarian Judeophobia. Slurs on the moral integrity of Jews and Judaism, previously based on medieval bigotry, were henceforth integrated into a "modern" antisemitism claiming so-called race science as its foundation. In this new format, ritual murder became an adjunct to xenophobia, "racial purity," and "Aryan supremacy."

—*Tom Kramer*

*See also* Beilis Case; Dreyfus Affair; Konitz Ritual Murder; Racism, Scientific; Ritual Murder (Medieval); Ritual Murder (Modern); Xanten Ritual Murder

**References**

Kramer, T. D. *From Emancipation to Catastrophe: The Rise and Holocaust of Hungarian Jewry* (Lanham, MD: University Press of America, 2000).

Patai, Raphael. *The Jews of Hungary: History, Culture, Psychology* (Detroit, MI: Wayne State University Press, 1996).

Stern, Edith. *The Glorious Victory of Truth: The Tiszaeszlar Blood Libel Trial, 1882–1883—A Historical-Legal-Medical Research* (Jerusalem: Rubin Mass, 1998).

## Tivoli Program (1892)

At the Tivoli congress, held in the Tivoli beer hall in suburban Berlin in December 1892, the German Conservative Party (DKP) embraced antisemitism as a means of making the party more popular. The congress came at a time of crisis within Conservative Party politics, when Otto von Bismarck's successor as German chancellor, Leo von Caprivi, began to dismantle the Bismarckian system of agricultural protection and pursue policies seen as favoring industrialists and unions. The highlight of the congress was a power struggle between traditional governmentalist Conservatives (led by prominent Prussian aristocrats) and more radical Conservatives (led by Wilhelm von Hammerstein and Court Chaplain Adolf Stoecker) who wanted to pursue policies opposed to those of the Caprivi government. The radicals also argued that, to be electorally successful and to compensate for its shrinking social base, the party needed to accept a more "populist" platform in place of the one drafted in 1876. According to James Retallack, this meant abandoning the traditional elitist disdain for antisemitic rabble-rousing and putting in place a more pronouncedly antisemitic agenda.

That agenda, however, was not forthcoming. The party's oligarchic leadership prepared a short, balanced clause for the program that read, "We combat the manifold upsurging and decomposing Jewish influence in our national life. . . . We condemn the excesses of antisemitism." In a floor vote, however, Stoecker and his allies succeeded in having the second clause dropped from the program. This defeat cost the leadership little—they retained the all-important control of the party apparatus, while taking the wind out of the sails of the independent antisemites. As Richard Levy has correctly observed, "Had the Conservative party chosen to take up the interests of peasants and *Mittelständler* [the lower middle class] and to develop an anti-Semitic program in earnest, the history of the independent anti-Semitic parties might have ended abruptly in 1892. However, the Conservatives made little actual use of Tivoli and usually ignored the implications of their anti-Semitic clause" (Levy 1975, 85).

—*George S. Vascik*

See also Agrarian League; Ahlwardt, Hermann; Antisemitic Political Parties; Stoecker, Adolf
**References**
Levy, Richard S. *The Downfall of the Anti-Semitic Political Parties in Imperial Germany* (New Haven, CT: Yale University Press, 1975).
Retallack, James N. *Notables of the Right* (Boston: Unwin Hyman, 1988).

# Toland, John (1670–1722)

Born in northern Ireland in 1670, John Toland fashioned a career characterized by constant conflict with recognized clerical authorities, the result of his outspoken views on the nature of religion. Educated as a Catholic, he converted to Protestantism in his youth. While pursuing his studies in Glasgow and Edinburgh and later in Utrecht and Leiden, he came under the influence of various secret societies and radical groups and the dissenting theological positions they professed. His unorthodox orientation to the Scriptures intensified after he spent time in London, socializing with various anti-Trinitarian figures and deists. In 1695, he anonymously published *Christianity Not Mysterious,* a controversial work that criticized conventional Christian theology and engendered heated controversy. This was the first of many works that continually earned him derogatory epithets, such as "heretic," "notorious Socinian," and "atheist."

After having campaigned in London in support of the Whig bill to naturalize foreign Protestants, he published *Reasons for Naturalizing the Jews in Great Britain and Ireland* (1714). Although this work failed to have a significant impact in its day, it became an important source for later advocates of the improvement of Jewish legal status. Toland's pamphlet considered and dismissed many of the common prejudices against Jews and called for their being placed "on the same foot with all other nations." Like the Jewish apologists before him (for example, Menasseh ben Israel and Simon Luzzatto), Toland rejected the claims that Jews could not be loyal residents of any country. Following John Locke's *Letter on Toleration,* he argued that since Jews had no country of their own and no foreign loyalties, unlike Catholics who were "bound to Rome," they would become completely devoted residents and refrain from any subversive political activity. If the English would put them on a par with other residents in society, Jews would be forever wedded to English society, as they had shown themselves to be dedicated to those countries that granted them the privilege to remain in their midst. Even though he miscalculated in finding that Jews were as numerous as the French and the Spanish, Toland was not deterred from advocating their immigration and naturalization.

He thought very highly of the Jews and of their "Mosaic Republic." In *Nazarenus, or Jewish, Gentile, and Mahometan Christianity* (1718), he even reckoned that the Jews would someday end their dispersion and return to Palestine and "by reason of their excellent constitution, be much more populous, rich, and powerful than any nation in the world." He thought it in the best interest of Christians to help them in this process. Toland's reasoning was clear: shorn of sovereignty and territory, Jews were prospectively ideal citizens.

—*Richard I. Cohen*

See also Dohm, Christian Wilhelm von; Emancipation; Grégoire, Henri-Baptiste; Jew Bill; Philosemitism
**References**
Cohen, Richard I. "Jews and the State: The Historical Context." In *Studies in Contemporary Jewry.* Edited by Ezra Mendelsohn. (2004): 19:3–16.

Sullivan, Robert E. *John Toland and the Deist Controversy: A Story in Adaptations* (Cambridge, MA: Harvard University Press, 1982).

# Torquemada, Tomás de (1420–1498)

Tomás de Torquemada was born in Valladolid, Spain, in 1420. Rumors and claims about his being of Jewish descent are very unreliable. One of his uncles was Cardinal Juan de Torquemada. In his early youth, Tomás became a Dominican monk in his hometown. In 1452, he was appointed prior of the Monastery of Santa Cruz at Segovia.

From February 1482, he worked for the recently established Castilian Inquisition, which had been authorized by the pope in 1482. Only one year later, he became general inquisitor, that is, chief of the Inquisition for Castile and then, in 1484, for Aragon as well. He was responsible for the nomination of new inquisitors, whom he chose mainly from among the Dominicans. Torquemada developed the Spanish Inquisition, which was under the control of not the pope but of the Spanish kings, into the first bureaucracy for all of Castile and Aragon. Tribunals were established in all important cities. In 1484, Torquemada convened a general assembly of all inquisitors in Seville. There, he presented uniform guidelines for the activity of the Inquisition. In 1488, he created the Supreme Council (Consejo Supremo) of the Spanish Inquisition, which he headed.

Torquemada gained the confidence of the Catholic rulers of Aragon and Castile, Ferdinand and Isabella, whom he served as father confessor and confidential adviser. The decree on the expulsion of all Jews in 1492 was mainly the result of his initiative. He justified this and other draconian measures with the argument that Jews who converted to Christianity lacked firmness and were prone to relapse into Judaism. This concern for the purity of the faith, rather than cruelty for its own sake, is probably what motivated him. Still, Torquemada stands in history as the inquisitor par excellence, a fanatic, and a relentless enemy of the Jews. Until his death in Ávila in 1498, the Inquisition pronounced several thousand death sentences, and he was known to have intervened repeatedly when he thought a sentence to be too mild.

—Bernd Rother

**See also** *Auto-da-fé;* Dominican Order; Inquisition
**References**
Netanyahu, Benzion. *The Origins of the Inquisition in Fifteenth Century Spain*. 2nd ed. (New York: New York Review Books, 2001).
Roth, Norman. *Conversos, Inquisition, and the Expulsion of the Jews from Spain* (Madison: University of Wisconsin Press, 1995).

# Toussenel, Alphonse (1803–1885)

A disciple of Charles Fourier, the journalist Alphonse Toussenel became the coeditor of the Fourierist movement's journal, *La Phalange,* in 1839 and helped found another, *La Démocratie pacifique,* in the 1840s. In the 1830s, he worked closely with the avowed anti-Jewish Catholic activist Louis Veuillot at the right-wing newspaper *La Paix.* Toussenel's most enduring work was his two-volume anti-Jewish tract entitled *The Jews, Kings of the Epoch: History of Financial Feudalism,* first published in 1845. Inspired by a unique combination of Fourierism and aspects of Ultramontane Catholicism, the work sparked little public debate at the time of its publication; it was not even reviewed in the Fourierist journals themselves. However, it became extremely significant later on when its main arguments were appropriated by Henri Gougenot des Mousseaux and then by the notorious antisemite Édouard Drumont in his best-selling work, *La France juive* (1886).

In *The Jews, Kings of the Epoch,* Toussenel identified Jews as new "aristocrats" comparable to the nobles of Old Regime France because, as usurious bankers and industrial capitalists, the Jews did not work but instead profited from the toil of the increasingly impoverished French people. In spite of its fiercely anti-Jewish content, the work was seen as relatively unimportant by the contemporary French Jewish press; Samuel Cahen, editor of *Les Archives israélites,* dismissed it as misguided socialism rather than true anti-Jewish prejudice in his 1845 review, perhaps because Toussenel's book departed in significant ways from traditional anti-Judaism. For example, it defined Jews not as adherents of the Jewish religion but rather as all who made a living in commerce, financial speculation, or industrial development, whatever their actual religion may have been. Toussenel's book foreshadowed late nineteenth-century antisemitic conspiracy theories, describing the numerous non-Jews involved in economic modernization as mere puppets who consciously or unconsciously did the Jews' bidding in their campaign to bring ruin on the French people. Toussenel's writing may have served other political motives, as well. His book attacked the Saint-Simonians, a rival socialist group that believed centrally organized banks and industry were the keystones to establishing a new world order. Toussenel's diatribe may well have been meant to discredit the Saint-Simonians as Jews and as aristocrats, since the group had attracted a small number of Jews to its inner circle. In addition, the book defined all Protestants as Jews; in this, Toussenel meant not only the small minority of Protestants in France but also the entire populations of the nearby nations of England and Holland and the Protestant regions of Switzerland and Germany. In this sense, his antisemitism also played on his readers' nationalist xenophobia.

The book's second edition, published in 1847, was even more fierce in its attacks on the Jews than the previous edition, including revised and expanded sections attacking the Saint-Simonians and the members of the Rothschild banking family.

—*Lisa Moses Leff*

**See also** Drumont, Édouard; Fourier, Charles; France; *France juive, La;* Gougenot des Mousseaux, Henri; Rothschilds; Socialists on Antisemitism; Ultramontanism; Veuillot, Louis

**References**

Poliakov, Léon. *The History of Anti-Semitism.* Translated by Richard Howard. 2 vols. (New York: Schocken Books, 1974).
Szajkowski, Zosa. "Jewish Saint-Simonians and Socialist Antisemites in France." In *Jews and the French Revolutions of 1789, 1830 and 1848* (New York: Ktav, 1970).

## Treitschke, Heinrich von (1834–1896)

One of the most prominent historians of Prussia and imperial Germany, Heinrich von Treitschke is best known for his five-volume *Deutsche Geschichte im 19. Jahrhundert* (German History in the Nineteenth Century [1879–1894]) and for his inauguration of what has come to be referred to as the *Berliner Antisemitismusstreit* (Berlin antisemitism controversy). From his position at the University of Berlin, Treitschke exercised great influence on German historians and the educated elite. Through his agency, antisemitism gained acceptability in the upper reaches of German society.

Born into a noble Saxon officer's family in Dresden, Treitschke studied political and cultural history in Bonn, Leipzig, Tübingen, and Freiburg. He then taught history at several universities until succeeding Leopold von Ranke (1874) at the most prestigious seat of German history, the University of Berlin. Beginning in 1858, Treitschke contributed regularly to the *Preußische Jahrbücher* (Prussian Yearbooks), a widely read and influential journal. Initially a supporter of many liberal positions, he rejected democratic representation as antithetical to German understandings of freedom, which, he argued, emphasized the state over the individual. Treitschke became increasingly conservative following German unification in 1871, an ideological metamorphosis reflected in his monumental *German History.* He served in the Reichstag from 1871 to 1884, first as a National Liberal and, after 1879, as an Independent. On Ranke's death in 1886, Treitschke succeeded him again, this time as historian of the Prussian state. Shortly before his own death, he was named the editor of the *Historische Zeitschrift* (Historical Journal).

Treitschke launched the Berlin antisemitism controversy with his sentence, "The Jews are our misfortune," which appeared in his regular monthly commentary for the *Prussian Yearbooks* in 1879; this and two succeeding columns were published as the pamphlet *A Word about Our Jews* in 1880. In it, Treitschke argued that German Jews clung to their group identity instead of truly integrating themselves in the German national community, which made them responsible for an assortment of injurious effects on state and society. He demanded that Jews become part of the German state and culture, although how they were to achieve such assimilation remained unclear. The article unleashed a storm. Jews and liberal-minded non-Jews, most notably Treitschke's colleague Theodor Mommsen, engaged him in a fierce debate about the Jewish Question. Nonetheless, by virtue of his academic reputation and position, Treitschke's article helped legitimate antisemitism in academic circles.

Treitschke's posthumous reputation fluctuated in subsequent German history. A Treitschke monument (later dismantled) was erected on the grounds of the University of Berlin in October 1909. In the early years of the Weimar Republic, his standing diminished before soaring again in the 1930s, especially after the Nazis took power. Treitschke's famous utterance, "The Jews are our misfortune," later adorned the masthead of Julius Streicher's antisemitic *Der Stürmer* (The Stormer).

—*Elizabeth A. Drummond*

**See also** Class, Heinrich; German Students, Association of; Hahn, Diedrich; *Stürmer, Der;* Weimar; *Word about Our Jews, A*

**References**

Davis, H. W. Carless. *The Political Thought of Heinrich von Treitschke* (Westport, CT: Greenwood Press, 1973).

Dorpalen, Andreas. *Heinrich von Treitschke* (Port Washington, NY: Kennikat Press, 1957).

Prolific novelist of the Victorian era, Anthony Trollope depicted Jews as symbols of the new commercial forces that threatened the stability of English society. (Bettmann/Corbis)

## Trollope, Anthony (1815–1882)

After a childhood disrupted by his father's mental illness and bankruptcy, Anthony Trollope worked in the postal service in Ireland during the famine of the 1840s and later in England. He achieved some renown with his Barsetshire novels of mild ecclesiastical satire, beginning in the 1850s. By the mid-1860s, he was a successful and prolific novelist and public affairs commentator, and in addition to publishing a series of political novels, he stood (unsuccessfully) as a Liberal candidate for Parliament in 1868. In his *Autobiography* (1883), Trollope linked his Liberal politics with his approach to fiction, claiming that in his writing, he did not take sides or espouse doctrine but aimed to represent a balanced viewpoint. Nonetheless, though he believed in a general "tendency towards equality," he also held that "inequality is the work of God."

This contradiction informs Trollope's representation of Jews. In his novels of the 1850s and 1860s, Jews are repeatedly presented as symbols of the new commercial forces that threatened the stable class structure of Victorian England. However, Trollope's narratives ultimately do not seek to exclude Jews; rather, they identify them and establish their rightful place within an hierarchically conceived social order. To this end, his writing deploys a racial discourse. In *Nina Balatka* (1867), the Jewish businessman Anton Trendellsohn has "jet black hair," dark skin—"no white man could be more dark and swarthy than Anton Trendellsohn"—and "eyes . . . too close together in his face"; "the movement of the man's body was the movement of a Jew." Such physiological features also have temperamental analogs, and the initially generous Anton reverts to the "inborn suspicion of his nature" rather than trusting to the goodness of his Christian lover, Nina Balatka. Critics have noted the similar names of the protagonist and his creator, suggesting that Trollope, conscious of his status as a commercial writer, saw himself similarly as an alien outsider seeking admission into a hostile society.

Trollope's ambivalence is evident in a range of his novels from the 1870s. In *The Eustace Diamonds* (1873) and *Phineas Redux* (1874), he reveals the true identity of the convert Joseph Emilius, who successfully tempts the English heroine, as a "foreigner and a Jew" and an "imposter." In contrast, it is precisely the indeterminacy of the racial identity of Trollope's villains that makes them so threatening. Augustus Melmotte, the cosmopolitan, fraudulent financier and pretender to parliamentary office and upper-class alliance in *The Way We Live Now* (1875), remains a hollow cipher throughout the text. He may or may not be a Jew, he may or may not have a criminal past, he may or may not be very rich. The Melmottes' reputation is built entirely on hearsay, but ultimately they are unsettling because "no one knows who they are, or where they came from." In contrast, the more reliably Jewish Ezekiel Brehgert, pursued by an impoverished, gold-digging aristocrat, forgoes the marriage and thus demonstrates to the reader his laudable sense of the inferior place of the Jews in relation to the ruling class.

—*Nadia Valman*

*See also* Britain; English Literature from Chaucer to Wells

*References*

Cheyette, Bryan. *Constructions of "the Jew" in English Literature and Society, 1875–1945* (Cambridge: Cambridge University Press, 1993).

Ragussis, Michael. *Figures of Conversion: "The Jewish Question" and English National Identity* (Durham, NC: Duke University Press, 1995).

# Twain, Mark (1835–1910)

For a century and a quarter, Mark Twain has remained America's best-known author. His stature is iconic, and his works have never gone out of print; by means of his sardonic wit, fresh idiom, and biting commentary, his high-spirited texts continue to provoke controversy. Whether in narrative or polemical format, he approached divisive matters with an unprecedented gaiety, often not shared by earnest critics. Recent interest in whether his Huck Finn was black (the word *nigger* appears 212 times in the classic) serves to raise an equally provocative inquiry—was Mark Twain Jewish? "*Der Jude Mark Twain*" (the Jew Mark Twain), charged Viennese antisemites when he published "Concerning the Jews" in 1899, the most cogently argued polemical essay in his writings.

Indeed, a case can be made for the "Jewish Mark Twain" or, more to the point, Mark Twain's intimate identification and concern for the Jews, both biblical and contemporary. Born Samuel Clemens in 1835 in Florida, Missouri, he lost his father in 1847, whereupon the family fell from modest comfort into poverty. Sam was placed in the trades without finishing school. His evangelical mother—loquacious and playful—nurtured her children in Bible literacy: the King James Bible influenced Twain more than any other. From early boyhood days, Jews captured his perverse imagination. The first Jews he met were at his local school, he recalled with a schoolboy's relish of those ridiculed, chased, and scorned by the Christian boys: "To my fancy they were clothed invisibly in the damp and cobwebby mold of antiquity. They carried me back to Egypt, and in imagination I moved among the Pharaohs and all the shadowy celebrities of that remote age" (*Autobiography* 2:218).

Twain was a southerner, not born to tolerance. Nevertheless, unlike his treatment of the Irish, Mexicans, and Native Americans, at whom he could poke merciless fun, he joked relatively little about Jews. It pleased him when his daughter Clara married a Jewish musician. His books, translated into Yiddish, were popular on New York's Lower East Side. When Sholem Aleichem, the humorist, was called the "Jewish Mark Twain," Twain replied, "Please tell him that I'm the American Sholem Aleichem" (in Kahn 1985, 24).

Invariably, Twain's humor was double-edged and bittersweet, skirting the edge of burlesque. No serious subject escaped unscathed, its value intact and its stupidity safe from humorous barbs. Twain's relationship to Jews (randomly named Israelites, Hebrews, and Jews) was no exception. Coming of age personally immersed in the everyday experiences of common trades—printer, pilot, miner, newspaperman, funnyman, travel writer, lecturer—Twain developed the best ear in American letters for colloquial speech. Vernacular was the underground spring for critical social observation. Employing prevalent Shylock allusions in casual speech—"to Jew down," "rich as a Jew"—he connected to his audience's folk knowledge. After a publishing deal gone bad with Bret Harte, he fumed in a letter: "Harte is a liar, a thief, a swindler, a snob, a sot, a sponge, a coward, a Jeremy Diddler, he is brim full of treachery, & he conceals his Jewish birth as carefully as if he considers it a disgrace" (*Mark Twain–Howells Letters* 1:135). In one early instance, Twain edited himself by not including his most extended sketch of a sleazy Jew in the final text of his best-selling first book, *Innocent's Abroad* (1869). Isaac, the "kinky-haired" Israelite, was an unctuous con man accompanying the gullible American pilgrims to the Holy Land.

Twain fashioned the grand tour as a sarcastic and amusing commentary on the commercial corruption of religious sites, venerated monuments, and consecrated saints—Catholicism, his favored target. Notably, the depictions of the Old World Israelites and Jews presented a significantly smaller target for Twain's arrows than Christianity and its vendors.

In late 1863 or early 1864, Twain met Adolph Sutro, an immigrant Jewish businessman who became enormously successful as a tough-minded and visionary mining entrepreneur on the Comstock Lode and, later, mayor of San Francisco. For Twain, Sutro represented the model of the no-nonsense, disciplined "brain" for worldly business and its power for accountability to both the economy and society. "I have always found something of Sutro in all the Jews whom I have personally known since," Twain professed in praise, proposing that "a part of Sutro is a sufficient equipment for an average man." The Jews, he said, have the best average brain of any people in the world "by long odds the most marvelous that the world has produced" (Twain to Charles Erskine Scott Wood 1885).

Twain maintained that "we do not satirize people whom we singularly respect" (Twain to Wood 1885). In 1899, he chose to publish a well-crafted polemical essay about the Jewish problem in *Harper's Magazine* instead of a short story in draft. Free of any patronizing or didacticism, the manuscript of "Randall's Story" was a tale about a Jew's admirable outwitting of an uncouth riverboat gambler over an ill-gotten female slave. However, the prosaic essay format better served Twain's immediate interest in direct argumentation. What was the "secret" of this people's "immortality," he asked? Complex and layered, "Concerning the Jews" drew together his feelings twisting back over two generations. In part, Jews continued to serve Twain as the biblical chosen people—the elect—in a personal quarrel with the hypocrisy of his own Christian nurture in the Golden Rule. In part, he was venting his fury at Dreyfus's treatment in France and his own resentment after a year-long residence in Vienna. Associating with a circle of Jewish writers, artists, and intellectuals, Twain himself had become the target of malicious antisemitic newspaper attacks. "The Jew article" was Twain's answer.

His analysis of the Jewish problem worked to provoke both antisemitic reactionaries and philosemitic liberals. "Neither Jew nor Christian will approve," he remarked with a defensive satisfaction (Twain to Henry H. Rogers 1898). Twain himself continued to propagate his impression that a group of commercial Jews surpassed even the Yankee at low cunning and sharp practice. However, he now hastened to address the historical context over two millennia, vigorously rejecting the paranoid antisemitic accusations of banking conspiracies, media controlling trusts, and the barbaric corruption of Anglo-Saxon civilization. The achievement of the historical Jewish community in mastering the business of money was real. Manipulated by both high-church nobility and low-church peasantry and hemmed in by ecclesiastical and state restrictions, Jews were largely compelled to survive by their wits as middlemen, traders, and artisans— the conduits of fluid capital. This tiny group beyond others made itself fit to function in the modern marketplace. In emancipated western European nations, the positive accomplishments of the Jewish communities—self-reliance, community trust, good citizenship, professional accomplishment, and creative intellectuals and artists— surpassed all the negatives.

Twain has never been forgiven for his transgression—focusing exclusively on the ubiquitous reputation of the Jew as money-getter. Jewish newspapers criticized him for a provincial ignorance of late nineteenth-century immigration, ghettos, factory work, and physical exertion, especially military service. But he stood by the common experience of his extensive travels that Jewish tramps, beggars, and manual laborers were seldom to be seen, primarily because the historical trajectory of the Jewish community was away from manual labor toward educated occupations and professions.

Twain was neither a temperamental optimist nor a political liberal. He forecast a grim future, part of which would consist of the permanent persecution of Jews in the West. At the turn of the new century, the vocabulary was changing. To Christians, Jews had always been "strangers" and "foreigners," the same word in German (*Fremde*). Now, the antisemites stigmatized them further—they became aliens. As the religious motives for theologically based Jew-hatred were subsiding, the racial motives for a modern, state-centered antisemitism were surging. Nurtured an evangelical, Twain accepted the immutable persistence of evil. "We may not pay Satan reverence," he perceived in "Concerning the Jews," "but we can at least respect his talents. A person who has during all the time maintained the imposing position of spiritual head of four-fifths of the human race, and political head of the whole of it, must be granted the possession of executive abilities of the loftiest order" (528).

At the time of its publication, Twain's essay was widely reviewed but then mostly forgotten. In 1938, he would have felt vindicated when Sigmund Freud, who had known Twain in Vienna in the early days of his psychoanalytic practice, abridged "Concerning the Jews" as a précis for his own essay entitled "A Comment on Antisemitism" (*Ein Wort zum Antisemitismus*).

On topics of enduring interest and controversy, Twain's legacy has been uncanny for resurfacing and casting fresh irreverence on familiar ideas.

—*Burton Bledstein*

**See also** Dreyfus Affair; English Literature of the Twentieth Century; Freud, Sigmund; Jewish Question; Norris, Frank; Populist Movement; Shylock

**References**
Dolmetsch, Carl. *"Our Famous Guest": Mark Twain in Vienna* (Athens: University of Georgia Press, 1992).
Foner, Philip S. *Mark Twain: Social Critic* (New York: International Publishers, 1958).
Kahn, Sholom J. "Mark Twain's Philosemitism: 'Concerning the Jews,'" *Mark Twain Journal* 23 (Fall, 1985), 24.
Paine, Albert B., ed. *Mark Twain's Autobiography*. 2 vols. (New York: Harper Brothers, 1924).
Smith, Henry N., and William M. Gibson, eds. *Mark Twain–Howells Letters: The Correspondence of Samuel L. Clemens and William D. Howells, 1872–1910*. 2 vols. (Cambridge, MA: Harvard University Press, 1970).
Twain, Mark. *Mark Twain Papers*. (Berkeley, California: Bancroft Library, University of California).
———. "Concerning the Jews," *Harper's New Monthly Magazine* 99 (September 1899). http://www.fordham.edu/halsall/mod/1898 twain-jews.html. (Accessed March 2, 2005).

## Twilight of Israel, The (1932)

Henryk Rolicki was the pseudonym of Tadeusz Gluzinski (1888–1940), a founding member of the extremist National Radical Camp (ONR). His *The Twilight of Israel* (1932) was a prominent example of the antisemitic propaganda of the extreme Right in interwar Poland, advancing its characteristic arguments. Republished in 1996 by the Ojczyzna (Fatherland) publishing house, it has resumed its leading place among publications of the Far Right in Poland.

The book purports to be a history of the Jews from antiquity to the modern age. Gluzinski argues that because of the concept of the promised land, the Jewish religion is by nature directed toward a secular political end: the creation of "God's kingdom on Earth," meaning world domination by the Jews. The Jews seek to achieve this aim through violent means, by fomenting revolutions: Gluzinski accuses Jewish financiers of having underwritten both the American and the Russian Revolutions (Gluzinski was antidemocratic as well as anticommunist). He follows in the tradition of eighteenth-century antisemitic writings in characterizing the Jews as a secret society similar to the Freemasons. According to this view, the true meanings of Jewish writings and thus the real aims of the Jews are known only to a small circle of initiates and passed on by word of mouth from one generation to the next. Ordinary Jews faithfully carry out their leaders' instructions, not knowing the final aim. Jews convert to Christianity in order to infiltrate and subvert Christian society; they retain their Jewish faith in secret, however, and often revert to it generations later. Thus, Gluzinski also belongs to the nineteenth-century "racial" antisemites, for whom assimilation and conversion, the traditional aims of Christian antisemitism, are inadequate. Gluzinski does not go so far as to recommend the physical destruction of the Jews, but he does advocate their removal through "voluntary" emigration. Antisemitic nationalism in Europe, he says, has exposed the secret plans of the Jews, which will therefore eventually be defeated; hence, the present age represents "the twilight of Israel."

—*Steven Paulsson*

**See also** Barruel, Augustin; Freemasonry; Gougenot des Mousseaux, Henri; Judeo-Bolshevism; National Democrats; Poland; Poland since 1989; *Protocols of the Elders of Zion*

**Reference**
Rolicki, Henryk. *Zmierzch Izraela* (The Twilight of Israel) (Warsaw: Ojczyzna, 1996).

# U

## Ukraine, Post-Soviet

On the collapse of the USSR in 1991, the anti-semitic policies propagated by Joseph Stalin and gradually dismantled under Mikhail Gorbachev came to an end. The turning away from state antisemitism, usually practiced under the cover of anti-Zionism, took place with greater transparency in the Ukraine than in Russia. Immediately after the failed coup of August 1991, President Leonid Kravchuk announced that his country would work with Western organizations to locate persons of Ukrainian nationality who had committed crimes against Jews during World War II and to bring them to justice. This confession of Ukrainian complicity in the Final Solution was accompanied by an annual commemoration of the Holocaust. These two gestures of atonement and reconciliation earned general approbation from the international community.

The honeymoon between Jews and Ukrainians, which continued after the election of the next president, Leonid Kuchma (in 1994), owed something to the country's wish to join the West and knowledge that this would require it to guarantee human rights and meet other international norms. But the slow pace of economic development disappointed many who had expected a rapid upsurge in the standard of living; from the middle of the 1990s, popular dissatisfaction began to be heard. Nationalist and right-wing extremist parties fed off the discontent and used it to sustain their movements. For historical reasons, these groups find most of their supporters in the western Ukraine (Galicia), where before World War II the greatest number of Jews lived and where during the war the Ukrainian independence movement was active. They take their lead from Symon Petliura, Dmytro Dontsov, and Stepan Bandera, the most important ideologues of Ukrainian independence of the interwar period. At the top of the agenda for the Congress of Ukrainian Nationalists, the Ukrainian Conservative Republican Party, and the Ukrainian National Assembly–Ukrainian Self-Defense is the emancipation of the country from the "Great Russian yoke." However, antisemitic slogans are also part of their repertoire.

The ultranationalist group State Independence of the Ukraine (DSU), which has no seats in parliament, speaks of the inevitable uniting of all ethnically Ukrainian regions, currently under the jurisdiction of other states—a pointed reference to Russia. The DSU's house organ, *Neskorena natsiia* (Invincible Nation), rails against both the Russians and the Jewish world conspiracy that aims at enslaving the Ukraine. The favorite sources of writers for *Nezborima natsiia* (Unconquered Nation), *Golos natsii* (Voice of the Nation), and *Za vilnu Ukrainu* (For a Free Ukraine) are the *Protocols of the Elders of Zion*, Henry Ford's *The International Jew*, Alfred Rosenberg's *Myth of the Twentieth Century*, and Adolf Hitler's *Mein Kampf*. Russian antisemitic works, from the Soviet and post-Soviet periods, provide (often contradictory) theses concerning the evil of the Jews. Jews, for example, bear the guilt for the October Revolution of 1917, the creation of the USSR, *and* its destruction.

Several Ukrainian extremists employ mythic and mystical elements in the construction of their ideology. Ukraine, they claim, was the land that gave birth to the Aryan race and from which all Indo-Germanic peoples derive. The country, therefore, has a special messianic task, the restoration of a Greater Ukraine that will do battle with evil, that is, with cosmopolitan Jews who would lead mankind into the abyss. In carrying out this Aryan-Ukrainian mission, Jesus himself becomes a Ukrainian and thereby makes the Moscow-oriented Russian Orthodox Church of the Ukraine an ideal ally against Freemason-Zionists, who are said to be working for the advent of the Antichrist and the destruction of Eastern Orthodoxy.

For a number of reasons, these nationalist groups play a relatively marginal role in the political life of the nation. Many hundreds of thousands of Jews have emigrated. Those who remain—the estimate fluctuates between 135,000 and 400,000—play only a modest role in politics, in contrast to the situation in Russia. Another difference is the absence of a "Red-Brown" alliance (of old line communists and nationalists or fascists) that can be seen at work among the antisemitic extremists in the Russian Duma. According to reliable sources, the desecrations of synagogues and Jewish cemeteries have diminished in recent years. Thanks to the positive attitude of the government and its good relations with Israel, there are numerous Jewish charitable and memorial organizations working in the country. Further, Kiev has its own institute of Jewish studies.

—*Matthias Messmer*
*Richard S. Levy, translation*

*See also* Antichrist; Anti-Zionism in the USSR; *Dearborn Independent* and *The International Jew;* Freemasonry; *Mein Kampf; Myth of the Twentieth Century, The;* Petliura, Symon; *Protocols of the Elders of Zion;* Russia, Post-Soviet; Russian Orthodox Church

**References**
Aster, Howard, and Peter J. Potichnyj, eds. *Ukrainian-Jewish Relations in Historical Perspective* (Edmonton: Canadian Institute of Ukrainian Studies, 1990).
Dymerskaya-Tsigelman, Liudmilla Finberg, and Leonid Finberg. *Antisemitism of the Ukrainian Radical Nationalists: Ideology and Policy* (Jerusalem: Vidal Sassoon International Center for the Study of Antisemitism, Hebrew University, 1999).
Messmer, Matthias. *Sowjetischer und postkommunistischer Antisemitismus: Entwicklungen in Russland, der Ukraine und Litauen* (Konstanz, Germany: Hartung-Gorre, 1997).

## Ultramontanism

Originally used as a geographic expression (*ultra montes,* meaning "on the other side of the mountains"), the word *Ultramontanism* became a polemical term in the late eighteenth century, used by liberal Catholics to describe supporters of strict papal supremacy. Especially in Germany during the second part of the nineteenth century, the term became a catchword used to write off Catholics in general. Protestants, politically and culturally dominant, doubted that the first loyalty of Catholics was or could be to the secular nation-state, given their allegiance to the pope "on the other side of the mountains." Today, historians, theologians, and sociologists argue about the meaning of Ultramontanism as a way of describing the main trend in Catholicism from the nineteenth century up to the Second Vatican Council (1962–1965).

Ultramontanism can be characterized by several elements: the church's submission to the increased power of the papacy in doctrine and governance; the struggle to keep the church absolutely independent of all forms of state interference; the revival of older forms of devotion (for example, the veneration of the Virgin Mary, processions, and pilgrimages); the reestablishment of holy orders, especially the restoration of the Jesuit Order; the foundation of new brotherhoods and communities; and finally and perhaps most important, the effective use of modern tools and techniques to defend the interests of Catholicism, including political parties, lay societies, grassroots organizations, and the extensive publishing of books, newspapers, and other periodicals.

The Ultramontanist movement would not have been possible without the social and mental shock caused by the French Revolution. Ultramontanism can best be understood as an attempt to cope with the radical changes of the time, in particular with the consequences of enlightenment and revolution. French Ultramontanism, for example, was the reaction to Napoleon's strategy of transforming the Catholic Church into an instrument of state policy. In France, Joseph de Maistre, Louis de Bonald, and Hugues de Lamennais agitated for a strictly centralized organization of the church in order to defend

Catholic interests against the modern and increasingly intrusive state.

In German-speaking Europe, Ultramontanism first formed in Munich, Vienna, and Mainz around Joseph von Görres and Clemens Maria Hofbauer and in journals such as *Historisch-politische Blätter* (Historical-Political Papers) and *Der Katholik* (The Catholic). Acrimonious controversies with the Prussian state over the issue of mixed marriages and the arrest of the archbishop of Cologne stiffened the defensive posture of the Ultramontanists. The liberal, modernizing agendas of the revolutions of 1830 and 1848 had the effect of popularizing the movement among Catholics. Originally established to keep liberal Catholics in check, Ultramontanism eventually pitted itself against all secular developments; the life-and-death struggle, according to this view of the world, had to begin with the internal strengthening of the church. The dogma of the Immaculate Conception (1854), the Syllabus of Errors (1864), and the First Vatican Council (1869–1870) announcing the doctrine of papal infallibility brought the Catholic Church into a deep opposition to modern society. Whether these changes strengthened the church or not, Ultramontanism became known far and wide as the most intransigent enemy of freedom of conscience and all human progress.

Generally speaking, during the nineteenth and twentieth centuries, Ultramontanism was the most important manifestation of Catholicism worldwide, not only in Germany, France, and Belgium but also in Italy, Switzerland, Poland, England, Ireland, and the United States. Once a movement of the laity, it fell increasingly under the control of the church hierarchy, especially during the pontificate of Pius IX (1846–1878). In its contradictory combination of antimodern ideas and modern methods, Ultramontanism was successful in establishing a specific Catholic countersociety, one that emphasized self-assertion in the name of stability. Some scholars have seen elements of democracy within the movement; others have highlighted its fundamentalist, antidemocratic character. Historically, it can be argued that Ultramontanism, while insulating the church from the threats of modernity, also allowed it to fend off the worst aspects of communist and fascist totalitarianism.

However, this discipline resulted in the Catholic Church's willful separation from and rejection of modern, pluralistic society. Ultramontanism remained, first and foremost, a movement against liberalism, nationalism, capitalism, and socialism. And insofar as Jews were regarded as protagonists of these new ideologies, Ultramontanism evinced a generalized hostility toward them. Nevertheless, to describe the movement as antisemitic in the modern sense is not warranted. No doubt, it helped keep alive among the Catholic faithful some old and harmful anti-Jewish prejudices. But Ultramontanism did not form a closed system in which modern and eventually lethal racial antisemitism could play a central role. The defenders of the church may have wished to create a monolithic Catholic community, but, in fact, there were a variety of politics to be found within it. In Germany, for example, some prominent individuals and intellectual organs advocated measures against Jews as the agents of soulless modernity and the enemies of Christ. But within all levels of the church hierarchy, in the Catholic Center Party, and among ordinary Catholics, there were also defenders of Jewish rights who were prepared to condemn antisemitic excesses within and outside the church.

—*Carsten Kretschmann*

**See also** Barruel, Augustin; Belloc, Hilaire; Center Party; Gougenot des Mousseaux, Henri; Jesuit Order; *Kulturkampf;* Mortara Affair; Papacy, Modern; Pius IX, Pope; Toussenel, Alphonse; Vatican Council, First; Vatican Council, Second; Veuillot, Louis

**References**

Blaschke, Olaf. *Katholizismus und Antisemitismus im Deutschen Kaiserreich* (Göttingen, Germany: Vandenhoeck and Ruprecht, 1997).

Kaufmann, Franz Xaver. *Religion und Modernität* (Tübingen, Germany: Mohr, 1989).

Mergel, Thomas. "Ultramontanism, Liberalism, Moderation: Political Mentalities and Political Behavior of the German Catholic *Bürgertum,* 1848–1914." *Central European History* 29 (1996): 151–174.

Von Arx, Jeffrey, ed. *Varieties of Ultramontanism* (Washington, DC: Catholic University Press, 1998).

## United States

Antisemitism has been part of the American Jewish experience since 1654, when Governor Peter Stuyvesant of New Amsterdam (Manhattan) attempted to expel the first small group of Jews to land on the North American continent. Although colonial Jews experienced prejudice and occasional harassment, they thrived in an atmosphere of overall social and economic equality. They had de facto and, in most places, de jure religious freedom. Various colonies imposed political disabilities, but these were inconsistently applied, and many Jews were active in civic life. All political disabilities were eliminated in the course of the nineteenth century.

Gentile attitudes emerged in a distinctive pattern: In the Protestant mind, Jews evoked an ambivalent image, compounded from inherited attitudes about the "mythical Jew" and new experiences with the "Jew next door." On the one hand, Jews were admired as descendants of the Old Testament people; on the other hand, they were suspect as dangerous to the Christian society that many Protestants assumed America was. On the one hand, Jews were admired for their success in business; on the other hand, they were suspected of sharp practice.

Although antebellum Jews had to cope with constant Christian religious condescension and the prevalence of Christianity in civic life, overt antisemitism was relatively rare. It might be deployed to attack Jewish public figures such as Mordecai Noah and Uriah Levy, but most American Jews lived in harmony with their non-Jewish neighbors. Despite widespread negative economic stereotypes, they prospered economically, which enabled the creation of a strong national network of Jewish religious, cultural, and social institutions.

The mid-nineteenth century gave evidence, however, that the balance of ambivalence could tilt toward antisemitism in times of social stress. Jews (most of them immigrants) suffered from the increase in nativist sentiment in the 1840s and 1850s, although most attacks were verbal, not physical. Before and during the Civil War, there was an escalation of both antisemitic rhetoric and action. Drawing on the classic Shylock image, gentiles scapegoated Jews, accusing them of war profiteering and smuggling. Most ominously, there were local expulsions of Jews in the South, including one ordered by Gen. Ulysses Grant in 1862. Yet these suspicions notwithstanding, Jews were successfully integrated into both armies.

Antisemitism, rhetorical and active, subsided after the war, but in the volatile climate of the later nineteenth century, it reemerged in new guises. In the Gilded Age, status-conscious, upwardly mobile gentiles deployed antisemitism as a tool for their own advancement. Soon, wealthy and middle-class Jews found themselves excluded from clubs and schools to which they had previously had access; by the 1890s, such social ostracism was pervasive. Antisemitism was also evident in the evangelical "Christian America" movement, in intellectual theories of so-called Anglo-Saxonism, and in the rhetoric of many agrarian radicals of the Populist movement. Immigration restrictionism often had antisemitic overtones; ironically, too, the increase in ethnic Catholic immigration intensified antisemitism of the traditional European variety, which often manifested itself violently in neighborhoods where poor Catholic and Jewish immigrants lived in close proximity. Taken together, these phenomena account for what Leonard Dinnerstein calls "the emergence of a full-fledged antisemitic society" by the end of the nineteenth century.

In the first half of the twentieth century, antisemitism was at its peak in the United States, constantly reconfigured to meet the needs of the historical moment. In the virulently racist climate of the South, a Jew, Leo Frank, was even lynched in 1915 on a false charge of murder. A new secularized antisemitism, based on the "scientific racism" exemplified by Madison Grant's *Passing of the Great Race* (1916), expressed the fear of many Americans of all classes that the country was being invaded by inferior peoples who would soon overwhelm the older population of the superior "Nordic" race. Such theories buttressed the conviction that many in the mass migration of the late nineteenth century—including two and a quarter million Jews who arrived, mostly from eastern Europe, between 1880 and 1920—were unassimilable and could never become truly American. The identification of Jewish immi-

A group of white men protest the integration of Montgomery, Alabama, high schools waving Confederate flags and antisemitic signs. (Flip Schulke/Corbis)

grants with Bolshevik radicalism was hysterically inflated from a minority phenomenon into a full-fledged threat. Under such influences, Congress passed laws in 1924 restricting the immigration of southern and eastern Europeans.

The intensity—and acceptability—of overt antisemitism increased in the 1920s and 1930s. No less a figure than automotive mogul Henry Ford propagated the libels of the *Protocols of the Elders of Zion*. The revived Ku Klux Klan, though primarily emphasizing moral reform and anti-Catholicism, included Jews on its list of enemies of Christian America. Between 1933 and 1941, over 100 new antisemitic organizations were created; some, such as the German-American Bund, William Dudley Pelley's Silver Shirts, Rev. Gerald Winrod's Defenders of the Christian Faith, and radio demagogue Fr. Charles Coughlin's Christian Front, had high public profiles and considerable followings. Right-wingers attacked the New Deal as a "Jew Deal," alleging a Jewish conspiracy behind Roosevelt's programs. In the years leading up to World War II, isolationists such as Charles Lindbergh often blamed Jews for the international crisis.

Jews continued to acculturate and to prosper in those areas of endeavor open to them. As the second generation of the east European migration came to maturity in the 1920s and 1930s, there was resistance to their entry into parts of American society. Many colleges and universities, alarmed at the influx of academically successful young Jews, established admissions quotas. So did many professional schools and professional societies, although Jews were still able to make remarkable progress in law and medicine. Explicit and implicit employment discrimination was rampant, as were restrictive housing covenants. During World War II, many Jews in the armed forces experienced discriminatory treatment. This overall atmosphere of domestic antisemitism was certainly among the factors that limited the U.S. response to the plight of European Jews.

World War II, however, seemed to stem the tide of antisemitism in the United States; the decline was noticeable even by the late 1940s. Nazism had made antisemitism disreputable and all forms of bigotry suspect, and the optimism and self-satisfaction of the postwar boom focused Americans' minds on building a prosperous and well-adjusted society. Discrimination in education, employment, and housing decreased sharply, sometimes because of legal sanction. Social exclusion also decreased. Antisemitic demagogues were relegated to the fanatical fringe. Even the 1953 case of the Rosenbergs—Jews who really were Soviet-style communists—did not evoke widespread antisemitism. Starting in the early 1960s, Protestant and Catholic thinkers began to grapple with the complicity of Christianity in historical antisemitism. Jewish defense organizations and the community relations movement worked hard to encourage these trends.

Though the postwar gains were real, undercurrents of antisemitic attitudes would still occasionally well up to the surface. Southern opponents of African American civil rights used antisemitism to smear the movement as "communistic" and "un-American." The radical New Left often seemed to many Jews, including participants, to be antisemitic in its dismissal of Jewish concerns and its "anti-imperialist" rhetoric against Israel. Ironically, too, African Americans have often singled out Jews in their critique of white society. Especially in changing urban neighborhoods in the 1960s, African Americans used the traditional antisemitic imagery to blame powerful Jewish exploiters for blocking African American advancement. Ambivalence about Jewish involvement in the civil rights movement added fuel to the fire, as did the increased participation of African Americans in Islam. The Nation of Islam, an American sect, distributed *The Secret Relationship between Blacks and Jews,* accusing Jews of dominating the slave trade.

Overall, by the turn of the twenty-first century, antisemitism was at an all-time low in the United States, though antisemitic attitudes no doubt remain more prevalent than antisemitic behavior. Pockets of prejudice exist on the political fringe (the White Power and Militia movements) and in some circles of the Christian Right. But active discrimination is virtually non-existent, and Jews are remarkably prominent in the professions, in academia, and in business. A powerful indicator of decreased hostility is the increase in intermarriage, amounting to almost half of the marriages entered into by Jews.

The benignity of the American experience has many causes. Jews as a group in the United States never experienced the strains of emancipation like European Jews (or, for that matter, African Americans); because the United States was always modern, there was no real backlash against Jews as representatives of modernity. Consensus politics has kept antisemitism and (usually) other extremisms out of mainstream political life. The practical demands of American capitalism, the political ideals of American individualism and egalitarianism, the social fluidity of a mobile society, and the facts of cultural pluralism and religious voluntarism have always acted as a restraint on the oppression of Jews and other (white) minorities. At various times, there has been more religious persecution of Baptists, Quakers, Catholics, and Mormons than of Jews. Even in the worst days of nativism, Jews suffered far less than Catholic or Asian immigrants. And antisemitism was never politically and socially institutionalized, as were the two most intractable American racisms—against African Americans and Native Americans.

Furthermore, Jews in the United States have always felt free to engage in self-defense. The first defense organization, the Board of Delegates of American Israelites, was founded in 1859. B'nai B'rith was an important force in the nineteenth century, and in 1913, it centralized its defense activities in the Anti-Defamation League (ADL). The ADL, the American Jewish Committee (1906), and the American Jewish Congress (1916) are active and powerful organizations today.

The future remains ambiguous. American Jews continue to perceive more antisemitism in society than they claim to have experienced personally. The ADL closely tracks attitudes it considers antisemitic and issues progress reports that quantify them. Critics have lambasted Jewish organizations for a continued obsession with a declining problem to the detriment of other pressing issues such as Jewish education. However, it is not unrealistic to see ominous signs in the current rhetoric of debate on the Middle East. In May 2002, pro-Israel demonstrators at San Francisco State University were met with calls of "Hitler didn't finish the job" from pro-Palestinian demonstrators; the student newspaper at another California campus ran an editorial cartoon fusing images of a Torah scroll and a machine gun.

Whatever future developments may be, it is impossible to disagree with historian Jonathan Sarna's succinct conclusion: "If [this] country has not been utter heaven for Jews, it has been as far from hell as Jews in the Diaspora have ever known" (Sarna 1986, 126).

—*Amy Hill Shevitz*

**See also** American Jewish Committee and Antidefamation Efforts in the United States; Colonial America; Coughlin, Charles E.; Ford, Henry; Frank, Leo; General Orders No. 11; German-American Bund; Immigration and Naturalization Laws; Judeo-Bolshevism; Ku Klux Klan; Lindbergh, Charles; Militia Movement; Nation of Islam; New Left; *Numerus Clausus* (United States); *Passing of the Great Race;* Pelley, William Dudley; *Protocols of the Elders of Zion;* Restricted Public Accommodations, United States; Restrictive Covenants; *Secret Relationship between Blacks and Jews, The;* Stuyvesant, Peter; Wharton, Edith; White Power Movement; Winrod, Gerald B.

**References**

Chanes, Jerome A., ed. *Antisemitism in America Today* (Secaucus, NJ: Birch Lane Press, 1995).

Dinnerstein, Leonard. *Antisemitism in America* (New York: Oxford University Press, 1994).

Gerber, David, ed. *Anti-Semitism in American History* (Urbana: University of Illinois Press, 1987).

Mayo, Louise A. *The Ambivalent Image: Nineteenth-Century America's Perception of the Jew* (Rutherford, NJ: Fairleigh Dickinson University Press, 1988).

Sarna, Jonathan. "American Anti-Semitism." In *History and Hate: The Dimensions of Anti-Semitism.* Edited by David Berger. (Philadelphia: Jewish Publication Society, 1986), 115–128.

## USSR

The Bolshevik Revolution of October 1917 brought a new regime to power in Russia, claiming to govern according to communist principles. Over the course of a four-year civil war, the Bolsheviks succeeded in expanding their rule to encompass neighboring regions, resulting in the formation of the Union of Soviet Socialist Republics (USSR). Several of the newly gained territories had large Jewish populations, of which the most significant were Ukraine and Belorussia (Belarus). According to the 1926 census, there were nearly 2.6 million Jews in the Soviet Union, of whom 21 percent lived in Russia, 61 percent in Ukraine, and 16 percent in Belorussia. Until its demise on Christmas Day 1991, the USSR struggled with its national constituency, in which Jews formed a significant minority. Antisemitism in the Soviet Union can be divided into two broad categories: popular and official. Popular antisemitism waxed and waned throughout the century but remained a constant undercurrent. Official attitudes toward the Jews also varied, from guarded benevolence to aggressive antisemitism.

The Bolsheviks rose to power during a period of total war and intense antisemitism in the Russian Empire. The influence of antisemitic propaganda that flourished under the tsarist regime was still being felt, such that many people were willing to blame the Jews for the misfortunes befalling the region. The monarchist White Guards, in particular, exploited the fact that there were many Jews among the Bolshevik leadership as evidence that the revolution was a Jewish plot akin to that described in the infamous *Protocols of the Elders of Zion*. In the confusion of war, pogroms swept through Jewish towns and villages. During the Russian Civil War, there were an estimated 2,000 pogroms, in which approximately 150,000 Jews lost their lives. In addition to the pogroms perpetrated by the White Guardists, other military factions involved in the fighting, including Ukrainian nationalists and anarchist revolutionaries, engaged in antisemitic violence. The Red Army, however, largely fought against the perpetrators of pogroms, gaining the sympathy of many Jews who believed that the Bolsheviks were the only people willing to fight against antisemitism.

In its early years, the Soviet government treated the Jewish population in much the same way it treated other national minorities. It hoped to assimilate the Jews eventually, but in the short term, it accorded them limited national rights, including the right to use Yiddish in official matters and the right to be administered by Jews. In accordance with this principle, Jewish Sections (*Evsektsii*) of the Communist Party were established. During the 1920s, the Evsektsii embarked on a series of campaigns against Zionism, the Jewish religion, and the Hebrew language. Between 1923 and 1933, tens of thousands of Zionist activists were arrested; many others were forced to flee the country. In the same period, some 650 synagogues were closed throughout the Soviet Union; thousands of rabbis, cantors, and ritual slaughterers were arrested or forced to flee; and antireligious campaigns were launched to discredit Judaism. About 1,000 *kheyders* (primary schools) were closed, and many of the leading Hebrew writers and activists were encouraged to emigrate. These campaigns are often regarded as antisemitic, but similar actions were carried out against other religious and ethnic groups, including the Russian Orthodox majority.

During the first decade of Soviet power, Jews were also subjected to popular antisemitism. The dissolution of the Pale of Settlement, which had limited Jewish residency rights, coupled with the ending of restrictions on Jewish enrollment in universities and governmental service—all of which occurred under the Provisional Government that ruled prior to the Bolshevik Revolution—led to a rapid increase in the presence of Jews in public life. Jews and non-Jews also began working side by side on an unprecedented scale. Having long imbibed antisemitic rhetoric from the tsarist government and the Orthodox Church, many non-Jews reacted to the increased presence of Jews in their lives with resentment. Local newspapers and governmental intelligence of the era were rife with reports of antisemitic incidents in the workplace, the universities, and the trade unions. These incidents usually took the form of public mockery and abuse, discrimination, and even sporadic violence. Jews were commonly accused of unfairly profiting from the revolution, monopolizing administrative positions, grabbing the best land, and shirking manual labor. Local governmental and party officials at times acted with antisemitic motivations, particularly regarding the allocation of living quarters and promotions. The central government, however, viewed antisemitism as counterrevolutionary. It regularly conducted investigations into reported incidents, and the more flagrant perpetrators were often judicially punished. The government also embarked on an educational propaganda campaign against antisemitism. By the mid-1930s, incidents of antisemitism had declined.

However, Stalin's launching of the Great Terror in 1936 led to a new wave of attacks on Jews, dramatically impacting Jewish party members and intellectuals. Many of the most prominent Jewish Communists were the first to be accused of "anti-Soviet sabotage," most notably Leon Trotsky, Lev Kamenev, Grigorii Zinoviev, and Karl Radek. The latter three were executed after dramatic show trials in which the tortured prisoners were forced to confess to outrageous crimes against the state. Within the next two years, the purges reached down to the lower ranks of the party, again affecting numerous Jews. Former members of the Evsektsii and other party activists prominent in Jewish affairs were arrested and executed. As accusations of foreign espionage engulfed the cultural intelligentsia, the Jews, with their suspect international contacts, became easy targets. Jews suffered disproportionately during the Great Terror, primarily because of their overrepresentation in the party apparatus and the intelligentsia rather than because of any outright discrimination on the basis of religion or nationality. Although the Terror was not motivated by official antisemitism, the troubled times had the effect of encouraging the overt expression of antisemitic attitudes among large segments of the population.

In June 1941, the German army entered Soviet territory and quickly overwhelmed Ukraine, Belorussia, and other regions with large Jewish populations. Nazi rule led ultimately to the murder of about 2.5 million Soviet Jews. Most were murdered by German Einsatzgruppen (mobile death squads) in ravines or forests in the vicinity of their hometowns. At Babi Yar, on the outskirts of Kiev, over 30,000 Jews were massacred during two days in September 1941. Others were forced into ghettos, where they starved to death or died of disease. About 1 million Jews survived by fleeing eastward from the advancing Germans.

Popular antisemitism also flourished during

the war and in its immediate aftermath. Anti-semitic propaganda had been spread widely in regions under Nazi control and reached beyond, as well. Further, many Soviet citizens in the Nazi-occupied territories benefited from the Nazi extermination of the Jews—taking over abandoned Jewish houses, stolen property, and vacated jobs. Some actively collaborated with the Germans, helping round up Jews for extermination or even killing Jews themselves. After the war ended, many of these people feared retribution or loss of the benefits reaped from Jewish absence if the Jewish refugees were permitted to return. As a result, the postwar period witnessed a renewal of pogroms in parts of Ukraine and a general rise of antisemitic incidents throughout the Soviet Union, fed by false rumors that Jews avoided military service and that they had dragged the USSR into the war in the first place.

Official antisemitism and Stalinist attacks against the Jews intensified in late 1948 and early 1949. During that time, the last remaining Jewish institutions in the Soviet Union were closed down. An anticosmopolitan campaign that had been brewing in the Soviet press was transformed into a deliberately antisemitic crusade. Dozens of leading Jewish political, cultural, and intellectual personalities were arrested, followed by a long-term campaign of persecution against Jewish journalists, academicians, artists, politicians, students, military personnel, and ordinary citizens. The charges ranged from cosmopolitanism to bourgeois nationalism. On August 12, 1952, known as the Night of the Murdered Poets, thirteen of the most prominent Jewish public figures, most of whom were associated with the Jewish Anti-Fascist Committee, were executed. In January 1953, a group of mostly Jewish doctors were accused of collaborating with Jewish organizations abroad to poison leading Kremlin officials. The Doctors' Plot was intended as a final purge against Soviet Jews, rumored to include the complete exile of all Soviet Jews to Siberia. They were saved only by Stalin's death two months later.

Official antisemitism following Stalin's death was mostly related to Soviet foreign policy in the Middle East and the rise of Jewish nationalism within the USSR. The Soviet alliance with the Arab countries was accompanied by the adoption of an anti-Israel stance. This diplomatic maneuvering was coupled with a harsh "anti-Zionism," an official Soviet euphemism that allowed for the deployment of well-worn antisemitic stereotypes. Stereotyping and criticism of Jews became more common in the official press. Informal quotas were placed on Jews in educational institutions, government service, and the professions. Jewish suffering during World War II and the Holocaust, never officially acknowledged, now became a taboo subject. Rising Jewish nationalism during the 1950s and again following the Six Days' War (in 1967) led to massive crackdowns on the Jewish population. The movement of Soviet Jews seeking to emigrate to Israel occasioned more government antisemitism. Jews who supported the state of Israel and sought to leave the USSR were accused of participating in an international Zionist plot to spread anti-Soviet propaganda. Those refused exit visas (*refusniks*) were harassed and discriminated against in their daily lives. Between 1977 and 1978, some of the most prominent Soviet Jewish dissidents were arrested and falsely accused of espionage on behalf of Western governments. Throughout the 1970s and early 1980s, the Soviet Union became a leading center of anti-Zionist and antisemitic propaganda, not only spreading it within the borders of the USSR but also exporting books and pamphlets abroad.

Mikhail Gorbachev's release of the most prominent refusnik, Anatoly Scharansky, in 1986, followed by the freeing of other imprisoned Jewish dissidents, signaled the end of official Soviet antisemitism. Popular antisemitism, however, remained. The increased freedoms of glasnost led to the appearance of numerous antisemitic publications and movements that often were even more aggressive and racist than those that had previously been permitted.

—*Jeffrey Veidlinger*

***See also*** Anti-Zionism in the USSR; Doctors' Plot; Einsatzgruppen; Jewish Anti-Fascist Committee; Judeo-Bolshevism; Pale of Settlement; Petliura, Symon; *Protocols of the Elders of Zion;* Purges, Soviet; Russia, Imperial; Russian Civil War; Russian Orthodox Church; Solzhenitsyn, Aleksandr; Stalin, Joseph

***References***
Gitelman, Zvi. *A Century of Ambivalence: The Jews of Russia and the Soviet Union, 1881 to the Present.*

2nd ed. (Bloomington: Indiana University Press, 2001).

Levin, Nora. *The Jews in the Soviet Union since 1917: A Paradox of Survival* (London: I. B. Taurus, 1988).

Pinkus, Benjamin. *The Jews of the Soviet Union: The History of a National Minority* (Cambridge: Cambridge University Press, 1988).

## Ustasha

Ustasha, or Ustaša in Croatian, was an extreme nationalist movement that ruled the Independent State of Croatia during World War II between 1941 and 1945. In 1929, when King Alexander I imposed a royal dictatorship promoting a unitary Yugoslavia and prohibiting separate national names, the Croatian nationalist leader Ante Pavelić fled to Italy, where he formed the Ustaša-Hrvatska Revolucionarna Organizacija (Ustasha Croatian Revolutionary Organization) in 1932. The basic aim of Ustasha ideology was to achieve Croatian independence from Yugoslavia, but in practice, this led to increasingly anti-Serb positions. The movement founded terrorist training centers in Italy and Hungary. To foment political crises in Yugoslavia, Ustasha activists attempted to incite a rebellion in the central Croatian region of Lika in 1932, the so-called Velebit uprising, and participated in the assassination of King Alexander of Yugoslavia in Marseille (1934). They were not able to achieve their ultimate goal until the Germans and Italians invaded and partitioned Yugoslavia in April 1941.

When the Germans could not persuade the leader of the strongest Croatian party to form a government—he did not wish to compromise himself by collaborating with the Nazis—the Ustasha got its opportunity to exercise power. The first government of the Independent State of Croatia (Nezavisna država Hrvatskaita [NDH]) was formed from most of the territory of Croatia, Bosnia, and Herzegovina, with Zagreb as its capital. Pavelić and about 600 Ustasha exiles returned to Croatia from Italy and other countries to be greeted by about 2,000 loyalists who had been working underground in the country. Pavelić took the title of *Poglavnik* (leader) of the NDH and became prime minister and foreign minister, as well. Opportunists immediately flocked to join the movement, so that by May 1941, 100,000 members had already sworn the Ustasha oath. The Ustasha drew most of its sympathizers from the lower, less educated classes and from some poor regions of the Dinaric Mountains, where Serbs and Croats lived in close proximity.

The Ustasha proceeded to establish a "New Order" that closely followed the Italian-German fascist model. As early as 1936, when Pavelić had moved closer to Nazi Germany, antisemitism had already become one of the important elements of his movement. Now, the NDH proclaimed racial laws similar to Nazi Germany's and then implemented them with a policy of isolation, concentration, and extermination; Serbs and Gypsies, along with Jews, were the principal victims. Pavelić's main lieutenant in the persecution of the Jews was chief of the Ustasha police, Eugen Dido Kvaternik (1910–1962); he was succeeded by Minister of Internal Affairs Andrija Artuković (1899–1988), who lived in the United States for many years. The murderousness of the Ustasha members became legendary. In terms of sheer brutality and sadism, they outdid the Nazis.

Although the crimes incited a strong antifascist movement in the country, the Ustasha remained in power with the help of its Italian and German allies until May 1945. When German power collapsed, Pavelić and his supporters fled before the Communist partisans. In Spain, Argentina, and other locales, separate and often antagonistic splinter groups operating under a variety of names kept some of the movement's traditions alive.

—*Ivo Goldstein*

**See also** Croatia; Croatia, Holocaust in; Holocaust; Ljotić, Dimitrije; Nuremberg Laws; Pavelić, Ante
**References**
Broszat, Martin. *Der Kroatische Ustascha-Staat* (Stuttgart, Germany: Deutsche Verlags-Anstalt, 1964).
Goldstein, Ivo. *Holokaust u Zagrebu* (Zagreb: Novi liber—Židovska Općina Zagreb, 2001).
Tomasevich, Jozo. *War and Revolution in Yugoslavia, 1941–1945: Occupation and Collaboration* (Stanford, CA: Stanford University Press, 2001).

A woodcut dating from 1531 depicts a farmer's visit to a Jewish moneylender, who sits at a desk with an abacus. (Christel Gerstenberg/Corbis)

## Usury

*Usury* is the derogatory term for lending money at interest. For some, this meant at any rate of interest at all; others defined it as interest over a certain "reasonable" amount. Charging a fee for the loan to one's brother is condemned in the Pentateuch (Exod. 2:25; Lev. 25:35–37; Deut. 23:19–20), and the Gospel of Luke insisted "lend, hoping for nothing in return" (6:35). Nevertheless, by the High Middle Ages, both Jews and Christians accepted the need for some form of credit. Theologians argued about what was an acceptable level of recompense and what was infamous gain. Those who charged for mak-

ing loans were condemned, but making loans was permitted to "aliens," so it became accepted that Jews, who were not considered "brothers," were allowed to make loans to Christians. Though Christians did, indeed, lend one another money in the Middle Ages, Jews were regarded as the prime usurers, and they were often excoriated by those who obliged them to practice the sin.

Even though Jews were not the only moneylenders nor even the most important ones in medieval society, their moneylending activities became the greatest focus of hatred. In the early Middle Ages, Jews specialized in occupations shunned by Christians in an agrarian society. Initially, their lending money at interest was closely allied to other forms of currency dealing—coinage, monetary exchange, and goldsmithing. The very things that suited them so well to such endeavors—the ability to pool capital, international contacts, common language, familiarity with trade routes—gave rise to suspicion. Over time and as other occupations were increasingly closed to Jews because of guild regulations and restrictions on landownership, they specialized in pawnbroking and moneylending; the loaning of small sums to individuals over short periods appears to have become the primary Jewish occupation of the late Middle Ages.

Traditionally, the rise of antisemitism has been attributed to the extensive credit transactions between Christians and Jews, but recent scholarship suggests the need for a more nuanced picture. Our view of the historical acrimony occasioned by Jewish moneylending may have been distorted by the sorts of evidence that have survived. Some Jewish creditors and their Christian borrowers had close personal relations that extended over decades. But the great body of existing evidence is purely financial in nature, telling of deals that went awry, debts unpaid, and lawsuits engendered.

Undoubtedly, the need for hard-pressed Christians to borrow from wealthy Jews caused great emotional distress, which sometimes issued in physical violence. The first accusation of ritual murder was made by a knight heavily indebted to a Jewish creditor (in 1144); the first expulsion from a town occurred in the context of burdensome debts to Jews (in 1181); and the butchery of the Jews of York was prompted by knights who wanted to burn records of what they owed in order to fend off foreclosure (in 1190). Subsequent ritual murder accusations and riots frequently resulted in or focused on the destruction of lending documents. Complaints against Jewish lending appear in the Magna Carta (in 1215), and requests for relief from Jewish creditors appear often in petitions to authorities. Debtors frequently sought and received protection from paying interest to Jewish moneylenders as the reward for services rendered to the Crown.

But rulers benefited in many ways, and even popes condoned Jewish lending. Many charters required Jews to borrow money from authorities at a set interest rate, with the understanding that they would, in turn, lend the money at higher interest rates to others. By the mid-twelfth century, Bernard of Clairvaux could use *Judaize* to mean "lend at interest." Much of the pressure for Christians to borrow came from rulers, who could suddenly impose feudal fines and other forms of taxation in which services could be exchanged for monetary payments. Knights, landowners, and members of the elite frequently turned to Jews to borrow money to pay such taxes to the king. As a guarantee, they would pledge land or property, and as the debt often escalated, the result could be foreclosure. Since Jews were not allowed to own land, they disposed of it quickly, often at low prices, to wealthy buyers. The distorted effect of such Jewish involvement in the land market often aggravated already tense social relations.

Increasingly, Jews competed with Christians who provided similar services, but Jews could be forced to take riskier clients and therefore charged higher rates of interest. Although they gained the reputation of preying on the poorest members of society, who pledged their clothes or the tools of their trade, the financial records suggest that the primary borrowers were nobles. Indeed, many Jews settled near aristocratic courts to provide them with various financial services. When nobles reneged on their debts or received permission not to repay, the Jews were forced to move. Attacks on Jewish usury deflected attention that could otherwise be focused on central governments. However, consumption loans to the lower classes in a society predominantly based on agriculture meant that even small debts piled up quickly, creating the perception that Jews wielded undue power over Christians, bleeding them dry both literally and figuratively.

Economic and religious motives for outbreaks of antisemitic hatred often coexisted. When Jewish loans were given for security on valuable liturgical vessels, Christians feared that Jews were mistreating sacred objects; loans to religious institutions put Christian clerics under the power of Jewish laypeople, undermining their spiritual authority. Canon law dictated that Jews were to be tolerated only in a subordinate position in Christendom. Moneylending confused their assigned social role.

Attitudes toward the actual operation of credit in the medieval economy and the role of the Jews differed widely, but symbolically, usury became closely associated with sin. Visually and rhetorically, Jews and money were inextricably linked in popular consciousness, and this theme was given special emphasis in sermon literature. The image of the Jew holding a moneybag became common in all artistic media. Usury was understood as the product of avarice. Lending at interest was deemed to be thievery and therefore sacrilege. Love of money was likewise associated with worship of the Golden Calf and idolatry. The Jewish moneylender—and, by extension, all Jews—was not only avaricious but also unclean and impure. In Christian iconography, the deicide Judas, who betrayed Jesus out of the love of money, was pictured as the typical Jew, holding a moneybag. Popular biblical images presented not only Jews but also Judaism itself as sinful. Bags of money came to signify Jewish sin as much or more than Jewish commercial activity.

In the early modern period, Jews provided the long-term credit for major construction projects and military initiatives at competitive market rates; only later did they concentrate on the high-interest, high-risk consumption loans for which they were demonized as usurers. The astoundingly high interest rates that often appear in the records were clearly never collected: Jewish creditors or the crown often settled for far less. Jews were limited to extending credit when the era of European economic expansion was drawing to a close, but by that time, there were few other outlets for them. In the early seventeenth century, Rabbi Leon de Modena lamented that if the Jews had any other way of making a living, they would not lend at interest.

—*Emily Rose*

**See also** Banker, Jewish; Capital: Useful vs. Harmful; Coin Clipping; Court Jews; Crusades; Iconography, Christian; Ritual Murder (Medieval); Shylock

**References**

Lipton, Sara. *Images of Intolerance: The Representations of Jews and Judaism in the Bible Moralisée* (Berkeley: University of California Press, 1999).

Little, Lester K. *Religious Poverty and the Profit Economy in Medieval Europe* (Ithaca, NY: Cornell University Press, 1983).

Nelson, Benjamin N. *The Idea of Usury: From Tribal Brotherhood to Universal Otherhood.* 2nd rev. and enlarged ed. (Chicago: University of Chicago Press, 1969).

# V

## Vallat, Xavier (1891–1972)

A much wounded and decorated World War I veteran, politician, lawyer, and self-proclaimed "serious antisemite," Xavier Vallat continued a French form of rural, Catholic antisemitism; reminiscent of Édouard Drumont, he stressed the impossibility of Jewish assimilation and the destructive influence of Jews on French life. During World War II, he served the Vichy state in several capacities, but he is remembered primarily as the first director of the Commissariat Général aux Questions Juives (General Commissariat for Jewish Affairs), a key institution of the Final Solution in France.

The tenth child born to a reactionary teacher and a peasant mother in the rural Ardèche, Vallat came of age during the Dreyfus Affair and the subsequent wave of anticlerical legislation. He read the antisemitic clerical press aimed at a rural audience and then discovered the writings of Charles Maurras, the chief ideologue of the monarchist and antisemitic *Action Française*. By age twenty, he had formed his worldview, composed of a defensive Catholic piety and an aggressive antisemitism.

Briefly a teacher, Vallat welcomed World War I, to which he sacrificed an eye and a leg. After the war, he earned a law degree and served as deputy for the Ardèche from the years 1919 to 1924 and 1928 to 1940, always as a member or ally of rightist factions. Although he had written anti-Jewish texts in the early 1920s, he did not become generally known as an antisemite until June 6, 1936, when, in front of a full parliament, he expressed his outrage toward the Jewish Léon Blum, the new head of government. Receiving numerous congratulatory letters, he convinced himself that he was competent—and destined—to pursue the Jewish Question.

Having served Marshal Henri Philippe Pétain as minister of veterans' affairs and secretary-general of the French Legion of Combatants, his own creation, Vallat returned to his area of "competence." In the spring of 1941, he became director of Vichy's newly created General Commissariat for Jewish Affairs. As director of the commissariat from April 1941 until his ouster in May 1942, Vallat was charged with applying Vichy's existing anti-Jewish legislation, creating new laws, and administering the liquidation of Jewish property in all French territories. Appalled by the laxity of the initial Jewish statute of October 3, 1940, the director set about widening the definition of Jews in a second statute, promulgated June 2, 1941 (and in a more draconian but unenacted third statute), to include race and religion with the goal of eliminating Jewish social and economic influence. Surprising even the Germans, he ordered a census of Jews in the unoccupied zone administered directly by Vichy and introduced Jewish identity cards in December 1942—both measures crucial to the later deportation and murder of Jews in France.

Although he was a fervent antisemite, it is unclear whether the Germanophobe Vallat foresaw the Final Solution in France and at least doubtful that he approved of it. Nonetheless, by legally defining and registering Jews, stripping them of citizenship and property and livelihood, and directly or indirectly blaming them as a group for the ills of French society, Xavier Vallat contributed significantly to the legislative and administrative apparatus that enabled the Final Solution in France.

—*Benn Williams*

*See also* *Action Française;* Dreyfus Affair; Drumont, Édouard; France; Holocaust; Jewish Question; Maurras, Charles; Ultramontanism; Vichy

*References*

Marrus, Michael R., and Robert O. Paxton. *Vichy France and the Jews* (New York: Basic Books, 1981).

Weisberg, Richard H. *Vichy Law and the Holocaust in France* (New York: New York University Press, 1996).

## Varnhagen von Ense, Rahel Levin (1771–1833)

Rahel Levin, often cited as the most famous case study of "Jewish self-hatred," denied her Jewishness in order to assimilate to the Prusso-German society of the early nineteenth century. In her own day, she was known primarily for hosting a salon that attracted many cultural luminaries to Berlin (between 1790 and 1806 and, less famously, from 1819).

Rahel habitually described herself as an outsider in society, often belittling herself and lamenting that no one truly understood her. In her letters and diaries, she created her own original poetic persona for future generations; there, she constructed an identity that rejected the very idea of having a stable identity. Hannah Arendt, one of the first to take Rahel seriously, read her life as a failure to escape from her Jewishness in the nationalistic climate of the Restoration. More recently, scholars such as Dagmar Barnouw have focused on a complex of factors that led to Rahel's constant projection of her social exclusion: her Jewish roots that could not be abandoned; her status as an unmarried woman (until 1814); and her need for approval, especially from the correspondents she unburdened herself to.

Rahel opened herself completely to her correspondents, in Rousseauian fashion; at the same time, she relied on her correspondents as authors of herself. On September 27, 1814, Rahel Levin married the Prussian diplomat Karl August Varnhagen von Ense. She saw in him the person who was able to understand her and who—as a congenial Christian and male companion—could complete her identity search. He partly accomplished this by publishing her work posthumously, beginning with *A Book of Remembrance for Her Friends* in 1834.

In 1806, when Rahel had to give up her first salon, she wrote: "How horrid it is to always have

Rahel Varnhagen von Ense (1771–1833), born Rahel Levin, hosted a salon at which the leading lights of German cultural life gathered. Her Jewish identity was a source of great personal turmoil for her. (Bildarchiv Preussischer Kulturbesitz/Art Resource, New York)

to legitimate yourself! That's why it is *hateful* to be a Jewess!!" (in Tewarson 1998, 102). This remark is often taken as decisive proof of her Jewish self-hatred, but it mainly documents Rahel's struggle with her roles as a Jew and as a woman to achieve her ideal of true communication.

The expression of Jewish self-hatred and cultural inferiority is personalized in Rahel's writing. On the one hand, she converted to Protestantism four days before her marriage and was baptized Friederike Antonie Varnhagen von Ense; on the other hand, she continued to use the name Rahel, obviously a denial of both her new and her old identity; she was somewhere in between, simultaneously maintaining and denying her roots. In the eyes of others, Rahel remained Jewish; they called her "the little Levi."

Besides the question of her own identity, Rahel's letters demonstrate her sharp intellect in analyzing the situation of the German Jews and the antisemitism they experienced as a result of Napoleon's defeat and occupation of Prussia after 1806. This ability can be seen in her precise descriptions of the Teplitz spa society and of the Christian-German Dining Society, which excluded women, Frenchmen, and Jews. In correspondence with her brother Ludwig Robert, she discussed critically the Hep-Hep Riots of 1819 and the wide-scale attacks on Jewish property. She distanced herself from the Jewish victims and seemed to be paradoxically included within and excluded from her Jewish roots.

Arendt argues that Rahel came to terms with her Jewishness at the end of her life, yet Rahel also expressed strong Christian beliefs at that time. So, if she came to terms with anything, it was with her own individual character, beyond any specific religious belief or confession.

—*Stephan Jaeger*

**See also** Arndt, Ernst Moritz; Burschenschaften; Dining Society, Christian-German; Emancipation; Heine, Heinrich; Hep-Hep Riots; Jewish Question; Self-Hatred, Jewish

**References**
Arendt, Hannah. *Rahel Varnhagen: The Life of a Jewish Woman* (London: East and West Library, 1957).
Barnouw, Dagmar. "Einzigartig: Rahel Varnhagen und die deutsch-jüdische Identität um 1800." In *Rahel Levin Varnhagen: Studien zu ihrem Werk im zeitgenössischen Kontext.* Edited by Sabina Becker (St. Ingbert, Germany: Röhrig, 2001), 81–117.
Tewarson, Heidi Thomann. *Rahel Levin Varnhagen: The Life and Work of a German Jewish Intellectual* (Lincoln: University of Nebraska Press, 1998).

# Vatican Council, First (1869–1870)

Pope Pius IX convened the First Vatican Council (Vatican I) on December 8, 1869, in the midst of considerable political turmoil in Europe, especially within the Italian states that were caught up in the forward movement of Italian unification. Close to 800 delegates assembled in Rome for the council and faced a heavy agenda, none of which was directly linked to the question of the Catholic Church's relationship to Judaism. In that sense, Vatican I bears no similarity to Vatican II, which made the Catholic-Jewish relationship an important discussion topic.

The council was suspended on September 1, 1870, after the surrender of the Papal States to the invading Italian armies. Its original agenda was far from completed at that point, with only 100 or so delegates present in its final weeks. The papacy was too preoccupied with its dramatically new political status to resume the council. Its temporal power had basically vanished as a result of Italian unification, and Pius IX considered himself a "prisoner of the Vatican."

During the time it was in session, Vatican I addressed two principal issues: how God is known and papal infallibility. The latter is its most noteworthy work. The notion of papal infallibility encountered some opposition in the council. (The bishop of Little Rock, Arkansas, for example, voted against the proposal.) The push for declaring the pope infallible was certainly a theological issue at the council. But it was also seen as a defensive measure, a way of enhancing the power of the papacy at a time when its political fortunes were in steep decline.

Since Vatican I did not address the Jewish Question specifically, it cannot be said that it directly contributed to the growth of antisemitism. But antisemitism was clearly on the rise at the time, and the council took no notice of this very disturbing reality. It did not see the increasing hostility toward Jews within Catholic circles in such countries as France, Italy, and Russian Poland as a major concern. Nor did it regard the celebrated kidnapping of Edgardo Mortara, the Jewish boy who had been baptized by a servant woman and made a personal ward of Pius IX, as any kind of stain on Catholicism. There is little doubt that the vast majority of the conciliar participants supported Pius IX's handling of the Mortara case, as well as his growing identification of Jews with the despised ideology of liberalism and Freemasonry.

The European push for liberal and democratic reforms in civil society since 1848 had a positive impact on the social situation of Jews, leading to their emancipation in several places and a greater degree of individual freedom for them. In supporting the intractable opposition to these political changes expressed by Pius IX and his predecessors, Vatican I clearly opposed a process that was enhancing the dignity and social status of European Jews.

Vatican I thus proved to be no friend of the Jewish community. It failed to confront the growing antisemitism in Europe or to use its influence among Catholics to counter this threat. At least indirectly, therefore, the council's unconcern seemed to condone the increasingly negative attitudes toward Jews in several Catholic-dominated countries.

—*John T. Pawlikowski*

*See also* Freemasonry; Mortara Affair; Papacy, Modern; Pius IX, Pope; Ultramontanism; Vatican Council, Second

**References**

Hughes, Philip. *The Church in Crisis: A History of the General Councils, 325–1870* (Garden City, NY: Hanover House, 1961).

Mooras, Ronald. *The Catholic Church and Anti-semitism: Poland, 1933–1939* (Chur, Switzerland: Harwood, 1994).

Schweitzer, Frederick M. *A History of the Jews since the First Century* A.D. (New York: Macmillan, 1971).

## Vatican Council, Second (1962–1965)

The Second Vatican Council (Vatican II) opened a new chapter in the history of Christian-Jewish relations. Unlike the First Vatican Council of 1869, the church's understanding of its relationship to Judaism became an important agenda item for the deliberations of the assembled bishops. The initial proposal for the council lacked any specific reference to the Jewish Question. But after a personal meeting with French Jewish historian Jules Isaac, Pope John XXIII decided that the council would take up the Catholic Church's understanding of the Jewish people.

The discussion took many turns in the course of the council. For a time, it seemed the effort would be scuttled because of opposition from conservative bishops and some representing dioceses in Arab-dominated societies. But in the end, the statement on the church and the Jewish people was approved overwhelmingly during the closing session of October 1965.

Differing viewpoints were raised during the council regarding the nature of the document on Jews and Judaism. Would it be a totally independent statement? Would it be combined with another declaration, such as the one on the nature of the church? Or would it be a more general document on interreligious relations? The third option prevailed, with the statement on Jews and Judaism becoming chapter four of the conciliar declaration on the church's relationship to non-Christians known by its Latin title, *Nostra Aetate* (which is often wrongly equated with chapter four).

The statement on the Jews argued three major propositions. First, neither Jews in the time of Jesus nor Jews of the present day can be held collectively responsible for the death of Christ. Second, the coming of Christ did not signal the displacement of the Jews from the covenant with God, which Christian theologians and church leaders—especially the very influential Patristic writers—had claimed in the past to be the case. Finally, *Nostra Aetate* asserted that Jesus, his apostles, and the early church were profoundly impacted in a constructive fashion by their Jewish context.

The conciliar declaration also had a significant effect on another major popular teaching throughout Christian history: the idea that refusal to accept Christ as the Messiah brought on the Jewish community a perpetual social condition of wandering and homelessness, with no prospect of ever again having a national homeland of its own. This teaching came to the fore within the church during the early years of the Zionist movement. Vatican II's elimination of Jewish blame for the murder of Christ totally undercut this classical teaching, even though it made no direct reference to it in *Nostra Aetate* itself.

In another companion document on religious liberty, Vatican II affirmed democratic notions of religious liberty and freedom of conscience, notions strongly opposed by Catholicism for over 100 years and often associated in the Catholic mind with a Freemasonry thought to be dominated by Jews. This document helped eliminate a more modern form of antisemitism that exercised strong influence in certain European countries such as France and Poland.

Vatican II set the Catholic Church on a totally new course in terms of its relationship with the Jewish community. The process begun in the council culminated in Pope John Paul II's naming of antisemitism as deeply sinful and offering an apology at the Western Wall in Jerusalem for its strong manifestation in the church for centuries. *Nostra Aetate* also inspired similar declarations in many Protestant denominations.

—*John T. Pawlikowski*

**See also** Augustine of Hippo; Church Fathers; Deicide; Freemasonry; Gospels; Papacy, Modern; Paul; Supersessionism; Ultramontanism; Vatican Council, First; Wandering Jew; Zionism

**References**
Gilbert, Arthur. *The Vatican Council and the Jews* (Cleveland, OH, and New York: World Publishing, 1968).
Oesterreicher, John M. *The New Encounter between Christians and Jews* (New York: Philosophical Library, 1986).
Pawlikowski, John T. *What Are They Saying about Christian-Jewish Relations?* (New York and Ramsey, NJ: Paulist Press, 1980).

## Verjudung

A central concept in modern antisemitic thought, *Verjudung* (Judaization or Jewification) refers to the supposed danger of a growing Jewish influence over surrounding Christian society. Allegations of Judaization were leveled at Jews particularly regarding the economy, culture, and politics, but the concept also carried broader connotations and could even take on mythic proportions. For certain commentators, Judaization came to represent almost any aspect of modern life to which they were opposed and brought with it its own promise of redemption through a process of *Entjudung*, or "de-Judaization." Although the roots of the idea can be traced back to early Christian polemics over the role of Judaism in the new church, it was principally during the nineteenth and early twentieth centuries and particularly in Germany that the idea of Jewification assumed programmatic importance.

Although the word *Verjudung* itself only came into use during the second half of the nineteenth century, the idea that gave it birth was already gaining prominence during the 1830s and 1840s amid intensifying debates about Jewish emancipation. Complaints about Jewish usury and economic domination could be heard among both opponents and proponents of emancipation and among liberals as well as conservatives. So, too, if less often, could worries about the role of an acculturated German Jewish intelligentsia in German cultural and political life. Above all among conservative opponents of emancipation who defended the idea of a Christian state and repudiated the growth of a modern commercial economy, Judaism at times came to symbolize everything secular and materialist that they hoped to stave off in modern life.

If the equation of Judaism with an unwanted middle-class modernity had already occurred on the Right, the same move was made even more uncompromisingly on the radical Left among the so-called Young Hegelians in the 1840s. By the early 1840s, certain disciples of G. W. F. Hegel, such as Bruno Bauer, Moses Hess, and Karl Marx, had emerged as radical critics of German society, with Hess and Marx going so far as to oppose the whole nascent capitalist social and economic order. Bauer came out against Jewish emancipation, deploying a battery of images from the prevailing anti-Jewish social and economic stereotype to buttress his position. Hess, himself a Jew, and Marx, a convert of Jewish origins, at once supported Jewish emancipation against Bauer yet warned of the increasing sway of "Judaism" in German society. For Hess and even more for Marx, Judaism embodied the entire world of capitalism, which meant that to overthrow the latter, it would be necessary to eradicate the former. Scholars still dispute whether Marx is to be read as fundamentally anti-Jewish or as simply anticapitalist, with an unfortunate choice of polemical rhetoric. It is, however, certainly the case that Marx's critique and others like it paved the way for the spread of such far-reaching attacks on Jewish influence in society later in the century.

The word *Verjudung* itself may have been coined in 1850 by the German composer and cultural critic Richard Wagner in his essay *Judaism in Music*. Wagner had roots among the radicals of the 1840s, but in the wake of the failed 1848 revolution in Germany, he turned against the democratic revolutionary outlook in favor of a more "German" revolution, to be achieved through overcoming the allegedly Jewish commercial spirit in German culture and society. Wagner's essay was thus not simply a bad review of certain acculturated German Jewish composers; rather, it was a broad critique of German culture itself and an attack on Jewish influence within it.

Although Wagner spelled out many of the presuppositions of anti-Jewish arguments based on the idea of Judaization in the 1850s, it was only in the 1870s and after that other polemicists made the notion a central part of their rhetoric. This move coincided with the more general rise of modern antisemitism in response to German unification and Jewish emancipation after 1870. Wilhelm Marr, for example, often said to have coined the word *antisemite*, stated in 1879 that one of the principal aims of his new Antisemites' League was to oppose the Verjudung of German society; for Marr in particular, that meant alleged Jewish control of the press and the spread of Jewish commercial values in the newly unified and industrializing Germany. Other antisemitic thinkers of Bismarckian and Wilhelmine Germany, such as Paul de Lagarde and Eugen Dühring, agreed. So, too, did many conservative groups, such as the Conservative Party and the ultranationalist Pan-German League. These latter organizations, although not first and foremost antisemitic in orientation, often did play the antisemitic card in their politics, and they did so with reference to ideas of Judaization. Even liberals of the era sometimes associated Jews with the "worship of Mammon" that they saw undermining German society in a variant of the myth of Jewification.

Scholars disagree about how far fears of economic and cultural Judaization may have fed into the racial and biological antisemitism of National Socialism. Marr, for example, specifically defined his antisemitism in opposition to the religious-based anti-Judaism of an older stamp and has therefore usually been seen as a racist antisemite. Others, however, have suggested that even Marr was still moving along more traditional lines. Debates about Wagner and Wagner's influence on Hitler are yet more conflicted. In considering the role of the Judaization concept in National Socialist ideology and practice, though, it is important to keep in mind that the racial interpretation by no means excluded the social, economic, cultural, and political. The notion of *Verjudung* can thus help explain not only the Nuremberg Laws of 1935 but also the prior programs of Aryaniza-tion of the government, civil service, the press and educational institutions, and ultimately business life, with which the Nazis began their regime. If it is still problematic to trace a direct line from the idea of a spiritual de-Judaization of German society to that of the physical Entjudung seen in the Final Solution, it is at least clear that the range of solutions to the Jewish Question in Nazi ideology owed a great deal to the myth of *Verjudung.*

—Brian Vick

**See also** Bauer, Bruno; Christian State; Dühring, Eugen; Emancipation; Fascist Intellectuals; Feuerbach, Ludwig; Glagau, Otto; Heine, Heinrich; Hitler, Adolf; Jewish Question; *Judaism as an Alien Phenomenon; Judaism in Music;* Lagarde, Paul de; Marr, Wilhelm; Marx, Karl; Nazi Cultural Antisemitism; Nazi Legal Measures against Jews; Nuremberg Laws; Pan-German League; Racial Laws; Rosenberg, Alfred; Tivoli Program; *Völkisch* Movement and Ideology; Wagener, Hermann; Wagner, Richard; Young Germany; Young Hegelians

**References**

Aschheim, Steven E. "'The Jew Within': The Myth of 'Judaization' in Germany." In *Culture and Catastrophe: German and Jewish Confrontations with National Socialism and Other Crises* (New York: New York University Press, 1996), 45–68.

Katz, Jacob. *From Prejudice to Destruction: Anti-Semitism, 1700–1933* (Cambridge, MA: Harvard University Press, 1980).

Rose, Paul Lawrence. *German Question/Jewish Question: Revolutionary Antisemitism in Germany from Kant to Wagner* (Princeton, NJ: Princeton University Press, 1992).

## Versailles Treaty

Jewish nationhood was not mentioned in the Versailles Treaty. Only in article 95 of the Treaty of Sèvres (1920), one of the five treaties negotiated in the suburbs of Paris that ended World War I, was vague reference made to the Balfour Declaration of November 2, 1917. Thus, the expectations of many Zionists among the Allied states were disappointed. Despite its silence, the Versailles Treaty nevertheless had a significant indirect impact on the Jews of Europe, above all in the impetus it gave to a violence-prone antisemitism in Germany.

Before and during the war, Jews had developed only a rudimentary common identity. They fought in all the contesting armies and fell at the front, not as Jews but as soldiers of the countries in which they served. In Germany, notwithstanding the humiliating Jew Census of 1916, the elite elements of the Jewish population fully supported the country and also supported its war aims. The Hamburg banker Max Warburg later boasted (correctly) that it was his bank, more than any other, that had cut through the thorny problems of financing the German war effort. Walther Rathenau rendered great service to the nation in the organization and management of the war economy. Similarly, Jews of the upper classes in France, England, and the United States demonstrated their allegiance to the nation-state and shared in the joy of the Allied victory.

In Germany, the Versailles Treaty met with universal rejection. All political groups, from the radical Right to the radical Left and even the pacifists, condemned its articles as impossible or intolerable. Immediately following the armistice and even before the treaty negotiations, a portion of the bourgeois Right in Germany reorganized itself and set about acquiring a mass base by means of antisemitic propaganda. The Pan-German League and other *völkisch* (racist-nationalist) organizations used Versailles as a catalyst in the process of self-definition. Sweepingly, German and International Jewry were held responsible for the German defeat and for the unconscionable harshness of the treaty. Quite purposefully, new racist antisemitic tropes were injected into German political discourse.

The initial targets for attack were the Jewish members of the German peace delegation who had attempted, from behind the scenes, to ameliorate the treaty conditions. In particular, Max Warburg and other financiers were sharply criticized for having supposedly caved in too easily to the demands of the Entente. Warburg's attempts to win sizable concessions for his country from the Allies were easily misunderstood by the public. Meanwhile, the treaty mobilized intense antisemitic sentiment, especially among some returning soldiers. Physical violence against Jews became more frequent. "Jewish war-profiteers" were accused of having grown rich off the German people during the war. Liberal newspapers were attacked because they had not unreservedly supported the extreme war aims of the government and had, according to the antisemites' logic, therefore served the interests of Jewry instead.

The Pan-German League opportunistically sought to exploit the antisemitism stirred up in Germany by the Versailles Treaty. The league's Bamberg Manifesto proclaimed the struggle against Jewry and officially declared a racial war. Pan-German leaders, almost all of them university educated, steered into existence the German Racial League for Defense and Defiance, which inundated Weimar Germany with primitive antisemitic manifestos aimed at the victims of war and economic turmoil. Versailles came to symbolize International Jewry's scheming to destroy Germany, and the treaty itself was represented as the triumph of the Jews. Multiple conspiracy theories fed off obscure writings and decontextualized quotations; the *Protocols of the Elders of Zion*, soon exposed as a fraud, nonetheless appeared in several editions and in large printings.

The treaty drew the ire of all social classes, but it was particularly on the extreme Right that anti-Versailles agitation was most intense throughout the 1920s. Hostility toward the treaty was not always antisemitic. But the radical rightist, ultra-nationalist, antisemitic, and, somewhat later, National Socialist agitators who sought to mobilize a mass following ceaselessly hammered into the public the supposedly inescapable associations of "defeat," "stab-in-the-back," "Versailles," and "International Jewry."

—*Boris Barth*
*Richard S. Levy, translation*

**See also** Central Association of German Citizens of Jewish Faith; *Culture-Antisemitism or Pogrom-Antisemitism?*; Freemasonry; German National People's Party; Hitler's Speeches (Early); Jew Census; "Jewish" Press; National Socialist German Workers' Party; Pan-German League; *Protocols of the Elders of Zion*; Rathenau, Walther; Scheunenviertel Pogrom; *Völkisch* Movement and Ideology; Weimar; Zionism

**References**

Barth, Boris. *Dolchstosslegenden und politische Desintegration: Das Trauma der deutschen Niederlage im Ersten Weltkrieg* (Düsseldorf, Germany: Droste, 2003).

Korinman, Michel. *Deutschland über alles: Le pangermanisme, 1890–1945* (Paris: Fayard, 1999).

Lohalm, Uwe. *Völkischer Radikalismus: Die Geschichte des Deutschvölkischen Schutz- und Trutz- Bundes, 1919–1923* (Hamburg, Germany: Leipniz-Verlag, 1970).

## Veuillot, Louis (1813–1883)

Journalist Louis Veuillot, lay exponent of extreme Ultramontane Catholicism, was considered by most Jewish leaders to be their most dangerous opponent in mid-nineteenth-century France. Veuillot's political activism began after his conversion to Catholicism, which took place in 1838 on a trip to Rome. Until that event, his politics had been moderate; he had been a supporter of François Guizot's *juste milieu* (balance between revolution and reacton). In 1843, Veuillot became the editor of the Catholic journal *L'Univers.* From this platform, he became the leading French exponent of Ultramontanism, which looked to the pope as the supreme authority and fought all efforts to separate church and state in France. An emotional writer remembered for his acerbic style, he waged his first battle against the state-run university, whose leaders attempted to limit the control of the church in education. His position on this issue also put him at odds with the moderate leaders of the French Catholic Church. After 1848, he focused his attacks on liberal Catholics, using the same ferocious language that he had previously reserved for non-Catholics. In 1853, Veuillot won the support of Pope Pius IX (r. 1846–1878) in his struggle against liberal Catholicism, thereby making it difficult for even moderate Catholics to censure him publicly.

As early as the 1840s, Veuillot wrote articles defaming Judaism in *L'Univers,* using traditional anti-Jewish tropes. He portrayed Jews as alien vagabonds, accused them of having killed Jesus, and asserted that Judaism (and especially the Talmud) taught Jews to hate all Christians. In response, Jewish leaders defended their religion in the mainstream French press, and they won the support of liberal journalists in their struggle. During the Mortara Affair of 1858, Veuillot's anti-Judaism and antiliberalism reached new heights and finally put him at odds with Emperor Napoleon III, whom he had previously supported. Veuillot was unrelenting in his attacks on both Jews and the emperor, who responded by suppressing *L'Univers* from 1859 to 1867; Veuillot only regained full control of the journal in the 1870s.

Although Veuillot's anti-Judaism was religiously motivated and thus traditional in content, his two-pronged struggle against Jews and liberalism, which eventually resulted in his total opposition to liberal state policy, foreshadowed the antirepublican form of the political antisemitism that began to thrive in France shortly after his death.

—*Lisa Moses Leff*

**See also** Deicide; Dreyfus Affair; France; Mortara Affair; Pius IX, Pope; Talmud; Ultramontanism
**References**
Brown, Marvin L. *Louis Veuillot: French Ultramontane, Catholic Journalist and Layman, 1813–1883* (Durham, NC: Moore, 1977).
Gurian, Waldemar. "Louis Veuillot," *Catholic Historical Review* 36 (January 1951): 385–414.

## Vichy

Anti-Jewish prejudice and persecution did not begin in France with the Vichy regime. The Dreyfus Affair was perhaps the episode that most prominently called the world's attention to French antisemitism, but as recently as the 1930s, Léon Blum, shortly before his election as the first Jewish prime minister in France, had been beaten savagely in the streets of Paris by a group of royalist students. In fact, constant verbal abuse and virulent antisemitic press campaigns against Blum by right-wing organizations were a notable feature of the Popular Front era. A surge of xenophobia and heightened antisemitism characterized the interwar years in France. Some observers find disturbing continuities between the policies dealing with foreigners and refugees instituted by the Third Republic in its last years and the wartime Vichy regime, but without discounting such links entirely, it seems more appropriate to highlight the distinctiveness of the Vichy years in the long and complex history of relations between Jews and non-Jews in France.

The signal distinction of French antisemitism during the Vichy era was that the French government, on its own initiative and without being pressured initially by the German Occupation authorities, erected an elaborate and comprehensive program of state-sanctioned antisemitism that included more than 100 laws and decrees and two versions of the *Statut des Juifs* (Jewish Statute). These laws defined Jews in a manner more stringent than the Germans had originally planned to apply in Paris and the Occupied Zone of northern France. In contrast to periodic, historical outbursts of popular antisemitism, Vichy integrated into official government policy the views of racist theorists on the extremist, antisemitic fringe. Since these measures were instituted by decrees—the French parliament was never called back into session after voting to grant full powers to Marshal Philippe Pétain in July 1940, and there was no free press or any other traditional marker of public opinion in free societies—it is easier to characterize and describe the behavior of Vichy officials than it is to gauge the reactions of the population at large to the blatant antisemitism.

Although, in practice, foreign Jews were significantly more injured by Vichy's antisemitism, Jews who were French citizens of long standing were also the target of sweeping discriminatory measures. The actions taken by the Vichy administration fell into four major categories: legal definitions of Jews as inferiors; exclusion and isolation from French society through special censuses and requirements to have their identity papers stamped "*JUIF*" (JEW) or "*JUIVE*" (JEWESS); economic and financial spoliation through the so-called Aryanization program; and finally, roundup and deportation.

Several months after their conquest of France, the Germans ordered Jews in Paris and the Occupied Zone to register at police stations, required yellow signs bearing the label "Jewish Enterprise" to be placed on windows or doors of all Jewish businesses, and began to assign non-Jewish "trustees" to manage all Jewish businesses that were destined for outright sale or for permanent control by non-Jews. Correctly assuming that this German Aryanization program was essentially a ruse to confiscate Jewish property and

"The true face of the Free French." This Vichy poster sought to discredit the leader of the Committee of National Liberation, Charles de Gaulle (face obscured by the microphone but clearly recognizable by his military cap). He is depicted as the "advance man" for the caricatured Jews who stand behind him, literally and figuratively. (Courtesy of Richard S. Levy)

wealth for transfer to Germany, French authorities adopted and systematically applied a similar policy through the General Commissariat for Jewish Affairs, a central agency that was created in March 1941 to deal with the Jewish Question. In the summer and early fall of 1940, before implementation of any German antisemitic measures, the Vichy government repealed a Third Republic prohibition (the Marchandeau Law) on "hate language" aimed especially at the Jews, rolled back thousands of naturalizations that had given Jews French citizenship in the interwar years, and subjected foreign Jews to internment in "special camps" or to forced residence under police surveillance in remote locations. Even before deportations began to the death camps in the East, 3,000 Jews died from malnutrition or disease in these camps.

From its earliest days, the Vichy regime began the process, codified and expanded by the two Jewish Statues of October 1940 and June 1941, of confining all Jews to an inferior status that excluded them from public function, leadership in the military, or significant participation in the liberal professions and restricted their access to higher education. In line with traditional stereotypes, the French Aryanization measures aspired to remove "excessive" Jewish influence in the economy. The goal was to limit Jewish employment opportunities to manual labor or minor office positions, thereby restricting Jews' contact with the public to the minimum and denying them all authority or influence over non-Jews. Despite wartime labor shortages, there was no guarantee of employment for Jews in even the most menial occupation—the gravedigger at Pere Lachaise Cemetery in Paris was fired because he was Jewish. By the summer of 1941, just one year into the Occupation, approximately half of the Jewish population in France was deprived of all means of existence, and the situation deteriorated rapidly thereafter for the other half. In addition to the sale or transfer of Jewish property to non-Jewish trustees, all Jewish bank accounts and other financial assets were frozen, allowing withdrawals of a bare pittance. Consequently, thousands of Jews came to depend for their survival on charities affiliated with the controversial Union Générale des Israélites de France (General Union of French Israelites [UGIF]), a Jewish council created by Vichy in November 1941. Meant to centralize all Jewish relief organizations, the UGIF eventually provided lists that would identify and facilitate the location of Jews targeted for deportation. Moreover, as it did most notoriously in December 1941 with a 1 billion franc fine levied in reprisal for the assassination of German officers by the Resistance, the UGIF offered the Germans a central agency through which to tax or levy fines on the French Jewish community.

The Holocaust was fundamentally a result of German policy, but the cooperation of the Vichy administration with German police authorities facilitated the success of the massive roundups and deportations from France in the summer and fall of 1942 and the spring of 1943. Approximately 80,000 Jews, few of whom survived, were deported from France to Auschwitz and other German concentration camps. The Vichy authorities gave the Germans the censuses of the Jewish population they had ordered the French police to conduct, they concentrated thousands of foreign Jews in camps and assigned them to forced residence, and they stamped identity papers with *JUIF* or *JUIVE*—all of which expedited the arrest of those targeted for deportation. Moreover, especially until the final year of the Occupation when Vichy's enthusiasm for cooperation in this endeavor with the Germans had cooled somewhat, the French police and gendarmerie provided the bulk of the manpower for the arrests. Despite occasional reports of a lack of enthusiasm among a few individual policemen, orders for arrests and deportation were executed routinely and with firm determination. As acknowledged formally by President Jacques Chirac in July 1995, France's partial responsibility for the victims of the Holocaust deported from French soil is undeniable.

More complex than this well-documented indictment of Vichy's state-sponsored antisemitism is the question of the general reaction of non-Jews in France to these policies. Most historians agree that in the early period of the Occupation, there was little resistance to the thrust of the Jewish Statutes or to Vichy's sweeping antisemitic program in the economic, legal, and social domains. Although public acts of antisemitic violence, such as vandalism of Jewish shops, were relatively rare and limited essentially to traditional antisemitic circles and although many Jews reported individual acts of kindness or expressions of sympathy from their non-Jewish neighbors, most French people seemed either indifferent to the fate of the Jews or preoccupied with their own concerns as they confronted the harsh realities of the Occupation. Only in the summer of 1942 did French public opinion seem to be sharply affected by the German imposition of the yellow star on Jews living in the Occupied Zone (which began in June) and especially by the mass deportations in all of France in the summer and fall of that year. From that point forward, many Jews who were in need of shelter were comforted by the public protests of leading clerics such as

Msgr. J.-G. Saliège, the bishop of Toulouse, and found assistance from non-Jews in French towns and villages in all parts of the country—the rescue of approximately 2,500 children by the Protestant villagers of Le Chambon-sur-Lignon being one of the most celebrated cases. In addition to the direct action that most Jews in France took to escape deportation, the individual and collective actions of many French people were instrumental in saving thousands of the approximately 240,000 Jews who escaped deportation from France during the war.

—*John F. Sweets*

**See also** Alsace; Aryanization; Crimes against Humanity (French Trials); Dreyfus Affair; Fascist Intellectuals; France; Holocaust; Vallat, Xavier; Yellow Star

**References**

Kaspi, André. *Les Juifs pendant l'Occupation* (Paris: Seuil, 1991).

Klarsfeld, Serge. *Vichy-Auschwitz*. 2 vols. (Paris: Fayard, 1983 and 1985).

Marrus, Michael R., and Robert O. Paxton. *Vichy France and the Jews* (New York: Basic Books, 1981).

Poznanski, Renée. *Jews in France during World War II* (Hanover, NH: Brandeis University Press, 2001).

## Victory of Jewry over Germandom, The (1879)

The seventeen years that elapsed between *A Mirror to the Jews* (*Der Judenspiegel*) in 1862 and *The Victory of Jewry over Germandom* (*Der Sieg des Judenthums über das Germanenthum*) in 1879 brought their author, Wilhelm Marr, a succession of personal and public miseries, which he invested with world-historical significance. The shipwreck that was his life in these years helps explain his deepening commitment to the idea of a Jewish world conspiracy and his attempt to politicize this myth in his sixtieth year.

After the indifferent reception of *Der Judenspiegel,* Marr stopped writing about the Jews, but it is clear from the greater depth and sophistication of *The Victory of Jewry* that he had been unable to put the subject aside. Although Marr once again posed as historian, literary critic, psychologist, philosophe, economist, and moralist, his story could no longer be confined to his original inspiration, the petty politics of Hamburg. *The Victory of Jewry* was grander in scope and passion, the chronicle of an epic struggle.

In 1879, Marr placed Jewish evil in a world-historical, racial, and conspiratorial framework. It was race that made that history explicable. More insistently than in 1862, it was race that explained the mutual hatred of Jews and Germans, indeed, of Jews and all other peoples. On the most superficial level, *The Victory of Jewry* rested squarely on the idea of racial determinism working through history. But even a cursory reading of the book raises doubts about the authenticity of Marr's interest in the historical record. As his many critics noted, his treatment of Jewish history was idiosyncratic and haphazard, to say the least. Only the most damning episodes were selected and then only because they cast a specially lurid light on the German present. Beginning with the Babylonian Captivity and proceeding up to the present moment, Marr showed his readers that the obnoxious behavior of Jews in the new German Empire was absolutely consistent with the entire previous history of the "Race." Again and again in history, Jews had been welcomed by other peoples—up to the point when their crimes made them unendurable. For 1,800 years, ever since their arrival in the West, they had waged a cowardly but unremitting war of revenge. Their weapons were no longer the biblical fire and sword but slyness, cunning, ruthless realism, subversion, and usury—all racially conditioned and perfected. But Marr defied the logic of his own argument by portraying Jews as anything but the helpless victims of their own genetic evil. They were, in fact, conscious, premeditating, disciplined destroyers of the good. Although he assured his readers that he was merely the dispassionate chronicler of the Jewish conquest and personally resigned to enter into slavery, there could be no mistaking his hatred or his intention of goading his readers to fury.

*The Victory of Jewry* went through twelve editions by the end of 1879. Its enthusiastic reception cannot be explained solely by the quality of its argument, however. The transformation of German life by a dynamic capitalism with its many social casualties, the visible thriving of German Jews, the threat of socialism, and the decline of traditional values had readied large segments of the population for Marr's message. For once in his long career of misadventures, his timing was perfect. He spoke directly to the desperate situation of the small farmer and the lower middle class, the two social groups that would provide the mass basis for all future antisemitic parties. With his best-seller, Marr also registered a changed perception in the nature of the Jewish danger. He proclaimed that the old sorts of casual anti-Jewish behavior—the occasional book, the occasional pogrom—were outmoded. Such measures had failed to halt the onslaught of the Jews. Now, after their emancipation (1871), it was too late for such intermittent and defensive gestures because the Jews had become so enormously powerful. To replace the ineffectual traditional methods, a continuous grassroots political effort would have to be mounted, institutionalized in parties, propaganda associations, and newspapers. The political action program was implicit in the book. It became explicit in Marr's next pamphlet, dashed off in late 1879, *Elect No Jews!* It bore the subtitle, "The Way to Victory of Germandom over Jewry," and it launched antisemitism into the political culture of Germany.

—*Richard S. Levy*

*See also* Antisemitic Political Parties; Emancipation; Marr, Wilhelm; *Mirror to the Jews, A*
**Reference**
Levy, Richard S., ed. *Antisemitism in the Modern World: An Anthology of Texts* (Lexington, MA: D. C. Heath, 1991).

## Visigothic Spain

Unlike most episodes in Jewish history, the story of the Jews in Visigothic Spain, in the century after 587 when the Visigothic King Recarred converted to Nicean Christianity, has drawn the attention of historians of many schools. Understanding Jewish fortunes in this period is integral to understanding life and rule in the Spanish realms as a whole. The problem scholars have posed is why the kings, beginning with Sisebut in 613, literally forced the Jews of Spain to convert and why subsequent kings eagerly enforced the policy. Some have suggested royal initiative, others that the kings were following an ecclesiastical lead. One has said the policy was checkered; some kings eased the pressure because, intermittently, Jews were royal allies.

Essential to the solution is that Jews were not viewed simply as members of a religious group. Rather, they were considered a *gens,* a legally privileged ethnic group entitled to permanent residence and a set of laws; for Jews, this was a combination of (surviving) Roman and Jewish law. Conversion, accordingly, did not eliminate Jewish ethnic identity, which explains why contemporary legal texts include alternating references to "Jews," "baptized Jews," and "sincerely baptized Jews."

The Visigothic kings sought to eradicate "Judaism," not the Jewish gens. They did so to ensure their rule. The Visigoths were not indigenous to Spain, nor were they ever a majority. To entrench what was really rule from the outside, they sought to put themselves at the top of a hierarchy: first, through establishing a single faith, and then, when this failed, through a unified law. Jews were forcibly converted, but they kept practicing Judaism. A series of oaths forcing Jews to swear to observe Christianity apparently achieved nothing. The Visigoths therefore enacted a new law code that was binding on all and annulled all previous codes, meaning that members of the Jewish gens no longer enjoyed the rights of Roman law and citizenship, even in the abbreviated forms in which these had survived. The Hispani, residents of the Iberian Peninsula during the Roman period who were Christian but not Visigoth, were also forced to cede legally. Jewry policy thus reflected royal policies of unification as a whole and, hence, their general importance. The law was draconian. Members of the Jewish gens were eventually declared slaves. All this came to an end, artificially, when the Arab conquest of Iberia ended Visigothic rule in 711.

Churchmen faced two problems. Forced baptism, though not unknown, was illegal. King Sisebut's decree of 613 was called an act of "hazy zeal." More difficult was "backsliding," the canonically repugnant return of a Christian to a prior faith. The solution, which was reaffirmed at a series of church councils held at Toledo over which the kings presided, set canonical precedent; the early modern Spanish Inquisition, nearly a millennium later, was still applying it directly. It was said that *quia constat* (to backslide)—since it was evident that the convert (forced or not) had observed Christian rites—was to apostize. This concept entered the later formal canon law, although some doubted its validity even in the sixteenth century.

—*Kenneth Stow*

**See also** Church Councils (Early); Inquisition; Islam and the Jews; Roman Empire
**References**
Bachrach, Bernard. *Early Medieval Jewish Policy in Western Europe* (Minneapolis: University of Minnesota Press, 1977).
Glick, T. F. *Islamic and Christian Spain in the Early Middle Ages* (Princeton, NJ: Princeton University Press, 1979).
Juster, J. *The Legal Condition of the Jews under the Visigothic Kings.* Translated and updated by A. M. Rabello (Jerusalem: Israel Law Review Association, 1976).
Stow, Kenneth. *Alienated Minority: The Jews of Medieval Latin Europe* (Cambridge, MA: Harvard University Press, 1994).

## *Völkisch* Movement and Ideology

The *völkisch* movement originated in the late nineteenth century in opposition to the modernizing trends of the Wilhelmian Empire. These trends included liberalism, democracy, socialism, and industrial capitalism, the growth of which *völkisch* ideologues attributed primarily to the subversive influence of the Jews. Drawing their inspiration and elements of their ideology from the romantic era and the War of Liberation against Napoleon, *völkisch* publicists celebrated the uniqueness and superiority of the German language, history, spirituality, and "race." The frustrations of German defeat in World War I and the widespread perception of the Weimar Republic as an "un-German" form of government imposed by the victorious Allies had the effect of shifting *völkisch* ideas and values from the margins into the mainstream of the German Right. The Nazi Party became the most popular and successful of the many *völkisch* organizations,

which it absorbed or superseded after assuming power in 1933.

In 1875, obsessed with purifying German language and culture of foreign influence, the linguist Hermann von Pfister-Schwaighusen (1836–1916) introduced the adjective *völkisch*, derived from the noun *Volk* (nation or people) as a German substitute for the Latin-rooted word *national*. The term came into widespread usage in the 1890s, a decade in which numerous nationalist and nativist organizations were formed to promote supposedly authentic German culture and racial awareness as a way of generating popular support for right-wing policies. Elements of *völkisch* ideology may be found in the works of such early nineteenth-century writers as the poet Ernst Moritz Arndt, the philosopher Johann Gottlieb Fichte, and the pioneer of physical education Friedrich Ludwig Jahn, all of whom sought to strengthen German ethnicity (*Volkstum*) and spoke disparagingly of Jews. However, the political objectives of the *völkisch* movement that emerged in the late nineteenth century were more extreme than the populist politics of their romantic predecessors. The main objective of the *völkisch* movement—never unified until the Nazi era—was to deepen Germans' sense of national solidarity through appeals to the mystical notion of a racial blood bond among all members of the ethnic community. This racial mythology was designed to overcome the many social, political, religious, cultural, and territorial divisions in the recently unified German Empire and to create a popular consensus for deeply reactionary and often contradictory policies. This agenda typically included the dissolution of the parliamentary system; the suppression of the liberal and socialist parties and partisan politics in general; the restoration of a precapitalist economic system based on agriculture, handicrafts, and small proprietorship; the "reform" of German institutions allegedly corrupted by commercialism and materialism; the creation of a specifically German religion (whether Protestant Christian or Nordic pagan); the regeneration of the nation through "racial hygiene"; the strengthening of a hierarchical, authoritarian, and militaristic state; the union of all ethnic Germans in a greater Reich; the conquest and colonization of foreign territories; and the total elimination of Jews from German society. The hallmark of the *völkisch* movement was the overriding significance that its adherents attached to the Jewish Question, defined as a problem of race. From the *völkisch* perspective, revocation of Jewish citizenship rights and expulsion of the Jews were the keys to the *völkisch* project of national regeneration and German expansion.

The principal source of the *völkisch* reaction lay in the transformation of a static agrarian society into a dynamic, competitive, urbanized, and industrial system following German unification, a process that coincided with the full emancipation of German Jews in 1869. Early *völkisch* culture critics, including Richard Wagner, Constantin Franz, and Paul de Lagarde, criticized the Bismarckian state in the 1870s for its economic liberalism, its adoption of parliamentary institutions, and its failure to create a unified national culture. Later *völkisch* ideologues, such as Julius Langbehn, Adolf Bartels, and Heinrich Class, held up the "Iron Chancellor" as a positive foil to Wilhelm II, under whose reign the modernization, commercialization, and "Judaization" of German society appeared irreversible. Although the antisemitic political parties certainly shared a *völkisch* orientation, the *völkisch* movement (also sometimes referred to as the *Deutschbewegung*, or German movement) is usually more closely identified with the extraparliamentary antisemitic pressure groups that emerged in the 1890s and 1900s. The Deutschbund (German Union), founded by Friedrich Lange in 1894, represented one of the first attempts to unify a movement that was made up of diverse racist groups, parties, cults, and sects, often in competition and rivalry with each other. Typically eccentric examples are the "arioheroic" cult of the Austrian Jörg Lanz von Liebenfels, the Theosophic racial doctrine of Guido von List, and the Mittgart-Bund founded in 1906 to propagate the selective breeding projects of Willibald Hentschel. There were tensions also between supporters of a Germanic Christianity, such as the racialists Houston Stewart Chamberlain, Ludwig Schemann, and Arthur Bonus, and advocates of an Aryan-German faith, such as Ludwig Fahrenkrog and Wilhelm Schwaner, founders of the *Deutschreligiöse*

*Glaubensgemeinschaft* (German faith community) in 1912. *Völkisch* ideas were also disseminated in such influential interest groups as the Agrarian League (1893), German National White Collar Employees Association (1893), Eastern Marches Society (1894), League of Industrialists (1895), German Naval League (1898), German Army League (1912), and especially the Pan-German League (1891/1894), which took a radically *völkisch* turn after Class's accession to its leadership in 1908. There were student and youth groups; women's organizations; and movements for "reform" in the arts, education, and the professions, all of which adopted *völkisch* ideology. The most extreme leadership cadres of various antisemitic organizations were joined in Theodor Fritsch's Imperial Hammer League (Reichshammerbund) in 1912. The German Union and the Imperial Hammer League were among the seventeen *völkisch* organizations that joined to form the Deutschvölkische Vereinigung in 1913.

Its populist, anticapitalist, and antiestablishment rhetoric and program relegated the *völkisch* movement to the political fringe of the Wilhelmian monarchy before World War I. But this situation began to change during the war. *Völkisch* publicists actively opposed the German peace initiative of 1917, the same year that the Munich-based publisher J. F. Lehmann launched the movement's most important postwar journal, *Deutschlands Erneuerung* (Germany's Renewal). After the November revolution and the collapse of the empire in 1918, the *völkisch* movement emerged from the relative isolation of the imperial era. Its counterrevolutionary and insurrectionist aims swiftly gathered support from a wide variety of rightists, including even the monarchical conservatives. Greater numbers and a more intransigent ideology, however, did not cure the movement's divisiveness. Though agreeing on the need to organize under the *Führerprinzip* (leadership principle), overthrow the republic, and establish a national dictatorship to create a *judenfrei* (Jew-free) Germany, *völkisch* leaders and organizations continued their cut-throat competition for control of the movement. Aspirants included Erich Ludendorff, the favorite of the *Wehrverbände* (military organizations); Konstantin von Gebsattel, backed by the Pan-Germans; Alfred Roth, the head of the largest postwar extraparliamentary *völkisch* organization, the German Racial League for Defense and Defiance (DSTB); Count Ernst zu Reventlow, head of the Deutschvölkische Freiheitspartei (German Racial Freedom Party); Reinhold Wulle, head of the Deutschvölkischer Arbeitsring (German Racial Working Circle) in Berlin; and Wolfgang Kapp, whose short-lived coup in March 1920 received support from all quarters of the *völkisch* movement.

Out of this welter of contestants, Adolf Hitler's tiny, Munich-based National Socialist German Workers' Party emerged as the strongest *völkisch* organization. From the start, its deliberate appeal to the working class made it appear less beholden to the wealthy bourgeoisie than many of its *völkisch* rivals. The banning of the DSTB in 1922 following the murder of the German foreign minister, Walther Rathenau, in which members of the DSTB were involved, left the field clear for the Nazis to absorb much of its membership. The Nazis also enjoyed what amounted to the protection of the Bavarian state, which refused to implement the Weimar government's laws restricting right-wing organizations. After his failed putsch attempt in November 1923, Hitler took a more pragmatic road to power, stressing organizational discipline, political activism, and practical propaganda. In *Mein Kampf,* he scorned his *völkisch* precursors for their sectarianism, lack of realism, and political ineffectiveness. Nonetheless, the preparatory work of the *völkisch* movement (both in Germany and in Austria) was indispensable to Hitler's eventual acquisition of power. The Nazis put into practice many of the long-standing *völkisch* goals, none more important than the elimination of Jews from German society.

—*Roderick Stackelberg*

**See also** Antisemitic Political Parties; Arndt, Ernst Moritz; Austria; Bartels, Adolf; Chamberlain, Houston Stewart; Class, Heinrich; Emancipation; Fichte, J. G.; Frantz, Constantin; Fritsch, Theodor; German National White Collar Employees Association; German Racial Freedom Party; German Racial League for Defense and Defiance; Hentschel, Willibald; Imperial Hammer League; Jewish Question; Lagarde, Paul de; Lange, Friedrich; Lanz von Liebenfels, Jörg; List, Guido von; Ludendorff, Erich; National Socialist German Workers' Party; Nazi Party Program; Pan-German League; Reventlow, Ernst zu; Roth, Alfred; Schemann, Ludwig; *Verjudung;* Wagner, Richard; Weimar

**References**

Hermand, Jost. *Old Dreams of a New Reich: Völkisch Utopias and National Socialism.* Translated by Paul Levesque with Stefan Soldovieri (Bloomington: Indiana University Press, 1992).

Mohler, Armin. *Die Konservative Revolution in Deutschland, 1918–1932: Ein Handbuch.* 5th ed. (Graz, Austria, and Stuttgart, Germany: Leopold Stocker Verlag, 1999).

Mosse, George L. *The Crisis of German Ideology: Intellectual Origins of the Third Reich* (New York: Grosset and Dunlap, 1964).

Puschner, Uwe. *Die völkische Bewegung im wilhelminischen Kaiserreich: Sprache—Rasse—Religion* (Darmstadt, Germany: Wissenschaftliche Buchgesellschaft, 2001).

Stern, Fritz. *The Politics of Cultural Despair: A Study in the Rise of the Germanic Ideology* (Berkeley: University of California Press, 1961).

## Vogelsang, Karl von (1818–1890)

Karl von Vogelsang was born in Silesia, the son of a Prussian army officer. After earning a law degree, he entered the Prussian civil service but resigned from his position to become a provincial landowner in Mecklenburg. He converted to Catholicism in 1850, and in 1860, he left Germany for Vienna.

In Austria, he became the leading intellectual figure of political Catholicism. Starting in 1875, he edited the Catholic newspaper *Vaterland,* representing the tradition of Catholic romanticism (Adam Müller) and conservative aristocrats. Vogelsang delved into the "social question," elaborating his ideas about social reform to improve the lot of the lower classes. In 1879, to promote these views, he founded the more academic journal *Österreichische Monatsschrift für christliche Sozialreform* (Austrian Monthly for Christian Social Reform).

During the 1880s, Vogelsang was an influential voice within the Christian Social Movement, which developed into one of the most important political parties of Austria. His intellectual impact on politicians such as Prince Alois Liechtenstein and Karl Lueger was significant. In addition to his journal, Vogelsang used an informal study group to spread his ideas about overcoming the dire consequences of industrialization and proletarianization.

His theoretical approach was antimodernist, socially interventionist, antisocialist, and antiliberal. His opposition to liberalism embraced a critique of capitalism, as well. He was one of the first and most prominent representatives of corporatism—the supplanting of class and class warfare by the institutionalized cooperation between status groups (*Stände*). Corporatism has often been seen as a kind of forerunner of fascism. Yet it is also the basis of democratic versions of systematic cooperation between employers and employees. Vogelsang linked his theories to the idea of a "social kingdom." Tying together the defense of monarchy with the promotion of social reforms, he attached his reactionary outlook to a progressive one. Vogelsang was a universalist, a man who believed that society and polity should be conceived of as an organic unity, not as the products of warring individualistic interests and interest articulation. He was not explicitly against democracy, but his understanding of politics did not leave much room for a competitive party system.

Vogelsang's double strategy of confronting both liberalism and socialism was underpinned by his antisemitism, which, in turn, had its roots in his antimodernism. The evils of pauperism and social volatility he laid at the door of economic and political liberalism. The Jews owed their emancipation to liberalism and were, according to Vogelsang, all too ready to profit from any of its damaging interventions. His ideal was the medieval world, imagined as an age of natural harmony, one not yet poisoned by enlightenment, rationalism, individualism, and the profit motive. He did not criticize Jews as a "race" or as a religion but as the vanguard of social changes destroying the natural order. Capitalism and socialism were both expressions of these changes, and both were prominently represented, according to Vogelsang, by Jews. He did not fight the Jews per se but the so-called Jewish press, Jewish capitalism, and Jewish

Marxism. At least in theory, he accepted the proposition that Jewish identity could be overcome by conversion to Christianity.

Vogelsang's personal, socially based antisemitic views were less significant in their own right than what became of them in the hands of some of his influential followers. The most important of these was Lueger, a politician with clear links to Vogelsang who justified his own crude antisemitism by referring to his mentor. Although not a Nazi, Anton Orel, among the more theoretically inclined of the Vogelsang school, represented what passed as "principled" antisemitism in the Austrian politics of the 1920s and 1930s. Vogelsang was not forward-looking enough to anticipate or prevent the "racist" interpretation of his social antisemitism. The limits of his vision—and his sympathies—are exemplified by the critique he felt impelled to level against Georg von Schönerer's Pan-German politics. He unhesitatingly rejected Schönerer's anti-Catholicism but not the Pan-Germans' radical antisemitism that paved the way for Hitler's. Vogelsang, in the tradition of Catholic antisemitism, showed little regard for the basic rights of Jews.

—*Anton Pelinka*

*See also* Austria; Capital: Useful vs. Harmful; Christian Social Party (Austria); "Jewish" Press; Linz Program; Lueger, Karl; Pan-Germans (Austria); Schönerer, Georg von

**References**

Bader, Erwin. *Karl v. Vogelsang: Die geistigen Grundlagen der christlichen Sozialreform* (Vienna: Herder, 1990).

Boyer, John W. *Political Radicalism in Late Imperial Vienna: Origins of the Christian Social Movement, 1848–1897* (Chicago: University of Chicago Press, 1981).

Pulzer, Peter. *The Rise of Political Anti-Semitism in Germany and Austria*. Rev. ed. (London: P. Halban, 1988).

# Voltaire, François-Marie-Arouet de (1694–1778)

The leading figure of the French Enlightenment, François-Marie Arouet Voltaire came from a middle-class background but later invented an aristocratic lineage and adopted the pen name

Voltaire. He became the most famous writer in eighteenth-century France, with works of history, drama, literature, and philosophy and on issues of the day. He also produced scientific studies with his mistress and collaborator, Mme. du Châtelet. His most famous writings include the *Philosophical Letters* (1734), *Zadig* (1747), *Candide* (1758), and the *Philosophical Dictionary* (1764). A great wit, Voltaire infused his works with satire, directed particularly against the Catholic Church, which he called "*l'infâme.*" His writings were viewed as dangerous to those in power, and he spent many years in exile or in hiding.

Voltaire is widely famed for his advocacy of philosophical and religious tolerance; though he did not actually say, "I disapprove of what you say, but I will defend to the death your right to say it," the quote—often attributed to him—expresses a central aspect of his thinking. His fervent support of freedom of thought did not prevent him, however, from ridiculing those whose beliefs he found wanting. Jews and Judaism were special objects of his derision. In his *Philosophical Dictionary,* he called the Jewish people "ignorant," "barbarous," and full of superstition. At the same time, he also criticized those who persecuted them, noting acerbically, "Still, we ought not to burn them."

Voltaire's fervent support of freedom of thought did not prevent him from ridiculing those whose beliefs he found wanting. Jews and Judaism were special objects of his derision. (Library of Congress)

These kinds of comments created a profound sense of ambivalence among Jews of his time, who otherwise admired the philosopher and appreciated his attacks on the Inquisition and on religious persecution. The Sephardi writer Isaac de Pinto wrote a famous open letter to Voltaire in 1762, in which he lamented that "horrid prejudices" were being "authorized by the greatest genius of the most enlightened age." Voltaire responded apologetically for having stereotyped all Jews and praised De Pinto, but the interchange did not alter his opinion of Jews in general.

De Pinto's ambivalence about Voltaire has endured among modern scholars. Some writers who revere Voltaire's general philosophy have argued that his comments on the Jews were no more than incidental prejudices left over from his Catholic education or results of unpleasant encounters with particular Jews. Others have maintained that Voltaire's attacks on the Old Testament were not criticisms of Judaism per se but

indirect attacks on Christianity, done in such a way as to escape the notice of censors. Yet others have taken a harsher view. Heinrich Graetz argued that Voltaire profoundly hated all Jews, whereas Arthur Hertzberg saw him as "the major link in Western intellectual history between the anti-Semitism of classic paganism and the modern age" (Herztberg 1968, 10). This view has been challenged by those who insist that Voltaire's ideas must be understood in context. Allan Arkush has argued that Voltaire actually spoke more favorably of Judaism than of Christianity. Harvey Chisick has noted that, though Voltaire had a flawed understanding of Jewish history and Judaism, his opposition was to what he perceived as its intolerance and exclusivism, ideals that were at odds with his own universalist ethics.

The debate on Voltaire is a central one in scholarship on Jewish history and on antisemitism because of his place in the European tradition and because of the conflicted nature of his statements on Jews. It is likely to endure, for it concerns a question of crucial significance in Jewish history: the place of Jews in modern, secular, universalist societies.

—*Alyssa Goldstein Sepinwall*

**See also** Diderot, Denis; Lavater, Johann Kaspar; Philosemitism

*References*

Chisick, Harvey. "Ethics and History in Voltaire's Attitudes towards the Jews," *Eighteenth Century Studies* 35 (2002): 577–600.

Hertzberg, Arthur. *The French Enlightenment and the Jews* (New York: Columbia University Press, 1968).

Sutcliffe, Adam. "Myth, Origins, Identity: Voltaire, the Jews and the Enlightenment Notion of Toleration," *Eighteenth Century* 39 (1998): 107–126.

# W

## Wagener, Hermann (1815–1889)

Hermann Wagener was born in Seeglitz near Neuruppin in Prussia, into the Pietistic and patriotic household maintained by his father, a Lutheran pastor. He studied law in Berlin and in 1838 joined the Prussian judicial administration. There, he quickly became a protégé, along with Otto von Bismarck, of Ernst Ludwig von Gerlach, the influential archconservative. In 1848, Wagener became the founding editor of the *Neue Preussische Zeitung* (New Prussian Newspaper, nicknamed the *Kreuzzeitung* because of the cross on its masthead), the leading paper of the Prussian Right. Forced to resign in 1854 after a conflict with the Berlin chief of police, Wagener won a seat in the Prussian Chamber of Deputies, where he became the leader of a small band of Christian Conservatives interested in social and political reform. In 1862, he became an unofficial adviser to Bismarck on social issues. His task, as he saw it, was to defeat liberalism, win over the emerging class of industrial workers to the Prussian monarchy, and restore their weakening Christian faith. He advocated equal male suffrage over the wealth-weighted Prussian franchise and the right of unions to strike. After German unification, Wagener was officially employed as an adviser in the Prussian Ministry of State. Again, he was forced to give up this position (as well as his parliamentary seats) in 1873, when he was involved in a scandal concerning the sale of railroad shares. Wagener was thereafter of diminished usefulness to Bismarck, although he regained some stature in the 1880s as the publicist whose writings prepared the way for Bismarck's social insurance reforms.

Wagener was not an original thinker. As editor of the *Kreuzzeitung* and the *Staats- und Gesellschaftslexikon* (Lexicon for State and Society) and frequent contributor to the *Berliner Revue,* he popularized already current ideas of a "social monarchy" that directly influenced the emergence of Court Chaplain Adolf Stoecker's Christian Social Party at the end of the 1870s. He, like Stoecker, regarded Jews as highly problematic for his vision of a harmonious German future. In the 1850s and 1860s, when few Germans showed much interest in the Jewish Question, Wagener used his access to various media outlets and his personal influence to keep the "problem of the Jews" before the public eye. He presented a motion in Prussian Chamber of Deputies in 1856 to revoke article 12 of the constitution, which stated religion was to be no bar to political and civic rights. The motion was seen at the time as aimed specifically at Jews (and roundly defeated). Wagener opened the pages of his *Lexicon* to a thoroughly antisemitic essay by Bruno Bauer (in 1862), blaming Jews for the deterioration of social unity, shameless exploitation of Germans, naked materialism, and many other sins. Well before it became widespread, the notion of a wide-reaching Jewish conspiracy could be found fully spelled out in the pages of the *Kreuzzeitung* under Wagener's editorship.

Wagener himself was not a racist, nationalist, or extreme antisemite, at least not when measured against late nineteenth- or early twentieth-century standards. He held Jews as essentially harmful but did not blame them exclusively for all the ills of German society or conceive of them as a terrifyingly powerful force for evil. In a Christian state, as he conceived of it, they simply could not participate as equals.

—*George Vascik*

**See also** Bauer, Bruno; Christian Social Party (Germany); Christian State; 1848; *Judaism as an Alien Phenomenon;* Stoecker, Adolf

**Reference**
Beck, Hermann. *The Origins of the Authoritarian Welfare State in Prussia* (Ann Arbor: University of Michigan Press, 1995).

## Wagner, Cosima (1837–1930)

Daughter of composer Franz Liszt, Cosima married Richard Wagner in 1869 and after his death assumed the directorship of the Bayreuth Festival dedicated to the performance of Wagner's works, which she held until 1906. Cosima's attitudes toward Jews were as elusive and contradictory as those of her husband, but her diaries and letters are a valuable source for determining not only her own but especially Richard's private feelings toward Jews, feelings that were often in conflict with their public actions.

Cosima's own paradoxical feelings are exemplified by a comment in her diary on G. E. Lessing's play about religious tolerance, *Nathan the Wise*, which, she wrote, "reminds one of the businesslike attitude of the Jews toward their God." This is immediately followed by an entry in which she noted how a Jewish saying had deeply moved her. Cosima was also apprehensive about Wagner's decision in 1869 to republish the anonymous antisemitic essay *Judaism in Music*, this time revealing his authorship, and her diary chronicles the reactions to the publication, both positive and negative. Her account details the growing admiration for Wagner among activists in the antisemitic movement, which she sometimes expressed as a vindication of Wagner's anti-Jewish pronouncements, as well as the harsh critiques and anonymous letters of protest. After Wagner's death, Cosima became quite taken with the writings of Houston Stewart Chamberlain and engaged in lively dialogue with him about his theories on Jews. Chamberlain, a longtime admirer of Wagner's antisemitic views, married the Wagners' daughter Eva in 1908 and drew the attention of a young Wagnerite named Adolf Hitler.

Cosima's writings also provide insights into Richard's private musings about Jews, often revealing a deep-seated revulsion toward "Jewish nature," but a revulsion sometimes commingled with admiration and even friendship. Cosima documented Wagner's tutelage of Josef Rubinstein, who, in a state of mental instability, took up residence in the Wagner home in the hope of being "redeemed" from his burdensome Judaism; the close relationship and frank discussions with the conductor and rabbi's son, Hermann Levi, and Wagner's frustrated attempts to convert him to Christianity before Levi was to conduct the premiere of Wagner's Christianity-based opera *Parsifal;* Wagner's reluctance to speak publicly about the Jews because of his many Jewish admirers; and his more conciliatory sentiment, repeated in various formulations, that the Jews were not to blame but merely came on the Germans too early, before the Germans had sufficient self-awareness to absorb the Jewish influence.

Despite such moments of conciliation, Cosima's testimonies also reveal the ulterior motives of such gestures, as when she attributed Wagner's refusal to sign a petition to revoke Jewish rights to his conviction that he had already done his part for the anti-Jewish cause. Cosima's diligence in recording her husband's thoughts also provided access to some of his most destructive notions, including his fascination toward the end of his life with the concept of the Jews as a race, his basic endorsement of their total expulsion from Germany, and his most shocking anti-Jewish remarks in which, on hearing about numerous Jewish casualties in a fire in Vienna, he proclaimed that all Jews should be burned at a performance of Lessing's *Nathan the Wise*.

—*Pamela M. Potter*

**See also** Antisemites' Petition; Antisemitic Political Parties; Bayreuth Circle; Chamberlain, Houston Stewart; Hitler, Adolf; *Judaism in Music;* Marr, Wilhelm; *Völkisch* Movement and Ideology; Wagner, Richard
**References**
Gregor-Dellin, Martin, and Dietrich Mack, eds. *Cosima Wagner's Diaries.* Translated by Geoffrey Skelton (New York and London: Harcourt Brace Jovanovich, 1978–1980).
Marek, George. *Cosima Wagner* (New York: Harper and Row, 1981).
Werner, Eric. "Jews around Richard and Cosima Wagner," *Musical Quarterly* 71 (1985): 172–199.

## Wagner, Richard (1813–1883)

One of the most influential German opera composers of the nineteenth century, Richard Wagner is linked to the development of German antisemitism through his writings, as well as the exploitation of his fame by other noted antisemites. The degree to which Wagner is to be credited with inspiring the Holocaust has long been the subject of heated controversy, compelling scholars to look beyond his anti-Jewish publications and to seek evidence of his antisemitism in his private life, relationships, and musical works. Above all, Adolf Hitler's deep admiration for Wagner's works, close association with the Wagner clan, and promotion of Wagner's music during the Third Reich have inspired many to find the blueprints for the physical destruction of the Jewish community in Wagner's life and works. The difficulties in assessing Wagner's own antisemitism, as distinct from the antisemitic image of him that developed after his death, stem from a number of contradictions in his actions. Wagner's politics and personal alliances often fluctuated according to whatever could benefit him most. Despite the support and assistance he had received from Jews, he published his antisemitic attack *Judaism in Music* in 1850, after his conversion from a revolutionary worldview and around the same time that like-minded conservatives had begun linking Jews as a group to democratic and revolutionary political movements. Most puzzling is the fact that he chose to publish the essay first under a pseudonym and then reissued it in 1869 under his own name, all the while maintaining close and fruitful relationships with Jews. A statement by Friedrich Nietzsche initially suggested that Wagner's antisemitism was a form of self-hatred stemming from a suspicion that his biological father was a Jew, but more systematic studies, especially that of Jacob Katz, have offered compelling arguments that Wagner's antisemitism grew out of an uncontrollable artistic paranoia rather than self-hatred, racism, or even a consistent political anti-Jewish agenda. Yet the coincidence of his public reissue of the essay with the impending rise of organized antisemitism in Germany made him appear as a pioneer of the movement and gave him occasion to exploit this position for his own self-advancement.

Prior to writing *Judaism in Music,* Wagner was not known to be an outspoken antisemite but instead an admirer and friend of a number of Jews. The essay arose out of a strained professional relationship with the successful Jewish composer of French operas Giacomo Meyerbeer, Wagner's own failures in Paris despite Meyerbeer's assistance, and Wagner's desire to liberate himself from this perceived subservience. Wagner's discomfort reached a climax when critics found striking similarities between his own musical works and those of Meyerbeer while simultaneously castigating Meyerbeer's music for its alleged "Hebraic" traits. Unwilling to attack Meyerbeer openly, Wagner never named him directly but instead expanded his object of criticism to include the inherent failings of all Jewish creations, and in the process, he compromised the work of artists he had previously admired, including Felix Mendelssohn and Heinrich Heine.

Thereafter, Wagner seems to have let his paranoia get the better of him, assuming that his identity as author must have been known and interpreting any negative reception of his music as a "Jewish conspiracy" in retribution for its publication. When he decided to republish the essay nineteen years later, it was as a gesture of openly confronting his imagined Jewish adversaries. Ironically, his identity as the author of the 1850 essay was not as widely known as he had assumed, and its republication sent shock waves through his many Jewish admirers. Yet Wagner's unveiling as the author of this extreme attack also had the opposite effect of attracting the attention of antisemitic writers such as Paul de Lagarde, Constantin Frantz, and his own future son-in-law, Houston Stewart Chamberlain, as well as that of the Jewish musician Josef Rubinstein, who successfully appealed to Wagner to aid him in finding "redemption" from his supposed Jewish failings. The establishment of the Bayreuth theater complex dedicated to the performance of Wagner's works later created a forum for antisemitic dialogue with the publication of the first *Bayreuther Blätter* (Bayreuth Pages) in 1878.

Wagner was emboldened to weave his antisemitic ideas into the arguments of later essays, such as "What Is German?" (1865/1878) and "Know Thyself" (1881). Yet even at the peak of his fame as a prophet of the antisemitic movement, he continued to cultivate close relationships with Jews, especially the conductor Hermann Levi. Realizing the importance of appeasing his Jewish admirers, Wagner cautiously refused to sign the Antisemites' Petition (of 1880) to revoke Jewish rights. With such gestures, he managed to maintain a public image of relative neutrality toward Jews, even though he was known at times to express shocking antisemitic sentiments in his private life, as documented in the diaries of his wife, Cosima.

Although Wagner came to know the racial theories of Joseph Arthur de Gobineau later in life, it is difficult to isolate a consistent racial conception of Jewishness in his own writings. Wagner's impact on later antisemitic views, however, was considerable, resonating in antisemitic publications in Germany and also in other countries thanks to numerous translations of *Judaism in Music*. Wagner's most notorious admirer, Adolf Hitler, was drawn not only to his music but also to the antisemitic writings of his son-in-law, Chamberlain, and he forged close ties to the Wagner family in the 1920s. Wagner's English-born daughter-in-law, Winifred, became an avid supporter of Hitler, and as chancellor, Hitler became a frequent guest at the Wagner home while channeling substantial funding to support the Bayreuth Festival. The links between Hitler and Wagner have become a source of a heated controversy in which Wagner has been, on the one hand, designated as a prophetic architect of the Third Reich and, on the other hand, exonerated as a mere mouthpiece of the commonplace anti-Jewish sentiments of his times.

The exaltation of Wagner in Nazi Germany provoked the exiled philosopher and music critic Theodor Adorno to write an extensive musical and sociological analysis of Wagner's impact on Germany in 1937. In this essay, Adorno was the first to detect antisemitism not only in Wagner's prose but also in several of his musical works. Almost simultaneously, there was a last-minute decision by the Palestine Symphony Orchestra in November 1938 to refrain from performing the overture to Wagner's *Meistersinger von Nürnberg* after learning of the Night of Broken Glass (the November 1938 pogrom). This decision grew into a hotly disputed ban on Wagner's music that has lasted to the present day. The ongoing controversy in Israel, combined with Adorno's suggestions that the roots of racial theory are laid out in Wagner's operas and that certain characters can be interpreted as antisemitic caricatures, have inspired a wealth of analyses that seek to expand or to discredit Adorno's assumptions and raise serious questions about the ethical implications of performing Wagner's music.

—*Pamela M. Potter*

***See also*** Antisemites' Petition; Bayreuth Circle; Chamberlain, Houston Stewart; Gobineau, Joseph Arthur de; Heine, Heinrich; Hitler, Adolf; *Judaism in Music;* Lagarde, Paul de; Marr, Wilhelm; Music, Nazi Purge of Jewish Influence in; Musicology and National Socialism; Nietzsche, Friedrich; Schemann, Ludwig; Self-Hatred, Jewish; *Verjudung;* Wagner, Cosima

***References***
Adorno, Theodor W. *In Search of Wagner.* Translated by Rodney Livingstone (New York: Verso, 1981).
Katz, Jacob. *The Darker Side of Genius: Richard Wagner's Anti-Semitism* (Hanover, NH, and London: Brandeis University Press, 1986).
Köhler, Joachim. *Wagner's Hitler: The Prophet and His Disciple.* Translated by Ronald Taylor (Oxford: Polity Press, 1999).
Sheffi, Na'ama. *The Ring of Myths: The Israelis, Wagner and the Nazis.* Translated by Martha Grenzeback (Brighton, UK: Sussex Academic Press, 2001).
Weiner, Marc A. *Wagner and the Anti-Semitic Imagination* (Lincoln: University of Nebraska Press, 1995).

## Waldheim Affair

The Waldheim affair grew out of the disclosures about the past of Kurt Waldheim, former secretary-general of the United Nations, during his campaign for the Austrian presidency in 1986. The affair raised broader questions relating to the history of antisemitism in Austria, the role Austrians played in the Nazi Final Solution, and the reemergence of appeals to antisemitic prejudice in Austrian politics.

Waldheim held various foreign service posts abroad and in Vienna after World War II, including foreign minister and delegate to the United Nations. From 1971 to 1981, he served as UN secretary-general. Shortly after he returned home, the Christian Democratic Austrian People's Party (ÖVP) nominated him as its candidate for the upcoming presidential elections. In March 1986, the Austrian weekly *Profil,* quickly followed by the World Jewish Congress (WJC) and the *New York Times,* published documents revealing that Waldheim had belonged to the Nazi Student Union and an equestrian unit of the Storm troopers while attending the Consular Academy in Vienna between 1937 and 1939. Other documents revealed that he had also served in Army Group E, based in Thessalonika, Greece. Army Group E had been involved in the deportations of Jews from Greece and had waged savage military operations against Yugoslav Partisans and their suspected civilian supporters.

Although the Waldheim affair became an international media extravaganza, the principal source of documents relating to Waldheim's past, as well as his most vocal critic, was the WJC, an organization based in New York. By April 1986, further research by the WJC and by independent journalists revealed that in 1948, Waldheim had been accused of war crimes by the Yugoslav War Crimes Commission and that these allegations had been reviewed and endorsed by the UN War Crimes Commission. Waldheim denied past membership in any Nazi organization. He conceded having served in Army Group E but denied participation in any atrocities committed by its units, claiming not to have known of the deportations of Jews. The more general strategy pursued by Waldheim and his supporters was to portray him as the victim of a coordinated international "defamation campaign," initiated by Austrian socialists, led by the WJC, and promoted by the international press, particularly the *New York Times.* In the course of the election campaign, the political invective marshaled by the Waldheim camp against the WJC helped legitimate antisemitic prejudice in public discourse to an extent unseen in Austria since 1945. Waldheim also attempted to identify his own fate with that of his generation and country by claiming that he, like thousands of other Austrians, had merely done his duty under the dominant Nazis, an appeal that won the sympathy of many Austrian voters.

Waldheim won the June 1986 runoff election with 53.9 percent of the votes. Contrary to his expectations, however, interest in the unanswered questions about his past did not dissipate after his election, even though three independent research efforts found nothing criminal in his behavior. Nonetheless, his pariah status was reinforced in April 1987, when the U.S. Department of Justice announced that it was placing him on the State Department's "watch list" of undesirable aliens. Throughout his presidency, Waldheim was largely snubbed by most foreign heads of state, and he continued to be controversial in Austria itself.

His personal biography personified for many Austrians their own ambiguous relationship to the Nazi past. Since Waldheim's election, however, successive Austrian governments have addressed issues of restitution to Jewish and non-Jewish victims of Nazism. The Waldheim affair thus became both the occasion and the impetus for a more open discussion of the legacy of antisemitism and National Socialism in Austria.

—*Richard Mitten*

See also Austria; Christian Social Party (Austria); Wiesenthal-Kreisky Controversy
**References**
Mitten, Richard. *The Politics of Antisemitic Prejudice: The Waldheim Phenomenon in Austria* (Boulder, CO: Westview Press, 1992).
Palumbo, Michael. *The Waldheim Files: Myth and Reality* (London and Boston: Faber and Faber, 1988).

# Wandering Jew

The nature of Jewish historical development and the quest to explain Jewish survival over three millennia explain the remarkable staying power of the legend of the Wandering Jew. The omnipresence of the Jews, a product of their historical migrations, survival of catastrophic crises, homelessness, and problematic relationship to Christ and Christianity, engaged the minds and imaginations of many; a wide range of explanations have been offered to unravel the mystery. These inquiries often fueled and found resonance in the constant reincarnations of the legend of the Wandering Jew that emerged in thirteenth-century Europe.

A central element in the creation of the myth was the story of Cain's slaying of his brother

*The Wandering Jew* (Juif errant), from popular wood-cut, France. (Bettmann/Corbis)

Abel, ending in God's curse that Cain be "a fugitive and a wanderer on the earth" (Gen. 4:8). In Christian tradition, the story prefigured the fate and status of the Jews. Jesus' words, according to Matthew 16:28—"Truly, I say to you, there are some standing here who will not taste death before they see the Son of man coming in his kingdom"—contributed another element to the construction of the Wandering Jew by prophesying that some of his (Jewish) disciples would not face death until his return. Eventually, these and other biblical references merged into a legend that revolved around Christ's encounter with an individual in Jerusalem on the way to Calvary. Seeking to rest his burden on the man's doorstep, Christ was callously driven away by the taunt "Walk faster!" Christ responded, "I go, but you will walk until I come again." This was to be the curse of the Wandering Jew, a symbolic, name-

less figure doomed to walk the earth until Christ's return.

Literary treatments of the myth abound in variations. In one of the earliest texts, the figure to become known as the Wandering Jew is named Cartaphilus, and he is identified as the individual who had slapped Jesus while he was being questioned by the high priest (John 18:22). Cartaphilus was but the first of many names. Others were Buttadeus, Botadeo, Juan de Vota Dios, Malchus, and Isaac Laquedem. From the 1602 publication of a German chapbook, *A Short Description and History of a Jew Named Ahasuerus,* that name became synonymous with the Wandering Jew. An immediate success, twenty editions of the pamphlet appeared within a single year in Germany, exposing a socially diverse and large audience to the legend.

In this seminal version, Ahasuerus was born in Jerusalem and worked as a shoemaker. Shabbily dressed and barefoot, tall, lean, and gaunt, with long, unkempt hair and ragged clothes, he had been present at the Crucifixion, but because he rejected Christ, he has been condemned to eternal wandering ever since. The traveler through many lands is sympathetically portrayed, distinguished by his grave demeanor, taciturnity, aversion to oaths and blasphemy, and charitable inclinations. Although his past deed was known, nothing damning is said about him. Constantly questioned by scholars in different languages, Ahasuerus responds in their tongue. On his return to Jerusalem, he will find the city destroyed, and thus, again homeless, he must wander on.

A variation on the German tale appeared in France in 1609 in the form of a popular lyrical lament. Known as a *complainte,* it circulated in both oral and written forms and in at least six versions. All of them place the Jew at the Crucifixion and condemn him to eternal wandering. Some of the more prominent ones mention that he had only 5 sous in his pocket (symbolic of the five injuries inflicted on Christ) and was poorly dressed and shabby looking. Respectable individuals engage him in conversation, but he refuses to be coaxed into joining them for a drink, claiming that he may never rest. He willingly relates his past to them, detailing his birth in Jerusalem and his long journeys in fulfillment of

Christ's prophecy. One of the most popular variants attached what may have been the first visual image, said to record the visit of the Wandering Jew to Brussels on April 22, 1774, at 6:00 p.m. Another widely disseminated version (in 1804) shows the Wandering Jew in the center, wearing a hat and holding a walking stick, while in the background three emblematic scenes are taking place: Christ confronting the Jew, Christ carrying the cross to Calvary, and the Wandering Jew conversing with two residents of the city he visits. Sold for a small sum as a broadsheet or in a chapbook by merchants and peddlers who often made their own supernatural embellishments to the text, the complainte was sung and read aloud in France and later translated into Flemish, Danish, and Dutch.

The myth flourished in seventeenth-century Europe. Dozens of folk renditions appeared in many lands, making the legend into a common cultural possession. By the nineteenth century, the power and familiarity of the image of the Wandering Jew allowed its frequent reconfiguration and application in a wide variety of literary and artistic treatments, some of which were not intrinsically related to Jews or their historical evolution. One such example was the hugely popular and much-translated anti-Jesuit satire of Eugène Sue, *The Wandering Jew* (1844–1845), which portrayed the mythic figure as a symbol of the downtrodden, himself the victim of the ruthless Jesuit villain. More typically, the legend also fed into a broad array of nineteenth-century antisemitic contexts and arguments, literary and visual. In these incarnations, Ahasuerus took on the malicious attributes commonly ascribed to Jews and Judaism. In response, Jewish interpreters, both literary and visual, countered this tendency by putting a different valuation on Ahasuerus's eternal wandering and ubiquity; these were to be admired because they bore witness to the endurance and uniqueness of the Jews.

In an attempt to come to terms with the complex cultural significance of the myth, the folklore scholar Galit Hasan-Rokem has suggested that the Wandering Jew's "simultaneous presentation as local and itinerant, almost autochthonous as a nature spirit and as exotic as a complete stranger . . . signal the paradoxical identity of European Jews in their own eyes and in the eyes of their Christian neighbors as at the same time completely local and familiar and on the other as deeply alien" (Hasan-Rokem and Dundes 1986, 52–53).

—*Richard I. Cohen*

**See also** Antichrist; Caricature, Anti-Jewish (Early); Doré, Gustave; Gospels; Iconography, Christian; Jesuit Order
**References**
Anderson, George K. *The Legend of the Wandering Jew* (Providence, RI: Brown University Press, 1965).
Hasan-Rokem, Galit, and Alan Dundes, eds. *The Wandering Jew: Essays in the Interpretation of a Christian Legend* (Bloomington: Indiana University Press, 1986).
Sigal-Klagsbald, Laurence, and Richard I. Cohen, eds. *Le Juif Errant: Un Témoin du temps* (Paris: Musée d'Art et d'Histoire du Judaïsme and Adam Biro, 2001).

# Wannsee Conference

A prevailing conception among historians is that the Final Solution of the Jewish Question (*Endlösung der Judenfrage*), the Nazi euphemism for the mass murder of European Jewry, was a vast technical undertaking, an unprecedented state-sponsored crime dependent on a meticulous administrative operation. No event more aptly captures that image of soulless, bureaucratic detachment than the Wannsee Conference, the name given (after the war) to a two-hour meeting convened by Reinhard Heydrich, in accordance with Hermann Göring's instruction of July 31, 1941. In attendance at the villa Am Grossen Wannsee on January 20, 1942, were party functionaries and bureaucratic representatives, gathered to discuss the technical details pertaining to the Final Solution.

Evidence documenting Hitler's decision-making role in the genocide is rare and difficult to interpret; no signed order for the Final Solution has yet been found. So, too, the competencies and lines of command of various agencies of the state and party are difficult to establish precisely. The Wannsee Conference is a part of this general pattern. One surviving copy of the minutes gives a suggestive though incomplete account of the meeting, identifying the presence of agencies and individuals responsible for administrative and legal jurisdiction in the exclusion and management of those deemed racially inferior, particularly the *Mischlinge* (Jews of mixed parentage) of the first and second degrees. Participants at the conference included representatives from the Reich Ministry for the Occupied Eastern Territories, the Interior Ministry, the Ministry of Justice, the Foreign Affairs Ministry, the Race and Settlement Main Office, the Security Police, and the Sicherheitsdienst (SD). Topics discussed included the achievements of past policies directed at the emigration of Jews and the benefits of those policies that were "of major significance to the coming Final Solution of the Jewish Question" (in Levy 1991, 254).

Adolf Eichmann, head of the IV B 4 of the Reich Security Main Office, supplied an inaccurate numerical breakdown of Jewish communities in Europe. The language used to indicate forced removal of Jews from these territories as "resettlement" sanitized the discussion of organizing mass murder. By the time of the conference, the bulk of eastern European Jewry had already been living in squalid ghettos for almost two years. The deportation of Jews to the East was camouflaged as "evacuation," a euphemism that masked the untold misery, separation from family, and mental anguish of the deported. Heydrich noted in the minutes that the Final Solution would require combing out the Jews of Europe from "west to east" and that the success of this sweep would depend on the coordination of foreign ministries and the appointment of persons responsible for "Jewish Affairs" in the various countries occupied by the Nazis or subject to their influence. Despite the euphemisms and language of high politics, those at the meeting could have had little doubt about the real meaning of their discussions. They raised logistical and technical objections but none of a moral nature.

Historians contest the significance of the Wannsee Conference. It is difficult to describe the event as reflective of Hitler's long-held desire for mass murder. If the conference were so important a moment in the realization of Hitler's plans for Jews, why was he not present? Why were members of his inner elite not invited to deliberate on matters that promised to have a direct impact on one of the regime's major projects—the solution of the Jewish Question? Why was the Wehrmacht not present? The Transport Ministry, on which the SS would depend to supply trains for the mass deportations of Polish Jews (in the summer of 1942), was notably absent. The timing of the conference adds another element of disagreement in regard to its exact significance. Invitations were sent out on November 29, 1941, for a conference that was to convene on December 9 but was postponed a further six weeks, scarcely an argument for its crucial significance. It is, in any case, unlikely that the purpose of the Wannsee Conference could have been to make the decision for mass murder. According to some historians, this was already under way, at least against Soviet Jewry, since the attack on the USSR in June 1941.

Although convincing answers to these questions are still lacking, the Wannsee Conference is nonetheless important for understanding the launching of the Final Solution. It offers valuable insight into the culture of decisionmaking in the Third Reich. Heydrich apparently felt the need to solicit approval from individuals and agencies with competing ideologies and perspectives, to secure their commitment to and coordination with the implementation of genocide. The conference also served to begin (or attempt to begin) the synchronization of what had so far been localized actions of mass murder into a single European-wide program of genocide. It is probably a mistake to overinterpret the Wannsee Conference as *the* critical moment in the unleashing of the Final Solution. At the very least, however, the meeting sought to remove or neutralize potential resistance—political, ideological, technical—from within the governmental agencies of the Third Reich, and thus, it symbolized another critical step toward the destruction of the Jews of Europe.

—*Simone Gigliotti*

**See also** Eichmann, Adolf; Eichmann Trial; Einsatzgruppen; Göring, Hermann; Himmler, Heinrich; Hitler, Adolf; Holocaust; Order Police

**References**

Gerlach, Christian. "The Wannsee Conference, the Fate of German Jews, and Hitler's Decision in Principle to Exterminate All European Jews," *Journal of Modern History* 70 (December 1998): 759–812.

Levy, Richard S., ed. *Antisemitism in the Modern World: An Anthology of Texts* (Lexington, MA: D. C. Heath, 1991), 250–258. Translation of the conference text.

Roseman, Mark. *The Wannsee Conference and the Final Solution: A Reconsideration* (New York: Metropolitan Books, 2002).

## Watson, Tom (1856–1922)

Tom Watson became one of the most infamous antisemites in the United States in the early twentieth century. He was a populist demagogue who played the leading role in inciting the lynching of Leo Frank. Frank's extrajudicial execution, in turn, was the most notorious antisemitic murder in U.S. history.

Born just outside Thomson, Georgia, Watson considered himself a proud southerner. Yet he broke away from prevailing regional loyalties and joined the agrarian rebellion against tyrannical landlords, corporate monopolists, and the "money power." Although elected to the House of Representatives in 1890 as a Democrat, he soon left his party and became the leading congressman of the People's (Populist) Party and its presidential nominee in 1904 and 1908.

Ironically, before turning to the politics of hate, Watson—at the risk of his life—advanced the cause of black-white political unity. But he never became a full antiracist, and like almost all populists, he refused to support the "social equality" of the races, condoning neither blacks' freedom to marry across the race line nor their right to live in the same neighborhood as whites. Still, his advocacy of the political freedom of African Americans was remarkable, coming during one of the worst periods of racial oppression in the history of the United States.

After the disintegration of the People's Party, Watson revived his political career by becoming an extreme racist, trading also in anti-Catholicism and antisemitism. Eventually, he returned to Congress, this time as a senator, on a platform that connected the hatred of minorities and the populist resentment of elites.

Crucial to his political revival was the lynching of Leo Frank. Frank had been convicted, on flimsy evidence, of murdering one of the employees in the Atlanta pencil factory he managed.

As liberal forces throughout the nation sought the commutation of Frank's death sentence, Watson used the pages of his newspaper, the *Jeffersonian,* to recommend lynching of this "typical young libertine Jew" (in Woodward 1938, 438). As the conflict over Frank's fate heated up, he thundered: "The next Jew who does what Frank did, is going to get exactly the same thing that we give to Negro rapists" (in Woodward 1938, 443). Nevertheless, Georgia's governor commuted Frank's death sentence. Watson ultimately got his wish, though, when a largely unmasked mob stormed into the state penitentiary and dragged Frank off to his death.

Why did Tom Watson turn out the way he did? This is perhaps the most difficult problem for those seeking to understand the populist legacy. C. Vann Woodward, in his magisterial *Tom Watson: Agrarian Rebel* (1938), argued that the violent intimidation and political betrayals that Watson and his followers suffered were, in the end, too much for almost any human being to endure. Watson, a learned historian and otherwise a sensitive soul, snapped, and his previously democratic search for the people's enemies turned sour—and deadly. Other scholars are not as charitable, seeing even in his search for a biracial alliance not an enlightened egalitarianism but evidence of a consistent political opportunism.

—*Robert D. Johnston*

**See also** Frank, Leo; Populist Movement; United States
**References**
Bryan, Ferald J. *Henry Grady or Tom Watson?: The Rhetorical Struggle for the New South, 1880–1890* (Macon, GA: Mercer University Press, 1994).
Shaw, Barton C. *The Wool-Hat Boys: Georgia's Populist Party* (Baton Rouge: Louisiana State University Press, 1984).
Woodward, C. Vann. *Tom Watson: Agrarian Rebel* (New York: Rinehart, 1938).

## Webb, Beatrice (1858–1943)

Beatrice Potter was born in 1858, the daughter of Richard Potter, who had railway and industrial interests, and his wife, Laurencina, the daughter of a Liverpool merchant. Beatrice received her early education at home, traveled on the Conti-

The writer and social activist Beatrice Webb. Across her lifetime she revealed a range of sentiments and a high degree of ambivalence concerning Jews. (Library of Congress)

nent, and then led a busy social life. But in her early twenties, various influences changed her life's direction. When her mother died, she became involved in her father's business, which broadened her outlook. She also became interested in working-class life and got involved in social problems through her contact with the social scientist Herbert Spencer, a family friend. The collection of her father's rents also led her into professional contact with her relative Charles Booth, a link that resulted in her contributing to his survey of life and labor in East London.

The most decisive step in her life came in January 1890 when she met and then married Sidney Webb. The two worked as a devoted team, with Beatrice's large unearned income to sustain their activities. They wrote and politicked unceasingly for social reform and change, assuming an increasingly important presence in the Labor Party and the Fabians.

Beatrice's early writings, at a time of Jewish immigration from Russian Poland into the East End of London, presented the newcomers as "a race of producers with an indefinitely low standard of life" and "apparently without the capacity for combination." At the same time, they had developed a "love of profit as distinct from other forms of money earning" (in Holmes 1979, 19–20). In short, she presented the Jew as the embodiment of David Ricardo's ideal "economic man," one who knew none but economic motives. The description was overdrawn and simplistic, but it mirrored the opinions of many of her contemporaries, including J. A. Hobson. Historians continue to debate whether her assessments were antisemitic.

Her later writings reveal a continuing interest in racial and ethnic matters, again in common with many of her contemporaries, who contributed to the then budding social sciences. Her unpublished diary was peppered with gratuitous references to the ethnic roots of the many Jews she met. However, she enjoyed good personal relationships with many prominent Jews, such as Sir Ernest Cassel, who helped to fund the London School of Economics, one of the Webbs' creations. A visit to the USSR, which led to the Webbs' *Soviet Communism: A New Civilisation?* (1931), brought her into contact with many Jews who had assumed senior positions in the Soviet Union. At about the same time, following the Palestine pogroms of 1929, she commented offensively to Chaim Weizmann: "I can't understand why the Jews make such a fuss over a few dozen of their people killed in Palestine. As many are killed every week in London in traffic accidents and no one pays attention" (in Weizmann, *Trial and Error,* 411). As these examples demonstrate, she revealed a range of sentiments and a high degree of ambivalence concerning Jews over her lifetime.

In her unpublished diary, she frequently spoke of being unwell and anticipated the approach of death long before it actually occurred at Passfield Corner in Hamprshire on April 30, 1943.

—*Colin Holmes*

*See also* Britain; British Brothers League; Hobson, J. A.; *Ostjuden;* Socialists on Antisemitism, Wells, H. G.

**References**

Harrison, R. *The Life and Times of Sidney and Beatrice Webb, 1858–1905: The Formative Years* (Basingstoke, UK: Macmillan, 2000).

Holmes, Colin. *Anti-Semitism in British Society, 1876–1939* (London: Edward Arnold, 1979).

## Webster, Nesta (1876–1960)

Nesta Helen Bevan Webster was a writer, antisemite, and world-conspiracy theorist, active in a number of British antisocialist, racist, and fascist organizations. She was born at the family estate of Trent Park, near Barnet in Herefordshire, England, the youngest of fourteen children. Her father was Robert Cooper Lee Bevan, a director of Barclay's Bank and a member of the Plymouth Brethren; her mother, Robert's second wife, was Frances Shuttleworth, the daughter of the bishop of Chichester. Nesta spent her childhood and youth in England and traveling in Europe and the British Empire and was educated for a short time at Westfield College in Hampstead, leaving in 1897 without a degree. In 1904, she married Arthur Webster (d. 1942), a district superintendent of police in Fatehgarh, India. They had two daughters.

She began her writing soon after marrying, eventually publishing three novels. But she is most famous for her historical polemics, which fleshed out her arcane conspiracy theories. Of the eight substantial volumes in this genre, the most influential was *Secret Societies and Subversive Movements* (1924). She wrote an autobiography, *Spacious Days* (1950), which detailed her life up to the outbreak of World War I and described her intellectual genealogy, including her fascination with the French Revolution, her interest in world religions, and her relationship to women's movements. Her skepticism about feminism, she explained, was the result of its infiltration by the forces of the world conspiracy. Yet she simultaneously claimed to reject Victorian notions of women's separate sphere.

The autobiography ends without a discussion of her activities following the war, when she emerged as a leading figure on the British extreme Right. During the 1920s, she was a regular contributor to *The Patriot,* the ultranationalist and xenophobic paper launched by the duke of Northumberland that publicized the *Protocols of the Elders of Zion* in Britain, and to *The Nineteenth Century and After.* Both venues allowed her to expatiate on the threats posed to civilization by scheming Freemasons, Illuminati, atheists, Bolsheviks, and world Jewry. She was also a member of the Anti-Socialist Union and the author of its handbooks.

It was in *The Patriot* that a recruitment article appeared for the newly formed British Fascisti (BF) in 1923. Webster became involved in this organization and sat on its Grand Council but left the BF to form her own Patriots' Enquiry Centre in 1927. Although she did not become a member of the British Union of Fascists, she shared its admiration for Nazi Germany during the 1930s, as evidenced in her 1938 pamphlet "Germany and England." She was approached by Sir Barry Domvile to help with the activities of the pro-German *The Link;* and she continued writing for *The Patriot* until it folded in 1950. Her work has had a considerable influence on extreme right-wing politics in the United States and is esteemed by Pat Robertson, the John Birch Society, and the militia and patriot movements.

—*Julie V. Gottlieb*

*See also* Barruel, Augustin; Britain; British Union of Fascists; Freemasonry; Judeo-Bolshevism; Militia Movement; *Protocols of the Elders of Zion*

**References**

Farr, B. Storm. *The Development and Impact of Right-Wing Politics in Britain, 1903–1932* (New York: Garland, 1987).

Webster, N. *Spacious Days: An Autobiography* (London: Hutchinson, 1950).

## Weimar

The Weimar Republic, Germany's first parliamentary democracy, came into being in 1919 following defeat in World War I and amid economic and political turmoil. For the next fourteen years, its enemies on the extreme Left—the Communists—and the extreme Right—ultimately the Nazis—sought its destruction. Although it survived its difficult first years and enjoyed comparative success and growing acceptance from 1924 to 1929, it could not survive the Great Depression and the Nazi onslaught. War, defeat, political radicalization, and economic crises combined to intensify and broaden antisemitism, particularly among a small minority of militant racists who attributed all of Germany's problems to the Jews. Drawing on ideas and institutions that predated 1919, these radical elements were most active during the troubled early and late years of the republic. More common, however, were moderate forms of antisemitism that stopped well short of wishing harm to the Jews but ultimately played into Hitler's hands.

The charges leveled at Jews by radical antisemites were not new; rather, they were old calumnies adapted to Weimar conditions. In the immediate postwar years, they stressed the Jews' alleged lack of patriotism. Figures based on a 1916 census of Jewish soldiers fighting for Germany were manipulated to show that they were underrepresented on the fighting fronts. The participation of Jews in leftist and antiwar agitation was held as proof that they had helped deliver a "stab in the back" to the German army in 1918. Later, the charges continued, Jewish socialists and communists such as Rosa Luxemburg and Kurt Eisner had tried to impose a Marxist dictatorship in Germany. When that failed, Jewish liberals had brought an "un-German" democratic system to the nation. That a Jewish law professor, Hugo Preuss, had helped write the Weimar constitution assured that radical antisemites would castigate it as the "Jew Republic." So, too, did Jewish support for Weimar democracy.

Radical antisemites were equally determined to saddle the Jews with Germany's economic woes. Long prominent as merchants, businesspeople, and bankers, the Jews were accused of taking excessive profits during the war and manipulating the postwar economy for their exclusive benefit. Hence, food shortages, reparations, farm and business bankruptcies, inflation, and unemployment were blamed on them. Small businesspeople and shopkeepers were susceptible to allegations of unfair Jewish competition, particularly from department stores. The presence in Germany of nearly 100,000 largely unassimilated eastern European Jewish refugees (*Ostjuden*) fueled complaints that they took jobs and resources from Germans. Other charges against the Jews included their alleged contempt for Christianity

and their pollution of German culture. Avantgarde productions by the composer Arnold Schoenberg, the playwright Ernst Toller, and the novelist Alfred Döblin were held up as proof that Jews promoted decadent modernism and undermined traditional values. In fact, Jews no more dictated German culture than they dominated politics or economy. But that did not stop anti-Jewish zealots from spreading the somewhat contradictory stereotypes of Jews as bloodthirsty radicals and as mercenary capitalists to every corner of postwar Germany.

Chiefly responsible for disseminating this radical message during the early years of the republic was a new organization, the Deutschvölkischer Schutz- und Trutz-Bund (German Racial League for Defense and Defiance). It was founded in February 1919 by the Pan-German League, which had expounded ultranationalist and anti-Jewish views for decades before the world war. The new organization distributed millions of leaflets and brochures and raised money for the cause, with additional funds provided by the military and political hoping to shift responsibility for the lost war and the collapse of imperial Germany to the Jews. By the time the government banned it in 1922, the organization had attracted 200,000 members. Also active in spreading antisemitism were new radical fringe parties, such as Adolf Hitler's tiny National Socialist German Workers' Party in Munich, as well as the racist wing of the much larger German National People's Party. The agitation doubtless won new converts to antisemitism and disrupted relations between Jews and gentiles, but it generated little actual violence. The only important exception occurred in Berlin at the peak of the hyperinflation in November 1923, when a mob of unemployed citizens attacked the Scheunenviertel, an inner-city district inhabited by eastern European Jews. The police were slow to react but ultimately restored order and prevented the loss of life. The June 1922 assassination of Germany's foreign minister, Walther Rathenau, by superpatriotic university students was carried out as much for his moderate policies as for his Jewishness, and non-Jewish republican leaders were targeted as well.

During the prosperous "good years" of the republic, from 1924 to 1929, radical antisemitism abated. The German National People's Party reined in its racist wing, which then seceded. Only Hitler's Nazi movement survived the shakeout of small parties on the extreme Right lunatic fringe, and it absorbed most of the racist militants. In 1928, the Nazi Party won a mere 2.6 percent of the votes in a national election. Two years later, that changed spectacularly as the Great Depression caused unemployment to surge and confidence in Weimar democracy to plummet. In 1932, the Nazis became the largest party, winning 37 percent of the vote. One year later, they came to power legally with the aid of Germany's conservative establishment, more the result of Germans' fear of the Communists than because of major concerns about the Jews.

Hitler seems to have sensed that anti-Jewish diatribes had limited popular appeal, and in contrast to his earlier speeches, he rarely mentioned the Jews during the last years of the Weimar Republic. The Nazi Party resorted to antisemitism in communities where it struck a chord but downplayed it elsewhere. Even when calling attention to the Jewish problem, Nazi propaganda offered no clear program for solving it. Statements by party leaders that law-abiding Jews had nothing to fear from a Nazi government seemed designed to allay public concern over isolated attacks by Nazi Storm troopers on Jews in Berlin and elsewhere in Germany. The inconsistency and lack of clarity that marked Nazi antisemitism from 1930 to 1933 left the impression of opportunism and discounted the importance of racism. Most of Hitler's new supporters came to him because they had lost confidence in the Weimar Republic and feared the Communists, not because they had converted to his views about the Jews. Insofar as they noticed those views at all, indifference toward the Jews and moderate antisemitism neutralized whatever aversion they might otherwise have felt for Nazi racism.

The small minority of radical antisemites that made up the core of the Nazi Party was opposed by an equally small minority of Germans who considered antisemitism a scandal and a threat. Some, such as those who belonged to the interconfessional Verein zur Abwehr des Antisemitismus (League against Antisemitism), did so in defense of Jewish rights. Others spoke out against antisemitism primarily in order to defend Weimar democracy. This was especially true of the Social Democratic Party, which understood that a Nazi victory based, in part, on anti-Jewish appeals would mean the end of civil rights for all, Jews and gentiles alike. All these groups cooperated with the Jewish self-defense organization, the Centralverein deutscher Staatsbürger jüdischen Glaubens (Central Association of German Citizens of the Jewish Faith), which countered racist propaganda and brought legal proceedings against antisemites in the courts.

More numerous by far than the minorities of radical antisemites and their opponents were citizens across a broad spectrum of German society who were influenced to varying degrees by moderate forms of antisemitism. Moderate antisemites shared some of the doubts about the Jews expressed by the radicals without being persuaded that they were central issues or required urgent action. Unevenly distributed among the classes and regions of Germany, moderate antisemitism could be found among workers who distrusted Jewish capitalists, peasants who disliked Jewish moneylenders and cattle dealers, and conservatives of all classes who were troubled by Jewish liberalism. The educated middle classes were particularly susceptible. University students excluded Jews from fraternities and other social organizations and unsuccessfully demanded limits to the numbers of Jews allowed to matriculate. Some of their professors shared the view that Jews were overcrowding professions such as law, medicine, and journalism. Other civil servants, many of them holdovers from the imperial era, displayed similar prejudices. Judges sometimes handed down the mildest possible sentences to antisemites, and police officers were not always swift to respond to complaints from Jews. The German army was a hotbed of militant nationalism and did not welcome Jewish recruits. The German churches advocated just treatment and conversion of the Jews but also criticized them for fostering liberalism, socialism, materialism, and secularism. Such moderate antisemitism did not promote violence or advocate placing significant limits on Jewish rights, but it weakened resistance to Nazism in the last years of the republic.

The victory of Nazism in 1933 meant the triumph of radical antisemitism, but few Germans realized it at the time. To most of them, even the large minority that voted for Hitler, Nazi antisemitism seemed unremarkable.

—*Donald L. Niewyk*

*See also* Aryan Paragraph; Central Association of German Citizens of Jewish Faith; Desecration of Cemeteries and Synagogues in Germany since 1919; Dinter, Artur; Fritsch, Theodor; German National People's Party; German Racial League for Defense and Defiance; Goebbels, Joseph; Hitler, Adolf; Jew Census; League against Antisemitism; National Socialist German Workers' Party; Nazi Party Program; *Ostjuden;* Pan-German League; Rathenau, Walther; Reventlow, Ernst zu; Rosenberg, Alfred; Scheunenviertel Pogrom; Socialists on Antisemitism; Thule Society

**References**

Fischer, Klaus P. *The History of an Obsession: German Judeophobia and the Holocaust* (New York: Continuum, 1998).

Niewyk, Donald L. *The Jews in Weimar Germany* (New Brunswick, NJ: Transaction Publishers, 2001).

## Weininger, Otto (1880–1903)

Born in Vienna in 1880, Otto Weininger is notorious as the Jewish thinker whom Hitler praised—for acting on the consequences of his thought by killing himself. Weininger shot himself in 1903 and is usually regarded as the classic example of a Jewish self-hater. This image is, however, superficial, and obfuscates valuable aspects of Weininger's thought, not least on the subject of antisemitism.

Weininger's main work, *Geschlecht und Charakter* (Sex and Character), was based on the idea that bisexuality is a universal phenomenon among human beings. Instead of men and women being distinct sexes, Weininger posited that there was some male and some female plasma in everyone, to varying degrees. He explained the complex spectrum of sexual types, including homosexuality, in terms of varying combinations of the ideal types of Man and Woman that lay behind empirical reality but were not of it.

He delineated these ideal types in terms redolent of conventional, misogynistic thinking on gender, strongly influenced by postromantic German thinkers such as Arthur Schopenhauer and Richard Wagner. Man became the rational, intellectual, and moral principle and the genius, whereas Woman represented the earthbound, instinctive, and sensual side of human existence. Hence, Weininger asserted that the only true emancipation of women was from Woman.

His thesis often broke down in navigating between the empirical and the theoretical, and it was especially marred by his insistence on the superiority of all men to women. Even so, Weininger's purpose was emancipatory. He ultimately demanded equal rights for women as human beings and blamed men and their sexual demands for women's inability to free themselves from their "unconscious" female existence.

Weininger's significance to the study of antisemitism rests on the chapter in his book entitled "*Das Judentum*" (inadequately translated as Judaism). He apparently added this to demonstrate the applicability of his method in other subjects but also to extend the consequences of his thinking into the realm of religion. His analysis of the ideal types of the "Jew" and the "Aryan," similar to that of Man and Woman and similarly flawed, posited a polar opposition between the positive ideal of the Aryan Man and the negative ideal of the Jew, which allowed Weininger to indulge many of the prejudices about Jews acquired from his upbringing and his reading of cultural antisemites such as Houston Stewart Chamberlain. There were many similarities between the character of the Jew and of Woman; ultimately, though, there were crucial differences. If Woman represented the unconscious material world, the Jew represented something even worse: unbelief and nihilism. The Jew was the person who did not believe in anything, but "belief is everything." Therefore, the only way that the Jew could be redeemed was for him to overcome himself and become a Christian. (Weininger converted to Protestantism in 1902.)

On the face of it, this was clearly at least cultural antisemitism, but there were two aspects that resulted in a surprising reversal of expected conclusions. First, antisemitism was "Jewish." As with Man and Woman, "the Jew" was not present as such in empirical reality but was instead a spiritual possibility for all individuals. Weininger stressed that his Jew was not to be confused with empirical Jews or even the Jewish religion but was a universal possibility (even if it might have found its strongest concentration in historical Judaism). Indeed, the antisemitism of Aryan artists such as Wagner was to be explained by their hatred of the Jew within themselves. Antisemitism, indeed, was doubly Jewish. It was a projection of the hatred of one's own Jewish self onto the Jewish other and, as such, illogical and immoral. Actual Jewish self-hatred, as the necessary starting point for redemptive self-overcoming, was good, but antisemitism diverted onto others the self-loathing that should have been tackled internally and was thus bad. Also, antisemitism by its very nature treated individuals in collective, generic terms, which went against Kantian, Aryan individualism and was a Jewish way of thinking.

Second, Weininger asserted, self-overcoming Jews were the hope of Mankind and were spiritually superior to non-Jewish Aryans. The discussion about Judaism became a discussion about Christianity, especially the meaning of Jesus Christ's being born a Jew. The Jew could never be a normal genius like an Aryan Man, but a self-overcoming Jew, such as Jesus Christ, could become the greatest genius of all—the founder of religion. The implication was that only Jews, most heavily concentrated among empirical Jewry, could have the truly Christian religious experience of self-struggle, in contrast to those purer and simpler Aryans who had a commensurately simpler approach to faith.

Weininger's approach to the Jewish Question universalized the Jewish problem as a general problem of nihilism, while also protecting Jews, including empirical Jewish individuals, from antisemitism by individualizing the problem's solution. Weininger's approach was clearly marked by conventional prejudices against Jewishness, but if this was antisemitism, it was a very strange form of it.

—*Steven Beller*

**See also** Chamberlain, Houston Stewart; Freud, Sigmund; Hirschfeld, Magnus; Nietzsche, Friedrich; Schnitzler, Arthur; Schopenhauer, Arthur; Self-Hatred, Jewish; Wagner, Richard

**Reference**
Harrowitz, Nancy A., and Barbara Hyams. *Jews and Gender: Responses to Otto Weininger* (Philadelphia: Temple University Press, 1995).

## Well Poisoning

In the twelfth century and earlier, Jews were frequently accused of poisoning individuals, especially in cases when the patients of Jewish doctors died. In conjunction with the charge of ritual murder, they were said to have thrown the bodies of their victims into wells. In 1308, 1316, and 1319, in scattered locales in southern France, these allegations culminated in the charge that Jews committed murder on a massive scale by poisoning wells. Jews and lepers were accused of conspiring to destroy Christendom. The charge appeared again during the 1320 Shepherds' Crusade (*pastoureaux*), when mobs of peasants attacked the Jews of southern France.

The stories grew increasingly fantastic, detailed, and wide-ranging. They also took on political overtones when Jews were said to conspire with foreign powers, the kings of Tunis and Granada. Chroniclers took these allegations seriously and claimed that Jews concocted their poisons from blood, urine, herbs, and spices. Other identified ingredients included snakes' heads, toads' legs, and women's hair. A Jew confessed under torture to having made poisons from frogs, lizards, and the flesh and hearts of Christians.

Jews were fined for the crime of *lèse-majesté* (insulting the sovereign) and had their possessions confiscated. Poor Jews were expelled on the basis of the charge; rich Jews were held for heavy ransom. In France, the context for these charges was a depleted treasury and a severe famine, which lasted from 1315 to 1322, exactly the years Jews had been allowed back into the country after their expulsion in 1306. Panic and greed created the atmosphere in which the myth could flourish.

Panic emerged again during the scourge of the Black Death in 1348, when widespread terror prompted a revival of the well poisoning charge. In areas where Jews appeared to die of the plague in fewer numbers than Christians, possibly because of better hygiene and greater isolation, lower mortality rates provided evidence of Jewish guilt. In cases where Jews suffered more, however, this was seen as proof that they were the source of the disease. The well poisoning accusation united potent fears of science, religion, and politics to produce deadly consequences for Jews. Many thousands were killed. The Jews of Chinon, France, were put to death. A mass suicide took place at Vitry. A further 60 large and 150 small Jewish communities were extinguished.

The original charges were centered in southern France in the fourteenth century, but accusations of well poisoning became commonplace in the literature of the early modern period and spread far and wide thereafter. Christopher Marlowe's protagonist in *The Jew of Malta* is portrayed as one who enjoys poisoning wells. Accusations of Jewish well poisoning, which were originally limited in the medieval period, have reappeared in modern times in literature that links Jews with poison in allegorical terms as dangers to public health. The charge is reiterated in antisemitic propaganda found on the Internet.

—*Emily Rose*

**See also** Doctors' Plot; Host Desecration; *Jew of Malta, The;* Middle Ages, High; Ritual Murder (Medieval); Sorcery/Magic

*References*
Barber, Malcolm. "Lepers, Jews and Moslems: The Plot to Overthrow Christendom in 1321," *History* 66 (1981): 1–17.
Brown, Elizabeth A. R. "Philip V, Charles IV, and the Jews of France: The Alleged Expulsion of 1322," *Speculum* 66 (1991): 294–329.

## Wells, H. G. (1866–1946)

The prolific English writer Herbert George Wells came from a lower-middle-class background. He made his name early in life with "scientific romances," such as his celebrated *Time Machine,* published in 1895. Being a professed Darwinist and socialist, he wrote numerous novels as well as sociological, political, and historical books in which he combined both outlooks. Generally, his works advocated a eugenically based scheme for a scientifically planned society in which an enlightened minority would lead humanity toward worldly salvation and thereby circumvent the dangers of racial degeneration. During the course of his life, Wells acquired a readership of mil-

lions. He became a public educator, who claimed to "have always refused to be enlightened and sympathetic about the Jewish question" (*Experiment in Autobiography,* 1934). Wells located the Jewish problem within a general framework of racial thinking that included colonized peoples as well as depraved sections of the gentile population he called the "rabble of the Abyss." Efficiency, he said, would be the test of whether peoples or alleged races had to "die out" so that a better future—that is, one in accord with Darwinian insights—could result (*Anticipations,* 1901).

Wells linked his ideas on degeneration, as the negative side of evolution, to a critique of modern capitalism; by this, he meant the spirit of commercialism, which, in turn, he held to be the essence of Jewishness. He argued that under the existing system, the "rat-like" and "intensely acquisitive" people would prevail like the "ignoble sort of Jew," whom he reproached as "the very type of it" (*New Worlds for Old,* 1908). He also spoke of a "racial Jewish commercialism" (*The Outline of History,* 1920).

On the basis of these ideas, Wells developed an outlook in which he constructed a dystopian societal vision of a Semitic England in the process of eroding traditional social unity and Anglo-Saxon values, replacing them with selfish individuality. The new money-defined and thus "pseudomorphous" (*Tono-Bungay,* 1909) Jewish gentry of Britain was eagerly learning the "art of breaking in Anglo-Saxon villagers." Some also used their connections to manipulate the London stock market (*Marriage,* 1912). Wells was certain that the Jewish people wanted to "bring the whole world at last under the benevolent but firm Jewish heel" (*The Outline of History,* 1920). He invoked an antisemitic dichotomy of a productive, caring capital against the conspiring Jewish money-grubbing that preyed parasitically on the social body politic.

Even though Wells took a stance against the persecution of Jews in Nazi Germany, he held that "one could never tell whether a Jew was being a citizen or just a Jew" and that "their peculiarities aroused bitter resentment" (*The Shape of Things to Come,* 1933). Wells was still accusing Jews of a refusal to assimilate in 1939 (*Travels of a Republican Radical in Search of Hot*

*Water*), thus blaming their inherent qualities for the existence of antisemitism. Wells's ambivalent relationship to anti-Jewish violence was on view early in his literary career. His *Invisible Man* (1897) fights the temptation to "hit" the "silly countenance" of his Polish Jewish landlord when threatened by eviction but sets the house on fire instead.

—*Sören Niemann-Findeisen*

*See also* Belloc, Hilaire; Britain; Capital: Useful vs. Harmful; Chesterton, G. K.; English Literature from Chaucer to Wells; English Literature of the Twentieth Century; Eugenics; Nordau, Max; *Protocols of the Elders of Zion;* Racism, Scientific; Social Darwinism; Webb, Beatrice

**References**
Batchelor, John. *H. G. Wells* (Cambridge: Cambridge University Press, 1985).
Cheyette, Bryan. *Constructions of 'The Jew' in English Literature and Society: Racial Representations, 1875–1945* (Cambridge: Cambridge University Press, 1993).
Coren, Michael. *The Invisible Man: The Life and Liberties of H. G. Wells* (London: Bloomsbury, 1993).
Niemann-Findeisen, Sören. *Weeding the Garden: Die Eugenik-Rezeption der frühen Fabian Society* (Münster, Germany: Westfälisches Dampfboot, 2004).

Edith Wharton. With a plot that introduces a rich Jewish bachelor into the patrician society of old New York, Wharton's novel, *The House of Mirth* (1905), is a revealing study in the language of antisemitism. (Bettmann/Corbis)

## Wharton, Edith (1862–1937)

A wealthy American writer born into New York's high society, Edith Wharton wrote her best work as an embittered satirist of that society: a society in which (in her view) women existed only to be married and the only object of marriage was money. With a plot that introduces a rich Jewish bachelor into this social system, Wharton's novel *The House of Mirth* (1905) is a revealing study in the language of antisemitism.

*The House of Mirth* tells the story of Lily Bart, a pure and good young woman destroyed by the Darwinian apparatus of sex and money. As the tragic plot unfolds, a measure of Lily's degradation is that she is forced to consider marrying the Jew. Now, this Jew is only one of the men in Lily's world, and Wharton's satire is no more merciless to him than it has been to the others. In fact, compared to such Christian characters as the friend who tries to rape Lily, Rosedale the Jew

shows up relatively well. He is a vulgarian and a calculating social climber, but his affection for Lily is real, and a glimpse of him in an unguarded moment of tenderness convinces her that he would be a good father.

But none of this matters to the character Lily Bart, to her creator Edith Wharton, or to the readers for whom Wharton wrote. Like every book, *The House of Mirth* is a language system operating under the rules of a social grammar, and in 1905, that grammar regarded it as an absurdity for a subject such as "Lily" to take the appositive "Mrs. Rosedale." When the plot of the novel brings Lily to the point of doing so anyway, she becomes a solecism in herself: a communication that is socially wrong, like saying "I seen." Halfway through the book, therefore, a change occurs in the grammar governing "Lily." The name begins falling under the usage rules of gossip. Having been used in sentences with the word "Jew," it is now a Jew-word.

> "When a girl 's as good-looking as that [remarks one of Lily's acquaintances, Ned Van Alstyne] she 'd better marry; then no questions are asked. In our imperfectly organized society there is no provision as yet for the young woman who claims the privilege of marriage without assuming its obligations."
>
> "Well, I understand Lily is about to assume them in the shape of Mr. Rosedale," Mrs. Fisher said with a laugh.
>
> "Rosedale—good heavens!" exclaimed Van Alstyne, dropping his eye-glass. "Stepney, that 's your fault for foisting the brute on us."
>
> "Oh, confound it, you know, we don't *marry* Rosedale in our family," Stepney languidly protested; but his wife, who sat in oppressive bridal finery at the other side of the room, quelled him with the judicial reflection: "In Lily's circumstances it 's a mistake to have too high a standard." (Bk. 1, chap. 14)

Since gossip now controls the word "Lily," it also controls the word's referent, the woman. Halfway through *The House of Mirth,* Lily has been able to reject Rosedale's proposal, but by the end—humiliated, impoverished, contaminated—she is forced to propose to him. With that act, Lily violates a social law of her world, and Rosedale reacts to her desperation in a hideously intimate way: by looking at and then speaking to her frankly, unmasked, as a man outside the law from birth—that is, as a Jew. Wharton introduces his speech with a descriptive passage written in the mercantile code language of traditional antisemitism: "He met this with a steady gaze of his small stock-taking eyes, which made her feel herself no more than some superfine human merchandise." Then she has him say:

> "Last year I was wild to marry you, and you wouldn't look at me: this year—well, you appear to be willing. Now, what has changed in the interval? Your situation, that 's

all. Then you thought you could do better; now—"

> "You think you can?" broke from her ironically.
>
> "Why, yes, I do: in one way, that is. . . . I want to have the run of the best houses; and I 'm getting it too, little by little. But I know the quickest way to queer yourself with the right people is to be seen with the wrong ones; and that 's the reason I want to avoid mistakes. . . .
>
> I'm more in love with you than ever, but if I married you now I 'd queer myself for good and all, and everything I've worked for all these years would be wasted." (Bk. 2, chap. 7)

The book will end with Lily's death, of course. But the preceding passage has prepared the reader to see that her death will not be unhappy. Lily has survived the utmost humiliation a Christian woman can endure: to contemplate herself not just in economic terms but also in Jewish economic terms. Surviving to die a Christian, she enables Edith Wharton to continue writing a language with a Christian social grammar. In *The House of Mirth,* the chronicler of a world where women are subordinate to men and men are subordinate to money has given us a female Christ who dies to establish the price of the word "Jew."

—*Jonathan Morse*

**See also** English Literature of the Twentieth Century; Restricted Public Accommodations, United States; Seligman-Hilton Affair

**References**

Auchincloss, Louis. *Edith Wharton: A Woman in Her Time* (New York: Viking, 1971).

Benstock, Shari, ed. *Edith Wharton, "The House of Mirth": Complete, Authoritative Text with Biographical and Historical Contexts, Critical History, and Essays from Five Contemporary Critical Perspectives* (Boston: Bedford–St. Martin's, 1994).

# White Power Movement

Members of the White Power movement commonly feel that the white race is losing or has lost its dominant position in American society and the world in general. At their rallies, they often chant "White Power, White Pride" as they call for a return of whites to their former influence. As Betty Dobratz and Stephanie Shanks-Meile have pointed out, some question whether this is a social movement or simply various fractionalized groups with limited direction, leadership, and resources (Dobratz and Shanks-Meile 1997, 9–17). Movement participants have been labeled white separatists, white supremacists, white nationalists, or white racialists, with subtle differences in the meanings of these terms. The many ideological divisions and strategic disagreements in the movement make generalizing difficult, but the Ku Klux Klan, National Socialists, and skinheads are major groupings. According to the Anti-Defamation League of B'nai B'rith, George Lincoln Rockwell started the American version of the neo-Nazi movement in 1958 when he formed the American Nazi Party, which later became the National Socialist White People's Party. Current National Socialist organizations in the United States support the policies of Hitler and the Third Reich to varying degrees and often celebrate Hitler's birthday on April 20. Others in the movement question such support and criticize those displaying the swastika at rallies.

Movement supporters are also divided by their religious beliefs. Some argue that religion is a personal matter and/or that "my race is my religion." Many espouse Christian Identity, others support the World Church of the Creator, and the number of racial paganists (for example, Odinists or Wotanists) associated with the occult is growing. These beliefs have been described as antisemitic by researchers. Michael Barkun identified three key tenets of Christian Identity: (1) white Aryans are the offspring of the tribes of Israel according to the Bible; (2) Jews are the children of the devil; and (3) the world is approaching a final apocalyptic struggle between good and evil, with Aryans battling to save the world from a Jewish conspiracy (Barkun 1997, x–xi). Christian Identity maintains that the white race is predominantly Semitic because it consists of descendants of the lost sheep of the House of Israel. Therefore, accusing white believers of being antisemitic is illogical. From the Christian Identity perspective, they may be anti-Jewish, but they are not antisemitic.

White Power advocates portray Jews differently from most other minorities. Jews are seen as powerful and formidable opponents; indeed, Jews who fill major positions in corporations, government, entertainment, international banking, and the media are frequently pictured as the archenemy harming the white race. Often, movement supporters use the acronym ZOG (Zionist Occupied Government) to describe the federal government. Others in the movement recognize that whites occupy the major political positions, and they call them race traitors because they do not promote the interests of the white race. Some focus on trying to wake up whites so they can develop racial consciousness and identity.

Mattias Gardell has argued that many movement organizations detect a major Jewish conspiracy to rule the world and assume "that the thoughts and acts of every Jew everywhere by nature are synchronized to the end of exterminating the Aryan race to secure global supremacy" (Gardell 2003, 103). White Power movement members typically espouse many of the common stereotypes regarding Jews, picturing them as greedy, dishonest, clannish, conceited, and pushy, as well as power hungry. Some, however, compliment Jews for maintaining their identity and creating a separatist state (Israel).

The White Power movement tends to advance certain views associated with Holocaust revisionism (although revisionist historians may not necessarily espouse White Power ideology). Using the term *Holohoax,* many in the White Power movement question whether 6 million Jews really died in the Holocaust. Others applaud the Holocaust, and still others are disappointed that Hitler did not completely exterminate the Jews.

Although Jews tend to support liberal policies and reject white separatist goals, Carol Swain was surprised to find that a few Jews have aligned themselves with certain white nationalist beliefs. She has attributed this to their anger at affirmative action and other race-based policies, disdain for African Americans, and the decreasing antisemitism in the broader American population (Swain 2002, 70, 236).

—*Betty A. Dobratz*

*See also* American Nazi Party; Antichrist; Christian Identity Movement; Holocaust Denial, Negationism, and Revisionism; Internet; Ku Klux Klan; Militia Movement; Nazi Rock; Neo-Nazism, German; Rockwell, George Lincoln; United States

**References**

Barkun, Michael. *Religion and the Racist Right* (Chapel Hill: University of North Carolina Press, 1997).

Dobratz, Betty A., and Stephanie L. Shanks-Meile. *"White Power, White Pride!" The White Separatist Movement in the United States* (Baltimore, MD: Johns Hopkins University Press, 1997).

Gardell, Mattias. *Gods of the Blood: The Pagan Revival and White Separatism* (Durham, NC: Duke University Press, 2003).

Swain, Carol M. *The New White Nationalism in America* (Cambridge: Cambridge University Press, 2002).

# White Slavery

Beginning about 1870, Jews played a conspicuous, if not a majority, role in white slavery, the dramatic contemporary term for the commercial prostitution that was the most extensive manifestation of organized crime in the pre–World War I era. Jewish procurers and brothel keepers were prominent in the cities of Poland, the Russian Pale, Hungary, Galicia, Bukovina, and Romania. Jews also trafficked gentile and Jewish women along every migratory route to western Europe, the Americas, Africa, and Asia. There were substantial colonies of "unclean ones," as they were called by their hostile coreligionists in such places as New York, Buenos Aires, Johannesburg, and Constantinople, and there were smaller settlements in dozens of cities from Chicago to Rio de Janeiro to Harbin, Manchuria.

Jewish leaders feared, with good cause, that white slavery would provide powerful material for the emerging antisemitic movement, which became attentive as early as 1869 when Henry Gougenot des Mousseaux sardonically proclaimed that this new development displayed the "morality of the Talmud in action" (Bristow 1982, 22). Édouard Drumont agreed, and in Germany, Otto Glagau and Theodor Fritsch reported on every incident in their papers and pamphlets. The 1892 trial of twenty-two traffickers in the Galician city of Lemberg, who were convicted of procuring girls and women for Constantinople, was a watershed that provoked antisemites in the Habsburg Empire. They ignored the fact that most of the victims were Jewish. Later, Hitler's lurid description of Viennese Jewish traffickers in *Mein Kampf* (1925) reflected the currency of this material.

There was a vigorous Jewish response to this dangerous *chillul hashem,* or "desecration of the Name," as some leaders described it, and to the victimization of Jewish women, a minority of whom were truly being entrapped. Jewish workers in Warsaw destroyed brothels in the celebrated 1905 *Alphonsenpogrom* (*Alphonse* was the slang term for pimp). Social ostracism caused the unclean ones to establish their own synagogue and cemetery both in Buenos Aires and in Constantinople. Jewish vigilantes worked against the traffickers in New York and Cardiff.

A systematic international effort emerged with two focal points. In England, the Jewish Association for the Protection of Girls and Women, founded in 1896 with ongoing support from the Jewish Colonization Association, organized protective and police work in South America. In Germany at about the same time, the B'nai B'rith chapters of Hamburg and Berlin made this work part of the movement for Jewish self-defense against antisemitism.

In addition to building their own network of vigilance committees, Jews were central to the general international volunteer movement against white slavery, work that was ultimately taken over by the League of Nations. Jewish efforts were responsible for legislation against procuring and juvenile prostitution in Britain, South Africa, and Illinois and Louisiana in the United States. Many Jewish victims were dramatically rescued. The issue became a rallying cry for Jewish feminists in Germany, Hungary, and the United States. Combating white slavery promoted communal solidarity in a number of places and led German Jews to organize social reconstruction in Galicia, where impoverished *Ostjuden* (eastern European Jews) sometimes became involved in the traffic.

Jewish white slavery was a self-limiting phenomenon tied to the breakup of traditional Jewish life, mass migration, poverty, and persecution. Except in South America, it had largely disappeared by 1939.

—*Edward Bristow*

**See also** Drumont, Édouard; Fritsch, Theodor; Glagau, Otto; Gougenot des Mousseaux, Henri; *Mein Kampf; Ostjuden;* Russia, Imperial; *Talmud Jew, The*

**References**

Bristow, Edward. *Prostitution and Prejudice: The Jewish Fight against White Slavery, 1870–1939* (Oxford: Clarendon Press, 1982).

Gardner, Lloyd. "Anglo-Jewry and the Jewish International Traffic in Prostitution, 1885–1914," *American Jewish Studies Review* 78 (1982): 129–178.

Van Onselen, Charles. "Jewish Marginality in the Atlantic World: Organized Crime in the Era of the Great Migrations," *South African Historical Journal* 43 (2000): 96–137.

## White Terror (Hungary)

The catastrophe of World War I generated social turmoil and political upheaval in the defeated Central Powers. In immediate postwar Hungary, an ineffective progressive government was supplanted in March 1919 by the Communist regime of Bela Kun, a dogmatic Bolshevik of Jewish origin. Although initially popular, the Soviet Republic Kun proclaimed in June 1919 quickly provoked a reactionary, xenophobic, anticommunist (White) reaction.

From March to August 1919, the doctrinaire and harsh communist regime nationalized private assets and liquidated 500 to 600 alleged "enemies of the working class." Even though the heavily middle-class Jewish community suffered proportionately greater losses than the population in general, the presence of thirty-two members of Jewish origin among the Soviet's forty-five commissars facilitated a fiercely antisemitic—and highly successful—propaganda campaign by the White junta. One of its abiding and fateful consequences was to implant in public opinion the notion that Hungarian Jewry and Kun's regime were synonymous. Jews were reviled as the spirit behind communist revolution.

Originally, the White leadership consisted of two factions, one based in Vienna, the other in Szeged in southern Hungary. Although both vehemently opposed the Soviet regime, the Vienna group, composed largely of aristocratic elements, advocated an authoritarian, neofeudal restoration of historic "Christian Hungary." In contrast, the southern contingent, consisting of less influential social groups, championed the Szeged Concept, an intransigent counterrevolutionary agenda of extreme nationalism, anticommunism, territorial revisionism, and virulent antisemitism. Unlike the aristocratic Whites, these lower-class elements also demanded a thorough restructuring of Hungary into a totalitarian state. The Szegeds later boasted that they pioneered fascism and Nazism in Hungary.

Despite his alignment with the Vienna group, Adm. Miklós Horthy, supremo of the 12,000-strong White militia, instituted the Szegeds's uncompromising strategy of "national purification and regeneration," a crusade to eliminate "alien Judeo-Bolshevik" elements in Hungary. In early August 1919, after Kun's Soviet fled interventionist Romanian forces, Horthy's militia intensified its terror campaign, massacring from 5,000 to 6,000 people, mainly Jews but also left-wingers and sundry other perceived traitors to Christian Hungary. The consciously intimidating nature of the White Terror was made clear by the public nature of the atrocities. Further, over 70,000 "suspects" were imprisoned in newly created concentration camps. The situation was so desperate that the traditionally patriotic Jews of Budapest felt impelled to submit a petition with 100,000 signatures to the Paris Peace Conference, begging the recent conquerors for the restoration of order in Hungary.

The relatively pragmatic Vienna Whites, concerned by the potentially disastrous financial and territorial consequences for Hungary at the peace talks, asked Horthy to restrain the extremists. Meanwhile, Hungarian Jewish leaders, with the notable exception of the Zionists, maintained their traditional stance of fervent patriotism, rejecting "international Jewry's" attempts to intervene in Hungary's internal affairs. Eventually, as domestic and foreign pressure forced Horthy to curb his fanatics, the violence diminished and finally ceased by late 1920. In retrospect, the White Terror can be seen as a first step toward the genocide of Hungarian Jewry.

—*Tom Kramer*

*See also* Horthy, Miklós; Hungary; Hungary, Holocaust in; Judeo-Bolshevism; Versailles Treaty
**References**
Braham, Randolph L. *The Politics of Genocide: The Holocaust in Hungary.* 2 vols. (New York: Columbia University Press, 1994).
Kramer, T. D. *From Emancipation to Catastrophe: The Rise and Holocaust of Hungarian Jewry* (Lanham, MD: University Press of America, 2000).
Patai, Raphael. *The Jews of Hungary: History, Culture, Psychology* (Detroit, MI: Wayne State University Press, 1996).
Sakmyster, Thomas. *Hungary's Admiral on Horseback: Miklos Horthy, 1918–44* (New York: Columbia University Press, 1994).

## Wiesenthal-Kreisky Controversy

The Wiesenthal-Kreisky controversy was a public argument in 1975 involving as the main actors the famed Nazi-hunter Simon Wiesenthal and Bruno Kreisky, then chancellor of Austria. In October 1975, when Wiesenthal revealed that Friedrich Peter, leader of the Austrian Freedom Party (FPÖ), had distorted the nature of his military service during the war, the Jewish Kreisky became his defender and Wiesenthal's most bitter critic. The controversy put on display many issues regarding Jewish identity in Austria, the relationship of the post–World War II Austrian political elite to Austria's Nazi past, and, more generally, the resilience of antisemitic stereotypes. It also rehearsed many of the major themes that resurfaced with even greater passion a decade later during the Waldheim affair.

From the late nineteenth century, political allegiance in Austria has been pledged to one of three major "camps" (*Lager*): the Christian Socials, the Social Democrats, and the German Nationalists. Although the politics of this third Lager had always been ardently nationalist and antisemitic, they became predominantly Nazi during the final years before the Third Reich annexed Austria in 1938. The FPÖ, founded in 1956, emerged as the principal electoral home for former Nazis who had been disfranchised in the 1945 elections as part of de-Nazification but whose rights were restored in a 1948 amnesty. Peter became leader of the FPÖ in 1958.

Although Peter claimed to have served in the Waffen-SS, Wiesenthal learned in early September 1975 that he actually had been a member of the First SS Infantry Brigade, infamous for its mass murders behind the lines of the eastern front. If, after the upcoming October election, Kreisky were to invite the FPÖ to form a coalition with his Social Democratic Party, Peter would become the country's vice-chancellor. To prevent this, Wiesenthal gave the Austrian president, who had to approve government ministers, a dossier on Peter's past. The Social Democrats won an absolute majority, making a coalition government with the FPÖ unnecessary. But four days after the election, Wiesenthal decided to go public with his information anyway. Peter immediately conceded his service in the SS Brigade but claimed not to have participated in or known about the mass shootings, having just done his "duty as a soldier."

The next day, Kreisky, who had lost family members in the Holocaust, publicly defended Peter and attacked Wiesenthal as the head of a "political mafia working against Austria." Over the next two months, Kreisky's verbal attacks escalated. He accused Wiesenthal of character assassination, of dishonest methods, and of "crypto-racism." He contemptuously referred to "that Wiesenthal" as an "alleged engineer"; intimated that Wiesenthal had fraudulently obtained his Austrian citizenship; held him responsible for the reemergence of antisemitism; and most notoriously, hinted that he had collaborated with the Gestapo. Wiesenthal sued Kreisky for defamation of character, and Peter sued Wiesenthal for the same.

Press commentary in Austria on this controversy mostly favored the chancellor, although many of his more inflammatory comments drew criticism from foreign observers. The affair ended almost as abruptly as it had begun. On December 3, 1975, Kreisky stated before parliament that he had "not characterized Wiesenthal as a Nazi collaborator"; the same day, Wiesenthal withdrew his lawsuit. Peter finally withdrew his suit against Wiesenthal in 1982. On the whole, the Austrian population supported Kreisky, not only because they agreed with what he said but also because of his Jewishness, which shielded him (but not them) from the charge of antisemitism. He was free to air many of their thoughts as well as their defensiveness about the Nazi past and also their uneasiness at being reminded of it. Kreisky's disdain for Wiesenthal reflected the traditional hostility of assimilated Viennese Jews, as well as Austrian gentiles, toward the *Ostjuden* (eastern European Jews) who immigrated to Vienna from the East. His insinuations about Wiesenthal's dishonesty, vengefulness, hypocrisy, and non-Austrian origins helped legitimate and revive public expression of deep-seated anti-Jewish stereotypes.

—*Richard Mitten*

**See also** Austria; Christian Social Party (Austria); Lueger, Karl; *Ostjuden;* Pan-Germans (Austria); Schönerer, Georg von; Waldheim Affair

**References**

Spira, Leopold. *Feindbild Jud'* (Vienna: Löcker Verlag, 1981).

Wistrich, Robert. "The Strange Case of Bruno Kreisky," *Encounter* (May 1979), 78–85.

Wodak, Ruth, Peter Nowak, Johanna Pellkan, Rudolf de Cillia, Helmut Gruber, and Richard Mitten. *"Wir sind alle unschuldige Täter!" Studien zum Nachkriegsantisemitismus* (Frankfurt am Main, Germany: Suhrkamp, 1990).

## William of Norwich (d. 1144)

St. William of Norwich was the first Christian victim alleged to have been killed by Jews in a ritual murder. His story was told by Thomas of Monmouth, a monk who arrived in Norwich shortly after William's death and devoted himself to promoting William's cult beginning in 1150. He completed the seven books of William's life and miracles around 1170, dedicating the work to the bishop of Norwich.

The monk claimed that William, a twelve-year-old apprentice leatherworker, was lured by some Jews into the archdeacon's kitchen under the pretense of offering him a job. Having accepted money to let her son go around Passover, which fell at the same time as Easter, the boy's mother then became suspicious and asked his sister to follow him into the Jewry. When William's body was later discovered in the woods outside Norwich, the Jews were blamed for torturing and killing him in mockery of Christ. The body was eventually reburied in the monks' cemetery, a shrine erected in the church, and William's feast day was celebrated on March 24.

It is clear from Thomas's work that many people in Norwich did not believe his tale. The Jewish community in the town was large and successful, and the accusation of ritual murder does not seem to have substantially affected it, although the monk said many left Norwich on that account. Unlike later accusations of ritual murder, William's cult was not endorsed by the English Crown, and it does not seem to have played an important role in local relations between Christians and Jews.

Thomas of Monmouth repeatedly claimed that William's shrine was a popular object of pilgrimage. William's death was recorded in a few English chronicles and in a German monastery, but otherwise, he did not receive much attention. He was not mentioned in any Jewish sources of the period. It is not clear what connection existed between this, the first accusation of ritual murder, and later ones. There is no record of another such charge for more than a decade.

The few images of William recorded around Norwich point to a brief revival of his cult in the late Middle Ages when a guild sprang up and St. William was portrayed as a schoolboy holding a satchel, perhaps meant to serve as a virtuous model for the young boys of the Norwich cathedral priory. The cathedral now features a prayer for victims of intolerance at the site of the former shrine.

William's cult developed in the wake of the failed Second Crusade and not long after the Civil War in England, a time of brutal attacks against Jews on the Continent and fierce but intermittent fighting in England. Some scholars see this as first example of an accusation of ritual murder in the context of the rising indebtedness of Christians to Jews, which was a source of economic tension; others view it in relation to Thomas of Monmouth's religious concerns.

—*Emily Rose*

**See also** Crusades; Deicide; Host Desecration; Hugh of Lincoln; Middle Ages, High; Middle Ages, Late; Ritual Murder (Medieval); Simon of Trent

**References**

Langmuir, Gavin. "Thomas of Monmouth: Detector of Ritual Murder." In *Toward a Definition of Antisemitism* (Berkeley: University of California Press, 1990), 209–236.

McCulloh, John M. "Jewish Ritual Murder: William of Norwich, Thomas of Monmouth, and the Early Dissemination of the Myth," *Speculum* 72 (1996): 698–740.

Rose, Emily. "The Cult of St. William of Norwich and the Accusation of Ritual Murder in Anglo-Norman England." Dissertation, Princeton University, 2001.

## Winrod, Gerald B. (1900–1957)

Gerald B. Winrod was born on March 7, 1900, in Wichita, Kansas. Converted at age eleven to evangelical Protestantism and armed with an elementary school education, he began preaching at seventeen. In 1925, he organized a coalition of conservative and fundamentalist Christians into the Defenders of the Faith to combat theological modernism, evolutionism, and higher criticism of the Bible. In April 1926, Winrod launched the *Defender Magazine,* a monthly that attracted powerful voices of American fundamentalism and advertisements from fundamentalist publishing houses. The *Defender*'s circulation grew to 100,000 in the 1930s.

Winrod's antisemitism, a function of his theology, developed into a coherent worldview. Although he had once praised Orthodox rabbis for repudiating modernism and evolution within Judaism and had scorned legends of Jewish ritual sacrifice of Christian children in the 1920s, he was, by 1933, elaborating an all-encompassing antisemitic philosophy of history grounded in scriptural prophecy. A dispensational premillenarian, he contended that history was divided into distinct epochs or dispensations. The current dispensation, initiated by Jesus Christ, was coming to an end as moral degeneration, the re-creation of the Roman Empire under Benito Mussolini (the most likely candidate for the Antichrist), and the return of Jews to Israel under the auspices of Zionism portended. Winrod prophesied the imminent return of Jesus Christ, who would defeat the Antichrist and reign over his millenarian kingdom. Within this prophetic scheme, apostate Jews stood at the center of Winrod's conspiratorial view of history.

In January 1933, Winrod published "Facing Ten Deadly Enemies at the Beginning of 1933" in the *Defender*. His decalogue comprised modernism, evolution, atheism, immorality, alcohol, communism, fascism, liberalism, war, and "the Hidden Hand." The following month, in "Unmasking the Hidden Hand—A Conspiracy," he introduced his readers to the *Protocols of the Elders of Zion,* elaborating a theory of subversion by apostate Jewry stretching back to King Solomon and reaching forward to Armageddon. The spiritual ancestors of the Elders were responsible for ancient Israel's disobedience, the murder of Jesus, the Roman persecution of the ancient Christian church, the diabolical Talmud, and anti-Christian ideas throughout the centuries. Winrod linked the Elders to the Illuminati and to the rise of European Freemasonry and Marxism, which produced the French and Russian Revolutions. The Soviet Union, liberalism, the depression, and the New Deal were Judaic inventions. The Elders of Zion overlapped with leaders of world Zionism. In light of this threat, Winrod, who had visited Nazi Germany for four days in 1935, praised Adolf Hitler's suppression of Jewish subversives.

In another of his magazines, the *Revealer* (1934–1937), Winrod buttressed his prophetic musings with a relentless assault on President Franklin D. Roosevelt and the New Deal. He claimed that apostate Jews were the descendants of the tribe of Dan, the son of Jacob. Roosevelt (and Mussolini) descended from this blood line. In 1938, Winrod muted his antisemitism to run for the U.S. Senate in the Kansas Republican primary. Hampered by unsubstantiated charges that he received funds from Nazi Germany, he won 53,149 votes and a third-place finish, campaigning as an economic conservative and isolationist.

In July 1942, Winrod led the list of twenty-eight defendants charged with sedition. In two subsequent indictments, the government claimed that his pro-Nazi propaganda cultivated insubordination in the armed forces and that he was part of an international Nazi conspiracy to subvert democracy. All three indictments were eventually dismissed.

After the war, the Defenders of the Faith, with an income of $276,272 in 1950, acquired larger headquarters; the *Defender* boasted 100,000 subscriptions. Winrod maintained his claim that "International Jewish Communism" was well on the way to undermining the nations and "exterminating of all Christians" (Roy 1953, 45). He spent his last years crusading on behalf of unconventional forms of medicine and cancer cures. He died of pneumonia on November 11, 1957.

—*Peter R. D'Agostino*

**See also** Antichrist; Freemasonry; Judeo-Bolshevism; Mussolini, Benito; *Protocols of the Elders of Zion;* Ritual Murder (Medieval); Ritual Murder (Modern); Talmud; Webster, Nesta; Zionism

**References**

Ribuffo, Leo P. *The Old Christian Right: The Protestant Far Right from the Great Depression to the Cold War* (Philadelphia: Temple University Press, 1983).

Roy, Ralph Lord. *Apostles of Discord: A Study of Organized Bigotry and Disruption on the Fringes of Protestantism* (Boston: Beacon Press, 1953).

## Women and British Fascism

An examination of the role of women in interwar British fascist and racist organizations suggests a more complex and complicated role for them than that of "breeders of race and nation." The history of this special relationship between women, British fascism, and antisemitism began in 1923, when the ultrapatriotic ex-servicewoman Rotha Lintorn-Orman (1895–1935) founded the first British fascist movement, the British Fascisti (BF). Nesta Webster, conspiracy theorist and antisemite, sat on the BF's Grand Council in the mid-1920s. In Fascist Children's Clubs, organized by the women of the movement, children were taught lessons about patriotism, the limits of imperial citizenship, and xenophobia with texts such as A. H. Lane's *The Alien Menace* (1928). Always wary of "foreigners," the BF adopted a policy of overt antisemitism only in the 1930s, when anti-Jewish attitudes generally began to harden on the Right.

Oswald Mosley, the founder of the British Union of Fascists (BUF), proclaimed that "we want men who are men, and women who are women" in the BUF, but women came to play far more activist roles than he had envisioned. They represented 25 percent of the membership, joined male Blackshirts on marches, served as stewards at meetings, sold fascist newspapers, and

Three female Blackshirts, members of the British Union of Fascists, salute as they leave their Chelsea headquarters for Birmingham, where they will attend a meeting addressed by their führer, Oswald Mosley. (Hulton-Deutsch Collection/Corbis)

canvassed for new members. They fully participated in the activities of the organization and its branches. The Women's Section was established in London in March 1933, first under the leadership of Mosley's mother, Maud Mosley (1874–1948); it functioned as a parallel paramilitary hierarchy and offered classes in speech making and fascist policy, as well as training in physical fitness and self-defense.

Full participation in the BUF also entailed active Jew-baiting on the part of women. They could, for example, be heard chanting: "The Yids, the Yids, we gotta get rid of the Yids." Women's antisemitism was clearly articulated in their contributions to the BUF's newspapers and journals and in their propaganda at election time. Anne Brock-Griggs, the candidate for Limehouse in the London County Council elections, denounced Jews as slumlords, evil financiers, pornographers, and polluters of the Christian blood line. The pitch of women's antisemitism became shriller still with the launch in February 1940 of their own Women's Peace Campaign against the "Jew's War."

Women were also well represented in other extreme Right and "Jew-Wise" organizations: Unity Mitford (1914–1948), who proudly proclaimed herself "a Jew-hater" in Julius Streicher's *Der Stürmer* in 1935, was a member of the BUF and the Anglo-German Fellowship, as well as Mosley's sister-in-law; women joined Arnold Leese's Imperial Fascist League; and the leading protagonist in Captain Archibald Ramsay's Right Club was Anna Wolkoff, who exhibited a degree of hysteria in her antisemitic outpourings. British women's antisemitism was often premised on antivivisectionist grounds and opposition to kosher slaughtering, as laid out by Mrs. Dudley Ward of the Nordic League and the British People's Party, in her vituperative booklet *Jewish "Kosher"* (1944).

The conflation of maternalist concerns with aggressive racism resulted in an ideology of "motherly hate." Judging from their actions in the first part of the twentieth century, women—and more than just a few of them—could become deeply complicit in British fascist and racist movements.

—*Julie V. Gottlieb*

**See also** Britain; Dietary Laws; Kosher Slaughtering; Mosley, Oswald; *Stürmer, Der;* Webster, Nesta

**References**

Durham, Martin. *Women and Fascism* (New York: Routledge, 1998).

Gottlieb, Julie V. *Feminine Fascism: Women in Britain's Fascist Movement, 1923–1945* (London: I. B. Tauris, 2000).

———. "'Motherly Hate': Gendering Anti-Semitism in the British Union of Fascists," *Gender & History,* 14/2 (August 2002): 294–320.

## Word about Our Jews, A (1880)

Heinrich von Treitschke (1834–1896), the doyen of German national historians, regularly used his editorship of the influential journal *Prussian Yearbooks* (*Preussische Jahrbücher*) to proclaim his views on public affairs. Reacting to the sensational best-seller *The Victory of Jewry over Germandom* (1879) by Wilhelm Marr, the noisy launching of Court Chaplain Adolf Stoecker's Christian Social Workers' Party in the national capital, and widespread anti-Jewish demonstrations elsewhere in the country, Treitschke spoke out on the Jewish Question in three successive monthly columns; in early 1880, he published them as the pamphlet, *A Word about Our Jews.*

Treitschke normally spoke with great authority on all matters affecting the well-being of the new German Empire. He approved of neither Marr, whom he had once called a windbag, nor Stoecker, whom he regarded as a shallow demagogue. He made a point of condemning the excesses of anti-Jewish agitation, its "coarseness and crudities," and the sort of extremism that blamed Jews for all the woes of the day. Far from a fanatic, Treitschke nevertheless went on to make his sympathies absolutely clear. The movement was fully justified, not as a return to the senseless Jew-baiting of earlier days but as a merited response of the *Volk* to the provocations of an ascendant Jewry. The "mammonism" of the Jews, their vulgarity, their sense of entitlement to full participation in German life—all these antagonized the *Praeceptor Germaniae* (moral guide of the Germans). Jewish preponderance in the press and in commerce, he warned, came at the expense of the authentic Germans and suggested a determination to take over. He made exceptions for a few of his favorites, but his generalized contempt for Germany's Jews was unmistakable. In a brutally dismissive phrase that later appeared on the mastheads of antisemitic newspapers and that the Nazis put on rubber stamps, Treitschke pronounced, "The Jews are our misfortune."

Long-established nations, such as France and England, could afford to talk about tolerance and scold the Germans for their prejudices, but Germany was too young and vulnerable to risk *Verjudung* (Jewification) or the creation of a mongrel culture. Treitschke demanded of Germany's Jews that they become "truly German," extinguishing the marks of their moribund religion and separate national identity. "Our Jewish fellow-citizens must resolve to be German without qualification, as so many of them have already done, to our benefit and their own. The task can never be wholly completed. A cleft has always existed between Occidental and Semitic essences." (in Levy 1991, 73). Such a sentiment, though deeply hurtful to Jews who thought that they had already—proudly and wholeheartedly—opted for *Deutschtum* (Germanism), distinguished Treitschke from the racist antisemites who were rising to prominence at that time. Although he occasionally employed a racist vocabulary, he was no racist; he thought Jews could become much more German, if only they wanted to. He also rejected as uncivilized what would shortly become the essential demand of the political antisemites, the revocation of Jewish emancipation.

Although he condemned rowdy antisemitism, antisemitic activists were vastly encouraged by this pamphlet from a member of the intellectual elite. More "refined" antisemites also drew encouragement. He inspired a generation of university students, Germany's future decisionmakers; the most prominent among them was Heinrich Class, later president of the racist-nationalist Pan-German League, who acknowledged the direct impact of his professor's lectures on his own mission. Treitschke was one of the "founding spirits" of the antisemitic Association of German Students. Whatever his intent in *A Word about Our Jews*, his immediate and long-term effect was to make an ideology of hatred reputable enough for the educated.

—*Richard S. Levy*

**See also** Berlin Movement; Class, Heinrich; Emancipation; German Students, Association of; Marr, Wilhelm; Pan-German League; Stoecker, Adolf; Treitschke, Heinrich von; *Verjudung; Victory of Jewry over Germandom, The*

**References**

Dorpalen, Andreas. *Heinrich von Treitschke* (New Haven, CT: Yale University Press, 1957).

Levy, Richard S., ed. *Antisemitism in the Modern World: An Anthology of Texts* (Lexington, MA: D. C. Heath, 1991).

# X

## Xanten Ritual Murder (1891–1892)

The murder of a five-year-old Christian boy on June 29, 1891, in the small town of Xanten, situated on the left bank of the Rhine not far from the German border with Holland, touched off a notorious case of ritual murder accusation.

A deeply Catholic town of about 4,000 people, Xanten was located in an area rich in ritual murder tales. These included a thirteenth-century case in Oberwesel, across the river, and two cases in the early nineteenth century: Dormagen in 1819 and Neuss in 1834. In 1891, the first person to accuse the Jews of killing the boy was a local Catholic butcher, Heinrich Junkermann, who on the morning after the murder leveled the accusation against his neighbor, Adolph Buschhoff, a Jewish butcher. By late afternoon, rumor and gossip spread through the town as countless people came forward to report on what they perceived as the suspicious behavior of Buschhoff.

The initial accusers were, by their own admission, antisemites, and, in the view of others, marginal to the community. But their accusations were supported by a local medical examiner and a local priest who gathered evidence against the Jews. The priest also helped the Catholic butcher compose a written affidavit attesting that the boy's throat had been cut according to the technique a kosher butcher would have employed. Local demonstrations against the Jews picked up pace, and antisemitic newspapers wrote about "an authentic ritual murder."

Recognizing their position as precarious, the Jews of Xanten petitioned the Prussian minster of the interior to send a qualified police inspector. If only the killer could be found, the tempest would pass, they hoped; in fact, it had just begun. When the Berlin inspector found rumors generated by the ritual murder myth credible, he indicted the Jewish butcher. A local judge, however, found the evidence specious.

The judge's dismissal of the case angered the antisemites. Populist newspapers, whether antisemitic, Catholic, or conservative, portrayed the release of Buschhoff as a travesty of justice. In the Prussian state parliament, legislators discussed the merits of the case, and in Xanten, local authorities were impressed by the hue and cry. With new evidence, they again arrested Buschhoff and his family, who were alleged to be his accomplices. But the trial by jury, which took place in Cleve District Court in July 1892, resulted in a verdict of not guilty.

The acquittal brought on a hail of criticism and begot another round of violence. In Xanten and the area around it, rioters desecrated Jewish cemeteries, tossed rocks smeared with blood through the windows of Jewish homes and businesses, and painted "blood-red crosses" on Jewish buildings. In nearby Grevenbroich, rioters vandalized the synagogue.

The Xanten case prompted the League against Antisemitism to count ritual murder accusations in Europe, and by 1900, they had listed over 100, distinguishing the last decade of the nineteenth century as particularly prone to this seemingly medieval superstition. Widely discussed in newspapers and political pamphlets, the Xanten case also helped antisemitic parties achieve significant successes in the Reichstag elections of 1893. Finally, the case suggests something of the rootedness of the ritual murder tale in the folklore of the Catholic Rhineland and the ease with which it could incite Christian townspeople against their Jewish neighbors.

—*Helmut Walser Smith*

**See also** *Antisemitic Correspondence;* Antisemitic Political Parties; Hep-Hep Riots; Kosher

Slaughtering; League against Antisemitism; Polná Ritual Murder; Ritual Murder (Medieval); Ritual Murder (Modern)

**Reference**

Klling, Bernd. "Blutige Illusionen: Ritualmorddiskurse und Antisemitismus im niederrheinischen Xanten am Ende des 19. Jahrhunderts." In *Agrarische Verfassung und politische Struktur: Studien zur Gesellschaftsgeschichte Preussens, 1700–1918*. Edited by Wolfgang Neugebauer and Ralf Prve (Berlin: Berlin Verlag Spitz, 1998), 349–382.

# Y

## Yellow Badge

In the Muslim world, specific markings were used to distinguish and humiliate individuals not belonging to the Islamic faith but dwelling within Muslim-dominated lands. The practice seems to have been introduced by the caliph Umar II in the early eighth century, although it was unevenly applied throughout the Middle Ages. In medieval Christendom, Jews were often forced to wear distinguishing marks or clothing. The earliest extant legislation mandating special signs of separation for Jews was canon 68 of the Fourth Lateran Council of 1215. According to this canon:

> In some Church provinces a difference in dress distinguishes the Jews and Saracens from the Christians, but in certain others such a confusion has grown up that they cannot be distinguished by any difference. Thus it happens at times that through error Christians have relations with the women of Jews or Saracens, and Jews and Saracens with Christian women. Therefore, that they may not, under pretext of error of this sort, resort to excusing themselves in the future for the excesses of such accursed intercourse, we decree that such [Jews and Saracens] of both sexes in every province and at all times shall be marked off in the eyes of the public from other peoples through the character of their dress. Particularly, since it may be read [in *Numbers* 15:37–41] that this very law has been enjoined on them by Moses.

Throughout medieval Europe, there was great divergence in the extent to which such legislation was enforced and a good deal of diversity regarding the types of markings—hats, patches, and so on. Colors also varied. Although yellow was most typical, some sources mention or depict other colors; in early modern Venice, for example, mention is made of the color red. Although Jews were consciously singled out, in some places other marginal groups, most especially heretics and prostitutes, were also forced to wear distinguishing marks.

The application of the distinction seems to have waned in Europe during the early modern period, and it was abrogated in most places at the end of the eighteenth or beginning of the nineteenth century as Jewish emancipation spread. The badge was reintroduced by the National Socialists in Germany in the late 1930s.

—*Dean Phillip Bell*

**See also** Ghetto; Innocent III; Islam and the Jews; Lateran Council, Fourth; Middle Ages, Early; Middle Ages, High; Middle Ages, Late; Nazi Legal Measures against Jews; Yellow Star

**References**

Cohen, Mark. *Under Crescent and Cross: The Jews in the Middle Ages* (Princeton, NJ: Princeton University Press, 1994).

Kisch, Guido. "The Yellow Badge in History." *Historia Judaica* 19, no. 2 (October 1957): 89–146.

Ravid, Benjamin. "From Yellow to Red: On the Distinguishing Head-Covering of the Jews of Venice." *Jewish History* 6, nos. 1–2 (1992): 179–210.

## Yellow Star

In reaction to the Nazi boycott of April 1, 1933, Robert Weltsch, editor of the *Jüdische Rundschau*, wrote: "Wear It with Pride, the Yellow Spot." At that moment, however, there was still no system of obligatory physical markers for Jews in Germany. Weltsch probably drew his

A Jewish couple in the Budapest ghetto. Ordered to wear yellow stars prominently displayed on their clothing, Hungarian Jews were first identified, then isolated, and finally murdered in the spring and summer of 1944. (Yevgeny Khaldei/Corbis)

metaphor from the antisemitic graffiti and pamphlets that accompanied the boycott.

Historically, of course, Jews in and beyond Europe had been compelled to wear distinguishing markings of a certain shape or color on their clothes, hats, or shoes to make them instantly identifiable to other populations or religious groups. Often, this requirement was meant to be humiliating. Yellow was the color that designated Jews in Muslim realms. The practice was frequently adopted in Christian lands, although the reason for the choice of color has never been established.

The markings began to disappear from Christian Europe in the modern era and were fully done away with as Jews achieved emancipation during the course of the nineteenth century. It was Reinhard Heydrich who, shortly after the Night of Broken Glass pogrom of November 1938, first suggested imposing special signs for German Jews. During the campaign in Poland,

German occupying authorities issued random orders to disclose Jewish businesses through special symbols. Soon, Jews were ordered to wear signs on their clothing. In Lublin, for example, the ordinance called for a yellow insignia to be worn on the left breast, bearing the inscription "Jew." On November 23, 1939, Hans Frank decreed that all Jews in the General Gouvernement of Poland over the age of twelve would wear a white armband with a blue Jewish Star of David. Jews received the same order in the annexed parts of Silesia, where the armband was replaced by an insignia. In the city of Kalisz, the chief administrator ordered the wearing of an armband 4 centimeters in width and "of a Jew-yellow color." A month later, he changed his mind, ruling in favor of a 10-centimeter yellow Star of David to be worn on the right breast and back.

Following the invasion of the USSR, the same measures for the physical identification of Jews were implemented. Gradually, the yellow star became the preferred symbol in all locales. Jews who failed to wear the insignia or observe the appropriate regulations for its display were fined, jailed, or, in extreme cases, killed. In ghettos and concentration camps, variations of the star identified members of the Jewish police or Jewish council personnel. Inmates in concentration camps were classified by triangles of various colors, designating the reasons for their incarceration: homosexuals (pink), "asocials" (black), Jehovah's Witnesses (purple), and so on. Jews always wore two superimposed triangles (to make a Star of David), one of them yellow with letters displaying their "racial" origins and the other indicating their "crimes."

From the end of September 1938, Jewish passports were stamped with a large red *J*. Ration cards were first marked with a *J* and, in September 1942, imprinted with *Jew*. The yellow star, applied in the German-controlled regions of Europe beginning in 1939, did not become obligatory in the Old Reich until September 1941. At all times, every Jew over the age of six was to wear a "securely sewn, palm-sized, black-bordered, and six-sided star of yellow cloth" on the left breast of his or her outer clothing. On the star, in faux Hebrew lettering, stood the word *Jew*. Covering or obscuring the symbol was a punishable offense. In March 1942, Jews also had to affix the star to the doors of their dwellings.

The classification of Jews by means of visible signs completed both their social and their legal isolation. The system allowed authorities, particularly the police, to identify Jews easily; arrest them more effortlessly; and exercise control over their habitations, movements, and general behavior. The non-Jewish population was simultaneously transformed into an auxiliary police force, able to monitor the actions and presence of Jews at all times. The Jewish victims were paralyzed by the sense of being under permanent scrutiny. Trying to get around the system risked denunciation by one's neighbors; few Jews were willing to take that chance. Their inescapable visibility rendered them less and less likely to resist the overwhelming forces that controlled their lives.

—Matthias Brosch
Richard S. Levy, translation

*See also* Boycott of Jewish Shops, Germany; Emancipation; Islam and the Jews; J Stamp; Nazi Legal Measures against Jews; Night of Broken Glass (November 1938 Pogrom); Yellow Badge
**Reference**
Klemperer, Victor. *I Will Bear Witness*. Translated by Martin Chalmers. 2 vols. (New York: Random House, 1998).

## Young Germany

In opposition to the post-Napoleonic restoration's intensification of political oppression and especially of censorship after 1815, a number of dissident writers emerged in the 1830s who were collectively known as Young Germany. The term was applied to them almost by accident, for they were not revolutionary like the contemporary Young Italy movement, nor were they bound to one another in an organized conspiracy. The group has been variously defined, but all definitions include at least four writers—Ludolf Wienbarg (1802–1872), Heinrich Laube (1806–1884), Theodor Mundt (1808–1861), and Karl Gutzkow (1811–1878)—whose works were banned in a decree of the Germanic Confederation of December 10, 1835. At the insistence of the Austrian chancellor, Prince Metternich, the name of Heinrich Heine (1797–1856) was added. An occasion for depoliticizing government action against the dissidents was provided by Gutzkow's novel *Wally, die Zweiflerin* (Wally the Skeptic [1835]), which challenged conventional views on religion and sexual relations. The author was consequently prosecuted and jailed on grounds of blasphemy and pornography. Providing middle-class support for the ban (though not the instigator of it, as has been believed) with a campaign against the novel was the influential critic Wolfgang Menzel, who—for reasons still imperfectly understood—just at that time mutated from a liberal literary historian to a conservative, nationalistic ideologue with a pronounced antisemitic tendency. He began to refer to Young Germany as Young Palestine, even though none of the Young Germans proper was Jewish. In so doing, he was attempting to devalue them by association with their older models of Jewish origin, Heine and Ludwig Börne, and with immoral, frivolous, and unpatriotic—that is, French—ideas.

In fact, the Young Germans exhibited, in various ways, the typical attitudes of enlightened liberalism: pleasant associations with individual Jews, lack of interest in or knowledge of Judaism as a consequence of having left traditional religious belief behind, support of emancipation in the interest of dissolving Jewish identity in assimilation, and a readiness to accept commonplace prejudices about the Jews as a collectivity. Wienbarg, who advocated the Norwegian constitution of 1814 as a model for a democratic Germany, was untroubled by its ban of Jews (and Jesuits) from the kingdom. Gutzkow, with his tendency to extreme convictions, was a particularly convoluted case. He had close associations with Jewish contemporaries and was a strong admirer of Börne, whose biography he wrote (thus incidentally making him an enemy of Heine), though at one point, he was astonished to discover that Börne was Jewish. Gutzkow's *Uriel Acosta* (1846) was the first German drama with a serious Jewish protagonist in the fifty-seven years since Gotthold Ephraim Lessing's *Nathan the Wise*. Acosta (or D'Acosta, 1590–1640), a dissident *marrano* (crypto-Jew) from Portugal who was twice excommunicated and finally driven to suicide by the Orthodox Jewish authorities in Amsterdam, is presented as an inspiration to the young Benedict Spinoza (1632–1677), who had become important to the pantheistic thought of German culture. The drama was staged throughout the nineteenth century and beyond, although critics have long recognized that it has little to do with Jews, as Gutzkow himself agreed; it is a demonstration in favor of freedom of thought for modern religious skepticism directed against the oppressors of the author's own time. Gutzkow was strongly opposed to the preservation of Jewish identity, insisting that there not be any more "tribes" and that all spirituality be dissolved in a universal world religion. Although supporting emancipation in the expectation that it would eradicate Jewishness, in many writings he expressed intense hostility toward the Jews as they so exasperatingly continued to be. The Jewish author Berthold Auerbach pronounced him an "intimate enemy of the Jews." However, since he ultimately came to hate everyone, it is hard to tell whether this was a particular animosity. At the end of his life, he suffered from mental illness, believing that the Jews were persecuting him.

Friendliest to the Jews among the Young Germans was Laube, who was Heine's most faithful supporter until they had a breach over politics in 1848. Laube remained grateful for warm experiences with charitable Jews in his impoverished youth. His novel about the Polish revolution of 1831, *Die Krieger* (The Warriors [1837]), portrays a Jewish youth who tries to become a modern man through progressive political commitment but finds he is allowed no human relationship among the revolutionary aristocrats, the democrats, or the rebellious people; in bitterness, he reverts to the role of a traditional peddler. In German fiction, Laube's work is the most empathic portrayal of modern Jewish identity before Auerbach's early novels. Yet even Laube fell back into conventional prejudice on one occasion. The incident concerned his 1844 drama *Struensee,* the performance of which was blocked by the powerful composer Giacomo Meyerbeer in the interest of protecting his late brother Michael Beer's twenty-year-old drama on the same subject, even though it was regarded as unplayably old-fashioned. Laube took Meyerbeer's notoriety for applying his personal wealth to the advancement of his career as license to declare competitive commercialism an un-German trait of a foreign Jewish element forcing itself into literature, especially in Berlin. In the introduction to his drama, Laube devoted a few pages to a demand for radical emancipation to make Jews less foreign—Auerbach is said to be proof that a Jew can be completely Germanized—but in his rage, he permitted himself an outburst that rings ominously in retrospect: "Either we must be barbarians and drive out the Jews to the last man, or we must incorporate them." The intemperate expression has been linked to Richard Wagner's antisemitic invective that was formulated a few years later and was also at least partly motivated by resentment of Meyerbeer. Although Laube's overall record should not be dissolved in this one episode, it indicates how readily antisemitic atavisms surfaced in moments of frustration.

—*Jeffrey L. Sammons*

**See also** Emancipation; Heine, Heinrich; *Judaism in Music;* Wagner, Richard

*References*

Lea, Charlene A. *Emancipation, Assimilation and Stereotype: The Image of the Jew in German and Austrian Drama, 1800–1850* (Bonn, Germany: Bouvier, 1978).

Sammons, Jeffrey L. *Six Essays on the Young German Novel* (Chapel Hill: University of North Carolina Press, 1972).

# Young Hegelians

Following the repressive Carlsbad Decrees (of 1819), G. W. F. Hegel censored himself and muted potentially subversive pronouncements to avoid open conflict with the Prussian authorities. This invariably lent additional ambiguity to the meaning and implications of his complex philosophical system and rendered the conflicts emerging among his students and followers soon after his death in 1831 all the more acrimonious.

Hegel contended that philosophy and religion were but two distinct modes of understanding and expressing truth. Putting them on the same footing was seen, by some, as heretical, ultimately privileging the god of the philosophers over the god of the theologians. Hegel also suggested that his thought and the form of Protestantism he envisaged reflected the imminent consummation of the identity of the real and the rational. This philosophical argument had potentially important consequences, for Hegel implied or seemed to imply that the Prussian bureaucracy was the universal class whose objective task was to facilitate this process. Had Hegel's relevant remarks been of a factual or of a normative nature? Had he suggested that the contemporary Prussian state was on the verge of perfection, or had he instead tried to cajole the authorities into doing their historical/philosophical duty?

Either way, the very thing that signaled the threat of Hegel's system to his critics on the Right represented its promise to his more radical adherents on the Left—the Young (or Left) Hegelians. On both fronts, Hegel's more conformist disciples, the Old (or Right) Hegelians, sought to defend him against the suggestion he had been anything other than an orthodox Protestant or loyal and enthusiastic subject of the Prussian regime.

It was not only the inherent ambiguities of Hegel's thought, however, that rendered the ensuing controversy so vehement that any notion of a unitary Hegelian school became impossible. The circumstances of the dispute contributed directly to this outcome. Although the Old Hegelians, perhaps, stood a chance of appeasing the establishment, their ostensible defense of Hegel could only radicalize the Young Hegelians. For them, that defense misrepresented Hegel's thought and led to an overt affirmation of the current state of affairs that betrayed Hegel's vision. The accession of Friedrich Wilhelm IV in 1840, who soon professed a bizarre Christian romanticism and a loathing for Hegelianism of any kind, seemed to underscore just how groundless the claims of the Old Hegelians had been.

The Young Hegelians soon began to question (in principle) the role that they had hitherto assigned the Prussian state in facilitating the identity of the real and the rational. Beyond that, they also increasingly abandoned the whole notion that reality was the outgrowth of an overarching rational idea or set of ideas and instead began to examine ideas as reflections of an independent, objective reality. Most prominent among them were David Friedrich Strauss (whose *Life of Jesus* [1835] was a milestone in the formulation of the Young Hegelian challenge), the publisher Arnold Ruge, August von Cieszkowski, Max Stirner, Ludwig Feuerbach, Bruno Bauer, and the young Karl Marx.

The Jewish Question was not a primary concern of the Young Hegelians and was not treated in a consistent fashion by them, although the debate on Jewish legal status in the early 1840s obviously caught their attention and prompted some of them to comment publicly. Their ambiguities and conventional prejudices notwithstanding, they generally inclined toward perceiving Jewish emancipation as a test case for emancipation more generally. They tended to direct many of the criticisms previously associated specifically with Judaism against religion in general. Given their Hegelian roots, they nevertheless felt the need to maintain the notion of a relative superiority of Christianity over Judaism. Thus, they were left with fewer but all the more negative stereotypes at their disposal to explain the distinction between Judaism and Christianity. On the whole, however, the religious rather than ethnic or racial focus of these stereotypes and the heavy philosophical diction of the Young Hegelians rendered their writing of limited use to emerging modern antisemitism.

—Lars Fischer

**See also** Bauer, Bruno; Emancipation; Feuerbach, Ludwig; Hegel, G. W. F.; Jewish Question; *Jewish Question, The* (1843); Marx, Karl

**References**

Carlebach, Julius. *Karl Marx and the Radical Critique of Judaism* (London: Littman/Routledge and Kegan Paul, 1978).

Stepelevich, Lawrence S., ed. *The Young Hegelians: An Anthology* (Cambridge: Cambridge University Press, 1983).

# Youth Movement (German)

In the words of Walter Laqueur, one of its many historians, the German youth movement should be studied as a virtual microcosm of twentieth-century Germany. The movement that emerged at the close of the nineteenth century as a simple ramblers' club for high school and college students swiftly developed into a multifaceted sociological and cultural phenomenon.

The German youth movement unfolded in two phases: the initial *Wandervogel* (literally, migratory bird) period, from about 1896 to 1919, and the era of the youth leagues (*Bünde*), dating from approximately 1920 to 1933. In both stages, the reaction to political and ideological developments within the general youth movement varied markedly. During the initial phase, political and religious neutrality was a stated goal. In the era of the leagues, this neutrality vanished.

Scholarly literature on the youth movement frequently describes it as part of a generational conflict, a reaction by the younger generation against the outmoded social norms of the German Empire and the alienation that it bred. Urgent questions about "a new identity" and the search for "authentic culture" formed the background. The youthful community's rambling into the countryside and the movement's emotionally charged special events were not seen as ends in themselves but rather as expressions of longing for a new, emancipatory design for living. The idealism of the educated bourgeoisie and the life reform movement, spontaneity, and an overly romantic enthusiasm blended together into an identifiable youth culture.

The bourgeois youth movement was not revolutionary. Despite its declared political-religious neutrality, it remained the captive of its social base and brought its values to bear on the social and political conflicts of the age. Among these were the antisemitic tendencies widely present in the middle classes of Wilhelmine Germany.

An early "age of innocence" came to an end as *völkisch* (racist-nationalist) ideology conquered the bourgeois youth movement. Under the leadership of Karl Fischer, a striking change of direction took place, leading to the cultivation of "old German values" (*Altdeuschtum*) and a delving into the mythic past. In fact, the leaders of the movement fashioned their ideals from their parental homes and from the literature that inculcated national pride and patriotic thinking. The movement's periodicals set the tone, giving pride of place to *völkisch* writers. The *völkisch* trend and the more or less accentuated antisemitism it always contained resulted in the public "antisemitism debate" of 1912 and 1913. A collective youth movement position on the Jewish Question is difficult to determine, however, because the great majority of the members did not speak out in any consistent way and most simply had no well-considered opinion on the issue.

If, however, the few prominent individuals, leaders of key constituent groups, favored authors, and other individuals who often functioned in the public sphere are taken into consideration, then the conclusion would be a different one. These leaders provided the influential role models for impressionable young people; they were the "insiders" capable of presenting youth culture to the none-too-friendly outside world, and they exerted a decisive influence on attitudes in the process of being formed. This dedicated *völkisch* stratum dominated the movement and—fatefully—introduced a destructive antisemitism into its outlook. And it is noteworthy that this negative image of Jews was not of the old-fashioned kind—the product of religious, political, or economic conflicts—but rather one founded on racism. The Jew, they argued, was the "other," irreparably alienated from Nature, the German landscape, the German peasant, and the ancient Germanic ceremonies.

Until just before the outbreak of World War I, there seems to have been no fixed policy with regard to Jewish membership in the various bourgeois youth groups. But when a Jewish girl was denied membership on the basis of her descent by the Zittau (Saxony) chapter of the Wandervogel in 1913, it led to an expansive, clarifying discussion of the Jewish Question. At that juncture, antisemitism strengthened its hold over the movement. Counteractions by individual leaders, local groups, or regional organizations had little or no effect. The Central Association of German Citizens of Jewish Faith, true to its assimilationist principles, urged Jewish young people to persevere in their efforts to stay in the Wandervogel or to join it and not "to return to the ghetto." However, to escape the stigma of antisemitic agitation and the arbitrary exclusiveness of the Wandervogel leadership, Zionist-oriented groups recruited vigorously for their own Jewish hiking clubs, especially the Blue and Whites (Blau-Weiss Bünde), which experienced a large increase in membership at this time.

The end of the war ushered in the next phase of the youth movement, the league era. Many of the crucial questions concerning this phase of development have yet to be studied in a thorough way. How was *völkisch* ideology imported into the youth movement of the Weimar Republic? Which of the individual youth organizations were open to and/or disposed toward antisemitic tendencies and practices? And finally, how did *völkisch* and antisemitic ideologies within the youth leagues play into the synthesizing National Socialist movement?

—*Andreas Winnecken*
*Richard S. Levy, translation*

**See also** Central Association of German Citizens of Jewish Faith; Jewish Question; National Socialist German Workers' Party; *Völkisch* Movement and Ideology; Weimar; Zionism

**References**

Laqueur, Walter. *Young Germany: A History of the German Youth Movement* (New Brunswick, NJ: Transaction Books, 1982; orig. 1962).
Winnecken, Andreas. *Ein Fall von Antisemitismus: Zur Geschichte und Pathogenese der deutschen Jugendbewegung vor dem ersten Weltkrieg* (Cologne, Germany: Verlag Wissenschaft und Politik, 1991).

# Z

## Zionism

Zionism is the Jewish nationalist movement that began in the nineteenth century, led to the founding of the state of Israel, and continues to support Israel's existence today. Its basic tenet is that the Jews constitute a nation and that, as such, they should have a Jewish state as their national homeland in Eretz Israel (Palestine).

A persistent myth about the foundation of Zionism was that it was a direct response to antisemitism. This myth is embodied in the claim that Theodor Herzl was "converted" to Zionism because of his experience of the Dreyfus Affair in 1895. However, the relation between antisemitism and Zionism is more complicated than this.

Zionism was the combination of two movements, one centered on western and central Europe and the other on eastern Europe, primarily Russia. "Political" Zionism began as the response of highly acculturated central European Jews, most notably Herzl and his right-hand man, Max Nordau, to what they saw as the failure of legal emancipation to provide real integration of Jews into their respective national societies because of the emergence of modern antisemitism. Zionism, for them, was a means not merely of escaping antisemitism but also of reforming what they saw as the many social and even moral problems of so-called modern European Jewry. Once they had "rediscovered" their own Jewish national identity, both insisted that they had found their authentic selves and that their Zionism was now quite independent of antisemitism.

Practical and cultural Zionism, centered largely in Russia, antedated the political variant by over a decade, tracing its roots to the Hibbat Zion movement of the early 1880s. Leo Pinsker's *Autoemancipation* (1882) anticipated most of Herzl's later thought. This first Zionist movement had also been a response to an outbreak of anti-Jewish violence in the wave of pogroms of the 1880s, but it was based on a strong, prior sense of Jewish ethnic identity, even Jewish secular nationality, as expressed in the work of Perez Smolenskin in the 1860s. Cultural Zionists, such as Ahad Ha'am (Asher Ginzberg), were already writing in the 1880s.

Zionism only achieved real momentum in the late 1890s, when Herzl's political movement combined with the Zionism already active, but inchoate, in Russia and eastern Europe. Antisemitism thus played a *necessary* role in the movement's success, by persuading first Herzl and his Western followers and later still a large part of western, eastern, and central European Jewry of the impossibility of a true integration of Jews into European society. Moreover, antisemitism's durability was central to the political Zionists' logic. It explained why Western assimilated Jews were suffering and would continue to suffer an existential moral crisis because it made real assimilation impossible; antisemitism could also be blamed for the dire material condition of the Eastern Jewish masses. If antisemitism was a permanent condition, then the only long-term solution to both crises was the creation of a Jewish state or homeland.

Antisemitism was not, however, a *sufficient* cause of Zionism, even in its political form. Cultural Zionists had a Jewish nationalist program concerning the reform of traditional Jewish society and culture and the development of an "authentic" Jewish language, modern Hebrew, that was quite independent from considerations of antisemitism. Political Zionists also had plans for modernizing European Jewry that were much more than an attempt to counter antisemitism and that originated in the original ideology of emancipation and the Jewish Enlightenment that preceded it.

Some of the Zionist critique of European Jewry has been seen as an internalized form of antisemitism, but in most cases, it was the result of internally generated, intra-Jewish considerations. Ahad Ha'am's desire to reform the language Jews speak, for instance, giving up Yiddish for modern Hebrew, can be viewed as independent of antisemitic attacks on the "impure" language of the Jews. Nordau's call for a "muscle Jewry" can similarly be viewed as having more to do with his own views as a physician and the author of *Degeneration* and with general contemporary concerns about national physical fitness, rather than with an internalization of antisemitic stereotypes about puny Jews.

Part of the confusion about the parallels between Zionist and antisemitic thought concerning Jews is that Zionism and antisemitism drew much of their inspiration and logic from the same source: nationalism. As an emancipatory nationalism, albeit for a Diasporic nation, Zionism shared the ideas of other nationalisms. Political Zionists such as Nordau, for instance, accepted the notion that it was natural for nations not to want to tolerate "foreign" groups within their borders and that members of minorities, such as the Jews, therefore had to choose *either* total assimilation *or* leaving to form their own nation.

The links between Zionist and antisemitic thought through nationalist ideology should be carefully considered, however. Although Nordau and Herzl might have accepted some of the central tenets of European nationalism in asserting that the Jews were a nation and could only realize themselves as a nation in their own Jewish state, they also saw the future Zionist state as being an exemplar of cosmopolitan pluralism— a model that would free the world from the sort of exclusive nationalism that had created modern antisemitism.

—*Steven Beller*

**See also** Degeneration; Dreyfus Affair; Emancipation; Herzl, Theodor; Jewish Question; Masculinity; Nordau, Max; Pale of Settlement; Pogroms; Schnitzler, Arthur; Self-Hatred, Jewish
**References**
Beller, Steven. *Herzl* (London: Halban, 1991).

Hertzberg, Arthur. *The Zionist Idea* (New York: Atheneum, 1959).
Shimoni, Gideon. *The Zionist Ideology* (Hanover, NH: Brandeis University Press, 1995).

## Zola, Émile (1840–1902)

With the publication of his essay collection, *The Experimental Novel* (1880), and *L'Assommoir: The Dram Shop, Nana,* and *Germinal,* part of the Rougon-Macquart cycle of novels (1877–1885), the French writer Émile Zola became the major voice of literary naturalism. Worldwide fame also came to him as a result of the Dreyfus Affair. The highpoint of his engagement in the case was marked by "J'accuse" (I accuse), his open letter of January 13, 1898, addressed to the president of the Third Republic.

Zola became involved in the case of Alfred Dreyfus rather late, after the captain had already been convicted and deported to Devil's Island. Following a long conversation with the vice-president of the *Senat,* Auguste Scheurer-Kestner, Zola published three articles between late November and early December 1897 in *Figaro,* detailing the current state of the affair and its ideological and political background. He subjected the popular notion of a "Jewish Syndicate" to scathing irony. In his article "Protocol," he denounced antisemitism and the "despicable exploitation of patriotism" by the press. The immediate occasion for the open letter to the president of the Third Republic was the acquittal by a military court of Maj. Ferdinand Walsin-Esterhazy—since revealed as the true guilty party.

Zola's long article took up the entire first page and a part of the second of the newspaper *L'Aurore.* It was considered the first thorough portrayal of the course of the affair. In its concluding litany of charges, all of which began with "I accuse," he indicted the leadership of the French army, the judges of the military courts, prominent members of the government, and even President Felix Faure for knowingly having condemned an innocent man or for having illegally covered up the grounds for his conviction. Zola's stand represented an act of civil courage, and it was a defining moment in the emergence of the "engaged intellectual." "J'accuse" brought the Dreyfus Affair to the point of moral and politi-

French novelist Émile Zola. On January 13, 1898, during the height of the Dreyfus Affair, Émile Zola challenged anti-Dreyfusards with the publication of his "J'Accuse" letter in a French newspaper. (Library of Congress)

In it, he labeled antisemitism as monstrous and senseless, declaring that it would throw France back to the era of the wars of religion. Biological racism, he argued, was only a pretext for socially and economically motivated antisemitism, which he regarded as the main evil. If Jews actually dominated economic life—and there were certainly Christian exploiters as well—then this was the fault of a society that had ostracized them for centuries and hindered their complete assimilation. Blaming Jews for social shortcomings was nothing more than a hypocritical, mendacious, and misguided sort of socialism.

Zola's engagement in the Dreyfus Affair, part of a long public career on behalf of unpopular causes, was not without its personal costs. In the violent wave of antisemitism following "I accuse," he was reproached with his Italian parentage (his father was a Venetian), his patriotism was impugned, and he was accused of being in the pay of the Jews. It is not impossible that his death in 1902 by carbon monoxide poisoning, from a blocked chimney, was an assassination carried out by a nationalist fanatic.

—*Karl Zieger*
*Richard S. Levy, translation*

**See also** Dreyfus Affair; Drumont, Édouard; France; *France juive, La;* Hollywood, Treatment of Antisemitism in; Lienhard, Friedrich

**References**
Brown, Frederick. *Zola—A Life* (New York: Farrar Straus Giroux, 1995).
Burns, Michael. *Dreyfus: A Family Affair* (New York: HarperCollins, 1991).
Mitterand, Henri. *Zola.* Vol. 3, *L'Honneur, 1893–1902* (Paris: Fayard, 2002).
Oriol, Philippe. *"J'Accuse . . . !" Emile Zola et l'Affaire Dreyfus* (Paris: Librio, 1998).

cal crisis and had repercussions far beyond the borders of France. Zola was convicted of slander and assessed a large fine, but he avoided imprisonment by going into exile in England (in July 1898), where he stayed nearly a year before returning to France.

That Zola should risk his lofty reputation and his chance of being named to the French Academy was, at least at first glance, somewhat surprising. In at least a few of his novels, there are antisemitic stereotypes of an economic and "intellectual" nature that were commonplace in that era. The parliamentary deputy Kahn, a banker's son, in *His Excellency* is undoubtedly an antisemitic characterization, as is Steiner, the Jewish banker in *Nana,* and especially Gundermann, another Jewish banker, from *Money.*

Nonetheless, Zola reacted angrily against the antisemitism being spread by Édouard Drumont's *La France juive* (1886) and his newspaper, *La Libre parole.* In May 1896, well before his involvement in the Dreyfus case, he wrote an article for *Figaro* entitled "On Behalf of the Jews."

## Zündel, Ernst (1939– )

The neo-Nazi, antisemite, and Holocaust denier Ernst Christof Friedrich Zündel was born to a family of simple, pious Christians—his father was a woodcutter and served as a medic in World War II—in Calmbach, a village in the Black Forest region of Germany. He emigrated to Canada in 1958 and settled in Toronto in the 1960s, where he ran a successful photo-retouching business for magazines. The Canadian Nazi Adrien

Arcand, who had spent World War II in prison, shared his racist, antisemitic library with Zündel and introduced him to white supremacist groups in Canada and abroad. Zündel cowrote with Eric Thomson *The Hitler We Loved and Why* (1977). Together, they portrayed Hitler as "this humble, totally dedicated savior" who "saved White civilization" and had "the vision to create a happy and sound society," meaning no Jews or other "race-defilers": "We love you, Adolph [*sic*] Hitler," they gushed.

By the early 1980s, Zündel's extremist antisemitism, Holocaust denial, and Nazi agitation were too blatant to be ignored. Attempts to prosecute him began in 1985, when the Holocaust survivor Sabina Citron brought suit against him. He was found guilty in a jury trial for knowingly spreading "false news" that was likely to do harm to a recognizable group of people; he was sentenced to fifteen months in jail. In 1987, the Appeals Court found that the law making false news punishable was constitutional, but it granted a retrial due to judicial irregularities. At the second trial in 1988, no Holocaust survivors testified, and historian Christopher Browning (replacing Raul Hilberg) served as the leading expert witness. Zündel was found guilty again and sentenced this time to nine months of imprisonment. In 1990, the Appeals Court upheld the decision, the sentence, and the constitutionality of the false news law. In 1992, however, the Supreme Court overturned Zündel's conviction, finding the law too vague and therefore unconstitutional.

Zündel celebrated his "victory for free speech" by renewing the barrage of antisemitic hatred and Holocaust denial. The Canadian Human Rights Commission brought an action against him in "a hearing on the merits." The hearing before a tribunal of three persons (reduced to two when the academic member had to return to his university) ran fifty-five days but dragged on over five years (from 1996 to 2001), thanks largely to the defense counsel's delaying tactics. Frederick M. Schweitzer, the commission's principal expert witness, established that over many centuries, there was a correlation between antisemitic propaganda and persecution of Jews, that Zündel's antisemitic writings repli-cated classic lethal antisemitism, and that therefore Zündel's antisemitic attacks would likely injure Jews. Although he never took the witness stand, Zündel was invariably present at the hearing until February 2001, when he fled to the United States. There, he married his third wife, a U.S. citizen, and swiftly resumed disseminating hate literature on the Internet.

Meanwhile, the tribunal's decision (of January 18, 2002) barring Zündel from the Internet hinged on its perception of his propaganda as "hate messages" that were "likely to expose a person or persons to hatred or contempt by reason of the fact that that person or those persons are identifiable on the basis of a prohibited ground [religion, race, and so on] of discrimination." The decision placed a stigma on Zündel, as it did on those so-called experts summoned to testify on his behalf, all of whom were rejected by the tribunal as "unreliable" and "unqualified." These included Robert Countess, Robert Faurisson, and Tony Martin, a professor who accuses Jews of being the principal architects of the Atlantic slave trade. Mark Weber, editor of the denier *Journal of Historical Review,* was allowed to testify only on his knowledge of how Holocaust deniers operate.

For overstaying his U.S. visa, Zündel was deported back to Canada in February 2003. In May of that year, a Canadian federal judge declared him a threat to national security. In March 2005, the Canadian Appeals Court, declaring him a threat to the international community of nations, deported him to Germany where he was immediately arrested and where he remains subject to prosecution for hate speech and Holocaust denial. Prone to self-dramatization, Zündel has dressed in a bulletproof vest and carried a cross "like Jesus on his way to Calvary." Reportedly, he has also derived great personal profit from his massive distribution of antisemitic and Holocaust denial propaganda in all its forms.

—*Frederick M. Schweitzer*

***See also*** Auschwitz Lie; Holocaust Denial, Negationism, and Revisionism; Institute for Historical Review; Internet; Irving, David; Leuchter Report; Neo-Nazism, German; *Secret Relationship between Blacks and Jews, The;* Slave Trade and the Jews; White Power Movement

**Reference**

Perry, Marvin, and Frederick M. Schweitzer. "Canada's Attempts to Curb Ernst Zündel's Antisemitic Actions as a Public Danger." In *Antisemitism: Myth and Hate from Antiquity to the Present* (New York: Palgrave Macmillan, 2002), app. 2: 269–277, 301, and works cited there.

# INDEX

Donnelley, Ignatius (1831–1901), 511

Dontsov, Dmytro (1883–1973), 717

**Doré, Gustave** (1832–1883**), 186–187**, 207

Doriot, Jacques (1898–1945), 224, 591

**Dostoevsky, Fyodor** (1821–1881), 168, **187–188**, 551, 569, 628, 632, 681

**Dracula, 188–189**, 205
*See also* Degeneration

Drexler, Anton (1884–1942), 486, 706

**Dreyfus Affair,** 28, 63, **189–191**, 238, 370, 379
in French politics, 1, 10, 15, 58, 192, 448, 594, 667, 788–789
and foreign opinion, 2, 65, 115, 148, 232, 668, 684, 714
and Jewish response to, 11, 300, 315–316, 787
*See also* Drumont, Édouard; Herzl, Theodor; Maurras, Charles; Zola, Émile

Dreyfus, Alfred (1859–1935), 106, 189, 240

Drieu la Rochelle, Pierre (1893–1945), 57, 224, 591

Droste-Hülshoff, Annette von (1797–1848), 383–384

**Drumont, Édouard** (1844–1917), 10, 15, 31, 55, **191–192**, 240–241, 681, 700, 768
and the Dreyfus Affair, 189–191, 192, 789
*See also* France juive, La

Du Maurier, George (1834–1896), 205, 207, 691

Dubnow, Simon (1860–1941), 400, 451, 553, 631

DuBois, W. E. B. (1868–1919), 5, 661

Dubrovin, A. I., 71, 581

Dugin, Aleksandr (1962–), 633

**Dühring, Eugen** (1833–1921), **192–193**, 290, 386, 495, 587, 667, 681, 736
his radical solutions of the Jewish Question, 276, 381–382

**Duke, David** (1950–), 108, **193–194**, 349

Duma, 71, 79, 405, 581–582, 631, 633, 634–635, 718

Durban Conference on Racism and Xenophobia (2001), 26

Düsseldorf, 154, 171, 270–271, 293, 476–477

Dutch West India Company, 133, 688

Eastern Orthodox Church, 4, 690, 718

Eckart, Dietrich (1868–1923), 73, 480, 493, 706

Ecker, Jakob (d. 1912), 78, 564

École Normale Supérieure, 57, 81, 223, 639

Edison, Thomas Alva (1847–1931), 315, 349, 705

Edward I, King of England (1239–1307), 132, 216, 327

Egypt (modern), 31, 33, 160–161, 361, 483

Ehrenburg, Ilya (1891–1967), 373

**Eichmann, Adolf** (1906–1962), 74–75, 90, **195–196**, 506, 662, 756
and the Holocaust in Hungary, 323, 331–332

**Eichmann Trial,** 36, **196–197**, 697

**1848, 197–199**, 232
anti-Jewish violence in, 15
in France, 277, 571
and Jewish emancipation, 203, 445
Jewish emancipation, opposition to, 39, 386. 644, 749
Jews' exploitation of revolutions of, 61, 386, 466
in the German states, 60–61, 91, 165, 232, 286, 400, 601, 735
in Hungary, 327
and the papacy, 548, 719, 733

**Einsatzgruppen,** 125, 135, **199–200**, 302, 318, 428, 555, 724
*See also* Commissar Order, Order Police, Wannsee Conference

Einstein, Albert (1879–1955), 421, 545–547

Einstein, Alfred (1880–1952), 476, 477

Einstein, Carl (1885–1940), 65

Eisenhower, Dwight D. (1890–1969), 17, 471, 472, 623, 663

Eisler, Hanns (1898–1962), 228

Eisner, Kurt (1867–1919), 706, 760

*Election, An* (1754), 312–314

Elghanian, Habib (d. 1979), 352, 398

**Eliot, T. S.** (1888–1965), **200–201**, 208, 562

Elisabeth, Empress of Austria (1837–1898), 295

**Emancipation,**
*See also* Antisemitic Political Parties (Germany, 1879–1914); Dohm, Christian Wilhelm von; 1848; Grégoire, Henri-Baptiste; Jew Bill of 1753; Jewish Question; Nuremberg Laws; Philosemitism

Emicho of Flonheim (d. 1139), 153

Eminescu, Mihai (1850–1889), 157, 617

*Encyclopédie*, 177, 456

Endeks. *See* National Democrats (Poland)

Engels, Friedrich (1820–1895), 27, 97, 447, 452, 667–668
and Dühring, Eugen, 192, 667
*See also* Socialists on Antisemitism

**English Literature from Chaucer to Wells, 204–206**

**English Literature of the Twentieth Century, 206–209**

*Entdecktes Judenthum* (1700, 1711), **209–210**, 609, 700
*See also* Reformation, Talmud, *Talmud Jew, The*

**Erasmus, Desiderius** (1466–1536), **210–211**, 544

Erfurt, 98, 171, 218, 437

Eriksson, Elof (1883–1965), 693

Erzberger, Matthias (1875–1921), 111, 270

*Essay on the Inequality of the Human Races* (1853–1855), 62, 277, 586, 640

Esterhazy, Ferdinand Walsin (1847–1923). *See* Walsin-Esterhazy, Marie Charles Ferdinand

Ethiopia, 203, 432, 480, 566

Eudoxia, Empress (d. 404 CE), 122

**Eugenics, 211–212**, 239, 665
in the United States, 38, 212, 472

Leo XII, Pope (1760–1820), 531

Leo XIII, Pope (1878–1903), 64, 407, 531

Leon de Modena, Rabbi (1571–1648), 729

**Léon, Abram** (1918–1944), **417–418**

*See also* Socialists on Antisemitism

**Leskov, Nikolai Semenovich** (1831–1895), **418–419**

Lessing, Gotthold Ephraim (1729–1781), 396

*Die Juden*, 458

on Jewish Emancipation, 202

*Nathan the Wise*, 232, 545, 655, 750, 782

*See also* Emancipation; Philosemitism

Lessing, Theodor (1872–1933), 648

***Leuchter Report***, 45, 225, 321, **419–420**, 354

Leuchter, Fred (1943–), 419

Leutheuser, Julius (b. 1900), 172

Levenson, J. C. (1922–), 2

Leveridge, Richard (1670–1758), 312

Levi, Hermann (1839–1900), 750, 752

Levinson, Barry (1942–), 209

Levy, Abraham (1878–1957), 672

Levy, Uriah P. (1792–1862), 37

Lewis, C. S. (1898–1963), 115

Libanius (314–ca. 394), 121

**Liberty Lobby,** 107, 320, 348, **420–421**

*Libre parole, La*, 189, 191, 240, 789

**LICA—International League against Antisemitism**
(Ligue Internationale Contre l'Antisémitisme), **421**

Lichtenberg, Bernhard (1875–1943), 127, 313

Licinius, Emperor (250–325), 137

Lieber, Ernst (1838–1902), 111

**Liebermann von Sonnenberg, Max** (1848–1911), 22–23, 66, 236, 276, 296–297, 403, **422**

and ideas on harmful versus useful capital, 97–98,

Liebknecht, Wilhelm (1826–1900), 403

Liebold, Ernest G. (1884–1956), 163, 233

Liechtenstein, Alois (1846–1920), 746

**Lienhard, Friedrich** (1865–1929), 63, **422–423**

*Life of Jesus* (Strauss, 1835), 783

*Life of Jesus* (Renan, 1863), 594

Lillienblum, Moshe Leib (1843–1910), 630

Lincoln, Abraham (1809–1865), 663

**Lindbergh, Charles** (1902–1974), **423–424**, 721

Lindsey, Hal (1929–), 20

Lingen, Theo (1903–1978), 703

Lintorn-Orman, Rotha (1895–1935), 773

**Linz Program** (1882), 49, **424–425**, 643

Lippert, Julius (1895–1956), 18

Lissitzky, El (1890–1941), 631

**List, Guido von** (1848–1919), 269, 412, **425–426**, 474, 682, 744

Liszt, Franz (1811–1886), 750

**Lithuania,** 276, **426–428**, 527, 564–565, 605, 630, 677

**Lithuania, Holocaust in,** 251, 365, **428–429**

**Lithuania, Post-Soviet, 429–430**

Lithuanian Activist Front (LAF), 429

**Liutostanskii, Ippolit** (1835–1915/1918?), **430–431**

**Ljotić, Dimitrije** (1891–1945), **431–432**

Locke, John (1632–1704), 709

Lodz Ghetto, 229, 318, 555

Lösener, Bernhard (1890–1952), 516

Löwenfeld, Raphael (1854–1910), 112

Löwenstein, Rudolf (1819–1891), 400

Löwith, Karl (1897–1973), 292

Lombardy, Duchy of, 216, 257

Lombroso, Cesare (1835–1909), 167, 188, 191

London, 55, 80, 87, 163, 188, 206, 311, 399, 450, 566, 606, 773, 576

and the East End, 86, 473, 758

medieval and early modern, 99, 132–133, 154, 313–314, 372, 626–627, 652, 709

London School of Economics, 758

**Long, Breckinridge** (1881–1958), **432–433**

Long, Huey (1893–1935), 663

López, Rodrigo (d. 1593), 652–653

*Lorelei*, 294, 295

Lorenz, Alfred (1868–1939), 477

Lorre, Peter (1904–1964), 228

Louis Philippe, King of France (1830–1848), 239

Louis the Pious, Holy Roman Emperor (768–840), 6

Louis VII, King of France (ca. 1120–1180), 542

Louis IX, King of France (1214–1270), 216–217

Louis XIII, King of France (1601–1643), 102

Louis XVI, King of France (1754–1793), 13

Louisiana, 661, 663, 768

Lowell, A. Lawrence (1856–1943), 514

Loyola, Ignatius (1491–1556), 369

Lübeck, 272, 344

Lucan (39–65 CE), 613

Lucis Trust, 53, 351, 502

Lucretius (ca. 99– ca. 55 BCE), 612

**Ludendorff, Erich** (1865–1937), 265, **433–434**, 744

and Hitler, 113, 434

as promoter of the *Protocols of the Elders of Zion*, 705

and Tannenberg League, 60

*See also Völkisch* Movement and Ideology

**Ludendorff, Mathilde** (1877–1966), 433, **434–435**

**Ludendorff Publishing House** (Volkswarte-Verlag), 434, **435–436**

**Lueger, Karl** (1844–1910), 40–41, 229, **436–437**, 474

and the Christian Social movement, 49, 118, 247, 379

Hitler's admiration for, 118, 531

influence of Vogelsang, Karl von on, 746

and Schönerer, Georg von, 643

*See also* Aryan Theater; Austria; Christian Social Party (Austria)

Lundén, Barthold (d. 1932), 693

**Luther, Martin** (1483–1546), 247, 388, **437–439**, 454, 592–593, 690, 749

appropriation by Nazis, 520

Ploetz, Berthold von (1844–1898), 263–264

**Pobedonostsev, Constantine Pavlovich** (1827–1907), 419, **551**, 629

Pogroms,
absence of, 89, 94, 358
Alexandrian, 9, 29, 130–131, 176, 610
and the *Alliance Israélite Universelle*, 11, 160–161
in Baghdad, 221, 337
and the Black Death, 218
in Buenos Aires, 36, 88–89
in Constantine, 10, 139–140
during the Crusades, 152–154, 169
in Damascus, 11, 31–32, 160–161, 294, 470, 545, 605–606
in Germany,
Hitler's views on, 157, 255–256, 575
and Marr, Wilhelm, rejection of, 742
in Neustettin, 296, 500–501
Night of Broken Glass (November 1938 pogrom), 89, 157, 171, 229, 488, 506–508, 752
and Pudor, Heinrich, advocacy of, 575
in the Scheunenviertel (Berlin), 641
Hep-Hep Riots, 297–299, 733
in Hungary, 333–334, 390
in Tiszaeszlar, 707–708
in Lithuania, 428
in medieval Spain, 219, 673
in Poland, 532
Jedwabne, 366–367
Kielce, 311, 398–399
Prague Massacre (1389), 563–564
during revolutions of 1848, 198
during the Rindfleisch Massacres, 602
in Russia,
and the Black Hundreds, 71, 634
1903–1905, 71, 635
Lenin's denunciation of, 668
in Kishinev, 399–400, 405
Odessa, 519
during the Russian Civil War, 636, 723
during World War II, carried out by Romanian troops, 619

*See also* Pogroms (Russian, 1881) and Stalininization of eastern Europe, 183, 679
*See also Culture-Antisemitism or Pogrom-Antisemitism?*; Gemlich Letter; Hep-Hep Riots; Pogroms (Russian, 1881)

**Pogroms (Russian, 1881)**, 315, 419, 523, **552–553**, 668, 787
governmental complicity, debate over, 519, 553, 629–630
*See also* Immigration and Naturalization Laws (U.S.); Leskov, Nikolai; May Laws; *Ostjuden*; Pale of Settlement; Russia, Imperial; Zionism

Polak, H. (1868–1943), 498

**Poland**, 96, 426–427, 459, 527, **553–556**, 592, 605
*See also* Boycott of 1912 (Poland); Dmowski, Roman; Ghetto Benches; Jedwabne; Kielce Pogrom; National Democrats (Poland); Purge of 1968 (Poland); Stalinization of Eastern Europe

**Poland since 1989, 557**

Poliakov, Leon (1910–), 317

Polish Institute of National Memory, 366

Pollasky, Marcus, 513

**Polná Ritual Murder, 557–558,** 607

Pompey (106–48 BCE), 610, 612–615

Pompidou, Georges (1911–1974), 144

Popular Front (France), 10, 15, 82, 146, 240, 667, 682, 738

**Populist Movement, 558–559**
and Norris, Frank, 511–513
and Watson, Tom, 757
*See also* Agrarian League; Banker, Jewish; Capital: Useful versus Harmful; Ford, Henry

**Pork, 559–562**
*See also* Caricature, Anti-Jewish (Early); *Judensau*

Portugal, 82, 216, 219, 348, 369, 661, 675, 782

Posse Comitatus, 465

Poujade, Pierre (1920–2003), 415

**Pound, Ezra** (1885–1972), 201, 208, **562–563**

Poznania (Posen), 198, 260, 310, 493

**Prague Massacre** (1389), **563–564**

**Pranaitis, Justinas** (1861–1917), **564–565**

Preuss, Hugo (1860–1925), 760

**Preziosi, Giovanni** (1881–1945), **565–567**
*See also Manifesto of the Racial Scientists*; Mussolini, Benito; *Protocols of the Elders of Zion*; Racial Laws (Italy)

Primo de Rivera, Miguel (1870–1930), 674

Project Reinhard, 555

***Protocols of the Elders of Zion***, 11, 69–70, 368, 456, **567–569**, 584
and the Antichrist, 20
and anti-Zionism, 27
in Brazil, 83
in Britain, 85, 108, 286
in Fascist Italy, 443
and Freemasonry, 245, 456, 565–566
in Japan, 251, 364–365
and Judeo-Bolshevism, 390, 723
in the Muslim world, 31, 47, 107, 289, 359–361, 483
in Nazi propaganda, 568, 569–570, 600, 621–622, 737
promotional efforts of Fritsch, Theodor, 250, 290
role in death of Rathenau, Walther, 705–706
in Russia, Imperial, 405, 431, 509, 567, 584, 630
in Russia, Post-Soviet, 632, 637
in the Russian Civil War, 636
and the Russian Orthodox Church, 637
on trial in South Africa, 672
in the U.S., 38, 141, 465, 663, 721, 772
and Henry Ford's sponsorship of, 162–164, 233–234, 390
and Webster, Nesta, 759
*See also* Barruel, Augustin; *Biarritz*; *Cause of World Unrest, The*; *Dearborn Independent* and *The International Jew*; Freemasonry; Fritsch,

Yolanda, Queen of Aragon (d. 1443), 225
Yom Kippur War (1973), 365
Young England, 136
**Young Germany, 781–783**
**Young Hegelians, 783–784**
    *See also* Bauer, Bruno; Feuerbach, Ludwig; Marx, Karl
Young Italy, 781
Young Plan, 262, 305, 326
Young, Andrew (1932–), 5
**Youth Movement, 784–785**
Yrigoyen, Hipolito (1852–1933), 89
Yudovin, Solomon (1892–1954), 631
Yurovsky, Yakov (1878–1938), 389, 638
Yushkevich, Semyon (1868–1907), 631

Zagreb, 147–150, 539–540, 726
Zangwill, Israel (1864–1926), 475
Zankov, Alexandăr (1879–1959), 90
Zbor, 431–432
Zemstvo, 581
Zeno of Verona (d. 380), 169
Zhdanov, A. (1896–1948), 182–183
Zhirinovsky, Vladimir (1946–), 633
Ziegler, Adolf (1892–1959), 166
Ziegler, Hans Severus (b. 1893), 476, 702
Zinoviev, Grigorii (1883–1936), 724
Zion, Daniel, 90
**Zionism,** 240, 418, 443, 545, 668, **787–788**
    *See also* Anti-Zionism; Caricature, Anti-Jewish (Modern); Herzl, Theodor; Nordau, Max

ZOG (Zionist Occupied Government), 465, 767
**Zola, Emile** (1840–1902), 168, 190, 232, 423, **788–789**
    falsely identified as Jewish, 40, 148
    film treatment of, 315–316
    and *J'accuse!,* 190, 788–789
Zoroastrians, 30, 352, 357
**Zündel, Ernst** (1939–), 173, 349, **790–791**
    and the Auschwitz Lie, 45
    Canadian trials of, 225, 420, 790
    *See also* Holocaust Denial, Negationism and Revisionism; Internet; *Leuchter Report;* Neo-Nazism, German
Zuviria, Gustavo Martinez (1882–1962), 36
Zwingli, Ulrich (1884–1531), 592
Zyklon B, 420, 496